Directions in

AMERICAN POLITICAL THOUGHT

Kenneth M. Dolbeare

ASSOCIATE PROFESSOR OF POLITICAL SCIENCE
UNIVERSITY OF WISCONSIN

JOHN WILEY & SONS, INC.

New York • London • Sydney • Toronto

Directions in American Political Thought

Preface

I have profited immeasurably from participating with students in their determined effort to understand American political ideas and directions, past and present. Operating from a contemporary and personalized focus, but readily grasping the necessity for historical perspective and rigorous analytical methods, students have shown me that it is possible to use political theory as a basic intellectual tool for judgment and action in politics today.

Because of this experience, I have been encouraged to attempt to serve some specialized goals in this book. Valuable results are produced by analyzing the works of political theorists as a kind of history of ideas, or by assessing the linkages between ideas and action, or by employing theory as a vehicle for gaining insight into the abstract and eternal problems of political order. But I have sought to achieve three other goals. First, I want to employ political theory as the organizing framework for coming to terms with the major alternatives of political power, purpose, and change that currently face citizens of the United States. Next, I have sought to promote development of individual intellectual skills of analysis and evaluation and sophisticated understanding of the nature of politics. Finally, I seek to show the relevance and utility of extracts from major empirical research for purposes of testing contemporary prescriptions. Each of these purposes deserves some further comment.

Nothing in politics is neutral: constitutions, institutions, traditions—all confer advantages, reflect values, and militate toward some ends to the exclusion of others. Very little that we now know as the American political system was as inevitable as it now appears. One set of values, or one priority ranking among values, has triumphed over other possible values or rankings of values. A focus on value conflict, past and present, can reveal vital aspects of the ongoing nature of American politics. The central concerns of political theory serve to alert one to the value components of action in ways unequalled by other approaches to the study of politics.

But in order to identify value choices, and to make rational judgments and take timely and effective action, one must develop the intellectual skills of analysis and evaluation. This can only be accomplished by confronting original materials and searching out the premises from which authors begin, the assumptions that are implicit in their work, and the values that have dictated their prescriptions. It also requires individuals to develop their own independent definitions of what is important in politics, their own explicit value ordering, and the capacity to select from the work of others to build a new and personal posture for political judgment and action. To do less is to consent to being controlled by the arguments of others.

Empirical research, when properly employed, can provide a descriptive base from which prescription may be attempted. Every bit of knowledge gained about the "is" of the present enhances one's capacity to decide between competing prescriptions for the future, and to devise ways of getting from the unsatisfactory present to the preferable future. Not all empirical findings are equally useful, however, and so it is necessary to set up criteria for extracting the most revealing and relevant landmarks of knowledge about contemporary politics before entering this body of research.

I hope it is clear that I am neither probehavioral nor antibehavioral, and that I do not seek to revive the tired argument between classical political theorists and empirical political scientists over which is the sounder approach to the study of politics. Empirical studies have much to contribute to understanding of the politics of the present—to the descriptive side of political thought. *Assumptions are no substitute for evidence.* To the extent that we have reliable evidence available (and it needs only to be good evidence, not necessarily utterly comprehensive or fully scientific) we are better able to focus our attention on the value preference questions, clarify what it is that divides us, assess the implications of various alternative solutions, and make our judgments about what actions to take. Issues of value preference, of course, must be recognized for what they are, and treated as such. *"Facts" are no substitute for hard thinking about moral and ethical choices.* Empirical studies can contribute, but in the prescriptive aspects of political thought, all men are on their own, and their judgments and actions must be based on their value preferences. Probably all would agree to this point in the abstract: the problem comes when men seek to distinguish between facts and values in specific situations, and we shall have to face this problem when we take up particular empirical studies. For the moment, I am merely pointing out that the inclusion of empirical materials is part of an effort to adapt this body of research into the mainstream of evolving political ideas in the United States, and to make use of these findings for the purpose of making better judgments about American political processes, public policies, and contemporary prescriptions for their improvement.

Thus, this book attempts to trace the evolution of American political ideas and ideology and to assess their present character; to explore the "reality" of power distribution and usage in the United States today through selective employment of landmarks of empirical research; and to use this background of knowledge, and the intellectual skills developed in the process of acquiring that knowledge, to critically evaluate contemporary prescriptions for improvement of the American political system.

As I look upon it now, this was a bold endeavor, and I hope some of my shortcomings may be attributed to that fact. The effort to integrate empirical findings with prescriptive materials required much more analysis and interpretation from me than I had originally planned, and my essays began to rival the contributors' essays in length. The decision to issue the empirical section as a paperback supplement, taken chiefly because of the bulk of the combined materials, places another obstacle in the way of accomplishing integration. I hope that readers will be generous enough to acknowledge the potential in that goal, and to dip into that collection *(Power and Change in the United States: Empirical Findings and Their Implications)* to see for themselves whether it has been fulfilled.

I am aware of some other problems created by my particular choice of goals for this book. Concern for the development of individual intellectual skills, in my eyes, requires inclusion of relatively lengthy selections from each author. Brief snippets of a thinker's work will not suffice; he must be granted the opportunity to present and develop his ideas as he would wish, and the student may then form his own impression of a man who had a more or less coherent set of values and programs. Original works are readily available, of course. There are ample paperback materials for several courses in American political thought, but few students have that much time to devote to this area of knowledge. Further, use of original works in their entirety is inefficient, because the time required to read one complete book still may result in less than complete understanding of that author, in addition to reducing the time available for other authors. I have tried to resolve this dilemma by presenting rather substantial selections from several (but still relatively few) thinkers, in hopes that it might be possible to cover more ground without sacrificing the opportunity to come to intimate grips with each and to develop useful intellectual skills.

This accommodation obliges me to state the criteria of selection employed— for I anticipate that neither teachers nor students will be entirely satisfied with the authors represented and selections employed. First, I have sought to present the makers and carriers of the American political tradition, the thinkers who exemplify both the central components and the boundaries of American political thought and who are chiefly responsible for the character of our political ideas and ideology today. Thus, there should be available not only some key individuals but also some continuing threads or themes that serve to integrate them and fit them into a coherent framework of developing doctrine. Because these thinkers are no more than such a central core, I assume that supplementary materials will be used as individual viewpoints and definitions of the field suggest. This explains why, for example, there are relatively few excerpts from the *Federalist Papers* included: no original source in American political ideas is more readily available in more inexpensive editions than the *Federalist Papers*. In the contemporary selections, I have tried to make up for the orthodox approach of the earlier section by taking a very wide frame of reference. "Where do we go from here?" is a question the answer to which may well take us outside the liberal tradition as we now understand it, and the full range of possibilities ought to be examined. Once again, however, there is opportunity for readers to select, substitute, supplement, and omit as they see fit. This book will have achieved its purpose if it provides the beginning base from which such actions can be taken.

I would like to add one or two additional comments about the plan of this book. I have made no effort to present comprehensive historical contexts for individual selections, nor have I sought to provide extensive descriptions of preceding or intervening events or ideas, or to take up commentators' authoritative interpretations. There are several more than adequate secondary sources and historical texts that describe and interpret such matters, and I shall consider my responsibilities in this respect fulfilled by referring to specific locations where information may be found. I see no utility in oversimplifying or compressing history that readily can be found elsewhere, so I have set for myself only the tasks mandatory to the political thought focus of the book: furnishing with each selection only those basic facts about the author and his work that are essential to an understanding of it, and, in my own essays, raising what seem to me to be the critical issues concerning the substance of selections and relating these to one or two continuing themes concerning evolving liberalism. I think there are clear and continuing regularities in the ideas of American political thinkers, and that a coherent line of interpretation and explanation is, therefore, possible— and I shall try to demonstrate this throughout the book. At the same time, I wish to avoid structuring conclusions for others, or becoming so unique and personal that no others can use this book. So I have declared my own views, and referred the reader to sources that disagree. The reader should stand warned that my essays necessarily reflect my subjective interpretations, and be guided accordingly. When it comes to the contemporary writers and problems, of course, I have had sense enough to remain silent, and it is every man for himself.

Finally, the political focus of the book means that it is lacking in at least one other respect of which I am acutely aware: there is little or no explicit inquiry into ethical abstracts as such—into the nature of the good life, the nature of obligation, the meaning of justice, and so forth. One reason is that

American political thinkers have not given much time to explicit consideration of such questions, although they have, of course, been obliged to make assumptions or to work with implicit answers. (We shall assess their efforts, and press toward consideration of these questions, however, out of necessity, because one cannot make evaluative judgments without doing so.) The second reason is that it seems preferable to me to leave these dimensions (as separate areas of study) to the individual proclivities of teachers and students. My concentration has been on facilitating the development of the analytical and evaluative skills that are specially political in character, for which the experience and training of political science are most applicable. History, sociology, economics, and philosophy are all inevitably involved here, too, but they are brought to bear secondarily, and for the purpose of better developing intellectual skills in thinking about and making judgments about political prescriptions. These are tasks grand enough for several shelves of books, and I see no real reason to apologize for what has not been attempted.

Many people have made important contributions to this book, and many of its better qualities result from their suggestions which, in most cases, were accepted. Hank Lufler and Jon Lampman, graduate students in political science, provided much of the early intellectual testing and bibliographical research that went into choice of selections. Douglas Dague, Cynthia Ingols, Sheila Brigham, and Joan Sturmthal, also graduate students, were very capable researchers, bibliographers, and administrators. Immensely useful reviews were provided by my publisher's reviewers Lane Davis, Robert P. Boynton, and Robert Pranger. My colleagues Booth Fowler, Judy Stiehm, and Stuart Scheingold read all of my essays with widely varying but uniformly helpful reactions, and supplemented these with continuing availability as I worked my way toward a final version. Joel Brenner, former editor of the Wisconsin Daily Cardinal, proved specially adept at both editorial and substantive criticism. The encouragement and assistance of Jerry Papke and the editorial staff of John Wiley & Sons was essential to timely completion of the task. Typists too numerous to name shared faithfully in the burden of preparing the manuscript. I wish to thank all of these people for the integral contributions that they made to a book that simply would not have been possible without them.

My most demanding critic has been my wife Pat, whose professional convictions still diverge from several interpretations in my essays. The book is dedicated, however, to my students at the University of Wisconsin. Many of them will disagree with my arguments, as usual, but I would be well satisfied if this book reflected some of the intellectual stimulation I have drawn from their wide-ranging and skeptical confrontation with the directions of American political thought. It is a constant challenge, and a continuing satisfaction, to engage in political inquiry with such students.

K. M. D.

Contents

CHAPTER 1

Political Thought in the United States: An Overview

THE insistent public problems of the last third of the twentieth century—race relations, foreign policy, economic distributions, urban deterioration, technological change—confront the American political system with deep-cutting value questions.

1. To what extent are commitments to orderly processes, property rights, and established power distributions compatible with timely attainment of justice by black Americans?

2. What do freedom and equality mean, if not the possession of tangible and proportionate shares of wealth and power on the part of all members of the society?

3. What are the standards by which a purportedly democratic nation should determine its foreign policy, and how far can definitions of the national interest legitimate intervention overseas without vitiating the claim to democracy at home?

4. What happens to the individual and his personal growth and fulfillment in this complex, specialized, and not altogether pleasant world?

It is simply absurd to blithely assume that, having always managed to muddle through in the past, the pragmatic American political system will somehow respond again with incremental changes sufficient to cope with these problems. To understate the matter somewhat, dominant American political ideas may not be equal to these problems. Indeed, perhaps they are more a limiting than a facilitating factor in the process of reaching judgments about what course of action to take under present conditions. We can readily demonstrate that the pace of environmental change, the depth and danger of international problems, the complexity and specialized nature of the society, and the sheer multitude of persons and claims within it, have never existed before. Past experience does *not* lend assurance for the present: our inability to cope with race relations problems, for example, produced a Civil War that only succeeded in deferring the real problem to the present; and "muddling through" for the past decades produced the present circumstances of our existence. Surely these are times that mandate the examination of political ideas and directions at the most fundamental level.

We must acquire the knowledge, and the skills of analysis and evaluation, which are requisite to judgment and action in politics today. We must try to understand the present context of political ideas, the present distribution of political power, and the nature of political change in the United States. Armed with such knowledge, and with the intellectual skills generated in the process of acquiring it, we shall be prepared to confront contemporary political problems and prescriptions, and to make judgments and take action in a rational and effective manner. The design of this book reflects a strategy to reach these goals.

First, we shall seek to understand the origins, character, and evolution of contemporary political ideas and ideology. In exploring these aspects of political development, we shall be dealing speculatively with political values and problems of political theory in the traditional sense. This analysis will not necessarily tell us how the American political system worked, works, or should work. But it will illustrate the range of questions and the varying solutions that individuals who have engaged in serious political thinking have found it necessary to entertain, and we can attempt to reach judgments about the relevance of the questions posed and the answers advanced for our contemporary problems. In addition, these theorists' ideas probably help to shape the present political thinking (and perhaps behavior) of elites, and possibly of larger numbers of Americans as well. Even if these ideas are merely a gloss by which elites explain and justify their actions, analysis will help in understanding the nature of our present political discourse.

Second, we shall employ this knowledge, and the skills of analysis and evaluation developed along the way, in critically evaluating contemporary American political problems and the prescriptions of those who urge particular types of change today. Individuals must rely upon their own evolved concepts, skills, and value priorities to reach judgments and decide on courses of action—but we can identify some of the questions and problems that we and other prescriptive thinkers must all face in the process.

A subordinate purpose runs through the book, as should already be evident. This is a self-conscious emphasis on developing the individual's intellectual skills of analysis and evaluation, including a sophisticated appreciation of the characteristic problems of politics. If we know what questions to ask, and when the evidence is adequate for an answer, we shall surely be on the way to rational judgment. Still needed to fill out criteria of judgment and action, of course, is careful consideration of value preferences and priorities to be applied to the state of facts found to exist. Although this is chiefly an individual responsibility, an understanding of politics and political theory can aid in raising questions that are useful in reaching one's own stand on an issue.

A second subordinate purpose, more fully explained in the preface, is represented by the paperback supplement to this volume entitled *Power and Change in the United States.* This is the somewhat unorthodox effort to merge empirical research with more traditional political theory in order to provide the clearest possible understanding of present and potential directions in American politics. Knowledge of the "is"—the important, structuring realities of power, politics, and change— is needed before one can decide *whether* and *how* to seek improvement in this political system. Those without either time or inclination to engage in this subordinate effort, however, should find that they can still profit significantly from developing a body of knowledge about the origins and evolution of political ideas and using this knowledge to confront contemporary proposals for change in our political system. The process of inquiry marked out here is a self-contained attempt to facilitate individual development of the knowledge and skills requisite to rational and effective political judgment and action. We shall begin by setting forth some of the intellectual tools appropriate to the analysis of political ideas, and sketching some of the historical background of American political thought.

I. APPROACHES TO THE ANALYSIS OF POLITICAL IDEAS

"Politics" is activity that has to do with the acquisition and usage of power in such a manner as to affect the nature and behavior of government. "Government" in turn signifies those institutions and processes that dominant elements in a society have established and staffed for the purposes of maintaining order, accommodating conflicts, and promoting preferred domestic and foreign goals. Politics necessarily involves ethical choices, societal relationships, environmental conditions, and interaction among such factors. It is thus a more comprehensive and less tangible concept than government. Nevertheless, the central concerns of politics can be summed up in the inclusive question "Who should rule, and why should others obey?" One who would be a political theorist—in short, one who would tell others how and why to organize their governments in a particular fashion—must respond to certain fundamental questions, specification of which may serve both to elaborate upon our understanding of the nature of politics and as a basis for analyzing the authors whose work follows this chapter.

In the course of centuries of observation and speculation on such issues, political theorists have generated a series of questions to which answers must be found if a system is to be designed in which men can expect to live together. The questions are formulated differently by different theorists, partly because they see their subject distinctively, and partly because they have favored varying answers over the years. (Of course, the answers given by different theorists have varied even more widely, because their values and preferences have diverged sharply; it is in the giving of answers that we see their principles most clearly and find our grounds for judgments.) But the questions asked, and our own understanding of the nature of the subject, can be fused together to articulate three sets of questions that we may use as beginning bases from which to analyze American thinkers.

What Is the Nature of Man and the Condition of His Existence?

This is surely one of the most fundamental questions that can be raised. If men, or most men, are generally rational, capable, and willing to take part in public affairs, imbued with public spiritedness—then one set of goals and procedures is possible and probably desirable. But, if men are emotional, likely to put selfish motives and personal pleasures ahead of public needs, and likely to make mistakes—then other necessities follow. The second part of the question raises another spectrum of issues: Is man irretrievably what he is today? Is he himself inevitably, or is he the product of his environment? If the latter, to what extent can he control his environment and direct his own development? If he can control his own development, then one range of possible goals is attainable; if not, he must prepare to do the best he can under the circumstances.

These are questions that theorists were at first forced to deal with through impressions or assumptions, neither of which could be proved either true or false. No matter how closely one observed man, he could not observe enough men in enough situations with enough objectivity to convince others that he had a conclusive verdict on man's nature. But it is at least theoretically possible now for important parts of this question to be answered with empirical evidence. The problem is that not enough evidence has been assembled to lay to rest the critical questions of degree that are the real cutting points. While we know from fairly persuasive and consistent evidence that environment plays a significant part in shaping the values and attitudes and nature of man, we do not know how completely his nature can be shaped, or what conditions are requisite to success in such a venture, or what elements in his nature are indeed endemic to his very existence. Wide areas of this issue remain open to assumptions based on guesses or preference or history, and there is little that can be done at present to reduce it to a provable state. Therefore, the important question for us to raise with each author is, what specific and/or unique assumptions does he make with regard to the nature of man and the condition of his existence? How does he envision the human animal? The author's answer may not tell us anything about the nature of man, but it will tell us a great deal about the point of view from which the author operates, and much about the nature of his values.

What Are the Goals of Political Organization?

Few people consider political organization a discretionary luxury, and so the question follows as to what goals (or, perhaps, what priorities among generally shared goals) should be acknowledged. Nor can the issue be avoided under the assumption that government can be neutral: even if that were possible, which the experience of centuries suggests it is not, it would mean only that sources of private power were freed thereby to work their will as they saw fit, and citizens would be handed from one controlling power to another not very different one. Every political thinker and every polity must reach conclusions as to which goals it considers paramount and which are to be secondary, since not all can be attained at the same time and, even with a short priority list, there is likely to be conflict at any given moment between desirable goals.

What we are concerned with, then, is the priority of goals established by the political thinker. We may expect that all thinkers will endorse roughly the same goals, at least in the abstract, and the telling analytical dimension, therefore, is likely to be the order of priority in which the thinker ranks his goals. Once again, this will tell us little about the relative desirability of the goals themselves, but much about the values of the author. Nor will the author be likely to perform this ranking for us: we shall have to sort out his relative attachments from the language he uses and the depth of commitment he displays in regard to each. One of the most revealing approaches and, again, one in which the author will not deliberately be of assistance, is to single out some key concepts and definitions that the author employs. Perhaps unconsciously, a political thinker frequently reveals himself in the implicit meanings he assigns to such concepts as freedom, equality, justice, democracy, and so forth. "Freedom" may mean freedom from, in the sense of freedom from government interference with the opportunity of the individual to seek maximum return from his property; or it may mean freedom to, in the sense of government action that releases the individual to seek his own development through removal of the fetters placed upon him by established educational or opportunity levels, or outside sources of power. "Equality" may mean equality of opportunity, in the sense of a right to compete along with others using whatever one has in the way of talent or other advantages to gain ultimate goals; or it may mean equality of opportunity defined as everybody starting with deliberately equalized levels of education and financial resources; or it may mean political equality without regard to economic status at all; or it may mean utter equality of economic, social, and, therefore, political, status. Similar ranges may exist in definitions of other key concepts. In each case, the political thinker is sometimes deliberately, sometimes inadvertently, providing his readers with cues to his basic values and priorities. Together, they add up to his view of what the good life consists of, and by what general routes it is to be attained.

It should be clear that there are no empirical components of this category of questions. Each of these definitions, and the priority of goals that they represent, is a product of a value preference on the part of the thinker. We cannot ask whether these are demonstrable one way or the other, and indeed it is profitless to argue whether a concept itself "really means" one thing or another. The concept means what the author says it means, as far as his usage is concerned. Its importance to us lies in what it reveals of his preference and priorities, and our only evaluative question is the private one of whether we happen to agree with him or not.

What Are the Means By Which the Thinker Proposes to Reach His Goals?

Once we have identified the thinker's assumptions about the nature of man and the proper goals of political organization, we have but to ask how he plans to get from the former to the latter. This is, of course, the point where political prescriptions most often go aground: even a journeyman political thinker can paint a rosy picture of the goals of social life, and many have obviously sincere and reasonable postulates about the nature of man from which to start, but the act of designing institutions and processes to reach from one to the other leads them to prescribe hopelessly impractical, unattractive, or unworkable mechanisms. In considering possible prescriptions in this area, of course, I do not mean to assume that all political thinkers proceed with logical rigor in moving from assumptions about the nature of man to the proper goals of society. We may well suspect that most thinkers decide on their goals and then fit their assumptions of the nature of man to those goals, and that many have fixed assumptions about the workability or nonworkability of certain institutional arrangements and, therefore, design their means and goals around those as landmarks. I am suggesting only that the inquiries we direct at their prescriptions should focus on the consistency and internal logic of these means as a separate set of questions.

This area is clearly one where experience and evidence is useful for both analytical and evaluative purposes. We know something about how institutions work, and about the consequences of particular political mechanisms. If the thinker's prescriptions are contrary to evidence, or to the assumptions about man that are fundamental to his other positions, we can legitimately consider him vulnerable. In addition to simple workability in the light of evidence as to present operating characteristics, we shall also see new dimensions of his value preferences in this area. For example, we should be interested in his conception of the proper role of elites. Does he consider elite rule (how complete a preponderance, by what sorts of people, does he envision?) inevitable and desirable, or inevitable and regrettable, or preventable? In the event that he is resigned to an elite role of some kind, we come to some critical and revealing questions: How are elites selected? How much influence over their policy determinations is retained by masses? In what ways is such influence wielded, and what are the vehicles, and who controls *them?* The whole area of mass-elite linkages and the means by which they are related to each other provides one of the best opportunities to understand both the thinker's value preferences and his capacity to ground his prescriptions in the realities of the present. Somehow, we must get from what now is to what he says should be: Has he faced and effectively dealt with this problem?

Another revealing direction of inquiry is to ask where the thinker proposes to place authority for determining the proper standards for behavior and policy within his proposed new system. Where will decisive decisions be made, and on what basis? If he argues that answers are to be found in natural law, or in history, by whom are they to be ascertained—by elites, judges, historians? Whoever has such capacity is probably the body most favored as having good judgment by the thinker himself, which again tells us little about the residence of good judgment but much about the thinker's values. Or perhaps the ultimate interpretation of the constitution or other source of final authority is placed in the hands of the people of the times, which says something quite different about the thinker.

These are by no means the only questions to be directed at the authors whose work follows this chapter. If we knew more about the essential characteristics of politics, no doubt we could formulate more perceptive and subtly characterizing questions. One of our tasks in the course of examining the original works of American political history is to refine and develop these crude approaches. The more sophisticated our sense of the nature of politics, the more searching the challenges that we can pose to political prescribers, and the better our own ultimate judgments about both present and future.

II. LEVELS OF POLITICAL THINKING

Not all political thinking involves such relatively fundamental reflections, of course. Real people vary widely in the comprehensiveness and sophistication of their political ideas. One way in which these distinctions may be taken into account is to think of three levels of sophistication at which political ideas may be held: ideology, political thought, and political theory. Ideology is the least sophisticated, most widely experienced of the three levels. By "ideology" I mean the operative myths (true or false, it matters not) actually held by most members of the polity concerning the way in which their government does and should work. Much simplified from (or even at variance with) the relaties of the political system, such beliefs support the established system and lend confidence that things have and will continue to work out properly. Ideology does not make for real consideration of why particular procedures are followed, nor does it involve a complex sense of the relationship between values, goals, and policies. It says, in effect, that if people subscribe to certain basic values, all will be well. This usage of "ideology" includes only those basic political beliefs that are supportive of the established order, regardless of whether such beliefs are accurate; many other (perhaps more accurate) political beliefs are probably held by various segments of the population, but these are not meant to be included within this characterization of "ideology."

Political thought is an intermediate level, at which more comprehensive—but still not truly fundamental—examination of premises and purposes occurs. Typical examples of political thought may be found in candidates' speeches, or in the reports of study commissions, in which some guiding principles are stated (though usually with several unstated premises and little real reexamination of the "first principles" underlying the present form of political or social organization itself) and some policy proposals made. Political thought may include elements of ideology, as in the case of unrecognized assumptions about what is or should be within a particular system. Much of the usage of the terms "liberal" and "conservative" which are familiar to us from issue-related, popular, or newspaper headline usage falls within the range of being political thought. For many scholars of classical political theory, there is very little in the American political experience that raises more fundamental or comprehensive value questions than those involved at the political thought level. Few college or university courses in American political ideas are bold enough to claim the title of "American political theory" for just this reason: American political thinking does not seem to go deep enough into fundamental questions to qualify.

As suggested in the foregoing, the term "political theory" is usually reserved for comprehensive original works in which a man of rare genius articulates a complete political philosophy—from an examination of the nature of man to the qualities of the good life and the means to attaining justice in the world. Some works of political theory are distinguished by their insight into the established order, some by the vision they display as to what might be; all assume the obligation to consider the basic values and principles that underlie (or should underlie) all political organization and activity, and then proceed deductively to show how these might be applied in the circumstances of the times to gain the ends considered most desirable. Political theory is the only level at which truly independent judgment and rethinking of fundamental principles takes place. The comprehensiveness and sophistication required imply that not many works of political theory are ever produced, perhaps only a few each century. It follows that, in the view of many scholars, and because of the American penchant for acceptance of givens from the liberal tradition, not much of the writing of American political thinkers meets these criteria, thus deserving only the label of "political thought."

This does not mean, of course, that American political thinking is simply dismissable for lack of profundity. American political ideas make a great deal of difference to those who must live within the American political system and, under present circumstances, to the rest of the world as well. Furthermore, while American thinkers have not explicitly considered some of the "first principles" questions that qualify in the minds of scholars as political theory, they frequently have done so implicitly or in a less coherently arranged manner—a characteristic that merely means that the analyst has a more difficult task to perform. For the record, we may place American political thinking—of the kind with which we shall be concerned in this book—at the more rudimentary level of political theory. It is surely more complex and fundamental than mere political thought (as defined above), but, just as clearly, less so than Plato or Aristotle. As may be apparent, I do not consider the issue of where American political thinking falls to be an important question. The point that *is* important is that there are levels of depth and sophistication of political ideas, which bear generally agreed labels that analysts can use to communicate with each other—if they are careful in their definitions.

Although distinguishable in these ways, ideology, political thought, and political theory are related to each other. Ideas, once produced in a work of political theory, may come into the everyday discourse of educated men, eventually forming part of the premises with which they discuss public problems and debate policies, in which case we have "political thought." After simplified versions of these ideas have been articulated often enough by leaders, and when government actions are interpreted in these terms, the average citizen may come to adopt them as his political values and as his understanding of how the system works—in which case the ideas have been translated into ideology. As ideology, they are perpetuated through a variety of means such as the public school, the mass media, and the family, to the point where they may bear little reference to reality in the political system but, nevertheless, remain politically potent for purposes of social control and as operative myths on which actions are based.

Let us imagine ideology as having two parts: basic political values and specific political manifestations of those values. The basics are such familiar political values as individualism, limited government, and natural rights such as property and equality. The political manifestations are concrete applications of the political values that shape the practices and institutions of the political system. They range from rules of procedure or political practices such as campaigning and voting to separation of powers in the institutions of the government, or to concepts of government as a neutral arbiter. Persons with the most rudimentary ideology may see no connections between these values and such applications within the political system; they may simply adhere to some few of each with little perception of their relationships. A more fully developed form of ideology would result in the person seeing more links between values and procedures and institutions. Such a person might understand institutions to have the form they do because of or in furtherance of particular values. An even more highly developed sense of ideology would more completely fill out this sense of relationships between values and procedures and institutions and result in the person understanding new problems by fitting their elements into his well-developed scheme of the interconnections. This last stage of the development of ideology spills over into the category of political thought, which is not much more than the application of highly developed ideology to new problems, together with a capacity to speculate upon the effects of doing things in various ways and to explain proposed actions in terms of aspects of ideology and the merits of the situation.

III. RECURRING COMPONENTS OF AMERICAN POLITICAL THOUGHT

Political thought in the United States displays some recurring elements, a preliminary identification of which may facilitate our analysis. These components are readily identifiable at this relatively elite level, and it is at least probable that some of them have been promulgated and have taken hold over the years as ideology. The latter is an empirical question, of course, for which we as yet have no evidence. But we shall see that many of the elements of American political thought do recur in the thinkers in this part; to a considerable extent, this is because American ideas share a single principal origin.

In one of the ironies of which politics is capable, John Locke's *Second Treatise on Government,*[1] written for 17th century England, had only marginal impact there at any time but came to dominate political thinking and action in 18th, 19th, and 20th century America. Published shortly after the Glorious Revolution of 1688, the book stressed the rights of men accruing to them for no other reason than their existence. Individuals in the state of nature were held to have been unable to conveniently enforce noninterference by others with their natural rights, and so by means of a contract they instituted government to better carry out this function. Crucial to this design is the assumption of the individual as the starting point, with natural rights pertaining to him. These natural rights were definable by the exercise of man's reason, although presumably there was a natural law that specified them and established the proper relationship between men, their rights, and their government. Paramount among these rights were those of life, liberty, and estate, which Locke called by the generic label "property."

The concept of property was central to Locke and is the same to his American followers. Locke envisioned men in the state of nature as mixing their labor with natural resources to produce an improved product that had much greater value than before. Such men deserved to have assurance of security in their possessions; without confidence that they would be able to retain and enjoy the fruits of their work, they might not engage in productive enterprise. Threats to this security appeared inevitable, both from powerful aristocrats, sometimes operating through government, and from the redistributive avarice of peasants and laboring masses. To reduce these threats, Locke and his followers sought to minimize the power of government and to make

---

[1] John Locke, *Two Treatises on Government.* New York: Hafner Publishing Company, 1947.

it into a "neutral" enforcer of law and order. Fearing the loss of their property in the event of violence and physical coercion, they emphasized the organizing and distributive capacities of the economic marketplace. This apparently noncoercive mechanism was seen as a replacement for the otherwise necessary (but ever-threatening) mobilizations of coercive power in government. Not that government was to be inconsequential: both society and economy, however, were anterior to politics and government, and the latter was to be the agent of the former, enforcing general compliance by the recalcitrant with the distributions and achievements wrought through the "natural" operations of society and economy.

Thus, neither Locke nor his American followers were radicals—they were businessmen concerned with their possessions and distrustful of power. The emphasis placed on economics as the distributor, and on the right to possess as property that with which one had mixed his labor and invested his personality, created correspondingly materialist standards of judgment in all spheres of activity including politics. But to justify the attainment of such ends and the primacy of such values, some principles about the role of government had to be articulated. Locke himself had to both defend the Glorious Revolution and discourage further opposition to established order. He did so by admitting the *right* of revolution in cases where government had failed to serve individuals' natural rights and had instead itself invaded those rights, but then stressed the unwisdom of exercise of such a right except in the most extreme cases. At the time of the American Revolution, dominant elites were narrowly divided as to whether circumstances were such as to constitute a sufficiently extreme case, and since then most American thinkers have reduced the "right" to one applicable only to "nondemocratic" countries. But the language is there in Locke, and in the Declaration of Independence, and it has a latent radicalizing potential.[2]

Why did Locke's ideas generate such complete acceptance by Englishmen on the American continent and not in England? Perhaps it was the empirical verification of the individual in the state of nature who entered into contractual relationships creating governments that led to adoption of the Lockean premises. Conditions of life were surely different than they were in England, where the traditions of generations attributed the origins of the state, not inaccurately, to the actions of the king. Possibly the Lockean assumptions about individuals, their rational nature, and their rights were simply attractive rationalizations for profit-oriented and acquisitive colonists who sought to make

---

[2] For a useful summary of political thought in this period, see Carl J. Friedrich and Robert McCloskey, *From the Declaration of Independence to the Constitution.* New York: The Liberal Arts Press, 1954.

the most of their risk-taking. It is also clear that an independent strain of similar thinking had developed on the American continent, particularly in some parts of New England, as a result of the religious controversies of the 17th and early 18th centuries. In any event, the substance of Locke's ideas became the foundation of American political thinking to the extent that after Jefferson wrote the Declaration of Independence, he could dismiss the achievement as being "but the common sense of the thing."

The origins of American political thinking, then, lie in the heritage of Locke. Specifically, most American thinkers proceed from the individual as the focal point, with government as the contractual creature of action by many individuals. Society, as a collectivity, is but a large number of individuals, though nevertheless an entity superior to government. The central purpose of government is to facilitate the individual's own self-development, by administering the laws that prevent others from intruding upon the individual's rights. Because the major threat to individual attainment was considered to be government itself—for which there was ample historical evidence—the principal form taken by the effort to secure individual rights was to erect a set of prohibitions against government actions. Bills of Rights were a key part of this effort. Notice that the Bill of Rights in the Constitution, for example, does not declare rights existing in individuals as such, but only prohibits government from doing things contrary to these rights. Although a citizen has the "right" of free speech, he has it (even today) only against actions by government to prevent speech; other individuals or other private sources of power can prevent him from speaking as much as they want to, without ever calling constitutional rights into play. The focus on government as the chief threat to the individual leads to the limited government principle. Effectuation is by contractual arrangement, as was the origin of government itself, and for the sake of clarity, of course, contracts are written.

Converging with this emphasis on written limitations is the application of the higher law basis of natural rights. In searching for a way to define the substance of the rights men were supposed to have, Locke had placed their source in the "natural law," a law discoverable by the reason of man but which had its roots in the state of nature. This law was above the acts of men and unaffected by them, but every man was (at least theoretically) equally capable of interpreting what that natural law required in the way of rights. Thus, there was a source of authority higher than governments, which were the tangible creations of men. The next step was to see the written contract of limitation on government as an embodiment of the higher law and a means of applying the natural rights against the actions of others. Thus, there developed the idea that certain rights were fundamental and applicable against all comers, including majorities.

At the same time, emphasis on individualism led to at least a rhetorical belief in political equality and raised the prospect of continuing thrust toward democracy. All men were possessed of reason and had the same rights, among which was the right to take part in the making of government and the direction of its actions. Although there could be disagreement about how widespread the actual distribution of voting rights should be, there was no dispute about the principle that when the authorized participants were divided, the greater number should prevail. Majority rule was thus established as a part of the components of liberalism from the outset. But majority rule may be inconsistent on particular occasions with the principle of minority rights enforced by the higher law-based limitations of the written constitution. Either one has majority rule, which means that the majority gets what it wants, or one has minority rights, which means that the majority gets what it wants except when the minority claims it has rights. If the majority still wins, of course, the minority does not really have the rights it thought it did; but if the majority must yield to the minority, then *it* does not have majority rule. The two principles are logically inconsistent. Nor can a nation really have both, no matter how glibly they are run together in a Fourth of July address. To be sure, we could assume that some body of men has magical power to harmonize the two. If that were the case, of course, it would be worth speculating how the role of such a body of men could be equated with "democracy." That we have not recognized this inconsistency may be a tribute to the dexterity of the Supreme Court in clouding the issue,[3] or to a national tolerance for ambiguity, or to a lack of really fundamental conflict within the country. It does not really matter: we carry both as part of the substance of our ideas.

Accompanying the emphasis on contractual relationships and written limitations on governments is a strong emphasis on the law, legalism, and lawyers. Important questions of policy with significant value components are converted into "legal" issues to be decided by courts; the language and concepts of the law become the vocabulary of politics; and issues are not really resolved until lawyers' interpretations or drafting have been applied. What cannot be spelled out by contracts is in danger of being considered nonexistent, and contracts constitute fixed commitments that may not be modified no matter what the exigencies. The high place accorded to property rights (which are only one of many "natural rights") comes into play here also: one of the primary purposes of the law is to render property safe, to secure repayment of debts, and to facilitate commerce.

---

[3] Robert McCloskey has elaborated this theme effectively in his *The American Supreme Court.* (Chicago: University of Chicago Press, 1960.)

We have identified several components of American political thought already: individualism, natural rights (particularly in the sense of property rights), limited government with written prohibitions, legalism, and a commitment to the individual's self-fulfillment. In addition to these core values are some associated characteristics of temperament or outlook that may well be noted. American thinkers have taken a relatively optimistic view of the capabilities of men, viewing them in the abstract as essentially good or at least improvable, rational, and capable of participation in politics. Though far from complacent about the capacities of ordinary citizens to direct the course of government action, American thinkers have articulated a faith in reason as the basis for public decision making. Hasty or faulty action by mass publics is more likely to be attributed to misunderstanding or lack of full knowledge than to inherent emotionalism or incapacity. Indeed, at times the declared faith in reason and adherence to evidence-based decisions appears to obscure the value choices or mere applications of power that determine results. But confidence in man's capacity to rationally shape his future has been high; generally, change is deemed to be in the direction of progress. In part, this may be due to the strong strand of business profit-orientation that forms part of the American ethic: new methods of production, based on new technologies, lead in all probability to greater sales and greater profit, which is a large part of the definition of progress.

Historically (but perhaps not logically or necessarily) associated with these components of American political thinking, is the political value of supremacy over nonwhite races. Recent studies have demonstrated the racism of both the early founders and their contemporary successors. Political manifestations of this principle, however inconsistent with at least some definitions of equality, are too numerous to require itemization. Racism is a national rather than merely a regional characteristic, and as such must be included within our catalogue of components of American political thought.

IV. LIBERALISM, CONSERVATISM, AND RADICALISM IN THE UNITED STATES

The elements just described appear in the writings of nearly all major American thinkers. But political thinkers hold these commitments with varying degrees of intensity, and they attach different priority rankings to them. For purposes of summary reference, we may group distinctive constellations of intensity and priority rankings regarding these component elements into three roughly defined packages to which we can apply the still-meaningful labels of liberalism, conservatism, and radicalism. The great majority of American political thinkers fall within the liberal category, and only a few display some of the characteristics of conservatism or radicalism; in view of its predominance, we shall first explore the characteristics of liberalism.

Like so many terms in the language of politics, "liberalism" has almost as many meanings as it has users. No single meaning is authoritative, or necessarily better than another, for no one holds a copyright on the definition. Indeed, one way to gain quick insight into the values and priorities of a political thinker is to analyze his definitions of key words and concepts, such as "equality," "freedom," "democracy," and so forth. But we must establish some agreed meaning for "liberalism" here, in order to be able to communicate clearly about crucial values and viewpoints in political thought. Although I cannot hope to avoid all disagreement, I shall suggest a definition that I believe has the utility of providing continuity with the pre-American usage and essential consistency with the work of major commentators on the American political tradition, particularly that of Louis Hartz.[4] I do not mean to imply that this definition is narrow, fixed, or that it has clear-cut boundaries. It is a general definition, within the range of which men may display sharp disagreements.

I shall use the term liberalism to refer to a political value system that:

1. Begins with individualism, natural rights (including both property rights and other civil or human rights such as equality), and limited government.

2. Emphasizes legalism, materialism, and individual self-fulfillment.

3. Displays faith in the uses of reason and in the capacity of the economic market to achieve the fairest and least coercive distribution of wealth, status, and power.

Liberalism in this definition is a center position, reflecting the needs of a middle class of small businessmen and entrepreneurs. In Europe, it served to defend their prerogatives and property against potential incursions from the landed power of upper class aristocrats and the claims of peasantry and proletariat. In the United States, where there was no comparable feudal residue to give rise to either a powerful aristocracy or a deprived peasantry of ex-serfs on the European model, the liberalism of the dominant middle class merchants and financiers reigned virtually unchallenged.

Because there were no effective challenges to the liberalism developed out of the heritage of Locke, some scholars have seen controversies in American

---

[4] Louis Hartz, *The Liberal Tradition in America.* New York: Harcourt Brace and World, Inc., 1955.

political thought as taking place within an unrecognizedly narrow range.[5] Sharing so many similar commitments, and neither hearing nor perceiving other possibilities, Americans exaggerated differences in positions that were, on any absolute scale of possibilities, not very far removed from each other. Other nonliberal arguments, such as socialism or classical conservatism, were either ignored or repressed as un-American.

The principal tension within the liberal tradition has been conflict over the priorities to be assigned among the natural rights of individuals. To most, property rights were paramount, with resulting emphasis on law, contracts, procedural regularity, and stability. To some, human rights and equality in first political and then social and economic dimensions were uppermost, with commensurately greater concern for participation, justice, and change. All liberals, of course, believe that property rights are important, but some are willing to reduce the priority assigned to property in favor of human rights in more circumstances than others. Much of the conflict in American political history has been over just this issue, and it has been bitter more often than not. That this conflict is real in the eyes of the contestants, however, should not obscure the fact that there is still a large body of agreement between them as to other fundamental questions. We should admit the possibility that the American spectrum is relatively narrow, lacking a real conservative or radical alternative to the centrist liberal tradition. What looks to us like a wide range of political viewpoints in the United States may be simply our own culture-bound failure to perceive the real range of possible alternatives.

It may be argued that the differences between American "liberals"—between those who emphasize human rights and those who emphasize property rights—is so great that it is not meaningful to characterize them all as "liberals." It seems to me that this is a question of what frame of reference we want to employ: if we are content to consider only what Americans have actually argued about in their politics, in a kind of culture-bound acceptance of self-imposed limitations, then the definition is indeed only a meaningless preliminary to decisive specifics. But if we wish to consider the entire range of possibilities, and to see the implications for past and future of those very self-limitations, we must work with definitions that provide such comparative dimensions—and also permit local subcategorization for what men have actually said in this context. I shall demonstrate the importance of defining liberalism this way, and the extent to which liberalism has predominated in the United States, by contrasting liberalism with a definition of conservatism

---

[5] Ibid. See also the discussion of various perspectives on the American political tradition in Chapter 14 following.

drawn from its modern source, Edmund Burke, and somewhat modified to fit with Clinton Rossiter's *Conservatism in America.*[6]

Conservatism begins from a quite different focus, and this leads to a different view of the relationship between men and their governments. Conservatism posits the society first, as having an independent existence apart from the individuals who make it up. The independent entity that is the society is a continuing organism with a life of its own, progressing through centuries. The individuals who happen to make up its population today are but transients, changing from day to day as deaths and births take place. They have no claims prior to the society's, and no rights except what the society gives them in furtherance of its needs. Because they are emotional and frequently irrational, they need order, and liberty is the product of an ordered society in which men are able to do that which is right and desirable for them to do. Conservatism does not deny the inevitability of change, but neither does it believe that change has merits for its own sake; the kind of change that is appropriate is that for which the society is ready and that which fits the established traditions of the society. If one imagines a long line moving from past through present and into the future, change that fits on the line is the appropriate kind; this same analogy may be used to connect generations—a partnership of the living with the dead and the unborn—and suggest the relative consideration given to the individual and to the society's needs. Government in this design cannot be either the creature or the servant of the people who happen to make up the society at any given moment, for it is an agent of the society. Further, because of the inherent inequalities in distribution of talents, some men are better qualified than others to decide what government policies should be; therefore, either the franchise should be limited, or other means devised to insure that men of talent predominate. Both political equality and majority rule are, therefore, considered either illusory or undesirable. Those with the requisite talent decide what government must do on behalf of the society, and individuals' lives are directed accordingly. Because one of the purposes for which the society exists is the betterment of the culture and the attainments of the society, individuals frequently derive very significant benefits and satisfactions from their lives within such a system; conservatives would argue that this is the only way in which, given the realities of mens' characteristics, the amenities of life are ever to be realized.

Does it not now appear that liberalism is a distinctive set of beliefs? And that we have indeed had but few conservatives in the American political tradition? We do gain perspective in our past and present from comparison with a different pattern of beliefs. To view the main body of American thinkers as

---

[6] Clinton Rossiter, *Conservatism in America.* New York: Random House, 1955, 1962.

representing a wide range of opposing political positions is to miss the whole remaining spectrum of what might have been and, at least theoretically, still could be. And it is well to bear in mind that conservatism is only a moderately differing variant, not far from liberalism in Western political ideas.

Of course, we have had a few conservatives in the United States, although they are sometimes not recognized as such. This is because, at any given moment, their views on particular issues (for example, what should be done to reform the Congress, so that it may more effectively perform as a representative institution) may coincide with those of liberals. Another reason may be that dominant liberalism has simply ignored or failed to understand their arguments. Or it may be because, in their efforts to conserve the hallowed traditions of the society, they look back and find nothing to conserve but elements of liberalism. This is not only frustrating for conservative thinkers, but it confuses observers as well. Nevertheless, we shall try to point up those rare thinkers and positions throughout American political history that show signs of being conservative in character, if only to mark the boundaries and occasions where liberalism has not been uniformly endorsed.

On the opposite side of liberalism from conservatism, there has been an occasional outcropping of radical thought from time to time. It is very fragile and usually ignored, but nonetheless worth defining at this point. I suggest that the term *radicalism* be reserved for use in regard to those ideas and men who meet two criteria. *First,* they proceed from premises that emphasize the good qualities of mens' natures, and, therefore, see men as entitled to an integrated package of human, social, economic, and political rights exclusively by virtue of their existence. Equality of distribution in all these dimensions would be sought. No rewards would be dependent upon immediate evaluations of the individual's contribution to general well-being, but solely upon the fact that of the individual's personal existence. There would be no personal ownership of property in the sense of a right to exclude others from its enjoyment, and personal acquisitiveness would be replaced by community consciousness. Fraternity and interpersonal trust within the community would be highly valued. *Second,* the implications of these values and goals would be a drastic reworking of the existing social and economic, as well as political, structures. Maximum possible weight would be accorded to participation and decision making by autonomous individuals. Government would be available and employed for the purpose of creating the conditions that would permit such attainments, but thereafter reduced to marginal functions. Dominant thinkers and other pragmatic and property-conscious Americans have impatiently rejected (or, even more devastating, ignored) such apparently idealistic arguments on those occasions when they have been granted a hearing at all. In some instances, radicals have concluded that the attainment of their goals will require that they "force others to be free" by temporarily employing revolutionary or coercive means. An enduring source of division and conflict among radicals has been the question of what means are justifiable in search of their idealistic ends.

Contrasting liberalism with conservatism and radicalism, two of its nearer alternatives, has enabled us to sharpen our definition somewhat. Another way to clarify this conception of liberalism is to trace its evolution through time to the present. Let us do this by envisioning liberalism in two parts: a central core of unchanging basic values and purposes, and a surrounding penumbra of time-specific issue positions and tactically flexible orientations toward the use of government.[7] In the central core of unchanging values are the key elements already described, such as individualism, limited government, natural rights (emphasizing property rights), and legalism. Also in this central core is the assumption that the individual is prior to government, and that government exists for the purpose of permitting that individual to best serve his own needs and attain his personal fulfillment. These values and commitments have remained essentially constant from the earliest days of the Republic to the present.

But there has been change in the surrounding penumbra of issue positions and orientations toward the use of government. Indeed, these changes, made unconsciously (at least in some cases) in response to perceived changes in social, economic, and political conditions, have amounted to almost a complete reversal in the view of some liberals toward the propriety of the use of government. Most of the early liberals believed that the chief threat to individuals' capacities to develop themselves to the utmost lay in government action, and so they both bound government down with prohibitions and practiced *laissez-faire* as a basic policy. This position endured for at least the first century, with some exceptions made by those who found government a convenient device for advancing their own interests; these latter were able to rationalize their particular use of government as being necessitated by particular circumstances, without raising questions about the basic general policy of laissez-faire. Toward the end of the 19th century, however, two related developments led some liberals to question the desirability of following a nearly absolute laissez-faire policy. One development was the rise of corporate and personal economic power, to the point where it became clear to many that government was no longer the chief threat to individual attainment. The presence of accumulations of "private" power, and the leverage that this power gave to some to direct and affect the lives of others, led some liberals to feel

---

[7] I am indebted for this image to Gene DeFelice, then a student and now (as then) a teacher.

that government could be used to redress the balance and restore the individual to some semblance of equal opportunity. Granger laws, rate regulations, and trust-busting are examples of such uses of government, and they are entirely consistent with the core values of seeking to promote the individual's capacity to serve his own ends and reach personal fulfillment.

The second development was the awakening of concern for human rights and social welfare as opposed to an exclusive emphasis on property rights. All liberals acknowledged the importance of property and economic rights—the rights of individuals to maximize the profit attainable from use of their property, and the propriety of economic motivations generally. Classic economic liberalism of the Adam Smith brand had legitimated individual profit-seeking as the best way to advance the economy and ultimately to raise the standard of living of all. In addition, property had always been seen as the basis of individual political independence. The man who owned his own land would be dependent upon no other man's favor, and would be able to vote his conscience in elections; sufficient property would give men a stake in the society, and lead them away from rash acts toward moderate and stable political behavior. But toward the end of the 19th century, the emphasis by some liberals on individual profiteering and self-aggrandizement, rationalized by the application of Darwinian natural selection analogies, produced a reaction from others not so exclusively devoted to property and economic rights. For one thing, the conditions of existence of many people were so marginal that action seemed necessary merely to preserve their existence. The by-products of industrialization, urbanization, and monopoly control over key fields such as transportation included impoverishment, unemployment, and severe practical limitations on economic opportunities. In addition, the pre-Civil War agitation over the plight of the Negro had contributed to a focus by some on the conditions of the less successful individuals within the society. For these reasons, a split developed between those liberals who saw natural rights in civil rights and human rights social welfare terms, and those who continued in an exclusively property rights view.

The first group began to see government as a useful tool for freeing individuals from the external forces that bore in on them and limited them from attaining their ends, and they have used government more and more for this purpose in the 20th century. The second group, whose priorities continued to place economic rights foremost—frequently due to the conviction that this remains the best way to advance the standard of living of all in the long run, and not just for personal self-interest—have steadily resisted government "interference." Aside from the acknowledged difference in relative priority of economic and human rights, however, all remain steadfast as to the core values of individualism, limited government, and so forth. Issue positions have shifted, among the majority of liberals, to produce an almost complete reversal as to the propriety of the use of government—but there has been little or no change in the core values or in the basic commitment to the individual and the attempt to make his self-development possible. This is both indicative of the flexibility inherent in liberal thought, and part of the explanation of the present confusions in the use of the term "liberal." Let us look at some other reasons for terminological uncertainty in the course of a brief review of the contemporary status of liberalism.

V. LIBERALISM IN CONTEMPORARY USAGE

The foregoing analysis suggests the need to detach ourselves from much popular and newspaper headline usage of the terms "liberal" and "conservative." I shall reserve the latter term for political thinking that displays some of the characteristics described in the paragraphs contrasting conservatism with liberalism. The concept of liberalism, of course, must be employed with realization of the variations in issue-positions and orientations toward government that may flow from similar core values. In the usage I have suggested, contemporary advocates of laissez-faire and individualism such as Barry Goldwater are representative of the property-rights brand of liberalism and emphatically not of conservatism. I shall use the term "Manchester liberal" to refer to that variant of liberal thinking, for the historical reason that the "Manchester (England) school" of liberalism represented the most extreme and noteworthy version of such late 19th century thought. The social welfare (but still property rights-oriented and individual-oriented) variant of liberalism will be referred to as welfare-state liberalism.

Without attempting to explore thoroughly the varieties of popular usages of the terms liberalism and conservatism, some comments nevertheless seem appropriate if only to underscore the distinctiveness of the usage contemplated here. I have sought to develop a definition that is applicable to a range of thinking that includes certain distinct values and commitments. For this reason, the definition is not to be found illustrated in most specific issues or people; persons who fit equally well within the range of liberalism as I have defined it may disagree with each other and be on opposite sides of any issue, and some persons do not respond to issues in these terms at all. Here is one of the points of divergence from contemporary popular usage. For convenience, headline writers or the general public may wish to characterize any given issue as having a "liberal" and a "conservative" side to it, but the issue itself may be too specific or too narrow to engage the basic value differences that divide liberals and conservatives, and, therefore, such characterization is misleading. Many people take sides exclusively on grounds of economic self-interest, or party, or personal reactions to other supporters or opponents —and some people pay no attention at all. The issue may be really nothing more than a question of how far to go in a particular direction already marked out, and while some may wish to go slower than others, or to include a group of beneficiaries that others do not want included, these are relatively superficial differences unworthy of the label liberal or conservative.

What is needed, then, is a definition that focuses on relatively fundamental value differences and relatively sophisticated and well-articulated political thinking, a definition at a more basic level than issue-oriented journalistic terms. I think it is essential that we not be distracted by popular usages, because they will do more to confuse than to clarify. For example, if we think we must be able to relate liberalism/conservatism to a willingness to employ government, we would have to emerge with different characterizations for the same people depending on what issue we happened to be talking about. In the case of international affairs, upper class people are usually more receptive to government action such as foreign aid or technical assistance; lower class people are more inclined to believe that government should attend to business at home. In the case of civil rights action, upper classes again seem to be more supportive of government action than lower classes. But when it comes to social security, regulation of business, or other government action that aids less advantaged people, the situation is reversed and upper classes oppose while lower classes strongly favor the use of government. Any particular individual may shift back and forth in totally random fashion. If we try to apply labels of liberal or conservative according to attitudes toward the use of government, we must specify what issue is at stake, and then we still end up with the same person being a liberal one moment and a conservative the next. The only way to maintain consistency and to find utility in these concepts is to focus exclusively on basic political values and the reasons behind specific positions taken, not on the positions themselves. That means we must avoid using issues as bases of categorization unless we are sure that positions on the issue reflect basic political thinking of the fundamental level at which our definitions are operative.

Even at this level, there are some possibilities of confusion. One is that, perhaps ironically, contemporary conditions have themselves contributed to the undermining of the clarity of the distinction between liberalism and conservatism except at precisely formulated fundamental levels. Liberals, who used to be so unanimously and adamantly attached to individualism and laissez-faire, have increasingly begun to talk in terms of conscious use of government in behalf of the totality of individuals—or a collectivity. Conservatives, who used to talk of just such a collectivity under the label of "society" and who readily subscribed to the conscious use of government as an agent of the society, have increasingly employed the language of individualism and limited government in an attempt to prevent what they consider an unwise and manipulative use of government.

This situation again raises the question of whether there is utility in the use of these concepts at all. I still insist that there is, and that the question really comes down to how broad a frame of reference one wishes to take, and the level at which one intends to make his analysis. If we seek to gain perspective on American political thinking, and not to be contained by the generally shared assumptions that are central to liberalism, the concepts as defined are functional. As soon as we accept the notion that definitions should be bounded by what the main body of American political thinkers have said and written, we lose analytical perspective, judgmental capacity, and prescriptive opportunity. Should we contain ourselves to the range between Hamilton and Jefferson, in the last third of the 20th century? I think we should not. Nor am I so anxious for immediate policy-issue relevance that I am willing to forego the chance to probe as deeply as possible into the values and assumptions that set men off in various political directions in this country. We cannot understand political thinkers' motivations and purposes except by exploring their most fundamental values, for wholly different premises might lead to similar positions on specific issues.

The pervasiveness of liberalism should be evident in the selections that follow. Although there are traces of conservatism from time to time, particularly in the works of Adams, Calhoun, and Croly, and of a special brand of radicalism, particularly in the works of Paine, Thoreau, and Emerson, for the most part the authors range across the span of liberalism from nearly exclusive commitment to property rights to a considerable inclusion of human rights and equality. The evolution of liberalism to the point of accommodating pragmatically to modern problems and the use of government may be seen clearly in the last four selections, from Sumner to Berle and Means. Further analysis must await completion of these materials.

GENERAL BIBLIOGRAPHY

Anderson, Thornton. *Development of American Political Thought.* New York: Appleton-Century, 1961. A collection of 84 historical documents and writings with introductory remarks by the author.

Blau, Joseph L. *Social Theories of Jacksonian Democracy.* New York: Hafner, 1947. A collection of 26 representative essays written during the period of 1825-1850.

Boorstein, Daniel. *The Genius of American Politics.* Chicago: University of Chicago Press, 1953. A descriptive work concerning the absence of an "American Philosophy" resulting from the uniqueness of the American experience.

✗ Bryce, James. *The American Commonwealth*. New York: Capricorn, 1959. An Englishman's impression in 1888 of American political thought and expression; emphasis is
placed on elements of unity and stability.

✗ Chamberlain, John. *Farewell to Reform*. Gloucester, Mass.: Day, 1932. A study of the
rise and fall of Progressivism, arguing the weakness of liberalism as a viable force.

✗ Commager, Henry Steele. *The American Mind*. New Haven: Yale University Press, 1959.
Provides a descriptive interpretation of the American way of thought as displayed
from 1880 to 1940.

Curti, Merle. *The Growth of American Thought*. New York: Harper, 1943. A social
history of American thought with emphasis on the characteristic ideas of successive
eras from Colonial to mid-20th century America.

Faulkner, Harold Underwood. *American Political and Social History*. New York: Appleton-
Century, 1948. A one-volume survey of American political history with coverage of
the less dominant phases included.

Fish, Carl. *The Rise of the Common Man*. New York: Macmillan, 1935. A social interpretation of Jacksonian Democracy seen as a reaction against the aristocratic heritage
of the United States.

Gabriel, Ralph Henry. *The Course of American Democratic Thought*. New York: Ronald
Press, 1940. An evolutionary history of American intellectual thought from 1815
to 1940.

Grimes, Alan Pendleton. *American Political Thought*. New York: Holt, Rinehart, and
Winston, 1960. A survey of American political development with special regard to
the relation of American political thought to Western political philosophy.

✗ Hartz, Louis. *The Liberal Tradition in America*. New York: Harcourt, 1955. America's
lack of an aristocratic and feudal tradition is the backdrop in this description of the
liberal influence in American history.

Hicks, John. *The Populist Revolt*. Minneapolis: University of Minnesota Press, 1931. An
analysis of the Populist Movement and the resulting political contributions of governmental regulation and popular rule.

✗ Hofstadter, Richard. *The American Political Tradition*. New York: Knopf, 1948. A series
of 12 essays critically examining leading representatives of major American political
movements.

Jacobson, J. Mark. *The Development of American Political Thought*. New York: Century,
1932. A documentary history of American political thought with emphasis placed on
relating theory to reality.

Josephson, Matthew. *The Politicos*. New York: Harcourt, 1938. A critical but comprehensive analysis of the political system during the Gilded Age.

✝ Mason, Alpheus Thomas. *Free Government in the Making*. New York: Oxford University Press, 1956. A collection of 153 original writings in the development of
American political thought with introductory remarks by the author.

Merriam, Charles Edward. *A History of American Political Theories*. New York: Macmillan, 1928. A description and analysis of the major political theories from Colonial
to World War I America in relation to the environmental forces under which they
were formulated.

✗ Minar, David W. *Ideas and Politics*. Homewood, Ill.: The Dorsey Press, 1964. A survey of
American political development with emphasis on relating political thought to institutions and action.

Parrington, Vernon. *Main Currents in American Thought*. New York: Harcourt, 1930. A three-volume work relating writings of leading American figures to the conflicts in American life with emphasis on the tension between agrarianism and capitalism.

Rossiter, Clinton, *Conservatism in America*. New York: Knopf, 1955. A study of the occasions, substance, and role of conservative political thinking in the U.S., concluding that true conservatism is hard to find in this context.

Rossiter, Clinton. *Seedtime of the Republic*. New York: Harcourt, 1953. An historical approach to the men and events that formulated the political ideas of Colonial and Revolutionary America.

de Tocqueville, Alexis. *Democracy in America*. New York: Knopf, 1963. A Frenchman's view in 1834 of the American democratic system with special regard to its potential for universal application.

Turner, Frederick Jackson. *The Frontier in American History*. New York: Holt, 1920. A classic study of the frontier's influence on the creation of a uniquely American way of life.

Wiltse, Charles Maurice. *The Jeffersonian Tradition in American Democracy*. Chapel Hill: University of North Carolina Press, 1935. The Jeffersonian system; an analysis of its origins, applications, and contribution to the American political process.

CHAPTER 2

Thomas Paine

Norfolk!

THOMAS Paine (1737-1809), born in Thetford, England, to a poor Quaker corset maker, went to school until the age of thirteen, when poverty made it necessary to apprentice him to the family trade. At nineteen he left home and, for the next twenty years, Paine moved from town to town dabbling at various trades.

In 1774, Paine decided to try the new world; he arrived in Philadelphia and very quickly fell into journalism. His first year's work ranged from articles on inventions to the abolition of slavery.

Common Sense made its appearance in January 1776 as an anonymous, two-shilling pamphlet; its success was amazing. It sold over 120,000 copies in a few months. Paine's authorship became known very quickly.

In mid-1776 Paine enlisted in the army and, in December, he wrote the first section of the *Crisis,* which begins with the famous words "These are the times that try men's souls. . . . " Eleven other parts to the *Crisis* appeared in the course of the war.

Paine filled several government posts from 1777 to 1780. In 1781, he went to France for several months in search of financial aid for the revolution. For the next five years, he lived in New Jersey, writing and working on various inventions. In 1786, he published *Dissertations on Government, The Affairs of the Bank,* and *Paper Money.*

Paine's restless nature led him to return to Europe in 1787. Burk's condemnation of the French Revolution in 1790 prompted Paine to reply, in early 1791, with his first part of the *Rights of Man.* The second part followed in 1792. The same year, French citizenship was conferred upon Paine by the Assembly; by late 1793, however, the political scene had changed so much that Paine was arrested and imprisoned as a citizen of a country at war with France. During his imprisonment, Paine composed part of the *Age of Reason.*

Released from prison in late 1794, Paine continued to live in Paris. During this period, he published *Dissertation on First-Prin-*

ciples of Government (1795), "Agrarian Justice" (1797), and *The Letter to George Washington* (1796).

In 1802 Paine returned to America. The last seven years of his life were spent in poverty, declining health, and social ostracism. He died in New York in June 1809.

From Common Sense

OF THE ORIGIN AND DESIGN OF GOVERNMENT IN GENERAL, WITH CONCISE REMARKS ON THE ENGLISH CONSTITUTION

Some writers have so confounded society with government as to leave little or no distinction between them, whereas they are not only different but have different origins. Society is produced by our wants, and government by our wickedness; the former promotes our happiness *positively* by uniting our affections, the latter *negatively* by restraining our vices. The one encourages intercourse, the other creates distinctions. The first is a patron, the last a punisher.

Society in every state is a blessing, but government even in its best state is but a necessary evil, in its worst state an intolerable one; for when we suffer or are exposed to the same miseries *by a government* which we might expect in a country *without government,* our calamity is heightened by reflecting that we furnish the means by which we suffer. Government, like dress, is the badge of lost innocence; the palaces of kings are built on the ruins of the bowers of paradise. For were the impulses of conscience clear, uniform, and irresistibly obeyed, man would need no other lawgiver; but that not being the case, he finds it necessary to surrender up a part of his property to furnish means for the protection of the rest, and this he is induced to do by the same prudence which in every other case advises him out of two evils to choose the least. Wherefore, security being the true design and end of government, it unanswerably follows that whatever form thereof appears most likely to ensure it to us, with the least expense and greatest benefit, is preferable to all others.

In order to gain a clear and just idea of the design and end of government, let us suppose a small number of persons settled in some sequestered part of the earth, unconnected with the rest; they will then represent the first peopling of any country, or of the world. In this state of natural liberty, society will be their first thought. A thousand motives will excite them thereto; the strength of one man is so unequal to his wants and his mind so unfitted for perpetual solitude that he is soon obliged to seek assistance and relief of another, who in his turn requires the same. Four or five united would be able to raise a tolerable dwelling in the midst of a wilderness, but one might labor out the common period of life without accomplishing anything; when he had felled his timber, he could not remove it, nor erect it after it was removed; hunger in the meantime would urge him from his work and every different want call him a different way. Disease, nay even misfortune, would be death; for though neither might be mortal, yet either would disable him from living and reduce him to a state in which he might rather be said to perish than to die.

Thus necessity, like a gravitating power, would soon form our newly arrived emigrants into society, the reciprocal blessings of which would supersede and render the obligations of law and government unnecessary while they remained perfectly just to each other; but as nothing but Heaven is impregnable to vice, it will unavoidably happen that in proportion as they surmount the first difficulties of emigration, which bound them together in a common cause, they will begin to relax in their duty and attachment to each other, and this remissness will point out the necessity of establishing some form of government to supply the defect of moral virtue.

Some convenient tree will afford them a statehouse, under the branch of which the whole colony may assemble to deliberate on public matters. It is more than probable that their first laws will have the title only of regulations and be enforced by no other penalty than public disesteem. In this first parliament every man by natural right will have a seat.

But as the colony increases, the public concerns will increase likewise, and the distance at which the members may be separated will render it too inconvenient for all of them to meet on every occasion as at first when their number was small, their habitations near, and the public concerns few and trifling. This will point out the convenience of their consenting to leave the legislative part to be managed by a select number chosen from the whole body, who are supposed to have the same concerns at stake which those have who appointed them and who will act in the same manner as the whole body would act were they present. If the colony continue increasing, it will become necessary to augment the number of representatives; and that the interest of every part of the colony may be attended to, it will be found best to divide the whole into convenient parts, each part sending its proper number; and that the *elected* might never form to themselves an interest separate from the *electors,* prudence will point out the propriety of having elections often, because as the elected might by that means return and mix again with the general body of the *electors* in a few months, their fidelity to the public will be secured by the prudent reflection of not making a rod for themselves. And as this frequent interchange will establish a common interest with every part of the community,

they will mutually and naturally support each other, and on this (not on the unmeaning name of King) depends the *strength of government and the happiness of the governed.*

Here then is the origin and rise of government, namely, a mode rendered necessary by the inability of moral virtue to govern the world; here too is the design and end of government, viz., freedom and security. And however our eyes may be dazzled with show or our ears deceived by sound, however prejudice may warp our wills or interest darken our understanding, the simple voice of nature and reason will say it is right.

I draw my idea of the form of government from a principle in nature which no art can overturn, viz., that the more simple anything is, the less liable it is to be disordered and the easier repaired when disordered; and with this maxim in view I offer a few remarks on the so much boasted constitution of England. That it was noble for the dark and slavish times in which it was erected is granted. When the world was overrun with tyranny, the least remove therefrom was a glorious rescue. But that it is imperfect, subject to convulsions, and incapable of producing what it seems to promise is easily demonstrated.

Absolute governments (though the disgrace of human nature) have this advantage with them: that they are simple; if the people suffer, they know the head from which their suffering springs, know likewise the remedy, and are not bewildered by a variety of causes and cures. But the constitution of England is so exceedingly complex that the nation may suffer for years together without being able to discover in which part the fault lies; some will say in one and some in another, and every political physician will advise a different medicine.

I know it is difficult to get over local or longstanding prejudices; yet if we will suffer ourselves to examine the component parts of the English constitution, we shall find them to be the base remains of two ancient tyrannies, compounded with some new republican materials:

First, the remains of monarchical tyranny in the person of the king.

Secondly, the remains of aristocratical tyranny in the persons of the peers.

Thirdly, the new republican materials in the persons of the Commons, on whose virtue depends the freedom of England.

The two first, by being hereditary, are independent of the people; wherefore, in a *constitutional sense,* they contribute nothing toward the freedom of the state.

To say that the constitution of England is a *union* of three powers, reciprocally *checking* each other, is farcical; either the words have no meaning or they are flat contradictions.

To say that the Commons is a check upon the kind presupposes two things:

First, that the king is not to be trusted without being looked after, or, in other words, that a thirst for absolute power is the natural disease of monarchy.

Secondly, that the Commons, by being appointed for that purpose, are either wiser or more worthy of confidence than the crown.

But as the same constitution which gives the Commons a power to check the king by withholding the supplies gives afterward the king a power to check the Commons by empowering him to reject their other bills, it again supposes that the king is wiser than those whom it has already supposed to be wiser than him. A mere absurdity!

There is something exceedingly ridiculous in the composition of monarchy; it first excludes a man from the means of information, yet empowers him to act in cases where the highest judgment is required. The state of a king shuts him from the world, yet the business of a king requires him to know it thoroughly; wherefore the different parts, by unnaturally opposing and destroying each other, prove the whole character to be absurd and useless. . . .

OF MONARCHY AND HEREDITARY SUCCESSION

. . . To the evil of monarchy we have added that of hereditary succession; and as the first is a degradation and lessening of ourselves, so the second, claimed as a matter of right, is an insult and imposition on posterity. For all men being originally equals, no one by birth could have a right to set up his own family in perpetual preference to all others forever; and though himself might deserve some desent degree of honors of his co-contemporaries, yet his descendants might be far too unworthy to inherit them. One of the strongest natural proofs of the folly of hereditary right in kings is that nature disapproves it; otherwise she would not so frequently turn it into ridicule by giving mankind an *ass for a lion.*

Secondly, as no man at first could posess any other public honors than were bestowed upon him, so the givers of these honors could have no power to give away the right of posterity, and though they might say "We choose you for our head," they could not without manifest injustice to their children say "that your children and your children's children shall reign over ours forever." Because such an unwise, unjust, unnatural compact might (perhaps) in the next succession put them under the government of a rogue or a fool. Most wise men in their private sentiments have ever treated hereditary right with contempt; yet it is on of those evils which when once established is not easily removed; many submit from fear, others from superstition, and the more powerful part shares with the king the plunder of the rest.

This is supposing the present race of kings in the world to have had an honorable origin; whereas it is more than probable that, could we take off the dark covering of antiquity and trace them to their first rise, that we should find the first of them nothing better than the principal ruffian of some restless gang, whose savage manners or pre-eminence in subtilty obtained him the title of chief among plunderers and who, by increasing in power and extending his depredations, overawed the quiet and defenseless to purchase their safety by frequent contributions. Yet his electors could have no idea of giving hereditary right to his descendants, because such a perpetual exclusion of themselves was incompatible with the free and unrestrained principles they professed to live by. Wherefore hereditary succession in the early ages of monarchy could not take place as a matter of claim, but as something casual or complemental; but as few or no records were extant in those days, the traditionary history stuffed with fables, it was very easy, after the lapse of a few generations, to trump up some superstitious tale conveniently times, Mahometlike, to cram hereditary right down the throats of the vulgar. Perhaps the disorders which threatened or seemed to threaten, on the decease of a leader and the choice of a new one (for elections among ruffians could not be very orderly) induced many at first to favor hereditary pretensions; by which means it happened, as it has happened since, that what at first was submitted to as a convenience was afterward claimed as a right. . . .

But it is not so much the absurdity as the evil of hereditary succession which concerns mankind. Did it insure a race of good and wise men, it would have the seal of divine authority, but as it opens a door to the *foolish* and *wicked,* and the *improper,* it has in it the nature of oppression. Men who look upon themselves born to reign and others to obey soon grow insolent. Selected from the rest of mankind, their minds are early poisoned by importance; and the world they act in differs so materially from the world at large that they have but little opportunity of knowing its true interests and, when they succeed to the government, are frequently the most ignorant and unfit of any throughout the dominions. . . .

If we inquire into the business of a king, we shall find that in some coun-tries they have none; and after sauntering away their lives without pleasure to themselves or advantage to the nation, withdraw from the scene and leave their successors to tread the same idle round. In absolute monarchies the whole weight of business, civil and military, lies on the king; the children of Israel in their request for a king urged this plea, "that he may judge us, and go out before us and fight our battles." But in the countries where he is neither a judge nor a general, as in England, a man would be puzzled to know what *is* his business. . . .

In England a king has little more to do than to make war and give away places, which, in plain terms, is to impoverish the nation and set it together by the ears. A pretty business indeed for a man to be allowed eight hundred thousand sterling a year for, and worshiped into the bargain! Of more worth, is one honest man to society, and in the sight of God, than all the crowned ruffians that ever lived.

THOUGHTS ON THE PRESENT STATE OF AMERICAN AFFAIRS

In the following pages I offer nothing more than simple facts, plain arguments, and common sense; and have no other preliminaries to settle with the reader than that he will divest himself of prejudice and prepossession, and suffer his reason and his feelings to determine for themselves; that he will put on, or rather that he will not put off, the true character of a man, and generously enlarge his views beyond the present day.

Volumes have been written on the subject of the struggle between England and America. Men of all ranks have embarked in the controversy, from different motives and with various designs; but all have been ineffectual, and the period of debate is closed. Arms as the last resource decide the contest; the appeal was the choice of the king, and the continent has accepted the challenge. . . .

The sun never shined on a cause of greater worth. 'Tis not the affair of a city, a county, a province, or a kingdom, but of a continent—of at least one-eighth part of the habitable globe. 'Tis not the concern of a day, a year, or an age; posterity are virtually involved in the contest, and will be more or less affected even to the end time by the proceedings now. Now is the seed-time of continental union, faith, and honor. The least fracture now will be like a name engraved with the point of a pin on the tender rind of a young oak; the wound would enlarge with the tree, and posterity read it in full-grown characters.

By referring the matter from argument to arms, a new era for politics is struck— a new method of thinking has arisen. All plans, proposals, etc. prior to the nineteenth of April, i.e., to the commencement of hostilities, are like the almanacs of the last year, which, though proper then, are superseded and useless now. Whatever was advanced by the advocates on either side of the question then terminated in one and the same point, viz., a union with Great Britain; the only difference between the parties was the method of effecting it—the one proposing force, the other friendship; but it has so far happened that the first has failed, and the second has withdrawn her influence.

As much has been said of the advantages of reconciliation, which, like an agreeable dream, has passed away and left us as we were, it is but right that we should examine the contrary side of the argument and inquire into some of the many material injuries which these colonies sustain, and always will sustain, by being connected with and dependent on Great Britain. To examine that connection and dependence on the principles of nature and common sense; to see what we have to trust to, if separated, and what we are to expect, if dependent. . . .

I challenge the warmest advocate for reconciliation to show a single advantage that this continent can reap by being connected with Great Britain. I repeat the challenge; not a single advantage is derived. Our corn will fetch its price in any market in Europe, and our im-

ported goods must be paid for, buy them where we will.

But the injuries and disadvantages we sustain by that connection are without number, and our duty to mankind at large, as well as to ourselves, instruct us to renounce the alliance; because any submission to or dependence on Great Britain tends directly to involve this continent in European wars and quarrels and sets us at variance with nations who would otherwise seek our friendship and against whom we have neither anger nor complaint. As Europe is our market for trade, we ought to form no partial connection with any part of it. It is the true interest of America to steer clear of European connections, which she never can do while, by her dependence on Britain, she is made the makeweight in the scale of British politics.

Europe is too thickly planted with kingdoms to be long at peace; and whenever a war breaks out between England and any foreign power, the trade of America goes to ruin *because of her connection with Britain*. The next war may not turn out like the last; and should it not, the advocates for reconciliation now will be wishing for separation then, because neutrality in that case would be a safer convoy than a man-of-war. Everything that is right or natural pleads for separation. The blood of the slain, the weeping voice of nature cries, " '*Tis time to part.*" . . .

Men of passive tempers look somewhat lightly over the offenses of Great Britain and, still hoping for the best, are apt to call out, "Come, come, we shall be friends again for all this." But examine the passions and feelings of mankind, bring the doctrine of reconciliation to the touchstone of nature, and then tell me whether you can hereafter love, honor, and faithfully serve the power that has carried fire and sword into your land? If you cannot do all these, then are you only deceiving yourselves, and by your delay bringing ruin upon posterity. Your future connection with Britain, whom you can neither love nor honor, will be forced and unnatural, and being formed only on the plan of present convenience will, in a little time, fall into a relapse more wretched than the first. But if you say you still can pass the violations over, then I ask, has your house been burned? Has your property been destroyed before your face? Are your wife and children destitute of a bed to lie on or bread to live on? Have you lost a parent or a child by their hands, and yourself the ruined and wretched survivor? If you have not, then are you not a judge of those who have. But if you have and can still shake hands with the murderers, then are you unworthy the name of husband, father, friend, or lover; and whatever may be your rank or title in life, you have the heart of a coward and the spirit of a sycophant.

This is not inflaming or exaggerating matters, but trying them by those feelings and affections which nature justifies and without which we should be incapable of discharging the social duties of life or enjoying the felicities of it. I mean not to exhibit horror for the purpose of provoking revenge, but to awaken us from fatal and unmanly slumbers, that we may pursue determinately some fixed object. It is not in the power of Britain or Europe to conquer America, if she does not conquer herself by delay and timidity. The present winter is worth an age if rightly employed, but if lost or neglected the whole continent will partake of the misfortune; and there is no punishment which that man will not deserve, be he who or what or where he will, that may be the means of sacrificing a season so precious and useful. . . .

A government of our own is our natural right; and when a man seriously reflects on the precariousness of human affairs, he will become convinced that it is infinitely wiser and safer to form a Constitution of our own in a cool, deliberate manner while we have it in our power than to trust such an interesting event to time and chance. If we omit it now, some Massanello may hereafter arise, who laying hold of popular disquietudes, may collect together the desparate and the discontented, and by assuming to themselves the powers of government may sweep away the liberties of the continent like a deluge. Should the government of America return again into the hands of Britain, the tottering situation of things will be a temptation for some desperate adventurer to try his fortune, and in such a case what relief can Britain give? Ere she could hear the news, the fatal business might be done, and ourselves suffering like the wretched Britons under the oppression of the conqueror. Ye that oppose independence now, ye know not what ye do; yet are opening a door to eternal tyranny by keeping vacant the seat of government. There are thousands and tens of thousands who would think it glorious to expel from the continent that barbarous and hellish power which has stirred up the Indians and Negroes to destroy us; the cruelty has a double guilt: it is dealing brutally by us and treacherously by them.

To talk of friendship with those in whom our reason forbids us to have faith and our affections, wounded through a thousand pores, instruct us to detest is madness and folly. Every day wears out the little remains of kindred between us and them; and can there be any reason to hope that, as the relationship expires, the affection will increase, or that we shall agree better when we have ten times more and greater concerns to quarrel over than ever?

Ye that tell us of harmony and reconciliation, can ye restore to us the time that is past? Can ye give to prostitution its former innocence? Neither can ye reconcile Britain and America. The last cord now is broken, the people of England are presenting addresses against us. There are injuries which nature cannot forgive; she would cease to be nature if she did. As well can the lover forgive the ravisher of his mistress as the continent forgive the murderers of Britain. The Almighty has implanted in us these unextinguishable feelings for good and wise purposes. They are the guardians of his image in our hearts. They distinguish us from the herd of common animals.

The social compact would dissolve and justice be extirpated [from] the earth, or have only a casual existence, were we callous to the touches of affection. The robber and the murderer would often escape unpunished did not the injuries which our tempers sustain provoke us into justice.

O ye that love mankind! Ye that dare oppose not only the tyranny but the tyrant, stand forth! Every spot of the Old World is overrun with oppression. Freedom has been hunted round the globe. Asia and Africa have long expelled her. Europe regards her like a stranger, and England has given her warning to depart. O! receive the fugitive, and prepare in time an asylum for mankind.

The American Crisis I

These are the times that try men's souls. The summer soldier and the sunshine patriot will, in this crisis, shrink from the service of their country, but he that stands it *now* deserves the love and thanks of man and woman. Tyranny, like hell, is not easily conquered; yet we have this consolation with us that, the harder the conflict, the more glorious the triumph. What we obtain too cheap, we esteem too lightly; it is dearness only that gives everything its value. Heaven knows how to put a proper price upon its goods, and it would be strange indeed if so celestial an article as freedom should not be highly rated. Britain, with an army to enforce her tyranny, has declared that she has a right *(not only to tax)* but *to bind us in all cases whatsoever;* and if being *bound in that manner* is not slavery, then is there not such a thing as slavery upon earth. Even the expression is impious, for so unlimited a power can belong only to God.

Whether the independence of the continent was declared too soon or delayed too long I will not now enter into as an argument; my own simple opinion is that, had it been eight months earlier, it would have been much better. We did not make a proper use of last winter, neither could we while we were in a dependent state. However, the fault, if it were one, was all our own; we have none to blame but ourselves. But no great deal is lost yet. All that Howe has been doing for this month past is rather a ravage than a conquest, which the spirit of the Jerseys, a year ago, would have quickly repulsed, and which time and a little resolution will soon recover.

I have as little superstition in me as any man living, but my secret opinion has ever been and still is that God Almighty will not give up a people to military destruction or leave them unsupportedly to perish who have so earnestly and so repeatedly sought to avoid the calamities of war by every decent method which wisdom could invent. Neither have I so much of the infidel in me as to suppose that He has relinquished the government of the world and given us up to the care of devils, and as I do not I cannot see on what grounds the King of Britain can look up to heaven for help against us; a common murderer, a highwayman, or a housebreaker has as good a pretense as he. . . .

. . . I turn with the warm ardor of a friend to those who have nobly stood and are yet determined to stand the matter out; I call not upon a few but upon all— not on *this* state or *that* state, but on *every* state—up and help us, lay your shoulders to the wheel, better have too much force than too little when so great an object is at stake. Let it be told to the future world that in the depth of winter, when nothing but hope and virtue could survive, that the city and the country, alarmed at one common danger, came forth to meet and to repulse it. Say not that thousands are gone, turn out your tens of thousands; throw not the burden of the day upon Providence, but "show your faith by your works," that God may bless you. It matters not where you live or what rank of life you hold, the evil or the blessing will reach you all. The far and the near, the home counties and the back, the rich and the poor will suffer or rejoice alike. The heart that feels not now is dead; the blood of his children will curse his cowardice who shrinks back at a time when a little might have saved the whole and made *them* happy. I love the man that can smile in trouble, that can gather strength from distress and grow brave by reflection. "Tis the business of little minds to shrink, but he whose heart is firm and whose conscience approves his conduct will pursue his principles unto death." My own line of reasoning is to myself as straight and clear as a ray of light. Not all the treasures of the world, so far as I believe, could have induced me to support an offensive war, for I think it murder; but if a thief breaks into my house, burns and destroys my property, and kills or threatens to kill me or those that are in it and to "bind me in all cases whatsoever" to his absolute will, am I to suffer it? What signifies it to me whether he who does it is a king or a common man, my countryman or not my countryman; whether it be done by an individual villain or an army of them? If we reason to the root of things, we shall find no difference; neither can any just cause be assigned why we should punish in the one case and pardon in the other. Let them call me rebel and welcome, I feel no concern from it; but I should suffer the misery of devils were I to make a whore of my soul by swearing allegiance to one whose character is that of a sottish, stupid, stubborn, worthless, brutish man. I conceive likewise a horrid idea in receiving mercy from a being who, at the last day, shall be shrieking to the rocks and mountains to cover him and fleeing with terror from the orphan, the widow, and the slain of America.

There are cases which cannot be overdone by language, and this is one. There are persons, too, who see not the full extent of the evil which threatens them; they solace themselves with hopes that the enemy, if he succeed, will be merciful. It is the madness of folly to expect mercy from those who have refused to do justice; and even mercy, where conquest is the object, is only a trick of war; the cunning of the fox is as murderous as the violence of the wolf, and we ought to guard equally against both.

The American Crisis XIII

THOUGHTS ON THE PEACE AND THE PROBABLE ADVANTAGES THEREOF

"The times that tried men's souls" are over, and the greatest and completest revolution the world ever knew gloriously and happily accomplished.

But to pass from the extremes of danger to safety, from the tumult of war to the tranquillity of peace, though sweet in contemplation, requires a gradual composure of the senses to receive it. Even calmness has the power of stunning, when it opens too instantly upon us. The long and ranging hurricane that should cease in a moment would leave us in a state rather of wonder than enjoyment, and some moments of recollection must pass before we could be capable of tasting the felicity of repose. There are but few instances in which the mind is fitted for sudden transitions; it takes in its pleasures by reflection and comparison, and those must have time to act before the relish for new scenes is complete.

In the present case, the mighty magnitude of the object, the various uncertainties of fate it has undergone, the numerous and complicated dangers we have suffered or escaped, the eminence we now stand on, and the vast prospect before us must all conspire to impress us with contemplation.

To see it in our power to make a world happy, to teach mankind the art of being so, to exhibit on the theater of the universe a character hitherto unknown, and to have, as it were, a new creation entrusted to our hands are honors that command reflection and can neither be too highly estimated nor too gratefully received.

In this pause then of recollection, while the storm is ceasing and the long-agitated mind vibrating to a rest, let us look back on the scenes we have passed and learn from experience what is yet to be done.

Never, I say, had a country so many openings to happiness as this. Her setting out in life, like the rising of a fair morning, was unclouded and promising. Her cause was good. Her principles just and liberal. Her temper serene and firm. Her conduct regulated by the nicest steps, and everything about her wore the mark of honor. It is not every country (perhaps there is not another in the world) that can boast so fair an origin. Even the first settlement of America corresponds with the character of the revolution. Rome, once the proud mistress of the universe, was originally a band of ruffians. Plunder and rapine made her rich, and her oppression of millions made her great. But America need never be ashamed to tell her birth, nor relate the stages by which she rose to empire.

The remembrance, then, of what is past, if it operates rightly, must inspire her with the most laudable of all ambition, that of adding to the fair fame she began with. The world has seen her great in adversity; struggling, without a thought of yielding beneath accumulated difficulties, bravely, nay proudly, encountering distress; and rising in resolution as the storm increased. All this is justly due to her, for her fortitude has merited the character. Let then the world see that she can bear prosperity and that her honest virtue in time of peace is equal to the bravest virtue in time of war.

She is now descending to the scenes of quiet and domestic life. Not beneath the cypress shade of disappointment, but to enjoy in her own land and under her own vine the sweet of her labors and the reward of her toil. In this situation, may she never forget that a fair national reputation is of as much importance as independence. That it possesses a charm that wins upon the world and makes even enemies civil. That it gives a dignity which is often superior to power, and commands reverence where pomp and splendor fail.

It would be a circumstance ever to be lamented and never to be forgotten were a single blot, from any cause whatever, suffered to fall on a revolution which to the end of time must be an honor to the age that accomplished it, and which has contributed more to enlighten the world and diffuse a spirit of freedom and liberality among mankind than any human event (if this may be called one) that ever preceded it.

It is not among the least of the calamities of a long-continued war that it unhinges the mind from those nice sensations which at other times appear so amiable. The continual spectacle of woe blunts the finer feelings, and the necessity of bearing with the sight renders it familiar. In like manner are many of the moral obligations of society weakened, till the custom of acting by necessity becomes an apology where it is truly a crime. Yet let but a nation conceive rightly of its character, and it will be chastely just in protecting it. None ever began with a fairer than America, and none can be under a greater obligation to preserve it. . . .

It is with confederated states as with individuals in society: something must be yielded up to make the whole secure. In this view of things we gain by what we give and draw an annual interest greater than the capital. I ever feel myself hurt when I hear the union, that great palladium of our liberty and safety, the least irreverently spoken of. It is the most sacred thing in the constitution of America and that which every man should be most proud and tender of. Our citizenship in the United States is our national character. Our citizenship in any particular state is only our local distinction. By the latter we are known at home, by the former to the world.

Our great title is *Americans;* our inferior one varies with the place.

So far as my endeavors could go, they have all been directed to conciliate the affections, unite the interests, and draw and keep the mind of the country together; and the better to assist in this foundation work of the revolution. I have avoided all places of profit or office, either in the state I live in or in the United States, kept myself at a distance from all parties and party connections, and even disregarded all private and inferior concerns; and when we take into view the great work which we have gone through and feel, as we ought to feel, the just importance of it, we shall then see that the little wranglings and indecent contentions of personal parley are as dishonorable to our characters as they are injurious to our repose.

It was the cause of America that made me an author. The force with which it struck my mind and the dangerous condition the country appeared to me in, by courting an impossible and an unnatural reconciliation with those who were determined to reduce her, instead of striking out into the only line that could cement and save her—*a declaration of independence*—made it impossible for me, feeling as I did, to be silent; and if, in the course of more than seven years, I have rendered her any service, I have likewise added something to the reputation of literature by freely and disinterestedly employing it in the great cause of mankind and showing that there may be genius without prostitution.

Independence always appeared to me practicable and probable, provided the sentiment of the country could be formed and held to the object; and there is no instance in the world where a people so extended and wedded to former habits of thinking, and under such a variety of circumstances were so instantly and effectually pervaded by a turn in politics as in the case of independence, and who supported their opinion, undiminished, through such a succession of good and ill fortune till they crowned it with success.

But as the scenes of war are closed and every man preparing for home and happier times, I therefore take my leave of the subject. I have most sincerely followed it from beginning to end and through all its turns and windings; and whatever country I may hereafter be in, I shall always feel an honest pride at the part I have taken and acted, and a gratitude to nature and providence for putting it in my power to be of some use to mankind.

From Rights of Man— Part One

There never did, there never will, and there never can exist a Parliament, or any description of men, or any generation of men, in any country, possessed of the right or the power of binding and controlling posterity to the "end of time," or of commanding forever how the world shall be governed or who shall govern it; and therefore all such clauses, acts, or declarations by which the makers of them attempt to do what they have neither the right nor the power to do, nor the power to execute, are in themselves null and void.

Every age and generation must be as free to act for itself, *in all cases,* as the ages and generation which preceded it. The vanity and presumption of governing beyond the grave is the most ridiculous and insolent of all tyrannies.

Man has no property in man; neither has any generation a property in the generations which are to follow. The Parliament or the people of 1688, or of any other period, had no more right to dispose of the people of the present day, or to bind or to control them *in any shape whatever,* than the Parliament or the people of the present day have to dispose of, bind, or control those who are to live a hundred or a thousand years hence.

Every generation is and must be competent to all the purposes which its occasions require. It is the living, and not the dead, that are to be accommodated. When man ceases to be, his power and his wants cease with him; and having no longer any participation in the concerns of this world, he has no longer any authority in directing who shall be its governors, or how its government shall be organized or how administered.

I am not contending for nor against any form of government, nor for nor against any party here or elsewhere. That which a whole nation chooses to do it has a right to do. Mr. Burke says, No. Where then does the right exist? I am contending for the rights of the *living,* and against their being willed away and controlled and contracted for by the manuscript assumed authority of the dead; and Mr. Burke is contending for the authority of the dead over the rights and freedom of the living.

There was a time when kings disposed of their crowns by will upon their death-beds and consigned the people, like beasts of the field, to whatever successor they appointed. This is now so exploded as scarcely to be remembered and so monstrous as hardly to be believed. But the parliamentary clauses upon which Mr. Burke builds his political church are of the same nature. . . .

The error of those who reason by precedents drawn from antiquity, respecting the rights of man, is that they do not go far enough into antiquity. They do not go the whole way. They stop in some of the intermediate stages of a hundred or a thousand years and produce what was then done as a rule for the present day. This is no authority at all.

If we travel still further into antiquity, we shall find a directly contrary opinion and practice prevailing; and if antiquity is to be authority, a thousand such authorities may be produced, successively contradicting each other; but if we proceed on, we shall at least come out right; we shall come to the time when man came from the hand of his Maker. What was he then? Man. Man was his high and only title, and a higher cannot be given him. But of titles I shall speak hereafter.

We have now arrived at the origin of man and at the origin of his rights. As to the manner in which the world has been governed from that day to this, it is no further any concern of ours than to make a proper use of the errors or the improvements which the history of it presents. Those who lived a hundred or a thousand years ago were then moderns as we are now. They had *their* ancients, and those ancients had others, and we also shall be ancients in our turn.

If the mere name of antiquity is to govern in the affairs of life, the people who are to live a hundred or a thousand years hence may as well take us for a precedent, as we make a precedent of those who lived a hundred or a thousand years ago.

The fact is that portions of antiquity, by proving everything, established nothing. It is authority against authority all the way, till we come to the divine origin of the rights of man at the creation. Here our inquiries find a resting place and our reason finds a home. . . .

The illuminating and divine principle of the equal rights of man (for it has its origin from the Maker of man) relates not only to the living individuals, but to generations of men succeeding each other. Every generation is equal in rights to the generations which preceded it, by the same rule that every individual is born equal in rights with his contemporary.

Every history of the creation and every traditionary account, whether from the lettered or unlettered world, however they may vary in their opinion or belief of certain particulars, all agree in establishing one point, *the unity of man;* by which I mean that men are all of *one degree,* and consequently that all men are born equal and with equal natural rights, in the same manner as if posterity had been continued by *creation* instead of *generation,* the latter being only the mode by which the former is carried forward; and consequently every child born into the world must be considered as deriving its existence from God. The world is as new to him as it was to the first man that existed, and his natural right in it is of the same kind.

The Mosaic account of the creation, whether taken as divine authority or merely historical, is fully up to this point, *the unity or equality of man.* The expressions admit of no controversy. "And God said, let us make man in our own image. In the image of God created he him; male and female created he them." The distinction of sexes is pointed out, but no other distinction is even implied. If this be not divine authority, it is at least historical authority and shows that the equality of man, so far from being a modern doctrine, is the oldest upon record. . . .

Hitherto we have spoken only (and that but in part) of the natural rights of man. We have now to consider the civil rights of man and to show how the one originates from the other. Man did not enter into society to become *worse* than he was before, nor to have fewer rights than he had before, but to have those rights better secured. His natural rights are the foundation of all his civil rights. But in order to pursue this distinction with more precision, it is necessary to make the different qualities of natural and civil rights.

A few words will explain this. Natural rights are those which appertain to man in right of his existence. Of this kind are all the intellectual rights, or rights of the mind, and also all those rights of acting as an individual for his own comfort and happiness which are not injurious to the natural rights of others. Civil rights are those which appertain to man in right of his being a member of society.

Every civil right has for its foundation some natural right pre-existing in the individual, but to the enjoyment of which his individual power is not in all cases sufficiently competent. Of this kind are all those which relate to security and protection.

From this short review it will be easy to distinguish between that class of natural rights which man retains after entering into society and those which he throws into the common stock as a member of society.

The natural rights which he retains are all those in which the *power* to execute is as perfect in the individual as the right itself. Among this class, as was before mentioned, are all the intellectual rights, or rights of the mind; consequently religion is one of those rights.

The natural rights which are not retained are all those in which, though the right is perfect in the individual, the power to execute them is defective. They answer not his purpose. A man, by natural rights, has a right to judge in his own cause, and so far as the right of the mind is concerned he never surrenders it; but what avails it him to judge if he has not power to redress? He therefore deposits his right in the common stock of society and takes the arm of society, of which he is a part, in preference and in addition to his own. Society *grants* him nothing. Every man is proprietor in society and draws on the capital as a matter of right.

From these premises, two or three certain conclusions will follow:

First, that every civil right grows out of a natural right; or, in other words, is a natural right exchanged.

Secondly, that civil power, properly considered as such, is made up of the aggregate of that class of the natural rights of man which becomes defective in the individual in point of power and answers not his purpose, but when collected to a focus becomes competent to the purpose of everyone.

Thirdly, that the power produced from the aggregate of natural rights, imperfect in power in the individual, cannot be applied to invade the natural rights which are retained in the individual and in which the power to execute is as perfect as the right itself.

We have now, in a few words, traced man from a natural individual to a member of society and shown, or endeavored to show, the quality of the natural rights retained and those which are exchanged for civil rights. Let us now apply those principles to governments.

In casting our eyes over the world, it is extremely easy to distinguish the governments which have arisen out of society, or out of the social compact, from those which have not; but to place this in a clearer light than what a single glance may afford, it will be proper to take a review of the several sources from which the governments have arisen and on which they have been founded.

They may be all comprehended under three heads. *First,* superstition. *Secondly,* power. *Thirdly,* the common interests of society and the common rights of man.

The first was a government of priestcraft, the second, of conquerors, and the third, of reason. . . .

We have now to review the governments which arise out of society, in contradistinction to those which arose out of superstition and conquest.

It has been thought a considerable advance toward establishing the principles of freedom to say that government is a compact between those who govern and those who are governed, but this cannot be true, because it is putting the effect before the cause; for as a man must have existed before governments existed, there necessarily was a time when governments did not exist, and consequently there could originally exist no governors to form such a compact with.

The fact therefore must be that the *individuals themselves,* each in his own personal and sovereign right, *entered into a compact with each other* to produce a government; and this is the only mode in which governments have a right to arise and the only principle on which they have a right to exist. . . .

A constitution is not a thing in name only, but in fact. It has not an ideal, but a real existence; and wherever it cannot be produced in a visible form, there is none. A constitution is a thing *antecedent* to a government, and a government is only the creature of a constitution. The constitution of a country is not the act of its government, but of the people constituting a government.

It is the body of elements to which you can refer and quote article by article, and which contains the principles on which the government shall be etablished, the manner in which it shall be organized, the powers it shall have, the mode of elections, the duration of parliaments or by what other name such bodies may be called, the powers which the executive part of the government shall have, and, in fine, everything that relates to the complete organization of a civil government and the principles on which it shall act and by which it shall be bound.

A constitution, therefore, is to a government what the laws made afterward by that government are to a court of judicature. The court of judicature does not make the laws, neither can it alter them; it only acts in conformity to the laws made, and the government is in like manner governed by the constitution. . . .

From Dissertation on First Principles of Government

The true and only true basis of representative government is equality of rights. Every man has a right to one vote and no more in the choice of representatives. The rich have no more right to exclude the poor from the right of voting or of electing and being elected than the poor have to exclude the rich, and wherever it is attempted or proposed on either side it is a question of force and not of right. Who is he that would exclude another? That other has a right to exclude him.

That which is now called aristocracy implies an inequality of rights, but who are the persons that have a right to establish this inequality? Will the rich exclude themselves? No. Will the poor exclude themselves? No. By what right then can any be excluded? It would be a question if any man or class of men have a right to exclude themselves, be this as it may, they cannot have the right to exclude another. The poor will not delegate such a right to the rich nor the rich to the poor, and to assume it is not only to assume arbitrary power but to assume a right to commit robbery.

Personal rights, of which the right of voting for representatives is one, are a species of property of the most sacred kind; and he that would employ his pecuniary property or presume upon the influence it gives him to dispossess or rob another of his property or rights uses that pecuniary property as he would use firearms and merits to have it taken from him.

Inequality of rights is created by a combination in one part of the community to exclude another part from its rights. Whenever it be made an article of a constitution or a law that the right of voting or of electing and being elected shall appertain exclusively to persons possessing a certain quantity of property, be it little or much, it is a combination of the persons possessing that quantity to exclude those who do not possess the same quantity. It is investing themselves with powers as a self-created part of society, to the exclusion of the rest.

It is always to be taken for granted that those who oppose an equality of rights never mean the exclusion should take place on themselves; and in this view of the case, pardoning the vanity of the thing, aristocracy is a subject of laughter. This self-soothing vanity is encouraged by another idea not less selfish, which is that the opposers conceive they are playing a safe game, in which there is a chance to gain and none to lose; that, at any rate, the doctrine of equality includes them and that, if they cannot get more rights than those whom they oppose and would exclude, they shall not have less.

This opinion has already been fatal to thousands who, not contented with *equal rights,* have sought more till they lost all, and experienced in themselves the degrading *inequality* they endeavored to fix upon others.

In any view of the case, it is dangerous and impolitic, sometimes ridiculous and always unjust, to make property the criterion of the right of voting. If the sum or value of the property upon which the right is to take place be considerable, it will exclude a majority of the people and unite them in a common interest against the government and against those who support it; and as the power is always with the majority, they can overturn such a government and its supporters whenever they please.

If, in order to avoid this danger, a small quantity of property be fixed as the criterion of the right, it exhibits liberty in disgrace by putting it in competition with accident and insignificance. When a broodmare shall fortunately produce a foal or a mule that, by being worth the sum in question, shall convey to its owner the right of voting or by its death take it from him, in whom does the origin of such a right exist? Is it in the man or in the mule? When we consider how many ways property may be acquired without merit and lost without crime, we ought to spurn the idea of making it a criterion of rights.

But the offensive part of the case is that this exclusion from the right of voting implies a stigma on the moral character of the persons excluded, and this is what no part of the community has a right to pronounce upon another part. No external circumstance can justify it; wealth is no proof of moral character, nor poverty of the want of it.

On the contrary, wealth is often the presumptive evidence of dishonesty and poverty the negative evidence of innocence. If therefore property, whether little or much, be made a criterion, the means by which that property has been acquired ought to be made a criterion also. . . .

In a political view of the case, the strength and permanent security of government is in proportion to the number of people interested in supporting it. The true policy, therefore, is to interest the whole by an equality of rights, for the danger arises from exclusions. It is possible to exclude men from the right of voting, but it is impossible to exclude them from the right of rebelling against that exclusion; and when all other rights are taken away, the right of rebellion is made perfect. . . .

That property will ever unequal is certain. Industry, superiority of talents, dexterity of management, extreme frugality, fortunate opportunities or the opposite, or the means of those things, will ever produce that effect, without having recourse to the harsh, ill-sounding names of avarice and oppression; and besides this there are some men who, though they do not despise wealth, will not stoop to the drudgery or the means of acquiring it nor will be troubled with it beyond their wants or their independence, while in others there is an avidity to obtain it by every means not punishable—it makes the sole business of their lives, and they follow it as a religion. All that is required with respect to property is to obtain it honestly and not employ it criminally, but it is always criminally employed when it is made a criterion for exclusive rights.

In institutions that are purely pecuniary, such as that of a bank or a commercial company, the rights of the members composing that company are wholly created by the property they invest therein, and no other rights are represented in the government of that company than what arise out of that property; neither has that government cognizance of *anything but property*.

But the case is totally different with respect to the institution of civil government, organized on the system of representation. Such a government has cognizance of *everything* and of *every man* as a member of the national society, whether he has property or not; and therefore the principle requires that *every man* and *every kind of right* be represented, of which the right to acquire and to hold property is but one, and that not of the most essential kind.

The protection of a man's person is more sacred than the protection of property, and besides this the faculty of performing any kind of work or services by which he acquires a livelihood or maintaining his family is of the nature of property. It is property to him; he has acquired it, and it is as much the object of his protection as exterior property, possessed without that faculty, can be the object of protection in another person.

I have always believed that the best security for property, be it much or little, is to remove from every part of the community, as far as can possibly be done, every cause of complaint and every motive to violence, and this can only be done by an equality of rights. When rights are secure, property is secure in consequence. But when property is made a pretense for unequal or exclusive rights, it weakens the right to hold the property, and provokes indignation and tumult; for it is unnatural to believe that property can be secure under the guarantee of a society injured in its rights by the influence of that property. . . .

It is at all times necessary, and more particularly so during the progress of a revolution and until right ideas confirm themselves by habit, that we frequently refresh our patriotism by reference to first principles. It is by tracing things to their origin that we learn to understand them, and it is by keeping that line and that origin always in view that we never forget them.

An inquiry into the origin of rights will demonstrate to us that *rights* are not *gifts* from one man to another, nor from one class of men to another; for who is he who could be the first giver, or by what principle or on what authority could he possess the right of giving?

A declaration of rights is not a creation of them nor a donation of them. It is a manifest of the principle by which they exist, followed by a detail of what the rights are; for every civil right has a natural right for its foundation, and it includes the principle of a reciprocal guarantee of those rights from man to man. As, therefore, it is impossible to discover any origin of rights otherwise than in the origin of man, it consequently follows that rights appertain to man in right of his existence only, and must therefore be equal to every man.

The principle of an *equality of rights* is clear and simple. Every man can understand it, and it is by understanding his rights that he learns his duties; for where the rights of men are equal, every man must finally see the necessity of protecting the rights of others as the most effectual security for his own. . . .

Next to matters of *principle* are matters of *opinion,* and it is necessary to distinguish between the two. Whether the rights of men shall be equal is not a matter of opinion but of right, and consequently of principle; for men do not hold their rights as grants from each other, but each one in right of himself. Society is the guardian but not the giver. And as in extensive societies, such as America and France, the right of the individual in matters of government cannot be exercised but by election and representation, it consequently follows that the only system of government consistent with principle, where simple democracy is impracticable, is the representative system. . . .

In all matters of opinion, the social compact, or the principle by which society is held together, requires that the majority of opinions becomes the rule for the whole and that the minority yields practical obedience thereto. This is perfectly comfortable to the principle of equal rights; for, in the first place, every man has *a right to give an opinion,* but no man has a right that his opinion should *govern the rest.* In the second place, it is not supposed to be known beforehand on which side of any question, whether for or against, any man's opinion will fall. He may happen to be in a majority upon some questions and in a minority upon others, and by the same rule that he expects obedience in the one case he must yield it in the other. . . .

It will sometimes happen that the minority are right and the majority are wrong, but as soon as experience proves this to be the case, the minority will increase to a majority, and the error will reform itself by the tranquil operation of freedom of opinion and equality of rights. Nothing, therefore, can justify an insurrection; neither can it ever be necessary where rights are equal and opinions free. . . .

I shall conclude this discourse with offering some observations on the means of *preserving* liberty; for it is not only necessary that we establish it, but that we preserve it.

It is, in the first place, necessary that we distinguish between the means made use of to overthrow despotism, in order to prepare the way for the establishment of liberty, and the means to be used after the despotism is overthrown.

The means made use of in the first case are justified by necessity. Those means are, in general, insurrections; for while the established government of despotism continues in any country, it is scarcely possible that any other means can be used. It is also certain that, in the commencement of a revolution, the revolutionary party permit to themselves a *discretionary exercise of power* regulated more by circumstances than by principle, which, were the practice to continue, liberty would never be established, or if established would soon be overthrown. It is never to be expected in a revolution that every man is to change his opinion at the same moment.

There never yet was any truth or any principle so irresistibly obvious that all men believed it at once. Time and reason must cooperate with each other to the final establishment of any principle, and therefore those who may happen to be first convinced have not a right to persecute others on whom conviction operates more slowly. The moral principle of revolutions is to instruct, not to destroy.

Had a constitution been established two years ago (as ought to have been done). the violences that have since desolated France and injured the character of the Revolution would, in my opinion, have been prevented. The nation would then have had a bond of union, and every individual would have known the line of conduct he was to follow. But instead of this, a revolutionary government, a thing without their principle or authority, was substituted in its place; virtue and crime depended upon accident, and that which was patriotism one day became treason the next.

All these things have followed from the want of a constitution: for it is the nature and intention of a constitution to *prevent governing by party* by establishing a common principle that shall limit and control the power and impulse of party, and that says to all parties, *thus far shalt thou go and no further.* But in the absence of a constitution, men look entirely to party; and instead of principle governing party, party governs principle.

An avidity to punish is always dangerous to liberty. It leads men to stretch, to misinterpret, and to misapply even the best of laws. He that would make his own liberty secure must guard even his enemy from oppression; for if he violates this duty, he establishes a precedent that will reach to himself.

THOMAS PAINE

Paris, July, 1795

WORKS OF THOMAS PAINE

The Complete Writings of Thomas Paine. Edited by Philip S. Foner. New York: The Citadel Press, 1945. A collection of Paine's works including scientific writings, letters, essays, and pamphlets.

Paine, Thomas. *The Age of Reason.* Paris, 1794. Fighting against the reactionary clergy, Paine presents his theological views, showing the necessity of destroying myth with reason thus escaping the tyranny of the dogmatic religious viewpoint.

_____. *Agrarian Justice, Opposed to Agrarian Law, and to Agrarian Monopoly.* Paris, 1796. A proposal for guaranteed financial security to all members of society through a system of land redistribution and societal control.

_____. *The American Crisis.* London, 1777. A collection of the fourteen pamphlets by the same name, which portray Paine's work as a popularizer of the ideas behind the American Revolution.

_____. *The Decline and Fall of the English System of Finance.* Paris, 1796. A prediction of the bankruptcy of the English resulting from increasing dissatisfaction with the hereditary form of government and the increasing economic drain resulting from foreign wars.

_____. *Dissertation on First-Principles of Government.* London, 1795. Governments of hereditary succession have no right to exist, while governments of election and representation must be based on equal rights guaranteed by equality of the vote under a common constitution.

_____. *A Letter addressed to the Abbe Raynal on the Affairs of North America; in which the Mistakes in the Abbe's Account of the Revolution of America are corrected and cleared up.* London, 1783. Refuting the Abbe's position, Paine describes the American Revolution as a unique event in history due to its widening of civilization through the ending of prejudice.

_____. *Miscellaneous Articles.* London, 1792. A collection of eight letters and articles reflecting Paine's views on various political subjects.

MAJOR SOURCES ON THOMAS PAINE

Berthold, S.M. *Thomas Paine: America's First Liberal.* Boston: Meador, 1938. An enthusiastic but poorly written biography bordering on near fiction with its hero-worship aura.

Clark, Harry Hayden. *Thomas Paine: Representative Selections.* New York: Hill, 1961. A collection of Paine's works with introductory remarks by the author.

Clark, Harry Hayden. "Toward a Reinterpretation of Thomas Paine," *American Literature,* Vol. 5 (1933), pp. 133–145. A description of Paine as an ideologue rejecting historical relativism and precedence and seeking only Universal Truths.

Conway, Moncure Daniel. *The Life of Thomas Paine.* London: Watts, 1909. One of the best biographies available; asserts that Paine can be understood only in terms of his intense Quakerism.

Elder, Brother Dominic. "The Common Man Philosophy of Thomas Paine." Doctoral dissertation. Notre Dame University, 1951. A carefully written analysis of the man and his works showing Paine as a popularizer motivated by the forces of Deism.

Maxey, Chester C. "Thomas Paine," in *Political Philosophies.* New York: Macmillan, 1938. Neither a theorist nor politician, Paine, the commoner, gave new scope and dimension to the Social Compact and in so doing popularized political democracy.

Merriam, C.E. "The Political Theories of Thomas Paine," *Political Science Quarterly,* Vol. 14 (1899), pp. 389–404. Shows Paine not as a political theorist, but as an agitator, a popularizer of radical political thought.

Penniman, Howard. "Thomas Paine—Democrat," *American Political Science Review,* Vol. 37 (1943), pp. 244–262. A discussion of several basic concepts in the subject's political philosophy, all of which portray Paine as a "majority-rule democrat."

Sykes, Norman. "Paine" in Hearnshaw, ed., *Social and Political Ideas of Some Representatives of the Revolutionary Era.* New York: Barnes & Noble, 1967. An essay emphasizing the relationship of natural religion and democratic thought in Paine's political ideology.

CHAPTER 3

Thomas Jefferson

THOMAS Jefferson (1743–1829), born into a well-established Virginia family, received a classical education. In 1760, he entered the College of William and Mary, from which he graduated two years later. The next five years were devoted to studying and, after passing the Virginia bar, he subsequently established a law practice.

Jefferson's public life began in 1769 when he took his seat as a member of the Virginia House of Burgesses. By the decisive year of 1774, Jefferson was known throughout Virginia; mid-1775 found him seated in Congress where fellow members soon noted his extraordinary knowledge and ability. In June 1776, a committee of five was appointed to write a draft of the Declaration of Independence; as chairman of the committee, Jefferson was asked to write the document.

Having thus linked his name with the birth of the nation, Jefferson resigned his seat in Congress because of the ill health of his wife. For the next two years he lived at Monticello, revising the Virginia laws to conform with a republican government.

In January 1779, the Virginia legislature elected Jefferson as governor of the State; his two years as governor proved to be one of the severest trials of his public life. Jefferson was next elected to Congress in 1783. As chairman of a committee on currency, he was largely responsible for the decimal currency used in the United States.

In 1785, Jefferson was appointed minister plenipotentiary to France, where he spent five years. Upon returning to the United States, Jefferson became the first Secretary of State. He soon found himself at odds over almost every policy advanced by Hamilton, who dominated Washington's cabinet. Although Washington tried to use his influence to induce the Secretary of State to remain in his post, Jefferson resigned in 1794.

In 1796, Jefferson was almost elected President; he received sixty-eight electoral votes to John Adams' seventy-one votes. As the law then stood, Jefferson became vice-president.

Jefferson was elected President in 1800. During his administration, he assured the physical greatness of this country and the future success of his party by purchasing the Louisiana Territory. During his second administration, Jefferson faced innumerable difficulties as head of a neutral nation in time of a general European war.

During the last seventeen years of his life, Jefferson did not venture far from Monticello. His chief concern during those days was education; under his guidance the University of Virginia developed.

From his Autobiography

. . . When I left Congress, in 1776, it was in the persuasion that our whole code must be reviewed, adapted to our republican form of government; and, now that we had no negatives of Councils, Governors, and Kings to restrain us from doing right, that it should be corrected, in all its parts, with a single eye to reason, and the good of those for whose govern ment it was framed. Early, therefore, in the session of 1776, to which I returned, I moved and presented a bill for the revision of the laws, which was passed on the 24th of October; and on the 5th of November, Mr. Pendleton, Mr. Wythe, George Mason, Thomas L. Lee, and myself, were appointed a committee to execute the work. We agreed to meet at Fredericksburg to settle the plan of operation, and to distribute the work. We met there accordingly, on the 13th of January, 1777. The first question was, whether we should propose to abolish the whole existing system of laws, and prepare a new and complete Institute, or preserve the general system, and only modify it to the present state of things. Mr. Pendleton, contrary to his usual disposition in favor of ancient things, was for the former proposition, in which he was joined by Mr. Lee. To this it was objected, that to abrogate our whole system would be a bold measure, and probably far beyond the views of the legislature; that they had been in the practice of revising, from time to time, the laws of the colony, omitting the expired, the repealed, and the obsolete, amending only

those retained, and probably meant we should now do the same, only including the British statutes as well as our own: that to compose a new Institute, like those of Justinian and Bracton, or that of Blackstone, which was the model proposed by Mr. Pendleton, would be an arduous undertaking, of vast research, of great consideration and judgment; and when reduced to a text, every word of that text, from the imperfection of human language, and its incompetence to express distinctly every shade of idea, would become a subject of question and chicanery, until settled by repeated adjudications; and this would involve us for ages in litigation and render property uncertain, until, like the statutes of old, every word has been tried and settled by numerous decisions, and by new volumes of reports and commentaries; and that no one of us, probably, would undertake such a work, which to be systematical, must be the work of one hand. This last was the opinion of Mr. Wythe, Mr. Mason, and myself. When we proceeded to the distribution of the work, Mr. Mason excused himself, as, being no lawyer, he felt himself unqualified for the work, and he resigned soon after. Mr. Lee excused himself on the same ground, and died, indeed, in a short time. The other two gentlemen, therefore, and myself divided the work among us. The common law and statutes to the 4 James I (when our separate legislature was established) were assigned to me; the British statutes, from that period to the present day, to Mr. Wythe; and the Virginia laws to Mr. Pendleton. As the law of Descents, and the criminal law fell of course within my portion, I wished the committee to settle the leading principles of these, as a guide for me in framing them; and, with respect to the first, I proposed to abolish the law of primogeniture, and to make real property descendible in parcenary to the next of kin, as personal property is, by the statute of distribution. Mr. Pendleton wished to preserve the right of primogeniture, but seeing at once that that could not prevail, he proposed we should adopt the Hebrew principle, and give a double portion to the elder son. I observed, that if the eldest son could eat twice as much, or do double work, it might be a natural evidence of his right to a double portion; but being on a par in his powers and wants, with his brothers and sisters, he should be on a par also in the partition of the patrimony; and such was the decision of the other members.

On the subject of the Criminal law, all were agreed, that the punishment of death should be abolished, except for treason and murder; and that, for other felonies, should be substituted hard labor in the public works, and in some cases, the *Lex talionis.* How this last revolting principle came to obtain our approbation I do not remember. There remained, indeed, in our laws, a vestige of it in a single case of a slave; it was the English law, in the time of the Anglo-Saxons, copied probably from the Hebrew law of "an eye for an eye, a tooth for a tooth," and it was the law of several ancient people; but the modern mind had left it far in the rear of its advances. These points, however, being settled, we repaired to our respective homes for the preparation of the work.

In the execution of my part, I thought it material not to vary the diction of the ancient statutes by modernizing it, nor to give rise to new questions by new expressions. The text of these statutes had been so fully explained and defined, by numerous adjudications, as scarcely ever now to produce a question in our courts. I thought it would be useful, also, in all new draughts, to reform the style of the later British statutes, and of our

own acts of Assembly; which, from their verbosity, their endless tautologies, their involutions of case within case, and parenthesis within parenthesis, and their multiplied efforts at certainty, by *saids* and *aforesaids,* by *ors* and by *ands,* to make them more plain, are really rendered more perplexed and incomprehensible, not only to common readers, but to the lawyers themselves. We were employed in this work from that time to February, 1779, when we met at Williamsburg, that is to say, Mr. Pendleton, Mr. Wythe and myself; and meeting day by day, we examined critically our several parts, sentence by sentence, scrutinizing and amending, until we had agreed on the whole. We then returned home, had fair copies made of our several parts, which were reported to the General Assembly, June 18, 1779, by Mr. Wythe and myself, Mr. Pendleton's residence being distant, and he having authorized us by letter to declare his approbation. We had, in this work, brought so much of the Common law as it was thought necessary to alter, all the British statutes from *Magna Charta* to the present day, and all the laws of Virginia, from the establishment of our legislature, in the 4th Jac. I. to the present time, which we thought should be retained, within the compass of one hundred and twenty-six bills, making a printed folio of ninety pages only. Some bills were taken out, occasionally, from time to time, and passed; but the main body of the work was not entered on by the legislature until after the general peace, in 1785, when, by the unwearied exertions of Mr. Madison, in opposition to the endless quibbles, chicaneries, perversions, vexations and delays of lawyers and demi-lawyers, most of the bills were passed by the legislature, with little alteration.

The bill for establishing religious freedom, the principles of which had, to a certain degree, been enacted before, I had drawn in all the latitude of reason and right. It still met with opposition; but, with some mutilations in the preamble, it was finally passed; and a singular proposition proved that its protection of opinion was meant to be universal. Where the preamble declares, that coercion is a departure from the plan of the holy author of our religion, an amendment was proposed, by inserting the word "Jesus Christ," so that it should read, "a departure from the plan of Jesus Christ, the holy author of our religion"; the insertion was rejected by a great majority, in proof that they meant to comprehend, within the mantle of its protection, the Jew and the Gentile, the Christian and Mahometan, the Hindoo, and Infidel of every denomination.

Beccaria, and other writers on crimes and punishments had satisfied the reasonable world of the unrightfulness and inefficacy of the punishment of crimes by death; and hard labor on roads, canals, and other public works, had been suggested as a proper substitute. The Revisors had adopted these opinions; but the general idea of our country had not yet advanced to that point. The bill, therefore, for proportioning crimes and punishments, was lost in the House of Delegates by a majority of a single vote. I learned afterwards, that the substitute of hard labor in public, was tried (I believe it was in Pennsylvania) without success. Exhibited as a public spectacle, with shaved heads and mean clothing, working on the high roads, produced in the criminals such a prostration of character, such an abandonment of self-respect, as, instead of reforming, plunged them into the most desperate and hardened depravity of morals and character. . . .

The acts of Assembly concerning the College of William and Mary, were properly within Mr. Pendleton's portion of our work; but these related chiefly to its revenue, while its constitution, organization and scope of science, were derived from its charter. We thought that on this subject, a systematical plan of general .education should be proposed, and I was requested to undertake it. I accordingly prepared three bills for the Revisal, proposing three distinct grades of education, reaching all classes. First, elementary schools, for all children generally, rich and poor. Second, colleges, for a middle degree of instruction, calculated for the common purposes of life, and such as would be desirable for all who were in easy circumstances. And, third, an ultimate grade for teaching the sciences generally, and in their highest degree. The first bill proposed to lay off every county into Hundreds, or Wards, or a proper size and population for a school, in which reading, writing, and common arithmetic should be taught; and that the whole State should be divided into twenty-four districts, in each of which should be a school for classical learning, grammar, geography, and the higher branches of numerical arithmetic. The second bill proposed to amend the constitution of William and Mary College, to enlarge its sphere of science, and to make it in fact a University. The third was for the establishment of a library. These bills were not acted on until the same year, 1796, and then only so much of the first as provided for elementary schools. The College of William and Mary was an establishment purely of the Church of England; the Visitors were required to be all of that Church; the Professors to subscribe to its thirty-nine Articles; its Students to learn its Catechism; and one of its fundamental objects was declared to be, to raise up Ministers for that church. The religious jealousies, therefore, of all the dissenters, took alarm lest this might give an ascendancy to the Anglican sect, and refused acting on that bill. Its local eccentricity, too, and unhealthy autumnal climate, lessened the general inclination towards it. And in the Elementary bill, they inserted a provision which completely defeated it; for they left it to the court of each county to determine for itself, when this act should be carried into execution, within their county. One provision of the bill was, that the expenses of these schools should be borne by the inhabitants of the county, every one in proportion to his general tax rate. This would throw on wealth the education of the poor; and the justices, being generally of the more wealthy class, were unwilling to incur that burden, and I believe it was not suffered to commence in a single county. I shall recur again to this subject, towards the close of my story, if I should have life and resolution enough to reach that term; for I am already tired of talking about myself.

The bill on the subject of slaves, was a mere digest of the existing laws respecting them, without any intimation of a plan for a future and general emancipation. It was thought better that this should be kept back, and attempted only by way of amendment, whenever the bill should be brought on. The principles of the amendment, however, were agreed on, that is to say, the freedom of all born after a certain day, and deportation at a proper age. But it was found that the public mind would not yet bear the proposition, nor will it bear it even at this day. Yet the day is not distant when it must bear and adopt it, or worse will follow. Nothing is more certainly written in the book of fate, than that these people are to be free; nor is it less certain that the two races, equally free, cannot live in the same government. Nature, habit, opinion have drawn indelible lines of distinction between them. It is still in our power to direct the process of emancipation and deportation, peaceably, and in such slow degree, as that the evil will wear off insensibly, and their place be, *pari passu,* filled up by free white laborers. If, on the contrary, it is left to force itself on, human nature must shudder at the prospect held up. We should in vain look for an example in the Spanish deportation or deletion of the Moors. This precedent would fall far short of our case.

I considered four of these bills, passed or reported, as forming a system by which every fibre would be eradicated of ancient or future aristocracy; and a foundation laid for a government truly republican. The repeal of the laws of entail would prevent the accumulation and perpetuation of wealth, in select families, and preserve the soil of the country from being daily more and more absorbed in mort-main. The abolition of primogeniture, and equal partition of inheritances, removed the feudal and unnatural distinctions which made one member of every family rich, and all the rest poor, substituting equal partition, the best of all Agrarian laws. The restoration of the rights of conscience relieved the people from taxation for the support of a religion not theirs; for the establishment was truly of the religion of the rich, the dissenting sects being entirely composed of the less wealthy people; and these, by the bill for a general education, would be qualified to understand their rights, to maintain them, and to exercise with intelligence their parts in self-government; and all this would be effected, without the violation of a single natural right of any one individual citizen. To these, too, might be added, as a further security, the introduction of the trial by jury, into the Chancery courts, which have already ingulfed, and continue to ingulf, so great a proportion of the jurisdiction over our property.

On the 1st of June, 1779, I was appointed Governor of the Commonwealth, and retired from the legislature. . . .

A Bill Concerning Slaves (1779)

SECTION I. Be it enacted by the General Assembly, that no persons shall, henceforth, be slaves within this commonwealth, except such as were so on the first day of this present session of Assembly, and the descendants of the females of them.

SECTION II. Negroes and mulattoes which shall hereafter be brought into this commonwealth and kept therein one whole year, together, or so long at different times as shall amount to one year, shall be free. But if they shall not depart the commonwealth within one year thereafter they shall be out of the protection of the laws.

SECTION III. Those which shall come into this commonwealth of their own accord shall be out of the protection of the laws; save only such as being seafaring persons and navigating vessels hither, shall not leave the same while here more than twenty four hours together.

SECTION IV. It shall not be lawful for any person to emancipate a slave but by deed executed, proved and recorded as in required by law in the case of a conveyance of goods and chattels, on consideration not deemed valuable in law, or by last will and testament, and with the free consent of such slave, expressed in presence of the court of the county wherein he resides. And if such slave, so emancipated, shall not within one year thereafter, depart the commonwealth, he shall be out of the protection of the laws. All conditions, restrictions and limitations annexed to any act of emancipation shall be void from the time such emancipation is to take place.

SECTION V. If any white woman shall have a child by a Negro or mulatto, she and her child shall depart the commonwealth within one year thereafter. If they shall fail so to do, the woman shall be out of the protection of the laws, and the child shall be bound out by the Aldermen of the county, in like manner as poor orphans are by law directed to be, and within one year after its terms of service expired shall depart the commonwealth, or on failure so to do, shall be out of the protection of the laws.

SECTION VI. Where any of the persons before described shall be disabled from departing the commonwealth by grievous sickness, the protection of the law shall be continued to him until such disability be removed: And if the county shall in the meantime, incur any expense in taking care of him, as of other county poor, the Aldermen shall be entitled to recover the same from his master, if he had one, his heirs, executors and administrators.

SECTION VII. No Negro or mulatto shall be a witness except in pleas of the commonwealth against Negroes or mulattoes, or in civil pleas wherein Negroes or mulattoes alone shall be parties.

SECTION VIII. No slave shall go from the tenements of his master, or other person with whom he lives, without a pass, or some letter or token whereby it may appear that he is proceeding by authority from his master, employer, or overseer: If he does, it shall be lawful for any person to apprehend and carry him before a Justice of the Peace, to be by his order punished with stripes, or not in his direction.

SECTION IX. No slaves shall keep any arms whatever, nor pass, unless with written orders from his master or employer, or in his company, with arms from one place to another. Arms in possession of a slave contrary to this prohibition shall be forfeited to him who will seize them.

SECTION X. Riots, routs, unlawful assemblies, trespasses and seditious speeches by a Negro or mulatto shall be punished with stripes at the discretion of a Justice of the Peace; and he who will may apprehend and carry him before such a Justice.

A Bill for Proportioning Crimes and Punishments (1779)

Whereas, it frequently happens that wicked and dissolute men, resigning themselves to the dominion of inordinate passions, commit violations on the lives, liberties, and property of others, and, the secure enjoyment of these having principally induced men to enter into society, government would be defective in its principal purpose, were it not to restrain such criminal acts, by inflicting due punishments on those who perpetrate them; but it appears at the same time, equally deducible from the purposes of society, that a member thereof, committing an inferior injury, does not wholly forfeit the protection of his fellow citizens, but, after suffering a punishment in proportion to his offence, is entitled to their protection from all greater pain, so that it becomes a duty in the legislature to arrange, in a proper scale, the crimes which it may be necessary for them to repress, and to adjust thereto a corresponding gradation of punishments.

And whereas, the reformation of offenders, though an object worthy the attention of the laws, is not effected at all by capital punishments, which exterminate instead of reforming, and should be the last melancholy resource against those whose existence is become inconsistent with the safety of their fellow citizens, which also weaken the State, by cutting off so many who, if reformed, might be restored sound members to society, who, even under a course of correction, might be rendered useful in various labors for the public, and would be living and long-continued spectacles to deter others from commiting the like offences.

And forasmuch as the experience of all ages and countries hath shown, that cruel and sanguinary laws defeat their own purpose, by engaging the benevolence of mankind to withhold prosecutions, to smother testimony, or to listen to it with bias, when, if the punishment were only proportioned to the injury, men would feel it their inclination, as well as their duty, to see the laws observed.

For rendering crimes and punishments, therefore, more proportionate to each other:

Be it enacted by the General Assembly, that no crime shall be henceforth punished by the deprivation of life or limb, except those hereinafter ordained to be so punished.

If a man do levy war against the Commonwealth [*in the same*], or be adherent to the enemies of the Commonwealth [*within the same*], giving to them aid or comfort in the Commonwealth, or elsewhere, and thereof be convicted of open deed, by the evidence of two sufficient witnesses, or his own voluntary confession, the said cases, and no other, shall be adjudged treasons which extend to the Commonwealth, and the person so convicted shall suffer death, by hanging, and shall forfeit his lands and goods to the Commonwealth.

If any person commit petty treason, or a husband murder his wife, a parent his child, or a child his parent, he shall suffer death by hanging, and his body be delivered to anatomists to be dissected.

Whosoever committeth murder by poisoning shall suffer death by poison.

Whosoever committeth murder by way of duel shall suffer death by hanging; and if he were the challenger, his body, after death, shall be gibbetted. He who removeth it from the gibbet shall be guilty of a misdemeanor; and the officer shall see that it be replaced

Whosoever shall commit murder in any other way shall suffer death by hanging.

And in all cases of petty treason and murder, one half of the lands and goods of the offender, shall be forfeited to the next of kin to the person killed, and the other half descend and go to his own representatives. Save only, where one shall slay the challenger in a duel, in which case, no part of his lands or goods shall be forfeited to the kindred of the party slain, but, instead thereof, a moiety shall go to the Commonwealth.

The same evidence shall suffice, and order and course of trial be observed in cases of petty treason, as in those of other murderers.

Whosoever shall be guilty of manslaughter, shall, for the first offence, be condemned to hard labor for seven years in the public works, shall forfeit one half of his lands and goods to the next of kin to the person slain; the other half to be sequestered during such term, in the hands and to the use of the Common-wealth, allowing a reasonable part of the profits for the support of his family. The second offence shall be deemed murder.

And where persons, meaning to commit a trespass only, or larceny, or other unlawful deed, and doing an act from which involuntary homicide hath ensued, have heretofore been adjudged guilty of manslaughter, or of murder, by transferring such their unlawful intention to an act, much more penal than they could have in probable contemplation; no such case shall hereafter be deemed manslaughter, unless manslaughter was intended, nor murder, unless murder was intended.

In other cases of homicide, the law will not add to the miseries of the party, by punishments and forfeitures.

However sentence of death shall have been pronounced against any person for treason or murder, execution shall be done on the next day but one after such sentence, unless it be Sunday, and then on the Monday following.

Whosoever shall be guilty of rape, polygamy, or sodomy, with man or woman, shall be punished, if a man, by castration, if a woman, by cutting through the cartilage of her nose a hole of one half inch in diameter at the least.

But no one shall be punished for polygamy, who shall have married after probable information of the death of his or her husband or wife, or after his or her husband or wife, hath absented him or herself, so that no notice of his or her being alive hath reached such person for seven years together, or hath suffered the punishments before prescribed for rape, polygamy, or sodomy.

Whosoever on purpose, and of malice forethought, shall maim another, or shall disfigure him, by cutting out or disabling the tongue, slitting or cutting off a nose, lip, or ear, branding, or otherwise, shall be maimed, or disfigured in like sort: or if that cannot be, for want of the same part, then as nearly as may be, in some other part of at least equal value

and estimation, in the opinion of a jury, and moreover, shall forfeit one half of his lands and goods to the sufferer. . . .

A Bill for the More General Diffusion of Knowledge (1779)

SECTION I. Whereas it appeareth that however certain forms of government are better calculated than others to protect individuals in the free exercise of their natural rights, and are at the same time themselves better guarded against degeneracy, yet experience hath shewn, that even under the best forms, those entrusted with power have, in time, and by slow operations, perverted it into tyranny; and it is believed that the most effectual means of preventing this would be, to illuminate, as far as practicable, the minds of the people at large, and more especially to give them knowledge of those facts, which history exhibiteth, that, possessed thereby of the experience of other ages and countries, they may be enabled to know ambition under all its shapes, and prompt to exert their natural powers to defeat its purposes; And whereas it is generally true that that people will be happiest whose laws are best, and are best administered, and that laws will be wisely formed, and honestly administered, in proportion as those who form and administer them are wise and honest; whence it becomes expedient for promoting the public happiness that those persons, whom nature hath endowed with genius and virtue, should be rendered by liberal education worthy to receive, and able to guard the sacred deposit of the rights and liberties of their fellow citizens, and that they should be called to that charge without regard to wealth, birth or other accidental condition or circumstance; but the indigence of the greater number disabling them from so educating, at their own expence, those of their children whom nature hath fitly formed and disposed to become useful instruments for the public, it is better that such should be sought for and educated at the common expence of all, than that the happiness of all should be confined to the weak or wicked:

SECTION II. Be it therefore enacted by the General Assembly, that in every county within this commonwealth, there shall be chosen annually, by the electors qualified to vote for Delegates, three of the most honest and able men of their country, to be called the Alderman of the county; and that the election of the said Aldermen shall be held at the same time and place, before the same persons, and notified and conducted in the same manner as by law is directed, for the annual election of Delegates for the county.

SECTION III. The person before whom such election is holden shall certify to the court of the said county the names of the Aldermen chosen, in order that the same may be entered of record, and shall give notice of their election to the said Aldermen within a fortnight after such election.

SECTION IV. The said Aldermen on the first Monday in October, if it be fair, and if not, then on the next fair day, excluding Sunday, shall meet at the court-house of their county, and proceed to divide their said county into hundreds, bounding the same by water courses, mountains, or limits, to be run and marked, if they think necessary, by the county surveyor, and at the county expence, regulating the size of the said hundreds, according to the best of their discretion, so as that they may contain a convenient number of children to make up a school, and be of such convenient size that all the children within each hundred may daily attend the school to be established therein, and distinguishing each hundred by a particular name; which division, with the names of the several

hundreds, shall be returned to the court of the county and be entered of record, and shall remain unaltered until the increase or decrease of inhabitants shall render an alteration necessary, if the opinion of any succeeding Alderman, and also in the opinion of the court of the county.

SECTION V. The electors aforesaid residing within every hundred shall meet on the third Monday in October after the first election of Aldermen, at such place within their hundred, as the said Aldermen shall direct, notice thereof being previously given to them by such person residing within the hundred as the said Aldermen shall require who is hereby enjoined to obey such requisition on pain of being punished by amercement and imprisonment. The electors being so assembled shall choose the most convenient place within their hundred for building a school-house. If two or more places, having a greater number of votes than any others, shall yet be equal between themselves, the Aldermen, or such of them as are not of the same hundred, on information thereof, shall decide between them. The said Aldermen shall forthwith proceed to have a school-house built at the said place, and shall see that the same shall be kept in repair, and, when necessary, that it be rebuilt; but whenever they shall think necessary that it be rebuilt, they shall give notice as before directed, to the electors of the hundred to meet at the said school-house on such a day as they shall appoint, to determine by vote, in the manner before directed, whether it shall be rebuilt at the same, or what other place in the hundred.

SECTION VI. At every of those schools shall be taught reading, writing, and common arithmetick, and the books which shall be used therein for instructing the children to read shall be such as will at the same time make them acquainted with Graecian, Roman, English and American history. At these schools all the free children, male and female, resident within the respective hundred, shall be intitled to receive tuition gratis, for the term of three years, and as much longer, at their private expence, as their parents, guardians, or friends shall think proper.

SECTION VII. Over every ten of these schools (or such other number nearest thereto, as the number of hundreds in the county will admit, without fractional divisions) an overseer shall be appointed annually by the aldermen at their first meeting, eminent for his learning, integrity, and fidelity to the commonwealth, whose business and duty it shall be, from time to time, to appoint a teacher to each school, who shall give assurance of fidelity to the commonwealth, and to remove him as he shall see cause; to visit every school once in every half year at the least; to examine the scholars; see that any general plan of reading and instruction recommended by the visitors of William and Mary College shall be observed; and to superintend the conduct of the teacher in everything relative to his school. . . .

SECTION IX. And in order that grammer schools may be rendered convenient to the youth in every part of the commonwealth, be it therefore enacted, that on the first Monday in November, after the first appointment of overseers for the hundred schools, if fair, and if not, then on the next fair day, excluding Sunday, after the hour of one in the afternoon, the said overseers. . . shall fix on such place in some one of the counties in their district as shall be most proper for situation a grammer school-house, endeavoring that the situation be as central as may be to the inhabitants of the said counties, that it be furnished with good water, convenient to plentiful supplies of provision and fuel, and more than all things that it be healthy. And if a majority of the overseers present should not concur in their choice of any one place proposed, the method of determining shall be as follows: If two places only were proposed, and the votes be divided, they shall decide between them by fair and equal lot; if more than two places were proposed, the question shall be put on those two which on the first division had the greater number of votes; or if no two places had a greater number of votes than the other, then it shall be decided by fair and equal lot (unless it can be agreed by a majority of votes) which of the places having equal numbers shall be thrown out of the competition, so that the question shall be put on the remaining two, and if on this ultimate question the votes shall be equally divided, it shall then be decided finally by lot. . . .

SECTION XIII. In either of these grammar schools shall be taught the Latin and Greek languages, English Grammer, geography, and the higher part of numerical arithmetick, to wit, vulgar and decimal fractions, and the extrication of the square and cube roots. . . .

SECTION XVI. Every overseer of the hundred schools shall, in the month of September annually, after the most diligent and impartial examination and inquiry, appoint from among the boys who shall have been two years at the least at some one of the schools under his superintendance, and whose parents are too poor to give them farther education, some one of the best and most promising genius and disposition, to proceed to the grammar school of his district; which appointment shall be made in the court-house of the county, and on the court day for that month if fair, and if not, then on the next fair day, excluding Sunday, in the presence of the Aldermen, or two of them at least, assembled on the bench for that purpose, the said overseer being previously sworn by them to make such appointment, without favor or affection, according to the best of his skill and judgment, and being interrogated by the said Aldermen, either on their own motion, or on suggestions from their parents, guardians, friends, or teachers of the children, competitors for such appointment; which teachers the parents shall attend for the information of the Aldermen. On which interrogatories the said Aldermen, if they be not satisfied with the appointment proposed, shall have right to negative it; whereupon the said visiter may proceed to make a new appointment, and the said Aldermen again to interrogate and negative, and so *toties quoties* until an appointment be approved.

SECTION XVII. Every boy so appointed shall be authorized to proceed to the grammer school of his district, there to be educated and boarded during such time as is hereafter limited; and his quota of the expences of the house together with a compensation to the master or usher for his tuition, at the rate of twenty dollars by the year, shall be paid by the Treasurer quarterly on warrant from the Auditors.

SECTION XVIII. A visitation shall be held, for the purpose of probation, annually at the said grammer school on the last Monday in September, if fair, and if not, then on the next fair day, excluding Sunday, at which one third of the boys sent thither by appointment of the said overseers, and who shall have been there one year only, shall be discontinued as public foundationers, being those who, on the most diligent examination and enquiry, shall be thought to be the least promising genius and disposition; and of those who shall have been there two years, all shall be discontinued save one only the best in genius and disposition, who shall be at liberty to continue there four years longer on the public foundation, and shall thence forward be deemed a senior.

SECTION XIX. The visitors for the district which, or any part of which, be southward and westward of James river, as known by that name, or by the names of Fluvanna and Jackson's river, in every other year, to wit, at the probation meetings held in the years, distinguished in the Christian computation by odd numbers, and the visiters for all the other districts at their said meetings to be held in those years, distinguished by even numbers, after diligent examination and enquiry as before directed, shall chuse one among the said seniors, of the best learning and most hopeful genius and disposition, who shall be authorized by them to proceed to William and Mary

College; there to be educated, boarded, and clothed, three years; the expence of which annually shall be paid by the Treasurer on warrant from the Auditors.

A Bill for Establishing Religious Freedom (1779)

SECTION I. Well aware that the opinions and belief of men depend on their own will, but follow involuntarily the evidence proposed to their minds; that Almighty God hath created the mind free, and manifested his supreme will that free it shall remain by making it altogether insusceptible of restraint; that all attempts to influence it by temporal punishments, or burthens, or by civil incapacitations, tend only to beget habits of hypocrisy and meanness, and are a departure from the plan of the holy author of our religion, who being lord both of body and mind, yet choose not to propogate it by coercions on either, as was in his Almighty power to do, but to exalt it by its influence on reason alone; that the impious presumption of legislature and ruler, civil as well as ecclesiastical, who, being themselves but fallible and uninspired men, have assumed dominion over the faith of others, setting up their own opinions and modes of thinking as the only true and infallible, and as such endeavoring to impose them on others, hath established and maintained false religions over the greatest part of the world and through all time: That to compel a man to furnish contributions of money for the propagation of opinions which he disbelieves and abhors, is sinful and tyrannical; that even the forcing him to support this or that teacher of his own religious persuasion, is depriving him of the comfortable liberty of giving his contributions to the partcular pastor whose morals he would make his pattern, and whose powers he feels most persuasive to righteousness; and is withdrawing from the ministry those temporary rewards, which proceeding from an approbation of their personal conduct, are an additional incitement to earnest and unremitting labours for the instruction of mankind; that our civil rights have no dependance on our religious opinions, any more than our opinions in physics or geometry; and therefore the proscribing any citizen as unworthy the public confidence by laying upon him an incapacity of being called to offices of trust or emolument, unless he profess or renounce this or that religious opinion, is depriving him unjudiciously of those privileges and advantages to which, in common with his fellow-citizens, he has a natural right; that it tends also to corrupt the principles of that very religion it meant to encourage, by bribing with a monopoly of worldly honours and emoluments, those who will externally profess and conform to it; that though indeed these are criminals who do not withstand such temptation, yet neither are those innocent who lay the bait in their way; that the opinions of men are not the object of civil government, nor under its jurisdiction; that to suffer the civil magistrate to intrude his powers into the field of opinion and to restrain the profession or propagation of principles on supposition of their ill tendency is a dangerous fallacy, which at once destroys all religious liberty, because he being of course judge of that tendency will make his opinions the rule of judgment, and approve or condemn the sentiments of others only as they shall square with or suffer from his own; that it is time enough for the rightful purposes of civil government for its officers to interfere when principles break out into overt acts against peace and good order; and finally, that truth is great and will prevail if left to herself; that she is the proper and sufficient antagonist to error, and has nothing to fear from the conflict unless by human interposition disarmed of her

natural weapons, free argument and debate; errors ceasing to be dangerous when it is permitted freely to contradict them.

SECTION II. We the General Assembly of Virginia do enact that no man shall be compelled to frequent or support any religious worship, place, or ministry whatsoever, nor shall be enforced, restrained, molested, or burthened in his body or goods, or shall otherwise suffer, on account of his religious opinions or belief; but all men shall be free to profess, and by argument to maintain, their opinions in matters of religion, and that the same shall in no wise diminish, enlarge, or affect their civil capacities.

SECTION III. And though we well know that this Assembly, elected by the people for their ordinary purposes of legislation only, have no power to restrain the acts of succeeding Assemblies, constituted with powers equal to our own, and that therefore to declare this act to be irrevocable would be of no effect in law; yet we are free to declare, and do declare, that the rights hereby asserted are of the natural rights of mankind, and that if any act shall be hereafter passed to repeal the present or to narrow its operations, such act will be an infringement of natural right.

Notes on Virginia (Freedom of Religion), 1785

The error seems not sufficiently eradicated that the operations of the mind, as well as the acts of the body, are subject to the coercion of the laws. But our rulers can have authority over such natural rights only as we have submitted to them. The rights of conscience we never submitted, we could not submit. We are answerable for them to our God.

The legitimate powers of government extend to such acts only as are injurious to others. But it does me no injury for my neighbor to say there are twenty gods or no God. It neither picks my pocker nor breaks my leg. If it be said his testimony in a court of justice cannot be relied on, reject it then, and be the stigma on him. Constraint may make him worse by making him a hypocrite, but it will never make him a truer man. It may fix him obstinately in his errors but will not cure them. Reason and free inquiry are the only effectual agents against error. Give a loose rein to them, they will support the true religion by bringing every false one to their tribunal, to the test of their investigation. They are the natural enemies of error, and of error only. Had not the Roman government permitted free inquiry, Christianity could never have been introduced. Had not free inquiry been indulged at the era of the Reformation, the corruptions of Christianity could not have been purged away. If it be restrained now, the present corruptions will be protected and new ones encouraged. Were the government to prescribe to us our medicine and diet, our bodies would be in such keeping as our souls are now. Thus in France the emetic was once forbidden as a medicine, and the potato as an article of food. Government is just as infallible, too, when it fixes systems in physics. Galileo was sent to the Inquisition for affirming that the earth was a sphere; the government had declared it to be as flat as a trencher, and Galileo was obliged to abjure his error. This error, however, at length prevailed; the earth became a globe, and Descartes declared it was whirled round its axis by a vortex. The government in which he lived was wise enough to see that this was no question of civil jurisdiction, or we should all have been involved by authority in vortices. In fact, the vortices have been exploded, and the Newtonian principle of gravitation is now more firmly established, on the basis of reason, than it would be were the government to step in and to make it an article of necessary faith. Reason and experiment have been indulged, and error has fled before them. It is error alone which needs the support of government. Truth can stand by itself. Subject opinion to coercion: whom will you make your inquisitors? Fallible men; men governed by bad passions, by private as well as public reasons. And why subject it to coercion? To produce uniformity. But is uniformity of opinion desirable? No more than of face and stature. Introduce the bed of Procrustes then; and, as there is danger that the large men may beat the small, make us all of a size by lopping the former and stretching the latter. Difference of opinion is advantageous in religion. The several sects perform the office of *censor morum* over each other. Is uniformity attainable? Millions of innocent men, women, and children, since the introduction of Christianity, have been burned, tortured, fined, imprisoned; yet we have not advanced one inch toward uniformity. What has been the effect of coercion? To make one half the world fools and the other half hypocrites; to support roguery and error all over the earth. Let us reflect that it is inhabited by a thousand millions of people; that these profess probably a thousand different systems of religion; that ours is but one of that thousand; that if there be but one right, and ours that one, we should wish to see the nine hundred and ninety-nine wandering sects gathered into the fold of truth. But against such a majority we cannot effect this by force. Reason and persuasion are the only practicable instruments. To make way for these, free inquiry must be indulged; and how can we wish others to indulge it while we refuse it ourselves? But every state, says an inquisitor, has established some religion. No two, say I, have established the same. Is this a proof of the infallibility of establishments? Our sister States of Pennsylvania and New York, however, have long subsisted without any establishment at all. The experiment was new and doubtful when they made it. It has answered beyond conception. They flourish infinitely. Religion is well supported; of various kinds, indeed, but all good enough; all sufficient to preserve peace and order; or if a sect arises whose tenets would subvert morals, good sense has fair play, and reasons and laughs it out of doors without suffering the state to be troubled with it. They do not hang more malefactors than we do. They are not more disturbed with religious dissensions. On the contrary, their harmony is unparalleled and can be ascribed to nothing but their unbounded tolerance, because there is no other circumstance in which they differ from every nation on earth. They have made the happy discovery that the way to silence religious disputes is to take no notice of them. Let us too give this experiment fair play and get rid, while we may, of those tyrannical laws. It is true we are as yet secured against them by the spirit of the times. I doubt whether the people of this country would suffer an execution for heresy, or a three years' imprisonment for not comprehending the mysteries of the Trinity. But is the spirit of the people an infallible, a permanent reliance? Is it government? Is this the kind of protection we receive in return for the rights we give up? Besides, the spirit of the times may alter, will alter. Our rulers will become corrupt, our people careless. A single zealot may commence persecutor, and better men be his victims. It can never be too often repeated that the time for fixing every essential right on a legal basis is while our rulers are honest and ourselves united. From the conclusion of this war we shall be going downhill. It will not then be necessary to resort every moment to the people for support. They will be forgotten, therefore, and their rights disregarded. They will forget themselves but in the sole faculty of making money, and will never think of uniting to effect a due respect for their rights. The shackles, therefore, which shall not be knocked off at the conclusion of this war will remain on us long, will be made heavier and heavier, till our rights shall revive or expire in a convulsion.

Letter to William S. Smith, November 1787

God forbid we should ever be twenty years without such a rebellion [Shays's Rebellion]. The people cannot be all, and always, well-informed. The part which is wrong will be discontented in proportion to the importance of the facts they misconceive. If they remain quiet under such misconceptions, it is a lethargy, the forerunner of death to the public liberty. We have had thirteen States independent for eleven years. There has been one rebellion. That comes to one rebellion in a century and a half for each State. What country before ever existed a century and a half without a rebellion? And what country can preserve its liberties if its rulers are not warned from time to time that this people preserve the spirit of resistance? Let them take arms. The remedy is to set them right as to facts, pardon and pacify them. What signify a few lives lost in a century or two? The tree of liberty must be refreshed from time to time with the blood of patriots and tyrants. It is its natural manure. Our convention has been too much impressed by the insurrection of Massachusetts, and on the spur of the moment they are setting up a kite to keep the hen yard in order.

Letter to James Madison, Paris, December 1787

Dear Sir, . . . The season admitting only of operations in the Cabinet, and these being in a great measure secret, I have little to fill a letter. I will therefore make up the deficiency by adding a few words on the Constitution proposed by our Convention. I like much the general idea of framing a government which should go on of itself peaceably, without needing continual recurrence to the state legislatures. I like the organization of the government into Legislative, Judiciary and Executive. I like the power given the Legislature to levy taxes, and for that reason solely approve of the greater house being chosen by the people directly. For tho' I think a house chosen by them will be very illy qualified to legislate for the Union, for foreign nations etc. yet this evil does not weigh against the good of preserving inviolate the fundamental principle that the people are not to be taxed but by representatives chosen immediately by themselves. I am captivated by the compromise of the opposite claims of the great and little states, of the latter to equal, and the former to proportional influence. I am much pleased too with the substitution of the method of voting by persons, instead of that of voting by states: and I like the negative given to the Executive with a third of either house, though I should have liked it better had the Judiciary been associated for that purpose, or invested with a similar and separate power. There are other good things of less moment. I will now add what I do not like. First the omission of a bill of rights providing clearly and without the aid of sophisms for freedom of religion, freedom of the press, protection against standing armies, restriction against monopolies, the eternal and unremitting force of the habeas corpus laws, and trials by jury in all matters of fact triable by the laws of the land and not by the law of nations. To say, as Mr. Wilson does that a bill of rights was not necessary because all is reserved in the case of the general government which is not given, while the particular ones all is given which is not reserved, might do for the audience to whom it was addressed, but is surely a *gratis dictum,* opposed by strong inferences from the body of the instrument, as well as from the omission of the clause of our present confederation which had declared

that in express terms. It was a hard conclusion to say because there has been no uniformity among the states as to the cases triable by jury, because some have been so incautious as to abandon this mode of trial, therefore the more prudent states shall be reduced to the same level of calamity. It would have been much more just and wise to have concluded the other way that as most of the states had judiciously preserved this palladium, those who had wandered should be brought back to it, and to have established general right instead of general wrong. Let me add that a bill of rights is what the people are entitled to against every government on earth, general or particular, and what no just government should refuse, or rest on inferences. The second feature I dislike, and greatly dislike, is the abandonment in every instance of the necessity of rotation in office, and most particularly in the case of the President. Experience concurs with reason in concluding that the first magistrate will always be re-elected if the Constitution permits it. He is then an officer for life. This once observed, it becomes of so much consequence to certain nations to have a friend or a foe at the head of our affairs that they will interfere with money and with arms. A Galloman or an Angloman will be supported by the nation he befriends. If once elected, and at a second or third election out voted by one or two votes, he will pretend false votes, foul play, hold possession of the reins of government, be supported by the States voting for him, especially if they are the central ones lying in a compact body themselves and separating their opponents: and they will be aided by one nation of Europe, while the majority are aided by another. The election of a President of America some years hence will be much more interesting to certain nations of Europe than ever the election of a king of Poland was. Reflect on all the instances in history ancient and modern, of elective monarchies, and say if they do not give foundation for my fears. The Roman emperors, the popes, while they were of any importance, the German emperors till they became hereditary in practice, the kings of Poland, the Deys of the Ottoman dependences. It may be said that if elections are to be attended with these disorders, the seldomer they are renewed the better. But experience shews that the only way to prevent disorder is to render them uninteresting by frequent changes. An incapacity to be elected a second time would have been the only effectual preventative. The power of removing him every fourth year by the vote of the people is a power which will not be exercised. The king of Poland is removable every day by the Diet, yet he is never removed.—Smaller objections are the Appeal in fact as well as law, and the binding all persons Legislative Executive and Judiciary by oath to maintain that constitution. I do not pretend to decide what would be the best method of procuring the establishment of the manifold good things in this constitution, and of getting rid of the bad. Whether by adopting it in hopes of future amendment, or, after it has been duly weighed and canvassed by the people, after seeing the parts they generally dislike, and those they generally approve, to say to them "We see now what you wish. Send together your deputies again, let them frame a constitution for you omitting what you have condemned, and establishing the powers you approve. Even these will be a great addition to the energy of your government."—At all events I hope you will not be discouraged from other trials, if the present one should fail of its full effect.—I have thus told you freely what I like and dislike: merely as a matter of curiosity, for I know your own judgment has been formed on all these points after having heard everything which could be urged on them. I own I am not a friend to a very energetic government. It is always oppressive. The late rebellion in Massachusetts has given more alarm than I think it should have done. Calculate that one rebellion in 13 states in the course of 11 years, is but one for each state in a century and a

half. No country should be so long without one. Nor will any degree of power in the hands of government prevent insurrections. France, with all its despotism, and two or three hundred thousand men always in arms has had three insurrections in the three years I have been here in every one of which greater numbers were engaged than in Massachusetts and a great deal more blood was spilt. In Turkey, which Montesquieu supposes more despotic, insurrections are the events of every day. In England, where the hand of power is lighter than here, but heavier than with us they happen every half dozen years. Compare again the ferocious depredations of their insurgents with the order, the moderation and the almost self extinguishment of ours.—After all, it is my principle that the will of the majority should always prevail. If they approve the proposed Convention in all its parts, I shall concur in it chearfully, in hopes that they will amend it whenever they shall find it work wrong. I think our governments will remain virtuous for many centuries; as long as they are chiefly agricultural; and this will be as long as there shall be vacant lands in any part of America. When they get piled upon one another in large cities, as in Europe, they will become corrupt as in Europe. Above all things I hope the education of the common people will be attended to; convinced that on their good sense we may rely with the most security for the preservation of a due degree of liberty. I have tired you by this time with my disquisitions and will therefore only add assurances of the sincerity of those sentiments of esteem and attachment with which I am Dear Sir your affectionate friend and servant.

P.S. The instability of our laws is really an immense evil. I think it would be well to provide in our constitutions that there shall always be a twelve-month between the ingrossing a bill and passing it: that it should then be offered to its passage without changing a word: and that if circumstances should be thought to require a speedier passage, it should take two thirds of both houses instead of a bare majority.

been the firmest bulwarks of English liberty. Were I called upon to decide whether the people had best be omitted in the legislative or judiciary department, I would say it is better to leave them out of the legislature. The execution of the laws is more important than the making of them. However, it is best to have the people in all the three departments, where that is possible.

Letter to the Abbe Arnoux, Paris, July 1789

We think, in America, that it is necessary to introduce the people into every department of government as far as they are capable of exercising it, and that is the only way to insure a long continued and honest administration of its powers.

1. They are not qualified to exercise themselves the executive department, but they are qualified to name the person who shall exercise it. 2. They are not qualified to legislate. With us, therefore, they only choose the legislators. 3. They are not qualified to judge questions of *law,* but they are capable of judging questions of *fact.* In the form of juries, therefore, they determine all matters of fact, leaving to the permanent judges to decide the law resulting from those facts. But we all know that permanent judges acquire an *esprit de corps;* that, being known, they are liable to be tempted by bribery; that they are misled by favor, by relationship, by a spirit of party, by a devotion to the executive or legislative power; that it is better to leave a cause to the decision of cross and pile than to that of a judge biased to one side; and that the opinion of twelve honest jurymen gives still a better hope of right than cross and pile does. It is left, therefore, to the juries, if they think the permanent judges are under any bias whatever in any cause, to take on themselves to judge the law as well as the fact. They never exercise this power but when they suspect partiality in the judges, and by the exercise of this power they have

The Kentucky Resolutions (November 1798)

1. *Resolved,* That the several States composing the United States of America, are not united on the principle of unlimited submission to their general government; but that, by a compact under the style and title of a Constitution for the United States, and of amendments, thereto, they constituted a general government for special purposes—delegated to that government certain definite powers, reserving, each State to itself, the residuary mass of right to their own self-government; and that whensoever the general government assumes undelegated powers, its acts are unauthoritative, void, and of no force: that to this compact each State acceded as a State, and as an integral party, its co-States forming, as to itself, the other party: that the government created by this compact was not made the exclusive or final judge of the extent of the powers delegated to itself; since that would have made its discretion, and not the Constitution, the measure of its powers; but that, as in all other cases of compact among powers having no common judge, each party has an equal right to judge for itself, as well of infractions as of the mode and measure of redress.

2. *Resolved,* That the Constitution of the United States, having delegated to Congress a power to punish treason, counterfeiting the securities and current coin of the United States, piracies, and felonies committed on the high seas, and offences against the law of nations, and no other crimes whatsoever; and it being true as a general principle, and one of the amendments to the Constitution having also declared, that "the powers not delegated to the United States by the Constitution, nor prohibited by it to the States, are reserved to the States respectively, or to the people," therefore the act of Congress, passed on the 14th day of July, 1798, and intituled "An Act in addition to the act intituled An Act for the punishment of certain crimes aginst the United States," as also the act passed by them on the — day of June, 1798, intituled "An Act to punish frauds committed on the bank of the United States," (and all their other acts which assume to create, define, or punish crimes, other than those so enumerated in the Constitution,) are altogether void, and of no force; and that the power to create, define and punish such other crimes is reserved, and, of right, appertains solely and exclusively to the respective States, each within its own territory.

3. *Resolved,* That it is true as a general principle, and is also expressly declared by one of the amendments to the Constitution, that "the powers not delegated to the United States by the Constitution, nor prohibited by it to the States, are reserved to the States respectively, or to the people"; and that no power over the freedom of religion, freedom of speech, or freedom of the press being delegated to the United States by the Constitution, nor prohibited by it to the States, all lawful powers respecting the same did of right remain, and were reserved to the States or the people: that thus was manifested their determination to retain to themselves the right of judging how far the licentiousness of speech and of the press may be abridged without lessening their useful freedom, and

how far those abuses which cannot be separated from their use should be tolerated, rather than the use be destroyed. And thus also they guarded against all abridgement by the United States of the freedom of religious opinions and exercises, and retained to themselves the right of protecting the same, as this State, by a law passed on the general demand of its citizens, had already protected them from all human restraint or interference. And that in addition to this general principle and express declaration, another and more special provision has been made by one of the amendments to the Constitution, which expressly declares, that "Congress shall make no law respecting an establishment of religion, or prohibiting the free exercise thereof, or abridging the freedom of speech or of the press": thereby guarding in the same sentence, and under the same words, the freedom of religion, of speech, and of the press: insomuch, that whatever violated either, throws down the sanctuary which covers the others, and that libels, falsehood, and defamation, equally with heresy and false religion, are withheld from the cognizance of federal tribunals. That, therefore, the act of Congress of the United States, passed on the 14th day of July, 1798, intituled "An Act in addition to the act intituled An Act for the punishment of certain crimes against the United States," which does abridge the freedom of the press, is not law, but is altogether void, and of no force.

4. *Resolved,* That alien friends are under the jurisdiction and protection of the laws of the State wherein they are: that no power over them has been delegated to the United States, nor prohibited to the individual States, distinct from their power over citizens. And it being true as a general principle, and one of the amendments to the Constitution having also declared, that "the powers not delegated to the United States by he Constitution, nor prohibited by it to the States, are reserved to the States respectively, or to the people," the act of the Congress of the United States, passed on the — day of July, 1798, intituled "An

Act concerning aliens," which assumes powers over alien friends, not delegated by the Constitution, is not law, but is altogether void, and of no force.

5. *Resolved,* That in addition to the general principle, as well as the express declaration, that powers not delegated are reserved, another and more special provision, inserted in the Constitution from abundant caution, has declared that "the migration or importation of such persons as any of the States now existing shall think proper to admit, shall not be prohibited by the Congress prior to the year 1808": that this commonwealth does admit the migration of alien friends, described as the subject of the said act concerning aliens: that a provision against prohibiting their migration, is a provision against all acts equivalent thereto, or it would be nugatory: that to remove them when migrated, is equivalent to a prohibition of their migration, and is, therefore, contrary to the said provision of the Constitution and void.

6. *Resolved,* That the imprisonment of a person under the protection of the laws of this commonwealth, on his failure to obey the simple *order* of the President to depart out of the United States, as is undertaken by said act intituled "An Act concerning aliens," is contrary to the Constitution, one amendment to which has provided that "no person shall be deprived of liberty without due progress of law"; and that another having provided that "in all criminal prosecutions the accused shall enjoy the right to public trial by an impartial jury, to be informed of the nature and cause of the accusation, to be confronted with the witnesses against him, to have compulsory process for obtaining witnesses in his favor, and to have the assistance of counsel for his defence," the same act, undertaking to authorize the President to remove a person out of the United States, who is under the protection of the law, on his own suspicion, without accusation, without jury, without public trial, without confrontation of the witnesses against him, without hearing witnesses in his fa-

vor, without defence, without counsel, is contrary to the provision also of the Constitution, is therefore not law, but utterly void, and of no force:; that transferring the power of judging any person, who is under the protection of the laws, from the courts to the President of the United States, as is undertaken by the same act concerning aliens, is against the article of the Constitution which provides that "the judicial power of the United States shall be vested in courts, the judges of which shall hold their offices during good behavior"; and that the said act is void for that reason also. And it is further to be noted, that this transfer of judiciary power is to that magistrate of the general government who already possesses all the Executive, and a negative on all Legislative powers.

7. *Resolved,* That the construction applied by the General Government (as is evidenced by sundry of their proceedings) to those parts of the Constitution of the United States which delegate to Congress a power "to lay and collect taxes, duties, imports, and exercises, to pay the debts, and provide for the common defence and general welfare of the United States," and "to make all laws which shall be necessary and proper for carrying into execution the powers vested by the Constitution in the government of the United States, or in any department or office thereof," goes to the destruction of all limits prescribed to their power by the Constitution: that words meant by the instrument to be subsidiary only to the execution of limited powers, ought not to be so construed as themselves to give unlimited powers, nor a part to be so taken as to destroy the whole residue of that instrument: that the proceedings of the General Government under color of these articles, will be a fit and necessary subject of revisal and correction, at a time of greater tranquillity, while those specified in the preceding resolutions call for immediate redress.

8. *Resolved,* That a committee of conference and correspondence be appointed, who shall have in charge to communicate

the preceding resolutions to the Legislatures of the several States; to assure them that this commonwealth continues in the same esteem of their friendship and union which it has manifested from that moment at which a common danger first suggested a common union: that it considers union, for specified national purposes, and particularly to those specified in their late federal compact, to be friendly to the peace, happiness and prosperity of all the States: that faithful to that compact, according to the plain intent and meaning in which it was understood and acceded to by the several parties, it is sincerely anxious for its preservation: that it does also believe, that to take from the States all the powers of self-government and transfer them to a general and consolidated government, wihout regard to the special delegations and reservations solemnly agreed to in that compact, is not for the peace, happiness or prosperity of these States; and that therefore this commonwealth is determined, as it doubts not its co-States are, to submit to undelegated, and consequently unlimited powers in no man, or body of men on earth: that in cases of an abuse of the delegated powers, the members of the general government, being chosen by the people, a change by the people would be the constitutional remedy; but, where powers are assumed which have not been delegated, a nullification of the act is the rightful remedy: that every State has a natural right in cases within the compact, (casus non foederis,) to nullify of their own authority all assumptions of power by others within their limits: that without this right, they would be under the dominion, absolute and unlimited, of whosoever might exercise this right of judgment for them: that nevertheless, this commonwealth, from motives of regard and respect for its co-States, has wished to communicate with them on the subject: that with them alone it is proper to communicate, they alone being parties to the compact, and solely authorized to judge in the last resort of the powers exercised under it, Congress being not a party, but merely

the creature of the compact, and subject as to its assumptions of power to the final judgment of those by whom, and for whose use itself and its powers were all created and modified: that if the acts before specified should stand, these conclusions would flow from them; that the general government may place any act they think proper on the list of crimes, and punish it themselves whether enumerated or not enumerated by the constitution as cognizable by them: that they may transfer its cognizance to the President, or any other person, who may himself be the accuser, counsel, judge and jury, whose suspicions may be the evidence, his order the sentence, his officer the executioner, and his breast the sole record of the transaction: that a very numerous and valuable description of the inhabitants of these States being, by this precedent, reduced, as outlaws, to the absolute dominion of one man, and the barrier of the Constitution thus swept away from us all, no rampart now remains against the passions and the powers of a majority in Congress to protect from a like exportation, or other more grievous punishment, the minority of the same body, the legislatures, judges, governors and counsellors of the States, nor their other peaceable inhabitants, who may venture to reclaim the constitutional rights and liberties of the States and people, or who for other causes, good or bad, may be obnoxious to the views, or marked by the suspicions of the President, or be thought dangerous to his or their election, or other interests, public or personal: that the friendless alien has indeed been selected as the safest subject of a first experiment; but the citizen will soon follow, or rather, has already followed, for already has a sedition act marked him as its prey: that these and successive acts of the same character, unless arrested at the threshold, necessarily drive these States into revolution and blood, and will furnish new calmunies against republican government, and new pretexts for those who wish it to be believed that man cannot be governed by by a rod of iron: that it would be a dangerous delusion were a confidence in the men of our choice to silence our fears for the safety of our rights: that confidence is everywhere the parent of despotiem—free government is founded in jealousy, and not in confidence; it is jealousy and not confidence which prescribes limited constitutions, to bind down those whom we are obliged to trust with power: that our Constitution has accordingly fixed the limits to which, and no further, our confidence may go; and let the honest advocate of confidence read the Alien and Sedition acts, and say if the Constitution has not been wise in fixing limits to the government it created, and whether we should be wise in destroying those limits. Let him say what the government is, if it be not a tyranny, which the men of our choice have conferred on our President, and the President of our choice has assented to, and accepted over the friendly strangers to whom the mild spirit of our country and its law have pledged hospitality and protection: that the men of our choice have more respected the bare *suspicions* of the President, than the solid right of innocence, the claims of justification, the sacred force of truth, and the forms and substance of law and justice. In questions of power, then, let no more be heard of confidence in man, but bind him down from mischief by the chains of the Constitution. That this commonwealth does therefore call on its co-States for an expression of their sentiments on the acts concerning aliens, and for the punishment of certain crimes herein before specified, plainly declaring whether these acts are or are not authorized by the federal compact. And it doubts not that their sense will be so announced as to prove their attachment unaltered to limited government, whether general or particular. And that the rights and liberties of their co-States will be exposed to no dangers by remaining embarked in a common bottom with their own. That they will concur with this commonwealth in considering the said acts as so palpably against the Constitution as to amount to an undisguised declaration that that com-

pact is not meant to be the measure of the powers of the General Government, but that it will proceed in the exercise over these States, of all powers whatsoever: that they will view this as seizing the rights of the States, and consolidating them in the hands of the General Government, with a power assumed to bind the States (not merely as the cases made federal, *casus foederis* but), in all cases whatsoever, by laws made, not with their consent, but by others against their consent: that this would be to surrender the form of government we have chosen, and live under one deriving its powers from its own will, and not from our authority; and that the co-States, recurring to their natural right in cases not made federal, will concur in declaring these acts void, and of no force, and will each take measures of its own for providing that neither these acts, nor any others of the General Government not plainly and intentionally authorized by the Constitution, shall be exercised within their respective territories.

9. *Resolved,* That the said committee be authorized to communicate by writing or personal conferences, at any times or places whatever, with any person or persons who may be appointed by any one or more co-States to correspond or confer with them; and that they lay their proceedings before the next session of Assembly.

Kentucky Resolutions as passed in November 1798, Sections 8 and 9

VIII. Resolved, that the preceding Resolutions be transmitted to the Senators and Representatives in Congress from this Commonwealth, who are hereby enjoined to present the same to their respective Houses, and to use their best endeavours to procure at the next session of Congress, a repeal of the aforesaid unconstitutional and obnoxious acts.

IX. Resolved lastly, that the Governor of this Commonwealth be, and is hereby authorised and requested to communicate the preceding Resolutions to the Legislatures of the several States, to assure them that this Commonwealth considers Union for specified National purposes, and particularly for those specified in their late Federal Compact, to be friendly to the peace, happiness, and prosperity of all the States: that faithful to that compact, according to the plain intent and meaning in which it was understood and acceded to by the several parties, it is sincerely anxious for its preservation: that it does also believe, that to take from the States all the powers of self government, and transfer them to a general and consolidated Government, without regard to the special delegations and reservations solemnly agreed to in that compact, is not for the peace, happiness, or prosperity of these States: And that therefore, this Commonwealth is determined, as it doubts not its co-States are, namely to submit to undelegated & consequently unlimited powers in no man or body of men on earth: that if the acts before specified should stand, these conclusions would flow from them; that the General Government may place any act they think proper on the list of cries & punish it themselves, whether enumerated or not enumerated by the Constitution as cognizable by them: that they may transfer its cognizance to the President or any other person, who may himself be the accuser, counsel, judge, and jury, whose *suspicions* may be the evidence, his order the sentence, his officer the executioner, and his breast the sole record of the transaction: that a very numerous and valuable description of the inhabitants of these States, being by this precedent reduced as outlaws to the absolute dominion of one man and the barrier of the Constitution thus swept away from us all, no rampart now remains against the passions and the power of a majority of Congress, to protect from a like exportation or other more grievous punishment the minority of the same body, the Legislatures, Judges, Governors, & Counsellors of the States, nor their other peaceable inhabitants who may venture to reclaim the constitutional rights & liberties of the States & people, or who for other causes, good or bad, may be obnoxious to the views or marked by the suspicions of the President, or be thought dangerous to his or their elections or other interests public or personal: that the friendless alien has indeed been selected as the safest subject of a first experiment: but the citizen will soon follow, or rather has already followed; for, already has a Sedition Act marked him as its prey: that these and successive acts of the same character, unless arrested on the threshold, may tend to drive these States into revolution and blood, and will furnish new calumnies against Republican Governments, and new pretexts for those who wish it be be believed, that man cannot be governed but by a rod of iron: that it would be a dangerous delusion were a confidence in the men of our choice to silence our fears for the safety of our rights: that confidence is every where the parent of despotism: free government is founded in jealousy and not in confidence; it is jealousy and not confidence which prescribes limited Constitutions to bind down those whom we obliged to trust with power: that our Constitution has accordingly fixed the limits to which and no further our confidence may go; and let the honest advocate of confidence read the Alien and Sedition Acts, and say if the Constitution has not been wise in fixing limits to the Government it created, and whether we should be wise in destroying those limits? Let him say what the Government is if it be not a tyranny, which the men of our choice have conferred on the President, and the President of our choice has assented to, and accepted over the friendly strangers, to whom the mild spirit of our Country and its laws had pledged hospitality and protection: that the men of our choice have more respected the bare suspicions of the President than the solid rights of innocence, the claims of justification, the sacred force of truth, and the forms & substance of law and justice. In questions of power then let no more be heard of confidence in man, but bind him down from mischief by the chains of the Constitution. That this Commonwealth does therefore call on its co-States for an expression of their sentiments on the acts concerning Aliens, and for the punishment of certain crimes herein before specified, plainly declaring whether these acts are or are not authorized by the Federal Compact? And it doubts not that their sense will be so announced as to prove their attachment unaltered to limited Government, whether general or particular, and that the rights and liberties of their co-States will be exposed to no dangers by remaining embarked on a common bottom with their own: That they will concur with this Commonwealth in considering the said acts as so palpably against the Constitution as to amount to an undisguised declaration, that the Compact is not meant to be the measure of the powers of the General Government, but that it will proceed in the exercise over these States of all powers whatsoever: That they will view this as seizing the rights of the States and consolidating them in the hands of the General Government with a power assumed to bind the States (not merely in cases made federal) but in all cases whatsoever, by laws made, not with their consent, but by others against their consent: That this would be to surrender the form of Government we have chosen, and to live under one deriving its powers from its own will, and not from our authority; and that the co-States recurring to their natural right in cases not made federal, will concur in declaring these acts void and of no force, and will each unite with this Commonwealth in requesting their repeal at the next session of Congress.

First Inaugural Address, March 1801

FRIENDS AND FELLOW CITIZENS: Called upon to undertake the duties of the first executive office of our country, I avail myself of the presence of that portion of my fellow citizens which is here assembled, to express my grateful thanks for the favor with which they have been pleased to look toward me, to declare a sincere consciousness that the task is above my talents, and that I approach it with those anxious and awful presentiments which the greatness of the charge and the weakness of my powers so justly inspire. A rising nation, spread over a wide and fruitful land, traversing all the seas with the rich productions of their industry, engaged in commerce with nations who feel power and forget right, advancing rapidly to destinies beyond the reach of mortal eye—when I contemplate these transcendent objects, and see the honor, the happiness, and the hopes of this beloved country committed to the issue and the auspices of this day, I shrink from the contemplation, and humble myself before the magnitude of the undertaking. Utterly indeed, should I despair, did not the presence of many whom I here see remind me, that in the other high authorities provided by our constitution, I shall find resources of wisdom, of virtue, and of zeal, on which to rely under all difficulties. To you, then, gentlemen, who are charged with the sovereign functions of legislation, and to those associated with you, I look with encouragement for that guidance and support which may enable us to steer with safety the vessel in which we are all embarked amid the conflicting elements of a troubled world.

During the contest of opinion through which we have passed, the animation of discussion and of exertions has sometimes worn an aspect which might impose on strangers unused to think freely and to speak and to write what they think; but this being now decided by the voice of the nation, announced according to the rules of the constitution, all will, of course, arrange themselves under the will of the law, and unite in common efforts for the common good. All, too, will bear in mind this sacred principle, that though the will of the majority is in all cases to prevail, that will, to be rightful, must be reasonable; that the minority possess their equal rights, which equal laws must protect, and to violate which would be oppression. Let us, then, fellow-citizens, unite with one heart and one mind. Let us restore to social intercourse that harmony and affection without which liberty and even life itself are but dreary things. And let us reflect that having banished from our land that religious intolerance under which mankind so long bled and suffered, we have yet gained little if we countenance a political intolerance as despotic, as wicked, and capable of as bitter and bloody persecutions. During the throes and convulsions of the ancient world, during the agonizing spasms of infuriated man, seeking through blood and slaughter his long-lost liberty, it was not wonderful that the agitation of the billows should reach even this distant and peaceful shore; that this should be more felt and feared by some and less by others; that this should divine opinions as to measures of safety. But every difference of opinion is not a difference of principle. We have called by different names brethren of the same principle. We are all reupblicans—we are federalists. If there be any among us who would wish to dissolve this Union or to change its republican form, let them stand undisturbed as monuments of the safety with which error of opinion may be tolerated where reason is left free to combat it. I know, indeed, that some honest men fear that a republican government cannot be strong; that this government is not strong enough. But would the honest patriot, in the full tide of successful experiment abandon a government which has so far kept us free and firm, on the theoretic and visionary fear that this government, the world's best hope, may by possibility want energy to preserve itself? I trust not. I believe this, on the contrary, the strongest government on earth. I believe it is the only one where every man, at the call of the laws, would fly to the standard of the law, and would meet invasions of the public order as his own personal concern. Sometimes it is said that man cannot be trusted with the government of himself. Can he, then, be trusted with the government of others? Or have we found angels in the forms of kings to govern him? Let history answer this question.

Let us, then, with courage and confidence pursue our own federal and republican principles, our attachment to our union and representative government. Kindly separated by nature and a wide ocean from the exterminating havoc of one quarter of the globe; too high-minded to endure the degradations of the others; possessing a chosen country, with room enough for our descendants to the hundredth and thousandth generation; entertaining a due sense of our equal right to the use of our own faculties, to the acquisitions of our industry, to honor and confidence from our fellow citizens, resulting not from birth but from our actions and their sense of them; enlightened by a benign religion, professed, indeed, and practiced in various forms, yet all of them including honesty, truth, temperance, gratitude, and the love of man; acknowledging and adoring an overruling Providence, which by all its dispensations proves that it delights in the happiness of man here and his greater happiness hereafter; with all these blessings, what more is necessary to make us a happy and prosperous people? Still one thing more, fellow citizens—a wise and frugal government, which shall restrain men from injuring one another, which shall leave them otherwise free to regulate their own pursuits of industry and improvement, and shall not take from the mouth of labor the bread it has earned. This is the sum of good government, and this is necessary to close the circle of our felicities.

About to enter, fellow citizens, on the exercise of duties which comprehend everything dear and valuable to you, it is proper that you should understand what I deem the essential principles of our government, and consequently those which ought to shape its administration. I will compress them within the narrowest compass they will bear, stating the general principle, but not all its limitations. Equal and exact justice to all men, of whatever state or persuasion, religious or political; peace, commerce, and honest friendship with all nations—entangling alliances with none; the support of the State governments in all their rights, as the most competent administrations for our domestic concerns and the surest bulwarks against anti-republican tendencies; the preservation of the general government in its whole constitutional vigor, as the sheet anchor of our peace at home and safety abroad; a jealous care of the right of election by the people—a mild and safe corrective of abuses which are lopped by the sword of the revolution where peaceable remedies are unprovided; absolute acquiescence in the decisions of the majority—the vital principle of republics, from which there is no appeal but to force, the vital principle and immediate parent of despotism; a well-disciplined milita—our best reliance in peace and for the first moments of war, till regulars may relieve them; the supremacy of the civil over the military authority; economy in the public expense, that labor may be lightly burdened; the honest payment of our debts and sacred preservation of the public faith; encouragement of agriculture, and of commerce as its handmaid; the diffusion of information and the arraignment of all abuses at the bar of public reason; freedom of religion; freedom of the press; freedom of person under the protection of the *habeas corpus;* and trial by juries impartially selected—these principles form the bright constellation which has gone before us, and guided our steps through an age of revolution and reformation. The wisdom of our sages and the blood of our heroes have been devoted to their attainment. They should be the creed of our political faith—the text of civil instruction—the touchstone by which to try the services of those we trust; and should we wander from them in moments of error or alarm, let us hasten to retrace our steps and to regain the road which alone leads into peace, liberty, and safety.

I repair, then, fellow citizens, to the post you have assigned me. With experience enough in subordinate offices to have seen the difficulties of this, the greatest of all, I have learned to expect that it will rarely fall to the lot of imperfect man to retire from this station with the reputation and the favor which bring him into it. Without pretensions to that high confidence reposed in our first and great revolutionary character, whose preeminent services had entitled him to the first place in his country's love, and destined for him the fairest page in the volume of faithful history, I ask so much confidence only as may give firmness and effect to the legal administration of your affairs. I shall often go wrong through defect of judgment. When right, I shall often be thought wrong by those whose positions will not command a view of the whole ground. I ask your indulgence for my own errors, which will never be intentional; and your support against the errors of others, who may condemn what they would not if seen in all its parts. The approbation implied by your suffrage is a consolation to me for the past; and my future solicitude will be to retain the good opinion of those who have bestowed it in advance, to conciliate that of others by doing them all the good in my power, and to be instrumental to the happiness and freedom of all.

Relying, then, on the patronage of your good will, I advance with obedience to the work, ready to retire from it whenever you become sensible how much better choice it is in your power to make. And may that Infinite Power which rules the destinies of the universe, lead our councils to what is best, and give them a favorable issue for your peace and prosperity.

Second Inaugural Address, March 1805

Proceeding, fellow citizens, to that qualification which the constitution requires, before my entrance on the charge again conferred upon me, it is my duty to express the deep sense I entertain of this new proof of confidence from my fellow citizens at large, and the zeal with which it inspires me, so to conduct myself as may best satisfy their just expectations.

On taking this station on a former occasion, I declared the principles on which I believed it my duty to administer the affairs of our commonwealth. My conscience tells me that I have, on every occasion, acted up to that declaration, according to its obvious import, and to the understanding of every candid mind.

In the transaction of your foreign affairs, we have endeavored to cultivate the friendship of all nations, and especially of those with which we have the most important relations. We have done them justice on all occasions, favored where favor was lawful, and cherished mutual interests and intercourse on fair and equal terms. We are firmly convinced, and we act on that conviction, that with nations, as with individuals, our interests soundly calculated, will ever be found inseparable from our moral duties; and history bears witness to the fact, that a just nation is taken on its word, when recourse is had to armaments and wars to bridle others.

At home, fellow citizens, you best know whether we have done well or ill. The suppression of unnecessary offices, of useless establishments and expenses, enabled us to discontinue our internal taxes. These covering our land with officers, and opening our doors to their intrusions, had already begun that process of domiciliary vexation which, once entered, is scarcely to be restrained from reaching successively every article of produce and property. If among these taxes some minor ones fell which had not been inconvenient, it was because their amount would not have paid the officers who collected them, and because, if they had any merit, the state authorities might adopt them, instead of others less approved.

The remaining revenue on the consumption of foreign articles, is paid cheerfully by those who can afford to add foreign luxuries to domestic comforts, being collected on our seaboards and frontiers only, and incorporated with the transactions of our mercantile citizens, it may be the pleasure and pride of an American to ask, what farmer, what mechanic, what laborer, ever sees a tax-gatherer of the United States? These contributions enable us to support the current expenses of the government, to fulfil contracts with foreign nations, to extinguish the native right of soil within our limits, to extend those limits, and to apply such a surplus to our public debts, as places at a short day their final redemption, and that redemption once affected, the revenue thereby liberated may, by a just repartition among the states, and a corresponding amendment of the constitution, be applied, *in time of peace,* to rivers, canals, roads, arts, manufactures, education, and other great objects within each state. *In time of war,* if injustice, by ourselves or others, must sometimes produce war, increased as the same revenue will be increased by population and consumption, and aided by other resources reserved for that crisis, it may meet within the year all the expenses of the year, without encroaching on the rights of future generations, by burdening them with the debts of the past. War will then be but a suspension of useful works, and a return to a state of peace, a return to the progress of improvement.

I have said, fellow citizens, that the income reserved had enabled us to extend our limits; but that extension may possibly pay for itself before we are called on, and in the meantime, may keep down the accruing interest; in all events, it will repay the advances we have made. I know that the acquisition of

Louisiana has been disapproved by some, from a candid apprehension that the enlargement of our territory would endanger its union. But who can limit the extent to which the federative principle may operate effectively? The larger our association, the less will it be shaken by local passions; and in any view, is it not better that the opposite bank of the Mississippi should be settled by our own brethren and children, than by strangers of another family? With which shall we be most likely to live in harmony and friendly intercourse?

In matters of religion, I have considered that its free exercise is placed by the constitution independent of the powers of the general government. I have therefore undertaken, on no occasion, to prescribe the religious exercises suited to it; but have left them, as the constitution found them, under the direction and discipline of state or church authorities acknowledged by the several religious societies.

The aboriginal inhabitants of these countries I have regarded with the commiseration their history inspires. Endowed with the faculties and the rights of men, breathing an ardent love of liberty and independence, and occupying a country which left them no desire but to be undisturbed, the stream of overflowing population from other regions directed itself on these shores; without power to divert, or habits to contend against, they have been overwhelmed by the current, or driven before it; now reduced within limits too narrow for the hunter's state, humanity enjoins us to teach them agriculture and the domestic arts; to encourage them to that industry which alone can enable them to maintain their place in existence, and to prepare them in time for that state of society, which to bodily comforts adds the improvement of the mind and morals. We have therefore liberally furnished them with the implements of husbandry and household use; we have placed among them instructors in the arts of first necessity; and they are covered with the aegis of the law against aggressors from among ourselves.

But the endeavors to enlighten them on the fate which awaits their present course of life, to induce them to exercise their reason, follow its dictates, and change their pursuits with the change of circumstances, have powerful obstacles to encounter; they are combated by the habits of their bodies, prejudice of their minds, ignorance, pride, and the influence of interested and crafty individuals among them, who feel themselves something in the present order of things, and fear to become nothing in any other. These persons inculcate a sanctimonious reverence for the customs of their ancestors; that whatsoever they did, must be done through all time; that reason is a false guide, and to advance under its counsel, in their physical, moral, or political condition, is perilous innovation; that their duty is to remain as their Creator made them, ignorance being safety, and knowledge full of danger; in short, my friends, among them is seen the action and counteraction of good sense and bigotry; they, too, have their anti-philosophers, who find an interest in keeping things in their present state, who dread reformation, and exert all their faculties to maintain the ascendency of habit over the duty of improving our reason, and obeying its mandates.

In giving these outlines, I do not mean, fellow citizens, to arrogate to myself the merit of the measures; that is due, in the first place, to the reflecting character of our citizens at large, who, by the weight of public opinion, influence and strengthen the public measures; it is due to the sound discretion with which they select from among themselves those to whom they confide the legislative duties; it is due to the zeal and wisdom of the characters thus selected, who lay the foundations of public happiness in wholesome laws, the execution of which alone remains for others; and it is due to the able and faithful auxiliaries, whose patriotism has associated with me in the executive functions.

During this course of administration, and in order to disturb it, the artillery of the press has been levelled against us, charged with whatsoever its licentiousness could devise or dare. These abuses of an institution so important to freedom and science, are deeply to be regretted, inasmuch as they tend to lessen its usefulness, and to sap its safety; they might, indeed, have been corrected by the wholesome punishments reserved and provided by the laws of the several States against falsehood and defamation; but public duties more urgent press on the time of public servants, and the offenders have therefore been left to find their punishment in the public indignation.

Nor was it uninteresting to the world, that an experiment should be fairly and fully made, whether freedom of discussion, unaided by power, is not sufficient for the propagation and protection of truth—whether a government, conducting itself in the true spirit of its constitution, with zeal and purity, and doing no act which it would be unwilling the whole world should witness, can be written down by falsehood and defamation. The experiment has been tried; you have witnessed the scene; our fellow citizens have looked on, cool and collected; they saw the latent source from which these outrages proceeded; they gathered around their public functionaries, and when the constitution called them to the decision by suffrage, they pronounced their verdict, honorable to those who had served them, and consolatory to the friend of man, who believes he may be intrusted with his own affairs.

No inference is here intended, that the laws, provided by the State against false and defamatory publications, should not be enforced; he who has time, renders a service to public morals and public tranquility, in reforming these abuses by the salutary coercions of the law; but the experiment is noted, to prove that, since truth and reason have maintained their ground against false opinions in league with false facts, the press, confined to truth, needs no other legal restraint; the public judgment will correct false reasonings and opinions, on a full hearing of all parties; and no other definite line can be drawn between the inestimable liberty of the press and its demoralizing licentiousness. If there be still improprieties which this rule would not restrain, its supplement must be sought in the censorship of public opinion.

Contemplating the union of sentiment now manifested so generally, as auguring harmony and happiness to our future course, I offer to our country sincere congratulations. With those, too, not yet rallied to the same point, the disposition to do so is gaining strength; facts are piercing through the veil drawn over them; and our doubting brethren will at length see, that the mass of their fellow citizens, with whom they cannot yet resolve to act, as to principles and measures, think as they think, and desire what they desire; that our wish, as well as theirs, is, that the public efforts may be directed honestly to the public good, that peace be cultivated, civil and religious liberty unassailed, law and order preserved, equality of rights maintained, and that state of property, equal or unequal, which results to every man from his own industry, or that of his fathers. When satisfied of these views, it is not in human nature that they should not approve and support them; in the meantime, let us cherish them with patient affection; let us do them justice, and more than justice, in all competitions of interest; and we need not doubt that truth, reason, and their own interests, will at length prevail, will gather them into the fold of their country, and will complete their entire union of opinion, which gives to a nation the blessing of harmony, and the benefit of all its strength.

I shall now enter on the duties to which my fellow citizens have again called me, and shall proceed in the spirit of those principles which they have approved. I fear not that any motives of interest may lead me astray; I am sensible of no passion which could seduce me knowingly from the path of justice; but the weakness of human nature, and the limits of my own understanding, will produce errors of judgment sometimes injurious to your interests. I shall need, therefore, all the indulgence I have heretofore experienced—the want of it will certainly not lessen with increasing years. I shall need, too, the favor of that Being in whose hands we are, who led our forefathers, as Israel of old, from their native land, and planted them in a country flowing with all the necessaries and comforts of life; who has covered our infancy with his providence, and our riper years with his wisdom and power; and to whose goodness I ask you to join with me in supplications, that he will so enlighten the minds of your servants, guide their councils, and prosper their measures, that whatsoever they do, shall result in your good, and shall secure to you the peace, friendship, and approbation of all nations.

Letter to John Adams, October 1813

. . . The passage you quote from Theognis, I think has an ethical rather than a political object. The whole piece is a moral *exhortation*, . . . and this passage particularly seems to be a reproof to man, who while with his domestic animals he is curious to improve the race, by employing always the finest male, pays no attention to the improvement of his own race, but intermarries with the vicious, the ugly, or the old, for considerations of wealth or ambition. It is in conformity with the principle adopted afterwards by the Pythagoreans, and expressed by Ocellus in another form; . . . [at this point, Jefferson quotes the original Greek.—Ed.] which as literally as intelligiability will admit, may be thus translated: "concerning the interprocreation of men, how, and of whom it shall be in a perfect manner, and according to the laws of modesty and sanctity, conjointly, this is what I think right. First to lay it down that we do not commix for the sake of pleasure, but of the procreation of children. For the powers, the organs and desires for coition have not been given by God to man for the sake of pleasure, but for the procreation of the race. For as it were incongruous, for a mortal born to partake of divine life, the immortality of the race being taken away, God fulfilled the purpose by making the generations uninterrupted and continuous. This, therefore, we are especially to lay down as a principle, that coition is not for the sake of pleasure." But nature, not trusting to this moral and abstract motive, seems to have provided more securely for the perpetuation of the species, by making it the effect of the *oestrum* implanted in the constitution of both sexes. And not only has the commerce of love been indulged on this unhallowed impulse, but made subservient also to wealth and ambition by marriage, without regard to the beauty, the healthiness, the understanding, or virtue of the subject from which we are to breed. The selecting the best male for a Harem of well chosen females also, which Theognis seems to recommend from the example of our sheep and asses, would doubtless improve the human, as it does the brute animal, and produce a race of revitable *aristoi*. For experience proves, that the moral and physical qualities of man, whether good or evil, are transmissible in a certain degree from father to son. But I suspect that the equal rights of men will rise up against this privileged Solomon and his Harem, and oblige us to continue acquiescence . . . and to content ourselves with the accidental *aristoi* produced by the fortuitious concourse of breeders.

For I agree with you that there is a natural aristocracy among men. The grounds of this are virtue and talents.

Formerly, bodily powers gave place among the *aristoi*. But since the invention of gunpowder has armed the weak as well as the strong with missile death, bodily strength, like beauty, good humor, politeness and other accomplishments, has become but an auxiliary ground of distinction. There is also an artificial aristocracy, founded on wealth and birth, without either virtue or talents; for with these it would belong to the first class. The natural aristocracy I consider as the most precious gift of nature, for the instruction, the thrusts, and government of society. And indeed, it would have been inconsistent in creation to have formed man for the social state, and not to have provided virtue and wisdom enough to manage the concerns of the society. May we not even say, that the form of government is the best, which provides the most effectually for a pure selection of these natural aristoi into the offices of government? The artificial aristocracy is a mischievous ingredient in government, and provision should be made to prevent its ascendency. On the question, what is the best provision, you and I differ; but we differ as rational friends, using the free exercise of our own reason, and mutually indulging its errors. You think it best to put the psuedo-aristoi into a separate chamber of legislation, where they may be hindered from doing mischief by their co-ordinate branches, and where, also, they may be a protection to wealth against the Agrarian and plundering enterprises of the majority of the people. I think that to give them power in order to prevent them from doing mischief, is arming them for it, and increasing instead of remedying the evil. For if the co-ordinate branches can arrest their action, so may they that of the co-ordinates. Mischief may be done negatively as well as positively. Of this, a cabal in the Senate of the United States, has furnished many proofs. Nor do I believe them necessary to protect the wealthy; because enough of these will find their way into every branch of the legislation, to protect themselves. From fifteen to twenty legis-

latures of our own, in action for thirty years past, have proved that no fears of an equalization of property are to be apprehended from them. I think the best remedy is exactly that provided by all our constitutions, to leave to the citizens the free election and separation of the aristoi from the pseudo-aristoi, of the wheat from the chaff. In general they will elect the really good and wise. In some instances, wealth may corrupt, and birth blind them; but not in sufficient degree to endanger the society.

It is probable that our difference of opinion may, in some measure, be produced by a difference of character in those among whom we live. From what I have seen of Massachusetts and Connecticut myself, and still more from what I have heard, and the character given of the former by yourself, who know them so much better, there seems to be in those two States a traditionary reverence for certain families, which has rendered the offices of the government nearly hereditary in those families. I presume that from an early period of your history, members of those families happening to possess virtue and talents, have honestly exercised them for the good of the people, and by their services have endeared their names to them. In coupling Connecticut with you, I mean it politically only, not morally. For having made the Bible the common law of their land, they seem to have modeled their morality on the story of Jacob and Laban. But although this hereditary succession to office with you, may, in some degree, be founded in real family merit, yet in a much higher degree, it has proceeded from your strict alliance of Church and State. These families are canonised in the eyes of the people on common principles, "you tickle me, and I will tickle you." In Virginia we have nothing of this. Our clergy, before the revolution, having been secured against rivalship by fixed salaries, did not give themselves the trouble of acquiring influence over the people. Of wealth, there were great accumulations in particular families, handed down from generation to generation, under the English law of entails. But the only object of ambition for the wealthy was a seat in the King's Council. All their court then was paid to the crown and its creatures; and they Philipised in all collisions between the King and the people. Hence they were unpopular; and that unpopularity continues attached to their names. A Randolph, a Carter, or a Burwell must have great personal superiority over a common competitor to be elected by the people even at this day. At the first session of our legislature after the Declaration of Independence, we passed a law abolishing entails. And this was followed by one abolishing the privilege primogeniture, and dividing the lands of intestates equally among all their children, or other representatives. These laws, drawn by myself, laid the axe to the foot of pseudo-aristocracy. And had another which I prepared been adopted by the legislature, our work would have been complete. It was a bill for the more general diffusion of learning. This proposed to divide every county into wards of five or six miles square, like your townships; to establish in each ward a free school for reading, writing and common arithmetic; to provide for the annual selection of the best subjects from these schools, who might receive, at the public expense, a higher degree of education at a district school; and from these district schools to select a certain number of the most promising subjects, to be completed at an University, where all the useful sciences should be taught. Worth and genius would thus have been sought out from every condition of life, and completely prepared by education for defeating the competition of wealth and birth for public trusts. My proposition had, for a further object, to impart to these wards those portions of self-government for which they are best qualified, by confiding to them the care of their poor, their roads, police, elections, the nomination of jurors, administration of justice in small cases, elementary exercises of militia; in short, to have made them little republics, with a warden at

the head of each, for all those concerns which, being under their eye, they would better manage than the larger republics of the county or State. A general call of ward meetings by their wardens on the same day through the State, would at any time produce the genuine sense of the people on any required point, and would enable the State to act in mass, as your people have so often done, and with so much effect by their town meetings. The law for religious freedom, which made a part of this system, having put down the aristocracy of the clergy, and restored to the citizen the freedom of the mind, and those of entails and descents nurturing an equality of condition among them, this on education would have raised the mass of the people to the high ground of moral respectability necessary to their own safety, and to orderly government; and would have completed the great object of qualifying them to select the veritable aristoi, for the trusts of government, to the exclusion of the pseudalists; . . . . Although this law has not yet been acted on but in a small and inefficient degree, it is still considered as before the legislature, with other bills of the revised code, not yet taken up, and I have great hope that some patriotic spirit will, at a favorable moment, call it up, and make it the keystone of the arch of our government.

With respect to aristocracy, we should further consider, that before the establishment of the American States, nothing was known to history but the man of the old world, crowded within limits either small or overcharged, and steeped in the vices which that situation generates. A government adapted to such men would be one thing; but a very different one, that for the man of these States. Here everyone may have land to labor for himself, if he chooses; or, preferring the exercise of any other industry, may exact for it such compensation as not only to afford a comfortable subsistence, but wherewith to provide for a cessation from labor in old age.

Everyone, by his property, or by his satisfactory situation, is interested in the support of law and order. And such men may safely and advantageously reserve to themselves a wholesome control over their public affairs, and a degree of freedom, which, in the hands of the *canaille* of the cities of Europe, would be instantly perverted to the demolition and destruction of everything public and private. The history of the last twenty-five years of France, and of the last forty years in America, nay of its last two hundred years, proves the truth of both parts of this observation.

But even in Europe a change has sensibly taken place in the mind of man. Science had liberated the ideas of those who read and reflect, and the American example had kindled feelings of right in the people. An insurrection has consequently begun, or science, talents, and courage, against rank and birth, which have fallen into contempt. It has failed in its first effort, because the mobs of the cities, the instrument used for its accomplishment, debased by ignorance, poverty, and vice, could not be restrained to rational action. But the world will recover from the panic of this first catastrophe. Science is progressive, and talents and enterprise on the alert. Resort may be had to the people of the country, a more governable power from their principles and subordination; and rank, and birth, and tinsel-aristocracy will finally shrink into insignificance, even there. This, however, we have no right to meddle with. It suffices for us, if the moral and physical condition of our own citizens qualifies them to select the able and good for the direction of their government, with a recurrence of elections at such short periods as will enable them to displace an unfaithful servant, before the mischief he meditates may be irremediable.

I have thus stated my opinion on a point on which we differ, not with a view to controversy, for we are both too old to change opinions which are the result of a long life of inquiry and reflection; but on the suggestions of a former letter of yours, that we ought not to die before we have explained ourselves to each other. We acted in perfect harmony, through a long and perilous contest for our liberty and independence. A constitution has been acquired, which, though neither of us thinks perfect, yet both consider as competent to render our fellow citizens the happiest and the securest on whom the sun has ever shone. If we do not think exactly alike as to its imperfections, it matters little to our country, which, after devoting to it long lives of disinterested labor, we have delivered over to our successors in life, who will be able to take care of it and of themselves. . . .

Letter to Pierre Samuel Dupont de Nemours, Poplar Forest, April 1816

I received, my dear friend, your letter covering the constitution for your Equinoctial republics. . . . I suppose it well-formed for those for whom it was intended, and the excellence of every government is its adaptation to the state of those to be governed by it. For us it would not do. Distinguishing between the structure of the government and the moral principles on which you prescribe its administration, with the latter we concur cordially, with the former we should not. We of the United States, you know, are constitutionally and conscientiously democrats. We consider society as one of the natural wants with which man has been created; that he has been endowed with faculties and qualities to effect its satisfaction by concurrence of others having the same want; that when, by the exercise of these faculties, he has procured a state of society, it is one of his acquisitions which he has a right to regulate and control, jointly indeed with all those who have concurred in the procurement, whom he cannot exclude from its use or direction more than they him. We think experience has proved it safer, for the mass of individuals composing the society, to reserve to themselves personally the exercise of all rightful powers to which they are competent, and to delegate those to which they are not competent to deputies named, and removable for unfaithful conduct by themselves immediately. Hence, with us, the people (by which is meant the mass of individuals composing the society) being competent to judge of the facts occurring in ordinary life, they have retained the functions of judges of facts under the name of jurors; but being unqualified for the management of affairs requiring intelligence above the common level, yet competent judges of human character, they chose, for their management, representatives, some by themselves immediately, others by electors chosen by themselves. . . .

But when we come to the moral principles on which the government is to be administered, we come to what is proper for all conditions of society. I meet you there in all the benevolence and rectitude of your native character, and I love myself always most where I concur most with you. Liberty, truth, probity, honor are declared to be the four cardinal principles of your society. I believe with you that morality, compassion, generosity are innate elements of the human constitution; that there exists a right independent of force; that a right to property is founded in our natural wants, in the means with which we are endowed to satisfy these wants, and the right to what we acquire by those means without violating the similar rights of other sensible beings; that no one has a right to obstruct another exercising his faculties innocently for the relief of sensibilities made a part of his nature; that justice is the fundamental law of society; that the majority, oppressing an individual, is guilty of a crime, abuses its strength, and by acting on the law of the strongest breaks up the foundations of society; that action by the citizens in person, in affairs within their reach and competence, and in all others by representatives, chosen immediately and removable by themselves, constitutes the essence of a republic; that all governments are more or less republican in proportion as this principle enters more or less into their composition; and that a government by representation is capable of extension over a greater surface of country than one of any other form. These, my friend, are the essentials in which you and I agree; however, in our zeal for their maintenance we may be perplexed and divaricate as to the structure of society most likely to secure them.

In the constitution of Spain, as proposed by the late Cortes, there was a principle entirely new to me and not noticed in yours, that no person born after that day should ever acquire the rights of citizenship until he could read and write. It is impossible sufficiently to estimate the wisdom of this provision. Of all those which have been thought of for securing fidelity in the administration of the government, constant ralliance to the principles of the constitution, and progressive amendments with the progressive advances of the human mind or changes in human affairs, it is the most effectual. Enlighten the people generally, and tyranny and oppressions of body and mind will vanish like evil spirits at the dawn of day. Although I do not with some enthusiasts believe that the human condition will ever advance to such a state of perfection as that there shall no longer be pain or vice in the world, yet I believe it susceptible of much improvement, and most of all in matters of government and religion, and that the diffusion of knowledge among the people is to be the instrument by which it is to be effected.

Letter to John Taylor, Monticello, May 1816

Besides much other good matter (in your *Enquiry into the Principles of Our Government*), it settles unanswerably the right of instructing representatives and their duty to obey. The system of banking we have both equally and ever reprobated. I contemplate it as a blot left in all our constitutions, which, if not covered, will end in their destruction, which is already hit by the gamblers in corruption and is sweeping away in its progress the fortunes and morals of our citizens. Funding I consider as limited, rightfully, to a redemption of the debt within the lives of a majority of the generation contracting it; every generation coming equally, by the laws of the Creator of the world, to the free possession of the earth he made for their subsistence, unencumbered by their predecessors, who, like them, were but tenants for life. You have successfully and completely pulverized Mr. Adams' system of orders and his opening the mantle of republicanism to every government of laws, whether consistent or not with natural right. Indeed, it must be acknowledged that the term "republic" is of very vague application in every language. Witness the self-styled republics of Holland, Switzerland, Genoa, Venice, Poland. Were I to assign to this term a precise and definite idea, I would say purely and simply it means a government by its citizens in mass, acting directly and personally, according to rules established by the majority, and that every other government is more or less republican in proportion as it has in its composition more or less of this ingredient of the direct action of the citizens. Such a government is evidently restrained to very narrow limits of space and population. I doubt if it would be practicable beyond the extent of a New England township. . . . Other shades of republicanism may be found in other forms of government where the executive,

judiciary, and legislative functions, and the different branches of the latter, are chosen by the people more or less directly for longer terms of years, or for life, or made hereditary; or where there are mixtures of authorities, some dependent on, and others independent of, the people. The further the departure from direct and constant control by the citizens, the less has the government of the ingredient of republicanism; evidently none where the authorities are hereditary, as in France, Venice, etc., or self-chosen, as in Holland, and little, where for life, in proportion as the life continues in being after the act of election.

The purest republican feature in the government of our own State is the House of Representatives. The Senate is equally so the first year, less the second, and so on. The Executive still less, because not chosen by the people directly. The Judiciary seriously anti-republican, because for life, and the national arm wielded, as you observe, by military leaders irresponsible but to themselves. Add to this the vicious constitution of our county courts (to whom the justice, the executive administration, the taxation, police, the military appointments of the county, and nearly all our daily concerns are confided), self-appointed, self-continued, holding their authorities for life, and with an impossibility of breaking in on the perpetual succession of any faction once possessed of the bench. They are in truth the executive, the judiciary, and the military of their respective counties, and the sum of the counties makes the State. And add also that one half of our brethren who fight and pay taxes are excluded like helots from the rights of representation, as if society were instituted for the soil and not for the men inhabiting it, or one half of these could dispose of the rights and the will of the other half without their consent.

What constitutes a State?
Not high-raised battlements, or labor'd
  mound,
Thick wall, or moated gate;
Not cities proud, with spires and turrets
  crown'd;

No! men, high-minded men;
Men, who their duties know;
But know their rights; and knowing, dare
    maintain;
These constitute a State.

In the General Government, the House of Representatives is mainly republican; the Senate scarcely so at all, as not elected by the people directly and so long secured even against those who do elect them; the Executive more republican than the Senate, from its shorter term, its election by the people in *practice,* (for they vote for A only on an assurance that he will vote for B), and because, *in practice also,* a principle of rotation seems to be in a course of establishment; the judiciary independent of the nation, their coercion by impeachment being found nugatory.

If, then, the control of the people over the organs of their government be the measure of its republicanism, and I confess I know no other measure, it must be agreed that our governments have much less of republicanism than ought to have been expected; in other words, that the people have less regular control over their agents than their rights and their interests require. And this I ascribe, not to any want of republican dispositions in those who formed these constitutions, but to a submission of true principle to European authorities, to speculators on government, whose fears of the people have been inspired by the populace of their own great cities and were unjustly entertained against the independent, the happy, and therefore orderly citizens of the United States. . . .

On this view of the import of the term "republic," instead of saying, as has been said, "that it may mean anything or nothing," we may say with truth and meaning that governments are more or less republican as they have more or less of the element of popular election and control in their composition; and believing as I do that the mass of the citizens is the safest depository of their own rights, and especially that the evils flowing from the duperies of the people are less injurious than those from the egoism

of their agents, I am a friend to that composition of government which has in it the most of this ingredient. And I sincerely believe with you that banking establishments are more dangerous than standing armies, and that the principle of spending money to be paid by posterity, under the name of funding, is but swindling futurity on a large scale.

Letter to Samuel Kercheval, Monticello, July 1816

Sir,—I duly received your favor of June the 13th, with the copy of the letters on the calling a convention, on which you are pleased to ask my opinion. I have not been in the habit of mysterious reserve on any subject, nor of buttoning up my opinions within my own doublet. On the contrary, while in public service especially, I thought the public entitled to frankness, and intimately to know whom they employed. But I am now at the helm, and ask but for rest, peace and good will. The question you propose, on equal representation, has become a party one, in which I wish to take no public share. Yet, if it be asked for your own satisfaction only, and not to be quoted before the public, I have no motive to withhold it, and the less from you, as it coincides with your own. At the birth of our republic, I committed that opinion to the world, in the draught of a constitution annexed to the *Notes on Virginia,* in which a provision was inserted for a representation permanently equal. The infancy of the subject at that moment, and our inexperience of self-government, occasioned gross departures in that draught from genuine republican canons. In truth, the abuses of monarchy had so much filled all the space of political contemplation, that we imagined everything republican which not monarchy. We had not yet penetrated to the mother principle, that "governments are republican only in proportion as they embody the will of their people, and execute it." Hence, our first constitutions had really no leading principles in them. But experience and reflection have but more and more confirmed me in the particular importance of the equal representation then proposed. On that point, then, I am entirely in sentiment with your letters; and only lament that a copy-right of your pamphlet prevents their appearance in the newspapers, where alone they would be generally read, and produce general effect. The present vacancy, too, of other matter, would give them place in every paper, and bring the question home to every man's conscience.

But inequality of representation in both Houses of our legislature, is not the only republican heresy in this first essay of our revolutionary patriots at forming a constitution. For let it be agreed that a government is republican in proportion as every member composing it has his equal voice in the direction of its concerns (not indeed in person, which would be impracticable beyond the limits of a city, or small township, but) by representatives chosen by himself, and responsible to him at short periods, and let us bring to the test of this canon every branch of our constitution.

In the legislature, the House of Representatives is chosen by less than half the people, and not at all in proportion to those who do choose. The Senate are still more disproportionate, and for long terms of irresponsibility. In the Executive, the Governor is entirely independent of the choice of the people, and of their control; his Council equally so, and at best but a fifth wheel to a wagon. In the Judiciary, the judges of the highest courts are dependent on none but themselves. In England, where judges were named and removable at the will of an hereditary executive, from which branch most misrule was feared, and has flowed, it was a great point gained, by fixing them for life, to make them independent of that executive. But in a government founded on the public will, this principle operates in an opposite direction, and against that will. There, too, they were still removable on a concurrence of the executive and legislative branches. But we have made them independent of the nation itself. They are irremovable, but by their own body, for any depravities of conduct, and even by their own body for the imbecilities of dotage. The justices of the inferior courts are self-chosen, are for life, and perpetuate their own body in succession forever, so that a faction once possessing themselves of the bench of a county, can never be broken up, but hold their county in chains, forever indissoluble. Yet these justices are the real executive as well as judiciary, in all our minor and most ordinary concerns. They tax us at will; fill the office of sheriff, the most important of all the executive officers of the county; name nearly all our military leaders, which leaders, once names, are removable but by themselves. The juries, our judges of all fact, and of law when they choose it, are not selected by the people, nor amenable to them. They are chosen by an officer named by the court and executive. Chosen, did I say? Picked up by the sheriff from the loungings of the court yard, after everything respectable has retired from it. Where then is our republicanism to be found? Not in our constitution certainly, but merely in the spirit of our people. That would oblige even a despot to govern us republicanly. Owing to this spirit, and to nothing in the form of our constitution, all things have gone well. But this fact, so triumphantly misquoted by the enemies of reformation, is not the fruit of our constitution, but has prevailed in spite of it. Our functionaries have done well, because generally honest men. If any were not so, they feared to show it.

But it will be said, it is easier to find faults than to amend them. I do not think their amendment so difficult as is pretended. Only lay down true principles, and adhere to them inflexibly. Do not be frightened into their surrender by the alarms of the timid, or the croakings of wealth against the ascendency of the people. If experience be called for, appeal to that of our fifteen or twenty governments for forty years, and show me where the people have done half the mischief in these forty years, that a single despot would have done in a single year; or show half the riots and rebellions, the crimes and the punishments, which have taken place in any single nation, under kingly government, during the same period. The true foundation of republican government is the equal right of every citizen, in his person and property, and in their management. Try by this, as a tally, every provision of our constitution, and see if it hangs directly on the will of the people. Reduce your legislature to a convenient number for full, but orderly discussion. Let every man who fights or pays, exercise his just and equal right in their election. Submit them to approbation or rejection at short intervls. Let the executive be chosen in the same way, and for the same term, by those whose agent he is to be; and leave no screen of a council behind which to skulk from responsibility. It has been thought that the people are not competent electors of judges *learned in the law*. But I do know that this is true, and, if doubtful, we should follow principle. In this, as in many other elections, they would be guided by reputation, which would not err oftener, perhaps, than the present mode of appointment. In one State of the Union, at least, it has long been tried, and with the most satisfactory success. The judges of Connecticut have been chosen by the people every six months, for nearly two centuries, and I believe there has hardly ever been an instance of change; so powerful is the curb of incessant responsibility. If prejudice, however, derived from a monarchical institution, is still to prevail against the vital elective principle of our own, and if the existing example among ouselves of periodical election of judges by the people be still

mistrusted, let us at least not adopt the evil, and reject the good, of the English precedent; let us retain amovability on the concurrence of the executive and legislative branches, and nomination by the executive alone. Nomination to office is an executive function. To give it to the legislature, as we do, is a violation of the principle of the separation of powers. It swerves the members from correctness, by temptations to intrigue for office themselves, and to a corrupt barter of votes; and destroys responsibility by dividing it among a multitude. By leaving nomination in its proper place, among executive functions, the principle of the distribution of power is preserved, and responsibility weighs with its heaviest force on a single head.

The organization of our county administrations may be thought more difficult. But follow principle, and the knot unties itself. Divide the counties into wards of such size as that every citizen can attend, when called on, and act in person. Ascribe to them the government of their wards in all things relating to themselves exclusively. A justice, chosen by themselves, in each, a constable a military company, a patrol, a school, the care of their own poor, their own portion of the public roads, the choice of one or more jurors to serve in some court, and the delivery, within their own wards, of their own votes for all elective officers of higher sphere, will relieve the county administration of nearly all its business, will have it better done, and by making every citizen an acting member of the government, and in the offices nearest and most interesting to him, will attach him by his strongest feelings to the independence of his country, and its republican constitution. The justices thus chosen by every ward, would constitute the county court, would do its judiciary business, direct roads and bridges, levy county and poor rates, and administer all the matters of common interest of the whole country. These wards, called townships in New England, are the vital principles of their governments, and have proved themselves the wisest invention ever devised by the wit of man for the perfect exercise of self-government, and for its preservation. We should thus marshal our government into (1) the general federal republic, for all concerns foreign and federal; (2) that of the State, for what related to our own citizens exclusively; (3) the county republics, for the duties and concerns of the county; and (4) the ward republics, for the small, and yet numerous and interesting concerns of the neighborhood; and in government, as well as in every other business of life, it is by division and subdiivsion of duties alone, that all matters, great and small, can be managed to perfection. And the whole is cemented by giving to every citizen, personally, a part in the administration of the public affairs.

The sum of these amendments is (1) General suffrage, (2) equal representation in the legislature, (3) an executive chosen by the people, (4) judges elective or amovable, (5) justices, jurors, and sheriffs elective, (6) ward divisions, and (7) periodical amendments of the constitution.

I have thrown out these as loose heads of amendment, for consideration and correction; and their object is to secure self-government by the republicanism of our constitution, as well as by the spirit of the people; and to nourish and perpetuate that spirit. I am not among those who fear the people. They, and not the rich, are our dependence for continued freedom. And to preserve their independence, we must not let our rulers load us with perpetual debt. We must make our election between *economy and liberty,* or *profusion and servitude.* If we run into such debts, as that we must be taxed in our meat and in our drink, in our necessaries and our comforts, in our labors and our amusements, for our callings and our creeds, as the people of England are, our people, like them, must come to labor sixteen hours in the twenty-four, give the earnings of fifteen of these to the government for their debts and daily expenses; and the sixteenth

being insufficient to afford us bread, we must live, as they now do, on oatmeal and potatoes; have no time to think, no means of calling the mismanagers to account; but be glad to obtain subsistence by hiring ourselves to rivet their chains on the necks of our fellow-sufferers. Our landholders, too, like theirs, retaining indeed the title and stewardship of estates called theirs, but held really in trust for the treasury, must wander, like theirs, in foreign countries, and be contented with penury, obscurity, exile, and the glory of the nation. This example reads to us the salutary lesson, that private fortunes are destroyed by public as well as by private extravagance. And this is the tendency of all human governments. A departure from principle in one instance becomes a precedent for a second; that second for a third; and so on, till the bulk of the society of reduced to be mere automatons of misery, and to have so sensibilities left but for sinning and suffering. Then begins, indeed, the *bellum omnium in omnia,* which some philosophers observing to be so general in this world, have mistaken it for the natural, instead of the abusive state of man. And the fore horse of this frightful team is public debt. Taxation follows that, and in its train wretchedness and oppression.

Some men look at constitutions with sanctimonious reverence, and deem them like the arc of the covenant, too sacred to be touched. They ascribe to the men of the preceding age a wisdom more than human, and suppose what they did to be beyond amendment. I knew that age well; I belonged to it, and labored with it. It deserved well of its country. It was very like the present, but without the experience of the present; and forty years of experience in government is worth a century of book-reading; and this they would say themselves, were they to rise from the dead. I am certainly not an advocate for frequent and untried changes in laws and constitutions. I think moderate imperfections had better be borne with; because, when once known, we accommodate ourselves to them, and find practical means of correcting their ill effects. But I know also, that laws and institutions must go hand in hand with the progress of the human mind. As that becomes more developed, more enlightened, as new discoveries are made, new truths disclosed, and manners and opinions change with the change of circumstances, institution must advance also, and keep pace with the times. We might as well require a man to wear still the coat which fitted him when a boy, as civilized society to remain ever under the regimen of their barbarous ancestors. It is this preposterous idea which has lately deluged Europe in blood. Their monarchs, instead of wisely yielding to the gradual change of circumstances, of favoring progressive accomodation to progressive improvement, have clung to old abuses, entrenched themselves behind steady habits, and obliged their subjects to seek through blood and violence rash and ruinous innovations, which, had they been referred to the peaceful deliberations and collected wisdom of the nation, would have been put into acceptable and salutary forms. Let us follow no such examples, nor weakly believe that one generation is not as capable as another of taking care of itself, and of ordering its own affairs. Let us, as our sister States have done, avail ourselves of our reason and experience, to correct the crude essays of our first and unexperienced, although wise, virtuous, and well-meaning councils. And lastly, let us provide in our constitution for its revision at stated periods. What these periods should be, nature herself indicates. By the European tables of mortality, of the adults living at any one moment of time, a majority will be dead in about nineteen years. At the end of that period, then, a new majority is come into place; or, in other words, a new generation. Each generation is as independent as the one preceding, as that was of all which had gone before. It has then, like them, a right to choose for itself the form of government it believes most promotive of its own happiness; consequently, to accommodate to the circumstances in which it finds itself,

that received from its predecessors; and it is for the peace and good of mankind that a solemn opportunity of doing this every nineteen or twenty years, should be provided by the constitution; so that it may be handed on, with periodical repairs, from generation to generation, to the end of time, if anything human can so long endure. It is now forty years since the constitution of Virginia was formed. The same tables inform us, that, within that period, two-thirds of the adults then living are now dead. Have then the remaining third, even if they had the wish, the right to hold in obedience to their will, and to laws heretofore made by them, the other two-thirds, who, with themselves compose the present mass of adults? If they have not, who has? The dead? But the dead have no rights. They are nothing; and nothing cannot own something. Where there is no substance, there can be no accident. This corporeal globe, and everything upon it, belong to its present corporeal inhabitants, during their generation. They alone have a right to direct what is the concern of themselves, alone, and to declare the law of that direction; and this declaration can only be made by their majority. That majority, then, has a right to depute representatives to a convention, and to make the constitution what they think will be the best for themselves. But how collect their voice? This is the real difficulty. If invited by private authority, or county or district meetings, these divisions are so large that few will attend; and their voice will be imperfectly, or falsely pronounced. Here then, would be one of the advantages of the ward divisions I have proposed. The mayor of every ward, on a question like the present, would call his ward together, take the simple yea or nay of its members, convey these to the county court, who would hand on those of all its wards to the proper general authority; and the voice of the whole people would be thus fairly, fully, and peaceably expressed, discussed, and decided by the common reason of the society. If this avenue be shut to the call of suffrance, it will make itself heard through that of force, and we shall go on, as other nations are doing, in the endless circle of oppression, rebellion, reformation; and oppression, rebellion, reformation, again; and so on forever.

These, Sir, are my opinions of the governments we see among men, and of the principles by which alone we may prevent our own from falling into the same dreadful track. I have given them at greater length than your letter called for. But I cannot say things by halves; and I confide them to your honor, so to use them as to preserve me from the gridiron of the public papers. If you shall approve and enforce them, as you have done that of equal representation, they may do some good. If not, keep them to yourself as the effusions of withered age and useless time. I shall, with not the less truth, assure you of my great respect and consideration.

Letter to Samuel Kercheval, Monticello, September 1816

The article, however, nearest my heart is the division of counties into wards. These will be pure and elementary republics, the sum of all which taken together composes the State, and will make of the whole a true democracy as to the business of the wards, which is that of nearest and daily concern. The affairs of the larger sections: of counties, of States, and of the Union, not admitting personal transaction by the people, will be delegated to agents elected by themselves, and representation will thus be substituted where personal action becomes impracticable. Yet, even over these representative organs, should they become corrupt and perverted, the division into wards, constituting the people in their

wards a regularly organized power, enables them by that organization to crush, regularly and peaceably, the usurpations of their unfaithful agents, and rescues them from the dreadful necessity of doing its insurrectionally. In this way we shall be as republican as a large society can be and secure the continuance of purity in our government by the salutary, peaceable, and regular control of the people. No other depositories of power have ever yet been found which did not end in converting to their own profit the earnings of those committed to their charge. . . .

. . . I have been told that on the question of equal representation, our fellow citizens in some sections of the State claim peremptorily a right of representation for their slaves. Principle will, in this as in most other cases, open the way for us to correct conclusion. Were our State a pure democracy in which all its inhabitants should meet together to transact all their business, there would yet be exluded from their deliberations: (1) infants, until arrived at years of discretion; (2) women, who, to prevent depravation of morals and ambiguity of issue, could not mix promiscuously in the public meetings of men; (3) slaves, from whom the unfortunate state of things with us takes away the rights of will and of property. Those then who have no will could be permitted to exercise none in the popular assembly, and, of course, could delegate none to an agent in a representative assembly.

Letter to William Johnson, Monticello, June 1823

You request me confidentially, to examine the question, whether the Supreme Court has advanced beyond its constitutional limits, and trespassed on those of the State authorities? I do not undertake, my dear Sir, because I am unable. Age and the wane of mind consequent on it, had disqualified me from investigations so severe, and researches so laborious. And it is the less necessary in this case, as having been already done by others with a logic and learning to which I could add nothing. On the decision of the case of Cohen vs. The State of Virginia, in the Supreme Court of the United States, in March, 1821, Judge Roane, under the signature of Algernon Sidney, wrote for the Enquirer a series of papers on the law of that case. I considered these papers maturely as they came out, and confess that they appeared to me to pulverize every word which had been delivered by Judge Marshall, of the extra-judicial part of his opinion; and all was extra-judicial, except the decision that the act of Congress had not purported to give to the corporation of Washington the authority claimed by their lottery law, of controlling the laws of the States within the States themselves. But unable to claim that case, he could not let it go entirely, but went on gratuitously to prove, that notwithstanding the eleventh amendment of the constitution, a State *could* be brought as a defendant, to the bar of his court; and again, that Congress might authorize a corporation of its territory to exercise legislation within a State, and paramount to the laws of that State.

I cite the sum and result only of his doctrines, according to the impression made on my mind at the time, and still remaining. If not strictly accurate in circumstances, it is so in substance. This doctrine was so completely refuted by Roane, that if he can be answered, I surrender human reason as a vain and useless faculty, given to bewilder, and not to guide us. And I mention this particular case as one only of several, because it gave occasion to that thorough examination of the constitutional limits between the General and State jurisdictions, which you have asked for. There were two other writers in the same paper, under the signatures of Fletcher of Saltoun, and Somers, who, in a few essays, presented some very luminous and striking view of the question. And there was a particular paper which recapitulated all the cases in which it was thought the federal court had usurped on the State jurisdictions. These essays will be found in the Enquirers of 1821, from May the 10th to July the 13th. It is not in my present power to send them to you, but if Ritchie can furnish them, I will procure and forward them. If they had been read in the other States, as they were here, I think they would have left, there as here, no dissentients from their doctrine. The subject was taken up by our legislature of 1821-1822, and two draughts of remonstrances were prepared and discussed. As well as I remember, there was no difference of opinion as to the matter of right; but there was as to the expediency of a remonstrance at that time, the general mind of the States being then under extraordinary excitement by the Missouri question; and it was dropped on that consideration. But this case is not dead, it only sleepeth. The Indian chief said he did not go to war for every petty injury by itself, but put it into his pouch, and when that was full, he then made war. Thank Heaven, we have provided a more peaceable and rational mode of redress.

This practice of Judge Marshall, of travelling out of his case to prescribe what the law would be in a moot case not before the court, is very irregular and very censurable. I recollect another instance, and the more particularly, perhaps, because it in some measure bore on myself. Among the midnight appointments of Mr. Adams, were commissions to some federal justices of the peace for Alexandria. These were signed and sealed by him, but not delivered. I found them on the table of the department of State, on my entrance into office, and forbade their delivery. Marbury, named in one of them, applied to the Supreme Court for a mandamus to the Secretary of State (Mr. Madison) to deliver the commission intended for him. The court determined at once, that being an original process, they had no cognizance of it; and therefore the question before them was ended. But the Chief Justice went on to lay down what the law would be, had they jurisdiction of the case, to wit: that they should command the delivery. The object was clearly to instruct any other court having the jurisdiction, what they should do if Marbury should apply to them. Besides the impropriety of this gratuitous interference, could anything exceed the perversion of law? For if there is any principle of law never yet contradicted it is that delivery is one of the essentials to the validity of the deed. Although signed and sealed, yet as long as it remains in the hands of the party himself, it is in *fieri* only, it is not a deed, and can be made so only by its delivery. In the hands of a third person it may be made an escrow. But whatever is in the executive offices is certainly deemed to be in the hands of the President; and in this case, was actually in my hands, because, when I countermanded them, there was as yet no Secretary of State. Yet this case of Marbury and Madison is continually cited by bench and bar, as if it were settled law, without any animadversion on its being merely an *obiter* dissertation of the Chief Justice.

It may be impracticable to lay down any general formula of words which shall decide at once, and with precision, in every case, this limit of jurisdiction. But there are two canons which will guide us safely in most of the cases. First, the capital and leading object of the constitution was to leave with the States all authorities which respected their own citizens only, and to transfer to the United States those which respected citizens of foreign or other States: to make us several as to ourselves, but one as to all others. In the latter case, then, constructions should lean to the general jurisdiction, if the words will bear it; and in favor of the States in the former, if possible to be so construed. And indeed, between citizens and citizens of the same State, and under their own laws, I know but a single case in which a jurisdiction is given to the General Government. That is, where anything but gold or silver is made a lawful tender, or the obligation of contracts is any otherwise impaired. The separate legislatures had so often abused that power, that the citizens themselves chose to trust it to the general, rather than to their own special authorities. Second, on every question of construction, carry ourselves back to the time when the constitution was adopted, recollect the spirit manifested in the debates, and instead of trying what meaning may be squeezed out of the text, or invented against it, conform to the probable one in which it was passed. Let us try Cohen's case by these canons only, referring always, however, for full argument, to the essays before cited.

1. It was between a citizen and his own State, and under a law of his State. It was a domestic case, therefore, and not a foreign one.

2. Can it be believed, that under the jealousies prevailing against the General Government, at the adoption of the constitution, the States meant to surrender the authority of preserving order, of enforcing moral duties and restraining vice, within their own territory? And this is the present case, that of Cohen being under the ancient and general law of gaming. Can any good be effected by taking from the States the moral rule of their citizens, and subordinating it to the general authority, or to one of their corporations, which may justify forcing the meaning of words, hunting after possible constructions, and hanging inference on inference, from heaven to earth, like Jacob's ladder? Such an intention was impossible, and such a licentiousness of construction and inference, if exercised by both governments, as may be done with equal right, would equally authorize both to claim all power, general and particular, and break up the foundations of the Union. Laws are made for men of ordinary understanding, and should, therefore, be construed only by the ordinary rules of common sense.

Their meaning is not to be sought for in metaphysical subtleties, which may make anything mean everything or nothing, at pleasure. It should be left to the sophisms of advocates, whose trade it is, to prove that a defendant is a plaintiff, though dragged into court, *torto collo,* like Bonaparte's volunteers, into the field in chains, or that a power has been given, because it ought to have been given, *et alia talia.* The States supposed that by their tenth amendment, they had secured themselves against constructive powers. They were not lessoned yet by Cohen's case, nor aware of the slipperiness of the eels of the law. I ask for no straining of words against the General Government, nor yet against the States. I believe the States can best govern our home concerns, and the General Government our foreign ones. I wish, therefore, to see maintained that wholesome distribution of powers established by the constitution for the limitation of both; and never to see all offices transferred to Washington, where, further withdrawn from the eyes of the people, they may more secretly be bought and sold as at market.

But the Chief Justice says, "there must be an ultimate arbiter somewhere." True, there must; but does that prove it is either party? The ultimate arbiter is the people of the Union, assembled by their deputies in convention, at the call of Congress, or of two-thirds of the States. Let them decide to which they mean to give an authority claimed by two of their organs. And it has been the peculiar wisdom and felicity of our constitution, to have provided this peaceable appeal, where that of other nations is at once to force.

WORKS BY THOMAS JEFFERSON

Jefferson, Thomas. *Autobiography of Thomas Jefferson.* New York: Capricorn, 1959. A humble, but solid, self-portrait emphasizing the political aspect of his life.

————. *History of the Expedition under the Command of Captains Lewis and Clarke.* Dublin: J. Christie, 1817. A vivid chronological description of the Lewis and Clarke expedition, giving accounts of both geography and Indian cultures.

————. *The Life and Morals of Jesus of Nazareth.* Washington, D.C.: Government Printing Office, 1904. Commonly known as the Jefferson Bible, the editor pieced together those sections that were free from myth and yet definitely the teachings of Christ.

————. *A Manual of Parliamentary Practice.* Philadelphia: Hogan and Thompson, 1850. Rules to be used by the Congressional bodies, which best allow the spirit and letter of the Constitution to be implemented.

————. *A Summary View of the Rights of British America.* New York: Scholar's Facsimiles and Reprints, 1943. Basing American claims for self-government upon the right of Expatriation, Jefferson calls for the end of England's denial of the natural rights of Americans.

The Jeffersonian Cyclopedia. Edited by J.P. Foley. New York: Funk and Wagnalls, 1900. A comprehensive collection of Jefferson's views on numerous subjects arranged alphabetically under 9000 headings.

Memoir, Correspondence, and Miscellanies, from the Papers of Thomas Jefferson. Edited by Thomas Jefferson Randolph. Boston: Gray and Bowen, 1830. A four volume collection put together by Jefferson's nephew, the Executor and Legatee of his Manuscript Papers.

The Writings of Thomas Jefferson. Edited by Andrew A. Libscomb, under the auspices of the Thomas Jefferson Memorial Association. Washington, D.C., 1904. A 20-volume work presenting the entire gamut of Jefferson's writings, both public and private.

MAJOR SOURCES ON THOMAS JEFFERSON

Boorstin, Daniel J. *The Lost World of Thomas Jefferson.* New York: Holt, 1948. An attempt to portray the Jeffersonian world of ideas with minimal emphasis upon its influences and sources.

Chinard, Gilbert. *Thomas Jefferson the Apostle of Americanism.* Boston: Little, Brown, and Co., 1939. Written superficially as a biography, an interpretation of the subject's ideas as he moves from a European to an uniquely American ideology.

Fisher, George P. "Jefferson and the Social Compact Theory," *Yale Review,* Vol. 11 (1894), pp. 403-417. A dull, pedantic portrayal of Jefferson's radical, "almost anarchical," interpretation of the Social Compact Theory.

Hofstadter, Richard. *The American Political Tradition.* New York: Knopf, 1948. Included in a series of essays on the representatives of dominant American political trends, a selection analyzing Jefferson's historic role as a statesman and political theorist.

Koch, Adrienne, and Peden, William. *The Life and Selected Writings of Thomas Jefferson.* New York: Random House, 1944. A comprehensive presentation of Jefferson through a collection of his writings with introductory remarks by the authors.

Koch, Adrienne. *The Philosophy of Thomas Jefferson.* New York: Columbia University Press, 1943. A presentation of Jefferson's ideology as a basis for understanding his political behavior.

Padover, Saul K. *Jefferson.* New York: Harcourt, 1942. A well-known biography, Jefferson is portrayed as a quasi-saint by the slightly awed author.

Patterson, Caleb Perry. *The Constitutional Principles of Thomas Jefferson.* Austin: University of Texas Press, 1953. A liberal presentation of Jefferson as a pragmatist rather than a doctrinaire as shown in his constitutional thoughts.

Wiltse, Charles M. "Jeffersonian Democracy; a Dual Tradition," *American Political Science Review,* Vol. XXVIII (1934), pp. 838-851. An analytic interpretation of the Jeffersonian system emphasizing its dual trends of individualism and socialism.

CHAPTER 4

James Madison

JAMES Madison (1751–1836), born to a wealthy Virginia family, graduated from Princeton in 1772 and then stayed another year to study Hebrew. Early in 1776, Madison was chosen as a delegate to the State convention where he was appointed to a special committee to write a constitution for the state. His chief contribution to this was a resolution that made the free exercise of religion a matter of right instead of toleration.

In 1780, the Assembly made Madison a delegate to the Continental Congress, a post he filled until the end of 1783. From 1784 to 1786, he was a member of the House of Delegates from Orange County, becoming a leader almost at once. Madison went to the Annapolis Convention of 1786 as a delegate from Virginia; he also was named as a delegate to the Philadelphia Convention. At the Convention, Madison took a prominent part from the beginning and became one of the acknowledged leaders of the group favoring a strong central government; his influence upon the Convention's work was so great that he has been called the "Father of the Constitution." After the Convention, Madison threw himself into the fight for the adoption of the Constitution; he cooperated with Hamilton and Jay in the series of essays later published as *The Federalist.*

Madison was elected to the first session of the House of Representatives. During his term in Congress, as he became increasingly critical of Hamilton's financial policies, Madison became a recognized leader of the Jeffersonian party. In 1797, Madison voluntarily retired from public life, expecting to devote his time to farming.

With the election of Jefferson in 1800, Madison was brought again into a prominent public position when he was appointed Secretary of State. The chief foreign policy problem during Madison's term of office was to maintain a neutral position between the warring states of Britain and France.

Madison became the fourth President of the United States in 1808. Unable to maintain a policy of nonintercourse indefinitely, war broke between the United States and Britain in 1812. Whatever opinion is held of the achievements or gains of the war for the United States, there is general agreement that the management of the war was very poor.

After the close of his second term in 1817, Madison retired to his estate at Montpelier, where he spent the last twenty years of his life. The most important work of these later years was the preparation for publication of his notes on the Federal Convention.

The Federalist No. 10

To the People of the State of New York:

Among the numerous advantages promised by a well constructed Union, none deserves to be more accurately developed than its tendency to break and control the violence of faction. The friend of popular governments never finds himself so much alarmed for their character and fate, as when he contemplates their propensity to this dangerous vice. He will not fail, therefore, to set a due value on any plan which, without violating the principles to which he is attached, provides a proper cue for it. The instability, injustice, and confusion introduced into the public councils, have, in truth, been the mortal diseases under which popular governments have everywhere perished; as they continue to be the favorite and fruitful topics from which the adversaries to liberty derive their most specious declamations. The valuable improvements made by the American constitutions on the popular models, both ancient and modern, cannot certainly be too much admired; but it would be an unwarrantable partiality, to contend that they have as effectually obviated the danger on this side, as was wished and expected. Complaints are everywhere heard from our most considerate and virtuous citizens, equally the friends of public and private faith, and of public and personal liberty, that our governments are too unstable, that the public good is disregarded in the conflicts of rival parties, and that measures are too often decided, not according to the rules of justice and the rights of the minor party, but by the superior force of an interested and overbearing majority. However anxiously we may wish that these complaints had no foundation, the evidence of known facts will permit us to deny that they are in some degree true. It will be found, indeed, on a candid review of our situation, that some of the distresses under which we labor have been erroneously charged on the operation of our governments, but it will be found, at the same time, that other causes will not alone account for many of our heaviest misfortunes; and, particularly, for that prevailing and increasing distrust of public engagements, and alarm for private rights, which are echoed from one end of the continent to the other. These must be chiefly, if not wholly, effects of the unsteadiness and injustice with which a factious spirit has tainted our public administrations.

By a faction, I understand a number of citizens, whether amounting to a majority or minority of the whole, who are united and actuated by some common impulse of passion, or of interest, adverse to the rights of other citizens, or to the permanent and aggregate interests of the community.

There are two methods of curing the mischiefs of faction: the one, by removing its causes; the other, by controlling its effects.

There are again two methods of removing the causes of faction: the one, by destroying the liberty which is essential to its existence; the other, by giving to every citizen the same opinions, the same passions, and the same interests.

It could never be more truly said than of the first remedy, that it was worse than the disease. Liberty is to faction what air is to fire, an ailment without which it instantly expires. But it could not be less folly to abolish liberty, which is essential to political life, because it nourishes faction, than it would be to wish the annihilation of air, which is essential to animal life, because it imparts to fire its destructive agency.

The second expedient is as impracticable as the first would be unwise. As long as the reason of man continues fallible, and he is at liberty to exercise it, different opinions will be formed. As long as the connection subsists between his reason and his self-love, his opinions and his passions will have a reciprocal influence on each other; and the former will be objects to which the latter will attach themselves. The diversity in the faculties of men, from which the rights of property originate, is not less an insuperable obstacle to a uniformity of interests. The protection of these faculties is the first object of government. From the protection of different and unequal faculties of acquiring property, the possession of different degrees and kinds of property immediately results; and from the influence of these on the sentiments and views of the respective proprietors, ensues a division of the society into different interests and parties.

The latent causes of faction are thus sown in the nature of man; and we see them everywhere brought into different degrees of activity, according to the different circumstances of civil society. A zeal for different opinions concerning religion, concerning government, and many other points, as well of speculation as of practice; an attachment to different leaders ambitiously contending for pre-eminence and power; or to persons of other descriptions whose fortunes have been interesting to the human passions, have, in turn, divided mankind into parties, inflamed them with mutual animosity, and rendered them much more disposed to vex and oppress each other than to cooperate for their common good. So strong is this propensity of mankind to fall into mutual animosities, that where no substantial occasion presents itself, the most frivolous and fanciful distinctions have been sufficient to

kindle their unfriendly passions and excite their most violent conflicts. But the most common and durable source of factions has been the various and unequal distribution of property. Those who hold and those who are without property have ever formed distinct interests in society. Those who are creditors, and those who are debtors, fall under a like discrimination. A landed interest, a manufacturing interest, a mercantile interest, a moneyed interest, with many lesser interests, grow up of necessity in civilized nations, and divide them into different classes, actuated by different sentiments and views. The regulation of these various and interfering interests forms the principal task of modern legislation, and involves the spirit of party and faction in the necessary and ordinary operations of the government.

No man is allowed to be a judge in his own cause, because his interest would certainly bias his judgment, and, not improbably, corrupt his integrity. With equal, nay with greater reason, a body of men are unfit to be both judges and parties at the same time; yet what are many of the most important acts of legislation, but so many judicial determinations, not indeed concerning the rights of single persons, but concerning the rights of large bodies of citizens? And what are the different classes of legislators but advocates and parties to the causes which they determine? Is a law proposed concerning private debts? It is a question to which the creditors are parties on one side and the debtors on the other. Justice ought to hold the balance between them. Yet the parties are, and must be, themselves the judges; and the most numerous party, or, in other words, the most powerful faction must be expected to prevail. Shall domestic manufactures be encouraged, and in what degree, by restrictions on foreign manufactures? [These] are questions which would be differently decided by the landed and the manufacturing classes, and probably by neither with a sole regard to justice and the public good. The apportionment of taxes on the various descriptions of property is an act which seems to require the most exact impartiality; yet there is, perhaps, no legislative act in which greater opportunity and temptation are given to a predominant party to trample on the rules of justice. Every shilling with which they overburden the inferior number, is a shilling saved to their own pockets.

It is in vain to say that enlightened statemen will be able to adjust these clashing interests, and render them all subservient to the public good. Enlightened statesmen will not always be at the helm. Nor, in many cases, can such an adjustment be made at all without taking into view indirect and remote considerations, which will rarely prevail over the immediate interest which one party may find in disregarding the rights of another or the good of the whole.

The inference to which we are brought is, that the *causes* of faction cannot be removed, and that relief is only to be sought in the means of controlling its *effects*.

If a faction consists of less than a majority, relief is supplied by the republican principle, which enables the majority to defeat its sinister views by regular vote. It may clog the administration, it may convulse the society; but it will be unable to execute and mask its violence under the forms of the Constitution. When a majority is included in a faction, the form of popular government, on the other hand, enables it to sacrifice to its ruling passion or interest both the public good and the rights of other citizens. To secure the public good and private rights against the danger of such a faction, and at the same time to preserve the spirit and the form of popular government, is then the great object to which our inquiries are directed. Let me add that it is the great desideratum by which this form of government can be rescued from the opprobrium under which it has so long labored, and be recommended to the esteem and adoption of mankind.

By what means is this object attainable? Evidently by one of two only.

Either the existence of the same passion or interest in a majority at the same time must be prevented, or the majority, having such coexistent passion or interest, must be rendered, by their number and local situation, unable to concert and carry into effect schemes of oppression. If the impulse and the opportunity be suffered to coincide, we well know that neither moral nor religious motives can be relied on as an adequate control. They are not found to be such on the injustice and violence of individuals, and lose their efficacy in proportion to the number combined together, that is, in proportion as their efficacy becomes needful.

From this view of the subject it may be concluded that a pure democracy, by which I mean a society consisting of a small number of citizens, who assemble and administer the government in person, can admit of no cure for the mischiefs of faction. A common passion or interest will, in almost every case, be felt by a majority of the whole; a communication and concert result from the form of government itself; and there is nothing to check the inducements to sacrifice the weaker party or an obnoxious individual. Hence it is that such democracies have ever been spectacles of turbulence and contention; have ever been found incompatible with personal security or the rights of property; and have in general been as short in their lives as they have been violent in their deaths. Theoretic politicians, who have patronized this species of government, have erroneously supposed that by reducing mankind to a perfect equality in their political rights, they would, at the same time, be perfectly equalized and assimilated in their possessions, their opinions, and their passions.

A republic, by which I mean a government in which the scheme of representation takes place, opens a different prospect, and promises the cure for which we are seeking. Let us examine the points in which it varies from pure democracy, and we shall comprehend both the nature of the cure and the efficacy which it must derive from the Union.

The two great points of difference between a democracy and a republic are: first, the delegation of the government, in the latter, to a small number of citizens elected by the rest; secondly, the greater number of citizens, and greater sphere of country, over which the latter may be extended.

The effect of the first difference is, on the one hand, to refine and enlarge the public views, by passing them through the medium of a chosen body of citizens, whose wisdom may best discern the true interest of their country, and whose patriotism and love of justice will be least likely to sacrifice it to temporary or partial considerations. Under such a regulation, it may well happen that the public voice, pronounced by the representatives of the people, will be more consonant to the public good than if pronounced by the people themselves, convened for the purpose. On the other hand, the effect may be inverted. Men of factious tempers, of local prejudices, or of sinister designs, may, by intrigue, by corruption, or by other means, first obtain the suffrages, and then betray the interests, of the people. The question resulting is, whether small or extensive republics are more favorable to the election of proper guardians of the public weal; and it is clearly decided in favor of the latter by two obvious considerations:

In the first place, it is to be remarked that, however small the republic may be, the representatives must be raised to a certain number, in order to guard against the cabals of a few; and that, however large it may be, they must be limited to a certain number, in order to guard against the confusion of a multitude. Hence, the number of representatives in the two cases not being in proportion to that of the two constituents, and being proportionally greater in the small republic, it follows that, if the proportion of fit characters be not less in the large than in the small republic, the former will present a greater option, and consequently a greater probability of a fit choice.

In the next place, as each representative will be chosen by a greater number of citizens in the large than in the small republic, it will be more difficult for unworthy candidates to practise with success the vicious arts by which elections are too often carried; and the suffrages of the people being more free, will be more likely to centre in men who possess the most attractive merit and the most diffusive and established characters.

It must be confessed that in this, as in most other cases, there is a mean, on both sides of which inconveniences will be found to lie. By enlarging too much the number of electors, you render the representative too little acquainted with all their local circumstances and lesser interests; as by reducing it too much, you render him unduly attached to these, and too little fit to comprehend and pursue great and national objects. The federal Constitution forms a happy combination in this respect; the great and aggregate interests being referred to the national, the local and particular to the State legislatures.

The other point of difference is, the greater number of citizens and extent of territory which may be brought within the compass of republican than of democratic government; and it is this circumstance principally which renders factious combinations less to be dreaded in the former than in the latter. The smaller the society, the fewer probably will be the distinct parties and interests composing it; the fewer the distinct parties and interests, the more frequently will a majority be found of the same party; and the smaller the number of individuals composing a majority, and the smaller the compass within which they are placed, the more easily will they concert and execute their plans of oppression. Extend the sphere and you take in a greater variety of parties and interests; you make it less probable that a majority of the whole will have a common motive to invade the rights of other citizens; or if such a common motive exists, it will be more difficult for all who feel it to discover their own strength, and to act in unison with each other. Besides other impediments, it may be remarked that, where there is a consciousness of unjust or dishonorable purposes, communication is always checked by distrust in proportion to the number whose concurrence is necessary.

Hence, it clearly appears, that the same advantage which a republic has over a democracy, in controlling the effects of faction, is enjoyed by a large over a small republic,—is enjoyed by the Union over the States composing it. Does the advantage consist in the substitution of representatives whose enlightened views and virtuous sentiments render them superior to local prejudices and to schemes of injustice? It will not be denied that the representation of the Union will be most likely to possess these requisite endowments. Does it consist in the greater security afforded by a greater variety of parties, against the event of any one party being able to outnumber and oppress the rest? In an equal degree does the increased variety of parties comprised within the Union, increase this security. Does it, in fine, consist in the greater obstacles opposed to the concert and accomplishment of the secret wishes of an unjust and interested majority? Here, again, the extent of the Union gives it the most palpable advantage.

The influence of factious leaders may kindle a flame within their particular States, but will be unable to spread a general conflagration through the other States. A religious sect may degenerate into a political faction in a part of the Confederacy; but the variety of sects dispersed over the entire face of it must secure the national councils against any danger from that source. A rage for paper money, for an abolition of debts, for an equal division of property, or for any other improper or wicked project, will be less apt to pervade the whole body of the Union than a particular member of it; in the same proportion as such a malady is more likely to taint a particular county or district, than an entire State.

In the extent and proper structure of the Union, therefore, we behold a republican remedy for the diseases most incident to republican government. And according to the degree of pleasure and pride we feel in being republicans, ought to be our zeal in cherishing the spirit and supporting the character of Federalist.

PUBLIUS

The Federalist No. 39

To the People of the State of New York:

The last paper having concluded the observations which were meant to introduce a candid survey of the plan of government reported by the convention, we now proceed to the execution of that part of our undertaking.

The first question that offers itself is, whether the general form and aspect of the government be strictly republican. It is evident that no other form would be reconcilable with the genius of the people of America; with the fundamental principles of the Revolution; or with that honorable determination which animates every votary of freedom, to rest all our political experiments on the capacity of mankind for self-government. If the plan of the convention, therefore, be found to depart from the republican character, its advocates must abandon it as no longer defensible.

What, then, are the distinctive characters of the republican form? Were an answer to this question to be sought, not by recurring to principles, but in the application of the term by political writers, to the constitutions of different States, no satisfactory one would ever be found. Holland, in which no particle of the supreme authority is derived from the people, has passed almost universally under the denomination of a republic. The same title has been bestowed on Venice, where absolute power over the great body of the people is exercised, in the most absolute manner, by a small body of hereditary nobles. Poland, which is a mixture of aristocracy and of monarchy in their worst forms, has been dignified with the same appellation. The government of England, which has one republican branch only, combined with an hereditary aristocracy and monarchy, has, with equal impropriety, been frequently placed on the list of republics. These examples, which are nearly as dissimilar to each other as to a genuine republic, show the extreme inaccuracy with which the term has been used in political disquisitions.

If we resort for a criterion to the different principles on which different forms of government are established, we may define a republic to be, or at least may bestow that name on, a government which derives all its powers directly or indirectly from the great body of the people, and is administered by persons holding their offices during pleasure, for a limited period, or during good behavior. It is *essential* to such a government that it be derived from the great body of the society, not from an inconsiderable proportion, or a favored class of it; otherwise a handful of tyrannical nobles, exercising their oppressions by a delegation of their powers, might aspire to the rank of republicans, and claim for their government the honorable title of republic. It is *sufficient* for such a government that the persons administering it be appointed, either directly or indirectly, by the people, and that they hold their appointments by either of the tenures just specified; otherwise every government in the United States, as well as every other popular government that has been or can be well organized or well executed, would be degraded from the republican character. According to the constitution of every State in the Union, some or other of the

officers of government are appointed indirectly only by the people. According to most of them, the chief magistrate himself is so appointed. And according to one, this mode of appointment is extended to one of the coordinate branches of the legislature. According to all the constitutions, also, the tenure of the highest offices is extended to a definite period, and in many instances, both within the legislative and executive departments, to a period of years. According to the provisions of most of the constitutions, again, as well as according to the most respectable and received opinions on the subject, the members of the judiciary department are to retain their offices by the firm tenure of good behavior.

On comparing the Constitution planned by the convention with the standard here fixed, we perceive at once that it is, in the most rigid sense, conformable to it. The House of Representatives, like that of one branch at least of all the State legislatures, is elected immediately by the great body of the people. The Senate, like the present Congress, and the Senate of Maryland, derives its appointment indirectly from the people. The President's is indirectly derived from the choice of the people, according to the example in most of the States. Even the judges with all other of the Union, will, as in the several States, be the choice, though a remote choice, of the people themselves. The duration of the appointments is equally comfortable to the republican standard, and to the model of State constitutions. The House of Representatives is periodically elective, as in all the States; and for the period of two years, as in the State of South Carolina. The Senate is elective, for the period of six years; which is but one year more than the period of the Senate of Maryland, and but two more than that of the Senates of New York and Virginia. The President is to continue in office for the period of four years; as in New York and Delaware the chief magistrate is elected for three years, and in South Carolina for two years. In the other

States the election is annual. In several of the States, however, no constitutional provision is made for the impeachment of the chief magistrate. And in Delaware and Virginia he is not impeachable till out of office. The President of the United States is impeachable at any time during his continuance in office. The tenure by which the judges are to hold their places, is, as it unquestionably ought to be, that of good behavior. The tenure of the ministerial offices generally, will be a subject of legal regulation, comformably to the reason of the case and the example of the State constitutions.

Could any further proof be required of the republican complexion of this system, the most decisive one might be found in its absolute prohibition of titles of nobility, both under the federal and the State governments; and in its express guaranty of the republican form to each of the latter.

"But it was not sufficient," say the adversaries of the proposed Constitution, "for the convention to adhere to the republican form. They ought, with equal care, to have preserved the *federal* form, which regards the Union as a *Confederacy* of sovereign states; instead of which, they have framed a *national* government, which regards the Union as a *consolidation* of the States." And it is asked by what authority this bold and radical innovation was undertaken? The handle which has been made of this objection requires that it should be examined with some precision.

Without inquiring into the accuracy of the distinction on which the objection is founded, it will be necessary to a just estimate of its force, first, to ascertain the real character of the government in question; secondly, to inquire how far the convention were authorized to propose such a government; and thirdly, how far the duty they owed to their country could supply any defect of regular authority.

First—In order to ascertain the real character of the government, it may be considered in relation to the foundation on which it is to be established; to the sources from which its ordinary powers are to be drawn; to the operation of those powers; to the extent of them; and to the authority by which future changes in the government are to be introduced.

On examining the first relation, it appears, on one hand, that the Constitution is to be founded on the assent and ratification of the people of America, given by deputies elected for the special purpose; but, on the other, that this assent and ratification is to be given by the people, not as individuals composing one entire nation, but as composing the distinct and independent States to which they respectively belong. It is to be the assent and ratification of the several States, derived from the supreme authority in each State,—the authority of the people themselves. The act, therefore, establishing the Constitution, will not be a *national,* but a *federal* act.

That it will be a federal and not a national act, as these terms are understood by the objectors; the act of the people, as forming so many independent States, not as forming one aggregate nation, is obvious from this single consideration, that it is to result neither from the decision of the *majority* of the people of the Union, nor from that of a *majority* of the States, It must result from the *unanimous* assent of the several States that are parties to it, differing no otherwise from their ordinary assent than in its being expressed, not by the legislative authority, but by that of the people themselves. Were the people regarded in this transaction as forming one nation, the will of the majority of the whole people of the United States would bind the minority, in the same manner as the majority in each State must bind the minority; and the will of the majority must be determined either by a comparison of the individual votes, or by considering the will of the majority of the States as evidence of the will of a majority of the people of the United States. Neither of these rules has been adopted. Each State, in ratifying the Constitution, is considered as a sovereign body, independent of all others, and only to be bound by its own voluntary act. In this relation, then, the new Constitution will, if established, be a *federal,* and not a *national* constitution.

The next relation is, to the sources from which the ordinary powers of government are to be derived. The House of Representatives will derive its powers from the people of America; and the people will be represented in the same proportion, and on the same principle, as they are in the legislature of a particular State. So far the government is *national,* not *federal.* The Senate, on the other hand, will derive its powers from the States, as political and coequal societies; and these will be represented on the principle of equality in the Senate, as they now are in the existing Congress. So far the government is *federal,* not *national.* The executive power will be derived from a very compound source. The immediate election of the President is to be made by the States in their political characters. The votes allotted to them are in a compound ratio, which considers them partly as unequal members of the same society. The eventual election, again, is to be made by that branch of the legislature which consists of the national representatives; but in this particular act they are to be thrown into the form of individual delegations, from so many distinct and coequal bodies politic. From this aspect of the government, it appears to be of a mixed character, presenting at least as many *federal* as *national* features.

The difference between a federal and national government, as it relates to the *operation* of the *government,* is supposed to consist in this, that in the former the powers operate on the political bodies composing the Confederacy, in their political capacities; in the latter, on the individual citizens composing the nation, in their individual capacities. On trying the Constitution by this criterion, it falls under the *national,* not the *federal* character; though perhaps not so completely as has been understood. In several cases, and particularly in the trial of contro-

versies to which States may be parties, they must be viewed and proceeded against in their collective and political capacities only. So far the national countenance of the government on this side seems to be disfigured by a few federal features. But this blemish is perhaps unavoidable in any plan; and the operation of the government on the people, in their individual capacities, in its ordinary and most essential proceedings, may, on the whole, designate it, in this relation, a *national* government.

But if the government be national with regard to the *operation* of its powers, it changes its aspect again when we contemplate it in relation to the extent of its powers. The idea of a national government involves in it, not only an authority over the individual citizens, but an indefinite supremacy over all persons and things, so far as they are objects of lawful government. Among a people consolidated into one nation, this supremacy is completely vested in the national legislature. Among communities united for particular purposes, it is vested partly in the general and partly in the municipal legislatures. In the former case, the local authorities are subordinate to the supreme; and may be controlled, directed, or abolished by it at pleasure. In the latter, the local or municipal authorities form distinct and independent portions of the supremacy, no more subject, within their respective spheres, to the general authority, than the general authority is subject to them, within its own sphere. In this relation, then, the proposed government cannot be deemed a *national* one; since its jurisdiction extends to certain enumerated objects only, and leaves to the several States a residuary and inviolable sovereignty over all other objects. It is true that in controversies relating to the boundary between the two jurisdictions, the tribunal which is ultimately to decide, is to be established under the general government. But this does not change the principle of the case. The decision is to be impartially made, according to the rules of the Constitution; and all the usual and most effectual precautions are taken to secure this impartiality. Some such tribunal is clearly essential to prevent an appeal to the sword and a dissolution of the compact; and that it ought to be established under the general rather than under the local governments, or to speak more properly, that it could be safely established under the first alone, is a position not likely to be combated.

If we try the Constitution by its last relation to the authority by which amendments are to be made, we find it neither wholly *national* nor wholly *federal*. Were it wholly national, the supreme and ultimate authority would reside in the *majority* of the people of the Union; and this authority would be competent at all times, like that of a majority of every national society, to alter or abolish its established government. Were it wholly federal, on the other hand, the concurrence of each State in the Union would be essential to every alteration that would be binding on all. The mode provided by the plan of the convention is not founded on either of these principles. In requiring more than a majority, and particularly in computing the proportion by *States,* not by *citizens,* it departs from the *national* and advances towards the *federal* character; in rendering the concurrence of less than the whole number of States sufficient, it loses again the *federal* and partakes of the *national* character.

The proposed Constitution, therefore, is, in strictness, neither a national nor a federal Constitution, but a composition of both. In its foundation it is federal, not national; in the sources from which the ordinary powers of the government are drawn, it is partly federal and partly national; in the operation of these powers, it is national, not federal; in the extent of them, again, it is federal, not national; and, finally, in the authoritative mode of introducing amendments, it is neither wholly federal nor wholly national.

PUBLIUS

From the New York Packet
Friday, February 1, 1788

The Federalist No. 48

To the People of the State of New York:

It was shown in the last paper that the political apothegm there examined does not require that the legislative, executive, and judiciary departments should be wholly unconnected with each other. I shall undertake, in the next place, to show that unless these departments be so far connected and blended as to give to each a constitutional control over the others, the degree of separation which the maximum requires, as essential to a free government, can never in practice be duly maintained.

It is agreed on all sides, that the powers properly belonging to one of the departments ought not to be directly and completely administered by either of the other departments. It is equally evident, that none of them ought to possess, directly or indirectly, an overruling influence over the others, in the administration of their respective powers. It will not be denied, that power is of an encroaching nature, and that it ought to be effectually restrained from passing the limits assigned to it. After discriminating, therefore, in theory, the several classes of power, as they may in their nature be legislative, executive, or judiciary, the next and most difficult task is to provide some practical security for each, against the invasion of the others. What this security ought to be, is the great problem to be solved.

Will it be sufficient to mark, with precision, the boundaries of these departments in the constitution of the government, and to trust to these parchment barriers against the encroaching spirit of power? This is the security which appears to have been principally relied on by the compilers of most of the American constitutions. But experience assures us, that the efficacy of the provision has been greatly overrated; and that some more adequate defence is indispensably necessary for the more feeble, against the more powerful, members of the government. The legislative department is everywhere extending the sphere of its activity, and drawing all power into its impetuous vortex.

The founders of our republics have so much merit for the wisdom which they have displayed, that no task can be less pleasing than that of pointing out the errors into which they have fallen. A respect for truth, however, obliges us to remark, that they seem never for a moment to have turned their eyes from the danger to liberty from the overgrown and all grasping prerogative of an hereditary magistrate, supported and fortified by an hereditary branch of the legislative authority. They seem never to have recollected the danger from legislative usurpations, which, by assembling all power in the same hands, must lead to the same tyranny as is threatened by executive usurpations.

In a government where numerous and extensive prerogatives are placed in the hands of an hereditary monarch, the executive department is very justly regarded as the source of danger, and watched with all the jealousy which a zeal for liberty ought to inspire. In a democracy, where a multitude of people exercise in person the legislative functions, and are continually exposed, by their incapacity for regular deliberation and concerted measures, to the ambitious intrigues of their executive magistrates, tyranny may well be apprehended, on some favorable emergency, to start up in the same quarter. But in a representative republic, where the executive magistracy is carefully limited, both in the extent and the duration of its power; and where the legislative power is exercised by an assembly, which is inspired, by a supposed influence over the people, with an intrepid confidence in its own strength; which is sufficiently numerous to feel all the passions which actuate a multitude, yet not so numerous as to be incapable of pursuing the objects of its passions, by means which reason prescribes; it is against the enterprising ambition of this department that the people ought to indulge all their jealousy and exhaust all their precautions.

The legislative department derives a superiority in our governments from other circumstances, Its constitutional powers being at once more extensive, and less susceptible of precise limits, it can, with the greater facility, mask, under complicated and indirect measures, the encroachments which it makes on the coordinate departments. It is not unfrequently a question of real nicety in legislative bodies, whether the operation of a particular measure will, or will not, extend beyond the legislative sphere. On the other side, the executive power being restrained within a narrower compass, and being more simple in its nature, and the judiciary being described by landmarks still less uncertain, projects of usurpation by either of these departments would immediately betray and defeat themselves. Nor is this all: as the legislative department alone has access to the pockets of the people, and has in some constitutions full discretion, and in all a prevailing influence, over the pecuniary rewards of those who fill the other departments, a dependence is thus created in the latter, which gives still greater facility to encroachments of the former.

I have appealed to our own experience for the truth of what I advance on this subject. Were it necessary to verify this experience by particular proofs, they might be multiplied without end. I might find a witness in every citizen who has shared in, or been attentive to, the course of public administrations. I might collect vouchers in abundance from the records and archives of every State in the Union. But as a more concise, and at the same time equally satisfactory, evidence, I will refer to the example of two States, attested by two unexceptionable authorities.

The first example is that of Virginia, a State which, as we have seen, has expressly declared in its constitution, that the three great departments ought not to be intermixed. The authority in support of it is Mr. Jefferson, who, besides his other advantages for remarking the operation of the government, was himself the chief magistrate of it. In order to convey fully the ideas with which his experience had impressed him on this subject, it will be necessary to quote a passage of some length from his very interesting "Notes on the State of Virginia," p. 195.

All the powers of government, legislative, executive, and judiciary, result to the legislative body. The concentrating these in the same hands, is precisely the definition of despotic government. It will be no alleviation, that these powers will be exercised by a plurality of hands, and not by a single one. One hundred and seventy-three despots would surely be as oppressive as one. Let those who doubt it, turn their eyes on the republic of Venice. As little will it avail us, that they are chosen by ourselves. An *elective despotism* was not the government we fought for; but one which should not only be founded on free principles, but in which the powers of government should be so divided and balanced among several bodies of magistracy, as that no one could transcend their legal limits, without being effectively checked and restrained by the others. For this reason, that convention which passed the ordnance of government, laid its foundation on this basis, that the legislative, executive, and judiciary departments should be separate and distinct, so that no person should exercise the powers of more than one of them at the same time. *But no barrier was provided between these several powers.* The judiciary and the executive members were left dependent on the legislative for their subsistence in office, and some of them for their continuance in it. If, therefore, the legislature assumes executive and judiciary powers, no opposition is likely to be made; nor, if made, can be effectual; because in that case they may put their proceedings into the form of acts of Assembly, which will render them obligatory on the other branches. They have accordingly, *in many instances, decided rights* which should have been left to *judiciary controversy,* and *the direction of the executive, during the whole time of their session, is becoming habitual and familiar.*

The other State which I shall take for an example is Pennsylvania; and the other

authority, the Council of Censors, which assembled in the years 1783 and 1784. A part of the duty of this body, as marked out by the constitution, was "to inquire whether the constitution had been preserved inviolate in every part; and whether the legislative and executive branches of government had performed their duty as guardians of the people, or assumed to themselves, or exercised, other or greater powers than they are entitled to by the constitution." In the execution of this trust, the council were necessarily led to a comparison of both the legislative and executive proceedings, with the constitutional powers of these departments; and from the facts enumerated, and to the truth of most of which both sides in the council subscribed, it appears that the constitution had been flagrantly violated, by the legislature in a variety of important instances.

A great number of laws had been passed, violating, without any apparent necessity, the rule requiring that all bills of a public nature shall be previously printed for the consideration of the people; although this is one of the precautions chiefly relied on by the constitution against improper acts of the legislature.

The constitutional trial by jury had been violated, and powers assumed which had not been delegated by the constitution.

Executive powers had been usurped.

The salaries of the judges, which the constitution expressly requires to be fixed, had been occasionally varied; and cases belonging to the judiciary department frequently drawn within legislative cognizance and determination.

Those who wish to see the several particulars falling under each of these heads, may consult the journals of the council, which are in print. Some of them, it will be found, may be imputable to peculiar circumstances connected with the war; but the greater part of them may be considered as the spontaneous shoots of an ill-constituted government.

It appears, also, that the executive department had not been innocent of frequent breaches of the constitution. There are three observations, however, which ought to be made on this head: *first,* a great proportion of the instances were either immediately produced by the necessities of the war, or recommended by Congress or the commander-in-chief; *secondly,* in most of the other instances, they conformed either to the declared or the known sentiments of the legislative department; *thirdly,* the executive department of Pennsylvania is distinguished from that of the other States by the number of members composing it. In this respect, it has as much affinity to a legislative assembly as to an executive council. And being at once exempt from the restraint of an individual responsibility for the acts of the body, and deriving confidence from mutual example and joint influence, unauthorized measures would, of course, be more freely hazarded, than where the executive department is administered by a single hand, or by a few hands.

The Federalist No. 51

To the People of the State of New York:

To what expedient, then, shall we finally resort, for maintaining in practice the necessary partition of power among the several departments, as laid down in the Constitution? The only answer that can be given is, that as all these exterior provisions are found to be inadequate, the defect must be supplied, by so contriving the interior structure of the government as that its several constituent parts may, by their mutual relations, be the means of keeping each other in their proper places. Without presuming to undertake a full development of this important idea, I will hazard a few general observations, which may

perhaps place it in a clearer light, and enable us to form a more correct judgment of the principles and structure of the government planned by the convention.

In order to lay a due foundation for that separate and distinct exercise of the different powers of government, which to a certain extent is admitted on all hands to be essential to the preservation of liberty, it is evident that each department should have a will of its own; and consequently should be so constituted that the members of each should have as little agency as possible in the appointment of the members of the others. Were this principle rigorously adhered to, it would require that all the appointments for the supreme executive, legislative, and judiciary magistracies should be drawn from the same fountain of authority, the people, through channels having no communication whatever with one another. Perhaps such a plan of constructing the several departments would be less difficult in practice than it may in contemplation appear. Some difficulties, however, and some additional expense would attend the execution of it. Some deviations, therefore, from the principle must be admitted. In the constitution of the judiciary department in particular, it might be inexpedient to insist rigorously on the principle; first, because peculiar qualifications being essential in the members, the primary consideration ought to be to select that mode of choice which best secures these qualifications; secondly, because the permanent tenure by which the appointments are held in that department, must soon destroy all sense of dependence on the authority conferring them.

It is equally evident, that the members of each department should be as little dependent as possible on those of the others, for the emoluments annexed to their offices. Were the executive magistrate, or the judges, not independent of the legislature in this particular, their independence in every other would be merely nominal.

But the great security against a gradual concentration of the several powers in the same department, consists of giving to those who administer each department the necessary constitutional means and personal motives to resist encroachments of the others. The provision for defence must in this, as in all other cases, be made commensurate to the danger of attack. Ambition must be made to counteract ambition. The interest of the man must be connected with the constitutional rights of the place. It may be a reflection on human nature, that such devices should be necessary to control the abuses of government. But what is government itself, but the greatest of all reflections on human nature? If men were angels, no government would be necessary. If angels were to govern men, neither external nor internal controls on government would be necessary. In framing a government which is to be administered by men over men, the great difficulty lies in this: you must first enable the government to control the governed; and in the next place oblige it to control itself. A dependence on the people is, no doubt, the the primary control on the government; but experience has taught mankind the necessity of auxiliary precautions.

This policy of supplying, by opposite and rival interests, the defect of better motives, might be traced through the whole system of human affairs, private as well as public. We see it particularly displayed in all the subordinate distributions of power, where the constant aim is to divide and arrange the several offices in such a manner as that each may be a check on the other—that the private interest of every individual may be a sentinel over the public rights. These inventions of prudence cannot be less requisite in the distribution of the supreme powers of the State.

But it is not possible to give to each department an equal power of self-defence. In republican government, the legislative authority necessarily predominates. The remedy for this inconveniency is to divide the legislature into different branches; and to render them, by different modes of election and different principles of action, as little connected with each other as the nature of their common functions and their common dependence on the society will admit. It may even be necessary to guard against dangerous encroachments by still further precautions. As the weight of the legislative authority requires that it should be thus divided, the weakness of the executive may require, on the other hand, that it should be fortified. An absolute negative on the legislature appears, at first view, to be the natural defence with which the executive magistrate should be armed. But perhaps it would be neither altogether safe nor alone sufficient. On ordinary occasions it might not be exerted with the requisite firmness, and on extraordinary occasions it might be perfidiously abused. May not this defect of an absolute negative be supplied by some qualified connection between this weaker department and the weaker branch of the stronger department, by which the latter may be led to support the constitutional rights of the former, without being too much detached from the rights of its own department?

If the principles on which these observations are founded be just, as I persuade myself they are, and they be applied as a criterion to the several State constitutions, and to the federal Constitution, it will be found that if the latter does not perfectly correspond with them, the former are infinitely less able to bear such a test.

There are, moreover, two considerations particularly applicable to the federal system of America, which place that system in a very interesting point of view.

First. In a single republic, all power surrendered by the people is submitted to the administration of a single government; and the usurpations are guarded against by a division of the government into distinct and separate departments. In the compound republic of America, the power surrendered by the people is first divided between two distinct governments, and then the portion allotted to each subdivided among distinct and separate departments. Hence a double security arises to the rights of the people. The different governments will control each other, at the same time that each will be controlled by itself.

Second. It is of great importance in a republic not only to guard the society against the oppression of its rulers, but to guard one part of the society against the injustice of the other part. Different interests necessarily exist in different classes of citizens. If a majority be united by a common interest, the rights of the minority will be insecure. There are but two methods of providing against this evil: the one by creating a will in the community independent of the majority—that is, of the society itself; the other, by comprehending in the society so many separate descriptions of citizens as will render an unjust combination of a majority of the whole very impropable, if not impracticable. The first method prevails in all governments possessing an hereditary or self-appointed authority. This, at best, is but a precarious security; because a power independent of the society may as well espouse the unjust views of the major, as the rightful interests of the minor party, and may possibly be turned against both parties. The second method will be exemplified in the federal republic of the United States. Whilst all authority in it will be derived from and dependent on the society, the society itself will be broken into so many parts, interests and classes of citizens, that the rights of individuals, or of the minority, will be in little danger from interested combinations of the majority. In a free government the security for civil rights must be the same as that for religious rights. It consists in the one case in the multiplicity of interests, and in the other in the multiplicity of sects. The degree of security in both cases will depend on the number of interests and sects; and this may be presumed to depend on the extent of country and number of people comprehended

under the same government. This view of the subject must particularly recommend a proper federal system to all the sincere and considerate friends of republican government, since it shows that in exact proportion as the territory of the Union may be formed into more circumscribed Confederacies, or States, oppressive combinations of a majority will be facilitated; the best security, under the republican forms, for the rights of every class of citizens, will be diminished; and consequently the stability and independence of some member of the government, the only other security, must be proportionally increased. Justice is the end of government. It is the end of civil society. It ever has been and ever will be pursued until it be obtained, or until liberty be lost in the pursuit. In a society under the forms of which the stronger faction can readily unite and oppress the weaker, anarchy may as truly be said to reign as in a state of nature, where the weaker individual is not secured against the violence of the stronger; and as, in the latter state, even the stronger individuals are prompted, by the uncertainty of their condition, to submit to a government which may protect the weak as well as themselves; so, in the former state, will the more powerful factions or parties be gradually induced, by a like motive, to wish for a government which will protect all parties, the weaker as well as the more powerful. It can be little doubted that if the State of Rhode Island was separated from the Confederacy and left to itself, the insecurity of rights under the popular form of government within such narrow limits would be displayed by such reiterated oppressions of factious majorities that some power altogether independent of the people would soon be called for by the voice of the very factions whose misrule had proved the necessity of it. In the extended republic of the United States, and among the great variety of interests, parties, and sects which it embraces, a coalition of a majority of the whole society could seldom take place on any other principles than those of justice and the general good; whilst there being thus less danger to a minor from the will of a major party, there must be less pretext, also, to provide for the security of the former, by introducing into the government a will not dependent on the latter, or, in other words, a will independent of the society itself. It is no less certain than it is important, notwithstanding the contrary opinions which have been entertained, that the larger the society, provided it lie within a practical sphere, the more duly capable it will be of self-government. And happily for the *republican cause,* the practicable sphere may be carried to a very great extent, by a judicious modification and mixture of the federal principle.

PUBLIUS

Madison's Defense of the Kentucky-Virginia Resolutions

CONCLUDING SECTIONS, KENTUCKY RESOLUTION OF 1798

VIII. Resolved, that the preceding Resolutions be transmitted to the Senators and Representatives in Congress from this Commonwealth, who are hereby enjoined to present the same to their respective Houses, and to use their best endeavours to procure at the next session of Congress, a repeal of the aforesaid unconstitutional and obnoxious acts.

IX. Resolved lastly, that the Governor of this Commonwealth be, and is hereby authorised and requested to communicate the preceding Resolutions to the Legislatures of the several States, to assure them that this Commonwealth considers Union for specified National purposes, and particularly for those specified in their late Federal Compact, to be friendly to the peace, happiness, and prosperity of all the States: that faithful to that compact, according to the plain intent and meaning in which it was understood and acceded to by the several parties, it is sincerely anxious for its preservation: that it does also believe, that to take from the States all the powers of self government, and transfer them to a general and consolidated Government, without regard to the special delegations and reservations solemnly agreed to in that compact, is not for the peace, happiness or prosperity of these States: And that therefore, this Commonwealth is determined, as it doubts not its co-States are, namely to submit to undelegated & consequently unlimited powers in no man or body of men on earth: that if the acts before specified should stand, these conclusions would flow from them; that the General Government may place any act they think proper on the list of crimes & punish it themselves, whether enumerated or not enumerated by the Constitution as cognizable by them: that they may transfer its cognizance to the President or any other person, who may himself be the accuser, counsel, judge, and jury, whose *suspicions* may be the evidence, his order the sentence, his officer the executioner, and his breast the sole record of the transaction: that a very numerous and valuable description of the inhabitants of these States, being by this precedent reduced as outlaws to the absolute dominion of one man, and the barrier of the Constitution thus swept away from us all, no rampart now remains against the passions and the power of a majority of Congress, to protect from a like exportation or other more grievous punishment the minority of the same body, the Legislatures, Judges, Governors, & Counsellors of the States, nor their other peaceable inhabitants who may venture to reclaim the constitutional rights & liberties of the States & people, or who for other causes, good or bad, may be obnoxious to the views or marked by the suspicions of the President, or be thought dangerous to his or their elections or other interests public or personal: that the friendless alien has indeed been selected as the safest subject of a first experiment: but the citizen will soon follow, or rather has already followed; for, already has a Sedition Act marked him as its prey: that these and successive acts of the same character, unless arrested on the threshold, may tend to drive these States into revolution and blood, and will furnish new calumnies against Republican Governments, and new pretexts for those who wish it to be believed, that man cannot be governed but by a rod of iron: that it would be a dangerous delusion were a confidence in the men of our choice to silence our fears for the safety of our rights: that confidence is every where the parent of despotism: free government is founded in jealousy and not in confidence; it is jealousy and not confidence which prescribes limited Constitutions to bind down those whom we are obliged to trust with power that our Constitution has accordingly fixed the limits to which and no further our confidence may go; and let the honest advocate of confidence read the Alien and Sedition Acts, and say if the Constitution has not been wise in fixing limits to the Government it created, and whether we should be wise in destroying those limits? Let him say what the Government is if it be not a tyranny, which the men of our choice have conferred on the President, and the President of our choice has assented to and accepted over the friendly strangers, to whom the mild spirit of our Country and its laws had pledged hospitality and protection: that the men of our choice have more respected the bare suspicions of the President than the solid rights of innocence, the claims of justification, the sacred force of truth, and the forms & substance of law and justice. In questions of power then let no more be heard of confidence in man, but bind him down from mischief by the chains of the Constitution. That this Commonwealth does therefore call on its co-States for

an expression of their sentiments on the acts concerning Aliens, and for the punishment of certain crimes herein before specified, plainly declaring whether these acts are or are not authorized by the Federal Compact? And it doubts not that their sense will be so announced as to prove their attachment unaltered to limited Government, whether general or particular, and that the rights and liberties of their co-States will be exposed to no dangers by remaining embarked on a common bottom with their own: That they will concur with this Commonwealth in considering the said acts as so palpably against the Constitution as to amount to an undisguised declaration, that the Compact is not meant to be the measure of the powers of the General Government, but that it will proceed in the exercise over these States of all powers whatsoever: That they will view this as seizing the rights of the States and consolidating them in the hands of the General Government with a power assumed to bind the States (not merely in cases made federal) but in all cases whatsoever, by laws made, not with their consent, but by others against their consent: That this would be to surrender the form of Government we have chosen, and to live under one deriving its powers from its own will, and not from our authority; and that the co-States recurring to their natural right in cases not made federal, will concur in declaring these acts void and of no force, and will each unite with this Commonwealth in requesting their repeal at the next session of Congress.

Virginia Resolution of 1798

Resolved, That the General Assembly of Virginia, doth unequivocally express a firm resolution to maintain and defend the Constitution of the United States, and the Constitution of this State, against every aggression either foreign or domestic, and that they will support the government of the United States in all measures warranted by the former.

That this Assembly most solemnly declares a warm attachment to the Union of the States, to maintain which it pledges all its powers; and that for this end, it is their duty to watch over and oppose every infraction of those principles which constitute the only basis of that Union, because a faithful observance of them, can alone secure its existence and the public happiness.

That this Assembly doth explicitly and peremptorily declare, that it views the powers of the federal government, as resulting from the compact, to which the States are parties; as limited by the plain sense and intention of the instrument constituting that compact; as no further valid than they are authorized by the grants enumerated in that compact; and that in case of a deliberate, palpable, and dangerous exercise of other powers, not granted by the said compact, the States who are parties thereto, have the right, and are in duty bound, to interpose for arresting the progress of the evil, and for maintaining within their respective limits, the authorities, rights and liberties appertaining to them.

That the General Assembly doth also express its deep regret, that a spirit has in sundry instances, been manifested by the federal government, to enlarge its powers by forced constructions of the constitutional charter which defines them; and that indications have appeared of a design to expound certain general phrases (which having been copied from the very limited grant of powers in the former articles of confederation were the less liable to be misconstrued) so as to destroy the meaning and effect, of the particular enumeration which necessarily explains and limits the general phrases; and so as to consolidate the States by degrees, into one sovereignty, the obvious tendency and inevitable consequence of which would be,

to transform the present republican system of the United States, into an absolute, or at best a mixed morarchy.

That the General Assembly doth particularly protest against the palpable and alarming infractions of the Constitution, in the two late cases of the "Alien and Sedition Acts" passed at the last session of Congress; the first of which exercises a power nowhere delegated to the federal government, and which by uniting legislative and judicial powers to those of executive, subverts the general principles of free government, as well as the particular organization, and positive provisions of the federal Constitution; and the other of which acts, exercises in like manner, a power not delegated by the Constitution, but on the contrary, expressly and positively forbidden by one of the amendments thereto;—a power, which more than any other, ought to produce universal alarm, because it is leveled against that right of freely examining public characters and measures, and of free communication among the people thereon, which has ever been justly deemed, the only effectual guardian of every other right.

That this State having by its Convention, which ratified the Federal Constitution, expressly declared, that among other essential rights, "the Liberty of Conscience and of the Press cannot be cancelled, abridged, restrained, or modified by any authority of the United States," and from its extreme anxiety to guard these rights from every possible attack of sophistry or ambition, having with other States, recommended an amendment for that purpose, which amendment was, in due time, annexed to the Constitution; it would mark a reproachful inconsistency, and criminal degeneracy, if an indifference were now shewn, to the most palpable violation of one of the Rights, thus declared and secured; and to the establishment of a precedent which may be fatal to the other.

That the good people of this Commonwealth, having ever felt, and continuing to feel, the most sincere affection for their brethren of the other States; the truest anxiety for establishing and perpetuating the union of all; and the most scrupulous fidelity to that Constitution, which is the pledge of mutual friendship, and the instrument of mutual happiness, the General Assembly doth solemnly appeal to the like dispositions of the other States, in confidence that they will concur with this Commonwealth in declaring, as it does hereby declare, that the acts aforesaid, are unconstitutional; and that the necessary and proper measures will be taken by each, for cooperating with this State, in maintaining the Authorities, Rights, and Liberties, reserved to the States respectively or to the People.

That the Governor be desired, to transmit a copy of the foregoing Resolutions to the executive authority of each of the other States, with a request that the same may be communicated to the Legislature thereof; and that a copy be furnished to each of the Senators and Representatives representing this State in the Congress of the United States.

Agreed to by the Senate, December 24, 1798.

Madison's Report to the Virginia General Assembly, January 1800 (relevant to the responses of the other states to the foregoing Virginia Resolution)

Whatever room might be found in the proceedings of some of the States, who have disapproved of the resolutions of the General Assembly of this Commonwealth, passed on the 21st day of December, 1798, for painful remarks on the spirit and manner of those proceedings, it appears to the committee, most consistent with the duty, as well as dignity of the General Assembly, to hasten an oblivion of every circumstance, which might be construed into a diminution of mutual respect, confidence and affection, among the members of the union.

The committee have deemed it a more useful task, to revise with a critical eye, the resolutions which have met with this disapprobation; to examine fully the several objections and arguments which have appeared against them; and to enquire, whether there be any errors of fact, of principle, or of reasoning, which the candour of the General Assembly ought to acknowledge and correct. . . .

The third resolution is in the words following:

> That this Assembly doth explicitly and peremptorily declare, that it views the powers of the Federal Government, as resulting from the compact, to which the States are parties, as limited by the plain sense and intention of the instrument constituting that compact; as no farther valid than they are authorized by the grants enumerated in that compact; and that in case of a *deliberate, palpable* and *dangerous* exercise of other powers not granted by the said compact, the states who are parties thereto, have the right, and are in duty bound, to interpose, for arresting the progress of the evil, and for maintaining within their respective limits, the authorities, rights and liberties appertaining to them.

On this resolution, the committee have bestowed all the attention which its importance merits: They have scanned it not merely with a strict, but with a severe eye; and they feel confidence in pronouncing, that in its just and fair construction, it is unexceptionably in its several positions, as well as constitutional and conclusive in its inferences.

The resolution declares, first, that "it views the powers of the Federal Government, as resulting from the compact to which the States are parties," in other words, that the federal powers are derived from the Constitution, and that the Constitution is a compact to which the states are parties. . . .

It appears to your committee to be a plain principle, founded in common sense, illustrated by common practice, and essential to the nature of compacts; that where resort can be had to no tribunal superior to the authority of the parties, the parties themselves must be the rightful judges in the last resort, whether the bargin made, has been pursued or violated. The Constitution of the United States was formed by the sanction of the States, given by each in its sovereign capacity. It adds to the stability and dignity, as well as to the authority of the Constitution, that it rests on this legitimate and solid foundation. The States then being the parties to the constitutional compact, and in their sovereign capacity, it follows of necessity, that there can be no tribunal above their authority, to decide in the last resort, whether the compact made by them be violated; and consequently that as the parties to it, they must themselves decide in the last resort, such questions as may be of sufficient magnitude to require their interposition.

It does not follow, however, that because the States as sovereign parties to their constitutional compact, must ultimately decide whether it has been violated, that such a decision ought to be interposed either in a hasty manner, or on doubtful and inferior occasions. Even in the case of ordinary conventions between different nations, where, by the strict rule of interpretation, a breach of a part may be deemed a breach of the whole; every part being deemed a condition of every other part, and of the whole, it is always laid down that the breach must be both wilful and material to justify an application of the rule. But in the case of an intimate and constitutional union, like that of the United States, it is evident that the interposition of the parties, in their sovereign capacity, can be called for by occasions only, deeply and essentially affecting the vital principles of their political system. . . .

But it is objected that the judicial authority is to be regarded as the sole expositor of the Constitution, in the last resort; and it may be asked for what reason, the declaration by the General Assembly, supposing it to be theoretically true, could be required at the present day and in so solemn a manner.

On this objection it might be observed *first,* that there may be instances of usurped power, which the forms of the Constitution would never draw within the control of the Judicial Department: *secondly,* that if the decision of the judiciary be raised above the authority of the sovereign parties to the Constitution, the decisions of the other departments, not carried by the forms of the Constitution before the judiciary, must be equally authoritative and final with the decisions of that department. But the proper answer to the objection is, that the resolution of the General Assembly relates to those great and extraordinary cases, in which all the forms of the Constitution may prove ineffectual against infractions dangerous to the essential rights of the parties to it. The resolution supposes that dangerous powers not delegated, may not only be usurped and executed by the other departments, but that the Judicial Department also may exercise or sanction dangerous powers beyond the grant of the Constitution; and consequently that the ultimate right of the parties to the Constitution, to judge whether the compact has been dangerously violated, must extend to violations by one delegated authority, as well as by another; by the judiciary, as well as by the executive, or the legislature.

However true therefore it may be that the Judicial Department is, in all questions submitted to it by the forms of the Constitution, to decide in the last resort, this resort must necessarily be deemed the last in relations to the authorities of the other departments of the government; not in relation to the rights of the parties to the constitutional compact, from which the judicial as well as the other departments hold their delegated trusts. On any other hypothesis, the delegation of judicial power, would annul the authority delegating it; and the concurrence, of this department with the others in usurped powers, might subvert forever, and beyond the possible reach of any rightful remedy, the very Constitution, which all were instituted to preserve. . . .

The fourth resolution stands as follows:

That the General Assembly doth also express its deep regret, that a spirit has in sundry instances, been manifested by the Federal Government, to enlarge its powers by forced constructions of the Constitutional charter which defines them; and that indications have appeared of a design to expound certain general phrases, (which, having been copied from the very limited grant of powers in the former articles of confederation were the less liable to be misconstrued) so as to destroy the meaning and effect, of the particular enumeration which necessarily explains, and limits the general phrases; and so as to consolidate the States by degrees, into one sovereignty, the obvious tendency and inevitable result of which would be, to transform the present republican system of the United States, into an absolute, or at best a mixed monarchy. . . .

The other questions presenting themselves are: 1. Whether indications have appeared of a design to expound certain general phrases copied from the "articles of confederation," so as to destroy the effect of the particular enumeration explaining and limiting their meaning. 2. Whether this exposition would by degrees consolidate the States into one sovereignty. 3. Whether the tendency and result of this consolidation would be to transform the republican system of the United States into a monarchy.

1. The general phrases here meant must be those "or providing for the common defence and general welfare."

In the "articles of confederation" the phrases are used as follows, in article VIII. "All charges of war, and all other expences that shall be incurred *for the common defence and general welfare,*

and allowed by the United States in Congress assembled, shall be defrayed out of a common treasury, which shall be supplied by the several States, in proportion to the value of all land and within each State, granted to or surveyed for any person, as such land and the buildings and improvements thereon shall be estimated, according to such mode as the United States in Congress assembled, shall from time to time direct and appoint."

In the existing Constitution, they made the following part of section 8. "The Congress shall have power, to lay and collect taxes, duties, imposts and exercises to pay the debts, and provide for the common defence and general welfare of the United States."

This similarity in the use of these phrases in the two great federal charters, might well be considered, as rendering their meaning less liable to be misconstrued in the latter; because it will scarcely be said that in the former they were ever understood to be either a general grant of power, or to authorize the requisition or application of money by the old Congress to the common defence and general welfare, except in the cases afterwards enumerated which explained and limited their meaning; and if such was the limited meaning attached to these phrases in the very instrument revised and remodeled by the present Constitution, it can never be supposed that when copied into this Constitution, a different meaning ought to be attached to them.

That notwithstanding this remarkable security against misconstruction, a design has been indicated to expound these phrases in the Constitution so as to destroy the effect of the particular enumeration of powers by which it explains and limits them, must have fallen under the observation of those who have attended to the course of public transactions. Not to multiply proofs on this subject, it will suffice to refer to the debates of the Federal Legislature in which arguments have on different occasions been drawn, with apparent effect from these phrases in their indefinite meaning.

To these indications might be added without looking farther, the official report on manufactures by the late Secretary of the Treasury, made on the 5th of December, 1791; and the report of a committee of Congress in January, 1797, on the promotion of agriculture. In the first of these it is expressly contended to belong "to the discretion of the National legislature to pronounce upon the objects which concern the *general welfare,* and for which under that description, an appropriation of money is requisite and proper. And there seems to be no room for a doubt that whatever concerns the "general interests of LEARNING, of AGRICULTURE, of MANUFACTURES, and of COMMERCE, are within the sphere of the national councils, *as far as regards an application of money."* The latter report assumes the same lattitude of power in the national councils and applies it to the encouragement of agriculture, by means of a society to be established at the seat of government. Although neither of these reports may have received the sanction of a law carrying it into effect; yet, on the other hand, the extraordinary doctrine contained in both, has passed without the slightest positive mark of disapprobation from the authority to which it was addressed.

Now whether the phrases in question be construed to authorize every measure relating to the common defence and general welfare, as contended by some; or every measure only in which there might be an application of money, as suggested by the caution of others, the effect must substantially be the same, in destroying the import and force of the particular enumeration of powers, which follow these general phrases in the Constitution. For it is evident that there is not a single power whatever, which may not have some reference to the common defence, or the general welfare; nor a power of any magnitude which in its exercise does not involve or admit an application of money. The

government therefore which possesses power in either one or other of these extents, is a government without the limitations formed by a particular enumeration of powers; and consequently the meaning and effect of this particular enumeration, is destroyed by the exposition given to these general pharses.

This conclusion will not be affected by an attempt to qualify the power over the "general welfare," by referring it to cases where the *general welfare* is beyond the reach of *separate* provisions by the *individual States;* and leaving to these their jurisdictions in cases, to which their separate provisions may be competent. For as the authority of the individual States must in all cases be incompetent to general regulations operating through the whole, the authority of the United States would be extended to every object relating to the general welfare, which might by any possibility be provided for the general authority. This qualitying construction, therefore would have little, if any tendency, to circumscribe the power claimed under the lattitude of the terms "general welfare."

The true and fair construction of this expression, both in the original and existing Federal compacts appears to the committee too obvious to be mistaken. In both, the Congress is authorized to provide money for the common defence and *general welfare.* In both, is subjoined to this authority, an enumeration of the cases, to which their powers shall extend. Money cannot be applied to the *general welfare,* otherwise than by an application of it to some *particular* measure conducive to the general welfare. Whenever therefore, money has been raised by the general authority, and is to be applied to a particular measure, a question arises, whether the particular measure be within the enumerated authorities vested in Congress. If it be, the money requisite for it may be applied to it; if it be not, no such application can be made. This fair and obvious interpretation coincides with, and is enforced by, the clause in the Constitution which declares that "no money shall be drawn from the treasury, but in consequence of appropriations by law." An appropriation of money to the general welfare, would be deemed rather a mockery than an observance of this constitutional injunction.

2. Whether the exposition of the general phrases here combated, would not, by degrees consolidate the States into one sovereignty, is a question concerning which, the committee can perceive little room for difference of opinion. To consolidate the States into one sovereignty, nothing more can be wanted, than to supersede their respective sovereignties in the cases reserved to them, by extending the sovereignty of the United States to all cases of the "general welfare," that is to say, to *all cases whatever.*

3. That the obvious tendency and inevitable result of a consolidation of the State into one sovereignty, would be, to transform the republican system of the United States into a monarchy, is a point which seems to have been sufficiently decided by the general sentiment of America. . . .

The resolution next in order, is contained in the following terms:

That the General Assembly doth particularly protest against the palpable, and alarming infractions of the Constitution, in the two late cases of the "Alien and Sedition acts," passed at the last session of Congress; the first of which, exercises a power no where delegated to the Federal government; and which by winning legislative and judicial powers to those of executive, subverts the general principles of a free government, as well as the particular organization, and positive provisions of the Federal Constitution; and the other of which acts, exercises in like manner, a power not delegated by the Constitution, but on the contrary, expressly and positively forbidden by one of the amendments thereto;—a power, which more than any other, ought to produce universal alarm; because it is leveled against that right of freely examining public characters and measures, and of free communication among the people thereon, which has ever been justly deemed the only effectual guardian of every other right. . . .

In the administration of preventive justice, the following principles have been held sacred; that some probable ground of suspicion be exhibited before some judicial authority; that it be supported by oath or affirmation; that the party may avoid being thrown into confinement, by finding pledges or sureties for his legal conduct sufficient in the judgment of some judicial authority; that he may have the benefit of a writ of habeas corpus, and thus obtain his release, if wrongfully confined; and that he may at any time be discharged from his recognizance, or his confinement, and restored to his former liberty and rights, on the order of the proper judicial authority; if it shall see sufficient cause.

All these principles of the only preventive justice known to American jurisprudence, are violated by the Alien Act. The ground of suspicion is to be judged of, not by any judicial authority, but by the executive magistrate alone; no oath or affirmation is required; if the suspicion be held reasonable by the President, he may order the suspected alien to depart the territory of the United States, without the opportunity of avoiding the sentence, by finding pledges for his future good conduct; as the President may limit the time of departure as he pleases, the benefit of the writ of habeas corpus, may be suspended with respect to the party, although the Constitution ordains, that it shall not be suspended, unless when the public safety may require it in case of rebellion or invasion, neither of which existed at the passage of the act: And the party being, under the sentence of the President, either removed from the United States, or being punished by imprisonment, or disqualification ever to become a citizen on conviction of not obeying the order of removal, he cannot be discharged from the proceedings against him, and restored to the benefits of his former situation, although the *highest judicial authority* should see the most sufficient cause for it.

But, in the last place, it can never be admitted, that the removal of aliens, authorized by the act; is to be considered, not as punishment for an offence; but as a measure of precaution and prevention. If the banishment of an alien from a country into which he has been invited, as the asylum most auspicious to his happiness; a country, where he may have formed the most tender of connections, where he may have vested his entire property, and acquired property of the real and permanent, as well as the moveable and temporary kind; where he enjoys under the laws, a greater share of the blessings of personal security and personal liberty, than he can elsewhere hope for, and where he may have nearly completed his probationary title to citizenship; if moreover, in the execution of the sentence against him, he is to be exposed, not only to the ordinary dangers of the sea, but to the peculiar casualties incident to a crisis of war, and of unusual licentiousness on that element and possibly to vindictive purposes which his emigration itself may have provoked; if a banishment of this sort be not a punishment, and among the severest of punishments, it will be difficult to imagine a doom to which the name can be applied. And if it be a punishment, it will remain to be enquired, whether it can be constitutionally inflicted, on mere suspicion, by the single will of the executive magistrate, on persons convicted of no personal offence against the laws of the land, nor involved in any offence against the law of nations, charged on the foreign state of which they are members.

One argument offered in justification of this power exercised over aliens, is, that the admission of them into the country being of favor not of right, the favor is at all times revocable. . . .

But it can not be a true inference, that because the admission of an alien is a favor, the favor may be revoked at pleasure. A grant of land to an individual, may be of favor not of right; but the moment the grant is made, the favor becomes a right, and must be forfeited before it can be taken away. To pardon a malefactor may be a favor, but the pardon is not, on that account, the less irrevocable. To admit an alien to natural-

ization, is as much a favor, as to admit him to reside in the country; yet it cannot be pretended, that a person naturalized can be deprived of the benefit, any more than a native citizen can be disfranchised.

Again it is said, that aliens not being parties to the Constitution, the rights and privileges which it secures, cannot be at all claimed by them. . . .

But a more direct reply is, that it does not follow, because aliens are not parties to the Constitution, as citizens are parties to it, that whilst they actually conform to it, they have no right to its protection. Aliens are not more parties to the laws, than they are parties to the Constitution; yet it will not be disputed, that as they owe on one hand, a temporary obedience, they are entitled in return, to their protection and advantage.

If aliens had no rights under the constitution, they might not only be banished, but even capitally punished, without a jury or the other incidents to a fair trial. But so far has a contrary principle been carried, in every part of the United States, that except on charges of treason, an alien has, besides all the common privileges, the special one of being tried by a jury, of which one half may be also aliens. . . .

II. It is next affirmed of the Alien Act, that it unites legislative, judicial and executive powers in the hands of the President.

However difficult it may be to mark, in every case, with clearness and certainty, the line which divides legislative power, from the other departments of power; all will agree, that the powers referred to these departments may be so general and undefined, as to be of a legislative, not of an executive or judicial nature; and may for that reason be unconstitutional. Details, to a certain degree, are essential to the nature and character of a law; and, on criminal subjects, it is proper, that details should leave as little as possible to the discretion of those who are to apply and to execute the law. If nothing more were required, in exercising a legislative trust, that a general conveyance of authority, without laying down any precise rules, by which the authority conveyed, should be carried into effect; it would follow, that the whole power of legislation might be transferred by the legislature from itself, and proclamations might become substitutes for laws. A delegation of power in this latitude, would not be denied to be a union of the different powers.

To determine then, whether the appropriate powers of the distinct departments are united by the act authorizing the executive to remove aliens, it must be enquired whether it contains such details, definitions, and rules, as appertain to the true character of a law; especially, a law by which personal liberty is invaded, property deprived of its value to the owner, and life itself indirectly exposed to danger.

The Alien Act, declares, "that it shall be lawful for the President to order all such aliens as he shall judge *dangerous* to the peace and safety of the United States, or shall have reasonable grounds to *suspect,* are concerned in any treasonable, *or secret machinations,* against the government thereof, to depart," &c.

Could a power be well given in terms less definite, less particular, and less precise? To be *dangerous to the public safety;* to be *suspected of secret machinations* against the government; these can never be mistaken for legal rules or certain definitions. They leave every thing to the President. His will is the law.

But it is not a legislative power only that is given to the President. He is to stand in the place of the judiciary also. His suspicion is the only evidence which is to convict: his order the only judgment which is to be executed.

Thus it is the President whose will is to designate the offensive conduct; it is his will that is to ascertain the individuals on whom it is charged; and it is his will, that is to cause the sentence to be executed. It is rightly affirmed therefore, that the act unites legislative and judicial powers to those of the executive. . . .

The *second* object against which the resolution protests is the Sedition Act.

Of this act it is affirmed (1) that it exercises in like manner a power not delegated by the Constitution; (2) that the power, on the contrary, is expressly and positively forbidden by one of the amendments to the Constitution; (3) that this is a power, which more than any other ought to produce universal alarm; because it is leveled against that right of freely examining public characters and measures, and of free communication thereon; which has ever been justly deemed the only effectual guardian of every other right.

I. That it exercises a power not delegated by the Constitution.

Here, again it will be proper to recollect, that the Federal Government being composed of powers specifically granted, with a reservation of all others to the States or to the people, the positive authority under which the Sedition Act could be passed must be produced by those who assert its constitutionality. In what part of the Constitution then is this authority to be found?

Several attempts have been made to answer this question, which will be examined in their order. The committee will begin with one, which has filled them with equal astonishment and apprehension; and which, they cannot but persuade themselves, must have the same effect on all, who will consider it with coolness and impartiality, and with a reverence for our Constitution, in the true character in which it issued from the sovereign authority of the people. The committee refer to the doctrine lately advanced as a sanction to the Sedition Act: "that the common or unwritten law," a law of vast extent and complexity, and embracing almost every possible subject of legislation, both civil and criminal, "makes a part of the law of these States; in their united and national capacity."

The novelty, and in the judgment of the committee, the extravagance of this pretension, would have consigned it to the silence, in which they have passed by other arguments, which an extraordinary zeal for the act has drawn into the discussion. But the auspices, under which this innovation presents itself, have constrained the committee to bestow on it an attention, which other considerations might have forbidden.

In executing the task, it may be of use, to look back to the colonial state of this country, prior to the revolution; to trace the effect of the revolution which converted the colonies into independent States; to enquire into the import of the articles of confederation, the first instrument by which the union of the States was regularly established; and finally to consult the Constitution of 1788, which is the oracle that must decide the important question.

In the State prior to the revolution, it is certain that the common law under different limitations, made a part of the colonial codes. But whether it be understood that the original colonists brought the law with them, or made it their law by adoption; it is equally certain that it was the separate law of each colony within its respective limits, and was unknown to them, as a law pervading and operating through the whole, as one society.

It could not possibly be otherwise. The common law was not the same in any two of the colonies; in some, the modifications were materially and extensively different. There was no common legislature, by which a common will, could be expressed in the form of a law; nor any common magistracy, by which such a law could be carried into practice. The will of each colony alone and separately, had its organs for these purposes.

This stage of our political history, furnishes no foothold for the patrons of this new doctrine.

Did then, the principle or operation of the great event which made the colonies, independent states, imply or introduce the common law, as a law of the union?

The fundamental principle of the revolution was, that the colonies were co-ordinate members with each other, and with Great Britain; of an Empire, united by a common Executive Sovereign, but not united by any common Legislative Sovereign. The Legislative power was maintained to be as complete in each American Parliament, as in the British Parliament. . . .

Such being the ground of our revolution, no support nor colour can be drawn from it, for the doctrines that the common law is binding on these States as one society. The doctrine on the contrary, is evidently repugnant to the fundamental principle of the revolution.

The articles of confederation, are the next source of information on this subject.

In the interval between the commencement of the revolution, and the final ratification of these articles, the nature and extent of the union was determined by the circumstances of the crisis, rather than by any accurate delineation of the general authority. It will not be alleged that the "common law," could have had any legitimate birth as a law of the United States, during that state of things. If it came as such, into existence at all, the charter of confederation must have been its parent.

Here again, however, its pretensions are absolutely destitute of foundation. This instrument does not contain a sentence or syllable, that can be tortured into a countenance of the idea, that the parties to it were with respect to the objects of the common law, to form one community. No such law is named or implied, or alluded to, as being in force, or as brought into force by that compact. No provision is made by which such a law could be carried into operation; whilst on the other hand, every such inference or pretext is absolutely precluded, by article 2d, which declares, "that each State retains its sovereignty, freedom and independence, and every power, jurisdiction and right, which is not by this confederation expressly delegated to the United States, in Congress assembled."

Thus far it appears, that not a vestige of this extraordinary doctrine can be found, in the origin or progress of American institutions. The evidence against it, has, on the contrary, grown stronger at every step; till it has amounted to a formal and positive exclusion, by written articles of compact among the parties concerned.

Is this exclusion revoked, and the common law introduced as a national law, by the present Constitution of the United States? This is the final question to be examined.

It is readily admitted, that particular parts of the common law, may have a sanction from the Constitution, so far as they are necessarily comprehended in the technical pharses which express the powers delegated to the government; and so far also, as such other parts may be adopted as necessary and proper, for carrying into execution the powers expressly delegated. But the question does not relate to either of these portions of the common law. It relates to the common law, beyond these limitations.

The only part of the Constitution which seems to have relied on in this case, is the 2d sect. of art. III. The judicial power shall extend to all cases, *in law and equity,* arising *under this Constitution,* the "laws of the United States, and treaties made or which shall be made under their authority.". . .

The expression, cases in law and equity, is manifestly confined to cases of a civil nature; and would exclude cases of criminal jurisdiction. Criminal cases in law and equity, would be a language unknown to the law. . . .

From these considerations, it is evident, that this part of the Constitution, even if it could be applied at all, to the purpose for which it has been cited, would not include any cases whatever of a criminal nature; and consequently, would not authorise the inference from it, that the juricial authority extends to offences against the common law, as offences arising under the Constitution.

It is further to be considered, that even if this part of the Constitution could be strained into an application to every common law case, criminal as well as civil, it could have no affect in justifying the Sedition Act; which is an exercise of legislative, and not of judicial power: and it is the judicial power only of which the extent is defined in this part of the Constitution.

In aid of these objections, the difficulties and confusion inseparable from a constructive introduction of the common law, would afford powerful reasons against it.

Is it to be the common law with, or without the British statutes?

If without the statutory amendments, the vices of the code would be insupportable?

If with these amendments, what period is to be fixed for limiting the British authority over our laws?

Is it to be the date of the eldest or the youngest of the colonies?

Or are the dates to be thrown together, and a medium deduced?

Or is our independence to be taken for the date?

Is, again, regard to be had to the various changes in the common law made by the local codes of America?

Is regard to be had to such changes, subsequent, as well as prior, to the establishment of the Constitution?

Is regard to be had to future, as well as past changes?

Is the law to be different in every State, as differently modified by its code; or are the modifications of any particular State, to be applied to all?

And on the latter supposition, which among the State codes would form the standard?

Questions of this sort might be multiplied with as much ease, as there would be difficulty in answering them. . . .

From the review thus taken of the situation of the American colonies prior to their independence; of the effect of this event on their situation; of the nature and import of the articles of confederation; of the true meaning of the passage in the existing Constitution from which the common law has been deduced; of the difficulties and uncertainties incident to the doctrine; and of its vast consequences in extending the powers of the federal government and in superseding the authorities of the State governments; the committee feel the utmost confidence in concluding that the common law never was nor by any fair construction, ever can be, deemed a law for the American people as one community; and they indulge the strongest expectation that the same conclusion will finally be drawn, by all candid and accurate enquirers into the subject. It is indeed distressing to reflect, that it ever should have been made a question, whether the Constitution, on the whole face of which is seen so much labour to enumerate and define the several objects of federal power, could intend to introduce in the lump, in an indirect manner, and by a forced construction of a few phrases, the vast and multifarious jurisdiction involved in the common law; a law filling so many ample volumes; a law overspreading the entire field of legislation; and a law that would sap the foundation of the Constitution as a system of limited and specified powers. A severer reproach could not in the opinion of the committee be thrown on the Constitution, on those who framed, or on those who established it, than such a supposition would throw on them.

The argument then drawn from the common law, on the ground of its being adopted or recognized by the Constitution, being inapplicable to the Sedition Act, the committee will proceed to examine the other arguments which have been founded on the Constitution. . . .

The part of the Constitution which seems most to be recurred to, in defence of the "Sedition Act," is the last clause of the above section, empowering Congress "to make all laws which shall be necessary and proper for carrying into execution the foregoing powers, and all other powers vested by this Constitution in the government of the United States, or in any department or officer thereof."

The plain import of this clause is, that Congress shall have all the incidental or instrumental powers, necessary and proper for carrying into execution all the express powers; whether they be vested in the government of the United States, more collectively, or in the several departments, or officers thereof. It is not a grant of new powers to Congress, but merely a declaration, for the removal of all uncertainty, that the means of carrying into execution, those otherwise granted, are included in the grant.

Whenever, therefore, a question arises concerning the constitutionality of a particular power; the first question is, whether the power be expressed in the Constitution. If it be, the question is decided. If it be not expressed; the next enquiry must be, whether it is properly an incident to an express power, and necessary to its execution. If it be, it may be exercised by Congress. If it be not; Congress cannot exercise it.

Let the question be asked, then, whether the power over the press exercised in the "Sedition Act," be found among the powers expressly vested in the Congress? This is not pretended.

Is there any express power, for executing which, it is necessary and proper power?

The power which has been selected, as least remote, in answer to this question, is that of "suppressing insurrections," which is aid to imply a power to *prevent* insurrections, by punishing whatever may *lead* or *tend* to them. But it surely cannot, with the least plausibility, be said, that a regulation of the press, and a punishment of libels, are exercises of a power to suppress insurrections. The most that could be said, would be, that the punishment of libels, if it had the tendency ascribed to it, might prevent the occasion, of passing or executing laws, necessary and proper for the suppression of insurrections. . . .

II. The next point which the resolution requires to be proved is, that the power over the press exercised by the Sedition Act, is positively forbidden by one of the amendments to the Constitution.

The amendment stands in these words—"Congress shall make no law respecting the establishment of religion, or prohibiting the free exercise thereof, *or abridging the freedom of speech or of the press;* or the right of the people peaceably to assemble and to petition the government for a redress of grievances." . . .

In every state, probably, in the union, the press has exerted a freedom in canvassing the merits and measures of public men, of every description, which has not been confined to the strict limits of the common law.—On this footing, the freedom of the press has stood; on this footing it yet stands. And it will not be a breach, either of truth or of candour, to say, that no persons or presses are in the habit of more unrestained animadversions on the proceedings and functionaries of the State governments than the persons and presses most zealous, in vindicating the act of Congress for punishing similar animadversions on the government of the United States.

The last remark will not be understood, as claiming for the State governments, an immunity greater than they have heretofore enjoyed. Some degree of abuse is inseparable from the proper use of every thing; and in no instance is this more true, than in that of the press. It has accordingly been decided by the practice of the States, that it is better to leave a few of its noxious branches, to their luxuriant growth, than by pruning them away, to injure the vigor of those yielding the proper fruits. And can the wisdom of this policy be doubted by any who reflect, that to the press alone, chequered as it is with abuses, the world is indebted for all the triumphs which have been gained by reason and humanity, over error and oppression; who reflect that to the same beneficent source, the United States owe much of the lights which conducted them to the rank of a free and independent nation; and which have improved their political system, into a shape so auspicious to their happiness. Had "sedition acts," forbidding every publication that might bring the constituted agents into contempt or disrepute, or that might excite the hatred of the people against the authors of unjust or pernicious measures, been uniformly enforced against the press; might not the United States have been languishing at this day, under the infirmities of a sickly confederation? Might they not possibly be miserable colonies, groaning under a foreign yoke? . . .

When the Constitution was under the discussions which preceded its ratification, it is well known, that great apprehensions were expressed by many, lest the omission of some positive exception from the powers delegated, of certain rights, and of the freedom of press particularly, might expose them to the danger of being drawn by construction within some of the powers vested in Congress; more especially of the power to make all laws necessary and proper, for carrying their own powers into execution. In reply to this objection, it was invariably urged to be a fundamental and characteristic principle of the Constitution that all powers not given by it, were reserved; that no powers were given beyond those enumerated in the Constitution, and such as were fairly incident to them; that the power over the rights in question, and particularly over the press, was neither among the enumerated powers, nor incident to any of them; and consequently that an exercise of any such power, would be a manifest usurpation. It is painful to remark, how much the arguments now employed in behalf of the Sedition Act are at variance with the reasoning which then justified the Constitution, and invited its ratification.

From this posture of the subject, resulted the interesting question in so many of the conventions, whether the doubts and dangers ascribed to the Constitution should be removed by any amendments previous to the ratification or be postponed, in confidence that as far as they might be proper, they would be introduced in the form provided by the Constitution. The latter course was adopted, and in most of the States, the ratifications were followed by propositions, and instructions for rendering the Constitution more explicit, and more safe to the rights, not meant to be delegated by it. Among those rights, the freedom of the press, in most instances, is particularly and emphatically mentioned. The firm and very pointed manner, in which it is asserted in the proceedings of the convention of this State will be hereafter seen.

In pursuance of the wishes thus expressed, the first Congress that assembled under the constitution, proposed certain amendments which have since, by the necessary ratifications, been made a part of it; among which amendments is the article containing, among other prohibitions on the Congress, an express declaration that they should make no law abridging the freedom of the press.

Without tracing farther the evidence on this subject, it would seem scarcely possible to doubt, that no power whatever over the press, was supposed to be delegated by the Constitution, as it originally stood; and that the amendment was intended as a positive and absolute reservation of it. . . .

III. And in the opinion of the committee well may it be said, as the resolution concludes with saying, that the unconstitutional power exercised over the press by the "Sedition Act," ought "more than any other, to produce universal alarm; because it is leveled against that right of freely examining public characters and measures, and of free communication among the people thereon, which has ever been justly deemed the only effectual guardian of every other right."

Without scrutinizing minutely into all the provisions of the "Sedition Act," it will be sufficient to cite so much of section 2. as follows: "And be it further enacted, that if any person shall write, print, utter, or publish, or shall cause or procure to be written, printed, uttered or published, or shall knowingly and willingly assist or aid in writing, printing, uttering or publishing any false, scandalous, and malicious writing or writings against the government of the United States, or either house of the Congress of the United States, or the President of the United States, *with an intent to defame the said government, or either house of the said Congress, or the President, or to bring them, or either of them, into contempt or disrepute; or to excite against them, or either, or any of them, the hatred of the good people of the United States, &c. Then such person being thereof convicted before any court of the United States, having jurisdiction thereof, shall be punished by a fine not exceeding two thousand dollars, and by imprisonment not exceeding two years."* . . .

May it not be asked of every intelligent friend to the liberties of his country whether, the power exercised in such an act as this, ought not to produce great and universal alarm? Whether a rigid execution of such an act, in time past, would not have repressed that information and communication among the people, which is indispensable to the just exercise of their electoral rights? And whether such an act, if made perpetual, and enforced with rigor, would not, in time to come, either destroy our free system of government, or prepare a convulsion that might prove equally fatal to it.

In answer to such questions, it has been pleaded that the writings and publications forbidden by the act, are those only which are false and malicious, and intended to defame; and merit is claimed for the privilege allowed to authors to justify, by proving the truth of their publications, and for the limitations to which the sentence of fine and imprisonment is subjected. . . .

But whatever may have been the meritorious intentions of all or any who contributed to the Sedition Act, a very few reflections will prove, that its baneful tendency is little diminished by the privilege of giving in evidence the truth of the matter contained in political writings.

In the first place, where simple and naked facts alone are in question, there is sufficient difficulty in some cases, and sufficient trouble and vexation in all, of meeting a prosecution from the government, with the full and formal proof, necessary in a court of law.

But in the next place, it must be obvious to the plainest minds; that opinions, and inferences, and conjectural observations, are not only in many cases inseparable from the facts, but may often be more the objects of the prosecution than the facts themselves; or may even be altogether abstracted from particular facts; and that opinions and inferences, and conjectural observations, cannot be subjects of that kind of proof which appertains to facts, before a court of law. . . .

Let it be recollected, lastly, that the right of electing the members of the government, constitutes more particularly the essence of a free and responsible government. The value and efficiency of this right, depends on the knowledge of the comparative merits and demerits of the candidates for public trust; and on the equal freedom, consequently, of examining and discussing these merits and demerits of the candidates respectively. It has been seen that a number of important elections will take place whilst the act is in force; although it should not be continued beyond the term to which it is limited. Should there happen, then, as is extremely probable in relation to some or other of the branches of the government, to be competition between those who are, and those who are not, members of the government; what will be the situations of the competitors? Not equal; because the characters of the former will be covered by the "Sedition Act" from animadversions exposing them to disrepute among the people; whilst the latter may be exposed to the contempt and hatred of the people, without a violation of the act? What will be the situation of the people? Not free; because they will be compelled to make their election between competitors, whose pretensions they are not permitted by the act, equally to examine, to discuss, and to ascertain. And from both these situa-tions, will not those in power derive an undue advantage for continuing themselves in it; which by impairing the right of election, endangers the blessings of the government founded on it.

It is with justice, therefore, that the General Assembly hath affirmed in the resolution, as well that the right of freely examining public characters and measures, and of free communication thereon, is the only effectual guardian of every other right; as that this particular right is leveled at, by the power exercised in the "Sedition Act."

The resolution next in order is as follows:

> That this State having by its Convention, which ratified the Federal Constitution, expressly declared, that among other essential rights, "the liberty of conscience and of the press cannot be cancelled, abridged, restrained or modified by any authority of the United States," and from its extreme anxiety to guard these rights from every possible attack of sophistry and ambition, having with other States, recommended an amendment for that purpose, which amendment was, in due time, annexed to the Constitution; it would mark a reproachful inconsistency, and criminal degeneracy, if an indifference were not shown, to the most palpable violation of one of the rights, thus declared and secured; and to the establishment of a precedent, which may be fatal to the other. . . .

First, Both of these rights, the liberty of conscience and of the press, rest equally on the original ground of not being delegated by the Constitution, and consequently withheld from the government. Any construction therefore, that would attack this original security for the one must have the like effect on the other.

Secondly. They are both equally secured by the supplement to the Constitution; being both included in the same amendment, made at the same time, and by the same authority. Any construction or argument then which would turn the amendment into a grant or acknowledgment of power with respect to the press, might be equally applied to the freedom of religion.

Thirdly. If it be admitted that the extent of the freedom of the press secured by the amendment, is to be measured by the common law on this subject; the same authority may be resorted to, for the standard which is to fix the extent of the "free exercise of religion." It cannot be necessary to say what this standard would be; whether the common law be taken solely as the unwritten, or as varied by the written, law of England.

Fourthly. If the words and phrases in the amendment, are to be considered as chosen with a studied discrimination, which yields an argument for a power over the press, under the limitation that its freedom be not abridged; the same argument results from the same consideration, for a power over the exercise of religion, under the limitation that its freedom be not prohibited.

For if Congress may regulate the freedom of the press, provided they do not abridge it: because it is said only, "they shall not abridge it;" and is not said, "they shall make no law respecting it;" the analogy of reasoning is conclusive, that Congress may *regulate* and even *abridge* the free exercise of religion; provided they do not *prohibit* it; because it is said only "they shall not prohibit it;" and is *not* said, "they shall make no law *respecting* or no law *abridging* it."

The General Assembly were governed by the clearest reason, then, in considering the "Sedition Act," which legislates on the freedom of the press, as establishing a precedent that may be fatal to the liberty of conscience and it will be the duty of all, in proportion as they value the security of the latter, to take the alarm at every encoachment on the former. . . .

The extensive view of the subject thus taken by the committee, has led them to report to the house, as the result of the whole, the following resolution.

Resolved, That the General Assembly, having carefully and respectfully attended to the proceedings of a number of the States, in answer to their resolutions of December 21, 1798, and having accurately and fully re-examined and reconsidered the latter, find it to be their indispensable duty to adhere to the same, as founded in the truth, as consonant with the Constitution, and as conducive to its preservation; and more especially to be their duty, to renew, as they do hereby renew, their protest against "the Alien and Sedition Acts," as palpable and alarming infractions of the Constitution.

WORKS BY JAMES MADISON

Journal of the Federal Convention. Edited by E. H. Scott. Chicago: Albert, Scott, and Co., 1893. A record of the debates during the Federal Convention of 1787.

Madison, James. *A Discourse on the Death of General Washington.* Richmond: John Martin and Co., 1844. A stirring peroration proclaiming Washington, a gift from Heaven, as a worthy example for any man.

The Papers of James Madison. Edited by Henry D. Gilpin. 3 Vols. Washington: Lang and O'Sullivan, 1840. A three-volume collection of Madison's correspondence and a record of the debates during the Congress of the Confederation.

The Writings of James Madison. Edited by Gaillard Hunt, 9 Vols. New York: Putnam's Sons, 1900. A nine-volume work comprised of Madison's letters, documents, and writings.

MAJOR SOURCES ON JAMES MADISON

Bourne, Edward Gaylord. "Madison's Studies in the History of Federal Government," in *Essays in Historical Criticism.* New York: Scribner, 1901, pp. 163–170. Describes Madison's rejection of all past forms of federal constitutions thus necessitating new ideas and approaches.

Brant, Irving. *James Madison.* 6 Vols. New York: Bobbs-Merrill, 1950. A six-volume work; each volume dealing with a separate phase in Madison's life.

Brant, Irving. "James Madison and His Times," *The American Historical Re-*

view, Vol. 57, No. 4 (July, 1952), pp. 853–870. Reacting strongly against the image of Madison as an errand-boy for Jefferson, the author portrays a high principled man of great ability and numerous contributions.

Burns, Edward Mcnall. *James Madison: Philosopher of the Constitution.* New Brunswick, N.J.: Rutgers University Press. 1938. A descriptive analysis of Madison as a radical in politics and a conservative in economics: emphasis is given to his differences with the Federalists.

DeLeon, Daniel. *James Madison and Karl Marx.* New York: New York Labor News, 1920. A Marxian interpretation showing Madison attempting to eliminate class conflict by adapting the laws and institutions to future changes in society.

Hunt, Gaillard. *The Life of James Madison.* New York: Doubleday, 1902. Written with a liberal approach, this classic biography shows Madison as a man of enormous talent and extreme idealism.

Koch, Adrienne. *Jefferson and Madison.* New York: Knopf, 1950. Madison and Jefferson are described as complementary, but equal, partners in the ideological development of "Jeffersonian Democracy."

Rives, William C. *The Life and Times of James Madison.* Boston: Little, Brown, and Co., 1859. Couched in a chauvinistic style, this three-volume work portrays Madison as a republican within the conservative school.

CHAPTER 5

John Adams

JOHN Adams (1735–1826) was the eldest son of a Massachusetts family of moderate means. Adams graduated from Harvard in 1755, and in 1758 he began to practice law. When the Stamp Act of 1765 was passed, Adams played a prominent role in defending the colonists' action. It was during this period that Adams wrote four articles dealing with the constitutional rights of the people of New England, later published under the title "An Essay on the Canon and Feudal Law." In 1768, Adams moved his law practice to Boston and, in 1770, he was elected to the Massachusetts legislature.

Adams was a delegate to the first and second Continental Congresses. At the Congress of all the delegates, John Adams was one of the few convinced that matters had gone too far to have a reconciliation with England.

In 1777, Adams was sent to Europe and for ten years served the American government as a negotiator to secure Dutch recognition and a loan, and as a diplomat in the peace negotiations between America and Great Britain.

Adams returned home in 1788. Since the presidency fell to Washington, a Virginian, it seemed natural that the Vice-President should come from Massachusetts. As Vice-President Adams supported Washington's policies and considered himself to be a Federalist. In 1796, Adams became the second President of the Republic. His four years in office were quite stormy because of domestic strife and European troubles.

Adams spent the last twenty-five years of his life in peaceful seclusion. He lived to see his son become President of the United States; he died on the fiftieth anniversary of the Declaration of Independence.

Thoughts on Government in a Letter from a Gentleman to his Friend (1776)

My dear Sir: If I was equal to the task of forming a plan for the government of a colony, I should be flattered with your request and very happy to comply with it because, as the divine science of politics is the science of social happiness, and the blessings of society depend entirely on the constitutions of government, which are generally institutions that last for many generations, there can be no employment more agreeable to a benevolent mind than a research after the best.

Pope flattered tyrants too much when he said,

For forms of government let fools contest,
That which is best administered is best.
(Essay on Man)

Nothing can be more fallacious than this. But poets read history to collect flowers, not fruits; they attend to fanciful images, not the effects of social institutions. Nothing is more certain from the history of nations and nature of man than that some forms of government are better fitted for being well administered than others.

We ought to consider what is the end of government before we determine which is the best form. Upon this point all speculative politicians will agree that the happiness of the individual is the end of man. From this principle it will follow that the form of government which communicates ease, comfort, security, or, in one word, happiness to the greatest number of persons and in the greatest degree is the best.

All sober inquirers after truth, ancient and modern, pagan and Christian, have declared that the happiness of man, as well as his dignity, consists in virtue. Confucius, Zoraster, Socrates, Mahomet, not to mention authorities really sacred, have agreed in this.

If this is a form of government, then, whose principle and foundation is virtue, will not every sober man acknowledge it better calculated to promote the general happiness than any other form?

Fear is the foundation of most governments; but it is so sordid and brutal a passion and renders men in whose breasts it predominates so stupid and miserable that Americans will not be likely to approve of any political institution which is founded on it.

Honor is truly sacred but holds a lower rank in the scale of moral excellence than virtue. Indeed, the former is but a part of the latter and consequently has not equal pretensions to support a frame of government productive of human happiness.

The foundation of every government is some principle or passion in the minds of the people. The noblest principles and most generous affections in our nature, then, have the fairest chance to support the noblest and most generous models of government.

A man must be indifferent to the sneers of modern Englishmen to mention in their company the names of Sidney, Harrington, Locke, Milton, Nedham, Neville, Burnet, and Hoadly. No small fortitude is necessary to confess that one has read them. The wretched condition of this country, however, for ten or fifteen years past has frequently reminded me of their principles and reasonings. They will convince any candid mind that there is no good government but what is republican. That the only valuable part of the British constitution is so because the very definition of a republic is "an empire of laws, and not of men." That, as a republic is the best of governments, so that particular arrangement of the powers of society or, in other words, that form of government which is best contrived to secure an impartial and exact execution of the laws is the best of republics.

Of republics there is an inexhaustible variety because the possible combinations of the powers of society are capable of innumerable variations.

As good government is an empire of laws, how shall your laws be made? In a large society inhabiting an extensive country, it is impossible that the whole should assemble to make laws. The first necessary step, then, is to depute power from the many to a few of the most wise and good. But by what rules shall you choose your representatives? Agree upon the number and qualifications of persons who shall have the benefit of choosing or annex this privilege to the inhabitants of a certain extent of ground.

The principal difficulty lies, and the greatest care should be employed, in constituting this representative assembly. It should be in miniature an exact portrait of the people at large. It should think, feel, reason, and act like them. That it may be the interest of this assembly to do strict justice at all times, it should be an equal representation, or, in other words, equal interests among the people should have equal interests in it. Great care should be taken to effect this and to prevent unfair, partial, and corrupt elections. Such regulations, however, may be better made in times of greater tranquility than the present; and they will spring up themselves naturally when all the powers of government come to be in the hands of the people's friends. At present, it will be safest to proceed in all established modes to which the people have been familiarized by habit.

A representation of the people in one assembly being obtained, a question arises whether all the powers of government—legislative, executive, and judicial—shall be left in this body? I think a people cannot be long free, nor ever happy, whose government is in one assembly. My reasons for this opinion are as follow:

1. A single assembly is liable to all the vices, follies, and frailties of an individual—subject to fits of humor, starts of passion, flights of enthusiasm, partialities, or prejudice—and consequently productive of hasty results and absurd judgments. And all these errors ought to be corrected and defects supplied by some controlling power.

2. A single assembly is apt to be avaricious and in time will not scruple to exempt itself from burdens which it will lay without compunction on its constituents.

3. A single assembly is apt to grow ambitious and after a time will not hesitate to vote itself perpetual. This was one fault of the Long Parliament, but more remarkably of Holland, whose assembly first voted themselves from annual to septennial, then for life, and after a course of years, that all vacancies happening by death or otherwise should be filled by themselves without any application to constituents at all.

4. A representative assembly, although extremely well qualified and absolutely necessary as a branch of the legislative, is unfit to exercise the executive power for want of two essential properties, secrecy and dispatch.

5. A representative assembly is still less qualified for the judicial power because it is too numerous, too slow, and too little skilled in the laws.

6. Because a single assembly, possessed of all the powers of government, would make arbitrary laws for their own interest, execute all laws arbitrarily for their own interest, and adjudge all controversies in their own favor.

But shall the whole power of legislation rest in one assembly? Most of the foregoing reasons apply equally to prove that the legislative power ought to be more complex, to which we may add that if the legislative power is wholly in one assembly and the executive in another or in a single person, these two powers will oppose and encroach upon each other until the contest shall end in war, and the whole power, legislative and executive, by usurped by the strongest.

The judicial power, in such case, could not mediate or hold the balance between the two contending powers because the legislative would undermine it. And this shows the necessity, too, of giving the executive power a negative upon the legislative; otherwise this will be continually encroaching upon that.

To avoid these dangers, let a distinct assembly be constituted as a mediator between the two extreme branches of the legislature, that which represents the people and that which is vested with the executive power.

Let the representative assembly then elect by ballot, from among themselves or their constituents or both, a distinct assembly which, for the sake of perspicuity, we will call a council. It may consist of any number you please, say twenty or thirty, and should have a free and independent exercise of its judgment and consequently a negative voice in the legislature.

These two bodies, thus constituted and made integral parts of the legislature, let them unite and by joint ballot choose a governor, who, after being stripped of most of those badges of domination called prerogatives, should have a free and independent exercise of his judgment and be made also an integral part of the legislature. This, I know, is liable to objections; and, if you please, you may make him only president of the council, as in Connecticut. But as the governor is to be invested with the executive power with consent of council, I think he ought to have a negative upon the legislative. If he is annually elective, as he ought to be, he will always have so much reverence and affection for the people, their representatives and counsellors, that, although you give him an independent exercise of his judgment, he will seldom use it in opposition to the two houses, except in cases the public utility of which would be conspicuous; and some such cases would happen.

In the present exigency of American affairs, when by an act of Parliament we are put out of the royal protection and consequently discharged from our allegiance, and it has become necessary to assume government for our immediate security, the governor, lieutenant-governor, secretary, treasurer, commissary, attorney-general should be chosen by joint ballot of both houses. And these and all other elections, especially of representatives and counsellors, should be annual, there not being in the whole circle of the sciences a maxim more infallible than this, "where annual elections end, there slavery begins."

These great men, in this respect, should be once a year—

Like bubbles on the sea of matter borne,
They rise, they break, and to that sea return.

This will teach them the great political virtues of humility, patience, and moderation, without which every man in power becomes a ravenous beast of prey.

This mode of constituting the great offices of state will answer very well for the present; but if by experiment it should be found inconvenient, the legislature may at its leisure devise other methods of creating them; by elections of the people at large, as in Connecticut; or it may enlarge the term for which they shall be chosen to seven years, or three years, or for life; or make any other alterations which the society shall find productive of its ease, its safety, its freedom, or, in one word, its happiness.

A rotation of all offices, as well as of representatives and counsellors, has many advocates and is contended for with many plausible arguments. It would be attended no doubt with many advantages; and if the society has a sufficient number of suitable characters to supply the great number of vacancies which would be made by such a rotation, I can see no objection to it. These persons may be allowed to serve for three years and then be excluded three years, or for any longer or shorter term.

Any seven or nine of the legislative council may be made a quorum for doing business as a privy council, to advise the governor in the exercise of the executive branch of power and in all acts of state.

The governor should have the command of the militia and of all your armies. The power of pardons should be with the governor and council.

Judges, justices, and all other officers, civil and military, should be nominated and appointed by the governor with the advice and consent of council, unless you choose to have a government more popular; if you do, all officers, civil and military, may be chosen by joint ballot of both houses; or, in order to preserve the independence and importance of each house, by ballot of one house concurred in by the other. Sheriffs should be chosen by the freeholders of counties; so should registers of deeds and clerks of counties.

All officers should have commissions under the hand of the governor and seal of the colony.

The dignity and stability of government in all its branches, the morals of the people, and every blessing of society depend so much upon an upright and skillful administration of justice that the judicial power ought to be distinct from both the legislative and executive, and independent upon both, that so it may be a check upon both, as both should be checks upon that. The judges, therefore, should be always men of learning and experience in the laws, of exemplary morals, great patience, calmness, coolness, and attention. Their minds should not be distracted with jarring interests; they should not be dependent upon any man, or body of men. To these ends, they should hold estates for life in their offices; or, in other words, their commissions should be during good behavior and their salaries ascertained and established by law. For misbehavior the grand inquest of the colony, the house of representatives, should impeach them before the governor and council, where they should have time and opportunity to make their defense; but, if convicted, should be removed from their offices and subjected to such other punishment as shall be thought proper.

A militia law requiring all men, or with very few exceptions besides cases of conscience, to be provided with arms and ammunition, to be trained at certain seasons; and requiring counties, towns, or other small districts to be provided with public stocks of ammunition and entrenching utensils and with some settled plans for transporting provisions after the militia, when marched to defend their country against sudden invasions; and requiring certain districts to be provided with fieldpieces, companies of matrosses, and perhaps some regiments of light-horse is always a wise institution, and in the present circumstances of our country indispensable.

Laws for the liberal education of youth, especially of the lower class of people, are so extremely wise and useful that to a humane and generous mind no expense for this purpose would be thought extravagant.

The very mention of sumptuary laws will excite a smile. Whether our countrymen have wisdom and virtue enough to submit to them, I know not; but the happiness of the people might be greatly promoted by them, and a revenue saved sufficient to carry on this war forever. Frugality is a great revenue, besides curing us of vanities, levities, and fopperies, which are real antidotes to all great, manly, and warlike virtues.

But must not all commissions run in the name of a king? No. Why may they not as well run thus, "The colony of _____to A. B. greeting," and be tested by the governor?

Why may not writs, instead of running in the name of the king, run thus, "The colony of_____to the sheriff," etc., and be tested by the chief justice?

Why may not indictments conclude, "against the peace of the colony of_____ and the dignity of the same?"

A constitution founded on these principles introduces knowledge among the people and inspires them with a conscious dignity becoming freemen; a general emulation takes place which causes good humor, sociability, good manners, and good morals to be general. That elevation of sentiment inspired by such a government makes the common people brave and enterprising. That ambition which is inspired by it makes them sober, industrious, and frugal. You will find among them some elegance, perhaps, but more solidity; a little pleasure, but a great deal of business; some politeness, but more civility. If you compare such a country with the regions of domination, whether monarchical or aristocratical, you will fancy yourself in Arcadia or Elysium.

If the colonies should assume governments separately, they should be left entirely to their own choice of the forms; and if a continental constitution should be formed, it should be a congress containing a fair and adequate representation of the colonies, and its authority should sacredly be confined to these cases, namely; war, trade, disputes between colony and colony, the post office, and the unappropriated lands of the crown, as they used to be called.

These colonies, under such forms of government and in such a union, would be unconquerable by all the monarchies of Europe.

You and I, my dear friend, have been sent into life at a time when the greatest lawgivers of antiquity would have wished to live. How few of the human race have ever enjoyed an opportunity of making an election of government—more than of air, soil, or climate—for themselves or their children! When, before the present epocha, had three millions of people full power and a fair opportunity to form and establish the wisest and happiest government that human wisdom can contrive? I hope you will avail yourself and your country of that extensive learning and indefatigable industry which you possess to assist her in the formation of the happiest governments and the best character of a great people. For myself, I must beg you to keep my name out of sight; for this feeble attempt, if it should be known to be mine, would oblige me to apply to myself those lines of the immortal John Milton in one of his sonnets:

I did but prompt the age to quit their clogs
By the known rules of ancient liberty,

When straight a barbarous noise environs me
Of owls and cuckoos, asses, apes, and dogs.
· · ·

From a Defense of the Constitutions of the United States of America Against the Attack of M. Turgot (1787)

It is become a kind of fashion among writers to admit, as a maxim, that if you could be always sure of a wise, active, and virtuous prince, monarchy would be the best of governments. But this is so far from being admissible that it will forever remain true that a free government has a great advantage over a simple monarchy. The best and wisest prince, by means of a freer communication with his people and the greater opportunities to collect the best advice from the best of his subjects, would have an immense advantage in a free state over a monarchy. A senate consisting of all that is most noble, wealthy, and able in the nation, with a right to counsel the crown at all times, is a check to ministers and a security against abuses such as a body of nobles who never meet and have no such right can never supply. Another assembly composed of representatives chosen by the people in all parts gives free access to the whole nation and communicates all its wants, knowledge, projects, and wishes to government; it excites emulation among all classes, removes complaints, redresses grievances, affords opportunities of exertion to genius, though in obscurity, and gives full scope to all the faculties of man; it opens a passage for every speculation to the legislature to administration, and to the public; it gives a universal energy to the human character, in every part of the state, such as never can be obtained in a monarchy.

There is a third particular which deserves attention both from governments and people. In a simple monarchy the ministers of state can never know their friends from their enemies; secret cabals undermine their influence and blast their reputation. This occasions a jealousy, ever anxious and irritated, which never thinks the government safe without an encouragement of informers and spies throughout every part of the state, who interrupt the tranquility of private life, destroy the confidence of families in their own domestics and in one another, and poison freedom in its sweetest retirements. In a free government, on the contrary, the ministers can have no enemies of consequence but among the members of the great or little council, where every man is obliged to take his side and declare his opinions upon every question. This circumstance alone to every manly mind would be sufficient to decide the preference in favor of a free government. Even secrecy, where the executive is entire in one hand, is as easily and surely preserved in a free government as in a simple monarchy; and as to dispatch, all the simple monarchies of the whole universe may be defined to produce greater or more numerous examples of it than are to be found in English history. An Alexander or a Frederic, possessed of the prerogatives only of a king of England and leading his own armies, would never find himself embarrassed or delayed in any honest enterprise. He might be restrained, indeed, from running mad and from making conquests to the ruin of his nation merely for his own glory; but this is no argument against a free government.

There can be no free government without a democratical branch in the constitution. Monarchies and aristocracies are in possession of the voice and influence of every university and academy in Europe. Democracy, simple democracy, never had a patron among men of letters. Democratical mixtures in government have lost almost all the advocates they ever had out of England and America. Men of letters must have a great deal of praise and some of the necessaries, conveniences, and ornaments of life. Monarchies and aristocracies pay well and applaud liberally. The people have almost always expected to be served gratis and be paid for the honor of serving them; and their applauses and adorations are bestowed too often on artifices and tricks, on hypocrisy and superstition, on flattery, bribes, and largesses. It is no wonder then that democracies and democratical mixtures are annihilated all over Europe except on a barren rock, a paltry fen, an inaccessible mountain, or an impenetrable forest. The people of England, to their immortal honor, are hitherto an exception; but, to the humiliation of human nature, they show very often that they are like other men. The people in America have now the best opportunity and the greatest trust in their hands that Providence ever committed to so small a number since the transgression of the first pair, if they betray their trust, their guilt will merit even greater punishment than other nations have suffered and the indignation of Heaven. If there is one certain truth to be collected from the history of all ages, it is this: that the people's rights and liberties and the democratical mixture in a constitution can never be preserved without a strong executive, or, in other words, without separating the executive from the legislative power. If the executive power or any considerable part of it is left in the hands either of an aristocratical or a democratical assembly, it will corrupt the legislature as necessarily as rust corrupts iron or as arsenic poisons the human body; and when the legislature is corrupted, the people are undone.

The rich, the well-born, and the able require an influence among the people that will soon be too much for simple honesty and plain sense in a house of representatives. The most illustrious of them must, therefore, be separated from the mass and placed by themselves in a senate; this is, to all honest and useful intents, an ostracism. A member of a senate of immense wealth, the most respected birth, and transcendent abilities has no influence in the nation in comparison of what he would have in a single representative assembly. When a senate exists, the most powerful man in the state may be safely admitted into the house of representatives because the people have it in their power to remove him into the senate as soon as his influence becomes dangerous. The senate becomes the great object of ambition and the richest and the most sagacious wish to merit an advancement to it by services to the public in the house. When he has obtained the object of his wishes, you may still hope for the benefits of his exertions without dreading his passions; for the executive power being in other hands, he has lost much of his influence with the people and can govern very few votes more than his own among the senators. . . .

The United States of America have exhibited, perhaps, the first example of governments erected on the simple principles of nature; and if men are not sufficiently enlightened to disabuse themselves of artifice, imposture, hypocrisy, and superstition, they will consider this event as an era in their history. Although the detail of the formation of the American governments is at present little known or regarded either in Europe or in America, it may hereafter become an object of curiosity. It will never be pretended that any persons employed in that service had interviews with the gods or were in any degree under the inspiration of Heaven, more than those at work upon ships or houses, of laboring in merchandise or agriculture; it will forever be acknowledged that these governments were contrived merely by the use of reason and the senses. . . . Neither the people nor their conventions, committees, or subcommittees considered legislation in any other light than an ordinary arts and sciences, only more important. Called without

expectation, and compelled without previous inclination, though undoubtedly at the best period of time, both for England and America, suddenly to erect new systems of laws for their future government, they adopted the method of a wise architect in erecting a new palace for the residence of his sovereign. They determined to consult Vitruvius, Palladio, and all other writers of reputation in the art; to examine the most celebrated buildings, whether they remain entire or in ruins; to compare these with the principles of writers, and to inquire how far both the theories and models were founded in nature or created by fancy; and when this was done, so far as their circumstances would allow, to adopt the advantages and reject the inconveniences of all. Unembarrassed by attachments to noble families, hereditary lines and successions, or any considerations of royal blood, even the pious mystery of holy oil had no more influence than that other one of holy water. The people were universally too enlightened to be imposed on by artiface; and their leaders, or more properly followers, were men of too much honor to attempt it. Thirteen governments thus founded on the natural authority of the people alone, without a pretense of miracle or mystery, and which are destined to spread over the northern part of that whole quarter of the globe, are a great point gained in favor of the rights of mankind. The experiment is made and has completely succeeded; it can no longer be called in question whether authority in magistrates and obedience of citizens can be grounded on reason, morality, and the Christian religion, without the monkery of priests or the knavery of politicians. As the writer was personally acquainted with most of the gentlemen in each of the states who had the principal share in the first draughts, the following work was really written to lay before the public a specimen of that kind of reading and reasoning which produced the American constitutions. . . .

M. Turgot is offended because the customs of England are imitated in most of the new constitutions in America without any particular motive. But if we suppose English customs to be neither good nor evil in themselves and merely indifferent; and the people by their birth, education, and habits were familiarly attached to them—would not this be a motive particular enough for their preservation rather than to endanger the public tranquility or unanimity by renouncing them? If those customs were wise, just, and good, and calculated to secure the liberty, property, and safety of the people as well or better than any other institutions, ancient or modern, would M. Turgot have advised the nation to reject them merely because it was at that time justly incensed against the English government? What English customs has it retained which may with any propriety be called evil? M. Turgot has instanced only one, namely, "that a body of representatives, a council, and a governor have been established because there is in England a house of commons, a house of lords, and a king." It was not so much because the legislature in England consisted of three branches, that such a division of power was adopted by the states, as because their own assemblies had ever been so constituted. It was not so much from attachment by habit to such a plan of power that it was continued as from conviction that it was founded in nature and reason.

M. Turgot seems to be of a different opinion and is for "collecting all authority into one center, the nation." It is easily understood how all authority may be collected into "one center" in a despot or monarch; but how it can be done when the center is to be the nation is more difficult to comprehend. Before we attempt to discuss the notions of an author, we should be careful to ascertain his meaning. It will not be easy, after the most anxious research, to discover the true sense of this extraordinary passage. If after the pains of "collecting all authority into one center," that cen-

ter is to be the nation, we shall remain exactly where we began and no collection of authority at all will be made. The nation will be the authority, and the authority the nation. The center will be the circle, and the circle the center. When a number of men, women, and children are simply congregated together there is no political authority among them; nor any natural authority but that of the parents over their children. To leave the women and children out of the question for the present, the men will all be equal, free, and independent of each other. Not one will have any authority over any other. The first "collection" of authority must be an unanimous agreement to form themselves into a *nation, people, community,* or *body politic* and to be governed by the majority of suffrages or voices. But even in this case, although the authority is collected into one center, that center is no longer the nation but the majority of the nation. Did M. Turgot mean that the people of Virginia, for example, half a million of souls scattered over a territory of two hundred leagues square, should stop here and have no other authority by which to make or execute a law or judge a cause but by a vote of the whole people and the decision of a majority! Where is the plain large enough to hold them; and what are the means, and how long would be the time, necessary to assembly them together?

A simple and perfect democracy never yet existed among men. If a village of half a mile square and one hundred families is capable of exercising all the legislative, executive, and judicial powers in public assemblies of the whole by unanimous votes or by majorities, it is more than has ever yet been proved in theory or experience. In such a democracy, for the most part, the moderator would be king, the town-clerk legislator and judge, and the constable sheriff; and upon more important occasions, committees would be only the counsellors of both the former and commanders of the latter.

Shall we suppose, then, that M. Turgot intended that an assembly of representatives should be chosen by the nation and vested with all the powers of government; and that this assembly should be the center in which all the authority was to be collected and should be virtually deemed the nation? After long reflection I have not been able to discover any other sense in his words, and this was probably his real meaning. . . .

As we have taken a cursory view of these countries in Europe where the government may be called, in any reasonable construction of the word, republican, let us now pause a few moments and reflect upon what we have seen. . . .

In every republic—in the smallest and most popular, in the larger and more aristocratical, as well as in the largest and most monarchical—we have observed a multitude of curious and ingenious inventions to balance, in their turn, all those powers, to check the passions peculiar to them, and to control them from rushing into those exorbitancies to which they are most addicted. The Americans will then be no longer censured for endeavoring to introduce an equilibrium which is much more profoundly mediated and much more effectual for the protection of the laws than any we have seen, except in England. We may even question whether that is an exception.

In every country we have found a variety of *orders* with very great distinctions. In America there are different orders of *offices,* but none of *men.* Out of office, all men are of the same species and of one blood; there is neither a greater nor a lesser nobility. Why, then, are the Americans accused of establishing different orders of men? To our inexpressible mortification we must have observed that the people have preserved a share of power of an existense in the government in no country out of England except upon the tops of a few inaccessible mountains, among rocks and precipices, in territories so narrow that you may span them with a hand's breadth, where, living unenvied, in extreme poverty, chiefly among pasturage, destitute of manufactures and commerce, they still exhibit the most charming picture of life and the most dignified character of human nature.

Wherever we have seen a territory somewhat larger, arts and sciences more cultivated, commerce flourishing, or even agriculture improved to any great degree, an aristocracy has risen up in the course of time, consisting of a few rich and honorable families who have united with each other against both the people and the first magistrate, who have wrested from the former by art and by force all their participation in the government and have even inspired them with so mean an esteem of themselves and so deep a veneration and strong attachment to their rulers as to believe and confess them a superior order of beings.

We have seen these noble families, although necessitated to have a head, extremely jealous of his influence, anxious to reduce his power, and to constrain him to as near a level as possible with themselves, always endeavoring to establish a rotation by which they may all equally be entitled in turn to the preeminence, and likewise anxious to preserve to themselves as large a share as possible of power in the executive and judicial, as well as the legislative departments of the state.

These patrician families have also appeared in every instance to be equally jealous of each other and to have contrived by blending lot and choice, by mixing various bodies in the elections to the same offices, and even by a resort to the horrors of an inquisition, to guard against the sin that so easily besets them, of being wholly influenced and governed by a junto or oligarchy of a few among themselves.

We have seen no one government in which is a distinct separation of the legislative from the executive power and of the judicial from both, or in which any attempt has been made to balance these powers with one another, or to form an equilibrium between the one, the few, and the many, for the purpose of enacting and executing equal laws by common consent for the general interest, excepting in England.

Shall we conclude from these melancholy observations that human nature is incapable of liberty, that no honest equality can be preserved in society, and that such forcible causes are always at work as must reduce all men to a submission to despotism, monarchy, oligarchy, or aristocracy?

By no means. We have seen one of the first nations in Europe, possessed of ample and fertile territories at home and extensive dominions abroad, of a commerce with the whole world, immense wealth, and the greatest naval power which ever belonged to any nation, which has still preserved the power of the people by the equilibrium we are contending for, by the trial by jury, and by constantly refusing a standing army. The people of England alone, by preserving their share in the legislature at the expense of the blood of heroes and patriots, have enabled their king to curb the nobility without giving him a standing army.

After all, let us compare every constitution we have seen with those of the United States of America, and we shall have no reason to blush for our country. On the contrary, we shall feel the strongest motives to fall upon our knees in gratitude to heaven for having been graciously pleased to give us birth and education in that country and for having destined us to live under her laws! We shall have reason to exult if we make our comparison with England and the English constitution. Our people are undoubtedly sovereign; all the landed and other property is in the hands of the citizens; not only their representatives but their senators and governors are annually chosen; there are no hereditary titles, honors, offices, or distinctions; the legislative, executive, and judicial powers are carefully separated from each other;

the powers of the one, the few, and the many are nicely balanced in the legislatures; trials by jury are preserved in all their glory, and there is no standing army; the *habeas corpus* is in full force; the press is the most free in the world. Where all these circumstances take place, it is unnecessary to add that the laws alone can govern. . . .

We cannot presume that a man is good or bad merely because his father was one or the other; and we should always inform ourselves first whether the virtues and talents are inherited before we yield our confidence. Wise men beget fools, and honest men knaves; but these instances, although they may be frequent, are not general. If there is often a likeness in feature and figure, there is generally more in mind and heart because education contributes to the formation of these as well as nature. The influence of example is very great and almost universal, especially that of parents over their children. In all countries it has been observed that vices as well as virtues very often run down in families from age to age. Any man may go over in his thoughts the circle of his acquaintance, and he will probably recollect instances of a disposition to mischief, malice, and revenge, descending in certain breeds from grandfather to father and son. A young woman was lately convicted at Paris of a trifling theft, barely within the law which decreed a capital punishment. There were circumstances, too, which greatly alleviated her fault, some things in her behavior that seemed innocent and modest; every spectator, as well as the judges, was affected at the scene, and she was advised to petition for a pardon, as there was no doubt it would be granted. "No," says she, "my grandfather, father, and brother were all hanged for stealing; it runs in the blood of our family to steal and be hanged. If I am pardoned now, I shall steal again in a few months more inexcusably; and, therefore, I will be hanged now." An hereditary passion for the halter is a strong instance, to be sure, and cannot be very common; but something like it too often descends in certain breeds from generation to generation.

If vice and infamy are thus rendered less odious by being familiar in a family, by the example of parents and by education, it would be as unhappy as unaccountable if virtue and honor were not recommended and rendered more amiable to children by the same means.

There are, and always have been, in every state, numbers possessed of some degree of family pride, who have been invariably encouraged, if not flattered in it, by the people. These have most acquaintance, esteem, and friendship with each other and mutually aid each other's schemes of interest, convenience, and ambition. Fortune, it is true, has more influence than birth. A rich man of an ordinary family and common decorum of conduct may have greater weight than any family merit commonly confers without it.

It will be readily admitted there are great inequalities of merit, or talents, virtues, services, and what is of more moment, very often of reputation. Some in a long course of service in an army have devoted their time, health, and fortunes, signalized their courage and address, exposed themselves to hardships and dangers, lost their limbs, and shed their blood for the people. Others have displayed their wisdom, learning, and eloquence in council and in various other ways acquired the confidence and affection of their fellow citizens to such a degree that the public have settled into a king of habit of following their example and taking their advice.

There are a few in whom all these advantages of birth, fortune, and fame are united.

These sources of inequality, which are common to every people and can never be altered by any because they are founded in the constitution of nature—the natural aristocracy among mankind has been dilated upon because it is a fact essential to be considered in the institution of a government. It forms a body of men which contains the greatest collection of virtues and abilities in a free government, is the brightest ornament and glory of the nation, and may always be made the greatest blessing of society if it be judiciously managed in the constitution. But if this be not done, it is always the most dangerous; nay, it may be added, it never fails to be the destruction of the commonwealth. . . .

There is but one expedient yet discovered to avail the society of all the benefits from this body of men which they are capable of affording, and at the same time to prevent them from undermining or invading the public liberty; and that is to throw them all, or at least the most remarkable of them, into one assembly together, in the legislature, to keep all the executive power entirely out of their hands as a body; to erect a first magistrate over them, invested with the whole executive authority; to make them dependent on that executive magistrate for all public executive employments; to give that first magistrate a negative on the legislature, by which he may defend both himself and the people from all their enterprises in the legislature; and to erect on the other side an impregnable barrier against them in a house of commons, fairly, fully, and adequately representing the people, who shall have the power both of negativing all their attempts at encroachment in the legislature and of withholding from them and from the crown all supplies by which they may be paid for their services in executive offices, or even the public service may be carried on to the detriment of the nation. . . .

Our first attention should be turned to the proposition itself—"The people are the best keepers of their own liberties."

But who are the people?

"Such as shall be successively chosen to represent them."

Here is a confusion both of words and ideas, which, though it may pass with the generality of readers in a fugative pamphlet or with a majority of auditors in a popular harangue, ought, for that very reason, to be as carefully avoided in politics as it is in philosophy or mathematics. If by "the people" is meant the whole body of a great nation, it should never be forgotten that they can never act, consult, or reason together because they cannot march five hundred miles, nor spare the time, nor find a space to meet; and, therefore, the proposition that they are the best keepers of their own liberties is not true. They are the worst conceivable; they are no keepers at all. They can neither act, judge, think, or will, as a body politic or corporation. If by "the people" is meant all the inhabitants of a single city, they are not in a general assembly at all times the best keepers of their own liberties, nor perhaps at any time, unless you separate from them the executive and judicial power and temper their authority in legislation with the maturer counsels of the one and the few, If it is meant by "the people," as our author explains himself, a representative assembly, "such as shall be successively chosen to represent the people," still they are not the best keepers of the people's liberties or their own if you give them all the power—legislative, executive, and judicial. They would invade the liberties or their own if you give them all the power—legislative, executive, and judicial. They would invade the liberties of the people, at least the majority of them would invade the liberties of the minority, sooner and oftener than an absolute monarchy such as that of France, Spain, or Russia, or than a well-checked aristocracy like Venice, Bern, or Holland.

An excellent writer has said, somewhat incautiously, that "a people will never oppress themselves or invade their own rights." This compliment, if applied to human nature, or to mankind, or to any nation or people in being or in memory, is more than has been merited. If it should be admitted that a people will not unanimously agree to oppress themselves, it is as much as is ever, and more than is always, true. All kinds of experience show that great numbers of individuals do oppress great numbers of other individuals, that parties often, if not always, oppress other parties; and majorities almost universally minorities. All that this observation can mean then, consistently with any color of fact, is that the people will never unanimously agree to oppress themselves. But if one party agrees to oppress another, or the majority the minority, the people still oppress themselves, for one part of them oppress another.

"The people never think of usurping over other men's rights."

What can this mean? Does it mean that the people never *unanimously* think of usurping over other men's rights? This would be trifling; for there would by the supposition be no other men's rights to usurp. But if the people never, jointly nor severally, think of usurping the rights of others, what occasion can there be for any government at all? Are there no robberies, burglaries, murders, adultries, thefts, nor cheats? Is not every crime a usurpation over other men's rights? Is not a great part, I will not say the greatest part of men detected every day in some disposition or other, stronger or weaker, more or less, to usurp over other men's rights. There are some few, indeed whose whole lives and conversations show that, in every thought, word, and action, they conscientiously respect the rights of others. There is a larger body still, who in the general tenor of their thoughts and actions discover similar principles and feelings yet frequently err. If we should extend our candor so far as to own that the majority of men are generally under the dominion of benevolence and to their families, relations, personal friends, parish, village, city, county, province, and that very few indeed extend it impartially to the whole community. Now grant but this truth and the question is decided. If a majority are capable of preferring their own private interest or that of their families, counties, and party to that of the nation collectively, some provision must be made in the constitution in favor of justice to compel all to respect the common right, the public good, the universal law, in preference to all private and partial considerations.

The proposition of our author, then, should be reversed, and it should have been said that they mind so much their own that they never think of others. Suppose a nation, rich and poor, high and low, ten millions in number, all assembled together; not more than one or two millions will have lands, houses, or any personal property; if we take into the account the women and children, or even if we leave them out of the question, a great majority of every nation is wholly destitute of property except a small quantity of clothes and a few trifles of other movables. Would Mr. Nedham be responsible that, if all were to be decided by a vote of the majority, the eight or nine millions who have no property would not think of usurping over the rights of the one or two millions who have? Property is surely a right of mankind as really as liberty. Perhaps, at first prejudice, habit, shame or fear, principle or religion would restrain the poor from attacking the rich, and the idle from usurping on the industrious; but the time would not be long before courage and enterprise would come and pretexts be invented by degrees to countenance the majority in dividing all the property among them, or at least in sharing it equally with its present possessors. Debts would be abolished first; taxes laid heavy on the rich, and not at all on the others; and at last a downright equal division of everything be demanded, and voted. What would be the consequence of this? The idle, the vicious, the intemperate would rush into the utmost extravagance of debauchery, sell and spend all their share, and then demand a new division of those who purchased from them. The moment the idea is admitted into society that property is not as sacred as the laws of God, and that there is not a force of law and public justice to protect it, anarchy and tyranny commence. If "Thou shalt not covet" and "Thou shalt not steal" were not commandments of Heaven, they must be made inviolable precepts in every society before it can be civilized or made free.

If the first part of the proposition, namely, that "the people never think of usurping over other men's rights," cannot be admitted, is the second, namely, "they mind which way to preserve their own," better founded?

There is in every nation and people under heaven a large proportion of persons who take no rational and prudent precautions to preserve what they have, much less to acquire more. Indolence is the natural character of man to such a degree that nothing but the necessities of hunger, thirst, and other wants equally pressing can stimulate him to action, until education is introduced in civilized societies and the strongest motives of ambition to excel in arts, trades, and professions are established in the minds of all men. Until this emulation is introduced, the lazy savage holds property in too little estimation to give himself trouble for the preservation or acquisition of it. In societies the most cultivated and polished, vanity, fashion, and folly prevail over every thought of ways to preserve their own. They seem rather to study what means of luxury, dissipation, and extravagance they can invent to get rid of it. . . .

Though we allow benevolence and generous affections to exist in the human breast, yet every moral theorist will admit the selfish passions in the generality of men to be the strongest. There are few who love the public better than themselves, though all may have some affection for the public. We are not, indeed, commanded to love our neighbor better than ourselves. Self interest, private avidity, ambition, and avarice will exist in every state of society and under every form of government. A succession of powers and persons by frequent elections will not lessen these passions in any case, in a governor, senator, or representative, nor will the apprehension of any approaching election restrain them from indulgence if they have the power. The only remedy is to take away the power by controlling the selfish avidity of the governor by the senate and house, of the senate by the governor and house, and of the house by the governor and senate. Of all possible forms of government, a soveriegnty in one assembly, successively chosen by the people, is perhaps the best calculated to facilitate the gratification of self love, and the pursuit of the private interest of a few individuals, a few eminent conspicuous characters will be continued in their seats in the sovereign assembly from one election to another, whatever changes are made in the seats around them, by superior art, address, and opulence, by more splendid birth, reputations, and connections they will be able to intrigue with the people and their leaders, out of doors, until they worm out most of their opposers and introduce their friends; to this end, they will bestow all offices, contracts, privileges in commerce, and other emoluments on the latter and their connections, and throw every vexation and disappointment in the way of the former, until they establish such a system of hopes and fears throughout the state as shall enable them to carry a majority in every fresh election of the house. The judges will be appointed by them and their party and, of consequence, will be obsequious enough to their inclinations. The whole judicial authority, as well as the executive, will be employed, perverted and prostituted to the purposes of electioneering. No justice will be attainable, nor will innocence or virtue be safe, in the judicial courts but for the friends of the prevailing leaders; legal prosecutions will be instituted and carried on against opposers, to their vexation and ruin; and as they have the public purse at command, as well as the executive and judicial power, the public money will be expanded in the same way. No favors will be attainable but by those who will court the ruling demagogues in the house by voting for their friends and instruments; and pen-

sions and pecuniary rewards and gratifications, as well as honors and offices of every kind, will be voted to friends and partisans. The leading minds and most influential characters among the clergy will be courted, and the views of the youth in this department will be turned upon those men, and the road to promotion and employment in the church will be obstructed against such as will not worship the general idol. Capital characters among the physicians will not be forgotten, and the means of acquiring reputation and practice in the healing art will be to get the state trumpeters on the side of youth. The bar, too, will be made so subservient that a young gentleman will have no chance to obtain a character or clients but by falling in with the views of the judges and their creators. Even the theatres, and actors and actresses, must become politicians and convert the public pleasures into engines of popularity for the governing members of the house. The press, that great barrier and bulwark of the rights of mankind, when it is protected in its freedom by law, can now no longer be free; if the authors, writers, and printers will not accept of the hire that will be offered them, they must submit to the ruin that will be denounced against them. The presses, with much secrecy and concealment, will be made the vehicles of calumny against the minority, and of panegyric and empirical applauses of the leaders of the majority, and no remedy can possibly be obtained. In one word, the whole system of affairs and every conceivable motive of hope and fear will be employed to promote the private interests of a few and their obsequious majority; and there is no remedy but in arms. . . .

It is agreed that the people are the best keepers of their own liberties and the only keepers who can be always trusted; and therefore, the people's fair, full, and honest consent to every law, by their representatives, must be made an essential part of the constitution; but it is denied that they are the best keepers, or any keepers at all, of their own liberties when they hold, collectively or by representation, the executive and judicial power, or the whole and uncontrolled legislative; on the contrary, the experience of all ages has proved that they instantly give away their liberties into the hand of grandees or kings, idols of their own creation. The management of the executive and judicial powers together always corrupts them and throws the whole power into the hands of the most profligate and abandoned among themselves. The honest men are generally nearly equally divided in sentiment, and therefore, the vicious and unprincipled, by joining one party, carry the majority; and the vicious and unprincipled always follow the most profligate leader, him who bribes the highest and sets all decency and shame at defiance. It becomes more profitable, and reputable too, except with a very few, to be a party man than a public spirited one.

It is agreed that "the end of all government is the good and ease of the people in a secure enjoyment of their rights without oppression"; but it must be remembered that the rich are *people* as well as the poor; that they have rights as well as others; that they have as clear and as *sacred* right to their large property as others have to theirs which is smaller; that oppression to them is as possible and as wicked as to others; that stealing, robbing, cheating are the same crimes and sins, whether committed against them or others. The rich, therefore, ought to have an effectual barrier in the constitution against being robbed, plundered, and murdered, as well as the poor; and this can never be without an independent senate. The poor should have a bulwark against the same dangers and oppressions; and this can never be without a house of representatives of the people. But neither the rich nor the poor can be defended by their respective guardians in the constitution without an executive power, vested with a negative equal to either,

to hold the balance even between them and decide when they cannot agree. If it is asked, When will this negative be used? it may be answered, Perhaps never. The known existence of it will prevent all occasion to exercise it; but if it has not a being, the want of it will be felt every day. If it has not been used in England for a long time past, it by no means follows that there have not been occasions when it might have been employed with propriety. But one thing is very certain, that there have been many occasions since the Revolution when the constitution would have been overturned if the negative had not been an indubitable prerogative of the crown.

It is agreed that the people are "most sensible of their own burdens, and being once put into a capacity and freedom of acting are the most likely to provide remedies for their own relief." For this reason they are an essential branch of the legislature and have a negative on all laws, an absolute control over every grant of money, and an unlimited right to accuse their enemies before an impartial tribunal. Thus far they are most sensible of their burdens and are most likely to provide remedies. But it is affirmed that they are not only incapable of managing the executive power but would be instantly corrupted by it in such numbers as would destroy the integrity of all elections. It is denied that the legislative power can be wholly entrusted in their hands with a moment's safety. The poor and the vicious would instantly rob the rich and virtuous, spend their plunder in debauchery or confer it upon some idol, who would become the despot; or, to speak more intelligibly if not more accurately, some of the rich, by debauching the vicious to their corrupt interest, would plunder the virtuous and become more rich until they acquired all the property, or a balance of property and of power, in their own hands and domineered as despots in an oligarchy.

WORKS BY JOHN ADAMS

Adams, John. *A Defense of the Constitutions of the United States of America Against the Attack of M. Turgot in his Letter to Dr. Price.* 3 Vols. Philadelphia: Buddard Bartran, 1797. A three-volume work arguing for balanced and limited government as expressed in a three-branch system thereby maximizing democracy but minimizing corruption.

Correspondence of the Late President Adams. Boston: Everett and Munroe, 1809. Originally published in the *Boston Patriot,* the selections were composed to popularize some of Adams' thoughts on American development.

The Political Writings of John Adams: Representative Selections. Edited by George A. Peck, Jr. New York: The Liberal Arts Press, 1954. A collection of Adams' works with introductory notes by the editor.

MAJOR SOURCES ON JOHN ADAMS

Bowen, Catherine Drinker. *John Adams and the American Revolution.* Boston: Little, Brown, and Co., 1951. Complete with geneological tree, this biography portrays Adams first and foremost as a "political animal" and emphasizes his deep faith, creativity, and leadership qualities.

Chinard, Gilbert. *Honest John Adams.* Boston: Little, Brown, and Co., 1933. One of the best biographies of Adams; shows his inability to relate to the emerging country due to his pessimism and unwillingness to break with the European past.

Dauer, Manning J. *The Adams Federalists.* Baltimore: John Hopkins Press, 1953. An historical evaluation of Adams' ideas, the environment which shaped them, and the effect of their application on that environment.

Dauer, Manning J. "The Political Economy of John Adams," *Political Science Quarterly,* LVI (1941), pp. 545–572.

Handler, Edward. *America and Europe in the Political Thought of John Adams.* Cambridge, Mass.: Harvard University Press, 1964. An analysis of the European influence showing Adams' inability to reconciliate the differences between America and Europe.

Haraszti, Zoltan. *John Adams and the Prophets of Progress.* Cambridge, Mass.: Harvard University Press, 1952. A presentation of John Adams' political and social views heavily interspersed with notes and writings by the subject emphasizing the deep influence of European Liberalism on his thought.

Morse, Anson D. "The Politics of John Adams," *American Historical Review,* Vol. IV (1899), pp. 292–312. An essay showing religion as the basis of Adams' ideology with independence being not an end, but only a means for obtaining the "best character", the final essence of the subject's labor.

CHAPTER 6

Alexander Hamilton

ALEXANDER Hamilton (1757–1804) was born on the island of Nevis in the British West Indies. Contradictory stories exist over his birthdate and parentage, but the accepted version is that his father was a Scottish merchant and his mother a French woman. Hamilton's education was brief and desultory. At the age of twelve, Hamilton was placed in the office of a West Indian merchant; when he left this position, he was sent to New York to study with funds provided by relatives.

Once in New York, Hamilton soon became involved in the revolutionary activities of the day. Two pamphlets which he wrote, "A Full Vindication of the Measures of the Congress" and "The Farmer Refuted," attracted immediate attention. Early in 1776, Hamilton was given command of a company of artillery which he skillfully organized and disciplined. The company distinguished itself so much that Hamilton was invited to serve on Washington's staff. Hamilton accepted the offer and became indispensable to Washington.

At the Philadelphia Convention of 1787, Hamilton played a very small part; it was after the convention that Hamilton's work for the Constitution began. He conceived and started "The Federalist," of which he wrote at least fifty-one articles and three more in conjunction with Madison.

Washington appointed Hamilton the first Secretary of the Treasury in 1789. Hamilton, envisioning a strong federal government, outlined a financial program designed to make the federal government stronger than the states. Although Congress passed many of Hamilton's proposals, one of the results of the struggle over Hamilton's economic policies was the emergence of national political parties.

Tried by criticism, Hamilton left the cabinet in 1795. He did not sever his connection with the government, but continued as an unofficial advisor to Washington's cabinet. In 1796, Hamilton tried to throw the election to Thomas Pinckney instead of Adams.

Hamilton succeeded only in splitting his party. In 1800, Hamilton further alienated himself from his own party and virtually ended his public career when he supported his old Republican enemy, Jefferson.

Hamilton then turned his attention to his law practice and family. In 1804, Hamilton supposedly made uncomplimentary remarks about Aaron Burr; Burr challenged Hamilton to a duel, which Hamilton felt compelled to accept. Accordingly, the two antagonists met early on the morning of July 11, and Hamilton fell mortally wounded.

From Report Relative to a Provision for the Support of Public Credit (1790)

The Secretary of the Treasury, in obedience to the resolution of the House of Representatives, on the twenty-first day of September last, has, during the recess of Congress, applied himself to the consideration of a proper plan for the support of the public Credit, with all the attention which was due to the authority of the House, and to the magnitude of the object.

In the discharge of this duty, he has felt, in no small degree, the anxieties which naturally flow from a just estimate of the difficulty of the task, from a well-founded diffidence of his own qualifications for executing it with success, and from a deep and solemn cónviction of the momentous nature of the truth contained in the resolution under which his investigations have been conducted, "That an *adequate* provision for the support of the Public Credit, is a matter of high importance to the honor and prosperity of the United States."

With an ardent desire that his well-meant endeavors may be conducive to the real advantage of the nation, and with the utmost deference to the superior judgment of the House, he now respectfully submits the result of his enquiries and reflections, to their indulgent construction.

In the opinion of the Secretary, the wisdom of the House, in giving their explicit sanction to the proposition which has been stated, cannot but be applauded by all, who will seriously consider, and trace through their obvious consequences, these plain and undeniable truths.

That exigencies are to be expected to occur, in the affairs of nations, in which there will be a necessity for borrowing.

That loans in times of public danger, especially from foreign war, are found an indispensable resource, even to the wealthiest of them.

And that in a country, which, like this, is possessed of little active wealth, or in other words, little monied capital, the necessity for that resource, must, in such emergencies, be proportionably urgent.

And as on the one hand, the necessity for borrowing in particular emergencies cannot be doubted, so on the other, it is equally evident, that to be able to borrow upon *good terms,* it is essential that the credit of a nation should be well established.

For when the credit of a country is in any degree questionable, it never fails to give an extravagant premium in one shape or another, upon all the loans it has occasion to make. Nor does the evil end here; the same disadvantage must be sustained upon whatever is to be bought on terms of future payment.

From this constant necessity of *borrowing* and *buying dear,* it is easy to conceive how immensely the expences of a nation, in a course of time, will be augmented by an unsound state of the public credit.

To attempt to enumerate the complicated variety of mischiefs in the whole system of the social aeconomy, which proceed from a neglect of the maxims that uphold public credit, and justify the solicitude manifested by the House on this point, would be an improper intrusion on their time and patience.

In so strong a light nevertheless do they appear to the Secretary, that on their due observance at the present critical juncture, materially depends, in his judgment, the individual and aggregate prosperity of the citizens of the United States; their relief from the embarrassments they now experience; their character as a People; the cause of good government.

If the maintenance of public credit, then, be truly so important, the next enquiry which suggests itself is, by what means it is to be effected? The ready answer to which question is, by good faith, by punctual performance of contracts. States, like individuals, who observe their engagements, are respected and trusted: while the reverse is the fate of those, who pursue an opposite conduct. . . .

While the observance of that good faith, which is the basis of public credit, is recommended by the strongest inducements of political expediency, it is enforced by considerations of still greater authority. There are arguments for it, which rest on the immutable principles of moral obligation. And in proportion as the mind is disposed to comtemplate, in the order of Providence, as intimate connection between public virtue and public happiness, will be its repugnancy to a violation of those principles.

This reflection derives additional strength from the nature of the debt of the United States. It was the price of liberty. The faith of America has been repeatedly pledged for it, and with solemnities, that give peculiar force to the obligation. There is indeed reason to regret that it has not hitherto been kept; that the necessities of the war, conspiring with inexperience in the subjects of finance, produced direct infractions; and that the subsequent period has been a continued scene of negative violation, or non-compliance. But a diminution of this regret arises from the reflection, that the last seven years have exhibited an earnest and uniform effort, on the part of the government of the union, to retrieve the national credit, by doing justice to the creditors of the nation; and that the embarrassments of a defective constitution, which defeated this laudable effort, have ceased.

From this evidence of a favorable disposition, given by the former government, the institution of a new one, cloathed with powers competent to calling forth the resources of the community, has excited correspondent expectations. A general belief, accordingly, prevails, that the credit of the United States will quickly be established on the firm foundation of an effectual provision for the existing debt. The influence, which this has had at home, is witnessed by the rapid increase, that has taken place in the market value of the public securities. From January to November, they rose thirty-three and a third per cent, and from that period to this time, they have risen fifty per cent more. And the intelligence from abroad announces effects proportionably favourable to our national credit and consequence.

It cannot but merit particular attention, that among ourselves the most enlightened friends of good government are those, whose expectations are the highest.

To justify and preserve their confidence; to promote the increasing respectability of the American name; to answer the calls of justice; to restore landed property to its due value; to furnish new resources both to agriculture and commerce; to cement more closely the union of the states; to add to their security against foreign attack; to establish public order on the basis of an upright and liberal policy. These are the great and invaluable ends to be secured, by a proper and adequate provision, at the present period, for the support of public credit. . . .

Having now taken a concise view of the inducements to a proper provision for the public debt, the next enquiry which presents itself is, what ought to be the nature of such a provision? This requires some preliminary discussions.

It is agreed on all hands, that that part of the debt which has been contracted abroad, and is denominated the foreign debt, ought to be provided for, according to the precise terms of the contracts relating to it. The discussions, which can arise, therefore, will have reference essentially to the domestic part of it, or to that which has been contracted at home. It is to be regretted, that there is not the same unanimity of sentiment on this part as on the other.

The Secretary has too much deference for the opinions of every part of the community, not to have observed one, which has, more than once, made its appearance in the public prints, and which is occasionally to be met with in conversation. It involves this question, whether a discrimination ought not be made between original holders of the public securities, and present possessors, by purchase. Those who advocate a discrimination are for making a full provision for the securities of the former, at their nominal value; but contend, that the latter ought to receive no more than the cost to them, and the interest: And the idea is sometimes suggested of making good the difference to the primitive possessor.

In favor of this scheme, it is alledged, that it would be unreasonable to pay twenty shillings in the pound, to one who had not given more for it than three or four. And it is added, that it would be hard to aggravate the misfortune of the first owner, who, probably through necessity, parted with his property at so great a loss, by obliging him to contribute to the profit of the person, who had speculated on his distresses.

The Secretary, after the most mature reflection on the force of this argument, is induced to reject the doctrine it contains, as equally unjust and impolitic, as highly injurious, even to the original holders of public securities; as ruinous to public credit.

It is inconsistent with justice, because in the first place, it is a breach of contract; in violation of the rights of a fair purchaser.

The nature of the contract in its origin, is, that the public will pay the sum expressed in the security, to the first holder, or his *assignee*. The *intent*, in making the security assignable, is, that the proprietor may be able to make use of his property, by selling it for as much as it *may be worth in the market*, and that the buyer may be *safe* in the purchase.

Every buyer therefore stands exactly in the place of the seller, has the same rights with him to the identical sum expressed in the security, and having acquired that right, by fair purchase, and in conformity to the original *agreement* and *intention* of the government, his claim cannot be disputed, without manifest injustice.

That he is to be considered as a fair purchaser, results from this: Whatever necessity the seller may have been under, was occasioned by the government, in not making a proper provision for its debts. The buyer had no agency in it, and therefore ought not to suffer. He is not even chargeable with having taken an undue advantage. He paid what the commodity was worth in the market, and took the risks of reimbursement upon himself. He, of course, gave a fair equivalent, and ought to reap the benefit of his hazard; a hazard which was far from inconsiderable, and which, perhaps, turned on little less than a revolution in government.

That the case of those, who parted with their securities from necessity, is a hard one, cannot be denied. But whatever complaint of injury, or claim of redress, they may have, respects the government solely. They have not only nothing to object to the persons who relieved their necessities, by giving them the current price of their property, but they are even under an implied condition to contribute to the reimbursement of those persons. They knew, that by the terms of the contract with themselves, the public were bound to pay to those, to whom they should convey their title, the sums stipulated to be paid to them; and, that as citizens of the United States, they were to bear their proportion of the contribution for that purpose. This, by the act of assignment, they tacitly engage to do; and if they had an option, they could not, with integrity or good faith, refuse to do it, without the consent of those to whom they sold.

But though many of the original holders sold from necessity, it does not follow, that this was the case with all of them. It may well be supposed, that some of them did it either through want of confidence in an eventual provision, or from the allurements of some profitable speculation. How shall it be ascertained, in any case, that the money, which the original holder obtained for his security, was not more beneficial to him, than if he had held it to the present time, to avail himself of the provision which shall be made? How shall it be known, whether if the purchaser had employed his money in some other way, he would not be in a better situation, than by having applied it in the purchase of securities, though he should now receive their full amount? And if neither of these things can be known, how shall it be determined whether a discrimination, independent of the breach of contract, would not do a real injury to purchasers; and if it included a compensation to the primitive proprietors, would not give them an advantage, to which they had no equitable pretension.

It may well be imagined, also, that there are not wanting instances, in which individuals, urged by a present necessity, parted with the securities received by them from the public, and shortly after replaced them with others, as an indemnity for their first loss. Shall they be deprived of the indemnity which they have endeavoured to secure by so provident an arrangement?

Questions of this sort, on a close inspection, multiply themselves without end, and demonstrate the injustices of a discrimination, even on the most subtile calculations of equity, abstracted from the obligation of contract.

The difficulties too of regulating the details of a plan for that purpose, which would have even the semblance of equity, would be found immense. It may well be doubted whether they would not be insurmountable, and replete with such absurd, as well as inequitable consequences, as to disgust even the proposers of the measure. . . .

But there is still a point in view in which it will appear perhaps even more exceptionable, than in either of the former. It would be repugnant to an express provision of the Constitution of the United States. This provision is, that "all debts contracted and engagements entered into before the adoption of that Constitution shall be as valid against the United States under it, as under the confederation," which amounts to a constitutional ratification of the contracts respecting the debt, in the state in which they existed under the confederation. And resorting to that standard, there can be no doubt, that the rights of assignees and original holders, must be considered as equal. . . .

The Secretary concluding, that a discrimination, between the different classes of creditors of the United States, cannot with propriety be *made*, proceeds to examine whether a difference ought to be permitted to *remain* between them, and another description of public creditors—those of the states individually.

The Secretary, after mature reflection on this point, entertains a full conviction, that an assumption of the debts of the particular states by the union, and a like provision for them, as for those of the union, will be a measure of sound policy and substantial justice.

It would, in the opinion of the Secretary, contribute, in an eminent degree, to an orderly, stable and satisfactory arrangement of the national finances.

Admitting, as ought to be the case, that a provision must be made in some way or other, for the entire debt; it will follow, that no greater revenues will be required, whether that provision be made wholly by the United States, or partly by them, and partly by the states separately.

The principal question then must be, whether such a provision cannot be more conveniently and effectually made, by one general plan issuing from one authority, than by different plans or originating in different authorities. . . .

If all the public creditors receive their dues from one source, distributed with an equal hand, their interest will be the same. And having the same interests, they will unite in the support of the fiscal arrangements of the government: As these, too, can be made with more convenience, where there is no competition: These circumstances combined will insure to the revenue laws a more ready and more satisfactory execution.

If on the contrary there are distinct provisions, there will be distinct interests, drawing different ways. That union and concert of views, among the creditors, which in every government is of great importance to their security, and to that of public credit, will not only not exist, but will be likely to give place to mutual jealousy and opposition. And from this cause, the operation of the systems which may be adopted, both by the particular states, and by the union, with relation to their respective debts, will be in danger of being counteracted.

There are several reasons, which render it probable, that the situation of the state creditors would be worse, than that of the creditors of the union, if there be not a national assumption of the state debts. Of these it will be sufficient to mention two; one, that a principal branch of revenue is exclusively vested in the union; the other, that a state must always be checked in the imposition of taxes on articles of consumption, from the want of power to extend the same regulation to the other states, and from

the tendency of partial duties to injure its industry and commerce. Should the state creditors stand upon a less eligible footing than the others, it is unnatural to expect they would see with pleasure a provision for them. The influence which their dissatisfaction might have, could not but operate injuriously, both for the creditors, and the credit, of the United States. . . .

This sum may, in the opinion of the Secretary, be obtained from the present duties on imports and tonnage, with the additions, which without any possible disadvantages either to trade, or agriculture, may be made on wines, spirits, including those distilled within the United States, tea and coffee.

The Secretary conceives, that it will be sound policy, to carry the duties upon articles of this kind, as high as will be consistent with the practicability of a safe collection. This will lessen the necessity, both of having recourse to direct taxation, and of accumulating duties where they would be more inconvenient to trade, and upon objects, which are more to be regarded as necessaries of life.

That the articles which have been enumerated, will, better than most others, bear high duties, can hardly be a question. They are all of them, in reality—luxuries—the greatest part of them foreign luxuries; some of them, in the excess in which they are used, pernicious luxuries. And there is, perhaps, none of them, which is not comsumed in so great abundance, as may, justly, denominate it, a source of national extravagance and impoverishment. The consumption of ardent spirits particularly, no doubt very much on account of their cheapness, is carried to an extreme, which is truly to be regretted, as well in regard to the health and the morals, as to the aeconomy of the community.

Should the increase of duties tend to a decrease of the consumption of those articles, the effect would be, in every respect desirable. The saving which it would occasion, would leave individuals more at their ease, and promote a more favorable balance of trade. As far as this decrease might be applicable to distilled spirits, it would encourage the substitution of cyder and malt liquors, benefit agriculture, and open a new and productive source of revenue.

It is not however, probable, that this decrease would be in a degree, which would frustrate the expected benefit to the revenue from raising the duties. Experience has shewn, that luxuries of every kind, lay the strongest hold on the attachments of mankind, which, especially when confirmed by habit, are not easily alienated from them. . . .

Deeply impressed, as the Secretary is, with a full and deliberate conviction, that the establishment of public credit, upon the basis of a satisfactory provision, for the public debt is, under the present circumstances of this country, the true desideratum towards relief from individual and national embarrassments; that without it, these embarrassments will be likely to press still more severely upon the community—He cannot but indulge an anxious wish, that an effectual plan for that purpose may, during the present session, be the result of the united wisdom of the legislature.

From Opinion on the Constitutionality of the Bank (1791)

The Secretary of the Treasury having perused with attention the papers containing the opinions of the Secretary of State and Attorney General concerning the constitutionality of the bill for establishing a National Bank proceeds according to the order of the President to submit the reasons which have induced him to entertain a different opinion.

It will naturally have been anticipated that, in performing this task he would feel uncommon solicitude. Personal considerations alone arising from the reflection that the measure originated with him would be sufficient to produce it. The sense which he has manifested of the great importance of such an institution to the successful administration of the department under his particular care, and an expectation of serious ill consequences to result from a failure of the measure, do not permit him to be without anxiety on public accounts. But the chief solicitude arises from a firm persuasion, that principles of construction like those espoused by the Secretary of State and the Attorney General would be fatal to the just and indispensable authority of the United States.

In entering upon the argument it ought to be premised, that the objections of the Secretary of State and Attorney General are founded on a general denial of the authority of the United States to erect corporations. The latter indeed expressly admits, that if there be anything in the bill which is not warranted by the constitution, it is the clause of incorporation.

Now it appears to the Secretary of the Treasury, that this *general principle* is *inherent* in the very *definition* of *Government* and *essential* to every step of the progress to be made by that of the United States, namely—that every power vested in a Government is in its nature *sovereign,* and includes by *force* of the *term,* a right to employ all the *means* requisite, and fairly *applicable* to the attainment of the *ends of* such power; and which are not precluded by restrictions and exceptions specified in the constitution, or not immoral, or not contrary to the essential ends of political society.

This principle in its application to Government in general would be admitted as an axiom. And it will be incumbent upon those, who may incline to deny it, to *prove* a distinction and to shew that a rule which in the general system of things is essential to the preservation of the social order, is inapplicable to the United States.

The circumstances that the powers of sovereignty are in this country divided between the National and State Governments, does not afford the distinction required. It does not follow from this, that each of the *portions* of powers delegated to the one or to the other is not sovereign *with regard to its proper objects.* It will only *follow* from it, that each has sovereign power as to *certain things,* and not as to *other things.* To deny that the Government of the United States has sovereign power as to its declared purposes and trusts, because its power does not extend to all cases, would be equally to deny, that the State Governments have sovereign power in any case; because their power does not extend to every case. The tenth section of the first article of the constitution exhibits a long list of very important things which they may not do. And thus the United States would furnish the singular spectacle of a *political society* without *sovereignty,* or of a people *governed* without *government.*

If it would be necessary to bring proof to a proposition so clear as that which affirms that the powers of the federal Government, *as to its objects,* are sovereign, there is a clause of its constitution which would be decisive. It is that which declares, that the constiution and the laws of the United States made in pursuance of it, and all treaties made or which shall be made under their authority shall be the supreme law of the land. The power which can create the *Supreme law* of the land, in any case, is doubtless sovereign *as to such case.*

This general and indisputable principle puts at once and end to the *abstract* question. Whether the United Staes have power to *erect a corporation?* that is to say, to give a *legal* or *artificial* capacity to one or more persons, distinct from the natural. For it is unquestionably incident to *sovereign power* to erect corporations, and consequently to *that* of

the United States, in *relation to the objects* intrusted to the management of the government. The difference is this—where the authority of the government is general, it can create corporations in *all cases;* where it is confined to certain branches of legislation, it can create corporations only in those cases.

Here then as far as concerns the reasonings of the Secretary of State and the Attorney General, the affirmative of the constitutionality of the bill might be permitted to rest. It will occur to the President that the principle here advanced has been untouched by either of them.

For a more complete elucidation of the point nevertheless, the arguments which they had used against the power of the government to erect corporations, however foreign they are to the great and fundamental rule which has been stated, shall be particularly examined. And after shewing that they do not tend to impair its force, it shall also be shewn that the power of incorporation incident to the government in certain cases, does fairly extend to the particular case which is the object of the bill.

The first of these arguments is, that the foundation of the constitution is laid on this ground "that all powers not delegated to the United States by the Constitution, nor prohibited by it to the States are reserved to the States or to the people," whence it is meant to be inferred, that congress can in no case exercise any power not included in those enumerated in the constitution. And it is affirmed that the power of erecting a corporation is not included in any of the enumerated powers.

The main proposition here laid down, in its true signification is not to be questioned. It is nothing more than a consequence of the republican maxim, that all government is a delegation of power. But how much is delegated in each case, is a question of fact to be made out by fair reasoning and construction, upon the particular provisions of the constitution—taking as guides the general principles and general ends of government.

It is not denied, that there are *implied*, as well as *express powers*, and that the *former* are as effectually delegated as the latter. And for the sake of accuracy it shall be mentioned, that there is another class of powers, which may be properly denominated *resulting* powers. It will not be doubted that if the United States should make a conquest of any of the territories of its neighbours, they would possess sovereign jurisdiction over the conquered territory. This would rather be a result from the whole mass of the powers of the government and from the nature of political society, than a consequence of either of the powers specially enumerated.

But be this as it may, it furnishes a striking illustration of the general doctrine contended for. It shows an extensive case, in which a power of erecting corporations is either implied in, or would result from some or all of the powers, vested in the National Government. The jurisdiction acquired over such conquered territory would certainly be competent to every species of legislation.

To return it—it is conceded, that implied powers are to be considered as delegated equally with express ones.

Then it follows, that as a power of erecting a corporation may as well be *implied* as any other thing; it may as well be employed as an *instrument* or *means* of carrying into execution any of the specified powers, as any other instrument or mean whatever. The only question must be, in this as in every other case, whether the mean to be employed, or in this instance the corporation to be erected, has a natural relation to any of the asknowledged objects or lawful ends of the government. Thus a corporation may not be erected by congress, for superintending the police of the city of Philadelphia because they are not authorized to *regulate* the *police* of that city; but one may be erected in relation to the collection of taxes, or to the trade with foreign countries, or to the trade between the States, or with the Indian Tribes, because it is the province of the federal government to *regulate those objects* and because it is incident to a general *sovereign* or *legislative power* to *regulate* a thing, to employ as the means which relate to its regulation to the *best* and *greatest advantage.*

A strange fallacy seems to have crept into the manner of thinking and reasoning upon this subject. Imagination appears to have been unusually busy concerning it. An incorporation seems to have been regarded as some great, independent, substantive thing—as a political end of peculiar magnitude and moment; whereas it is truly to be considered as a *quality, capacity or means* to an end. Thus a mercantile company is formed with a certain capital for the purpose of carrying on a particular branch of business. Here the business to be prosecuted is the *end;* the association in order to form the requisite capital is the primary mean. Suppose that an incorporation were added to this; it would only be to add a new *quality* to that association; to give it an artificial capacity by which it would be enabled to prosecute the business with more safety and convenience. . . .

To this mode of reasoning respecting the right of employing all the means requisite to the execution of the specified powers of the Government, it is objected that none but *necessary* and proper means are to be employed, and the Secretary of State maintains, that no means are to be considered as *necessary,* but those without which the grant of the power would be *nugatory.* Nay so far does he go in his restrictive interpretation of the word, as even to make the case of *necessity* which shall warrant the constitutional exercise of the power to depend on *casual* and *temporary* circumstances; an idea which alone refutes the construction. The *expediency* of exercising a particular power, at a particular time, must indeed depend on *circumstances;* but the constitutional right of exercising it must be uniform and invariable—the same today as tomorrow.

All the arguments therefore against the constitutionality of the bill derived from the accidental existence of certain State banks—institutions which *happen* to exist today, and, for ought that concerns the government of the United States, may disappear tomorrow, must not only be rejected as falacious, but must be viewed as demonstrative, that there is a *radical* source of error in the reasoning.

It is essential to the being of the National government, that so erroneous a conception of the meaning of the word *necessary,* should be exploded.

It is certain, that neither the grammatical nor popular sense of the term requires that construction. According to both, *necessary* often means no more than *needful, requisite, incidental, useful,* or *conductive to.* It is a common mode of expression to say, that it is *necessary* for a government or a person to do this thing or that thing, when nothing more is intended or understood, than that the interests of the government or person require, or will be promoted, by the doing of this or that thing. The imagination can be at no loss for exemplifications of the use of the word in this sense.

And it is the true one in which it is to be understood as used in the constitution. The whole turn of the clause containing it indicates, that it was the intent of the convention, by that clause to give a liberal latitude to the exercise of the specified powers. The expressions have peculiar comprehensiveness. They are, "to make *all laws,* necessary and proper for *carrying into execution* the foregoing powers and *all other powers* vested by the constitution in the *government* of the United States, or in any *department* or *officer* thereof." To understand the word as the Secretary of State does, would be to depart from its obvious and popular sense, and to give it a *restrictive* operation; an idea never before entertained. It would be to give it the same force as if the word *absolutely* or *indispensably* had been prefixed to it.

Such a construction would beget endless uncertainty and embarrassment. The cases must be palpable and extreme in which it could be pronounced with certainty that a measure was absolutely necessary, or one without which the exercise of a given power would be nugatory. There are few measures of any government, which would stand so severe a test. To insist upon it, would be to make the criterion of the exercise of any implied power *a case of extreme necessity;* which is rather a rule to justify the overleaping of the bounds of constitutional authority, than to govern the ordinary exercise of it.

It may be truly said of every government, as well as that of the United States, that it has only a right, to pass such laws as are necessary and proper to accomplish the objects intrusted to it. For no government has a right to do *merely what it pleases.* Hence by a process of reasoning similar to that of the Secretary of State, it might be proved, that neither of the State governments has the right to incorporate a bank. It might be shown, that all the public business of the State, could be performed without a bank, and inferring thence that it was unnecessary it might be argued that it could not be done, because it is against the rule which has been just mentioned. A like mode of reasoning would prove, that there was no power to incorporate the Inhabitants of a town, with a view to a more perfect police. For it is certain, that an incorporation may be dispensed with, though it is better to have one. It is to be remembered that there is no *express* power in any State constitution to erect corporations.

The *degree* in which a measure is necessary, can never be a test of the *legal* right to adopt it. That must be a matter of opinion; and can only be a test of expediency. The *relation* between the *measure* and the *end,* between the *nature of the mean* employed towards the execution of a power and the object of that power, must be the criterion of constitutionality not the more or less of *necessity* or *utility*. . . .

The doctrine which is contended for . . . leaves therefore a criterion of what is constitutional, and of what is not so. This criterion is the *end,* to which the measure relates as a *mean.* If the end can be clearly comprehended within any of the specified powers, and if the measure has an obvious relation to that end, and is not forbidden by any particular provision of the constitution—it may safely be deemed to come within the compass of the national authority. There is also this further criterion which may materially assist the decision: Does the proposed measure abridge a pre-existing right of any State, or of any individual? If it does not, there is a strong presumption in favour of its constitutionality; and slighter relations to any declared object of the constitution may be permitted to turn the scale. . . .

It is presumed to have been satisfactorily shewn in the course of the preceding observations

1. That the power of the government, *as to* the objects intrusted to its management, is in its nature sovereign.

2. That the right of erecting corporations is one, inherent in and inseparable from the idea of sovereign power.

3. That the position, that the government of the United States can exercise no power but such as is delegated to it by its constitution does not militate against this principle.

4. That the word *necessary* in the general clause can have no *restrictive* operation, derogating from the force of this principle; indeed, that the degree in which a measure is, or is not necessary, cannot be *a test of constitutional right,* but of expediency only.

5. That the power to erect corporations is not to be considered as an *independent* or *substantive* power but as an *incidental* and *auxiliary* one; and was therefore more properly left to implication, than expressly granted.

6. That the principle in question does not extend the power of the govern-

ment beyond the prescribed limits, because it only affirms a power to *incorporate* for *purposes within the sphere* of *the specified powers.*

And lastly that the right to exercise such a power, in certain cases, is unequivocally granted in the most *positive* and *comprehensive* terms.

To all which it only remains to be added that such a power has actually been exercised in two very imminent instances: namely in the erection of two governments, one, northwest of the river Ohio, and the other southwest— the *last, independent* of *any antecedent compact.* And there results a full and complete demonstration, that the Secretary of State and Attorney General are mistaken, when they deny generally the power of the National government to erect corporations.

It shall now be endeavoured to be shewn that there is a power to erect one of the kind proposed by the bill. This will be done, by tracing a natural and obvious relation between the institution of a bank, and the objects of several of the enumerated powers of the government; and by shewing that, *politically* speaking, it is necessary to the effectual execution of one or more of those powers. In the course of this investigation, various instances will be stated, by way of illustration of a right to erect corporation under those powers. . . .

A Bank relates to the collection of taxes in two ways; *indirectly,* by increasing the quantity of circulating medium and quickening circulation, which facilitates the means of paying—*directly,* by creating a *convenient species* of *medium* in which they are to be paid. . . .

A Bank has a direct relation to the power of borrowing money, because it is an usual and in sudden emergencies an essential instrument in the obtaining of loans to government.

A nation is threatened with war. Large sums are wanted, on a sudden, to make the requisite preparations. Taxes are laid for the purpose, but it requires time to obtain the benefit of them. Anticipation is indispensable. If there be a bank, the supply can, at once be had; if there be none loans from Individuals must be sought. The progress of these is often too slow for the exigency; in some situations they are not practicable at all. Frequently when they are, it is of great consequence to be able to anticipate the product of them by advances from a bank.

The essentiality of such an institution as an instrument of loans is exemplified at this very moment. An Indian expedition is to be prosecuted. The only fund out of which the money can arise consistently with the public engagements, is a tax which will only begin to be collected in July next. The preparations, however, are instantly to be made. The money must therefore be borrowed. And of whom could it be borrowed, if there were no public banks? . . .

The institution of a bank has also a natural relation to the regulation of trade between the States: In so far as it is conducive to the creation of a convenient medium of *exchange* between them, and to the keeping up a full circulation by preventing the frequent displacement of the metals in reciprocal remittances. Money is the very hinge on which commerce turns. And this does not mean merely gold and silver, many other things have served the purpose with different degrees of utility. Paper has been extensively employed. . . .

The very general power of laying and collecting taxes and appropriating their proceeds—that of borrowing money indefinitely—that of coining money and regulating foreign coins—that of making all needful rules and regulations respecting the property of the United States— these powers combined, as well as the reason and nature of the thing speak strongly this language: That it is the manifest design and scope of the constitution to vest in congress all the powers requisite to the effectual administration of the finances of the United States. As far as concerns this object, there appears to be no parsimony of power.

From Report on Manufactures (1791)

The Secretary of the Treasury, in obedience to the order of ye House of Representatives, of the 15th day of January, 1790, has applied his attention, at as early a period as his other duties would permit, to the subject of Manufactures; and particularly to the means of promoting such as will tend to render the United States, independent on foreign nations for military and other essential supplies. And he thereupon respectfully submits the following Report.

The expedience of encouraging manufactures in the United States, which was not long since deemed very questionable, appears at this time to be pretty generally admitted. The embarrassments, which have obstructed the progress of our external trade, have led to serious reflections on the necessity of enlarging the sphere of our domestic commerce: the restrictive regulations, which in foreign markets abridge the vent of the increasing surplus of our Agricultural produce, serve to beget an earnest desire, that a more extensive demand for that surplus may be created at home: And the complete success, which has rewarded manufacturing enterprise, in some valuable branches, conspiring with the promising symptoms, which attend some less mature essays, in others, justify a hope, that the obstacles to the growth of this species of industry are less formidable than they were apprehended to be, and that it is not difficult to find, in its further extension a full indemnification for any external disadvantages, which are or may be experienced, as well as an accession of resources, favorable to national independence and safety.

There still are, nevertheless, respectable patrons of opinions, unfriendly to the encouragement of manufactures. The following are, substantially, the arguments, by which these opinions are defended.

In every country (say those who entertain them) Agriculture is the most beneficial and *productive* object of human industry. This position, generally, if not universally true, applies with peculiar emphasis to the United States, on account of their immense tracts of fertile territory, uninhabited and unimproved. Nothing can afford so advantageous an employment for capital and labour, as the conversion of this extensive wilderness into cultivated farms. Nothing equally with this, can contribute to the population, strength and real riches of the country.

To endeavor, by the extraordinary patronage of Government, to accelerate the growth of manufactures, is, in fact, to endeavor, by force and art, to transfer the natural current of industry from a more, to a less beneficial channel. Whatever has such a tendency must necessarily be unwise. Indeed it can hardly ever be wise in a government, to attempt to give a direction to the industry of its citizens. This under the quicksighted guidance of private interest, will, if left to itself, infallibly find its own way to the most profitable employment: and 'tis by such employment, that the public prosperity will be most effectually prompted. To leave industry to itself, therefore, is, in almost every case, the soundest as well as the simplest policy.

This policy is, not only recommended to the United States, by considerations which affect all nations it is, in a manner, dictated to them by the imperious force of a very peculiar situation. The smallness of their population compared with their territory—the constant allurements to emigration from the settled to the unsettled parts of the country—the facility, with which the less independent condition of an artisan can be exchanged for the more independent condition of a farmer— these, and similar causes conspire to produce, and, for a length of time must continue to occasion, a scarcity of hands for manufacturing occupation, and dearness of labor generally. To these disadvantages for the prosecution of manufactures, a deficiency of pecuniary capital being added, the prospect of a successful competition with the manufactures of Europe must be regarded as little less than desperate. Extensive manufactures can only be the offspring of a redundant,

at least of a full population. Till the latter shall characterize the situation of this country, 'tis vain to hope for the former.

If contrary to the natural course of things, an unseasonable and premature spring can be given to certain fabrics, by heavy duties, prohibitions, bounties, or by other forced expedients; this will only be to sacrifice the interests of the community to those of particular classes. Besides the misdirection of labor, a virtual monopoly will be given to the persons employed on such fabrics; and an enhancement of price, the inevitable consequence of every monopoly, must be defrayed at the expense of the other parts of the society. It is far preferable, that those persons should be engaged in the cultivation of the earth, and that we should procure, in exchange for its productions, the commodities, with which foreigners are able to supply us in greater perfection, and upon better terms.

This mode of reasoning is founded upon facts and principles, which have certainly respectable pretensions. If it had governed the conduct of nations more generally, than it has done, there is room to suppose, that it might have carried them faster to prosperity and greatness, than they have attained, by the pursuit of maxims too widely opposite. Most general theories, however, admit of numerous exceptions, and there are few, if any, of the political kind, which do not blend a considerable portion of error, with the truths they inculcate.

In order to [reach] an accurate judgment how far that which has been just stated ought to be deemed liable to a similar inputation, it is necessary to advert carefully to the considerations, which plead in favour of manufactures, and which appear to recommend the special and positive encouragement of them; in certain cases, and under certain reasonable limitations.

It ought readily to be conceded that the cultivation of the earth—as the primary and most certain source of national supply—as the immediate and chief source of subsistence to man—as the principal source of those materials which constitute the nutriment of other kinds of labor—as including a state most favourable to the freedom and independence of the human mind—one, perhaps, most conducive to the multiplication of the human species—has *intrinsically a strong claim to pre-eminence over every other kind of industry.*

But that it has a title to any thing like an exclusive predilection, in any country, ought to be admitted with great caution. That it is even more productive than every other branch of Industry requires more evidence than has yet been given in support of the position. That its real interests, precious and important as without the help of exaggeration, they truly are, will be advanced, rather than injured by the due encouragement of manufactures, may, it is believed, be satisfactorily demonstrated. And it is also believed that the expedience of such encouragement in a general view may be shown to be recommended by the most cogent and persuasive motives of national policy. . . .

It is now proper to proceed a step further, and to enumerate the principal circumstances, from which it may be inferred—that manufacturing establishments not only occasion a positive augmentation of the Produce and Revenue of the Society, but that they contribute essentially to rendering them greater than they could possibly be, without such establishments. These circumstances are—

1. The division of labour.
2. An extension of the use of Machinery.
3. Additional employment to classes of the community not ordinarily engaged in the business.
4. The promoting of emigration from foreign Countries.
5. The furnishing greater scope for the diversity of talents and dispositions which discriminate men from each other.
6. The affording a more ample and various field for enterprize.

7. The creating in some instances a new, and securing in all, a more certain and steady demand for the surplus produce of the soil.

Each of these circumstances has a considerable influence upon the total mass of industrious effort in a community: Together, they add to it a degree of energy and effect, which are not easily conceived. Some comments upon each of them, in the order in which they have been stated, may serve to explain their importance.

I. AS TO THE DIVISION OF LABOUR

It has justly been observed, that there is a scarcely any thing of a greater moment in the aeconomy of a nation than the proper division of labour. The separation of occupations causes each to be carried to a much greater perfection, than it could possibly acquire, if they were blended. This arises principally from three circumstances—

1st. The greater skill and dexterity naturally resulting from a constant and undivided application to a single object. It is evident, that these properties must increase, in proportion to the separation and simplification of objects and the steadiness of the attention devoted to each; and must be less in proportion to the complication of objects, and the number among which the attention is distracted.

2nd. The aeconomy of time, by avoiding the loss of it, incident to a frequent transition from one operation to another of a different nature. This depends on various circumstances—the transition itself—the orderly disposition of the implements, machines and materials employed in the operation to be relinquished—the preparatory steps to the commencement of a new one—the interruption of the impulse, which the mind of the workman acquires, from being engaged in a particular operation—the distractions, hesitations and reluctances, which attend the passage from one kind of business to another.

3rd. An extension of the use of Machinery. A man occupied on a single object will have it more in his power, and will be more naturally led to exert his imagination in devising methods to facilitate and abridge labour, than if he were perplexed by a variety of independent and dissimilar operations. Besides this the fabrication of Machines, in numerous instances, becoming itself a distinct trade, the Artist who follows it, has all the advantages which have been enumerated, for improvement in his particular art; and in both ways the invention and application of machinery are extended.

And from these causes united, the mere separation of the occupation of the cultivator, from that of the Artificer, has the effect of augmenting the *productive powers* of labour, and with them, the total mass of the produce or revenue of a Country. In this single view of the subject, therefore, the utility of Artificers of Manufacturers, towards promoting an increase of productive industry, is apparent.

II. AS TO AN EXTENSION OF THE USE OF MACHINERY, A POINT WHICH, THOUGH PARTLY ANTICIPATED REQUIRES TO BE PLACED IN ONE OR TWO ADDITIONAL LIGHTS

The employment of Machinery forms an item of great importance in the general mass of national industry. 'Tis an artificial force brought in aid of the natural force of man; and, to all the purposes of labour, is an increase of hands; an accession of strength, *unencumbered too by the expense of maintaining the laborer.* May it not therefore be fairly inferred, that those occupations, which give greatest scope to the use of this auxiliary, contribute most to the general Stock of industrious effort, and in consequence, to the general product of industry?

It shall be taken for granted, and the truth of the position referred to observation, that manufacturing pursuits are susceptible in a greater degree of the application of machinery, than those of Agriculture. If so all the difference is lost to a community, which, instead of manufacturing for itself, procures the fabrics requisite to its supply from other Countries. The substantiation of foreign for domestic manufactures is a transfer to foreign nations of the advantages accruing from the employment of Machinery, in the modes in which it is capable of being employed, with most utility and to the greatest extent.

The Cotton Mill, invented in England, within the last twenty years, is a signal illustration of the general proposition, which has been just advanced. In consequence of it, all the different processes for spinning Cotton are performed by means of Machines, which are put in motion by water, and attended chiefly by women and Children; and by a smaller number of persons, in the whole, than are requisite in the ordinary mode of spinning. And it is an advantage of great moment, that the operations of this mill continue with convenience during the night as well as through the day. The prodigious effect of such a Machine is easily conceived. To this invention is to be attributed essentially the immense progress, which has been so suddenly made in Great Britain, in the various fabrics of cotton.

III. AS TO THE ADDITIONAL EMPLOYMENT OF CLASSES OF THE COMMUNITY, NOT ORIGINALLY ENGAGED IN THE PARTICULAR BUSINESS

This is not among the least valuable of the means, by which manufacturing institutions contribute to augment the general stock of industry and production. In places where those institutions prevail, besides the persons regularly engaged in them, they afford occasional and extra employment to industrious individuals and families, who are willing to devote the leisure resulting from the intermissions of their ordinary pursuits to collateral labours, as a resource for multiplying their acquisitions or their enjoyments. The husbandman himself experiences a new source of profit and support from the increased industry of his wife and daughters; invited and stimulated by the demands of the neighboring manufactories.

Besides this advantage of occasional employment to classes having different occupations, there is another, of a nature allied to it, and of a similar tendency. This is—the employment of persons who would otherwise be idle (and in many cases a burthen on the community) either from the bias of temper, habit, infirmity of body, or some other cause, indisposing or disqualifying them for the toils of the Country. It is worthy of particular remark, that, in general, women and Children are rendered more useful, and the latter more early useful by manufacturing establishments than they would otherwise be. Of the number of persons employed in the Cotton Manufactories of Great Britain, it is computed that four sevenths nearly are women and children; of whom the greatest proportion are children, and many of them of a very tender age.

And thus it appears to be one of the attributes of manufactures, and one of no small consequence, to give occasion to the exertion of a greater quantity of Industry, even by the *same number* of persons, where they happen to prevail, than would exist, if there were no such establishments.

IV. AS TO THE PROMOTING OF EMIGRATION FROM FOREIGN COUNTRIES

Men reluctantly quit one course of occupation and livelihood for another, unless invited to it by very apparent and proximate advantages. Many who would go from one country to another, if they had a prospect of continuing with more benefit the callings, to which they have been educated, will often not be tempted to change their situation by the hope of doing better, in some other way. Manufacturers, who, listening to the powerful invitations of a better price for their fabrics, or their labour, of greater cheapness of provisions and raw materials, of an exemption from the chief part of the taxes, burthens and restraints, which they endure in the old world, of greater personal independence and consequence, under the operation of a more equal government, and of what is far more precious than mere religious toleration—a perfect equality of religious privileges; would probably flock from Europe to the United States to pursue their own trades or professions, if they were once made sensible of the advantages they would enjoy, and were inspired with an assurance of encouragement and employment, will, with difficulty, be induced to transplant themselves, with a view to becoming Cultivators of Land.

If it be true then, that it is the interest of the United States to open every possible avenue to emigration from abroad, it affords a weighty argument for the encouragement of manufactures; which, for the reasons just assigned, will have the strongest tendency to multiply the inducements to it.

Here is perceived an important resource, not only for extending the population, and with it the useful and productive labour of the country, but likewise for the prosecution of manufactures, without deducting from the number of hands, which might otherwise be drawn to Tillage and even for the indemnification of Agriculture for such as might happen to be diverted from it. Many, whom Manufacturing views would induce to emigrate, would afterwards yield to the temptations, which the particular situation of this Country holds out to Agricultural pursuits. And while Agriculture would in other respects derive many signal and unmingled advantages, from the growth of manufactures, it is a problem whether it would gain or lose, as to the article of the number of persons employed in carrying it on.

V. AS TO THE FURNISHING GREATER SCOPE FOR THE DIVERSITY OF TALENTS AND DISPOSITIONS, WHICH DISCRIMINATE MEN FROM EACH OTHER

This is a much more powerful means of augmenting the fund of national Industry than may at first sight appear. It is a just observation, that minds of the strongest and most active powers for their proper objects fall below mediocrity and labour without effect, if confined to uncongenial pursuits. And it is thence to be inferred, that the results of human exertion may be immensely increased by diversifying its objects. When all the different kinds of industry obtain in a community, each individual can find his proper element, and can call into activity the whole vigour of his nature. And the community is benefitted by the services of its respective members, in the manner, in which each can serve it with most effect.

If there any any thing in a remark often to be met with—namely that there is, in the genius of the people of this country, a peculiar aptitude for mechanic improvements, it would operate as a forcible reason for giving opportunities to the exercise of that species of talent, by the propagation of manufacturers.

VI. AS TO THE AFFORDING A MORE AMPLE AND VARIOUS FIELD FOR ENTERPRISE.

This also is of greater consequence in the general scale of national exertion, than might perhaps on a superficial view be supposed, and has effects not altogether dissimilar from those of the circumstances last noticed. To cherish and stimulate the activity of the human mind, by multiplying the objects of enterprise, it is not among the least considerable of the expedients, by which the wealth of a nation may be promoted. Even things in themselves not positively advantageous, sometimes become so, by their tendency to provoke exertion. Every new scene which is opened to the busy nature of man to rouse and exert itself, is the addition of a new energy to the general stock of effort.

The spirit of enterprise, useful and prolific as it is, must necessarily be contracted or expanded in proportion to the simplicity or variety of the occupations and productions, which are to be found in a Society. It must be less in a nation of mere cultivators, than in a nation of cultivators and merchants; less in a nation of cultivators and merchants, than in a nation of cultivators, artificers and merchants.

VII. AS TO THE CREATING, IN SOME INSTANCES, A NEW, AND SECURING IN ALL A MORE CERTAIN AND STEADY DEMAND, FOR SURPLUS PRODUCE OF THE SOIL.

This is among the most important of the circumstances which have been indicated. It is a principal mean, by which the establishment of manufactures contributes to an augmentation of the produce or revenue of a country, and has an immediate and direct relation to the prosperity of Agriculture.

It is evident, that the exertions of the husbandman will be steady or fluctuating, vigorous or feeble, in proportion to the steadiness or fluctuation, adequateness or inadequateness, of the markets on which he must depend, for the vent of the surplus, which may be produced by his labor; and that such surplus in the ordinary course of things will be greater or less in the same proportion.

For the purpose of this vent, a domestic market is greatly to be preferred to a foreign one; because it is in the nature of things, far more to be relied upon.

It is a primary object of the policy of nations, to be able to supply themselves with subsistence from their own soils; and manufacturing nations, as far as circumstances permit, endeavor to procure from the same source, the raw materials necessary for their own fabrics. This disposition, urged by the spirit of monopoly, is sometimes even carried to an injudicious extreme. It seems not always to be recollected, that nations who have neither mines nor manufactures, can only obtain the manufactured articles, of which they stand in need, by an exchange of the products of their soils; and that if those who can best furnish them with such articles are unwilling to give a due course to this exchange, they must of necessity, make every possible effort to manufacture for themselves; the effect of which is that the manufacturing nations abridge the natural advantages of their situation, through an unwillingness to permit the Agricultural countries to enjoy the advantages of theirs, and sacrifice the interests of a mutually beneficial intercourse to the vain project of *selling every thing* and *buying nothing*.

But it is also a consequence of the policy, which has been noted, that the foreign demand for the products of Agricultural Countries is, in a great degree, rather casual and occasional, than certain or constant. To what extent injurious interruptions of the demand for some of the staple commodities of the United States, may have been experienced from that cause, must be referred to the judgment of those who are engaged in carrying on the commerce of the country; but it may be safely affirmed, that such interruptions are at times very inconveniently felt, and that cases not unfrequently occur, in which markets are so confined and restricted as to render the demand very unequal to the supply.

Independently likewise of the artificial impediments, which are created by the policy in question, there are natural causes tending to render the external demand for the surplus of Agricultural nations a precarious reliance. The differences of seasons, in the countries, which are the consumers, makes immense differences in the produce of their own soils, in different years; and consequently in the degrees of their necessity for foreign supply. Plentiful harvests with them, expecially if similar ones occur at the same time in the countries, which are the furnishers, occasion of course a glut in the markets of the latter.

Considering how fast and how much the progress of new settlements in the United States must increase the surplus produce of the soil, and weighing seriously the tendency of the system, which prevails among most of the commercial nations of Europe, whatever dependence may be placed on the force of natural circumstances to counteract the effects of an artificial policy, there appear strong reasons to regard the foreign demand for that surplus as too uncertain a reliance, and to desire a substitute for it, in an extensive domestic market.

To secure such a market, there is no other expedient, than to promote manufacturing establishments. Manufacturers who constitute the most numerous class, after the Cultivators of land, are for that reason the principal consumers of the surplus of their labour.

This idea of an extensive domestic market for the surplus produce of the soil is of the first consequence. It is, of all things, that which most effectually conduces to a flourishing state of Agriculture. If the effect of manufactories should be to detach a portion of the hands, which would otherwise be engaged in Tillage, it might possibly cause a smaller quantity of lands to be under cultivation; but, by their tendency to procure a more certain demand for the surplus produce of the soil, they would, at the same time, cause the lands which were in cultivation to be better improved and more productive. And while, by their influence, the condition of each individual farmer would be meliorated, the total mass of Agricultural production would probably be increased. For this must evidently depend as much, if not more, upon the degree of improvement than upon the number of acres under culture.

It merits particular observation, that the multiplication of manufactories not only furnishes a Market for those articles which have been accustomed to be produced in abundance in a country, but it likewise creates a demand for such as were either unknown or produced in inconsiderable quantities. The bowels as well as the surface of the earth are ransacked for articles which were before neglected. Animals, Plants and Minerals acquire a utility and a value which were before unexplored.

The foregoing considerations seem sufficient to establish, as general propositions, that it is the interest of nations to diversify the industrious pursuits of the individuals who compose them—that the establishment of manufactures is calculated not only to increase the general stock of useful and productive labour; but even to improve the state of Agriculture in particular, certainly to advance the interests of those who are engaged in it. There are other views, that will be hereafter taken of the subject, which, it is conceived, will serve to confirm these inferences. . . .

The remaining objections to a particular encouragement of manufacturers in the United States now require to be examined.

One of these turns on the proposition, that Industry, if left to itself, will naturally find its way to the most useful and profitable employment: whence it is inferred that manufacturers without the aid of government will grow up as soon and as fast, as the natural state of things and the interest of the community may require.

Against the solodity of this hypothesis, in the full lattitude of the terms, very cogent reasons may be offered. These have relation to—the strong influence

of habit and the spirit of imitation—the fear of want of success in untried enterprises—the intrinsic difficulties incident to first essays towards a competition with those who have previously attained to perfection in the business to be attempted—the bounties premiums and other artificial encouragements, with which foreign nations second the exertions of their own Citizens in the branches, in which they are to be rivalled.

Experience teaches, that men are often so much governed by what they are accustomed to see and practise, that the simplest and most obvious improvements, in the most ordinary occupations, are adopted with hesitation, reluctance, and by slow gradations. The spontaneous transition to new pursuits, in a community long habituated to different ones, may be expected to be attended with proportionably greater difficulty. When former occupations ceased to yield a profit adequate to the subsistence of their followers, or when there was an absolute deficiency of employment in them, owing to the superabundance of hands, changes would ensue; but these changes would be likely to be more tardy than might consist with the interest either of individuals or of the Society. In many cases they would not happen, while a bare support could be insured by an adherence to ancient courses; though a resort to a more profitable employment might be practicable. To produce the desirable changes as early as may be expedient, may therefore require the incitement and patronage of government.

The apprehension of failing in new attempts is perhaps a more serious impediment. There are dispositions apt to be attracted by the mere novelty of an undertaking—but these are not always the best calculated to give it success. To this, it is of importance that foreigners, should be excited. And to inspire this description of persons with confidence, it is essential, that they should be made to see in any project, which is new, and for that reason alone, if, for no other, precarious, the prospect of such a degree of countenance and support from government, as may be capable of overcoming the obstacles, inseparable from first experiments.

The superiority antecedently enjoyed by nations, who have pre-occupied and perfected a branch of industry, constitutes a more formidable obstacle, than either of those, which have been mentioned, to the introduction of the same branch into a country in which it did not before exist. To maintain between the recent establishments of one country and the long matured establishments of another country, a competition upon equal terms, both as to quality and price, is in most cases impracticable. The disparity, in the one or in the other, or in both, must necessarily be so considerable as to forbid a successful rivalship, without the extraordinary aid and protection of government.

The the greatest obstacle of all to the successful prosecution of a new branch of industry in a country, in which it was before unknown, consists, as far as the instances apply, in the bounties, premiums and other aids which are granted, in a variety of cases, by the nations, in which the establishments to be imitated are previously introduced. It is well known (and particular examples in the course of this report will be cited) that certain nations grant bounties on the exportation of particular commodities, to enable their own workmen to undersell and supplant all competitors in the countries to which those commodities are sent. Hence the undertakers of a new manufacture have to contend not only with the natural disadvantages of a new undertaking, but with the gratituities and remunerations which other governments bestow. To be enabled to contend with success, it is evident that the interference and aid of their own governments are indispensable.

Combinations by those engaged in a particular branch of business in one country, to frustrate the first efforts to introduce it into another, by temporary sacrifices, recompensed perhaps by extraordinary indemnifications of the government of such country, are believed to have existed, and are not to be regarded as destitute of probability. The existence or assurance of aid from the government of the country, in which the business is to be introduced, may be essential to fortify adventurers against the dread of such combinations—to defeat their efforts, if formed and to prevent their being formed, by demonstrating that they must in the end prove fruitless.

Whatever room there may be for an expectation that the industry of a people, under the direction of private interest, will upon equal terms find out the most beneficial employment for itself, there is none for a reliance that it will struggle against the force of unequal terms, or will of itself surmount all the adventitous barriers to a successful competition, which may have been erected either by the advantages naturally acquired from practice and previous possession of the ground, or by those which may have spring from positive regulations and an artificial policy. This general reflection might alone suffice as an answer to the objection under examination, exclusively of the weighty considerations which have been particularly urged. . . .

There remains to be noticed an objection to the encouragement of manufactures, of a nature different from those which question the probability of success. This is derived from its supposed tendency to give a monopoly of advantages to particular classes, at the expense of the rest of the community, who, it is affirmed, would be able to procure the requisite supplies of manufactured articles on better terms from foreigners, than from our own Citizens, and who, it is alleged, are reduced to the necessity of paying an enhanced price for whatever they want, by every measure, which obstructs the free competition of foreign commodities.

It is not an unreasonable supposition, that measures, which serve to abridge the free competition of foreign Articles, have a tendency to occasion an enhancement of prices and it is not to be denied that such is the effect, in a number of Cases; but the fact does not uniformly correspond with the theory. A reduction of prices has, in several instances, immediately succeeded the establishment of a domestic manufacture. Whether it be that foreign manufactures endeavour to supplant, by underselling our own, or whatever else be the cause, the effect has been such as is stated, and the reverse of what might have been expected.

But though it were true, that the immediate and certain effect of regulations controlling the competition of foreign with domestic fabrics was an increase of Price, it is universally true, that the contraty is the ultimate effect with every successful manufacture. When a domestic manufacture has attained to perfection, and has engaged in the prosecution of it a competent number of Persons, it invariably becomes cheaper. Being free from the heavy charges which attend the importation of foreign commodities, it can be afforded, and accordingly seldom or never fails to be sold Cheaper, in the process of time; than was the foreign Article for which it is a substitute. The internal competition, which takes place, soon does away [with] every thing like Monopoly, and by degrees reduces the price of the Article to the *minimum* of a reasonable profit on the Capital employed. This accords with the reason of the thing, and with experience. . . .

One more point of view only remains in which to Consider the expediency of encouraging manufactures in the United States.

It is not uncommon to meet with an opinion that though the promoting of manufactures may be the interest of a part of the Union, it is contrary to that of another part. The northern & southern regions are sometimes represented as having adverse interests in their respect. Those are called Manufacturing, these Agricultural states; and a species of opposition is imagined to subsist between the Manufacturing and Agricultural interests.

This idea of an opposition between those two interests is the common error of the early periods of every country; but experience gradually dissipates it. Indeed, they are perceived so often to Succor and to befriend each other, that they come at length to be considered as one: a supposition which has been frequently abused, and is not universally true. Particular encouragements of particular manufactures may be of a Nature to sacrifice the interests of landholders to those of manufactures. But it is nevertheless a maxim, well established by experience, and generally acknowledged where there has been sufficient experience, that the *aggregate* prosperity of manufactures, and the, *aggregate* prosperity of Agriculture are intimately connected. In the Course of the discussion which has had place, various weighty considerations have been adduced operating in support of that maxim. Perhaps the superior steadiness of the demand of a domestic market for the surplus produce of the soil, is alone a convincing argument of its truth.

Ideas of a contrariety of interests between the northern and southern regions of the Union, are in the Main as unfounded as they are mischievous. The diversity of Circumstances on which such contrariety is usually predicated, authorizes a directly contrary conclusion. Mutual wants constitute one of the strongest links of political connection, and the extent of these bears a natural proportion to the diversity in the means of mutual supply.

Suggestions of an opposite complexion are ever to be deplored, as unfriendly to the steady pursuit of one great common cause, and to the perfect harmony of all the parts. . . .

A full view having now been taken of the inducements to the promotion of Manufactures in the United States, accompanied with an examination of the principal objections which are commonly urged *in opposition,* it is proper, in the next phase, to consider the means, by which it may be effected, as introductory to a Specification of the objects, which in the present state of things appear the most fit to be encouraged, and of the particular measures which it may be advisable to adopt, in respect to each.

In order to a better judgment of the Means proper to be resorted to by the United States, it will be of use to Advert to those which have been employed with success in other Countries. The principal of these are—

I. Protecting duties—or duties on those foreign articles which are the rivals of the domestic ones intended to be encouraged. . . .

II. Prohibitions of rival articles, or duties equivalent to prohibitions. . . .

III. Prohibitions of the exportation of the materials and manufactures. . . .

IV. Pecuniary bounties.

This has been one of the most efficacious means of encouraging manufactures, and, is in some views, the best. Though it has not yet been practiced upon by the Government of the United States (unless the allowance on the exportation of dried and pickled Fish and salted meat could be considered a bounty), and though it is less favored by Public Opinion than some other modes. Its advantages are these—

1. It is a species of encouragement more positive and direct than any other, and for that very reason, has a more immediate tendency to stimulate and uphold new enterprises, increasing the chances of profit, and diminishing the risks of loss, in the first attempts.

2. It avoids the inconvenience of a temporary augmentation of price, which is incident to some other modes, or it produces it to a less degree, either by making no addition to the charges on the rival foreign article, as in the Case of protecting duties, or by making a smaller addition. . . .

3. Bounties have not, like high protecting duties, a tendency to produce scarcity. . . ,

4. Bounties are sometimes not only the best, but the only proper expedient for uniting the encouragement of a new

object of agriculture, with that of a new object of manufacture. It is the Interest of the farmer to have the production of the raw material promoted, by counteracting the interference of the foreign material of the same kind. It is the Interest of the manufacturer to have the material abundant and cheap. If prior to the domestic production of the Material, in sufficient quantity, to supply the manufacturer on good terms, a duty be laid upon the importation of it from abroad, with a view to promote the raising of it at home, the Interests both of the Farmer and Manufacturer will be disserved. By either destroying the requisite supply, or raising the price of the article beyond what can be afforded to be given for it, by the Conductor of an infant manufacture, it is abandoned or fails; and there being no domestic manufactories to create a demand for the raw material, which is raised by the farmer, it is in vain, that the Competition of the like foreign article may have been destroyed.

It cannot escape notice, that the duty upon the importation of an article can no otherwise aid the domestic production of it, than by giving the latter greater advantages in the home market. It can have no influence upon the advantageous sale of the article produced in foreign markets; no tendency, therefore, to promote its exportation.

The true way to conciliate these two interests is to lay a duty on foreign *manufactures* of the materiel, the growth of which is desired to be encouraged, and to apply the produce of that duty, by way of bounty, either upon the production of the material itself or upon its manufacture at home, or upon both. In this disposition of the thing, the Manufacturer commences his enterprise under every advantage which is attainable, as to quantity or price of the raw material: And the Farmer, if the bounty be immediately to him, is enabled by it to enter into a successful competition with the foreign material; if the bounty be to the manufacturer on so much of the domestic material as he consumes, the operation is nearly the same; he has a ,motive of interest to prefer the domestic Commodity, if of equal quality, even at a higher price than the foreign, so long as the difference of prices is any thing short of the bounty which is allowed upon the article.

Except the simple and ordinary kinds of household Manufacture, or those for which there are very commanding local advantages, pecuniary bounties are in most cases, indispensable to the introduction of a new branch. A stimulus and a support not less powerful and direct is generally speaking, essential to the overcoming of the obstacles which arise from the Competitions of superior skill and maturity elsewhere. Bounties are especially essential in regard to articles upon which those foreigners who have been accustomed to supply a Country are in the practice of granting them.

The continuance of bounties on manufactures long established must almost always be of questionable policy: Because a presumption would arise, in every such Case, that there were natural and inherent impediments to success. But in new undertakings, they are as justifiable as they are oftentimes necessary.

There is a degree of prejudice against bounties from an appearance of giving away the public money without an immediate consideration, and from a supposition that they serve to enrich particular classes, at the expence of the Community.

But neither of these sources of dislike will bear a serious examination. There is no purpose to which public money can be more beneficially applied than to the acquisition of a new and useful branch of industry; no Consideration more valuable than a permanent addition to the general stock of productive labour.

As the second source of objection it equally lies against other modes of encouragement, which are admitted to be eligible. As often as a duty upon a foreign article makes an addition to its price, it causes an extra expense to the Community for the benefit of the domestic manufacturer. A bounty does no more. But it is the Interest of the society in each case, to submit to the temporary expense, which is more than compensated, by an increase of industry and Wealth, by an augmentation of resources and independence, & by the circumstance of eventual cheapness, which has been noticed in another place.

It would deserve attention, however, in the employment of this special of encouragement in the United States, as a reason for moderating the degree of it in the instances, in which it might be deemed eligible, that the great distance of this country from Europe imposes very heavy charges on all the fabrics which are brought from thence, amounting to from 15 to 30 per cent on their value, according to their bulk.

A Question has been made concerning the Constitutional right of the Government of the United States to apply this species of encouragement, but there is certainly no good foundation for such a question. The National Legislature has express authority "To lay and Collect taxes, duties, imposts, and excises, to pay the Debts, and provide for the *Common defence* and *general welfare*" with no other qualifications than that "all duties, imposts, and excises shall be *uniform* throughout the United States, and that no capitation or other direct tax shall be laid unless in proportion to numbers ascertained by a census or enumeration taken on the principles prescribed in the Constitution," and that "no tax or duty shall be laid on articles exported from any States."

These three qualifications excepted the power to *raise money* is *plenary* and *indefinite,* and the objects to which it may be *appropriated* are no less comprehensive than the payment of the Public debts, and the providing for the common defence and *general Welfare.* The terms *"general Welfare"* were doubtless intended to signify more than was expressed or imported in those which Preceded; otherwise, numerous exigencies incident to the affairs of a nation would have been left without a provision. The phrase is as comprehensive as any that could have been used; because it was not fit that the constitutional authority of the Union to appropriate its revenues should have been restricted within narrower limits than the "General Welfare" and because this necessarily embraces a vast variety of particulars, which are susceptible neither of specification or of definition.

It is therefore of necessity left to the discretion of the National Legislature, to pronounce upon the objects, which concern the general Welfare, and for which under that description, an appropriation of money is requisite and proper. And there seems to be no room for a doubt that whatever concerns the general interests of *Learning,* of *Agriculture,* of *Manufactures,* and of *Commerce,* are within the sphere of the national Councils, *as far as regards an application of money*

The only qualification of the generality of the Phrase in question, which seems to be admissible, is this—That the object to which an appropriation of money is to be made be *General,* and not *local;* its operation extending in fact, or by possibility, throughout the Union, and not being confined to a particular spot.

No objection ought to arise to this construction from a supposition that it would imply a power to do whatever else should appear to Congress conducive to the General Welfare. A power to appropriate money with this lattitude which is granted too *in express terms* would not carry a power to do any other thing not authorized in the constitution, either expressly or by fair implication.

V. Premiums. . . .

VI. The exemption of the materials of manufactures from duty. . . .

VII. Drawbacks of the duties which are imposed on the materials of manufactures. . . .

VIII. The encouragement of new inventions and discoveries, at home, and of the introduction into the United States of such as may have been made in other countries; particularly those which relate to machinery. . . .

IX. Judicious regulations for the inspection of manufactured commodities. . . .

X. The facilitating of pecuniary remittance from place to place. . . .

XI. The facilitating of the transportation of commodities. . . .

The foregoing are the principal of the means, by which the growth of manufactures is ordinarily promoted. It is, however, not merely necessary that the measures of government which have a direct view to manufactures, should be calculated to assist and protect them, but that those which only collaterally affect them, in the general course of the administration, should be guarded from any peculiar tendency to injure them.

These are certain species of taxes, which are apt to be oppressive to difference parts of the community, and among other ill effects have a very unfriendly aspect towards manufacturers. All Poll or Capitation taxes are of this nature. They either proceed according to a fixed rate, which operates unequally, and injuriously to the industrious poor; or they vest a discretion in certain officers, to make estimates and assessments which are necessarily vague, conjectual and liable to abuse. They ought therefore to be abstained from, in all but cases of distressing emergency.

All such taxes (including all taxes on occupations) which proceed according to the amount of capital *supposed* to be employed in a business or of profits *supposed* to be made in it, are unavoidably hurtful to industry. It is in vain, that the evil may be endeavoured to be mitigated by leaving it, in the first instance, in the option of the party to be taxed, to declare the amount of his capital or profits.

Men engaged in any trade or business have commonly weighty reasons to avoid disclosures, which would expose, with any thing like accuracy the real state of their affairs. They most frequently find it better to risk oppression than to avail themselves of so inconvenient a refuge, and the consequence is, that they often suffer oppression.

When the disclosure too, if made, is not definitive, but controllable by the discretion, or in other words, by the passions & prejudices of the revenue officers, it is not only an ineffectual protection, but the possibility of its being so is an additional reason for not resorting to it.

Allowing to the public officers the most equitable dispositions, yet where they are to exercise a discretion without certain data, they cannot fail to be often misled by appearances. The quantity of business, which seems to be going on, is, in a vast number of cases, a very deceitful criterion of the profits which are made; yet it is perhaps the best they can have, and it is the one, on which they will most naturally rely. A business therefore which may rather require aid, from the government, than be in a capacity to be contributory to it, may find itself crushed by the mistaken conjectures of the Assessors of taxes.

Arbitrary taxes, under which denomination are comprised all those that leave the quantum of the tax to be raised on each person, to the discretion of certain officers, are as contrary to the genius of liberty as to the maxims of industry. In this light, they have been viewed by the most judicious observers on government, who have bestowed upon them the severest epithets of reprobation; as constituting one of the worst features usually to be met with in the practice of despotic governments.

It is certain at least, that such taxes are particularly inimical to the success of manufacturing industry, and ought carefully to be avoided by a government which desires to promote it. . . .

The possibility of a diminution of the revenue may also present itself, as an objection to the arrangements, which have been submitted.

But there is no truth, which may be more firmly relied upon, than that the interests of the revenue are promoted, by whatever promotes an increase of National industry and wealth.

In proportion to the degree of these, is the capacity of every country to contribute to the public Treasury; and where the capacity to pay is increased, or even is not decreased, the only consequence of measures, which diminish any particular resource is a change of the object. If by encouraging the manufacture of an article at home, the revenue, which has been wont to accrue from its importation, should be lessened, an indemnification, can easily be found, either out of the manufacture itself, or from some other object, which may be deemed more convenient.

The measures however, which have been submitted, taken aggregately, will for a long time to come rather augment than decrease the public revenue.

There is little room to hope, that the progress of manufactures, will so equally keep pace with the progress of population, as to prevent, even, a gradual augmentation of the product of the duties on imported articles.

As, nevertheless, an abolition in some instances, and a reduction in others of duties, which have been pledged for the public debt, is proposed, it is essential, that it should be accompanied with a competent substitute. In order to this, it is requisite, that all the additional duties which shall be laid, be appropriated in the first instance, to replace all defalcations, which may proceed from any such abolition or diminution. It is evident, at first glance, that they will not only be adequate to this, but will yield a considerable surplus.

This surplus will serve:

First, To constitute a fund for paying the bounties which shall have been decreed.

Secondly, To constitute a fund for the operations of a Board to be established, for promoting Arts, Agriculture, Manufactures and Commerce. Of this institution, different intimations have been given, in the course of this report. An outline of a plan for it shall now be submitted.

Let a certain annual sum, be set apart, and placed under the management of Commissioners, not less than three, to consist of certain officers of the Government and their Successors in Office.

Let these Commissioners be empowered to apply the fund confided to them to defray the expenses of the emigration of Artists and Manufacturers in particular branches of extraordinary importance—to induce the prosecution and introduction of useful discoveries, inventions, and improvements, by proportionate rewards, judiciously held out and applied—to encourage by premiums both honorable and lucrative the exertions of individuals, and of classes, in relation to the several objects they are charged with promoting—and to afford such other aids to those objects as may be generally designated by law.

The Commissioners to render to the Legislature an annual account of their transactions and disbursements; and all such sums as shall not have been applied to the purposes of their trust, at the end of every three years, to revert to the Treasury. It may also be enjoined upon them not to draw out the money, but for the purpose of some specific disbursement.

It may, moreover, be of use to authorize them to receive voluntary contributions, making it their duty to apply them to the particular objects for which they may have been made, if any shall have been designated by the donors.

There is reason to believe that the progress of particular manufactures has been much retarded by the want of skillful workmen. And it often happens, that the capitals employed are not equal to the purposes of bringing from abroad workmen of a superior kind. Here, in cases worthy of it, the auxiliary agency of Government would, in all probability, be useful. There are also valuable workmen in every branch, who are prevented from emigrating solely by the want of means. Occasional aids to such persons properly administered might be a source of valuable acquisitions to the country.

The propriety of stimulating by rewards, the invention and introduction of useful improvements, is admitted without difficulty. But the success of attempts in this way must evidently depend much on the manner of conducting them. It is probable, that the placing of the dispensation of those rewards under some proper discretionary direction, where they may be accompanied by *collateral expedients* will serve to give them the surest efficacy. It seems impracticable to apportion, by general rules, specific compensations for discoveries of unknown and disproportionate utility.

The great use which may be made of a fund of this nature, to procure and import foreign improvements is particularly obvious. Among these, the article of machines would form a most important item.

The operation and utility of premiums have been adverted to; together with the advantages which have resulted from their dispensation, under the direction of certain public and private societies. Of this some experience has been had, in the instance of Pennsylvania Society for Promotion of Manufactures and useful Arts, but the funds of that association have been too contracted to produce more than a very small portion of the good to which the principles of it would have led. It may confidently be affirmed that there is scarcely any thing which has been devised, better calculated to excite a general spirit of improvement than the institutions of this nature. They are truly invaluable.

In countries where there is great private wealth, much may be effected by the voluntary contributions of patriotic individuals; but in a community situated like that of the United States, the public purse must supply the deficiency of private resource. In what can it be so useful, as in prompting and improving the efforts of industry?

All which is humbly submitted.

Alexander Hamilton,
Secy of the Treasury

The Federalist No. 15

To the People of the State of New York:

In the course of the preceding papers, I have endeavored, my fellow-citizens, to place before you, in a clear and convincing light, the importance of Union to your political safety and happiness. I have unfolded to you a complication of dangers, to which you would be exposed, should you permit that sacred knot which binds the people of America together to be severed or dissolved by ambition or by avarice, by jealousy or by misrepresentation. In the sequel of the inquiry through which I propose to accompany you, the truths intended to be inculcated will receive further confirmation from facts and arguments hitherto unnoticed. If the road over which you will still have to pass should in some places appear to you tedious or irksome, you will recollect that you are in quest of information on a subject the most momentous which can engage the attention of a free people, that the field through which you have to travel is in itself spacious, and that the difficulties of the journey have been unnecessarily increased by the mazes with which sophistry has beset the way. It will be my aim to remove the obstacles from your progress in as compendious a manner as it can be done, without sacrificing utility to despatch.

In pursuance of the plan which I have laid down for the discussion of the subject, the point next in order to be examined in the "insufficiency of the present Confederation to the preservation of the Union." It may perhaps be asked what need there is of reasoning or proof to illustrate a position which is not either controverted or doubted, to which the understandings and feelings of all classes of men assent, and which in substance is admitted by the opponents as well as by the friends of the new Constitution. It must in truth be acknowledged that, however these may differ in other respects, they in general appear to harmonize in this sentiment, at least, that there are material imperfections in our national system, and that something is necessary to be done to rescue us from impending anarchy. The facts that support this opinion are no longer objects of speculation. They have forced themselves upon the sensibility of the people at large, and have at length exorted from those whose mistaken policy has had the principal share in precipitating the extremity at which we are arrived, a reluctant confession of the reality of those defects in the scheme of our federal government, which have been long pointed out and regretted by the intelligent friends of the Union.

We may indeed with propriety be said to have reached almost the last stage of national humiliation. There is scarcely any thing that can wound the pride or degrade the character of an independent nation which we do not experience. Are there engagements to the performance of which we are held by every tie respectable among men? These are the subjects of constant and unblushing violation. Do we owe debts to foreigners and to our own citizens contracted in a time of imminent peril for the preservation of our political existence? These remain without any proper or satisfactory provision for their discharge. Have we valuable territories and important posts in the possession of a foreign power which, by express stipulations, ought long since to have been surrendered? These are still retained, to the prejudice of our interests, not less than of our rights. Are we in a condition to resent or repel the aggression? We have neither troops, nor treasury, nor government. Are we even in a condition to remonstrate with dignity? The just imputations on our own faith, in respect to the same treaty, ought first to be removed. Are we entitled by nature and compact to a free participation in the navigation of the Mississippi? Spain excludes us from it. Is public credit an indispensable resource in time of public danger? We seem to have abandoned its cause as desperate and irretrievable.

Is commerce of importance to national wealth? Ours is at the lowest point of declension. Is respectability in the eyes of foreign powers a safeguard against foreign encroachments? The imbecility of our government even forbids them to treat with us. Our ambassadors abroad are the mere pageants of mimic sovereignty. Is a violent and unnatural decreace in the value of land a symptom of national distress? The price of improved land in most parts of the country is much lower than can be accounted for by the quantity of waste land at market, and can only be fully explained by that want of private and public confidence, which are so alarmingly prevalent among all ranks, and which have a direct tendency to depreciate property of every kind. Is private credit the friend and patron of industry? That most useful kind which relates to borrowing and lending is reduced within the narrowest limits, and this still more from an opinion of insecurity than from the scarcity of money. To shorten an enumeration of particulars which can afford neither pleasure nor instruction, it may in general be demanded, what indication is there of national disorder, poverty, and insignificance that could befall a community so peculiarly blessed with natural advantages as we are, which does not form a part of the dark catalogue of our public misfortunes.

This is the melancholy situation to which we have been brought by those very maxims and councils which would now deter us from adopting the proposed Constitution; and which, not content with having conducted us to the brink of a precipice, seem resolved to plunge us into the abyss that awaits us below. Here, my countrymen, impelled by every motive that ought to influence an enlightened people, let us make a firm stand for our safety, our tranquillity, our dignity, our reputation. Let us at last break the fatal charm which has too long seduced us from the paths of felicity and prosperity.

It is true, as has been before observed, that facts, too stubborn to be resisted, have produced a species of general assent to the abstract proposition that there exist material defects in our national system; but the usefulness of the concession, on the part of the old adversaries of federal measures, is destroyed by a strenuous opposition to a remedy, upon the only principles that can give it a chance of success. While they admit that the government of the United States is destitute of energy, they contend against conferring upon it those powers which are requisite to supply that energy. They seem still to aim at things repugnant and irreconcilable; at an augmentation of federal authority, without a diminution of State authority; at sovereignty in the Union, and complete independence in the members. They still, in fine, seem to cherish with blind devotion the political monster of an *imperium in imperio*. This renders a full display of the principal defects of the Confederation necessary, in order to show that the evils we experience do not proceed from minute or partial imperfections, but from fundamental errors in the structure of the building, which cannot be amended otherwise than by an alteration in the first principles and main pillars of the fabric.

The great and radical vice in the construction of the existing Confederation is in the principle of LEGISLATION for STATES or GOVERNMENTS, in their CORPORATE or COLLECTIVE CAPACITIES, and as contradistinguished from the INDIVIDUALS of which they consist. Though this principle does not run through all the powers delegated to the Union, yet it pervades and governs those on which the efficacy of the rest depends. Except as to the rule of apportionment, the United States has an indefinite discretion to make requisitions for men and money; but they have no authority to raise either, by regulations extending to the individual citizens of America. The consequence of this is, that though in theory their resolutions concerning those objects are laws, constitutionally binding on the members of the Union, yet in practice they are mere recommendations which the States observe or disregard at their option.

It is a singular instance of the capriciousness of the human mind, that after all the admonitions we have had from experience on this head, there there should still be found men who object to the new Constitution, for deviating from a principle which has been found the bane of the old, and which is in itself evidently incompatible with the idea of Government; a principle, in short, which, if it is to be executed at all, must substitute the violent and saguinary agency of the sword to the mild influence of the magistracy.

There is nothing absurd or impracticable in the idea of a league or alliance between independent nations for certain defined purposes precisely stated in a treaty regulating all the details of time, place, circumstance, and quantity; leaving nothing to future discretion; and depending for its execution on the good faith of the parties. Compacts of this kind exist among all civilized nations, subject to the usual vicissitudes of peace and war, of observance and non-observance, as the interests or passions of the contracting powers dictate. In the early part of the present century there was an epidemical rage in Europe for this species of compacts, from which the politicians of the times fondly hoped for benefits which were never realized. With a view to establishing the equilibrium of power and the peace of that part of the world, all the resources of negotiations were exhausted, and triple and quadruple alliances were formed; but they were scarcely formed before they were broken, giving an instructive but afflicting lesson to mankind, how little dependence is to be placed on treaties which have no other sanction than the obligations of good faith, and which oppose general considerations of peace and justice to the impulse of any immediate interest or passion.

If the particular States in this country are disposed to stand in a similar relation to each other, and to drop the project of a general DISCRETIONARY SUPERINTENDENCE, the scheme would indeed be pernicious, and would entail upon us all the mischiefs which have been enumerated under the first head; but it would have the merit of being, at least, consistent and practicable. Abandoning all views towards a confederate government, this would bring us to a simple alliance offensive and defensive; and would place us in a situation to be alternate friends and enemies of each other, as our mutual jealousies and rivalships, nourished by the intrigues of foreign nations, should prescribe to us.

But if we are unwilling to be placed in this perilous situation; if we still will adhere to the design of a national government, or, which is the same thing, of a superintending power, under the direction of a common council, we must resolve to incorporate into our plan those ingredients which may be considered as forming the characteristic difference between a league and a government; we must extend the authority of the Union to the persons of the citizens—the only proper objects of government.

Government implies the power of making laws. It is essential to the idea of a law, that it be attended with a sanction; or, in other words, a penalty or punishment for disobedience. If there be no penalty annexed to disobedience, the resolutions or commands which pretend to be laws will, in fact, amount to nothing more than advice or recommendation. This penalty, whatever it may be, can only be inflicted in two ways; by the agency of the courts and ministers of justice, or by military force; by the COERCION of the magistracy, or by the coercion of arms. The first kind can evidently apply only to men; the last kind must of necessity, be employed against bodies politic, or communities, or States. It is evident that there is no process of a court by which the observance of the laws can, in the last resort, be enforced. Sentences may be denounced against them for violations of their duty; but these sentences can only be carried into execution by the sword. In an associated where the general authority is confined to the collective bodies of the communities that compose it, every breach of the laws must involve a state of war; and military execution must become the only instrument of civil obedience. Such a state of things can certainly not deserve the name of government, nor would any prudent man choose to commit his happiness to it.

There was a time when we were told that breaches, by the States, of the regulations of the federal authority were not to be expected; that a sense of common interest would preside over the conduct of the respective members, and would beget a full compliance with all the constitutional requisitions of the Union. This language, at the present day, would appear as wild as a great part of what we now hear from the same quarter will be thought, when we shall have received further lessons from that best oracle of wisdom, experience. It at all times betrayed an ignorance of the true springs by which human conduct is actuated, and belief the original inducements to the establishment of civil power. Why has government been instituted at all? Because the passions of men will not conform to the dictates of reason and justice, without constraint. Has it been found that bodies of men act with more rectitude or greater disinterestedness than individuals? The contrary of this has been inferred by all accurate observers of the conduct of mankind; and the inference is founded upon obvious reasons. Regard to reputation has a less active influence, when the infamy of a bad action is to be divided among a number, than when it is to fall singly upon one. A spirit of faction, which is apt to mingle its poison in the deliberations of all bodies of men, will often hurry the persons of whom they are composed into improprieties and excesses, for which they would blush in a private capacity.

In addition to all this, there is, in the nature of sovereign power, an impatience of control, that disposes those who are invested with the exercise of it, to look with an evil eye upon all external attempts to restrain or direct its operations. From this spirit it happens, that in every political association which is formed upon the principle of uniting in a common interest a number of lesser sovereignties, there will be found a kind of eccentric tendency in the subordinate or inferior orbs, by the operation of which these will be a perpetual effort in each to fly off from the common centre. This tendency is not difficult to be accounted for. It has its origin in the love of power. Power controlled or abridged is almost always the rival and enemy of that power by which it is controlled or abridged. This simple proposition will teach us, how little reason there is to expect, that the persons intrusted with the administration of the affairs of the particular members of a confederacy will at all times be ready, with perfect, good humor, and an unbiased regard to the public weal, to execute the resolutions or decrees of the general authority. The reverse of this results from the constitution of human nature.

If, therefore, the measures of the Confederacy cannot be executed without the intervention of the particular administrations, there will be little prospect of their being executed at all. The rulers of the respective members, whether they have a constitutional right to do it or not, will undertake to judge of the propriety of the measures themselves. They will consider the conformity of the thing proposed or required to their immediate interests or aims; the momentary conveniences or inconveniences that would attend its adoption. All this will be done; and in a spirit of interested and suspicious scrutiny, without that knowledge of national circumstances and reasons of state, which is essential to a right judgment, and with that strong predilection in favor of local objects which can hardly fail to mislead the decision. The same process must be repeated in every member of which the body is constituted; and the execution of the plans, framed by the councils of the whole, will always fluctuate on the discretion of the ill-informed and prejudiced opinion of every part. Those who have been conversant in the proceedings of popular assemblies; who have seen how difficult it often is, where there is no exterior pressure of circumstances, to bring them to harmonious resolutions on important points, will readily conceive how impossible it must be to induce a number of such assemblies, deliberating at a distance from each other, at different times, and under different impressions, long to cooperate in the same views and pursuits.

In our case, the concurrence of thirteen distinct sovereign wills is requisite, under the Confederation, to the complete execution of every important measure that proceeds from the Union. It has happened as was to have been foreseen. The measures of the Union have not been executed; the delinquencies of the States have, step by step matured themselves to an extreme, which has, at length, arrested all the wheels of the national government, and brought them to an awful stand. Congress at this time scarcely possess the means of keeping up the forms of administration, till the States can have time to agree upon a more substantial substitute for the present shadow of a federal government. Things did not come to this desperate extremity at once. The causes which have been specified produced at first only unequal and disproportionate degrees of compliance with the requisitions of the Union. The greater deficiencies of some States furnished the pretext of example and the temptation of interest to the complying, or to the least delinquent States. Why should we do more in proportion than those who are embarked with us in the same political voyage? Why should we consent to bear more than our proper share of the common burden? These were suggestions which human selfishness could not withstand, and which even speculative men, who looked forward to remote conse-

quences, could not, without hesitation, combat. Each State, yielding to the persuasive voice of immediate interest or convenience, has successively withdrawn its support till the frail and tottering edifice seems ready to fall upon our heads, and to crush us beneath its ruins.

PUBLIUS

The Federalist No. 16

. . . Even in those confederacies which have been composed of members smaller than many of our counties, the principle of legislation for sovereign States, supported by military coercion, has never been found effectual. It has rarely been attempted to be employed, but against the weaker members; and in most instances attempts to coerce the refractory and disobedient have been the signals of bloody wars, in which one half of the confederacy has displayed its banners against the other half.

The result of these observations to an intelligent mind must be clearly this, that if it be possible at any rate to construct a federal government capable of regulating the common concerns and preserving the general tranquillity, it must be founded, as to the objects committed to its care, upon the reverse of the principle contended for by the opponents of the proposed Constitution. It must carry its agency to the persons of the citizens. It must stand in need of no intermediate legislations; but must itself be empowered to employ the arm of the ordinary magistrate to execute its own resolutions. The majesty of the national authority must be manifested through the medium of the courts of justice. The government of the Union, like that of each State, must be able to address itself immediately to the hopes and fears of individuals; and to attract to its support those passions which have the strongest influence upon the human heart. It must, in short, possess all the means, and have a right to resort to all the methods, of executing the powers with which it is entrusted, that are possessed and exercised by the governments of the particular States.

To this reasoning it may perhaps be objected, that if any State should be disaffected to the authority of the Union, it could at any time obstruct the execution of its laws, and bring the matter to the same issue of force, with the necessity of which the opposite scheme is reproached.

The plausibility of this objection will vanish the moment we advert to the essential difference between a mere NON-COMPLIANCE and a DIRECT and ACTIVE RESISTANCE. If the interposition of the State legislatures be necessary to give effect to a measure of the Union, they have only NOT TO ACT, or to ACT EVASIVELY, and the measure is defeated. This neglect of duty may be disguised under affected but unsubstantial provisions, so as not to appear, and of course not to excite any alarm in the people for the safety of the Constitution. The State leaders may even make a merit of their surreptitious invasions of it on the ground of some temporary convenience, exemption, or advantage.

But if the execution of the laws of the national government should not require the intervention of the State legislatures, if they were to pass into immediate operation upon the citizens themselves, the particular governments could not interrupt their progress without an open and violent exertion of an unconstitutional power. No omission nor evasions would answer the end. They would be obliged to act, and in such a manner as would leave no doubt that they had encroached on the national rights. An experiment of this nature would always be hazardous in the fact of a constitution in any degree competent to its own defence, and of a people

enlightened enough to distinguish between a legal exercise and an illegal usurpation of authority. The success of it would require not merely a factious majority in the legislature, but the concurrence of the courts of justice and of the body of the people. If the judges were not embarked in a conspiracy with the legislature, they would pronounce the resolutions of such a majority to be contrary to the supreme law of the land, unconstitutional, and void. If the people were not tainted with the spirit of their State representatives, they, as the natural guardians of the Constitution, would throw their weight into the national scale and give it a decided preponderancy in the contest. Attempts of this kind would not often be made with levity or rashness, because they could seldom be made without danger to the authors, unless in cases of a tyrannical exercise of the federal authority.

If opposition to the national government should arise from the disorderly conduct of refractory or seditious individuals, it could be overcome by the same means which are daily employed against the same evil under the State governments. The magistracy, being equally the ministers of the law of the land, from whatever source it might emanate, would doubtless be as ready to guard the national as the local regulations from the inroads of private licentiousness. As to those partial commotions and insurrections, which sometimes disquiet society, from the intrigues of an inconsiderable faction, or from sudden or occasional ill-humors that do not infect the great body of the community, the general government could command more extensive resources for the suppression of disturbances of that kind than would be in the power of any single member. And as to those mortal feuds, which, in certain conjunctures, spread a conflagration through a whole nation, or through a very large proportion of it, proceeding either from weighty causes of discontent given by the government or from the contagion of some violent popular paroxysm, they do not fall within any ordinary rules of calculation. When they happen, they commonly amount to the revolutions and dismemberments of empire. No form of government can always either avoid or control them. It is in vain to hope to guard against events too mighty for human foresight or precaution, and it would be idle to object to a government because it could not perform impossibilities.

PUBLIUS

The Federalist No. 21

To the People of the State of New York:

Having in the three last numbers taken a summary review of the principal circumstances and events which have depicted the genius and fate of other confederate governments, I shall now proceed in the enumeration of the most important of those defects which have hitherto disappointed our hopes from the system established among ourselves. To form a safe and satisfactory judgment of the proper remedy, it is absolutely necessary that we should be well acquainted with the extent and malignity of the disease.

The next most palpable defect of the subsisting Confederation is the total want of a SANCTION to its laws. The United States, as now composed, have no powers to exact obedience, or punish disobedience to their resolutions, either by pecuniary mulcts, by a suspension or divesture of privileges, or by any other constitutional mode. These is no express delegation of authority to them to use force against delinquent members; and if such a right should be ascribed to the federal head, as resulting from the nature of the social compact between the States, it must be by inference and construction, in the face of that part of the second article, by which it is declared, "that each State shall retain every power, jurisdiction and right, not *expressly* delegated to the United States in Congress assembled." There is, doubtless, a striking absurdity in supposing that a right of this kind does not exist, but we are reduced to the dilemma either by embracing that supposition, preposterous as it may seem, or of contravening or explaining away a provision, which has been of late a repeated theme of the eulogies of those who oppose the new Constitution; and the want of which, in that plan, has been the subject of much plausible animadversion, and severe criticism. If we are unwilling to impair the force of this applauded provision, we shall be obliged to conclude, that the United States afford the extraordinary spectacle of a government destitute even of the shadow of constitutional power to enforce the execution of its own laws. It will appear, from the specimens which have been cited, that the American Confederacy, in this particular, stands discriminated from every other institution of a similar kind, and exhibits a new and unexampled phenomenon in the political world.

The want of a mutual guaranty of the State government is another capital imperfection in the federal plan. There is nothing of this kind declared in the articles that compose it; and to imply a tacit guaranty from considerations of utility, would be a still more flagrant departure from the clause which has been mentioned, than to imply a tacit power of coercion from the like considerations. The want of a guaranty, though it might in its consequences endanger the Union, does not so immediately attack its existence as the want of a constitutional sanction of its laws.

Without a guaranty the assistance to be derived from the Union in repelling those domestic dangers which may sometimes threaten the existence of the State constitutions, must be renounced. Usurpation may rear its crest in each State, and trample upon the liberties of the people, while the national government could legally do nothing more than behold its encroachments with indignation and regret. A successful faction may erect a tyranny on the ruins of order and law, while no succor could constitutionally be afforded by the Union to the friends and supporters of the government. The tempestuous situation from which Massachusetts has scarcely emerged, evinces that dangers of this kind are not merely speculative. Who can determine what might have been the issue of her late convulsions, if the malcontents had been headed by a Caesar or by a Cromwell? Who can predict what effect a despotism, established in Massachusetts, would have upon the liberties of New Hampshire or Rhode Island, of Connecticut or New York?

The inordinate pride of State importance has suggested to some minds an objection to the principle of a guaranty in the federal government, as involving an officious interference in the domestic concerns of the members. A scruple of this kind would deprive us of one of the principal advantages to be expected from unions, and can only flow from a misapprehension of the nature of the provision itself. It could be no impediment to reforms of the State constitutions by a majority of the people in a legal and peaceable mode. This right would remain undiminished. The guaranty could only operate against changes to be effected by violence. Towards the preventions of calamities of this kind, too many checks cannot be provided. The peace of society and the stability of government depend absolutely on the efficacy of the precautions adopted on this head. Where the whole power of the government is in the hands of the people, there is the less pretence for the use of violent remedies in partial or occasional distempers of the State. The natural cure for an ill administration, in a popular or representative constitution, is a change of men. A guaranty by the national authority would be as much levelled against the usurpations

of rulers as against the ferments and outrages of faction and sedition in the community.

The principle of regulating the contributions of the States to the common treasury by QUOTAS is another fundamental error in the Confederation. Its repugnancy to an adequate supply of the national exigencies has been already pointed out, and has sufficiently appeared from the trial which has been made of it. I speak of it now solely with a view to equality among the States. Those who have been accustomed to contemplate the circumstances which produce and constitute national wealth, must be satisfied that there is no common standard or barometer by which the degrees of it can be ascertained. Neither the value of lands, nor the numbers of the people, which have been successively proposed as the rule of State contributions, has any pretension to being a just representative. If we compare the wealth of the United Netherlands with that of Russia or Germany, or even of France, and if we at the same time compare the total value of the lands and the aggregate population of that contracted district with the total value of the aggregate population of the immense regions of either of the three last-mentioned countries, we shall at once discover that there is no comparison between the proportion of either of these two objects and that of the relative wealth of those nations. If the like parallel were to be run between several of the American States, it would furnish a like result. Let Virginia be contrasted with North Carolina, Pennsylvania with Connecticut, or Maryland with New Jersey, and we shall be convinced that the respective abilities of those States, in relation to revenue, bear little or no analogy to their comparative stock in lands or to their comparative population. The position may be equally illustrated by a similar process between the counties of the same State. No man who is acquainted with the State of New York will doubt that the active wealth of

King's County bears a much greater proportion to that of Montgomery than it would appear to be if we should take either the total value of the lands or the total number of the people as a criterion!

The wealth of nations depends upon an infinite variety of causes. Situation, soil, climate, the nature of the productions, the nature of the government, the genius of the citizens, the degree of information they possess, the state of commerce, of arts, of industry,—these circumstances and many more, too complex, minute, or adventitious to admit of a particular specification, occasion differences hardly conceivable in the relative opulence and riches of different countries. The consequence clearly is that there can be no common measure of national wealth, and, of course, no general or stationary rule by which the ability of a state to pay taxes can be determined. The attempt, therefore, to regulate the contributions of the members of a confederacy by any such rule, cannot fail to be productive of glaring inequality and extreme oppression.

This inequality would of itself be sufficient in America to work the eventual destruction of the Union, if any mode of enforcing a compliance with its requisitions could be devised. The suffering States would not long consent to remain associated upon a principle which distributes the public burdens with so unequal a hand, and which was calculated to impoverish and oppress the citizens of some States, while those of others would scarcely be conscious of the small proportion of the weight they were required to sustain. This, however, is an evil inseparable from the principle of quotas and requisitions.

There is no method of steering clear of this inconvenience, but by authorizing the national government to raise its own revenues in its own way. Imposts, excises, and, in general, all duties upon articles of consumption, may be compared to a fluid, which will, in time, find its level with the means of paying them. The amount to be contributed by each citizen will in a degree be at his own option, and can be regulated by an attention to his resources. The rich may be extravagant, the poor can be frugal; and private oppression may always be avoided by a judicious selection of objects proper for such impositions. If inequalities should arise in some States from duties on particular objects, these will, in all probability, be counterbalanced by proportional inequalities in other States, from the duties on other objects. In the course of time and things, an equilibrium, as far as it is attainable in so complicated a subject, will be established everywhere. Or, if inequalities should still exist, they would neither be so great in their degree, so uniform in their operation, nor so odious in their appearance, as those which would necessarily spring from quotas, upon any scale that can possibly be devised.

It is a signal advantage of taxes on articles of consumption, that they contain in their own nature a security against excess. They prescribe their own limit; which cannot be exceeded without defeating the end proposed,—that is, an extension of the revenue. When applied to this object, the saying is as just as it is witty, that, "in political arithmetic, two and two do not always make four." If duties are too high, they lessen the consumption; the collection is eluded; and the product to the treasury is not so great as when they are confined within proper and moderate bounds. This forms a complete barrier against any material oppression of the citizens by taxes of this class, and is itself a natural limitation of the power of imposing them.

Impositions of this kind usually fall under the denomination of indirect taxes, and must for a long time constitute the chief part of the revenue raised in this country. Those of the direct kind, which principally relate to land and buildings, may admit of a rule of apportionment. Either the value of land, or the number of the people, may serve as a standard. The state of agriculture and the populousness of a country have been considered as nearly connected with each other. And, as a rule, for the purpose intended, numbers, in the view of simplicity and certainty, are entitled to the preference. In every country it is a herculean task to obtain a valuation of the land; in a country imperfectly settled and progressive in improvement, the difficulties are increased almost to impracticability. The expense of an accurate valuation is, in all situations, a formidable objection. In a branch of taxation where no limits to the discretion of the government are to be found in the nature of things, the establishment of a fixed rule, not incompatible with the end, may be attended with fewer inconveniences than to leave that discretion altogether at large.

PUBLIUS

The Federalist No. 22

To the People of the State of New York:

In addition to the defects already enumerated in the existing federal system, there are others of not less importance, which concur in rendering it altogether unfit for the administration of the affairs of the Union.

The want of a power to regulate commerce is by all parties allowed to be of the number. The utility of such a power has been anticipated under the first head of our inquiries; and for this reason, as well as from the universal conviction entertained upon the subject little need be added in this place. It is indeed evident, on the most superficial view, that there is no object, either as it respects the interest of trade, or finance, that more strongly demands a federal superintendence. The want of it has already operated as a bar to the formation of beneficial treaties with foreign powers, and has given occasions of dissatisfaction between the States. No nation acquainted with the nature of our political association would be unwise enough to enter into stipulations with the United States, by which they conceded privileges of any importance to them, while they were apprised that the engagements on the part of the Union might at any moment be violated by its members, and while they found from experience that they might enjoy every advantage they desired in our markets, without granting us any return but such as their momentary convenience might suggest. It is not, therefore, to be wondered at that Mr. Jenkinson, in ushering into the House of Commons a bill for regulating the temporary intercourse between the two countries, should preface its introduction by a declaration that similar provisions in former bills had been found to answer every purpose to the commerce of Great Britain, and that it would be prudent to persist in the plan until it should appear whether the American government was likely or not to acquire greater consistency.

Several States have endeavored, by separate prohibitions, restricts, and exclusions, to influence the conduct of that kingdom in this particular, but the want of concert, arising from the want of a general authority and from clashing and dissimilar views in the State, has hitherto frustrated every experiment of the kind, and will continue to do so as long as the same obstacles to a uniformity of measures continue to exist.

The interfering and unneighborly regulations of some States, contrary to the true spirit of the Union, have, in different instances, given just cause of umbrage and complaint to others, and it is to be feared that examples of this nature, if not restrained by a national control, would be multiplied and extended till they became not less serious sources of animosity and discord than injurious impediments to the intercourse between the different parts of the Confederacy. "The commerce of the German empire is in continual trammels from the multiplicity of the duties which the several princes and states exact upon the merchandises passing through their territories, by means of which the fine streams and navigable rivers with which Germany is so happily watered are rendered almost useless." Though the genius of the people of this country might never permit this description to be strictly applicable to us, yet we may reasonably expect, from the gradual conflicts of State regulations, that the citizens of each would at length come to be considered and treated by the others in no better light than that of foreigners and aliens.

The power of raising armies by the most obvious construction of the articles of the Confederation, is merely a power of making requisitions upon the States for quotas of men. This practice, in the course of the late war, was found replete with obstructions to a vigorous and to an economical system of defence. It gave birth to a competition between the States which created a kind of auction for men. In order to furnish the quotas required of them, they outbid each other till bounties grew to an enormous and insupportable size. The hope of a still further increase afforded an inducement to those who were disposed to serve to procrastinate their enlistment, and disinclined them from engaging for any considerable periods. Hence, slow and scanty levies of men, in the most critical emergencies of our affairs; short enlistments at an unparalleled expense; continual fluctuations in the troops, ruinous to their discipline and subjecting the public safety frequently to the perilous crisis of a disbanded army. Hence, also those oppressive expedients for raising men which were upon several occasions practised, and which nothing but the enthusiasm of liberty would have induced the people to endure.

This method of raising troops is not more unfriendly to economy and vigor than it is to an equal distribution of the burden. The States near the seat of war, influenced by motives of self-preservation, made efforts to furnish their quotas, which even exceeded their abilities; while those at a distance from danger were, for the most part, as remiss as the others were diligent, in their exertions. The immediate pressure of this inequality was not in this case, as in that of the contributions of money, alleviated by the hope of a final liquidation. The States which did not pay their proportions of money might at least be charged with their deficiencies; but no account could be formed of the deficiencies; but no account could be formed of the deficiencies in the supplies of men. We shall not, however, see much reason to regret the want of this hope, when we consider how little prospect there is, that the most delinquent States will ever be able to make compensation for their pecuniary failures. The system of quotas and requisitions, whether it be applied to men or money, is, in every view, a system of imbecility in the Union, and of inequality and injustice among the members.

The right of equal suffrage among the States is another exceptionable part of the Confederation. Every idea of proportion and every rule of fair representation conspire to condemn a principle, which gives to Rhode Island an equal weight in the scale of power with Massachusetts, or Connecticut, or New York; and to Delaware an equal voice in the national deliberations with Pennsylvania, or Virginia, or North Carolina. Its operation contradicts the fundamental maxim of republican government, which requires that the sense of the majority should prevail. Sophistry may reply, that sovereigns are equal, and that a majority of the votes of the States will be a majority of confederated America. But this kind of logical legerdemain will never counteract the plain suggestions of justice and commonsense. It may happen that this majority of States is a small minority of the people of America; and two thirds of the people of America could not long be persuaded, upon the credit of artificial distinction and syllogistic subtleties to submit their interests to the management and disposal of one third. The larger States would after a while revolt from the idea of receiving the law from the smaller. To acquiesce in such a privation of their due importance in the political scale, would be not merely to be insensible to the love of power, but even to sacrifice the desire of equality. It is neither rational to expect the first, nor just to require the last. The smaller states, considering how peculiarly their safety and welfare depend on union, ought readily to renounced a pretension which, if not relinquished, would prove fatal to its duration.

It may be objected to this, that not seven but nine States, or two thirds of the whole number, must consent to the most important resolutions; and it may be thence inferred, that nine States would always comprehend a majority of the Union. But this does not obviate the impropriety of an equal vote between States of the most unequal dimensions and populousness; nor is the inference accurate in point of fact; for we can enumerate nine States which contain less than a majority of the people; and it is constitutionally possible that these nine may give the vote. Besides, there are matters of considerable moment determinable by a bare majority; and there are others, concerning which doubts have been entertained, which, if interpreted in favor of the sufficiency of a vote of seven States, would extend its operation to interests of the first magnitude. In addition to this, it is to be observed that there is a probability of an increase in the number of States, and no provision for a proportional augmentation of the ratio of votes.

But this is not all; what at first sight may seem a remedy, is, in reality, a poison. To give a minority a negative upon the majority (which is always the case where more than a majority is requisite to a decision), is, in its tendency, to subject the sense of the greater number to that of the lesser. Congress,

from the nonattendance of a few States, have been frequently in the situation of a Polish diet, where a single VOTE has been sufficient to put a stop to all their movements. A sixtieth part of the Union, which is about the proportion of Delaware and Rhode Island, has several times been able to oppose an entire bar to its operations. This is one of those refinements which, in practice, has an effect the reverse of what is expected from it in theory. The necessity of unanimity in public bodies, or of something approaching towards it, has been founded upon a supposition that it would contribute to security. But its real operation is to embarrass the administration, to destroy the energy of the government, and to substitute the pleasure, caprice, or artifices of an insignificant, turbulent, or corrupt junto, to the regular deliberations and decisions of a respectable majority. In those emergencies of a nation, in which the goodness or badness, the weakness or strength of its government, is of the greatest importance, there is commonly a necessity for action. The public business must, in some way or other, go forward. If a pertinacious minority can control the opinion of a majority, respecting the best mode of conducting it, the majority, in order that something may be done, must conform to the views of the minority; and thus the sense of the smaller number will overrule that of the greater, and give a tone to the national proceedings. Hence, tedious delays; continual negotiation and intrigue; contemptible compromises of the public good. And yet, in such a system, it is even happy when such compromises can take place: for upon some occasions things will not admit of accommodation; and then the measures of government must be injuriously suspended, or fatally defeated. It is often, by the impracticability of obtaining the concurrence of the necessary number of votes, kept in a state of inaction. Its situation must always savor of weakness, sometimes border upon anarchy.

It is not difficult to discover, that a principle of this kind gives greater scope to foreign corruption, as well as to domestic faction, than that which permits the sense of the majority to decide; though the contrary of this has been presumed. The mistake has proceeded from not attending with due care to the mischiefs that may be occasioned by obstructing the progress of government at certain critical seasons. When the concurrence of a large number is required by the Constitution to the doing of any national act, we are apt to rest satisfied that all is safe, because nothing improper will be likely *to be done;* but we forget how much good may be prevented, and how much ill may be produced, by the power of hindering the doing what may be necessary, and of keeping affairs in the same unfavorable posture in which they may happen to stand at particular periods.

Suppose, for instance, we were engaged in a war, in conjunction with one foreign nation, against another. Suppose the necessity of our situation demanded peace, and the interest or ambition of our ally led him to seek the prosecution of war, with views that might justify us in making separate terms. In such a state of things, this ally of ours would evidently find it much easier, by his bribes and intrigues, to tie up the hands of government from making peace, where two thirds of all the votes were requisite to that object, than were a simple majority would suffice. In the first case, he would have to corrupt a smaller number; in the last, a greater number. Upon the same principle, it would be much easier for a foreign power with which we were at war to perplex our councils and embarrass our exertions. And, in a commercial view, we may be subjected to similar inconveniences. A nation, with which we might have a treaty of commerce, could with much greater facility prevent our forming a connection with her competitor in trade, though such a connec-tion should be ever so beneficial to ourselves.

Evils of this description ought not to be regarded as imaginary. One of the weak sides of republics, among their numerous advantages, is that they afford too easy an inlet to foreign corruption. An hereditary monarch, though often disposed to sacrifice his subjects to his ambition, has so great a personal interest in the government and in the external glory of the nation, that it is not easy for a foreign power to give him the equivalent for what he would sacrifice by treachery to the state. The world has accordingly been witness to few examples of this species of royal prostitution, though there have been abundant specimens of every other kind.

In republics, persons elevated from the mass of the community, by the suffrages of their fellow-citizens, to stations of great pre-eminence and power, may find compensations for betraying their trust, which, to any but minds animated and guided by superior virtue, may appear to exceed the proportion of interest they have in the common stock, and to overbalance the obligations of duty. Hence it is that history furnishes us with so many mortifying examples of the prevalency of foreign corruption in republican governments. How much this contributed to the ruin of the ancient commonwealths has been already delineated. It is well known that the deputies of the United Provinces have, in various instances, been purchased by the emissaries of the neighboring kingdoms. The Earl of Chesterfield (if my memory serves me right), in a letter to his court, intimates that his success in an important negotiation must depend on his obtaining a major's commission for one of those deputies. And in Sweden the parties were alternately bought by France and England in so barefaced and notorious a manner that it excited universal disgust in the nation, and was a principal cause that the most limited monarch in Europe, in a single day, without tumult, violence, or opposition, became one of the most absolute and uncontrolled.

A circumstance which crowns the defects of the Confederation remains yet to be mentioned,—the want of a judiciary power. Laws are a dead letter without courts to expound and define their true meaning and operation. The treaties of the United States, to have any force at all, must be considered as part of the law of the land. Their true import, as far as respects individuals, must, like all other laws, be ascertained by judicial determinations. To produce uniformity in these determinations, they ought to be submitted, in the last resort to one SUPREME TRIBUNAL. And this tribunal ought to be instituted under the same authority which forms the treaties themselves. These ingredients are both indispensable. If there is in each State a court of final jurisdiction, there may be as many different final determinations on the same point as there are courts. There are endless diversities in the opinions of men. We often see not only different courts but the judges of the same court differing from each other. To avoid the confusion which would unavoidably result from the contradictory decisions of a number of independent judicatories, all nations have found it necessary to establish one court paramount to the rest, possessing a general superintendence, and authorized to settle and declare in the last resort a uniform rule of civil justice.

This is the more necessary where the frame of the government is so compounded that the laws of the whole are in danger of being contravened by the laws of the parts. In this case, if the particular tribunals are invested with a right of ultimate jurisdiction, besides the contradictions to be expected from differences of opinion there will be much to fear from the bias of local views and prejudices, and from the interference of local regulations. As often as such an interference was to happen, there would be reason to apprehend that the provisions of the particular laws

might be preferred to those of the general laws; for nothing is more natural to men in office than to look with peculiar deference towards that authority to which they owe their official existence. The treaties of the United States, under the present Constitution, are liable to the infractions of thirteen different legislatures, and as many different courts of final jurisdiction, acting under the authority of those legislatures. The faith, the reputation, the peace of the whole Union, are thus continually at the mercy of the prejudices, the passions, and the interests of every member of which it is composed. Is it possible that foreign nations can either respect or confide in such a government? Is it possible that the people of America will longer consent to trust their honor, their happiness, their safety, on so precarious a foundation?

In this review of the Confederation, I have confined myself to the exhibition of its most material defects; passing over those imperfections in its details by which even a great part of the power intended to be conferred upon it has been in a great measure rendered abortive. It must be, by this time evident to all men of reflection, who can divest themselves of the prepossessions of preconceived opinions, that it is a system so radically vicious and unsound, as to admit not of amendment but by an entire change in its leading features and characters.

The organization of Congress is itself utterly improper for the exercise of those powers which are necessary to be deposited in the Union. A single assembly may be a proper receptacle of those slender, or rather fettered, authorities, which have been heretofore delegated to the federal head; but it would be inconsistent with all the principles of good government, to intrust it with those additional powers which, even the moderate and more rational adversaries of the proposed Constitution admit, ought to reside in the United States. If that plan should be able to withstand the ambitious aims of those men who may indulge magnificent schemes of personal aggrandizement from its dissolution, the probability would be, that we should run into the project of conferring supplementary powers upon Congress, as they are now constituted; and either the machine, from the intrinsic feebleness of its structure, will moulder into pieces, in spite of our ill-judged efforts to prop it; or, by successive augmentations of its force and energy, as necessity might prompt, we shall finally accumulate, in a single body, all the most important prerogatives of sovereignty, and thus entail upon our posterity one of the most execrable forms of government that human infatuation ever contrived. Thus we should create in reality that very tyranny which the adversaries of the new Constitution either are, or affect to be, solicitous to avert.

It has not a little contributed to the infirmities of the existing federal system, that it never had a ratification by the PEOPLE. Resting on no better foundation than the consent of the several legislatures, it has been exposed to frequent and intricate questions concerning the validity of its powers, and has, in some instances, given birth to the enormous doctrine of a right of legislative repeal. Owing its ratification to the law of a State, it has been contended that the same authority might repeal the law by which it was ratified. However gross a heresy it may be to maintain that a *party* to a *compact* has a right to revoke that *compact,* the doctrine itself has had respectable advocates. The possibility of a question of this nature proves the necessity of laying the foundations of our national government deeper than in the mere sanction of delegated authority. The fabric of American empire ought to rest on the solid basis of THE CONSENT OF THE PEOPLE. The streams of national power ought to flow immediately from that pure, original fountain of all legitimate authority.

PUBLIUS

The Federalist No. 23

To the People of the State of New York:

The necessity of a Constitution, at least equally energetic with the one proposed, to the preservation of the Union, is the point at the examination of which we are now arrived.

This inquiry will naturally divide itself into three branches—the objects to be provided for by the federal government, the quantity of power necessary to the accomplishment of those objects, the persons upon whom that power ought to operate. Its distribution and organization will more properly claim our attention under the succeeding head.

The principal purposes to be answered by union are these—the common defence of the members; the preservation of the public peace, as well against internal convulsions as external attacks; the regulation of commerce with other nations and between the States; the superintendence of our intercourse, political and commercial, with foreign countries.

The authorities essential to the common defence are these: to raise armies; to build and equip fleets; to prescribe rules for the government of both; to direct their operations; to provide for their support. These powers ought to exist without limitation, *because it is impossible to foresee or define the extent and variety of national exigencies, or the correspondent extent and variety of the means which may be necessary to satisfy them.* The circumstances that endanger the safety of nations are infinite, and for this reason no constitutional shackles can wisely be imposed on the power to which the care of it is committed. This power ought to be co-extensive with all the possible combinations of such circumstances; and ought to be under the direction of the same councils which are appointed to preside over the common defence.

This is one of those truths which, to a correct and unprejudiced mind, carries its own evidence along with it; and may be obscured, but cannot be made plainer by argument or reasoning. It rests upon axioms as simple as they are universal; the *means* ought to be proportioned to the *end;* the persons, from whose agency the attainment of any *end* is expected, ought to possess the *means* by which it is to be attained.

Whether there ought to be a federal government intrusted with the care of the common defence, is a question in the first instance, open for discussion; but the moment it is decided in the affirmative, it will follow, that that government ought to be clothed with all the powers requisite to complete execution of its trust. And unless it can be shown that the circumstances which may affect the public safety are reducible within certain determinate limits; unless the contrary of this position can be fairly and rationally disputed, it must be admitted, as a necessary consequence that there can be no limitation of that authority which is to provide for the defence and protection of the community, in any matter essential to its efficacy—that is, in any matter essential to the *formation, direction* or *support* of the NATIONAL FORCES.

Defective as the present Confederation has been proved to be, this principle appears to have been fully recognized by the framers of it; though they have not made proper or adequate provision for its exercise. Congress have an unlimited discretion to make requisitions of men and money; to govern the army and the navy; to direct their operations. As their requisitions are made constitutionally binding upon the States, who are in fact under the most solemn obligations to furnish the supplies required of them, the intention evidently was, that the United States should command whatever resources were by them judged requisite to the "common defence and general welfare." It was presumed that a sense of their true interests, and a regard to the dictates of good faith, would be found sufficient pledges for the punctual performance of the

duty of the members to the federal head.

The experiment has, however, demonstrated that this expectation was ill-founded and illusory; and the observations, made under the last head, will, I imagine, have sufficed to convince the impartial and discerning, that there is an absolute necessity for an entire change in the first principles of the system; that if we are in earnest about giving the Union energy and duration, we must abandon the vain project of legislating upon the States in their collective capacities; we must extent the laws of the federal government to the individual citizens of America; we must discard the fallacious scheme of quotas and requisitions, as equally impracticable and unjust. The result from all this is that the Union ought to be invested with full power to levy troops; to build and equip fleets; and to raise the revenues which will be required for the formation and support of an army and navy, in the customary and ordinary modes practised in other governments.

If the circumstances of our country are such as to demand a compound instead of a simple, a confederate instead of a sole, government, the essential point which will remain to be adjusted will be to discriminate the OBJECTS, as far as it can be done, which shall appertain to the different provinces or departments of power; allowing to each the most ample authority for fulfilling the objects committed to its charge. Shall the Union be constituted the guardian of the common safety? Are fleets and armies the guardian of the common safety? Are fleets and armies and revenues necessary to this purpose? The government of the Union must be empowered to pass all laws, and to make all regulations which have relation to them. The same must be the case in respect to commerce, and to every other matter to which its jurisdiction is permitted to extend. Is the administration of justice between the citizens of the same State the proper department of the local governments? These must possess all the authorities which are connected with this object, and with every other that may be allotted to their particular cognizance and direction. Not to confer in each case a degree of power commensurate to the end, would be to violate the most obvious rules of prudence and propriety, and improvidently to trust the great interests of the nation to hands which are disabled from managing them with vigor and success.

Who so likely to make suitable provisions for the public defence, as that body to which the guardianship of the public safety is confided; which, as the centre of information, will best understand the extent and urgency of the dangers that threaten; as the representative of the WHOLE, will feel itself most deeply interested in the preservation of every part; which, from the responsibility implied in the duty assigned to it, will be most sensibly impressed with the necessity of proper exertions; and which, by the extension of its authority throughout the States, can alone establish uniformity and concert in the plans and measures by which the common safety is to be secured? Is there not a manifest inconsistency in devolving upon the federal government the care of the general defense, and leaving in the State governments the *effective* powers by which it is to be provided for? Is not a want of cooperation the infallible consequence of such a system? And will not weakness, disorder, and undue distribution of the burdens and calamities of war, an unnecessary and intolerable increase of expense, be its natural and inevitable concomitants? Have we not had unequivocal experience of its effects in the course of the revolution which we have just accomplished?

Every view we may take of the subject, as candid inquirers after truth, will serve to convince us, that it is both unwise and dangerous to deny the federal government an unconfined authority, as to all those objects which are intrusted to its management. It will indeed deserve the most vigilant and careful attention of the people, to see that it be modelled in such a manner as to admit of its being safely vested with the requisite powers. If any plan which has been, or may be, offered to our consideration, should not, upon a dispassionate inspection, be found to answer this description, it ought to be rejected. A government, the constitution of which renders it unfit to be trusted with all the powers which a free people *ought to delegate to any government*, would be an unsafe and improper depositary of the NATIONAL INTERESTS. Wherever THESE can with propriety be confided, the coincident powers may safely accompany them. This is the true result of all just reasoning upon the subject. And the adversaries of the plan promulgated by the convention ought to have confined themselves to showing, that the internal structure of the proposed government was such as to render it unworthy of the confidence of the people. They ought not to have wandered into inflamatory declamations and unmeaning cavils about the extent of the powers. The POWERS are not too extensive for the OBJECTS of federal administration, or, in other words, for the management of our NATIONAL INTERESTS; nor can any satisfactory argument be framed to show that they are chargeable with such an excess. If it be true, as has been insinuated by some of the writers on the other side, that the difficulty arises from the nature of the thing, and that the extent of the country will not permit us to form a government in which such ample powers can safely be reposed, it would prove that we ought to contract our views, and resort to the expedient of separate confederacies, which will move within more practicable spheres. For the absurdity must continually stare us in the face of confiding to a government the direction of the most essential national interests, without daring to trust it to the authorities which are indispensable to their proper and efficient management. Let us not attempt to reconcile contradictions, but firmly embrace a rational alternative.

I trust, however, that the impracticability of one general system cannot be shown. I am greatly mistaken, if any thing of weight has yet been advanced of this tendency; and I flatter myself that the observations which have been made in the course of these papers have served to place the reverse of that position in as clear a light as any matter still in the womb of time and experience can be susceptible of. This, at all events, must be evident, that the very difficulty itself, drawn from the extend of the country, is the strongest argument in favor of an energetic government; for any other can certainly never preserve the Union of so large an empire. If we embrace the tenets of those who oppose the adoption of the proposed Constitution, as the standard of our political creed, we cannot fail to verify the gloomy doctrines which predict the impracticability of a national system pervading entire limits of the present Confederacy.

PUBLIUS

The Federalist No. 78

To the People of the State of New York:

We proceed now to an examination of the judiciary department of the proposed government.

In unfolding the defects of the existing Confederation, the utility and necessity of a federal judicature have been clearly pointed out. It is the less necessary to recapitulate the considerations there urged, as the propriety of the institution in the abstract is not disputed; the only questions which have been raised being relative to the manner of constituting it, and to its extent. To

these points, therefore, our observations shall be confined.

The manner of constituting it seems to embrace these several objects: First, the mode of appointing the judges. Second, the tenure by which they are to hold their places. Third, the partition of the judiciary authority between different courts, and their relations to each other.

First. As to the mode of appointing the judges; this is the same with that of appointing the officers of the Union in general, and has been so fully discussed in the two last numbers, that nothing can be said here which would not be useless repetition.

Second. As to the tenure by which the judges are to hold their places; this chiefly concerns their duration in office; the provisions for their support; the precautions for their responsibility.

According to the plan of the convention, all judges who may be appointed by the United States are to hold their offices *during good behavior;* which is conformable to the most approved of the State constitutions, and among the rest, to that of this State. Its propriety having been drawn into question by the adversaries of that plan, is no light symptom of the rage for objection, which disorders their imaginations and judgments. The standard of good behavior for the continuance in office of the judicial magistracy, is certainly one of the most valuable of the modern improvements in the practice of government. In a monarchy it is an excellent barrier to the despotism of the prince; in a republic it is no less excellent barrier to the encroachments and oppressions of the representative body. And it is the best expedient which can be devised in any government, to secure a steady, upright, and impartial administration of the laws.

Whoever attentively considers the different departments of power must perceive, that, in a government in which they are separated from each other, the judiciary, from the nature of its functions, will always be the least dangerous to the political rights of the Constitution; because it will be least in a capacity to annoy or injure them. The Executive not only dispenses the honors, but holds the sword of the community. The legislature not only commands the purse, but prescribes the rules by which the duties and rights of every citizen are to be regulated. The judiciary, on the contrary, has no influence over either the sword or the purse; no direction either of the strength or of the wealth of the society; and can take no active resolution whatever. It may truly be said to have neither FORCE nor WILL, but merely judgment; and must ultimately depend upon the aid of the executive arm even for the efficacy of its judgments.

This simple view of the matter suggests several important consequences. It proves incontestably, that the judiciary is beyond comparison the weakest of the three departments of power; that it can never attack with success either of the other two; and that all possible care is requisite to enable it to defend itself against their attacks. It equally proves, that though individual oppression may now and then proceed from the courts of justice, the general liberty of the people can never be endangered from that quarter; I mean so long as the judiciary remains truly distinct from both the legislature and the Executive. For I agree, that "there is no liberty, if the power of judging be not separated from the legislative and executive powers." And it proves, in the last place, that as liberty can have nothing to fear from the judiciary alone, but would have every thing to fear from its union with either of the other departments; that as all the effects of such a union must ensue from a dependence of the former on the latter, notwithstanding a nominal and apparent separation; that as, from the natural feebleness of the judiciary, it is in continual jeopardy of being overpowered, awed, or influenced by its coordinate branches; and that as nothing can contribute to much to its firmness and independence as permanency in office, this quality may therefore be justly regarded as an indispensable ingredient in its constitution, and, in a great measure,

as the citadel of the public justice and the public security.

The complete independence of the courts of justice is peculiarly essential in a limited Constitution. By a limited Constitution, I understand one which contains certain specified exceptions to the legislative authority; such, for instance, as that it shall pass no bills of attainder, no *ex-post-facto* laws, and the like. Limitations of this kind can be preserved in practice no other way than through the medium of courts of justice, whose duty it must be to declare all acts contrary to the manifest tenor of the Constitution void. Without this, all the reservations of particular rights or privileges would amount to nothing.

Some perplexity respecting the rights of the courts to pronounce legislative acts void, because contrary to the constitution, has arisen from an imagination that the doctrine would imply a superiority of the judiciary to the legislative power. It is urged that the authority which can declare the acts of another void, must necessarily be superior to the one whose acts may be declared void. As this doctrine is of great importance in all the American constitutions, a brief discussion of the ground on which it rests cannot be unacceptable.

There is no position which depends on clearer principles, than that every act of a delegated authority, contrary to the tenor of the commission under which it is exercised, is void. No legislative act, therefore, contrary to the Constitution, can be valid. To deny this, would be to affirm, that the deputy is greater than his principal; that the servant is above his master; that the representatives of the people are superior to the people themselves; that men acting by virtue of powers, may do not only what their powers do not authorize, but what they forbid.

If it be said that the legislative body are themselves the constitutional judges of their own powers, and that the construction they put upon them is conclusive upon the other departments, it may be answered, that this cannot be the natural presumption, where it is not to be collected from any particular provisions in the Constitution. It is not otherwise to be supposed, that the Constitution could intend to enable the representatives of the people to substitute their *will* to that of their constituents. It is far more rational to suppose, that the courts were designed to be an intermediate body between the people and the legislature, in order, among other things, to keep the latter within the limits assigned to their authority. The interpretation of the laws is the proper and peculiar province of the courts. A constitution is, in fact, and must be regarded by the judges, as a fundamental law. It therefore belongs to them to ascertain its meaning, as well as the meaning of any particular act proceeding from the legislative body. If there should happen to be an irreconcilable variance between the two, that which has the superior obligation and validity ought, of course, to be preferred; or, in other words, the Constitution ought to be preferred to the statute, the intention of the people to the intention of their agents.

Nor does this conclusion by any means suppose a superiority of the judicial to the legislative power. It only supposes that the power of the people is superior to both; and that where the will of the legislature, declared in its statutes, stands in opposition to that of the people, declared in the Constitution, the judges ought to be governed by the latter rather than the former. They ought to regulate their decisions by the fundamental laws, rather than by those which are not fundamental.

This exercise of judicial discretion, in determining between two contradictory laws, is exemplified in a familiar instance. It not uncommonly happens, that there are two statutes existing at one time, clashing in whole or in part with each other, and neither of them containing any repealing clause or expression. In such a case, it is the province of the courts to liquidate and fix their meaning and operation. So far

as they can, by any fair construction, be reconciled to each other, reason and law conspire to dictate that this should be done; where this is impracticable, it becomes a matter of necessity to give effect to one, in exclusion of the other. The rule which has obtained in the courts for determining their relative validity is, that the last in order of time shall be preferred to the first. But this is a mere rule of construction, not derived from any positive law, but from the nature and reason of the thing. It is a rule not enjoined upon the courts by legislative provision, but adopted by themselves, as consonant to truth and propriety, for the direction of their conduct as interpreters of the law. They thought it reasonable, that between the interfering acts of an *equal* authority, that which was the last indication of its will should have the preference.

But in regard to the interfering acts of a superior and subordinate authority, of an original and derivative power, the nature and reason of the thing indicate the converse of that rule as proper to be followed. They teach us that the prior act of a superior ought to be preferred to be subsequent act of an inferior and subordinate authority; and that accordingly, whenever a particular statute contravenes the Constitution, it will be the duty of the judicial tribunals to adhere to the latter and disregard the former.

It can be of no weight to say that the courts, on the pretence of a repugnancy, may substitute their own pleasure to the constitutional intentions of the legislature. This might as well happen in the case of two contradictory statutes; or it might as well happen in every adjudication upon any single statute. The courts must declare the sense of the law; and if they should be disposed to exercise WILL instead of JUDGMENT, the consequence would equally be the substitution of their pleasure to that of the legislative body. The observation, if it prove any thing, would prove that there ought to be no judges distinct from that body.

If, then, the courts of justice are to be considered as the bulwarks of a limited Constitution against legislative encroachments, this consideration will afford a strong argument for the permanent tenure of judicial offices, since nothing will contribute so much as this to that independent spirit in the judges which must be essential to the faithful performance of so arduous a duty.

This independence of the judges is equally requisite to guard the Constitution and the rights of individuals from the effects of those ill humors, which the arts of designing men or the influence of particular conjectures, sometimes disseminate among the people themselves, and which, though they speedily give place to better information, and more deliberate reflection, have a tendency, in the meantime, to occasion dangerous innovations in the government, and serious oppressions of the minor party in the community. Though I trust the friends of the proposed Constitution will never concur with its enemies, in questioning that fundamental principle of republican government, which admits the rights of the people to alter or abolish the established Constitution, whenever they find it inconsistent with their happiness, yet it is not to be inferred from this principle, that the representatives of the people, whenever a momentary inclination happens to lay hold of a majority of their constituents, incompatible with the provisions in the existing Constitution, would, on that account, be justifiable, in a violation of those provisions; or that the courts would be under a greater obligation to connive at infractions in this shape, than when they had proceeded wholly from the cabals of the representative body. Until the people have, by some solemn and authoritative act, annulled or changed the established form, it is binding upon themselves collectively, as well as individually; and no presumption or, even knowledge, of their sentiments, can warrant their representatives in a departure from it, prior to such an act. But it is easy to see, that it would re-

quire an uncommon portion of fortitude in the judges to do their duty as faithful guardians of the Constitution, where legislative invasions of it had been instigated by the major voice of the community.

But it is not with a view to infractions of the Constitution only, that the independence of the judges may be an essential safeguard against the effects of occasional ill humors in the society. These sometimes extend no farther than to the injury of the private rights of particular classes of citizens, by unjust and partial laws. Here also the firmness of the judicial magistracy is of vast importance in mitigating the severity and confining the operation of such laws. It not only serves to moderate the immediate mischiefs of those which may have been passed but it operates as a check upon the legislative body in passing them; who, perceiving that obstacles to the success of iniquitious intention are to be expected from the scruples of the courts, are in a manner compelled by the very motives of the injustices they mediate, to qualify their attempts. This is a circumstance calculated to have more influence upon the character of our governments, than but few may be aware of. The benefits of the integrity and moderation of the judiciary have already been felt in more States than one; and though they may have displeased those whose sinister expectations they may have disappointed, they must have commanded the esteem and applause of all the virtuous and disinterested. Considerate men, of every description, ought to prize whatever will tend to beget or fortify that temper in the courts; as no man can be sure that he may not be tomorrow the victim of a spirit of injustice, by which he may be a gainer today. And every man must now feel, that the inevitable tendency of such a spirit is to sap the foundations of public and private confidence, and to introduce in its stead universal distrust and distress. '

That inflexible and uniform adherence to the rights of the Constitution, and of individuals, which we perceive to be indispensable in the courts of justice, can certainly not be expected from judges who hold their offices by a temporary commission. Periodical appointments, however regulated, or by whomsoever made, would, in some way or other, be fatal to their necessary independence. If the power of making them was committed either to the Executive or legislature, there would be danger of an improper complaisance to the branch which possessed it; if to both, there would be an unwillingness to hazard the displeasure of either; if to the people, or to persons chosen by them for the special purpose, there would be too great a disposition to consult popularity, to justify a reliance that nothing would be consulted but the Constitution and the laws.

There is yet a further and a weightier reason for the permanency of the judicial offices, which is deducible from the nature of the qualifications they require. It has been frequently remarked, with great propriety, that a voluminous code of laws is one of the inconveniences necessarily connected with the advantages of a free government.˙ To avoid an arbitrary discretion in the courts, it is indispensable that they should be bound down by strict rules and precedents, which serve to define and point out their duty in every particular case that comes before them; and it will readily be conceived from the variety of controversies which grow out of the folly and wickedness of mankind, that the records of those precedents must unavoidably swell to a very considerable bulk, and must demand long and laborious study to acquire a competent knowledge of them. Hence, it is, that there can be but few men in the society who will have sufficient skill in the laws to qualify them for the stations of judges. And making the proper deductions for the ordinary depravity of human nature, the number must be still smaller of those who unite the requisite integrity with the requisite knowledge. These considerations apprise us, that the government can have no great option

between fit character; and that a temporary duration in office, which would naturally discourage such characters from quitting a lucrative line of practice to accept a seat on the bench, would have a tendency to throw the administration of justice into hands less able, and less well qualified, to conduct it with utility and dignity. In the present circumstances of this country, and in those in which it is likely to be for a long time to come, the disadvantages on this score would be greater than they may at first sight appear; but it must be confessed, that they are far inferior to those which present themselves under the other aspects of the subject.

Upon the whole, there can be no room to doubt that the convention acted wisely in copying from the models of those constitutions which have established *good behavior* as the tenure of their judicial offices, in point of duration; and that so far from being blameable on this account, their plan would have been inexcusably defective, if it had wanted this important feature of good government. The experience of Great Britain affords an illustrious comment on the excellence of the institution.

PUBLIUS

WORKS BY ALEXANDER HAMILTON

Hamilton, Alexander. "Defense of Mr. Jay's Treaty," Vols. 1, 2, and 3 of *American Remembrances.* Edited by Matthew Carey. Philadelphia: H. Tuckniss, 1795. With numerous selections in each of the three volumes, the author bases his support of the disputed treaty on constitutional and commercial grounds in hopes of creating a national sentiment and a strong central government.

_____. *Letters of Pacificus.* Philadelphia: Samuel E. Smith, 1796. A series of letters written in defense of Washington's proclamation of neutrality.

_____. *Observations on Certain Documents contained in No. V and VI of "The History of the United States for the year 1796" in which the Charge of Speculation against Alexander Hamilton, Late Secretary of the Treasury, is fully Refuted.* Philadelphia: John

Bioren, 1797. A refutation of both the charge of speculation and the spirit of Jacobinism.

The Works of Alexander Hamilton. Edited by Henry Cabot Lodge. New York: G.P. Putnam's Sons, 1904. A twelve-volume collection of Hamilton's speeches, writings and letters.

MAJOR SOURCES ON ALEXANDER HAMILTON

Charles, Joseph. "Hamilton and Washington: The Origins of the American Party System," *William and Mary Quarterly,* Vol. XII, No. 2 (1955), pp. 218–267. Hamilton, a member of the privileged class, despises democracy and desires a hierarchial system.

Hacker, Louis M. *Alexander Hamilton in the American Tradition.* New York: McGraw-Hill, 1957. An essay on the political and economic views of Hamilton showing his role in saving the Revolution and the Confederation by uniting private interests with public policy.

Kirk, Russell. *The Conservative Mind.* Chicago: Regnery Co., 1953. Shows Hamilton as a 17th century Mercantalist urging governmental assistance in aiding certain occupational classes.

Lodge, Henry Cabot. *Alexander Hamilton.* Boston: Houghton, 1882. A classic biography describing Hamilton as the paragon of conservatism.

Lunt, Edward C. "Hamilton as a Political Economist," *The Journal of Political Economy,* Vol. 3 (1894), pp. 289–310. A smugly written essay showing Hamilton as a great politician but a second-rate economist.

Mitchell, Broadus. *Heritage from Hamilton.* New York: Columbia University Press, 1957. A collection of lectures given at Columbia emphasizing Hamilton's economic principles in his political thought.

Morris, Richard B. (ed.). *Alexander Hamilton and the Founding of the Nation.* New York: Dial Press, 1957. A collection of Hamilton's writings with introductory comments by the editor.

Oliver, Frederick Scott. *Alexander Hamilton: an Essay on American Union.* New York: Putnam, 1928. Written by an Englishman, shows Hamilton, cut off from historical precedent, as the guiding spirit for the unification of the separate states.

Schachner, Nathan. *Alexander Hamilton.* New York: Appleton-Century, 1946. A well-written biography showing Halilton's ideology based on national rather than class interests.

CHAPTER 7

Ralph Waldo Emerson

RALPH Waldo Emerson (1803–1882) was by ancestory, education, and vocation, if not by wealth, a member of the Boston upper class. Like many of his ancestors before him, Emerson went into the ministry, having first prepared at Harvard. He took his degree from Harvard in 1821 at the age of 18. Then, by means of teaching and preaching, he finished a degree of divinity at Harvard Divinity School. He was ordained as a minister in 1829. In 1832, Emerson resigned his position, never to regularly resume the ministry. Emerson's next move was a trip to Europe; during this trip he met Coleridge, Wordsworth, and Thomas Carlyle.

Returning to the United States in 1834, Emerson settled in Concord permanently. In 1836, his book *Nature* appeared. During this period, Emerson became identified with the Transcendentalists. During the 1840's, Emerson was a strong proponent of many reforms, although he was not an active participant. It was only later that the slavery question called him from his solitude.

Emerson, lecturing more and more frequently, had become an institution toward the end of his life. In time, he was even called to lecture on philosophy and mount the pulpit of the divinity school at Harvard, a monumental achievement considering that Emerson was a persona non grata at Harvard for many years.

On Politics

In dealing with the State we ought to remember that its institutions are not aboriginal, through they existed before we were born; that they are not superior to the citizen; that every one of them was once the act of a single man; every law and usage was man's expedient to meet a particular case; that they all are imitable, all alterable; we may make as good, we may make better. Society is an illusion to the young citizen. It lies before him in rigid repose, with certain names, men and institutions rooted like oak-trees to the centre, round which all arrange themselves the best they can. But the old statesman knows that society is fluid; there are no such roots and centres, but any particle may suddenly become the centre of the movement and compel the system to gyrate round it; as every man of strong will, like Pisistratus or Cromwell, does for a time, and every man of truth, like Plato or Paul, does forever. But politics rest on necessary foundations, and cannot be treated with levity. Republics abound in young civilians who believe that the laws make the city; that grave modifications of the policy and modes of living and employments of the population, that commerce, education, and religion, may be voted in or out; and that any measure, though it were absurd, may be imposed on a people if only you can get sufficient voices to make it a law. But the wise know that foolish legislation is a rope of sand which perishes in the twisting: that the State must follow and not lead the character and progress of the citizen; the strongest usurper is quickly got rid of; and they only who build on Ideas, build for eternity; and that the form of government which prevails is the expression of what cultivation exists in the population which permits it. The law is only a memorandum. We are superstitious, and esteem the statute somewhat: so much life as it has in the character of living men is its force. The statute stands there to say, Yesterday we agreed so and so, but how feel ye this article to-day? Our statute is a currency which we stamp with our own portrait: it soon becomes unrecognizable, and in process of time will return to the mint. Nature is not democratic, nor limited-monarchical, but despotic, and will not be fooled or abated of any jot of her authority by the protest of her sons; and as fast as the public mind is opened to more intelligence, the code is seen to be brute and stammering. It speaks not articulately, and must be made to. Meantime the education of the general mind never stops. The reveries of the true and simple are prophetic. What the tender poetic youth dreams, and prays, and paints today, but shuns the ridicule of saying aloud, shall presently be the resolutions of public bodies; then shall be carried as grievance and bill of rights through conflict and war, and then shall be triumphant law and establishment for a hundred years, until it gives place in turn to new prayers and pictures. The history of the State sketches in coarse outline the progress of thought, and follows at a distance the delicacy of culture and of aspiration.

The theory of politics which has possessed the mind of men, and which they have expressed the best they could in their laws and in their revolutions, considers persons and property as the two objects for whose protection government exists. Of persons, all have equal rights, in virtue of being identical in nature. This interest of course with its whole power demands a democracy. Whilst the rights of all as persons are equal, in virtue of their access to reason, their rights in property are very unequal. One man owns his clothes, and another owns a county. This accident, depending primarily on the skill and virtue of the parties, of which there is every degree, and secondarily on patrimony, falls unequally, and its rights of course are unequal. Personal rights, universally the same, demand a government framed on the ratio of the census; property demands a government framed on the ratio of owners and of owning. Laban, who has flocks and herds, wishes them looked after by an officer on the frontiers, lest the Midianites shall drive them off; and pays a tax to that end. Jacob has no flocks or herds and no fear of the Midianites, and pays no tax to the officer. It seemed fit that Laban and Jacob should have equal rights to elect the officer who is to defend their persons, but that Laban and not Jacob should elect the officer who is to guard the sheep and cattle. And if questions arise whether additional officers or watchtowers should be provided, must not Laban and Isaac, and those who must sell part of their herds to buy protection for the rest, judge better of this, and with more right, than Jacob, who, because he is a youth and a traveller, eats their bread and not his own?

In the earliest society the proprietors made their own wealth, and so long as it comes to the owners in the direct way, no other opinion would arise in any equitable community than that property should make the law for property, and persons the law for persons.

But property passes through donation or inheritance to those who do not create it. Gift, in one case, makes it as really the new owner's, as labor made it the first owner's: in the other case, of patrimony, the law makes an ownership which will be valid in each man's view according to the estimate which he sets on the public tranquillity.

It was not however found easy to embody the readily admitted principle that property should make law for property, and persons for persons; since persons and property mixed themselves in every transaction. At last it seemed settled that the rightful distinction was that the proprietors should have more delective franchise than non-proprietors, on the Spartan principle of "calling that which is just, equal; not that which is equal, just."

That principle no longer looks so self-evident as it appeared in former times, partly because doubts have arisen whether too much weight had not been allowed in the laws to property, and such a structure given to our usages as allowed the rich to encroach on the poor, and to keep them poor; but mainly because there is an instinctive sense, however obscure and yet inarticulate, that the whole constitution of property, on its present tenures, is injurious, and its influence on persons deteriorating and degrading; that truely the only interest for the consideration of the State is persons; that property will always follow persons; that the highest end of government is the culture of men; and that if men can be educated, the institutions will share their improvement and the moral sentiment will write the law of the land.

If it be not easy to settle the equity of this question, the peril is less when we take note of our natural defenses. We are kept by better guards than the vigilence of such magistrates as we commonly elect. Society always consists in greatest part of young and foolish persons. The old, who have seen through the hypocrisy of courts and estatesmen, die and leave no wisdom to their sons. They believe their own newspaper, as their fathers did at their age. With such an ignorant and deceivable majority, States would soon run to ruin, but that there are limitations beyond which the folly and ambition of governors cannot go. Things have their laws, as well as men; and things refuse to be trifled with. Property will be protected. Corn will not grow unless it is planted and manured; but the farmer will not plant or hoe it unless the chances are a hundred to one that he will cut and harvest it. Under any forms, persons and property must and will have their just sway. They exert their power, as steadily as matter its attraction. Cover up a pound of earth never so cunningly, divide and subdivide it; melt it to liquid, convert it to gas; it will always weigh a pound; it will always attract and resist other matter by the full virtue of one pound weight:—and the attributes of a person, his wit and his moral energy, will exercise, under any law or extinguishing tyranny, their proper force,—if not overtly, then covertly; if not for the law, then against it; if not wholesomely, then poisonously; with right, or by might.

The boundaries of personal influence it is impossible to fix, as persons are organs of moral or supernatural force. Under the dominion of an idea which possesses the minds of multitudes, as civil freedom, or the religious sentiment, the powers of persons are no longer subjects of calculation. A nation of men unanimously bent on freedom or conquest can easily confound the arithmetic of statists, and achieve extravagant actions, out of all proportion to their means; as the Greeks, the Saracens, the Swiss, the Americans, and the French have done.

In like manner to every particle of property belongs its own attraction. A cent is the representative of a certain quantity of corn or other commodity. Its value is in the necessities of the animal man. It is so much warmth, so much bread, so much water, so much land. The law may do what it will with the owner of property; its just power will still attach to the cent. The law may in a mad freak say that all shall have power except the owners of property; they shall have no vote. Nevertheless, by á higher law, the property will, year after year, write every statute that respects property. The non-proprietor will be the scribe of the proprietor. What the owners wish to do, the whole power of property will do, either through the law or else in defiance of it. Of course I speak of all the property, not merely of the great estates. When the rich are outvoted, as frequently happens, it is the joint treasury of the poor which exceeds their accumulations. Every man owns something, if it is only a cow, or a wheel-barrow, or his arms, and so has that property to dispose of.

The same necessity which secures the rights of person and property against the malignity or folly of the magistrate, determines the form and methods of governing, which are proper to each nation and to its habit of thought, and nowise transferable to other states of society. In this country we are very vain of our political institutions, which are singular in this, that they sprung, within the memory of living men, from the character and condition of the people, which they still express with sufficient fidelity—and we ostentatiously prefer them to any other in history. They are not better, but only fitter for us. We may be wise in asserting the advantage in modern times of the democratic form, but to other states of society, in which religion consecrated the monarchical, that and not this was expedient. Democracy is better for us, because the religious sentiment of the present time accords better with it. Born democrats, we are nowise qualified to judge of monarchy which, to our fathers living in the monarchical idea, was also relatively right. But our institutions, though in coincidence with the spirit of the age, have not any exemption from the practical defects which have discredited other forms. Every actual State is corrupt. Good men must not obey the laws too well. What satire on government can equal the severity of censure conveyed in the world *politic,* which now for ages has signified *cunning,* intimating that the State is a trick?

The same benign necessity and the same practical abuse appear in the parties, into which each State divides itself, of opponents and defenders of the administration of the government. Parties are also founded on instincts, and have better guides to their own humble aims than the sagacity of their leaders. They have nothing perverse in their origin, but rudely mark some real and lasting relation. We might as wisely reprove the east wind or the frost, as a political party, whose members, for the most part, could give no account of their position, but stand for the defence of those interests in which they find themselves. Our quarrel with them begins when they quit this deep natural ground at the bidding of some leader, and obeying personal considerations, throw themselves into the maintenance and defence of points nowise belonging to their system. A party is perpetually corrupted by personality. Whilst we absolve the association from dishonesty, we cannot extend the same charity to their leaders. They reap the rewards of the docility and zeal of the masses which they direct. Ordinarily our parties are parties of circumstance, and not of principle; as the planting interest in conflict with the commercial; the party of capitalists and that of operatives; parties which are identical in their moral character, and which can easily change ground with each other in the support of many of their measures. Parties of principle, as, religious sects, or the party of free-trade, of universal sufferage, of abolition of slavery, of abolition of capital punishment,—degenrate into personalities, or would inspire enthusiasm. The vice of our leading parties in this country (which may be cited as fair specimen of these societies of opinion) is that they do not plant themselves on the deep and necessary grounds to which they are respectively entitled, but lash themselves to fury in the carrying of some local and momentary measure, nowise useful to the commonwealth. Of the two great parties which at this hour almost share the nation between them, I should say that one has the best cause, and the other contains the best man. The philosopher, the poet, or the religious man will of course wish to cast his vote with the democrat, for free-trade, for wide sufferage, for the abolition of legal cruelties in the penal code, and for facilitating in every manner the access of the young and the poor to the sources of wealth and power. But he can rarely accept the persons whom the so-called popular party propose to him as representatives of these liberalities. They have not at heart the ends which give to the name of democracy what hope and virtue are in it. The spirit of our American radicalism is destructive and aimless: it is not loving; it has no ulterior and divine ends, but is destructive only out of hatred and selfishness. On the other side, the conservative party, composed of the most moderate, able, and cultivated part of the population, is timid, and merely defensive of property. It vindicates no right, it aspires to no real good, it brands no crime, it proposes no generous policy; it does not build, nor write, nor cherish the arts, nor foster religion, nor establish schools, nor encourage science, nor emancipate the slave, nor befriend the poor, or the Indian, or the immigrant. From neither party, when in power, has the world any benefit to expect in science, art, or humanity, at all commensurate with the resources of the nation.

I do not for these defects despair of our republic. We are not at the mercy of any waves of chance. In the strife of ferocious parties, human nature always finds itself cherished; as the children of the convicts at Botany Bay are found to have as healthy a moral sentiment as other children. Citizens of feudal states are alarmed at our democratic institutions lapsing into anarchy, and the older and more cautious among ourselves are learning from Europeans to look with some terror at our turbulent freedom. It is said that in our license of constructing the Constitution, and in the despotism of public opinion, we have no anchor; and one foreign observer thinks he has found the safeguard in the sanctity of Marriage among us; and another thinks he has found it in our Calvanism. Fisher Ames expressed the popular security more wisely, when he compared a monarchy and a republic, saying that a monarchy is a merchant-man, which sails well, but will sometimes strike on a rock and go to the bottom; whilst a republic is a raft, which would never sink, but than your feet are always in water. No forms can have any dangerous importance whilst we are befriended by the laws of things. It makes no difference how many tons weight of atmosphere presses on our heads, so long as the same pressure resists it within the lungs. Augment the mass a thousand fold, it cannot begin to crush us, as long as reaction is equal to action. The fact of two poles, of two forces, centripetal and centrifugal, is universal, and each force by its own activity develops the other. Wild liberty, by strengthening law and decorum, stupefies conscience. "Lynch-law" prevails only where there is greater hardihood and self-subsistency in the leaders. A mob cannot be a permanency; everybody's interest requires that it should not exist, and only justice satisfies all.

We must trust infinitely to the beneficient necessity which shines through all laws. Human nature expresses itself in them as characteristically as in statutes, or songs, or railroads; and an abstract of the codes of nations would be a transcript of the common conscience. Governments have their origin in the moral identity of men. Reason for one is seen to be reason for another, and for every other. There is a middle measure which satisfies all parties, be they never so many or so resolute for their own. Every man finds a sanction for his simplest claims and deeds, in decisions of his own mind, which he calls Truth and Holiness. In these decisions all the citizens find a perfect agreement, and only in these; not in what is good to eat, good to wear, good use of time, or what amount of land or of public aid each is entitled to claim. This truth and justice men presently endeavor to make application of to the measuring of land, the apportionment of service, the protection of life and property. Their first endeavors, no doubt, are very awkward. Yet absolute right is the first governor; or, every government is an impure theocracy. The idea after which each community is aiming to make and mend its law, is the will of the wise man. The wise man it cannot find in nature, and it makes awkward but earnest efforts to secure his government by contrivance; as by causing the entire people to give their voices on every measure; or by a double choice to get the representation of the whole; or by a selection of the best citizens; or to secure the advantages of efficiency and internal peace by confiding the government to one, who may himself select his agents. All forms of government symbolize an immortal government, common to all dynasties and independent of numbers, perfect where two men exist, perfect where there is only one man.

Every man's nature is a sufficient advertisement to him of the character of his fellows. My right and my wrong is their right and their wrong. Whilst I do what is fit for me, and abstain from what is unfit, my neighbor and I shall often agree in our means, and work together for a time to one end. But whenever I find my dominion over myself not sufficient for me, and undertake the direction of him also, I overstep the truth, and come into false relations to him. I may have so much more skill or strength than he that he cannot express adequately his sense of wrong, but it is a lie, and hurts like a lie both him and me. Love and nature cannot maintain the assumption; it must be executed by a practical lie, namely by force. This undertaking for another is the blunder which stands in colossal ugliness in the governments of the world. It is the same thing in numbers, as in a pair, only not quite so intelligible. I can see well enough a great difference between my setting myself down to a self-control, and my going to make somebody else act after my views; but when a quarter of the human race assume to tell me what I must do, I may be too much disturbed by the circumstances to see so clearly the absurdity of their command. Therefore all public ends look vague and quixotic beside private ones. For any laws but those which men make for themselves, are laughable. If I put muself in the place of my child, and we stand in one thought and see that things are thus or thus, that perception is law for him and me. We are both there, both act. But if, without carrying him into the thought, I look over into his plot, and, guessing how it is with him, ordain this or that, he will never obey me. This is the history of governments,—one man does something which is to bind another. A man who cannot be acquainted with me taxes me; looking from afar at me ordains that a part of my labor shall go to this or that whimsical end,—not as I, but as he happens to fancy. Behold the consequence. Of all debts men are least willing to pay the taxes. What a satire is this on government. Everywhere they think they get their money's worth, except for these.

Hence the less government we have the better,—the fewer laws, and the less confided power. The antidote to this abuse of formal Government is the influence of private character, the growth of the Individual; the appearance of the principal to supersede the proxy; the appearance of the wise man; of whom the existing government is, it must be owned, but a shabby imitation. That which all things tend to educe; which freedom, cultivation, intercourse, revolutions, go to form and deliver, is character; that is the end of Nature, to reach unto this coronation of her king. To educate the wise man the State exists, and with the appearance of the wise man the State expires. The appearance of character makes the State unnecessary. The wise man is the State. He needs no army, fort, or navy,—he loves men too well; no bribe, or feast, or palace, to draw friends to him; no vantage ground, no favorable circumstance. He needs no library, for he has not done thinking; no church, for he is a prophet; no statute book, for he is the lawgiver, no money, for he is value; no road, for he is at home where is; no experience, for the life of the creator shoots through him, and looks from his eyes. He has no personal friends, for he who has the spell to draw the prayer and piety of all men unto him needs not husband and educate a few to share with him a select and poetic life. His relation to men is angelic; his memory is myrrh to them; his presence, frankincense and flowers.

We think our civilization near its meridian, but we are yet only at the cockcrowing and the morning star. In our barbarous society the influence of character is in its infancy. As a political power, as the rightful lord who is to tumble all rulers from their chairs, its presence is hardly yet suspected. Malthus and Ricardo quite omit it; the Annual Register is silent; in the Conversations' Lexicon it is not set down; the President's Message, the Queen's Speech, have not mentioned it; and yet it is never nothing. Every thought which genius and piety throw into the world, alters the world. The gladiators in the lists of power feel, through all their frocks of force and simulation, the presence of worth. I think the very strife of trade and ambition is confession of this divinity; and successes in those fields are the poor amends, the figleaf with which the shamed soul attempts to hide its nakedness. I find the like unwilling homage in all quarters. It is because we know how much is due from us that we are impatient to show some petty talent as a substitute for worth. We are haunted by a conscience of this right to grandeur of character, and are false to it. But each of us has some talent, can do somewhat useful, or graceful, or formidable, or amusing, or lucrative. That we do, as an apology to others and to ourselves for not reaching the mark of a good and equal life. But it does not satisfy *us,* whilst we thrust it on the notice of our companions. It may throw dust in their eyes, but does not smooth our own brow, or give us the tranquaillity of the strong when we walk abroad. We do penance as we go. Our talent is a sort of expiation, and we are constrained to reflect on our splendid moment with a certain humiliation, as somewhat too fine, and not as one act of many acts, a fair expression of our permanent energy. Most persons of ability meet in society with a kind of tacit appeal. Each seems to say, "I am not all here." Senators and presidents have climbed so high with pain enough, not because they think the place specially agreeable, but as an apology for real worth, and to vindicate their manhood in our eyes. This conspicious chair is their compensation to themselves for being of a poor, cold, hard nature. They must do what they can. Like one class of forest animals, they have nothing but a prehensile tail; climb they must, or crawl. If a man found himself so rich-natured that he could enter into strict relations with the best persons and make life serene around him by the dignity and sweetness of his behavior, could he afford to circumvent the favor of the caucus and the press, and covet relations so hollow and pompous as those of a politician? Surely nobody would be a charlatan who could afford to be sincere.

The tendencies of the times favor the idea of self-government, and leave the individual, for all code, to the rewards and penalties of his own constitution; which work with more energy than we believe whilst we depend on artificial restraints. The movement in this direction has been very marked in modern history. Much has been blind and discreditable, but the nature of the revolution is not affected by the vices of the revolters; for this is a purely moral force. It was never adopted by any party in history, neither can be. It separates the individual from all party, and unites him at the same time to the race. It promises a recognition of higher rights than those of personal freedom, or the security of property. A man has a right to be employed, to be trusted, to be loved, to be revered. The power of love, as the basis of a State, has never been tried. We must not imagine that all things are lapsing into confusion if every tender protestant be not compelled to bear his part in certain social conventions; nor doubt that roads can be built, letters carried, and the fruit of labor secured, when the government of force is at an end. Are our methods now so excellent that all competition is hopeless? Could not a nation of friends even devise better ways? On the other hand, let not the most conservative and timid fear anything from a premature surrender of the bayonet and the system of force. For, according to the order of nature, which is quite superior to our will, it stands thus; there will always be a government of force when men are selfish; and when they are pure enough to abjure the code of force they will be wise enough to see how these public ends of the post-office, of the highway, of commerce and the exchange of property, of museums and libraries, of institutions of art and science can be answered.

We live in a very low state of the world, and pay unwilling tribute to governments founded on force. There is not, among the most religious and instructed men of the most religious and civil nations, a reliance on the moral sentiment and a sufficient belief in the unity of things, to persuade them that society can be maintained without artificial restrains, as well as the solar system; or that the private citizen might be reasonable and a good neighbor, without a hint of a jail or a confiscation. What is strange too, there never was in any man sufficient faith in the power of rectitude to inspire him with the broad design of renovating the State on the principle of right and love. All those who have pretended this design have been partial reformers, and have admitted in some manner the supremacy of the bad State. I do not call to mind a single human being who has steadily denied the authority of the laws, on the simple ground of his own moral nature. Such designs, full of genius and full of faith as they are, are not entertained except avowedly as air-pictures. If the individual who exhbits them dare to think them practiceable, he disgusts scholars and churchmen; and men of talent and women of superior sentiments cannot hide their contempt. Not the less does nature continue to fill the heart of youth with suggestions of this enthusiasm, and there are now men,—if indeed I can speak in the plural number,—more exactly, I will say, I have just been conversing with one man, to whom no weight of adverse experience will make it for a moment appear impossible that thousands of human beings might exercise towards each other the grandest and simplest sentiments, as well as a knot of friends, or a pair of lovers.

WORKS BY RALPH WALDO EMERSON

Emerson, Ralph Waldo. *The Conduct of Life.* Boston: Houghton, Mifflin, and Co., 1896. A collection of nine essays in which Emerson, in a pragmatic and mellow style, shows the path to correct living.

_____. *English Traits.* Boston: Houghton, Mifflin, and Co., 1876. A description of the Englishman and his way of life, written in tones of admiration and respect.

_____. *Letters and Social Aims.* Boston: Osgood and Co., 1876. Eleven essays on various social and cultural virtues as expressed in the individual.

_____. *May-Day and Other Pieces.* Boston: Houghton, Mifflin, and Co., 1876. Forty-six poems divided into the categories: Miscellaneous, Nature and Life, and Elements.

_____. *Natural History of Intellect and Other Papers.* Boston: Houghton, Mifflin, and Co., 1895. A series of essays; the title one being a presentation of social psychology based on a transcendental spirit.

_____. *Nature.* Boston: Houghton, Mifflin, and Co., 1876. Brimming with optimism, Emerson makes Nature into an absolute Ideal without reconciling the dualism of mind and matter.

_____. *Poems.* Boston: Houghton, Mifflin, and Co., 1867. One hundred and seventy-three poems divided into various topics.

_____. *Representative Men.* Boston: Houghton, Mifflin, and Co., 1876. A series of biographical essays that attempt to illustrate Emerson's general ideas through specific individuals.

_____. *Society and Solitude.* Boston: Houghton, Mifflin, and Co., 1870. Written in his later life, this collection of essays merely reiterates his earlier views and reflections.

_____. *Success.* Boston: Houghton, Mifflin, and Co., 1870. Success is a personal subjective phenomenon accomplished through numerous failings and deep reflection.

Journals of Ralph Waldo Emerson. Edited by Edward Waldo Emerson. 4 Vols. Boston: Houghton, Mifflin, and Co., 1909. Representative selections from Emerson's *Journals* portraying the more personal side of the author.

Uncollected Lectures by Ralph Waldo Emerson. Edited by Clarence Gohdes. New York: William Rudge, 1932. A collection of seven essays: six on American life, the seventh on Natural Religion: with commentary by the editor.

The Works of Ralph Waldo Emerson. Edited by James Elliot Cabot. 14 Vols. Boston: Houghton, Mifflin, and Co., 1887. A collection of Emerson's writings with introductory remarks by the editor.

MAJOR SOURCES ON RALPH WALDO EMERSON

Cowan, Michael H. *City of the West: Emerson, America, and Urban Metaphor.* New Haven, Conn.: Yale University Press, 1967. A presentation of Emerson's dialectical approach as manifested in his writings on urban environments and problems.

Eliot, Charles W. "Emerson," in *Four American Leaders.* Boston: American Unitarian Association, 1906. A Christian interpretation of Emerson showing him as a progressive thinker, but well within the bounds of traditional Christianity.

Huggard, William Allen. "Emerson and the Problem of War and Peace," *University of Iowa Humanistic Studies,* Vol. V, No. 5 (1938), pp. 7–76. Ideally opposed to war, Emerson is shown as willing to resort to force when war emblemizes the moral will of the universe.

Kazin, Alfred, and Aaron, Daniel (ed.). *Emerson, A Modern Anthology.* New York: Houghton, Mifflin, and Co., 1960. Drawing from Emerson's *Essays, Journals,* and *Letters,* this collection emphasizes the poetic quality of Emerson.

McQuiston, Raymer. *The Relation of Ralph Waldo Emerson to Public Affairs.* Lawrence, Ohio: Ohio University Press, 1923. Tempering his extreme idealism with common sense, Emerson is shown as the leading exponent of the liberal tradition in America.

Paul, Sherman. *Emerson's Angle of Vision.* Cambridge, Mass.: Harvard University Press, 1952. An essay placing the concept of "correspondence" as the basis of Emerson's thought on the relation of man to the universe.

Sandeen, Ernest S. "Emerson's Americanism," *University of Iowa Humanistic Studies,* Vol. VI, No. 1 (1942), pp. 63–118. The American ideals of freedom and individualism are seen by Emerson as being based on religious and moral grounds.

Whicher, Stephen E. *Freedom and Fate.* Philadelphia: University of Pennsylvania Press, 1953. An essay attempting to trace Emerson's reflections into his mind.

Whicher, Stephen, and Speller, Robert, (ed.). *The Early Lectures of Ralph Waldo Emerson.* Cambridge, Mass.: Harvard University Press, 1960. A collection of twenty-two addresses given by Emerson after leaving the Unitarian ministry with commentary by the editors.

CHAPTER 8

Henry D. Thoreau

HENRY David Thoreau (1817–1862) was born in Concord, Massachusetts, where he lived most of his life.

Thoreau entered Harvard in 1833 and graduated in 1837, not at the top of his class, but perhaps the most well-read member of the group. While at Harvard he began keeping a journal, a practice that he continued until the end of his life.

After college, Thoreau and his brother John set up a school in Concord. The Thoreau brothers ran the school quite successfully until early 1841 when the school had to close because of John's health. At this time Henry went to live in the Emerson home. While residing with Emerson, Thoreau was introduced to the members of the Transcendental Club.

In 1845, Thoreau decided to build a small hut on Emerson's property on Walden Pond. Thoreau took up residence at the pond in July 1845, and stayed there until September 1847. During the summer of 1845, he was arrested for nonpayment of poll tax. Thoreau, protesting against slavery, chose "civil disobedience" as the most effective form of protest.

Between the publication of the *Week* (1849) and that of *Life in the Woods* (1854), Thoreau's friendships multiplied and the poet Ellery Channing replaced Emerson as the center of Thoreau's acquaintance. The year 1852 was probably the apex of Thoreau's career, for this was the time of his most fruitful journalizing.

In his later years, Thoreau became the scientific observer, working with weather records and ethnological studies of Indians. In 1861, Thoreau made a trip to Minnesota for his health, but instead of helping him the trip only exacerbated his condition. Thoreau died the following year.

Civil Disobedience

I heartily accept the motto, "That government is best which governs least;" and I should like to see it acted up to more rapidly and systematically. Carried out, it finally amounts to this, which also I believe—"That government is best which governs not at all;" and when men are prepared for it, that will be the kind of government which they will have. Government is at best but an expedient; but most governments are usually, and all governments are sometimes, inexpedient. The objections which have been brought against a standing army, and they are many and weighty, and deserve to prevail, may also at last be brought against a standing government. The standing army is only an arm of the standing government. The government itself, which is only the mode which the people have chosen to execute their will, is equally liable to be abused and perverted before the people can act through it. Witness the present Mexican war, the work of comparatively a few individuals using the standing government as their tool; for, in the outset, the people would not have consented to this measure.

This American government—what is it but a tradition, through a recent one, endeavoring to transmit itself unimpaired to posterity, but each instant losing some of its integrity? It has not the vitality and force of a single living man; for a single man can bend it to his will. It is a sort of wooden gun to the people themselves. But it is not the less necessary for this; for the people must have some complicated machinery or other, and hear its din, to satisfy that idea of government which they have. Governments show thus how successfully men can be imposed on, even impose on themselves, for their own advantage. It is excellent, we must all allow. Yet this government never of itself furthered any enterprise, but by the alacrity with which it got out of its way. It does not keep the country free. It does not settle the West. It does not educate. The character inherent in the American people has done all that has been accomplished; and it would have done somewhat more, if the government had not sometimes got in its way. For government is an expedient by which men would fain succeed in letting one another alone; and, as has been said, when it is most expedient, the governed are most let alone by it. Trade and commerce, if they were not made of india-rubber, would never manage to bounce over the obstacles which legislators are continually putting in their way; and, if one were to judge these men wholly by the effects of their actions and not partly by their intentions, they would deserve to be classed and punished with those mischievous persons who put obstructions on the railroads.

But, to speak practically and as a citizen, unlike those who call themselves no-government men, I ask for, not at once no government, but *at once* a better government. Let every man make known what kind of government would command his respect, and that will be one step toward obtaining it.

After all, the practical reason why, when the power is once in the hands of the people, a majority are permitted, and for a long period continue, to rule is not because they are most likely to be in the right, nor because this seems fairest to the minority, but because they are physically the stronger. But a government in which the majority rule in all cases cannot be based on justice, even as far as men understand it. Can there not be a government in which majorities do not virtually decide right and wrong, but conscience?—in which majorities decide only those questions to which the rule of expediency is applicable? Must the citizen ever for a moment, or in the least degree, resign his conscience to the legislator? Why has every man a conscience, then? I think that we should be men first, and subjects afterward. It is not desirable to cultivate a respect for the law, so much as for the right. The only obligation which I have a right to assume is to do at any time what I think right. It is truly enough said that a corporation has no conscience; but a corporation of conscientious men is a corporation with a conscience. Law never made men a whit more just; and, by means of their respect for it, even the well-disposed are daily made the agents of injustice. A common and natural result of an undue respect for law is, that you may see a file of soldiers, colonel, captain, corporal, privates, powder-monkeys, and all, marching in admirable order over hill and dale to the wars, against their wills, ay, against their common sense and consciences, which makes it very steep marching indeed, and produces a palpitation of the heart. They have no doubt that it is a damnable business in which they are concerned; they are all peaceably inclined. Now, what are they? Men at all? or small movable forts and magazines, at the service of some unscrupulous man in power? Visit the Navy-Yard, and behold a marine, such a man as an American government can make, or such as it can make a man with its black arts—a mere shadow and reminiscence of humanity, a man laid out alive and standing, and already, as one may say, buried under arms with funeral accompaniments, though it may be,

Not a drum was heard, not a funeral note,
    As his corse to the rampart we hurried;
Not a soldier discharged his farewell shot
    O'er the grave where our hero we buried.

The mass of men serve the state thus, not as men mainly, but as machines, with their bodies. They are the standing army; and the militia, jailers, constables, *posse comitatus*, etc. In most cases there is no free exercise whatever of the judgment or of the moral sense; but they put themselves on a level with wood and earth and stones; and wooden men can perhaps be manufactured that will serve the purpose as well. Such command no more respect than men of straw or a lump of dirt. They have the same sort of worth only as horses and dogs. Yet such as these even are commonly

esteemed good citizens. Others—as most legislators, politicians, lawyers, ministers, and office-holders—serve the state chiefly with their heads; and, as they rarely make any moral distinctions, they are as likely to serve the devil, without *intending* it, as God. A very few—as heroes, patriots, matryrs, reformers in the great *sense,* and *men*—serve the state with their consciences also, and so necessarily resist it for the most part; and they are commonly treated as enemies by it. A wise man will only be useful as a man, and will not submit to be "clay," and "stop a hole to keep the wind away," but leave that office to his dust at least:

I am too high-born to be propertied,
To be a secondary at control,
Or useful serving-man and instrument
To any sovereign state throughout the world.

He who gives himself entirely to his fellow-men appears to them useless and selfish; but he who gives himself partially to them is pronounced a benefactor and philanthropist.

How does it become a man to behave toward this American government today? I answer, that he cannot without disgrace be associated with it. I cannot for an instant recognize that political organization as *my* government which is the *slave's* government also.

All men recognize the right of revolution; that is, the right to refuse allegiance to, and to resist the government, when its tyranny or its inefficiency are great and unendurable. But almost all say that such is not the case now. But such was the case, they think, in the Revolution of '75. If one were to tell me that this was a bad government because it taxed certain foreign commodities brought to its ports, it is most probable that I should not make an ado about it, for I can do without them. All machines have their friction; and possibly this does enough good to counterbalance the evil. At any rate, it is a great evil to make a stir about it. But when the friction comes to have its machine, and oppression and robbery are organized, I say, let us not have such a machine any longer. In other words, when a sixth of the population of a nation which has undertaken to be the refuge of liberty are slaves, and a whole country is unjustly overrun and conquered by a foreign army, and subjected to military law, I think that it is not too soon for honest men to rebel and revolutionize. What makes this duty the more urgent is the fact that the country so overrun is not our own, but ours is the invading army.

Paley, a common authority with many on moral questions, in his chapter on the "Duty of Submission to Civil Government," resolves all civil obligation into expediency; and he proceeds to say that "so long as the interest of the whole society requires it, that is, so long as the established government cannot be resisted or changed without public inconvenience, it is the will of God . . . that the established government be obeyed—and no longer. This principle being admitted, the justice of every particular case of resistance is reduced to a computation of the quantity of the danger and grievance on the one side, and of the probability and expense of redressing it on the other." Of this, he says, every man shall judge for himself. But Paley appears never to have contemplated those cases to which the rule of expedience does not apply, in which a people, as well as an individual, must do justice, cost what it may. If I have unjustly wrested a plank from a drowning man, I must restore it to him though I drown myself. This, according to Paley, would be inconvenient. But he that would save his life, in such a case, shall lose it. This people must cease to hold slaves, and to make war on Mexico, though it cost them their existence as a people.

In practice, nations agree with Paley; but does any one think that Massachusetts does exactly what is right at the present crisis?

A drab of state, a cloth-o'-silver slut,
To have her train borne up,and her soul trail
    in the dirt.

Practically speaking, the opponents to a reform in Massachusetts are not a hundred thousand politicians at the South, but a hundred thousand merchants and farmers here, who are more interested in commerce and agriculture than they are in humanity, and are not prepared to do justice to the slave and to Mexico, *cost what it may.* I quarrel not with far-off foes, but with those who, near at home, cooperate with, and do the bidding of, those far away, and without whom the latter would be harmless. We are accustomed to say, that the mass of men are unprepared; but improvement is slow, because the few are not materially wiser or better than the many. It is not so important that many should be as good as you, as that there be some absolute goodness somewhere; for that will leaven the whole lump. There are thousands who are in *opinion* opposed to slavery and to the war, who yet in effect do nothing to put an end to them; who, esteeming themselves children of Washington and Franklin, sit down with their hands in their pockets, and say that they know not what to do, and do nothing; who even postpone the question of freedom to the question of free trade, and quietly read the prices—current along with the latest advices from Mexico, after dinner, and, it may be, fall asleep over them both. What is the price-current of an honest man and patriot today? They hesitate, and they regret, and sometimes they petition; but they do nothing in earnest and with effect. They will wait, well disposed, for others to remedy the evil, that they may no longer have it to regret. At most, they give only a cheap vote, and a feeble countenance and God-speed, to the right, as it goes by them. There are nine hundred and ninety-nine patrons of virtue to one virtuous man. But it is easier to deal with the real possessor of a thing than with the temporary guardian of it.

All voting is a sort of gaming, like checkers or backgammon, with a slight moral tinge to it, playing with right and wrong, with moral questions; and betting naturally accompanies it. The character of the voters is not staked. I cast my vote, perchance, as I think right; but I am not vitally concerned that that right should prevail. I am willing to leave it to the majority. Its obligation, therefore, never exceeds that of expedience. Even voting *for the right* is *doing* nothing for it. It is only expressing to men feebly your desire that it should prevail. A wise man will not leave the right to the mercy of chance, nor wish it to prevail through the power of the majority. There is but little virtue in the action of masses of men. When the majority shall at length vote for the abolition of slavery, it will be because they are indifferent to slavery, or because there is but little slavery left to be abolished by their vote. *They* will then be the only slaves. Only *his* vote can hasten the abolition of slavery who asserts his own freedom by his vote.

I hear of a convention to be held at Baltimore, or elsewhere, for the selection of a candidate for the Presidency, made up chiefly of editors, and men who are politicians by profession; but I think, what is it to any independent, intelligent, and respectable man what decision they may come to? Shall we not have the advantage of his wisdom and honesty, nevertheless? Can we not count upon some independent votes? Are there not many individuals in the country who do not attend conventions? But no: I find that the respectable man, so called, has immediately drifted from his position, and despaires of his country, when his country has more reason to despair of him. He forthwith adopts one of the candidates thus selected as the only *available* one, thus proving that he is of no more worth than that of any unprincipled foreigner or hierling native, who may have been bought. O for a man who is a *man,* and, as my neighbor says, has a bone in his back which you cannot pass your hand through! Our statistics are at fault: the population has been returned too large. How many men are there to a square thousand miles in this country? Hardly one. Does not

America offer any inducement for men to settle here? The American has dwindled into an Odd Fellow—one who may be known by the development of his organ of gregariousness, and a manifest lack of intellect and cheerful self-reliance; whose first and chief concern, on coming into the world, is to see that the almshouses are in good repair; and, before yet he has lawfully donned the virile garb, to collect a fund for the support of the widows and orphans that may be; who, in short, ventures to live only by the aid of the Mutual Insurance company, which has promised to bury him decently.

It is not a man's duty, as a matter of course, to devote himself to the radication of any, even the most enormous, wrong; he may still properly have other concerns to engage him; but it is his duty, at least, to wash his hands of it, and, if he gives it no thought longer, not to give it practically his support. If I devote myself to other pursuits and contemplations, I must first see, at least, that I do not pursue them sitting upon another man's shoulders. I must get off him first, that he may pursue his contemplations too. See what gross inconsistency is tolerated. I have heard some of my townsmen say, "I should like to have them order me out to help put down an insurrection of the slaves, or to march to Mexico;—see if I would go;" and yet these very men have each, directly by their allegiance, and so indirectly, at least, by their money, furnished a substitute. The soldier is applauded who refuses to serve in an injust war by those who do not refuse to sustain the unjust government which makes the war; is applauded by those whose own act and authority he disregards and sets at naught; as if the state were pentinent to that degree that it hired one to scourge it while it sinned, but not to that degree that it left off sinning for a moment. Thus, under the name of Order and Civil Government, we are all made at last to pay homage to and support our own meanness. After the first blush of sin comes its indifference; and from immortal it becomes, as it were, *un*moral, and not quite unnecessary to that life which we have made.

The broadest and most prevalent error requires the most disintersted virtue to sustain it. The slight reproach to which the virtue of patriotism is commonly liable, the noble are most likely to incur. Those who, while they disapprove of the character and measures of a government, yield to it their allegiance and support are undoubtedly its most conscientious supporters, and so frequently the most serious obstacles to reform. Some are petitioning the State to dissolve the Union, to disregard the requisitions of the President. Why do they not dissolve it themselves—the union between themselves and the State —and refuse to pay their quota into its treasury? Do not they stand in the same relation to the State that the State does to the Union? And have not the same reasons prevented the State from resisting the Union which have prevented them from resisting the State?

How can a man be satisfied to entertain an opinion merely, and enjoy *it?* Is there any enjoyment in it, if his opinion is that he is aggrieved? If you are cheated out of a single dollar by your neighbor, you do not rest satisfied with knowing that you are cheated, or with saying that you are cheated, or even with partitioning him to pay you your due; but you take effectual steps at once to obtain the full amount, and see that you are never cheated again. Action from principle, the perception and the performance of right, changes things and relations; it is essentially revolutionary, and does not consist wholly with anything which was. It not only divides States and churches, it divided families; ay, it divides the *individual,* separating the diabolical in him from the divine.

Unjust laws exist: shall we be content to obey them, or shall we endeavor to amend them, and obey them until we have succeeded, or shall we transgress them at once? Men generally, under such a government as this, think

that they ought to wait until they have persuaded the majority to alter them. They think that, if they should resist, the remedy would be worse than the evil. But it is the fault of the government itself that the remedy *is* worse than the evil. *It* makes it worse. Why is it not more apt to anticipate and provide for reform? Why does it not cherish its wise minority? Why does it cry and resist before it is hurt? Why does it not encourage its citizens to be on the alert to point out its faults, and *do* better than it would have them? Why does it always crucify Christ and excommunicate Copernicus and Luther, and pronounce Washington and Franklin rebels?

One would think, that a deliberate and practical denial of its authority was the only offence never contemplated by government; else, why has it not assigned its definite, its suitable and proportionate, penalty? If a man who has no property refuses but once to earn nine shillings for the State, he is put in prison for a period unlimited by any law that I know, and determined only by the discretion of those who placed him there; but if he should steal ninety times nine shillings from the State, he is soon permitted to go at large again.

If the unjustice is part of the necessary friction of the machine of government, let it go, let it go: perchance it will wear smooth—certainly the machine will wear out. If the unjustice has a spring, or a pulley, or a rope, or a crank, exclusively for itself, then perhaps you may consider whether the remedy will not be worse than the evil; but if it is of such a nature that it requires you to be the agent of unjustice to another, then, I say, break the law. Let your life be a counterfriction to stop the machine. What I have to do is to see, at any rate, that I do not lend myself to the wrong which I condemn.

As for adopting the ways which the State has provided for remedying the evil, I know not of such ways. They take too much time, and a man's life will be gone. I have other affairs to attend to. I came into this world, not chiefly to make this a good place to live in, but to live in it, be it good or bad. A man has not everything to do, but something; and because he cannot do *everything,* it is not necessary that he should do *something* wrong. It is not my business to be petitioning the Governor or the Legislature any more than it is theirs to petition me; and if they should not hear my petition, what should I do then? But in this case the State has provided no way: its very Constitution is the evil. This may seem to be harsh and stubborn and unconciliatory; but it is to treat with the utmost kindness and consideration the only spirit that can appreciate or deserve it. So is all change for the better, like birth and death, which convulse the body.

I do not hesitate to say, that those who call themselves Abolitionists should at once effectually withdraw their support, both in person and property, from the government of Massachusetts, and not wait till they constitute a majority of one, before they suffer the right to prevail through them. I think that it is enough if they have God on their side, without waiting for that other one. Moreover, any man more right than his neighbors constitutes a majority of one already.

I meet this American government, or its representative, the State government, directly, and face to face, once a year—no more—in the person of its tax-gatherer; this is the only mode in which a man situated as I am necessarily meets it; and it then says distinctly, Recognize me; and the simplest, the most effectual, and, in the present posture of affairs, the indispensablest mode of treating with it on this head, of expressing your little satisfaction with and love for it, is to deny it then. My civil neighbor, the tax-gatherer, is the very man I have to deal with—for it is, after all, with men and not with parchment that I quarrel—and he has voluntarily chosen to be an agent of the government. How shall he ever know well what he is and does as an officer of the government, or as a man, until he is obliged to consider whether he shall treat me, his neighbor, for whom he has respect, as a neighbor and well-disposed man, or as a maniac and disturber of the peace, and see if he can get over this obstruction to his neighborliness without a ruder and more impetuous thought or speech corresponding with his action. I know this well, that if one thousand, if one hundred, if ten men whom I could name—if ten *honest* men only—ay, if *one* HONEST man, in this State of Massachusetts, *ceasing to hold slaves,* were actually to withdraw from this copartnership, and be locked up in the county jail therefor, it would be the abolition of slavery in America. For it matters not how small the beginning may seem to be: what is once well done is done forever. But we love better to talk about it: that we say is our mission. Reform keeps many scores of newspapers in its service, but not one man. If my esteemed neighbor, the State's ambassador, who will devote his days to the settlement of the question of human rights in the Council Chamber, instead of being threatened with the prisons of Carolina, were to sit down the prisoner of Massachusetts, that State which is so anxious to foist the sin of slavery upon her sister—though at present she can discover only an act of inhospitality to be the ground of a quarrel with her—the Legislature would not wholly waive the subject the following winter.

Under a government which imprisons any unjustly, the true place for a just man is also a prison. The proper place today, the only place which Massachusetts has provided for her freer and less desponding spirits, is in her prisons, to be put out and locked out of the State by her own act, as they have already put themselves out by their principles. It is there that the fugitive slave, and the Mexican prisoner on parole, and the Indian come to plead the wrongs of his race should find them; on that separate, but more free and honorable, ground, where the State places those who are not *with* her, but *against* her—the only house in a slave State in which a free man can abide with honor. If any think that their influence would be lost there, and their voices no longer afflict the ear of the State, that they would not be as an enemy within its walls, they do not know by how much truth is stronger than error, nor how much more eloquently and effectively he can combat injustice who has experienced a little in his own person. Cast your whole vote, not a strip of paper merely, but your whole influence. A minority is powerless while it conforms to the majority; it is not even a minority then; but it is irresistible when it clogs by its whole weight. If the alternative is to keep all just men in prison, or give up war and slavery, the State will not hesitate which to choose. If a thousand men were not to pay their tax-bills this year, that would not be a violent and bloody measure, as it would be to pay them, and enable the State to commit violence and shed innocent blood. This is, in fact, the definition of a peaceable revolution, if any such is possible. If the tax-gatherer, or any other public officer, asks me, as one has done, "But what shall I do?" my answer is, "If you really wish to do anything, resign your office." When the subject has refused allegiance, and the officer has resigned his office, then the revolution is accomplished. But even suppose blood should flow. Is there not a sort of blood shed when the conscience is wounded? Through this would a man's real manhood and immortality flow out, and he bleeds to an everlasting death. I see his blood flowing now.

I have contemplated the imprisonment of the offender, rather than the seizure of his goods—though both will serve the same purpose—because they who assert the purest right, and consequently are most dangerous to a corrupt State, commonly have not spent much time in accumulating property. To such the State renders comparatively small service, and a slight tax is wont to appear exorbitant, particularly if they are obliged to earn it be special labor with their hands. If there were one who lived wholly without the use of money, the State itself would hesitate to demand it of him. But the rich man—not to make any invidious comparison—is always sold to the institution which makes him rich. Absolutely speaking, the more money, the less virtue; for money comes between a man and his objects, and obtains them for him; and it was certainly no great virtue to obtain it. It puts to rest many questions which he would otherwise be taxed to answer; while the only new question which it puts is the hard but superfluous one, how to spend it. Thus his moral ground is taken from under his feet. The opportunities of living are diminished in proportion as what are called the "means" are increased. The best thing a man can do for his culture when he is rich is to endeavor to carry out those schemes which he entertained when he was poor. Christ answered the Herodians according to their condition. "Show me the tribute-money," said he;—and one took a penny out of his pocket;—if you use money which has the image of Caesar on it, and which he has made current and valuable, that is, *if you are men of the State,* and gladly enjoy the advantages of Caesar's government, then pay him back some of his own when he demands it. "Render therefore to Caesar that which is Caesar's, and to God those things which are God's"—leaving them no wiser than before to which was which; for they did not wish to know.

When I converse with the freest of my neighbors, I perceive that, whatever they may say about the magnitude and seriousness of the question, and their regard for the public tranquility, the long and the short of the matter is, that they cannot spare the protection of the existing government, and they dread the consequences to their property and families of disobedience to it. For my own part, I should not like to think that I ever rely on the protection of the State. But, if I deny the authority of the State when it presents its tax-bill, it will soon take and waste all my property, and so harass me and my children without end. This is hard. This makes it impossible for a man to live honestly, and at the same time comfortably, in outward respects. It will not be worth the while to accumulate property; that would be sure to go again. You must hire or squat somewhere, and raise but a small crop, and eat that soon. You must live within yourself, and depend upon yourself always tucked up and ready for a start, and not have many affairs. A man may grow rich in Turkey even, if he will be in all respects a good subject of the Turkish government. Confucius said: "If a state is governed by the principles of reason, poverty and misery are subjects of shame; if a state is not governed by the principles of reason, riches and honors are the subjects of shame." No.: until I want the protection of Massachusetts to be extended to me in some distant Southern port, where my liberty is endangered, or until I am bent solely on building up an estate at home by peaceful enterprise, I can afford to refuse allegiance to Massachusetts, and her right to my property and life. It costs me less in every sense to incur the penalty of disobedience to the State than it would to obey. I should feel as if I were worth less in that case.

Some years ago, the State met me in behalf of the Church, and commanded me to pay a certain sum toward the support of a clergyman whose preaching my father attended, but never I myself. "Pay," it said, "or be locked up in the jail." I declined to pay. But, unfortunately, another man saw fit to pay it. I did not see why the schoolmaster should be taxed to support the priest, and not the priest the schoolmaster; for I was not the State's schoolmaster, but I supported myself by voluntary subscription. I did not see why the lyceum should not present its tax-bill, and have the State to back its demand, as well as the Church. However, at the request of the selectmen, I condescended to make some such statement as this in writing: —"Know all men by these presents, that I, Henry Thoreau, do not wish to be regarded as a member of any incorporated society which I have not

joined." This I gave to the town clerk; and he has it. The State, having thus learned that I did not wish to be regarded as member of that church, has never made a like demand on me since; though it said that it must adhere to its original presumption that time. If I had known how to name them, I should then have signed off in detail from all the societies which I never signed on to; but I did not know where to find a complete list.

I have paid no poll tax for six years. I was put into a jail once on this account, for one night; and, as I stood considering the walls of solid stone, two or three feet thick, the door of wood and iron, a foot thick, and the iron grating which strained the light, I could not help being struck with the foolishness of that institution which treated me as if I were mere flesh and blood and bones, to be locked up. I wondered that it should have concluded at length that this was the best use it could put me to, and had never thought to avail itself of my services in some way. I saw that, if there was a wall of stone between me and my townsmen, there was a still more difficult one to climb or break through before they could get to be as free as I was. I did not for a moment feel confined, and the walls seemed a great waste of stone and mortar. I felt as if I alone of all my townsmen had paid my tax. They plainly did not know how to treat me, but behaved like persons who are underbred. In every threat and in every compliment there was a blunder; for they thought that my chief desire was to stand the other side of stone wall. I could not but smile to see how industriously they locked the door on my meditations, which followed them out again without let or hindrance, and *they* were really all that was dangerous. As they could not reach me, they had resolved to punish my body, just as boys, if they cannot come at some person against whom they have a spite, will abuse his dog. I saw that the State was half-witted, that it was timid as a lone woman with her silver spoons, and that it did not know its friends from its foes, and I lost all my remaining respect for it, and pitied it.

Thus the State never intentionally confronts a man's sense, intellectual or moral, but only his body, his senses. It is not armed with superior wit or honesty, but with superior physical strength. I was not born to be forced. I will breathe after my own fashion. Let us see who is the strongest. What force has a multitude? They only can force me who obey a higher law than I. They force me to become like themselves. I do not hear of *men* being *forced* to live this way or that by masses of men. What sort of life were that to live? When I meet a government which says to me, "Your money or your life," why should I be in haste to give it my money? It may be in a great strait, and not know what to do: I cannot help that. It must help itself; do as I do. It is not worth the while to snivel about it. I am not responsible for the successful working of the machinery of society. I am not the son of the engineer. I perceive that, when an acorn and a chestnut fall side by side, the one does not remain inert to make way for the other, but both obey their own laws, and spring and grow and flourish as best they can, till one, perchance, over-shadows and destroys the other. If a plant cannot live according to its nature, it dies; and so a man.

The night in prison was novel and interesting enough. The prisoners in their shirt-sleeves were enjoying a chat and the evening air in the doorway, when I entered. But the jailer said, "Come, boys, it is time to lock up;" and so they dispersed, and I heard the sound of their steps returning into the hollow apartments. My room-mate was introduced to me by the jailer as "a first-rate fellow and a clever man." When the door was locked, he showed me where to hang my hat, and how he managed matters there. The rooms were whitewashed once a month; and this one, at least, was the whitest, most simply furnished, and probably the neatest apartment in the town. He naturally wanted to know where I came from, and what brought me there; and, when I had told him, I asked him in my turn how he came there, presuming him to be an honest man, of course; and, as the world goes, I believe he was. "Why" said he, "they accuse me of burning a barn; but I never did it." As near as I could discover, he had probably gone to bed in a barn when drunk, and smoked his pipe there; and so a barn was burnt. He had the reputation of being a clever man, had been there some three months waiting for his trial to come on, and would have to wait as much longer; but he was quite domesti-cated and contented, since he got his board for nothing, and thought that he was well treated.

He occupied one window, and I the other; and I saw that if one stayed there long, his principal business would be to look out the window. I had soon red all the tracts that were left there, and examined where former prisoners had broken out, and where a grate had been sawed off, and heard the history of the various occupants of that room; for I found that even here there was a history and a gossip which never cir-culated beyond the walls of the jail. Probably this is the only house in the town where verses are composed, which are afterward printed in a circular form, but not published. I was shown quite a long list of verses which were composed by some young men who had been de-tected in an attempt to escape, who avenged themselves by singing them.

I pumped my fellow-prisoner as dry as I could, for fear I should never see him again; but at length he showed me which was my bed, and left me to blow out the lamp.

It was like traveling into a far coun-try, such as I had never expected to behold, to lie there for one night. It seemed to me that I never had heard the town clock strike before, nor the evening sounds of the village; for we slept with the windows open, which were

inside the grating. It was to see my
native village in the light of the Middle
Ages, and our Concord was turned into
a Rhine stream, and visions of knights
and castles passed before me. They were
the voices of old burghers that I heard
in the streets. I was an involuntary
spectator and auditor of whatever was
done and said in the kitchen of the
adjacent village inn—a wholly new and
rare experience to me. It was a closer
view of my native town. I was fairly
inside of it. I never had seen its institutions before. This is one of its peculiar
institutions; for it is a shire town. I
began to comprehend what its inhabitants were about.

In the morning, our breakfasts were
put through the hole in the door, in
small oblong-square tin pans, made to
fit, and holding a pint of chocolate,
with brown bread, and an iron spoon.
When they called for the vessels again,
I was green enough to return what
bread I had left; but my comrade seized
it, and said that I should lay that up
for lunch or dinner. Soon after he was
let out to work at haying in a neighboring field, whither he went every day,
and would not be back till noon; so he
bade be goodday, saying that he doubted
if he should see me again.

When I came out of prison—for some
one interfered, and paid that tax—I did
not perceive that great changes had
taken place on the common, such as he
observed who went in a youth and
emerged a tottering and gray-headed
man; and yet a change had to my eyes
come over the scene—the town, and
State, and country—greater than any
that mere time could effect. I saw yet
more distinctly the State in which I
lived. I saw to what extent the people
among whom I lived could be trusted
as good neighbors and friends; that their
friendship was for summer weather only;
that they did not greatly propose to do
right; that they were a distinct race
from me by their prejudices and super-
stitions, as the Chinamen and Malays
are; that in their sacrifices to humanity
they ran no risks, not even to their

property; that after all they were not
so noble but they treated the thief as
he had treated them, and hoped, by a
certain outward observance and a few
prayers, and by walking in a particular
straight though useless path from time
to time, to save their souls. This may
be to judge my neighbors harshly; but
I believe that many of them are not
aware that they have such an institution
as the jail in their village.

It was formerly the custom in our
village, when a poor debtor came out
of jail, for his acquaintances to salute
him, looking through their fingers, which
were crossed to represent the grating of
a jail window, "How do ye do?" My
neighbors did not thus salute me, but
first looked at me, and then at one
another, as if I had returned from a
long journey. I was put into jail as I
was going to the shoemaker's to get a
shoe which was mended. When I was
let out the next morning, I proceeded
to finish my errand, and, having put
on my mended shoe, joined a huckle-
berry party, who were impatient to put
themselves under my conduct; and in
half an hour—for the horse was soon
tackled—was in the midst of a huckle-
berry field, on one of our highest hills,
two miles off, and then the State was
nowhere to be seen.

This is the whole history of "My
Prisons."

I have never declined paying the
highway tax, because I am as desirous
of being a good neighbor as I am of
being a bad subject; and as for supporting schools, I am doing my part to
educate my fellow-countrymen now. It
is for no particular item in the tax-bill
that I refuse to pay it. I simply wish
to refuse allegiance to the State, to
withdraw and stand aloof from it effectually. I do not care to trace the
course of my dollar, if I could, till it
buys a man or a musket to shoot one
with—the dollar is innocent—but I am
concerned to trace the effects of my
allegiance. In fact, I quietly declare war
with the State, after my fashion, though

I will still make what use and get what advantage of her I can, as is usual in such cases.

If others pay the tax which is demanded of me, from a sympathy with the State, they do but what they have already done in their own case, or rather they abet injustice to a greater extent than the State requires. If they pay the tax from a mistaken interest in the individual taxed, to save his property, or prevent his going to jail, it is because they have not considered wisely how far they let their private feelings interfere with the public good.

This, then, is my position at present. But one cannot be too much on his guard in such a case, lest his action be biased by obstinacy or an undue regard for the opinions of men. Let him see that he does only what belongs to himself and to the hour.

I think sometimes, Why, this people mean well, they are only ignorant; they would do better if they knew how: why give your neighbors this pain to treat you as they are not inclined to? But I think again, This is no reason why I should do as they do, or permit others to suffer much greater pain of a different kind. Again, I sometimes say to myself, When many millions of men, without heat, without ill will, without personal feelings of any kind, demand of you a few shillings only, without the possibility, such is their constitution, of retracting or altering their present demand, and without the possibility, on your side, of appeal to any other millions, why expose yourself to this overwhelming brute force? You do not resist cold and hunger, the winds and the waves, thus obstinately; you quietly submit to a thousand similar necessities. You do not put your head into the fire. But just in proportion as I regard this as not wholly a brute force, but partly a human force, and consider that I have relations to those millions as to so many millions of men, and not of mere brute or inanimate things, I see that appeal is possible, first and instantaneously, from them to the Maker of them, and, sec-

ondly, from them to themselves. But if I put my head deliberately into the fire, there is no appeal to fire or to the Maker of fire, and I have only myself to blame. If I could convince myself that I have any right to be satisfied with men as they are, and to treat them accordingly, and not according, in some respects, to my requisitions and expectations of what they and I ought to be, then, like a good Musselman and fatalist, I should endeavor to be satisfied with things as they are, and say it is the will of God. And, above all, there is this difference between resisting this and a purely brute or natural force, that I can resist this with some effect; but I cannot expect, like Orpheus, to change the nature of the rocks and trees and beasts.

I do not wish to quarrel with any man or nation. I do not wish to split hairs, to make fine distinctions, or set myself up as better than my neighbors. I seek rather, I may say, even an excuse for conforming to the laws of the land. I am but too ready to conform to them. Indeed, I have reason to suspect myself on this head; and each year, as the taxgatherer comes round, I find myself disposed to review the acts and position of the general and State governments, and the spirit of the people, to discover a pretext for conformity.

We must affect our country as our parents,
And if at any time we alienate
Our love or industry from doing it honor,
We must respect effects and teach the soul
Matter of conscience and religion,
And not desire of rule or benefit.

I believe that the State will soon be able to take all my work of this sort out of my hands, and then I shall be no better a patriot than my fellow-countrymen. Seen from a lower point of view, the Constitution, with all its faults, is very good; the law and the courts are very respectable; even this State and this American government, are, in many respects, very admirable, and rare things, to be thankful for, such as a great many have described them; but seen from a point of view a little higher, they are what I have described them; seen from a higher still, and the highest, who shall say what they are, or that they are worth looking at or thinking of at all?

However, the government does not concern me much, and I shall bestow the fewest possible thoughts on it. It is not many moments that I live under a government, even in this world. If a man is thought-free, fancy-free, imagination-free, that which *is not* never for a long time appearing *to be* to him, unwise rulers or reformers cannot fatally interrupt him.

I know that most men think differently from myself; but those whose lives are by profession devoted to the study of these or kindred subjects content me as little as any. Statesmen and legislators, standing so completely within the institution, never distinctly and nakedly behold it. They speak of moving society, but have no resting-place without it. They may be men of a certain experience and discrimination, and have no doubt invented ingenious and even useful systems, for which we sincerely thank them; but all their wit and usefulness lie within certain not very wide limits. They are wont to forget that the world is not governed by policy and expediency. Webster never goes behind government, and so cannot speak with authority about it. His words are wisdom to those legislators who contemplate no essential reform in the existing government; but for thinkers, and those who legislate for all time, he never once glances at the subject. I know of those whose serene and wise specualtions on this theme would soon reveal the limits of his mind's range and hospitality. Yet, compared with the cheap professions of most reformers, and the still cheaper wisdom and eloquence of politicians in general, his are almost the only sensible and valuable words, and we thank Heaven for him. Comparatively, he is always strong, original, and, above all, practical. Still, his quality is not wisdom, but prudence. The lawyer's truth is not Truth, but consistency or a consistent

expediency. Truth is always in harmony with herself, and is not concerned chiefly to reveal the justice that may consist with wrong-doing. He well deserves to be called, as he has been called, the Defender of the Constitution. There are really no blows to be given by him but defensive ones. He is not a leader, but a follower. His leaders are the men of '87. "I have never made an effort," he says, "and never propose to make an effort; I have never countenanced an effort, and never mean to countenance an effort, to disturb the arrangement as originally made, by which the various States came into the Union." Still thinking of the sanction which the Constitution gives to slavery, he says, "Because it was a part of the original compact— let it stand." Notwithstanding his special acuteness and ability, he is unable to take a fact out of its merely political relations, and behold it as it lies absolutely to be disposed of by the intellect—what, for instance, it behooves a man to do here in America today with regard to slavery—but ventures, or is driven, to make some such desperate answer as the following, while professing to speak absolutely, and as a private man—from which what new and singular code of social duties might be inferred? "The manner," says he, "in which the governments of those States where slavery exists are to regulate it is for their own consideration, under their responsibility to their constituents, to the general laws of propriety, humanity, and justice, and to God. Associations formed elsewhere, springing from a feeling of humanity, or any other cause, having nothing whatever to do with it. They have never received any encouragement from me, and they never will." (*Note.* These extracts have been inserted since the lecture was read.)

They who know of no purer sources of truth, who have traced up its stream no higher, stand, and wisely stand, by the Bible and the Constitution, and drink at it there with reverence and humility; but they who behold where it comes trickling into this lake or that pool, gird up their loins once more, and continue their pilgrimage toward its fountain-head.

No man with a genius for legislation has appeared in America. They are rare in the history of the world. There are orators, politicians, and eloquent men, by the thousand; but the speaker has not yet opened his mouth to speak who is capable of settling the much-vexed questions of the day. We love eloquence for its own sake, and not for any truth which it may utter, or any heroism it may inspire. Our legislators have not yet learned the comparative value of free trade and of freedom, of union, and of rectitude, to a nation. They have no genius or talent for comparatively humble questions of taxation and finance, commerce and manufactures and agriculture. If we were left solely to the wordy wit of legislators in Congress for our guidance, uncorrected by the reasonable experience and the effectual complaints of the people, America would not long retain her rank among the nations. For eighteen hundred years, though perchance I have no right to say it, the New Testament has been written; yet where is the legislator who has wisdom and practical talent enough to avail himself of the light which it sheds on the science of legislation?

The authority of government, even such as I am willing to submit to—for I will cheerfully obey those who know and can do better than I, and in many things even those who neither know nor can do so well—is still an impure one: to be strictly just, it must have the sanction and consent of the governed. It can have no pure right over my person and property but what I concede to it. The progress from an absolute to a limited monarchy, from a limited monarchy to a democracy, is a progress toward a true respect for the individual. Even the Chinese philosopher was wise enough to regard the individual as the basis of the empire. Is a democracy, such as we know it, the last improvement possible in government? Is it not

possible to take a step further towards recognizing and organizing the rights of man? There will never be a really free and enlightened State until the State comes to recognize the individual as a higher and independent power, from which all its own power and authority are derived, and treats him accordingly. I please myself with imagining a State at least which can afford to be just to all men, and to treat the individual with respect as a neighbor; which even would not think it inconsistent with its own repose if a few were to live aloof from it, not meddling with it, nor embraced by it, who fulfilled all the duties of neighbors and fellow-men. A State which bore this kind of fruit, and suffered it to drop off as fast as it ripened, would prepare the way for a still more perfect and glorious State, which also I have imagined, but not yet anywhere seen.

WORKS OF
HENRY DAVID THOREAU

The Correspondence of Henry David Thoreau. Edited by Walter Harding and Carl Bode. . New York: Washington Square, 1958. A thorough collection of Thoreau's letters.

The Heart of Thoreau's Journals. Edited by Odell Shepard. Boston: Houghton, Mifflin and Co., 1927. These representative selections provide a good cross section of the *Journal* in one volume.

The Journal of Henry D. Thoreau. Edited by Bradford Terrey and Francis H. Allen. 14 Vols. Cambridge, Massachusetts: Houghton, Mifflin and Co., 1906. A collection of Thoreau's diaries which contain the thoughts and feelings that were later to be developed into full-length essays.

Thoreau, Henry David. *Cape Cod.* Boston: Houghton, Mifflin and Co., 1893. A vivid and humorous description of the author's impression of the land and people of Cape Cod.

Thoreau, Henry David. *Excursions.* Boston: Houghton, Mifflin and Co., 1893. A collection of travel essays interspersed with philosophical comments and observations.

_____. *The Maine Woods.* Boston: Houghton, Mifflin and Co., 1864. Composed of three separate, but repetitive, essays describing both Indian folkways and the Maine country side.

————. *Walden.* 2 Vols. Boston: Houghton, Mifflin, and Co., 1854. Reflections on man's freedom and responsibilities developed in the solitude of nature.

————. *A Week on the Concord and Merrimack Rivers.* Boston: Houghton, Mifflin, and Co., 1867. Thoreau's Transcendentalism expressed through the medium of a travel book.

MAJOR SOURCES ON HENRY DAVID THOREAU

Channing, William Ellery. *Thoreau, The Poet-Naturalist.* Boston: Merrymount Press, 1902. Written by a close friend of Thoreau, this biography expresses the warmth and poetic qualities of the subject.

Dabbs, James McBride. "Thoreau: The Adventurer as Economist," *The Yale Review,* Vol. XXXVI, No. 4 (June, 1947), pp. 667-672. A mellow essay depicting Thoreau's concept of economy as applied to the personal life.

Derleth, August. *Concord Rebel.* Philadelphia: Chilton, 1962. A biography extolling the subject as an original and deeply profound thinker, completely alien to the American society.

Jackson, Holbrook. "Thoreau," in *Dreamers of Dreams.* London: Faber and Faber, pp. 211-254. Included in this work on 19th century Idealists, Thoreau demonstrates his ardent belief in Americanism by rejecting European thought due to its inadequacy in creating a "new" society.

Mackaye, James (ed.). *Thoreau: Philosopher of Freedom.* New York: Vanguard, 1930. Selections from the writings of Thoreau with introductory remarks by the editor.

Paul, Sherman. *The Shores of America.* Urbana, Ill.: University of Illinois Press, 1958. An analysis of Thoreau's Transcendentalism through an examination of his thoughts and actions.

Stoller, Leo. *After Walden.* Stanford: Stanford University Press, 1957. A study of Thoreau and his quest for social justice through legislation after having rejected mysticism and utopian impulses.

Van Doren, Mark. *Henry David Thoreau: A Critical Study.* New York: Russell, 1961. Thoreau is portrayed as a cynical hermit who is developed into a classic figure due to the periodic necessity of creating such a myth.

CHAPTER 9

John C. Calhoun

JOHN C. Calhoun (1782–1850), was born to a prosperous South
Carolinian family, graduated from Yale in 1804. In 1807, Calhoun
was admitted to the bar and in the following year entered the South
Carolina legislature.

Calhoun entered Congress in 1811 where he soon rose to national
attention by his outspoken support of the war with Great Britain.
In 1817, President Monroe asked Calhoun to be secretary of the
War Department. During his seven and a half years of tenure,
Calhoun improved the organization of the army and the Department
of War immensely.

In 1824, Calhoun accepted the nomination of his party for the
vice-presidency; with the election thrown into the House of Representatives, Adams and Calhoun were elected to the presidency and
vice-presidency respectively. In 1828, Calhoun was elected for a
second term as vice-president, this time with Andrew Jackson heading
the ticket. However, Calhoun and Jackson soon clashed over political,
social, and personal questions.

Returning to the Senate in the beginning of 1833, Calhoun came to
be regarded as the main source of arguments, plans, and inspiration
for the Southern bloc over the slavery question. In early 1844, President Tyler's secretary of state died and Calhoun was asked to fill
the vacancy. Calhoun accepted the position, but he was not asked
to remain in President Polk's cabinet. In the last years of his life,
Calhoun wrote two major works: "A Disquisition on Government,"
and "A Discourse on the Constitution and Government of the United
States."

From a Disquisition on Government

THE NATURE OF MAN AND THE ORIGIN OF GOVERNMENT

In order to have a clear and just conception of the nature and object of government, it is indispensable to understand correctly what that constitution or law of our nature is in which government originates, or to express it more fully and accurately—that law without which government would not and with which it must necessarily exist. Without this, it is as impossible to lay any solid foundation for the science of government as it would be to lay one for that of astronomy without a like understanding of that constitution or law of the material world according to which the several bodies composing the solar system mutually act on each other and by which they are kept in their respective spheres. The first question, accordingly, to be considered, What is that constitution or law of our nature without which government would not exist and with which its existence is necessary?

In considering this, I assume as an incontestable fact that man is so constituted as to be a social being. His inclinations and wants, physical and moral, irresistibly impel him to associate with his kind; and he has, accordingly, never been found, in any age or country, in any state other than the social. In no other, indeed, could he exist, and in no other—were it possible for him to exist—could he attain to a full development of his moral and intellectual faculties or raise himself, in the scale of being, much above the level of the brute creation.

I next assume also as a fact not less incontestable that, while man is so constituted as to make the social state necessary to his existence and the full development of his faculties, this state itself cannot exist without government. The assumption rests on universal ex-perience. In no age or country has any society or community ever been found, whether enlightened or savage, without government of some description.

Having assumed these as unquestionable phenomena of our nature, I shall, without further remark, proceed to the investigation of the primary and important question, What is that constitution of our nature which, while it impels man to associate with his kind, renders it impossible for society to exist without government?

The answer will be found in the fact (not less contestable than either of the others that, while man is created for the social state and is accordingly so formed as to feel what affects others as well as what affects himself, he is, at the same time, so constituted as to feel more intensely what affects him directly than what affects him indirectly through others, or, to express it differently, he is so constituted that his direct or individual affections are stronger than his sympathetic or social feelings. I intentionally avoid the expression "selfish feelings" as applicable to the former, because, as commonly used, it implies an unusual excess of the individual over the social feelings in the person to whom it is applied and, consequently, something depraved and vicious. My object is to exclude such inference and to restrict the inquiry exclusively to facts in their bearings on the subject under consideration, viewed as mere phenomena appertaining to our nature—constituted as it is; and which are as unquestionable as is that of gravitation or any other phenomenon of the material world.

In asserting that our individual are stronger than our social feelings, it is not intended to deny that there are instances, growing out of peculiar relations—as that of a mother and her infant—or resulting from the force of education and habit over peculiar constitutions, in which the latter have overpowered the former; but these instances are few and always regarded as something extraordinary. The deep impression they make, whenever they occur, is the strongest proof that they are regarded as exceptions to some general and well-understood law of our nature, just as some of the minor powers of the material world are apparently to gravitation. . . .

It follows, then, that man is so constituted that government is necessary to the existence of society, and society to his existence and the perfection of his faculties. It follows also that government has its origin in this two-fold constitution of his nature: the sympathetic or social feelings constituting the remote, and the individual or direct the proximate, cause.

If man had been differently constituted in either particular—if, instead of being social in his nature, he had been created without sympathy for his kind and independent of others for his safety and existence; or if, on the other hand, he had been so created as to feel more intensely what affected others than what affected himself (if that were possible) or even had this supposed interest been equal—it is manifest that in either case there would have been no necessity for government, and that none would ever have existed. But although society and government are thus intimately connected with and dependent on each other—of the two society is the greater. It is the first in the order of things and in the dignity of its object; that of society being primary—to preserve and perfect our race—and that of government secondary and subordinate—to preserve and perfect society. Both are, however, necessary to the existence and well-being of our race and equally of divine ordination. . . .

But government, although intended to protect and preserve society, has itself a strong tendency to disorder and abuse of its powers, as all experience and almost every page of history testify. The cause is to be found in the same constitution of our nature which makes government indispensable. The powers which it is necessary for government to possess in order to repress violence and

preserve order cannot execute themselves. They must be administered by men in whom, like others, the individual are stronger than the social feelings. And hence the powers vested in them to prevent injustice and oppression on the part of others will, if left unguarded, be by them converted into instruments to oppress the rest of the community. That by which this is prevented, by whatever name called, is what is meant by *constitution,* in its most comprehensive sense, when applied to *government.*

Having its origin in the same principle of our nature, *constitution* stands to *government* as *government* stands to *society;* and as the end for which society is ordained would be defeated without government, so that for which government is ordained would, in a great measure, be defeated without constitution. But they differ in this striking particular. There is no difficulty in forming government. It is not even a matter of choice whether there shall be one or not. Like breathing, it is not permitted to depend on our volition. Necessity will force it on all communities in some one form or another. Very different is the case as to constitution. Instead of a matter of necessity, it is one of the most difficult tasks imposed on man to form a constitution worthy of the name, while to form a perfect one—one that would completely counteract the tendency of government to oppression and abuse and hold it strictly to the great ends for which it is ordained—has thus far exceeded human wisdom, and possible ever will. From this another striking difference results. Constitution is the contrivance of man, while government is of divine ordination. Man is left to perfect what the wisdom of the Infinite ordained as necessary to preserve the race.

With these remarks I proceed to the consideration of the important and difficult question, How is this tendency of government to be counteracted? Or, to express it more fully, How can those who are invested with the powers of government be prevented from employing them as the means of aggrandizing themselves instead of using them to protect and preserve society? . . .

There is but one way in which this can possibly be done, and that is by such an organism as will furnish the ruled with the means of resisting successfully this tendency on the part of the rulers to oppression and abuse. Power can only be resisted by power— and tendency by tendency. Those who exercise power and those subject to its exercise—the rulers and the ruled— stand in antagonistic relations to each other. The same constitution of our nature which leads rulers to oppress the ruled—regardless of the object for which government is ordained—will, with equal strength, lead the ruled to resist when possessed of the means of making peaceable and effective resistance. Such an organism, then, as will furnish the means by which resistance may be systematically and peaceably made on the part of the ruled to oppression and abuse of power on the part of the rulers is the first and indispensable step toward *forming* a constitutional government. And as this can only be effected by or through the right of suffrage—the right on the part of the ruled to choose their rulers at proper intervals and to hold them thereby responsible for their conduct—the responsibility of the rulers to the ruled, through the right of suffrage, is the indispensable and primary principle in the *foundation* of a constitutional government. When this right is properly guarded, and the people sufficiently enlightened to understand their own rights and the interests of the community and duly to appreciate the motives and conduct of those appointed to make and execute the laws, it is all-sufficient to give to those who elect effective control over those they have elected.

I call the right of suffrage the indispensable and primary principle, for it would be a great and dangerous mistake to suppose, as many do, that it is, of itself, sufficient to form constitutional governments. . . .

The right of suffrage, of itself, can do more than give complete control to those who elect over the conduct of those they have elected. . . . The sum total, then, of its effects, when most successful, is to make those elected the true and faithful representatives of those who elected them—instead of irresponsible rulers, as they would be without it; and thus, by converting it into an agency, and the rulers into agents, to divest government of all claims to sovereignty and to retain it unimpaired to the community. But it is manifest that the right of suffrage in making these changes transfers, in reality, the actual control over the government from those who make and execute the laws to the body of the community and thereby places the powers of the government fully in the mass of the community as they would be if they, in fact, had assembled, made, and executed the laws themselves without the intervention of representatives or agents. The more perfectly it does this, the more perfectly it accomplishes its ends; but in doing so, it only changes the seat of authority without counteracting, in the least, the tendency of the government to oppression and abuse of its powers.

If the whole community had the same interests so that the interests of each and every portion would be so affected by the action of the government that the laws which oppressed or impoverished one portion would necessarily oppress and impoverish all others—or the reverse—then the right of suffrage, of itself, would be all-sufficient to counteract the tendency of the government to oppression and abuse of its powers, and, of course, would form, of itself, a perfect constitutional government. The interest of all being the same, by supposition, as far as the action of the government was concerned, all would have like interests as to what laws should be made and how they should be executed. All strife and struggle would cease as to who should be elected to make and execute them. The only question would be, who was most fit, who the wisest and most capable of understanding the common interest of the whole. This decided, the election would pass off quietly and without party discord, as no one portion could advance its own peculiar interest without regard to the rest by electing a favorite candidate.

But such is not the case. On the contrary, nothing is more difficult than equalize the action of the government in reference to the various and diversified interests of the community; and nothing more easy than to pervert its powers into instruments to aggrandize and enrich one or more interests by oppressing and impoverishing the others; and this, too, under the operation of laws couched in general terms and which, on their face, appear fair and equal. Nor is this the case in some particular communities only. It is so in all—the small and the great, the poor and the rich—irrespective of pursuits, productions, or degrees of civilization; with, however, this difference, that the more extensive and populous the country, the more diversified the condition and pursuits of its population; and the richer, more luxurious, and dissimilar the people, the more difficult it is to equalize the action of the government, and the more easy for one portion of the community to pervert its powers to oppress and plunder the other.

Such being the case, it necessarily results that the right of suffrage, by placing the control of the government in the community, must, from the same constitution of our nature which makes government necessary to preserve society, lead to conflict among its different interests—each striving to obtain possession of its powers as the means of protecting itself against the others or of advancing its respective interests regardless of the interests of others. For this purpose, a struggle will take place between the various interests to obtain a majority in order to control the government. If no one interest be strong enough, of itself, to obtain it, a combination will be formed between those

whose interests are most alike—each conceding something to the others until a sufficient number is obtained to make a majority. The process may be slow and much time may be required before a compact, organized majority can be thus formed, but formed it will be in time, even without preconcert or design, by the sure workings of that principle or constitution of our nature in which government itself originates. When once formed, the community will be divided into two great parties—a major and minor—between which there will be incessant struggles on the one side to retain, and on the other to obtain the majority and, thereby, the control of the government and the advantages it confers.

So deeply seated, indeed, is this tendency to conflict between the different interests or portions of the community that it would result from the action of the government itself, even though it were possible to find a community where the people were all of the same pursuits, placed in the same condition of life, and in every respect so situated as to be without inequality of condition or diversity of interests. The advantages of possessing the control of the powers of the government, and thereby of its honors and emoluments, are, of themselves, exclusive of all other considerations, ample to divide even such a community into two great hostile parties.

In order to form a just estimate of the full force of these advantages, without reference to any other consideration, it must be remembered that government— to fulfill the ends for which it is ordained, and more especially that of protection against external dangers— must in the present condition of the world be clothed with powers sufficient to call forth the resources of the community and be prepared at all times to command them promptly in every emergency which may possibly arise. For this purpose large establishments are necessary, both civil and military (including naval, where, from situation, that description of force may be required), with all the means necessary for prompt and effective action, such as fortifications, fleets, armories, arsenals, magazines, arms of all descriptions, with well-trained forces in sufficient numbers to wield them with skill and energy whenever the occasion requires it. The administration and management of a government with such vast establishments must necessarily require a host of employees, agents, and officers—of whom many must be vested with high and responsible trusts and occupy exalted stations accompanied with much influence and patronage. To meet the necessary expenses, large sums must be collected and disbursed, and for this purpose heavy taxes must be imposed, requiring a multitude of officers for their collection and disbursement. The whole united must necessarily place under the control of government an amount of honors and emoluments sufficient to excite profoundly the ambition of the aspiring and the cupidity of the avaricious, and to lead to the formation of hostile parties and violent party conflicts and struggles to obtain the control of the government. And what makes this evil remediless through the right of suffrage of itself, however modified or carefully guarded or however enlightened the people, is the fact that, as far as the honors and emoluments of the government and its fiscal action are concerned, it is impossible to equalize it. The reason is obvious. Its honors and emoluments, however great, can fall to the lot of but a few, compared to the entire number of the community and the multitude who will seek to participate in them. But without this there is a reason which renders it impossible to equalize the action of the government so far as its fiscal oepration extends— which I shall next explain. . . .

Some one portion of the community must pay in taxes more than it receives back in disbursements, while another receives in disbursements more than it pays in taxes. It is, then, manifest, taking the whole process together, that taxes must be, in effect, bounties to that portion of the community which receives more in disbursements than it pays in taxes, while to the other which pays in taxes more than it receives in disbursements they are taxes in reality—burthens instead of bounties. This consequence is unavoidable. It results from the nature of the process, be the taxes ever so equally laid and the disbursements ever so fairly made in reference to the public service. . . .

The necessary result, then, of the unequal fiscal action of the government is to divide the community into two great classes: one consisting of those who, in reality, pay the taxes and, of course, bear exclusively the burthen of supporting the government and the other, of those who are the recipients of their proceeds through disbursements, and who are, in fact, supported by the government; or, in fewer words, to divide it into tax-payers and tax-consumers.

But the effect of this is to place them in antagonistic relations in reference to the fiscal action of the government and the entire course of policy therewith connected. For the greater the taxes and disbursements, the greater the gain of the one and the loss of the other, and vice versa; and consequently, the more the policy of the government is calculated to increase taxes and disbursements, the more it will be favored by the one and opposed by the other.

The effect, then, of every increase is to enrich and strengthen the one, and impoverish and weaken the other. This, indeed, may be carried to such an extent that one class or portion of the community may be elevated to wealth and power, and the other depressed to abject poverty and dependence, simply by the fiscal action of the government; and this too through disbursements only— even under a system of equal taxes imposed for revenue only. If such may be the effect of taxes and disbursements when confined to their legitimate objects—that of raising revenue for the public service—some conception may be formed how one portion of the community may be crushed, and another elevated on its ruins, by systematically perverting the power of taxation and disbursement for the purpose of aggrandizing and building up one portion of the community at the expense of the other. That it *will* be so used, unless prevented, is, from the constitution of man, just as certain as that it *can* be so used; and that, if not prevented, it must give rise to two parties and to violent conflicts and struggles between them to obtain the control of the government, is, for the same reason, not less certain.

Nor is it less certain, from the operation of all these causes, that the dominant majority, for the time, would have the same tendency to oppression and abuse of power which, without the right of suffrage, irresponsible rulers would have. No reason, indeed, can be assigned why the latter would abuse their power, which would not apply, with equal force, to the former. The dominant majority, for the time, would in reality, through the right of suffrage, be the rulers—the controlling, governing, and irresponsible power; and those who make and execute the laws would, for the time, be in reality but *their* representatives and agents. . . .

As, then, the right of suffrage, without some other provision, cannot counteract the tendency of government, the next question for consideration is, What is that other provision? This demands the most serious consideration, for of all the questions embraced in the science of government it involves a principle, the most important and the least understood, and when understood, the most difficult of application in practice. It is, indeed, emphatically that principle which *makes* the constitution, in its strict and limited sense.

From what has been said, it is manifest that this provision must be of a character calculated to prevent any one interest or combination of interests from using the powers of government to aggrandize itself at the expense of others. Here lies the evil; and just in proportion as it shall prevent, or fail to prevent it, in the same degree it will effect, or fail to effect, the end intended to be accomplished. There is but one certain mode in which this result can be secured, and that is by the adoption of some restriction or limitation, which shall so effectually prevent any one interest or combination of interests from obtaining the exclusive control of the government as to render hopeless all attempts direct to that end. There is, again, but one mode in which this can be effected, and that is by taking the sense of each interest or portion of the community which may be unequally and injuriously affected by the action of the government separately, through its own majority of in some other way by which its voice may be fairly expressed, and to require the consent of each interest either to put or to keep the government in action. This, too, can be accomplished only in one way, and that is by such an organism of the government—and, if necessary for the purpose of the community also—as will, by dividing and distributing the powers of government, give to each division or interest, through its appropriate organ, either a concurrent voice in making and executing the laws or a veto on their execution. It is only by such an organism that the assent of each can be made necessary to put the government in motion, or the power made effectual to arrest its action when put in motion; and it is only by the one or the other that the different interests, orders, classes, or portions into which the community may be divided can be protected, and all conflict and struggle between them prevented—by rendering it impossible to put or to keep it in action without the concurrent consent of all.

Such an organism as this, combined with the right of suffrage, constitutes, in fact, the elements of constitutional government. The one, by rendering those who make and execute the laws responsible to those on whom they operate, prevents the rulers from oppressing the ruled; and the other, by making it impossible for any one in-interest or combination of interests, or class, or order, or portion of the community to obtain exclusive control, prevents any one of them from oppressing the other. It is clear that oppression and abuse of power must come, if at all, from the one or the other quarter. From no other can they come. It follows that the two, suffrage and proper organism combined, are sufficient to counteract the tendency of government to oppression and abuse of power and to restrict it to the fulfillment of the great ends for which it is ordained. . . .

It may be readily inferred, from what has been stated, the the effect of organism is neither to supersede nor diminish the importance of the right of suffrage, but to aid and perfect it. The object of the latter is to collect the sense of the community. The more fully and perfectly it accomplishes this, the more fully and perfectly it fulfills its end. But the most it can do, of itself, is to collect the sense of the greater number; that is, of the stronger interests or combination of interests, and to assume this to be the sense of the community. It is only when aided by a proper organism that it can collect the sense of the entire community, of each and all its interests—of each, through its appropriate organ, and of the whole through all of them united. This would truly be the sense of the entire community, for whatever diversity each interest might have within itself—as all would have the same interest in reference to the action of the government—the individuals composing each would be fully and truly represented by its own majority or appropriate organ, regarded in reference to the other interests. In brief, every individual of every interest might trust, with confidence, its majority or appropriate organ against that of every other interest.

THE NUMERICAL VERSUS THE CONCURRENT MAJORITY

It results, from what has been said, that there are two different modes in which the sense of the community may be taken: one, simply by the right of suffrage, unaided; the other, by the right through a proper organism. Each collects the sense of the majority. But one regards numbers only and considers the whole community as a unit having but one common interest throughout, and collects the sense of the greater number of the whole as that of the community. The other, on the contrary, regards interests as well as numbers—considering the community as made up of different and conflicting interests, as far as the action of the government is concerned—and takes the sense of each through its majority or appropriate organ, and the united sense of all as the sense of the entire community. The former of these I shall call the numerical or absolute majority, and the latter, the concurrent or constitutional majority. I call it the constitutional majority because it is an essential element in every constitutional government, be its form what it may. So great is the difference, politically speaking, between the two majorities that they cannot be confounded without leading to great and fatal errors; and yet the distinction between them has been so entirely overlooked that when the term "majority" is used in political discussions, it is applied exclusively to designate the numerical—as if there were no other. Until this distinction is recognized and better understood, there will continue to be great liability to error in properly constructing constitutional governments, especially of the popular form, and of preserving them when properly constructed. Until then, the latter will have a strong tendency to slide, first, into the government of the numerical majority, and finally, into absolute government of some other form. To show that such must be the case, and at the same time to mark more strongly the difference between the two in order to guard against the danger of overlooking it, I propose to consider the subject more at length.

THE NUMERICAL MAJORITY NOT THE PEOPLE

The first and leading error which naturally arises from overlooking the distinction referred to is to confound the numerical majority with the people, and this so completely as to regard them as identical. This is a consequence that necessarily results from considering the numerical as the only majority. All admit that a proper government, or democracy, is the government of the people, for the terms imply this. A perfect government of the kind would be one which would embrace the consent of every citizen or member of the community; but as this is impracticable in the opinion of those who regard the numerical as the only majority and who can perceive no other way by which the sense of the people can be taken, they are compelled to adopt this as the only true basis of popular government, in contradistinction to governments of the aristocratical or monarchial form. Being thus constrained, they are, in the next place, forced to regard the numerical majority as in effect the entire people; that is, the greater part as the whole, and the government of the greater part as the government of the whole. It is thus the two come to be confounded and a part made identical with the whole. And it is thus also that all the rights, powers, and immunities of the whole people come to be attributed to the numerical majority—and, among others, the supreme, sovereign authority of establishing and abolishing governments at pleasure.

This radical error, the consequence of confounding the two and of regarding the numerical as the only majority, has contributed more than any other cause to prevent the formation of popular constitutional governments and to destroy them even when they have been formed. It leads to the conclusion that in their formation and establishment nothing more is necessary than the right of suffrage and the allotment to each division of the community a representation in the government in proportion to numbers. If the numerical majority were really the people, and if to take its sense truly were to take the sense of the people truly, a government so constituted would be a true and perfect model of a popular constitutional government; and every departure from it would detract from its excellence. But as such is not the case, as the numerical majority, instead of being the people, is only a portion of them, such a government, instead of being a true and perfect model of the people's government, that is, a people self-governed, is but the government of a part over a part—the major over the minor portion.

But this misconception of the true elements of constitutional government does not stop here. It leads to others equally false and fatal, in reference to the best means of preserving and perpetuating them, when, from some fortunate combination of circumstances, they are correctly formed. For they who fall into these errors regard the restrictions which organism imposes on the will of the numerical majority as restrictions on the will of the people and, therefore, as not only useless but wrongful and mischievous. And hence they endeavor to destroy organism under the delusive hope of making government more democratic. . . .

Having now explained the reasons why it is so difficult to form and preserve popular constitutional government so long as the distinction between the two majorities is overlooked and the opinion prevails that a written constitution, with suitable restrictions and a proper division of its powers, is sufficient to counteract the tendency of the numerical majority to the abuse of its power—I shall next proceed to explain, more fully, why the concurrent majority is an indispensable element in forming constitutional governments, and why the numerical majority, of itself, must, in all cases, make governments absolute.

The necessary consequences of taking the sense of the community by the concurrent majority is, as has been explained, to give to each interest or portion of the community a negative on the others. It is this mutual negative among its various conflicting interests which invests each with the power of protecting itself, and places the rights and safety of each where only they can be securely placed, under its own guardianship. Without this there can be no systematic, peaceful, or effective resistance to the natural tendency of each to come into conflict with the others; and without this there can be no constitution. It is this negative power—the power of preventing or arresting the action of the government, be it called by what term it may, veto, interposition, nullification, check, or balance of power— which in fact forms the constitution. They are all but different names for the negative power. In all its forms, and under all its names, it results from the concurrent majority. Without this there can be no negative, and without a negative, no constitution. The assertion is true in reference to all constitutional governments, be their forms what they may. It is, indeed, the *negative* power which makes the constitution, and the *positive* which makes the government. The one is the power of acting, and the other the power of preventing or arresting action. The two, combined, make constitutional governments. . . .

Constitutional governments, of whatever form, are, indeed, much more similar to each other in their structure and character than they are, respectively, to the absolute governments, even of their own class. All constitutional governments, of whatever class they may be, take the sense of the community by its parts—each through its appropriate organ—and regard the sense of all its parts as the sense of the whole. They all rest on the right of suffrage and the responsibility of rulers, directly or indirectly. On the contrary, all absolute governments, of whatever form, concentrate power in one uncontrolled and irresponsible individual or body whose will is regarded as the sense of the community. And hence the great and broad distinction between governments is not that of the one, the few, or the many, but of the constitutional and the absolute.

From this there results another distinction which, although secondary in its character, very strongly marks the difference between these forms of government. I refer to their respective conservative principle—that is, the principle by which they are upheld and preserved. This principle in constitutional government is *compromise;* and in absolute governments is *force,* as will be next explained.

It has been already shown that the same constitution of man which leads those who govern to oppress the governed, if not prevented, will, with equal force and certainty, lead the latter to resist oppression when possessed of the means of doing so peaceably and successfully. But absolute governments, of all forms, exclude all other means of resistance to their authority than that of force, and, of course, leave no other alternative to the governed but to acquiesce in oppression, however great it may be, or to resort to force to put down the government. But the dread of such a resort must necessarily lead the government to prepare to meet force in order to protect itself, and hence, of necessity, force becomes the conservative principle of all such governments.

On the contrary, the government of the concurrent majority, where the organism is perfect, excludes the possibility of oppression by giving to each interest, or portion, or order—where there are established classes—the means of protecting itself by its negative against all measures calculated to advance the peculiar interests of others at its expense. Its effect, then, is to cause the different interests, portions, or orders, as the case may be, to desist from attempting to adopt any measure calculated to promote the prosperity of one, or more, by sacrificing that of others: and thus to force them to unite in such measures only as would promote the prosperity of all, as the only means to prevent the suspension of the action of the government, and thereby, to avoid anarchy, the greatest of all evils. It is by means of such authorized and effectual resistance that oppression is prevented and the necessity of resorting to force superseded in governments of the concurrent majority; and hence compromise, instead of force, becomes their conservative principle. . . .

In another particular, governments of concurrent majority have greatly the advantage. I allude to the difference in their respective tendency in reference to dividing or uniting the community, let its interests be ever so diversified or opposed, while that of the numerical is to divide it into two conflicting portions, let its interests be naturally ever so united and identified.

That the numerical majority will divide the community, let it be ever so homogeneous, into two great parties which will be engaged in perpetual struggles to obtain the control of the government has already been established. The great importance of the object at stake must necessarily form strong party attachments and party antipathies—attachments on the part of the members of each to their respective parties through whose efforts they hope to accomplish an object dear to all; and antipathies to the opposite party,

as presenting the only obstacle to success. . . .

The concurrent majority, on the other hand, tends to unite the most opposite and conflicting interests and to blend the whole in one common attachment to the country. By giving to each interest, or portion, the power of self-protection, all strife and struggle between them for ascendency is prevented, and thereby not only every feeling calculated to weaken the attachment to the whole is suppressed, but the individual and the social feelings are made to unite in one common devotion to country. Each sees and feels that is can best promote its own prosperity by conciliating the good will and promoting the prosperity of the others. And hence there will be diffused throughout the whole community kind feelings between its different portions and, instead of antipathy, a rivalry amongst them to promote the interests of each other, as far as this can be done consistently with the interest of all. . . .

If the two to be compared in reference to the ends for which government is ordained, the superiority of the government of the concurrent majority will not be less striking. These, as has been stated, are twofold: to protect and to perfect society. But to preserve society, it is necessary to guard the community against injustice, violence, and anarchy within, and against attacks from without. If it fail in either, it would fail in the primary end of government and would not deserve the name.

To perfect society, it is necessary to develop the faculties, intellectual and moral, with which man is endowed. But the mainspring to their development and civilization, with all their blessings, is the desire of individuals to better their condition. For this purpose liberty and security are indispensable. Liberty leaves each free to pursue the course he may deem best to promote his interest and happiness, as far as it may be compatible with the primary end for which government is ordained, while security gives assurance to each that he shall not be deprived of the fruits of his exertions to better his condition. These combined give to this desire the strongest impulse of which it is susceptible. For to extend liberty beyond the limits assigned would be to weaken the government and to render it incompetent to fulfill its primary end—the protection of society against dangers, internal and external. The effect of this would be insecurity; and of insecurity, to weaken the impulse of individuals to better their condition and thereby retard progress and improvement. On the other hand, to extend the powers of the government so as to contract the sphere assigned to liberty would have the same effect, by disabling individuals in their efforts to better their condition.

Herein is to be found the principle which assigns to power and liberty their proper spheres and reconciles each to the other under all circumstances. For if power be necessary to secure to liberty the fruits of its exertions, liberty, in turn repays power with interest—by increased population, wealth and other advantages which progress and improvement bestow on the community. By thus assigning to each its appropriate sphere, all conflicts between them cease, and each is made to cooperate with and assist the other in fulfilling the great ends for which government is ordained.

But the principle, applied to different communities, will assign to them different limits. It will assign a larger sphere to power and a more contracted one to liberty, or the reverse, according to circumstances. To the former, there must ever be allotted, under all circumstances, a sphere sufficiently large to protect the community against danger from without and violence and anarchy within. The residuum belongs to liberty. More cannot be safely or rightly allotted to it.

But some communities require a far greater amount of power than others to protect them against anarchy and ex-

ternal dangers; and, of course, the sphere of liberty in such must be proportionally contracted. The causes calculated to enlarge the one and contract the other are numerous and various. Some are physical—such as open and exposed frontiers surrounded by powerful and hostile neighbors. Others are moral—such as the different degrees of intelligence, patriotism, and virtue among the mass of the community, and their experience and proficiency in the art of self-government. Of these, the moral are by far the most influential. A community may possess all the necessary moral qualifications in so high a degree as to be capable of self-government under the most adverse circumstances, while, on the other hand, another may be so sunk in ignorance and vice as to be incapable of forming a conception of liberty or of living, even when most favored by circumstances, under any other than an absolute and despotic government.

The principle in all communities, according to these numerous and various causes, assigns to power and liberty their spheres. To allow to liberty, in any case, a sphere of action more extended than this assigns would lead to anarchy, and this, probably, in the end to a contraction instead of an enlargement of its sphere. Liberty, then, when forced on a people unfit for it, would, instead of a blessing, be a curse, as it would in its reaction lead directly to anarchy—the greatest of all curses. No people, indeed, can long enjoy more liberty than that to which their situation and advanced intelligence and morals fairly entitle them. If more than this be allowed, they must soon fall into confusion and disorder—to be followed, if not by anarchy and despotism, by a change to a form of government more simple and absolute, and therefore better suited to their condition. And hence, although it may be true that a people may not have as much liberty as they are fairly entitled to and are capable of enjoying, yet the reverse is unquestionably true—that no people can long possess more than they are fairly entitled to.

Liberty, indeed, though among the greatest of blessings, is not so great as that of protection, inasmuch as the end of the former is the progress and improvement of the race, while that of the latter is its preservation and perpetuation. And hence, when the two come into conflict, liberty must, and ever ought, to yield to protection, as the existence of the race is of greater moment than its improvement.

It follows, from what has been stated, that it is a great and dangerous error to suppose that all people are equally entitled to liberty. It is a reward to be earned, not a blessing to be gratuitously lavished on all alike—a reward reserved for the intelligent, the patriotic, the virtuous and deserving, and not a boon to be bestowed on a people too ignorant, degraded and vicious to be capable either of appreciating or of enjoying it. Nor is it any disparagement to liberty that such is and ought to be the case. On the contrary, its greatest praise—its proudest distinction is that an all-wise Providence has reserved it as the noblest and highest reward for the development of our faculties, moral and intellectual. A reward more appropriate than liberty could not be conferred on the deserving, nor a punishment inflicted on the undeserving more just than to be subject to lawless and despotic rule. This dispensation seems to be the result of some fixed law; and every effort to disturb or defeat it, by attempting to elevate a people in the scale of liberty above the point to which they are entitled to rise, must ever prove abortive, and end in disappointment. The progress of a people rising from a lower to a higher point in the scale of liberty is necessarily slow; and by attempting to precipitate, we either retard or permanently defeat it.

LIBERTY AND EQUALITY

There is another error, not less great and dangerous, usually associated with the one which has just been considered. I refer to the opinion that liberty and equality are so intimately united that liberty cannot be perfect without perfect equality.

That they are united to a certain extent, and that equality of citizens, in the eyes of the law, is essential to liberty in a popular government is conceded. But to go further and make equality of *condition* essential to liberty would be to destroy both liberty and progress. The reason is that inequality of condition, while it is a necessary consequence of liberty, is at the same time indispensable to progress. In order to understand why this is so, it is necessary to bear in mind that the mainspring to progress is the desire of individuals to better their condition, and that the strongest impulse which can be given to it is to leave individuals free to exert themselves in the manner they may deem best for that purpose, as far at least as it can be done consistently with the ends for which government is ordained, and to secure to all the fruits of their exertions. Now, as individuals differ greatly from each other in intelligence, sagacity, energy, perseverance, skill, habits of industry and economy, physical power, position and opportunity—the necessary effect of leaving all free to exert themselves to better their condition must be a corresponding inequality between those who may possess these qualities and advantages in a high degree and those who may be deficient in them. The only means by which this result can be prevented are either to impose such restrictions on the exertions of those who may possess them in a high degree as will place them on a level with those who do not, or to deprive them of the fruits of their exertions. But to impose such restrictions on them would be destructive of liberty, while to deprive them of the fruits of their exertions would be to destroy the desire of bettering their condition. It is, indeed, this inequality of condition between the front and rear ranks, in the march of progress, which gives so strong an impulse to the former to maintain their position, and to the latter to press forward into their files. This gives to progress its greatest impulse. To force the front rank back to the rear or to attempt to push forward the rear into line with the front, by the interposition of the government, would put an end to the impulse and effectually arrest the march of progress.

THE "STATE OF NATURE" PURELY HYPOTHETICAL

These great and dangerous errors have their origin in the prevalent opinion that all men are born free and equal—than which nothing can be more unfounded and false. It rests upon the assumption of a fact which is contrary to universal observation, in whatever light it may be regarded. It is, indeed, difficult to explain how an opinion so destitute of all sound reason ever could have been so extensively entertained unless we regard it as being confounded with another which has some semblance of truth, but which, when properly understood, is not less false and dangerous. I refer to the assertion that all men are equal in the state of nature, meaning by a state of nature a state of individuality supposed to have existed prior to the social and political state, and in which men lived apart and independent of each other. If such a state ever did exist, all men would have been, indeed, free and equal in it; that is, free to do as they pleased and exempt from the authority of control of others—as,

by supposition, it existed anterior to society and government. But such a state is purely hypothetical. It never did nor can exist, as it is inconsistent with the preservation and perpetuation of the race. It is, therefore, a great misnomer to call it "the state of nature." Instead of being the natural state of man, it is, of all conceivable states, the most opposed to his nature—most repugnant to his feelings and most incompatible with his wants. His natural state is the social and political—the one for which his Creator made him, and the only one in which he can preserve and perfect his race. As, then, there never was such a state as the so-called state of nature, and never can be, it follows that men, instead of being born in it, are born in the social and political state; and of course, instead of being born free and equal, are born subject, not only to parental authority, but to the laws and institutions of the country where born and under whose protection they draw their first breath. . . .

Such are the many and striking advantages of the concurrent over the numerical majority. Against the former but two objections can be made. The one is that it is difficult of construction, which has already been sufficiently noticed; and the other that it would be impracticable to obtain the concurrence of conflicting interests where they were numerous and diversified, or, if not, that the process for this purpose would be too tardy to meet with sufficient promptness the many and dangerous emergencies to which all communities are exposed. This objection is plausible and deserves a fuller notice than it has yet received.

The diversity of opinion is usually so great on almost all questions of policy that it is not surprising, on a slight view of the subject, it should be thought impracticable to bring the various conflicting interests of a community to unite on any one line of policy, or that a government founded on such a principle would be too slow in its movements and too weak in its foundation to succeed in practice. But plausible as it may seem at the first glance, a more deliberate view will show that this opinion is erroneous. It is true that, when there is no urgent necessity, it is difficult to bring those who differ to agree on any one line of action. Each will naturally insist on taking the course he may think best, and, from pride of opinion, will be unwilling to yield to others. But the case is different when there is an urgent necessity to unite on some common course of action, as reason and experience both prove. When something *must* be done—and when it can be done only by the united consent of all—the necessity of the case will force to a compromise, be the case of that necessity what it may. On all questions of acting, necessity, where it exists, is the overruling motive; and where, in such cases, compromise among the parties is an indispensable condition to acting, it exerts an overruling influence in predisposing them to acquiesce in some one opinion or course of action. . . .

But to form a juster estimate of the full force of this impulse to compromise, there must be added that in governments of the concurrent majority each portion, in order to advance its own peculiar interests, would have to conciliate all others by showing a disposition to advance theirs; and for this purpose each would select those to represent it whose wisdom, patriotism, and weight of character would command the confidence of the others. Under its influence—and with representatives so well qualified to accomplish the object for which they were selected—the prevailing desire would be to promote the common interests of the whole; and hence the competition would be, not which should yield the least to promote the common good, but which should yield the most. It is thus that concession would cease to be considered a sacrifice—would become a free-will offering on the altar of the country and lose the name of compromise. And herein is to be found that feature which distinguishes governments of the concurrent majority so strikingly from those of the numerical. In the latter, each faction, in the struggle to obtain the control of the government, elevates to power the designing, the artful, and unscrupulous who in their devotion to party—instead of aiming at the good of the whole—aim exclusively at securing the ascendency of party.

When traced to its source, this difference will be found to originate in the fact that in governments of the concurrent majority individual feelings are, from its organism, necessarily enlisted on the side of the social, and made to unite with them in promoting the interests of the whole as the best way of promoting the separate interests of each, while in those of the numerical majority the social are necessarily enlisted on the side of the individual and made to contribute to the interest of parties regardless of that of the whole. To effect the former—to enlist the individual on the side of the social feelings to promote the good of the whole—is the greatest possible achievement of the science of government, while to enlist the social on the side of the individual to promote the interest of parties at the expense of the good of the whole is the greatest blunder which ignorance can possibly commit.

To this also may be referred the greater solidity of foundation on which governments of the concurrent majority repose. Both ultimately rest on necessity, for force, by which those of the numerical majority are upheld, is only acquiesced in from necessity—in a necessity not more imperious, however, than that which compels the different portions in governments of the concurrent majority to acquiesce in compromise. There is, however, a great difference in the motive, the feeling, the aim which characterize the act in the two cases. In the one, it is done with that reluctance and hostility ever incident to enforced submission to what is regarded as injustice and oppression, accompanied by the desire and purpose to seize on the first favorable opportunity for resistance; but in the other, willingly and cheerfully, under the impulse of an exalted patriotism, impelling all to acquiesce in whatever the common good requires.

WORKS BY
JOHN C. CALHOUN

Calhoun: Basic Documents. Edited by John M. Anderson. Carroltown, Pa.: Bald Eagle Press, 1952. A collection of Calhoun's most representative works with commentary provided by the editor.

The Papers of John C. Calhoun, Edited by Robert L. Meriwether. Columbia, S.C.: University of South Carolina Press, 1959. The letters, speeches, and reports of Calhoun.

The Works of John C. Calhoun. Edited by Richard K. Cralle. 6 Vols. New York: D. Appleton and Co., 1859. The speeches, writings, reports and documents of Calhoun.

MAJOR SOURCES ON
JOHN C. CALHOUN

Dodd, William E. *Statesman of the Old South.* New York: Macmillan, 1936. Calhoun is shown as the extreme reactionary who reconciles nationalism with sectionalism in becoming the champion of slavery.

Heckscher, Gunnar, "Calhoun's Idea of 'Concurrent Majority'," *American Political Science Review,* Vol. XXXI (August, 1939), pp. 555-590. An analysis of Calhoun's ideas placing him in the same school of thought as European conservatives of the same age.

Hunt, Gaillard. *John C. Calhoun.* Philadelphia: Jacobs, 1907. A biography emphasizing Calhoun's leadership in the two opposing trends of nationalism and sectionalism.

Merriam, Charles E. "The Political Theory of John C. Calhoun," *American Journal of Sociology,* (March, 1902), pp. 577-594. While refuting past American political assumption, Calhoun is unable to create a new viable order due to his lack of understanding of historic forces.

Spain, August O. *The Political Theory of John C. Calhoun.* New York: Bookman, 1951. Calhoun, conscious of the trend towards centralization, develops his theories on universal political concepts rather than as a rationalization for the South's socio-economic system.

Styron, Arthur. *The Cast Iron Man.* New York: Longmans, 1935. A history of Calhoun's political career showing Calhoun as the last spokesman of 18th century Enlightenment in his reaction against the progress of middle-class aims.

Walker, J. H. "John C. Calhoun on Government," *Southern Quarterly Review* Vol. 26, (1864), pp 121-145. Written in 1884, this essay stresses Calhoun's premise that sovereignty lies not in the collective people of the United States, but in the individual states which compose that Union.

Wiltse, Charles M. *John C. Calhoun, Nationalist.* Indianapolis: Bobbs-Merrill, 1944. A well-written biography showing Calhoun's political development towards a system of federal rather than centralized government as the only means of preserving the Union.

CHAPTER 10

William Graham Sumner

WILLIAM G. Sumner (1840–1910) was born in Paterson, New Jersey. His father, an uneducated immigrant workman, but nevertheless a reader and a thinker, exerted a strong influence on his son. Educated in the public schools of Hartford, Connecticut, Sumner entered Yale in 1859. At Yale his outstanding academic record won him lasting prominent friends who helped him go abroad after graduation in 1863 for further study. For the next three years Sumner studied for the ministry at Geneva, Gottingen, and Oxford. Returning to the United States, he was an instructor at Yale from 1866 to 1869. During this same period Sumner was admitted to the deaconate of the Episcopal Church; by 1870 he had become rector of a church in Morristown, New Jersey.

As his interest turned increasingly to questions of social and political import, Sumner found that he could not express himself freely in the pulpit. Accordingly in 1872, he accepted the newly created chair of political and social science at Yale University where he remained for the rest of his academic career.

Sumner's activities were not confined to his academic duties. From 1873 to 1876 he was a member of New Haven's board of aldermen; from 1882 to 1910 he was an active member of the Connecticut State Board of Education and contributed much to the improvement of the public schools. His extensive research into the origins of institutions ranked Sumner among the foremost scholars in this field, and he did much to develop the academic study of sociology in the United States.

From What Social Classes Owe To Each Other

We are told every day that great social problems stand before us and demand a solution, and we are assailed by oracles, threats, and warnings in reference to those problems. There is a school of writers who are playing quite a role as the heralds of the coming duty and the coming woe. They assume to speak for a large, but vague and undefined, constituency, who set the task, exact a fulfillment, and threaten punishment for default. The task or problem is not specifically defined. Part of the task which devolves on those who are subject to the duty is to define the problem. They are told only that something is the matter; that it behooves them to find out what it is, and how to correct it, and then to work out the cure. All this is more or less truculently set forth.

After reading and listening to a great deal of this sort of assertion I find that the question forms itself with more and more distinctness in my mind: Who are those who assume to put hard questions to other people and to demand a solution of them? How did they acquire the right to demand that others should solve their world-problems for them? Who are they who are held to consider and solve all questions, and how did they fall under this duty?

So far as I can find out what the classes are who are respectively endowed with the rights and duties of posing and solving social problems, they are as follows: [Those who are bound to solve the problems are the rich, comfortable, prosperous, virtuous, respectable, educated, and healthy; those whose right it is to set the problems are those who have been less fortunate or less successful in the struggle for existence. The problem itself seems to be, How shall the latter be made as comfortable as the former? To solve this problem, and made us all equally well off, is assumed to be the duty of the former class; the

penalty, if they fail of this, is to be bloodshed and destruction. If they cannot make everybody else as well off as themselves, they are to be brought down to the same misery as others.]

During the last ten years I have read a great many books and articles, especially by German writers, in which an attempt has been made to set up "the State" as an entity having conscience, power, and will sublimated above human limitations, and as constituting a tutelary genius over us all. I have never been able to find in history or experience anything to fit this concept. I once lived in Germany for two years, but I certainly saw nothing of it there then. Whether the State which Bismarck is moulding will fit the notion is at best a matter of faith and hope. My notion of the State has dwindled with growing experience of life. As an abstraction, the State is to me only All-of-us. In practice—that is, when it exercises will or adopts a line of action—it is only a little group of men chosen in a very haphazard way by the majority of us to perform certain services for all of us. The majority do not go about their selection very rationally, and they are almost always disappointed by the results of their own operation. Hence "the State," instead of offering resources of wisdom, right reason, and pure moral sense beyond what the average of us possess, generally offers much less of all those things. Furthermore, it often turns out in practice that "the State" is not even the known and accredited servants of the State, but, as has been well said, is only some obscure clerk, hidden in the recesses of a Government bureau, into whose power the chance has fallen for the moment to pull one of the stops which control the Government machine. . . .]

The little group of public servants who, as I have said, constitute the State, when the State determines on anything, could not do much for themselves or anybody else by their own force. If they do anything, they must dispose of men, as in an army, or of capital, as in a treasury. But the army, or police, or *posse comitatus,* is more or less All-of-us, and the capital in the treasury is the product of the labor and saving of All-of us. Therefore, when the State means power-to-do it means All-of-us, as brute force or as industrial force.

[If anybody is to benefit from the action of the State it must be Some-of-us. If, then, the question is raised, What ought the State to do for labor, for trade, for manufactures, for the poor, for the learned professions? etc., etc.— that is, for class or an interest—it is really the question, What ought All-of-us to do for Some-of-us? But Some-of-us are included in All-of-us, and, so far as they get the benefit of their own efforts, it is the same as if they worked for themselves, and they may be cancelled out of All-of-us. Then the question which remains it, What ought Some-of-us to do for Others-of-us? or, What do social classes owe to each other?]

I now propose to try to find out whether there is any class in society which lies under the duty and burden of fighting the battles of life for any other class, or of solving social problems for the satisfaction of any other class; also, whether there is any class which has the right to formulate demands on "society"—that is, on other classes; also, whether there is anything but a fallacy and a superstition in the notion that "the State" owes anything to anybody except peace, order, and the guarantees of rights. . . .]

I. ON A NEW PHILOSOPHY: THAT POVERTY IS THE BEST POLICY

It is commonly asserted that there are in the United States no classes, and any allusion to classes is resented. On the other hand, we constantly read and hear discussions of social topics in which the existence of social classes is assumed as a simple fact. "The poor," "the weak," "the laborers," are expressions which are used as if they had exact and well-understood definition. Discussions are made to bear upon the assumed rights, wrongs, and misfortunes of certain social classes; and all public speaking and writing consists, in a large measure, of the discussion of general plans for meeting the wishes of classes of people who have not been able to satisfy their own desires. These classes are sometimes discontented, and sometimes not. Sometimes they are discontented and envious. They do not take their achievements as a fair measure of their rights. They do not blame themselves or their parents for their lot, as compared with that of other people. Sometimes they claim that they have a right to everything of which they feel the need for their happiness on earth. To make such a claim against God and Nature would, of course, be only to say that we claim a right to live on earth if we can. But God and Nature have ordained the chances and conditions of life on earth once for all. The case cannot be reopened. We cannot get a revision of the laws of human life. We are absolutely shut up to the need and duty, if we would learn how to live happily, of investigating the laws of Nature, and deducing the rules of right living in the world as it is. These are very wearisome and commonplace tasks. They consist in labor and self-denial repeated over and over again in learning and doing. When the people whose claims we are considering are told to apply themselves to these tasks they become irritated and feel almost insulted. [They formulate their claims as rights against society—that is, against some other men. In their view they have a right, not only to *pursue* happiness, but to *get* it; and if they fail to get, they think they have a claim to the aid of other men—that is, to the labor and self-denial of other men—to get it for them.] They find orators and poets who tell them that they have grievances, so long as they have unsatisfied desires. . . .

[Certain ills belong to the hardships of human life. They are natural. They are part of the struggle with Nature for existence. We cannot blame our fellow-men for our share of these. My neighbor and I are both struggling to free ourselves from these ills. The fact that my neighbor has succeeded in this struggle better than I constitutes no grievance for me. Certain other ills are due to the malice of men, and to the imperfections or errors of civil institutions. These ills are an object of agitation, and a subject of discussion. The former class of ills is to be met only by manly effort and energy; the latter may be corrected by associated effort. The former class of ills is constantly grouped and generalized, and made the object of social schemes. We shall see, as we go on, what that means. The second class of ills may fall on certain social classes, and reform will take the form of interference by other classes in favor of that one. The last fact is, no doubt, the reason why people have been led, not noticing distinctions, to believe that the same method was applicable to the other class of ills. The distinction here made between the ills which belong to the struggle and those which are due to the faults of human institutions is of prime importance. . . .

The humanitarians, philanthropists, and reformers, looking at the facts of life as they present themselves, find enough which is sad and unpromising in the condition of many members of society. They see wealth and poverty side by side. They note great inequality of social position and social chances. They eagerly set about the attempt to account for what they see, and to devise schemes for remedying what they do not like. In their eagerness to recommend the less fortunate classes to pity and consideration they forget all about the rights of other classes; they gloss over all the faults of the classes in question, and they exaggerate their misfortunes and their virtues. They invent new theories of property, distorting rights and perpetuating injustice, as anyone is sure to do who sets about the readjustment of social relations with the interests of one group distinctly before his mind,

and the interests of all other groups thrown into the background. When I have read certain of these discussions I have thought that it must be quite disreputable to be respectable, quite dishonest to own property, quite unjust to go one's own way and earn one's own living, and that the only really admirable person was the good-for-nothing. The man who by his own effort raises himself above poverty appears, in these discussions, to be of no account. The man who has done nothing to raise himself above poverty finds that the social doctors flock about him, bringing the capital which they have collected from the other class, and promising him the aid of the State to give him what the other had to work for. In all these schemes and projects the organized intervention of society through the State is either planned or hoped for, and the State is thus made to become the protector and guardian of certain classes. The agents who are to direct the State action are, of course, the reformers and philanthropists. Their schemes, therefore, may always be reduced to this type— that A and B decide what C shall do for D. It will be interesting to inquire, at a later period of our discussion, who C is, and what the effect is upon him of all these arrangements. In all the discussions attention is concentrated on A and B, the noble social reformers, and on D, the "poor man." I call C the Forgotten Man, because I have never seen that any notice was taken of him in any of the discussions. When we have disposed of A, B, and D we can better appreciate the case of C, and I think that we shall find that he deserves our attention, for the worth of his character and the magnitude of his unmerited burdens. Here it may suffice to observe that, on the theories of the social philosophers to whom I have referred, we should get a new maxim of judicious living: Poverty is the best policy. If you get wealth, you will have to support other people; if you do not get wealth, it will be the duty of other people to support you.

—No doubt one chief reason for the unclear and contradictory theories of class relations lies in the fact that our society, largely controlled in all its organization by one set of doctrines, still contains survivals of old social theories which are totally inconsistent with the former. In the Middle Ages men were united by custom and prescription into associations, ranks, guilds, and communities of various kinds. These ties endured as long as life lasted. Consequently society was dependent, throughout all its details, on status, and the tie, or bond, was sentimental. In our modern state, and in the United States more than anywhere else, the social structure is based on contract, and status is of the least importance. Contract, however, is rational—even rationalistic. It is also realistic, cold, and matter-of-fact. A contract relation is based on a sufficient reason, not on custom or prescription. It is not permanent. It endures only so long as the reason for it endures. In a state based on contract sentiment is out of place in any public or common affairs. It is relegated to the sphere of private and personal relations, where it depends not at all on class types, but on personal acquaintance and personal estimates. The sentimentalists among us always seize upon the survivals of the old order. They want to save them and restore them. Much of the loose thinking also which troubles us in our social discussions arises from the fact that men do not distinguish the elements of status and of contract which may be found in our society.

Whether social philosophers think it desirable or not, it is out of the question to go back to status or to the sentimental relations which once united baron and retainer, master and servant, teacher and pupil, comrade and comrade. That we have lost some grace and elegance is undeniable. That life once held more poetry and romance is true enough. But it seems impossible that any one who has studied the matter should doubt that we have gained immeasurably, and that our farther gains lie in going forward, not in going backward. The feudal ties can never be restored. If they could be restored they would bring back personal caprice, favoritism, sycophancy, and intrigue. A society based on contract is a society of free and independent men, who form ties without favor or obligation, and co-operate without cringing or intrigue. A society based on contract, therefore, gives the utmost room and chance for individual development, and for all the self-reliance and dignity of a free man. That a society of free men, co-operating under contract, is by far the strongest society which has ever yet existed; that no such society which has ever yet developed the full measure of strength of which it is capable; and that the only social improvements which are now conceivable lie in the direction of more complete realization of a society of free men united by contract, are points which cannot be controverted. It follows, however, that one man, in a free state, cannot claim help from and cannot be charged to give help to, another. To understand the full meaning of this assertion it will be worth while to see what a free democracy is. . . .

History is only a tiresome repetition of one story. Persons and classes have sought to win possession of the power of the State in order to live luxuriously out of the earnings of others. Autocracies, aristocracies, theocracies, and all other organizations for holding political power, have exhibited only the same line of action. It is the extreme of political error to say that if political power is only taken away from generals, nobles, priests, millionaires, and scholars, and given to artisans and peasants, these latter may be trusted to do only right and justice, and never to abuse the power; that they will repress all excess in others, and commit none themselves. They will commit abuse, if they can and dare, just as others have done. The reason for the excesses of the old governing classes lies in the vices and passions of human nature—cupidity, lust, vindictiveness, ambition, and vanity. These vices are confined to no nation, class, or age. They appear in the church, the academy, the workshop, and the hovel, as well as in the army or the palace. They have appeared in autocracies, aristocracies, theocracies, democracies, and ochlocracies, all alike. The only thing which has ever restrained these vices of human nature in those who had political power is law sustained by impersonal institutions. If political power be given to the masses who have not hitherto had it, nothing will stop them from abusing it but laws and institutions. To say that a popular government cannot be paternal is to give it a charter that it can do not wrong. The trouble is that a democratic government is in greater danger than any other of becoming paternal, for it is sure of itself, and ready to undertake anything, and its power is excessive and pitiless against dissentients. . . .

The notion of civil liberty which we have inherited is that of *a status created for the individual by laws and institutions, the effect of which is that each man is guaranteed the use of all his own powers exclusively for his own welfare.* It is not at all a matter of elections, or universal suffrage, or democracy. All institutions are to be tested by the degree to which they guarantee liberty. It is not to be admitted for a moment that liberty is a means to social ends, and that it may be impaired for major considerations. Any one who so argues has lost the bearing and relation of all the facts and factors in a free state. A human being has a life to live, a career to run. He is a centre of powers to work, and of capacities to suffer. What his powers may be—whether they can carry him far or not; what his chances may be, whether wide or restricted; what his fortune may be, whether to suffer much or little—are questions of his personal destiny which he must work out and endure as he can; but for all that concerns the bearing of the society and its institutions upon that man, and upon the sum of happiness to which he can attain during his life on earth, the product of all history and all philosophy up to this time is summed up in the doc-

trine, that he should be left free to do the most for himself that he can, and should be guaranteed the exclusive enjoyment of all that he does. If the society—that is to say, in plain terms, if his fellow-men, either individually, by groups, or in a mass—impinge upon him otherwise than to surround him with neutral conditions of security, they must do so under the strictest responsibility to justify themselves. Jealousy and prejudice against all such interferences are high political virtues in a free man. It is not at all the function of the State to make men happy. They must make themselves happy in their own way, and at their own risk. The functions of the State lie entirely in the conditions or chances can be affected by civil organization. Hence, liberty for labor and security for earnings are the ends for which civil institutions exist, not means which may be employed for ulterior ends. The free man who steps forward to claim his inheritance and endowment as a free and equal member of a great civil body must understand that his duties and responsibilities are measured to him by the same scale as his rights and his powers. He wants to be subject to no man. He wants to be equal to his fellows, as all sovereigns are equal. So be it; but he cannot escape the deduction that he can call no man to his aid. The other sovereigns will not respect his independence if he becomes dependent, and they cannot respect his equality if he sues for favors. The free man in a free democracy, when he cut off all the ties by which he might have made others pull him up. He must take all the consequences of his new status. He is, in a certain sense, an isolated man. The family tie does not bring to him disgrace for the misdeeds of his relatives, as it once would have done, but neither does it furnish him with the support which it once would have given. The relations of men are open and free, but they are also loose. A free man in a free democracy derogates from his rank if he takes a favor for which he does not render an equivalent.

A free man in a free democracy has no duty whatever toward other men of the same rank and standing, except respect, courtesy, and good-will. We cannot say that there are no classes, when we are speaking politically, and then say that there are classes, when we are telling A what it is his duty to do for B. [In a free state every man is held and expected to take care of himself and his family, to make no trouble for his neighbor, and to contribute his full share to public interests and common necessities. If he fails in this he throws burdens on others. He does not thereby acquire rights against the others. On the contrary, he only accumulates obligations toward them; and if he is allowed to make his deficiencies a ground of new claims, he passes over into the position of a privileged or petted person—emancipated from duties, endowed with claims. This is the inevitable result of combining democratic political theories with humanitarian social theories. It would be aside from my present purpose to show, but it is worth noticing in passing, that one result of such inconsistency must surely be to undermine democracy, to increase the power of wealth in the democracy, and to hasten the subjection of democracy to plutocracy; for a man who accepts any share which he has not earned in another man's capital cannot be an independent citizen. . . .]

[The aggregation of large fortunes is not at all a thing to be regretted. On the contrary, it is a necessary condition of many forms of social advance. If we should set a limit to the accumulation of wealth, we should say to our most valuable producers, "We do not want you to do us the services which you best understand how to perform, beyond a certain point," it would be like killing off our generals in war.] . . .

[Undoubtedly the man who possesses capital has a great advantage over the man who has no capital, in all the struggle for existence.] Think of two men who want to lift a weight, one of whom has a lever, and the other must apply his hands directly; think of two men tilling the soil, one of whom uses his hands or a stick, while the other has a horse and a plough; think of two men in conflict with a wild animal, one of whom has only a stick or a stone, while the other has a repeating rifle; think of two men who are sick, one of whom can travel, command medical skill, get space, light, air and water, while the other lacks all these things. This does not mean that one man has an advantage *against* the other, but that, when they are rivals in the effort to get the means of subsistence from Nature, the one who has capital has immeasurable advantages over the other. [If it were not so capital would not be formed. Capital is only formed by self-denial, and if the possession of it did not secure advantages and superiorities of a high order men would never submit to what is necessary to get it.] The first accumulation costs by far the most, and the rate of increase by profits at first seems pitiful. Among the metaphors which partially illustrate capital— all of which, however, are imperfect and inadequate—the snow-ball is useful to show some facts about capital. Its first accumulation is slow, but as it proceeds the accumulation becomes rapid in a high ratio, and the element of self-denial declines. This fact, also, is favorable to the accumulation of capital, for if the self-denial continued to be as great per unit when the accumulation had become great, there would speedily come a point at which further accumulation would not pay. [The man who has capital has secured his future, won leisure which he can employ in winning secondary objects of necessity and advantage, and emancipated himself from those things in life which are gross and belittling. The possession of capital is, therefore, an indispensable prerequisite of educational, scientific, and moral goods.] This is not saying that a man in the narrowest circumstances may not be a good man. It is saying that the extension and elevation of all the moral and metaphysical interests of the race are conditioned on that extension of civilization of which capital is the prerequisite, and that he who has capital can participate in and move along with the highest developments of his time. Hence it appears that the man who has his self-denial before him, however good may be his intention, cannot be as the man who has his self-denial behind him. Some seem to think that this is very unjust, but they get their notions of justice from some occult source of inspiration, not from observing the facts of this world as it has been made and exists.

The maxim, or injunction, to which a study of capital leads us is, Get capital. In a community where the standard of living is high, and the conditions of production are favorable, there is a wide margin within which an individual may practise self-denial and win capital without suffering, if he has not the charge of a family. That it requires energy, courage, perseverance, and prudence is not to be denied. Any one who believes that any good thing on this earth can be got without those virtues may believe in the philsopher's stone or the fountain of youth. It there were any Utopia its inhabitants would certainly be very insipid and characterless.

Those who have neither capital nor land unquestionably have a closer class interest than landlords or capitalists. If one of those who are in either of the latter classes is a spendthrift he loses his advantage. If the non-capitalists increase their numbers, they surrender themselves into the hands of the landlords and capitalists. They compete with each other for food until they run up the rent of land, and they compete with each other for wages until they give the capitalist a great amount of productive energy for a given amount of capital. If some of them are economical and prudent in the midst of a class which saves nothing and marries early, the few prudent suffer for the folly of the rest, since they can only get current rates of wages; and if these are low the margin out of which to make savings by special personal effort is narrow. No instance has yet been seen of a society composed of a class of great capitalists and class of laborers who had fallen into a caste of permanent drudges. Probbably no such thing is possible so long as landlords especially remain as a third class, and so long as society continues to develop strong classes of merchants, financiers, professional men, and other classes. If it were conceivable that noncapitalist laborers should give up struggling to become capitalists, should give way to vulgar enjoyments and passions, should recklessly increase their numbers, and should become a permanent caste, they might with some justice be called proletarians. The name has been adopted by some professed labor leaders, but it really should be considered insulting. If there were such a proletariat it would be hopelessly in the hands of a body of plutocratic capitalists, and a society so organized would, no doubt, be far worse than a society composed only of nobles and serfs, which is the worst society the world has been in modern times.

At every turn, therefore, it appears that the number of men and the quality of men limit each other, and that the question whether we shall have more men or better men is of most importance to the class which has neither land nor capital. . . .

The history of the human race is one long story of attempts by certain persons and classes to obtain control of the power of the State, so as to win earthly gratifications at the expense of others. People constantly assume that there is something metaphysical and sentimental about government. At bottom there are two chief things with which government has to deal. They are, the property of men and the honor of women. These it has to defend against crime. The capital which, as we have seen, is the condition of all welfare on earth, the fortification of existence, and the means of growth, is an object of cupidity. Some want to get it without paying the price of industry and economy. In ancient times they made use of force. They organized bands of robbers. They plundered laborers and merchants. Chief of all, however, they found that means of robbery which consisted in gaining control of the civil organization—the State—and using its poetry and romance as a glamour under cover of which they made robbery lawful. They developed highspun theories of nationality, patriotism, and loyalty. They took all the rank, glory, power, and prestige of the great civil organization, and they took all the rights. They threw on others the burdens and the duties. At one time, no doubt, feudalism was an organization which drew together again the fragments of a dissolved society; but when the lawyers had applied the Roman law to modern kings, and feudal nobles had been converted into an aristocracy of court nobles, the feudal nobility no longer served any purpose.

In modern times the great phenomenon has been the growth of the middle class out of the mediaeval cities, the accumulation of wealth, and the encroachment of wealth, as a social power, on the ground formerly occupied by rank and birth. The middle class has been obliged to fight for its rights against the feudal class, and it has, during three or four centuries, gradually invented and established institutions to guarantee personal and property rights against the arbitrary will of kings and nobles.

In its turn wealth is now becoming a power in three or four centuries, gradually invented and the State, and, like every other power, it is liable to abuse unless restrained by checks and guarantees. There is an insolence of wealth, as there is an insolence of rank. A plutocracy might be even far worse than an aristocracy. Aristocrats have always had their class vices and their class virtues. They have always been, as a class, chargeable with licentiousness and gambling. They have, however, as a class, despised lying and stealing. They have always pretended to maintain a standard of honor, although the definition and the code of honor have suffered many changes and shocking deterioration. The middle class has always abhorred gambling and licentiousness, but it has not

always been strict about truth and pecuniary fidelity. That there is a code and standard of mercantile honor which is quite as pure and grand as any military code, is beyond question, but it has never yet been established and defined by long usage and the concurrent support of a large and influential society. The feudal code has, through centuries, bred a high type of men, and constituted a caste. The mercantile code has not yet done so, but the wealthy class has attempted to merge itself in or to imitate the feudal class.

The consequence is, that the wealth-power has been developed, while the moral and social sanctions by which that power ought to be controlled have not yet been developed. A plutocracy would be a civil organization in which the power resides in wealth, in which a man might have whatever he could buy, in which the rights, interests, and feelings of those who could not pay would be overridden.

There is a plain tendency of all civilized governments toward plutocracy. The power of wealth in the English House of Commons has steadily increased for fifty years. The history of the present French Republic has shown an extraordinary development of plutocratic spirit and measures. In the United States many plutocratic doctrines have a currency which is not granted them anywhere else; that is, a man's right to have almost anything which he can pay for is more popularly recognized here than elsewhere. So far the most successful limitation on plutocracy has come from aristocracy, for the prestige of rank is still great wherever it exists. The social sanctions of aristocracy tell with great force on the plutocrats, more especially on their wives and daughters. It has already resulted that a class of wealthy men is growing up in regard to whom the old sarcasms of the novels and the stage about *parvenus* are entirely thrown away. They are men who have no superiors, by whatever standard one chooses to measure them. Such an interplay of social forces would, indeed, be a great and happy solution of a new social problem, if the aristocratic forces were strong enough for the magnitude of the task. If the feudal aristocracy, or its modern representative—which is, in reality, not at all feudal—could carry down into the new era and transmit to the new masters of society the grace, elegance, breeding, and culture of the past, society would certainly gain by that course of things, as compared with any such rupture between past and present as occurred in the French Revolution. The dogmatic radicals who assail "on principle" the inherited social notions and distinctions are not serving civilization. Society can do without patricians, but it cannot do without patrician virtues.

In the United States the opponent of plutocracy is democracy. Nowhere else in the world has the power of wealth come to be discussed in its political aspects as it is here. Nowhere else does the question arise as it does here. I have given some reasons for this in former chapters. Nowhere in the world is the danger of plutocracy as formidable as it is here. To it we appose the power of numbers as it is presented by democracy. Democracy itself, however, is new and experimental. It has not yet existed long enough to find its appropriate forms. It has no prestige from antiquity such as aristocracy possesses. It has, indeed, none of the surroundings which appeal to the imagination. On the other hand, democracy is rooted in the physical, economic, and social circumstances of the United States. This country cannot be other than democratic for an indefinite period in the future. Its political processes will also be republican. The affection of the people for democracy makes them blind and uncritical in regard to it, and they are as fond of the political fallacies to which democracy lends itself as they are of its sound and correct interpretation, or fonder. Can democracy develop itself and at the same time curb plutocracy? . . .

For now I come to the particular point which I desire to bring forward

against all the denunciations and complainings about the power of chartered corporations and aggregated capital. If charters have been given which confer undue powers, who gave them? Our legislators did. Who elected these legislators. We did. If we are a free, self-governing people, we must understand that it costs vigilance and exertion to be self-governing. It costs far more vigilance and exertion to be so under the democratic form, where we have no aids from tradition or prestige, than under other forms. If we are a free, self-governing people, we can blame nobody but ourselves for our misfortunes. No one will come to help us out of them. It will do no good to heap law upon law, or to try by constitutional provisions simply to abstain from the use of powers which we find we always abuse. How can we get bad legislators to pass a law which shall hinder bad legislators from passing a bad law? That is what we are trying to do by many of our proposed remedies. The task before us, however, is one which calls for fresh reserves of moral force and political virtue from the very foundations of the social body. Surely it is not a new thing to us to learn that men are greedy and covetous, and that they will be selfish and tyrannical if they dare. The plutocrats are simply trying to do what the generals, nobles, and priests have done in the past—get the power of the State into their hands, so as to bend the rights of others to their own advantage; and what we need to do is to recognize the fact that we are face to face with the same old foes—the vices and passions of human nature. One of the oldest and most mischievous fallacies in this country has been the notion that we are better than other nations, and that Government has a smaller and easier task here than elsewhere. This fallacy has hindered us from recognizing our old foes as soon as we should have done. Then, again, these vices and passions take good care here to deck themselves out in the trappings of democratic watchwords and phrases, so that they are more often greeted with cheers than with opposition when they first appear. The plan of electing men to represent us who systematically surrender public to private interests, and then trying to cure the mischief by newspaper and platform declamation against capital and corporations, is an entire failure.

The new foes must be met, as the old ones were met—by institutions and guarantees. The problem of civil liberty is constantly renewed. Solved once, it re-appears in a new form. The old constitutional guarantees were all aimed against king and nobles. New ones must be invented to hold the power of wealth to that responsibility without which no power whatever is consistent with liberty. The judiciary has given the most satisfactory evidence that it is competent to the new duty which devolves upon it. The courts have proved, in every case in which they have been called upon, that there are remedies, that they are adequate, and that they can be brought to bear upon the cases. The chief need seems to be more power of voluntary combination and cooperation among those who are aggrieved. Such cooperation is a constant necessity under free self-government; and when, in any community, men lose the power of voluntary cooperation in furtherance or defense of their own interests, they deserve to suffer, with no other remedy than newspaper denunciations and platform declamations. Of course, in such a state of things, political mountebanks come forward and propose fierce measures which can be paraded for political effect. Such measures would be hostile to all our institutions, would destroy capital, overthrow credit, and impair the most essential interests of society. On the side of political machinery there is no ground for hope, but only for fear. On the side of constitutional guarantees and the independent action of self-governing freemen there is every ground for hope. . .

Every man and woman in society has one big duty. That is, to take care of his or her own self. This is a social duty.

For, fortunately, the matter stands so that the duty of making the best of one's self individually is not a separate thing from the duty of filling one's place in society, but the two are one, and the latter is accomplished when the former is done. The common notion, however, seems to be that one has a duty to society, as a special and separate thing, and that this duty consists in considering and deciding what other people ought to do. Now, the man who can do anything for or about anybody else than himself is fit to be head of a family; and when he becomes head of a family he has duties to his wife and his children, in addition to the former big duty. Then, again, any man who can take care of himself and his family is in a very exceptional position, and his family is in a very exceptional position, if he does not find in his immediate surroundings people who need his care and have some sort of a personal claim upon him. If, now, he is able to fulfill all this, and to take care of anybody outside his family and his dependents, he must have a surplus of energy, wisdom, and moral virtue beyond what he needs for his own business. No man has this; for a family is a charge which is capable of infinite development, and no man could suffice to the full measure of duty for which a family may draw upon him. Neither can a man give to society so advantageous an employment of his services, whatever they are, in any other way as by spending them on his family. Upon this, however, I will not insist. I recur to the observation that a man who proposes to take care of other people must have himself and his family taken care of, after some sort of a fashion, and must have an as yet unexhausted store of energy.

The danger of minding other people's business is twofold. First, there is the danger that a man may leave his own business unattended to; and, second, there is the danger of an impertinent interference with another's affairs. The "friends of humanity" almost always run into both dangers. I am one of humanity, and I do not want any volunteer friends. I regard friendship as mutual, and I want to have my say about it. I suppose that other components of humanity feel in the same way about it. If so, they must regard any one who assumes the *role* of a friend of humanity as impertinent. The reference to the friend of humanity back to his own business is obviously the next step. . . .

The amateur social doctors are like the amateur physicians—they always begin with the question of *remedies,* and they go at this without any diagnosis or any knowledge of the anatomy or physiology of society. They never have any doubt of the efficacy of their remedies. They never take account of any ulterior effects which may be apprehended from the remedy itself. It generally troubles them not a whit that their remedy implies a complete reconstruction of society, or even a reconstitution of human nature. Against all such social quackery the obvious injunction to the quacks is, to mind their own business. . . .

The type and formula of most schemes of philanthropy or humanitarianism is this: A and B put their heads together to decide what C shall be made to do for D. The radical vice of all these schemes, from a sociological point of view, is that C is not allowed a voice in the matter, and his position, character, and interests, as well as the ultimate effects on society through C's interests, are entirely overlooked. I call C the Forgotten Man. For once let us look him up and consider his case, for the characteristic of all social doctors, is, that they fix their minds on some man or group of men whose case appeals to the sympathies and the imagination, and they plan remedies addressed to the particular trouble; they do not understand that all the parts of society hold together, and that forces which are set in action act and react throughout the whole organism, until an equilibrium is produced by a readjustment of all interests and rights. They therefore ignore entirely the source from which they must draw all the energy which they employ in their remedies, and they ignore all the effects on other members of society than the ones they have in view. They are always under the dominion of the superstition of government, and, forgetting that a government produces nothing at all, they leave out of sight the first fact to be remembered in all social discussion—that the State cannot get a cent for any man without taking it from some other man, and this latter must be a man who has produced and saved it. This latter is the Forgotten Man. . . .

There is a beautiful notion afloat in our literature and in the minds of our people that men are born to certain "natural rights." If that were true, there would be something on earth which was got for nothing, and this world would not be the place it is at all. The fact is, that there is no right whatever inherited by man which has not an equivalent and corresponding duty by the side of it, as the price of it. The rights, advantages, capital, knowledge, and all other goods which we inherit from past generations have been won by the struggles and sufferings of past generations; and the fact that the race lives, though men die, and that the race can by heredity accumulate within some cycle its victories over Nature, is one of the facts which make civilization possible. The struggles of the race as a whole produce the possessions of the race as a whole. Something for nothing is not to be found on earth.

If there were such things as natural rights, the question would arise, Against whom are they good? Who has the corresponding obligation to satisfy these rights? There can be no rights against Nature, except to get out of her what ever we can, which is only the fact of the struggle for existence stated over again. The common assertion is, that the rights are good against society; that is, that society is bound to obtain and secure them for the persons interested. Society, however, is only the persons interested plus some other persons; and as the persons interested have by the hypothesis failed to win the rights, we come to this, that natural rights are the claims which certain persons have by prerogative against some other persons) Such is the actual interpretation in practice of natural rights—claims which some people have by prerogative on other people.

[This theory is a very far-reaching one,] and of course it is adequate to furnish a foundation for a whole social philosophy. [n its widest extension it comes to mean that if any man finds himself uncomfortable in this world, it must be somebody else's fault, and that somebody is bound to come and make him comfortable.]Now, the people who are most uncomfortable in this world (for if we should tell all our troubles it would not be found to be very comfortable world for anybody) are those who have neglected their duties, and consequently have failed to get their rights. The people who can be called upon to serve the uncomfortable must be those who have done their duty, as the world goes, tolerably well. Consequently the doctrine which we are discussing turns out to be in practice only a scheme for making unjustice prevail in human society by reversing the distribution of rewards and punishments between those who have done their duty and those who have not.] . .

I have said something disparagingly in a previous chapter about the popular range against combined capital, corporations, corners, selling futures, etc., etc. The popular rage is not without reason, but it is sadly misdirected and the real things which deserve attack are thriving all the time. [The greatest social evil with which we have to contend is jobbery.]Whatever there is in legislative charters, watering stocks, etc., etc., which is objectionable, comes under the head of jobbery. Jobbery is any scheme which aims to gain, not by the legitimate fruits of industry and enterprise, but by extorting from somebody a part of his product under guise of some pretended industrial undertaking. Of course it is only a modification when the undertaking in question has some legitimate char-

acter, but the occasion is used to graft upon it devices for obtaining what has not been earned. [Jobbery is the vice of plutocracy, and it is the especial form under which plutocracy corrupts a democratic and republican form of government. The United States is deeply afflicted with it, and the problem of civil liberty here is to conquer it.]It affects everything which we really need to have done to such an extent that we have to do without public objects which we need through fear of jobbery. Our public public buildings are jobs—not always, but often. They are not needed, or are costly beyond all necessity or even decent luxury. Internal improvements are jobs. They are not made because they are needed to meet needs which have been experienced. They are made to serve private ends, often incidentally the political interests of the persons who vote the appropriations. Pensions have become jobs. In England pensions used to be given to aristocrats, because aristocrats had political influence, in order to corrupt them. Here pensions are given to the great democratic mass, because they have political power, to corrupt them. Instead of going out where there is plenty of land and making a farm there, some people go down under the Mississippi River to make a farm, and then they want to tax all the people in the United States to make dikes to keep the river off their farms. The California gold-miners have washed out gold, and have washed the dirt down into the rivers and on the farms below. They want the Federal Government to now clean out the rivers and restore the farms. The silver-miners found their product declining in value, and they got the Federal Government to go into the market and buy what the public did not want, in order to sustain (as they hoped) the price of silver. [The Federal Government is called upon to buy or hire unsalable ships, to build canals which will not pay, to furnish capital for all sorts of experiments, and to provide capital for enterprises of which private individuals will win the profits. All this is called "developing our resources," but it is, in truth, the great plan of all living on each other.] [The greatest job of all is a protective tariff.] It includes the biggest log-rolling and the widest corruption of economic and political ideas. It was said that there would be a rebellion if the taxes were not taken off whiskey and tobacco, which taxes were paid into the public Treasury. Just then the importations of Sumatra tobacco became important enough to affect the market. The Connecticut tobacco-growers at once called for an import duty on tobacco which would keep up the price of their product. So it appears that if the tax on tobacco is paid to the Federal Treasury there will be a rebellion, but if it is paid to the Connecticut tobacco-raisers there will be no rebellion at all. The farmers have long paid tribute to the manufacturers; now the manufacturing and other laborers are to pay tribute to the farmers. The system is made more comprehensive and complete, and we all are living on each other more than ever.

— [Now, the plan of plundering each other produces nothing.] It only wastes. All the material over which the protected interests wrangle and grab must be got from somebody outside of their circle.] The talk is all about the American laborer and American industry, but in every case in which there is not an actual production of wealth by industry there are two laborers and two industries to be considered—the one who gets and the one who gives. Every protected industry has to plead, as the major premise of its argument, that any industry which does not pay *ought* to be carried on at the expense of the consumers of the product, and, as its minor premise, that the industry in question does not pay; that is, that it cannot reproduce a capital equal in value to that which it consumes plus the current rate of profit. Hence every such industry must be a parasite on some other industry. What is the other industry? Who is the other man? This, the real question, is always overlooked.

— [In all jobbery the case is the same. There is a victim somewhere who is paying for it all.] The doors of waste and extravagance stand open, and there seems to be a general agreement to squander and spend. It all belongs to somebody. There is somebody who had to contribute it, and who will have to find more. Nothing is ever said about him. Attention is all absorbed by the clamorous interests, the importunate petitioners, the plausible schemers, the pitiless bores. Now, who is the victim? He is the Forgotten Man] If we go to find him, we shall find him hard at work tilling the soil to get out of it the fund for all the jobbery, the object of all the plunder, the cost of all the economic quackery, and the pay of all the politicians and statesmen who have sacrificed his interests to his enemies. We shall find him an honest, sober, industrious citizen, unknown outside his little circle, paying his debts and his taxes, supporting the church and the school, reading his party newspaper, and cheering for his pet politician. .). .

— [It is the Forgotten Man who is threatened by every extension of the paternal theory of government. It is he who must work and pay. When, therefore, the statesmen and social philosophers sit down to think what the State can do or ought to do, they really mean to decide what the Forgotten Man shall do. What the Forgotten Man wants, therefore, is a fuller realization of constitutional liberty. He is suffering from the fact that there are yet mixed in our institutions mediaeval theories of protection, regulation, and authority, and modern theories of independence and individual liberty and responsibility.] The consequence of this mixed state of things is, that those who are clever enough to get into control use the paternal theory by which to measure their own rights—that is, they assume privileges; and they use the theory of liberty to measure their own duties—that is, when it comes to the duties, they want to be "let alone." The

Forgotten Man never gets into control. He has to pay both ways. His rights are measured to him by the theory of liberty—that is, he has only such as he can conquer; his duties are measured to him on the paternal theory—that is, he must discharge all which are laid upon him, as is the fortune of parents.] In a paternal relation there are always two parties, a father and a child; and when we use the paternal relation metaphorically, it is of the first importance to know who is to be father and who is to be child. The *role* of parent falls always to the Forgotten Man. What he wants, therefore, is that ambiguities in our institutions be cleared up, and that liberty be more fully realized. . . .

We each owe to the other mutual redress of grievances. It has been said, in answer to my argument in the last chapter about the Forgotten Women and thread, that the tax on thread is "only a little thing," and that it cannot hurt the women much, and also that, if the women do not want to pay two cents a spool tax, there is thread of an inferior quality, which they can buy cheaper. These answers represent the bitterest and basest social injustice. Every honest citizen of a free state owes it to himself, to the community, and especially to those who are at once weak and wronged, to go to their assistance and to help redress their wrongs. Whenever a law or social arrangement acts so as to injure any one, and that one the humblest, then there is a duty on those who are stronger, or who know better, to demand and fight for redress and correction. When generalized this means that it is the duty of All-of-us (that is, the State) to establish justice for all, from the least to the greatest, and in all matters. This, however, is no new doctrine. It is only the old, true, and indisputable function of the State; and in working for a redress of wrongs and a correction of legislative abuses, we are only struggling to a fuller realization of it—that is, working to improve civil government.

We each owe it to the other to guarantee rights. Rights do not pertain to *results*, but only to *chances*. They pertain to the conditions of the struggle for existence, not to any of the results of it; to the *pursuit* of happiness, not to the possession of happiness. It cannot be said that each one has a right to have some property, because if one man had such a right some other man or men would be under a corresponding obligation to provide him with some property. Each has a right to acquire and possess property if he can. It is plain what fallacies are developed when we overlook this distinction. Those fallacies run through *all* socialistic schemes and theories. If we take rights to pertain to results, and then say that rights must be equal, we come to say that men have a right to be equally happy, and so on in all the details. Rights should be equal, because they pertain to chances, and all ought to have equal chances so far as chances are provided or limited by the action of society. This, however, will not produce equal results, but it is right just because it will produce unequal results—that is, results which shall be proportioned to the merits of individuals. We each owe it to the other to guarantee mutually the chance to earn, to possess, to learn, to marry, etc., etc., against any interference which would prevent the exercise to those rights by a person who wishes to prosecute and enjoy them in peace for the pursuit of happiness. If we generalize this, it means that All-of-us ought to guarantee rights to each of us. But our modern free, constitutional States are constructed entirely on the notion of rights, and we regard them as performing their functions more and more perfectly according as they guarantee rights in consonance with the constantly corrected and expanded notions of rights from one generation to another. Therefore, when we say that we owe it to each other to guarantee rights we only say that we ought to prosecute and improve our political science. . . .

From The Conquest of the United States by Spain

During the last year the public has been familiarized with descriptions of Spain and of Spanish methods of doing things until the name of Spain has become a symbol for a certain well-defined set of notions and policies. On the other hand, the name of the United States has always been, for all of us, a symbol for a state of things, a set of ideas and traditions, a group of views about social and political affairs. Spain was the first, for a long time the greatest, of the modern imperialistic states. The United States, by its historical origin, its traditions, and its principles, is the chief representative of the revolt and reaction against that kind of a state. I intend to show that, by the line of action now proposed to us, which we call expansion and imperialism, we are throwing away some of the most important elements of the American symbols and are adopting some of the most important elements of the Spanish symbol. We have beaten Spain in a military conflict, but we are submitting to be conquered by her on the field of ideas and policies. Expansionism and imperialism are nothing but the old philosophies of national prosperity which have brought Spain to where she now is. Those philosophies appeal to national vanity and national cupidity. They are seductive, especially upon the first view and the most superficial judgment, and therefore it cannot be denied that they are very strong for popular effect. They are delusions, and they will lead us to ruin unless we are hard-headed enough to resist them. . . .

War, expansion, and imperialism are questions of statesmanship and of nothing else. I disregard all other aspects of them and all extraneous elements which have been intermingled with them. . . . The original and prime cause of the war was that it was a move of partisan tactics in the strife of parties at Washington.

As soon as it seemed resolved upon, a number of interests began to see their advantage in it and hastened to further it. It was necessary to make appeals to the public which would bring quite other motives to the support of the enterprise and win the consent of classes who would never consent to either financial or political jobbery. Such appeals were found in sensational assertions which we had no means to verify, in phrases of alleged patriotism, in statements about Cuba and the Cubans which we now know to have been entirely untrue. . . .

We talk about "liberty" all the time in a big and easy way, as if liberty was a thing that men could have if they want it, and to any extent to which they want it. It is certain that a very large part of human liberty consists simply in the choice either to do a thing or to let it alone. If we decide to do it, a whole series of consequences is entailed upon us in regard to which it is exceedingly difficult, or impossible, for us to exercise any liberty at all. The proof of this from the case before us is so clear and easy that I need spend no words upon it. Here, then, you have the reason why it is a rule of sound statesmanship not to embark on an adventurous policy. . . .

There is another observation, however, about the war which is of far greater importance: that is, that it was a gross violation of self-government. We boast that we are a self-governing people, and in this respect, particularly, we compare ourselves with pride with older nations. What is the difference after all? The Russians, whom we always think of as standing at the opposite pole of political institutions, have self-government, if you mean by its acquiescence in what a little group of people at the head of the government agree to do. The war with Spain was precipitated upon us headlong, without reflection or deliberation, and without any due formulation of public opinion. Whenever a voice was raised in behalf of deliberation and the recognized maxims of statesmanship, it was howled down in a storm of vituperation and cant. Everything was done to make us throw away sobriety of thought and calmness of judgment and to inflate all expressions with sensational epithets and turgid phrases. It cannot be denied that everything in regard to the war has been treated in an exalted strain of sentiment and rhetoric very unfavorable to the truth. At present the whole periodical press of the country seems to be occupied in tickling the national vanity to the utmost by representations about the war which are extravagant and fantastic. There will be a penalty to be paid for all this. Nervous and sensational newspapers are just as corrupting, especially to young people, as nervous and sensational novels. The habit of expecting that all mental pabulum shall be highly spiced, and the corresponding loathing for whatever is soberly truthful, undermines character as much as any other vice. Patriotism is being prostituted into a nervous intoxication which is fatal to an apprehension of truth. It builds around us a fool's paradise, and it will lead us into errors about our position and relations just like those which we have been ridiculing in the case of Spain. . . .

There is not a civilized nation which does not talk about its civilizing mission just as grandly as we do. The English, who really have more to boast of in this respect than anybody else, talk least about it, but the Phariseeism with which they correct and instruct other people has made them hated all over the globe. The French believe themselves the guardians of the highest and purest culture, and that the eyes of all mankind are fixed on Paris, whence they expect oracles of thought and taste. The Germans regard themselves as charged with a mission, especially to us Americans, to save us from egoism and materialism. The Russians, in their books and newspapers, talk about the civilizing mission of Russia in language that might be translated from some of the finest paragraphs in our imperialistic newspapers. The first principle of Mohammedanism is that we Christians are dogs and

infidels, fit only to be enslaved or butchered by Moslems. It is a corollary that wherever Mohammedanism extends it carries, in the beliefs of its votaries, the highest blessings, and that the whole human race would be enormously elevated if Mohammedanism should supplant Christianity everywhere. To come, last, to Spain, the Spaniards have, for centuries, considered themselves the most zealous and self-sacrificing Christians, especially charged by the Almighty, on this account, to spread true religion and civilization over the globe. They think themselves free and noble, leaders in refinement and the sentiments of personal honor, and they despise us as sordid money-grabbers and heretics. I could bring you passages from peninsular authors of the first rank about the grand role of Spain and Portugal in spreading freedom and truth. Now each nation laughs at all the others when it observes these manifestations of national vanity. You may rely upon it that they are all ridiculous by virtue of these pretensions, including ourselves. The point is that each of them repudiates the standards of the others, and the outlying nations, which are to be civilized, hate all the standards of civilized men. We assume that what we like and practice, and what we think better, must come as a welcome blessing to Spanish-Americans and Filipinos. This is grossly and obviously untrue. They hate our ways. They are hostile to our ideas. Our religion, language, institutions, and manners offend them. They like their own ways, and if we appear amongst them as rulers, there will be social discord in all the great departments of social interest. The most important thing which we shall inherit from the Spaniards will be the task of suppressing rebellions. If the United States takes out of the hands of Spain her mission, on the ground that Spain is not executing it well, and if this nation in its turn attempts to be schoolmistress to others, it will shrivel up into the same vanity and self-conceit of which Spain now presents an example. To read our current literature one would think that we were already well on the way to it. Now, the great reason why all these enterprises which begin by saying to somebody else, We know what is good for you better than you know yourself and we are going to make you do it; are false and wrong is that they violate liberty; or, to turn the same statement into other words, the reason why liberty, of which we Americans talk so much, is a good thing is that it means leaving people to live out their own lives in their own way, while we do the same. If we believe in liberty, as an American principle, why do we not stand by it? Why are we going to throw it away to enter upon a Spanish policy of dominion and regulation? . . .

The question of imperialism, then, is the question whether we are going to give the lie to the origin of our own national existence by establishing a colonial system of the old Spanish type, even if we have to sacrifice our existing civil and political system to do it. I submit that it is a strange incongruity to utter grand platitudes about the blessings of liberty, etc., which we are going to impart to these people, and to begin by refusing to extend the Constitution over them, and still more, by throwing the Constitution into the gutter here at home. If you take away the Constitution, what is American liberty and all the rest? Nothing but a lot of phrases. . . .

Another phenomenon which deserves earnest attention from the student of contemporaneous history and of the trend of political institutions is the failure of the masses of our people to perceive *the inevitable effect of imperislism on democracy.* On the twenty-ninth of last November [1898] the Prime Minister of France was quoted in a cable dispatch as follows: "For twenty-eight years we have lived under a contradiction. The army and democracy subsist side by side. The maintenance of the traditions of the army is a menace to liberty, yet they assure the safety of the country and its most sacred duties." . . .

Everywhere you go on the continent of Europe at this hour you see the conflict between militarism and industrialism. You see the expansion of industrial power pushed forward by the energy, hope, and thrift of men, and you see the development arrested, diverted, crippled, and defeated by measures which are dictated by military considerations. At the same time the press is loaded down with discussions about political economy, political philosophy, and social policy. They are discussing poverty, labor, socialism, charity, reform, and social ideals, and are boasting of enlightenment and progress, at the same time that the things which are done are dictated by none of these considerations, but only by military interests. It is militarism which is eating up all the products of science and art, defeating the energy of the population, and wasting its savings. It is militarism which forbids the people to give their attention to the problems of their own welfare and to give their strength to the education and comfort of their children. It is militarism which is combating the grand efforts of science and art to ameliorate the struggle for existence.

The American people believe that they have a free country, and we are treated to grandiloquent speeches about our flag and our reputation for freedom and enlightenment. The common opinion is that we have these things because we have chosen and adopted them, because they are in the Declaration of Independence and the Constitution. We suppose, therefore, that we are sure to keep them and that the follies of other people are things which we can hear about with complacency. People say that this country is like no other; that its prosperity proves its exceptionality, and so on. These are popular errors which in time will meet with harsh corrections. The United States is in a protected situation. It is easy to have equality where land is abundant and where the population is small. It is easy to have prosperity where a few men have a great continent to exploit. It is easy to have liberty when you have no dangerous neighbors and when the struggle for existence is easy. There are no severe penalties, under such circumstances, for political mistakes. Democracy is not then a thing to be nursed and defended, as it is in an old country like France. It is rooted and founded in the economic circumstances of the country. The orators and constitution-makers do not make democracy. They are made by it. This protected position, however, is sure to pass away. As the country fills up with population, and the task of getting a living out of the ground becomes more difficult, the struggle for existence will become harder and the competition of life more severe. Then liberty and democracy will cost something, if they are to be maintained.

Now what will hasten the day when our present advantages will wear out and when we shall come down to the conditions of the older and densely populated nations? The answer is: war, debt, taxation, diplomacy, a grand governmental system, pomp, glory, a big army and navy, lavish expenditures, political jobbery—in a word, imperialism. In the old days the democratic masses of this country, who knew little about our modern doctrines of social philosophy, had a sound instinct on these matters, and it is no small ground of political disquietude to see it decline. They resisted every appeal to their vanity in the way of pomp and glory which they knew must be paid for. They dreaded a public debt and a standing army. They were narrow-minded and went too far with these notions, but they were, at least, right, if they wanted to strengthen democracy.

The great foe of democracy now and in the near future is plutocracy. Every year that passes brings out this antagonism more distinctly. It is to be the social war of the twentieth century. In that war militarism, expansion, and imperialism will all favor plutocracy. In the first place, war and expansion will favor jobbery, both in the dependencies and at home. In the second place, they will take away the attention of the people from what the plutocrats are doing. In the third place, they will cause large expenditures of the people's money, the return for which will not go into the treasury, but into the hands of a few schemers. In the fourth place, they will call for a large public debt and taxes, and these things especially tend to make men unequal, because any social burdens bear more heavily on the weak than on the strong, and so make the weak weaker and the strong stronger. Therefore expansion and imperialism are a grand onslaught on democracy.

The point which I have tried to make in this lecture is that expansion and imperialism are at war with the best traditions, principles, and interests of the American people, and that they will plunge us into a network of difficult problems and political perils, which we might have avoided while they offer us no corresponding advantage in return. . . .

Another answer which the imperialists make is that Americans can do anything. They say that they do not shrink from responsibilities. They are willing to run into a hole, trusting to luck and cleverness to get out. There are some things that Americans cannot do. Americans cannot $2 + 2 = 5$. You may answer that that is an arithmetical impossibility and is not in the range of our subject. Very well: Americans cannot collect two dollars a gallon tax on whisky. They tried it for many years and failed. That is an economic or political impossibility, the roots of which are in human nature. It is as absolute an impossibility on this domain as the former on the domain of mathematics. So far as yet appears, Americans cannot govern a city of one hundred thousand inhabitants so as to get comfort and convenience in it at a low cost and without jobbery. The fire department of this city is now demoralized by political jobbery—and Spain and all her possessions are not worth as much to you and me as the efficiency of the fire department of New Haven. The Americans in Connecticut cannot abolish the rotten borough system. The English abolished their rotten borough system seventy years ago, in spite of nobles and landlords. We cannot abolish ours in spite of the small towns. Americans cannot reform the pension list. Its abuses are rooted in the methods of democratic self-government, and no one dares to touch them. It is very doubtful indeed if Americans can keep up an army of one hundred thousand men in time of peace. Where can one hundred thousand men be found in this country who are willing to spend their lives as soldiers; or if they are found, what pay will it require to induce them to take this career? Americans cannot disentangle their currency from the confusion into which it was thrown by the Civil War, and they cannot put it on a simple, sure and sound basis which would give stability to the business of the country. This is a political impossibility. Americans cannot assure the suffrage to Negroes throughout the United States; they have tried it for thirty years and now, contemporaneously with this war with Spain, it has been finally demonstrated that it is a failure. Inasmuch as the Negro is now out of fashion, no further attempt to accomplish this purpose will be made. It is an impossibility on account of the complexity of our system of State and Federal government. If I had time to do so, I could go back over the history of Negro suffrage and show you how curbstone arguments, exactly analogous to the arguments about expansion, were used to favor it, and how objections were thrust aside in this same blustering senseless manner in which objections to imperialism are met. The ballot, we were told, was an educator and would solve all difficulties in its own path as by magic. Worse still, Americans cannot assure life, liberty, and the pursuit of happiness to Negroes inside of the United States. When the Negro postmaster's house was set on fire in the night in South Carolina, and not only he, but his wife and children, were murdered as they came out, and when moreover, this incident passed without legal

investigation or punishment, it was a bad omen for the extension of liberty, etc. to Malays and Tagals by simply setting over them the American flag. Upon a little serious examination the off-hand disposal of an important question of policy by the declaration that Americans can do anything proves to be only a silly piece of bombast, and upon a little reflection we find that our hands are quite full at home of problems by the solution of which the peace and happiness of the American people could be greatly increased. The laws of nature and of human nature are just as valid for Americans as for anybody else, and if we commit acts we shall have to take consequences, just like other people. Therefore prudence demands that we look ahead to see what we are about to do, and that we gauge the means at our disposal, if we do not want to bring calamity on ourselves and our children. We see that the peculiarities of our system of government set limitations on us. We cannot do things which a great centralized monarchy could do. The very blessings and special advantages which we enjoy, as compared with others, bring disabilities with them. That is the great fundamental cause of what I have tried to show throughout this lecture, that we cannot govern dependencies consistently with our political system, and that, if we try it, the State which our fathers founded will suffer a reaction which will transform it into another empire just after the fashion of all the old ones. That is what imperialism means. That is what it will be; and the democratic republic, which has been, will stand in history, like the colonial organization of earlier days, as a mere transition form.

WORKS BY WILLIAM GRAHAM SUMNER

The Challenge of Facts and Other Essays By William Graham Sumner. Edited by Albert Galloway Keller. New Haven Conn.: Yale University Press, 1914. Thirty-four essays dealing primarily with the American political system; the title work is a rebuttal of socialism due to its nonevolutionary character.

Earth-Hunger and Other Essays by William Graham Sumner. Edited by Albert Galloway Keller. New Haven, Conn.: Yale University Press, 1913. Forty-five essays divided under the headings: Liberty, Fantasies and Facts, and Democracy; "Earth-Hunger" proclaims the irrationality and destructiveness of rampant imperialism.

The Forgotten Man and Other Essays by William Graham Sumner. Edited by Albert Galloway Keller. New Haven, Conn.: Yale University Press, 1919. Twenty-four essays, the title one describing how social reform destroys the liberty of its victims (producers) since it upsets the equilibrium between rights and duties.

Sumner, William Graham. *Andrew Jackson.* Boston: Houghton, Mifflin and Co., 1899. A study in the development and institutionalizing of Americans as expressed in the political life of Jackson.

———. *Folkways.* Boston: Antheneum press, 1907. The formulation of the theory of cultural relativism through viewing individual behavior as formed by the cultural mores that define correct action.

———. *A History of American Currency.* New York: Holt, 1874. A factual history with minimal comment and interpretation by the author.

———. *Lectures on the History of Protection in the United States.* New York: Putnam's Sons, 1888. A history of tariff legislation followed by arguments favoring a free trade policy that will maximize productivity.

———. *Problems in Political Economy.* New York: Holt, 1888. Thousands of questions, divided into various categories, attempt to define the basic problems of political economy.

———. *Protection and Revenue in 1887.* New York: Putnam's Sons, 1878. A statistical report showing how a policy of free trade would increase both the production and trading potential of the United States.

———. *Protectionism.* New York: Holt, 1888. A moral and economic rebuttal of the protectionist policy written for the common man.

———. *Robert Morris.* New York: Dodd, Mead and Co., 1892. A well-written biography, describing Morris, a man driven by economic pursuits, as being of high repute and ability.

Sumner, William Graham, and Keller, Albert Galloway. *The Science of Society.*

4 Vols. New Haven, Conn.: Yale University Press, 1927. Written prior to Folkways, these earlier sociological writings portray his movement towards the concept of mores.

War and Other Essays by William Graham Sumner. Edited by Albert Galloway Keller. New Haven, Conn.: Yale University Press, 1911. A collection of seventeen essays, the title essay proclaiming that war arises not from a struggle for existence, but from a competition for life.

MAJOR SOURCES ON WILLIAM GRAHAM SUMNER

Barnes, Harry Elmer. "Two Representative Contributors of Sociology to Political Theory," *The American Journal of Sociology.* Vol. XXV, No. 1 (July, 1919), pp. 1-23. Sumner is portrayed as a rabid exponent of the laissezfaire doctrine, rejecting any hope of social reform through political action.

Chamberlain, John. "Sumner's 'Folkways'," *The New Republic,* Vol. LXXXIX, No. 1278 (May 31, 1939), pp. 93-96. Describing the basis of Sumner's theory as ever-changing mores, the author shows Sumner's economic policy as relevant only to that era in history.

Davie, Maurice R. (ed.). *William Graham Sumner.* New York: Crowell, 1940. A collection of sociological essays by the subject with commentary by the editor.

Healy, Sister Mary Edward. "Society and Social Change in the Writings of St. Thomas, Ward, Sumner, and Croly," *The Catholic University of America Studies in Sociology,* Vol. 27., Washington, D.C.: Catholic University of America Press, 1948. A presentation of the writers sociological theories followed by a critical analysis of Sumner's "materialistic monism."

Keller, A. G. "The Discovery of the Forgotten Man," *The American Mercury,* Vol. XXVII, No. 107 (Nov., 1952), pp. 00-00. A romantic presentation of Sumner as a far-sighted reformer, challenging rather than defending laissez-faire, desiring intelligent manipulation by the State rather than chaotic meddling.

McClosky, Robert Green. *American Conservatism.* Cambridge, Mass.: Harvard University Press, 1951. An illustration of how the transformation towards a conservative value system in American society during the laissez-faire period is reflected in the social theories of Sumner.

Page, Charles Hunt. "William Graham Sumner," *Class and American Sociology,* New York: The Dial Press, 1940, pp. 73-100. Through an analysis of Sumner's method, the class phenomena as expressed in societal structure and change is shown as basic to the subject's ideology.

Smith, Mortimer. "William Graham Sumner: The Forgotten Man," *The American Mercury,* Vol. LXXI, No. 321 (September, 1950), pp. 357-366. A great liberal intellectual who rabidly defended capitalism against the encroachments of state power, Sumner neglected to condemn similar misused power by capitalists.

CHAPTER 11

Herbert Croly

HERBERT Croly (1869–1930), son of a former editor of *The World* and of *The Graphic,* was born in New York City. After spending a year at the College of the City of New York, he studied for a year at Harvard, leaving to return again in 1895; Croly left Harvard in 1899 after an undistinguished career. He obtained a position with *The Architectural Record* the same year, and was its editor from 1900 to 1906, continuing as a member of its staff until 1913. He published his influential The Promise of American Life in 1909. The book had significant impact, particularly on Theodore Roosevelt, and Croly was established as a leading intellectual.

In 1914 *The New Republic* made its appearance with Croly as editor-in-chief. Croly announced that the magazine was a weekly review of current political and social events; the object of the magazine was not to lead, but to provide discussion among its readers. Croly remained the editor-in-chief of *The New Republic* until his death in 1930.

From The Promise of American Life

RECONSTRUCTION; ITS CONDITIONS AND PURPOSES

The best method of approaching a critical reconstruction of American political ideas will be by means of an analysis of the meaning of democracy. A clear popular understanding of the contents of the democratic principle is obviously of the utmost practical political importance to the American people. Their loyalty to the idea of democracy, as they understand it, cannot be questioned. Nothing of any considerable political importance is done or left undone in the United States, unless such action or inaction can be plausibly defended on democratic grounds; and the only way to secure for the American people the benefit of a comprehensive and consistent political policy will be to derive it from a comprehensive and consistent conception of democracy.

Democracy as most frequently understood is essentially and exhaustively defined as a matter of popular government; and such a definition raises at once a multitude of time-honored, but by no means superannuated, controversies. The constitutional liberals in England, in France, and in this country have always objected to democracy as so understood, because of the possible sanction it affords for the substitution of a popular despotism in the place of the former royal or oligarchic despotisms. From their point of view individual liberty is the greatest blessing which can be secured to a people by a government; and individual liberty can be permanently guaranteed only in case political liberties are in theory and practice subordinated to civil liberties. Popular political institutions constitute a good servant, but a bad master. When introduced in moderation they keep the government of a country in close relation with well-informed public opinion, which is a necessary condition of political sanitation; but if carried too far, such institutions compromise the security of the individual and the integrity of the state. They erect a power in the state, which in theory is unlimited and which constantly tends in practice to dispense with restrictions. A power which is theoretically absolute is under no obligation to respect the rights either of individuals or minorities; and sooner or later such power will be used for the purpose of oppressing the individual. The only way to secure individual liberty is, consequently, to organize a state in which the Sovereign power is deprived of any rational excuse or legal opportunity of violating certain essential individual rights.

The foregoing criticism of democracy, defined as popular government, may have much practical importance; but there are objections to it on the score of logic. It is not a criticism of a certain conception of democracy, so much as of democracy itself. Ultimate responsibility for the government of a community must reside somewhere. If the single monarch is practically dethroned, as he is by these liberal critics of democracy, some Sovereign power must be provided

to take his place. In England Parliament, by means of a steady encroachment on the royal prerogatives, has gradually become Sovereign; but other countries, such as France and the United States, which have wholly dispensed with royalty, cannot, even if they would, make a legislative body Sovereign by the simple process of allowing it to usurp power once enjoyed by the Crown. France did, indeed, after it had finally dispensed with Legitimacy, make two attempts to found governments in which the theory of popular Sovereignty was evaded. The Orleans monarchy, for instance, through the mouths of its friends, denied Sovereignty to the people, without being able to claim it for the King; and this insecurity of its legal framework was an indirect cause of a violent explosion of effective popular sovereignty in 1848. The apologists for the Second Empire admitted the theory of a Sovereign people, but claimed that the Sovereign power could be safely and efficiently used only in case it were delegated to one Napoleon III—a view the correctness of which the results of the Imperial policy eventually tended to damage. There is in point of fact no logical escape from a theory of popular Sovereignty—once the theory of divinely appointed royal Sovereignty is rejected. An escape can be made, of course, as in England, by means of a compromise and a legal fiction; and such an escape can be fully justified from the English national point of view; but countries which have rejected the royal and aristocratic tradition are forbidden this means of escape—if escape it is. They are obliged to admit the doctrine of popular Sovereignty. They are obliged to proclaim a theory of unlimited popular powers.

To be sure, a democracy may impose rules of action upon itself—as the American democracy did in accepting the Federal Constitution. But in adopting the Federal Constitution the American people did not abandon either its responsibilities or rights as Sovereign. Difficult as it may be to escape from the legal framework defined in the Constitution, that body of law in theory remains merely an instrument which was made for the people and which if necessary can and will be modified. A people, to whom was denied the ultimate responsibility for its welfare, would not have obtained the prime condition of genuine liberty. Individual freedom is important, but more important still is the freedom of a whole people to dispose of its own destiny; and I do not see how the existence of such an ultimate popular political freedom and responsibility can be denied by any one who has rejected the theory of a divinely appointed political order. The fallibility of human nature being what it is, the practical application of this theory will have its grave dangers; but these dangers are only evaded and postponed by a failure to place ultimate political responsibility where it belongs. While a country in the position of Germany or Great Britain may be fully justified from the point of view of its national tradition in merely compromising with democracy, other countries, such as the United States and France, which have earned the right to dispense with these compromises, are at least building their political structure on the real and righteous source of political authority. Democracy may mean something more than a theoretically absolute popular government, but it assuredly cannot mean anything less.

If, however, democracy does not mean anything less than popular Sovereignty, it assuredly does mean something more. It must at least mean an expression of the Sovereign will, which will not contradict and destroy the continuous existence of its own Sovereign power. Several times during the political history of France in the nineteenth century, the popular will has expressed itself in a manner adverse to popular political institutions. Assemblies have been elected by universal suffrage, whose tendencies have been reactionary and undemocratic, and who have been supported in this reactionary policy by an effective public opinion. Or the French people have by means of a plebiscite delegated their

Sovereign power to an Imperial dictator, whose whole political system was based on a deep suspicion of the source of his own authority. A particular group of political institutions or course of political action may, then, be representative of the popular will, and yet may be undemocratic. Popular Sovereignty is self-contradictory, unless it is expressed in a manner favorable to its own perpetuity and integrity.

The assertion of the doctrine of popular Sovereignty is, consequently, rather the beginning than the end of democracy. There can be no democracy where the people do not rule; but government by the people is not necessarily democratic. The popular will must in a democratic state be expressed somehow in the interest of democracy itself; and we have not traveled very far towards a satisfactory conception of democracy until this democratic purpose has received some definition. In what way must a democratic state behave in order to contribute to its own integrity?

The ordinary American answer to this question is contained in the assertion of Lincoln, that our government is "dedicated to the proposition that all men are created equal." Lincoln's phrasing of the principle was due to the fact that the obnoxious and undemocratic system of Negro slavery was uppermost in his mind when he made his Gettysburg address; but he meant by his assertion of the principle of equality substantially what is meant today by the principle of "equal rights for all and special privileges for none." Government by the people has its natural and logical complement in government for the people. Every state with a legal framework must grant certain rights to individuals; and every state, in so far as it is efficient, must guarantee to the individual that his rights, as legally defined, are secure. But an essentially democratic state consists in the circumstance that all citizens enjoy these rights equally. If any citizen or any group of citizens enjoys by virtue of the law any advantage over their fellow-citizens, then the most sacred principle of democracy is violated. On the other hand, a community in which no man or no group of men are granted by law any advantage over their fellow-citizens is the type of the perfect and fruitful democratic state. Society is organized politically for the benefit of all the people. Such an organization may permit radical differences among individuals in the opportunities and possessions they actually enjoy; but no man would be able to impute his own success or failure to the legal framework of society. Every citizen would be getting a "Square Deal."

Such is the idea of the democratic state, which the majority of good Americans believe to be entirely satisfactory. It should endure indefinitely, because it seeks to satisfy every interest essential to associated life. The interest of the individual is protected, because of the liberties he securely enjoys. The general social interest is equally well protected, because the liberties enjoyed by one or by a few are enjoyed by all. Thus the individual and the social interests are automatically harmonized. The virile democrat in pursuing his own interest "under the law" is contributing effectively to the interest of society, while the social interest consists precisely in the promotion of these individual interests, in so far as they can be equally exercised. The divergent demands of the individual and the social interest can be reconciled by grafting the principle of equality on the thrifty tree of individual rights, and the ripe fruit thereof can be gathered merely by shaking the tree.

It must be immediately admitted, also, that the principle of equal rights, like the principle of ultimate popular political responsibility is the expression of an essential aspect of democracy. There is no room for permanent legal privileges in a democratic state. Such privileges may be and frequently are defended on many excellent grounds. They may unquestionably contribute for a time to social and economic efficiency and to individual independence. But whatever advantage may be derived from such permanent discriminations must be abandoned by a democracy. It cannot afford to give any one class of its citizens a permanent advantage or to others a permanent grievance. It ceases to be a democracy, just as soon as any permanent privileges are conferred by its institutions or its laws; and this equality of right and absence of permanent privilege is the expression of a fundamental social interest.

But the principle of equal rights, like the principle of ultimate popular political responsibility, is not sufficient; and because of its insufficiency results in certain dangerous ambiguities and self-contradictions. American political thinkers have always repudiated the idea that by equality of rights they meant anything like equality of performance or power. The utmost varieties of individual power and ability are bound to exist and are bound to bring about many different levels of individual achievement. Democracy both recognizes the right of the individual to use his powers to the utmost, and encourages him to do so by offering a fair field and, in case of success, an abundant reward. The democratic principle requires an equal start in the race, while expecting at the same time an unequal finish. But Americans who talk in this way seem wholly blind to the fact that under a legal system which holds private property sacred there may be equal rights, but there cannot possibly be any equal opportunities for exercising such rights. The chance which the individual has to compete with his fellows and take a prize in the race is vitally affected by material conditions over which he has no control. It is as if the competitor in a Marathon cross country run were denied proper nourishment or proper training, and was obliged to toe the mark against rivals who had every benefit of food and discipline. Under such conditions he is not as badly off as if he were entirely excluded from the race. With the aid of exceptional strength and intelligence he may overcome the odds against him and win out. But it would be absurd to claim that, because all the rivals toed the same mark, a man's victory or defeat depended exclusively on his own efforts. Those who have enjoyed the benefits of wealth and thorough education start with an advantage which can be overcome only by very exceptional men,—men so exceptional, in fact, that the average competitor without such benefits feels himself disqualified for the contest.

Because of the ambiguity indicated above, different people with different interests, all of them good patriotic Americans, draw very different inferences from the doctrine of equal rights. The man of conservative ideas and interests means by the rights, which are to be equally exercised, only those rights which are defined and protected by the law—the more fundamental of which are the rights to personal freedom and to private property. The man of radical ideas, on the other hand, observing, as he may very clearly, that these equal rights cannot possibly be made really equivalent to equal opportunities, bases upon the same doctrine a more or less drastic criticism of the existing economic and social order and sometimes of the motives of its beneficiaries and conservators. The same principle, differently interpreted, is the foundation of American political orthodoxy and American political heterodoxy. The same measure of reforming legislation, such as the new Interstate Commerce Law, seems to one party a wholly inadequate attempt to make the exercise of individual rights a little more equal, while it seems to others an egregious violation of the principle itself. What with reforming legislation on the one hand and the lack of it on the other, the once sweet air of the American political mansion is soured by complaints. Privileges and discriminations seem to lurk in every political and economic corner. The "people" are appealing to the state to protect them against the usurpations of the corporations and the Bosses. The government is appealing to the courts to protect the shippers against the railroads. The corporations are appealing to the Federal courts to protect them from

the unfair treatment of state legislatures. Employers are fighting trades-unionism, because it denies equal rights to their employers. The unionists are entreating public opinion to protect them against the unfairness of "government by injunction." To the free trader the whole protectionist system seems a flagrant discrimination on behalf of a certain portion of the community. Everybody seems to be clamoring for a "Square Deal" but nobody seems to be getting it.

The ambiguity of the principle of equal rights and the resulting confusion of counsel are so obvious that there must be some good reason for their apparently unsuspected existence. The truth is that Americans have not readjusted their political ideas to the teaching of their political and economic experience. For a couple of generations after Jefferson had established the doctrine of equal rights as the fundamental principle of the American democracy, the ambiguity resident in the application of the doctrine was concealed. The Jacksonian Democrats, for instance, who were constantly nosing the ground for a scent of unfair treatment, could discover no example of political privileges, except the continued retention of their offices by experienced public servants; and the only case of economic privilege of which they were certain was that of the National Bank. The fact is, of course, that the great majority of Americans were getting a "Square Deal" as long as the economic opportunities of a new country had not been developed and appropriated. Individual and social interest did substantially coincide as long as so many opportunities were open to the poor and untrained man, and as long as the public interest demanded first of all the utmost celerity of economic development. But, as we have seen in a preceding chapter, the economic development of the country resulted inevitably in a condition which demanded on the part of the successful competitor either increasing capital, improved training, or a larger amount of ability and energy. With the advent of comparative economic and social maturity, the exercise of certain legal rights became substantially equivalent to the exercise of a privilege; and if equality of opportunity was to be maintained, it could not be done by virtue of non-interference. The demands of the "Higher Law" began to diverge from the results of the actual legal system.

Public opinion is, of course, extremely loth to admit that there exists any such divergence of individual and social interest, or any such contradiction in the fundamental American principle. Reformers no less than conservatives have been doggedly determined to place some other interpretation upon the generally recognized abuses; and the interpretation on which they have fastened is that some of the victors have captured too many prizes, because they did not play fair. There is just enough truth in this interpretation to make it plausible, although, as we have seen, the most flagrant examples of apparent cheating were due as much to equivocal rules as to any fraudulent intention. But orthodox public opinion is obliged by the necessities of its own situation to exaggerate the truth of its favorite interpretation; and any such exaggeration is attended with grave dangers, precisely because the ambiguous nature of the principle itself gives a similar ambiguity to its violations. The cheating is understood as disobedience to the actual law, or as violation of a Higher Law, according to the interests and preconceptions of the different reformers; but however it is understood, they believe themselves to be upholding some kind of a Law, and hence endowed with some kind of sacred mission.

Thus the want of integrity in what is supposed to be the formative principle of democracy results, as it did before the Civil War, in a division of the actual substance of the nation. Men naturally disposed to be indignant at people with whom they disagree come to believe that their indignation is comparable to that of the Lord. Men naturally disposed to be envious and suspicious of others more fortunate than themselves come to con-fuse their suspicions with a duty to the society. Demagogues can appeal to the passions aroused by this prevailing sense of unfair play for the purpose of getting themselves elected to office or for the purpose of passing blundering measures of repression. The type of admirable and popular democrat ceases to be a statesman, attempting to bestow unity and health on the body politic by prescribing more wholesome habits of living. He becomes instead a sublimated District Attorney, whose duty it is to punish violations both of the actual and the "Higher Law." Thus he is figured as a kind of an avenging angel; but (as it happens) he is an avenging little angel who can find little to avenge and who has no power of flight. There is an enormous discrepancy between the promises of these gentlemen and their performances, no matter whether they occupy an executive office, the editorial chairs of yellow journals, or merely the place of public prosecutor; and it sometimes happens that public prosecutors who have played the part of avenging angels before election, are, as Mr. William Travers Jerome knows, themselves prosecuted after a few years of office by their aggrieved constituents. The truth is that these gentlemen are confronted by a task which is in a large measure impossible, and which, so far as possible, would be either disappointing or dangerous in its results.

Hence it is that continued loyalty to a contradictory principle is destructive of a wholesome public sentiment and opinion. A wholesome public opinion in a democracy is one which keeps a democracy sound and whole; and it cannot prevail unless the individuals composing it recognize mutual ties and responsibilities which lie deeper than any differences of interest and idea. No formula whose effect on public opinion is not binding and healing and unifying has any substantial claim to consideration as the essential and formative democratic idea. Belief in the principle of equal rights does not bind, heal, and unify public opinion. Its effect rather is confusing, distracting, and at worst, disintegrating. A democratic political organization has no immunity from grievances. They are a necessary result of a complicated and changing industrial and social organism. What is good for one generation will often be followed by consequences that spell deprivation for the next. What is good for one man or one class of men will bring ills to other men or classes of men. What is good for the community as a whole may mean temporary loss and a sense of injustice to a minority. All grievances from any cause should receive full expression in a democracy, but, inasmuch as the righteously discontented must be always with us, the fundamental democratic principle should, above all, counsel mutual forbearance and loyalty. The principle of equal rights encourages mutual suspicion and disloyalty. It tends to attribute individual and social ills, for which general moral, economic, and social causes are usually in large measure responsible, to individual wrong-doing; and in this way it arouses and intensifies that personal and class hatred, which never in any society lies far below the surface. Men who have grievances are inflamed into anger and resentment. In claiming what they believe to be their rights, they are in their own opinion acting on behalf not merely of their interests, but of an absolute democratic principle. Their angry resentment becomes transformed in their own minds into righteous indignation; and there may be turned loose upon the community a horde of self-seeking fanatics—like unto those soldiers in the religious wars who robbed and slaughtered their opponents in the service of God.

DEMOCRACY AND DISCRIMINATION

The principle of equal rights has always appealed to its more patriotic and sensible adherents as essentially an impartial rule of political action—one that held a perfectly fair balance between the individual and society, and between different and hostile individual and class interests. But as a fundamental principle of democratic policy it is as ambiguous in this respect as it is in other respects. In its traditional form and expression it has concealed an extremely partial interest under a formal proclamation of impartiality. The political thinker who popularized it in this country was not concerned fundamentally with harmonizing the essential interest of the individual with the essential popular or social interest. Jefferson's political system was intended for the benefit only of a special class of individuals, viz., those average people who would not be helped by any really formative rule or method of discrimination. In practice it has proved to be inimical to individual liberty, efficiency, and distinction. An insistent demand for equality, even in the form of a demand for equal rights, inevitably has a negative and limiting effect upon the free and able exercise of individual opportunities. From the Jeffersonian point of view democracy would incur a graver danger from a violation of equality than it would profit from a triumphant assertion of individual liberty. Every opportunity for the edifying exercise of power, on the part either of an individual, a group of individuals, or the state is by its very nature also an opportunity for its evil exercise. The political leader whose official power depends upon popular confidence may betray the trust. The corporation employing thousands of men and supplying millions of people with some necessary service or commodity may reduce the cost of production only for its own profit. The state may use its great authority chiefly for the benefit of special interests. The advocate of equal rights is preoccupied by these opportunities for the abusive exercise of power, because from his point of view rights exercised in the interest of inequality have ceased to be righteous. He distrusts those forms of individual and associated activity which give any individual or association substantial advantages over their associates. He becomes suspicious of any kind of individual and social distinction with the nature and effects of which he is not completely familiar.

A democracy of equal rights may tend to encourage certain expressions of individual liberty; but they are few in number and limited in scope. It rejoices in the freedom of its citizens, provided this freedom receives certain ordinary expressions. It will follow a political leader, like Jefferson or Jackson, with a blind confidence of which a really free democracy would not be capable, because such leaders are, or claim to be in every respect, except their prominence, one of the "people." Distinction of this kind does not separate a leader from the majority. It only ties them together more firmly. It is an acceptable assertion of individual liberty, because it is liberty converted by its exercise into a kind of equality. In the same way the American democracy most cordially admired for a long time men, who pursued more energetically and successfully than their fellows, ordinary business occupations, because they believed that such familiar expressions of individual liberty really tended towards social and industrial homogeneity. Herein they were mistaken; but the supposition was made in good faith, and it constitutes the basis of the Jeffersonian Democrat's illusion in reference to his own interest in liberty. He dislikes or ignores liberty, only when it looks in the direction of moral and intellectual emancipation. In so far as his influence has prevailed, Americans have been encouraged to think those thoughts and to perform those acts which everybody else is thinking and performing.

The effect of a belief in the principle of "equal rights" on freedom is, however, most clearly shown by its attitude toward Democratic political organization and policy. A people jealous of their rights are not sufficiently afraid of special individual efficiency and distinction to take very many precautions against it. They greet it oftener with neglect than with positive coercion. Jeffersonian Democracy is, however, very much afraid of any examples of associated efficiency. Equality of rights is most in danger of being violated when the exercise of rights is associated with power, and any unusual amount of power is usually derived from the association of a number of individuals for a common purpose. The most dangerous example of such association is not, however, a huge corporation or a labor union; it is the state. The state cannot be bound hand and foot by the law, as can a corporation, because it necessarily possesses some powers of legislation; and the power to legislate inevitably escapes the limitation of the principle of equal rights. The power to legislate implies the power to discriminate; and the best way consequently for a good democracy of equal rights to avoid the danger of discrimination will be to organize the state so that its power for ill will be rigidly restricted. The possible preferential interference on the part of a strong and efficient government must be checked by making the government feeble and devoid of independence. The less independent and efficient the several departments of the government are permitted to become, the less likely that the government as a whole will use its power for anything but a really popular purpose.

In the foregoing type of political organization, which has been very much favored by the American democracy, the freedom of the official political leader is sacrificed for the benefit of the supposed freedom of that class of equalized individuals known as the "people," but by the "people" Jefferson and his followers have never meant all the people or the people as a whole. They have meant a sort of apotheosized majority—the people in so far as they could be generalized and reduced to an average. The interests of this class were conceived as inimical to any discrimination which tended to select peculiarly efficient individuals or those who were peculiarly capable of social service. The system of equal rights, particularly in its economic and political application *has* worked for the benefit of such a class, but rather in its effect upon American intelligence and morals, then in its effect upon American political and economic development. The system, that is, has only partly served the purpose of its founder and his followers, and it has failed because it did not bring with it any machinery adequate even to its own insipid and barren purposes. Even the meager social interest which Jefferson concealed under cover of his demand for equal rights could not be promoted without some effective organ of social responsibility; and the Democrats of to-day are obliged, as we have seen, to invoke the action of the central government to destroy those economic discriminations which its former inaction had encouraged. But even so the traditional democracy still retains its dislike of centralized and socialized responsibility. It consents to use the machinery of the government only for a negative or destructive object. Such must always be the case as long as it remains true to its fundamental principle. That principle defines the social interest merely in the terms of an indiscriminate individualism—which is the one kind of individualism murderous to both the essential individual and the essential social interest.

The net result has been that wherever the attempt to discriminate in favor of the average or indiscriminate individual has succeeded, it has succeeded at the expense of individual liberty, efficiency, and distinction; but it has more often failed than succeeded. Whenever the exceptional individual has been given any genuine liberty, he has inevitably conquered. That is the whole meaning of the process of economic and social development traced in certain preceding chapters. The strong and capable men not only conquer, but they seek to perpetuate their conquests by occupying all the strategic points in the economic and political battlefield—whereby they obtain certain more or less permanent advantages over their fellow-democrats. Thus in so far as the equal rights are

freely exercised, they are bound to result in inequalities; and these inequalities are bound to make for their own perpetuation, and so to provoke still further discrimination. Wherever the principle has been allowed to mean what it seems to mean, it has determined and encouraged its own violation. The marriage which it is supposed to consecrate between liberty and equality gives birth to unnatural children, whose nature it is to devour one or the other of their parents.

The only way in which the thoroughgoing adherent of the principle of equal rights can treat these tendencies to discrimination, when they develop, is rigidly to repress them; and this tendency to repression is now beginning to take possession of those Americans who represent the pure Democratic tradition. They propose to crush out the chief examples of effective individual and associated action, which their system of democracy has encouraged to develop. They propose frankly to destroy, as far as possible, the economic organization which has been built up under stress of competitive conditions; and by assuming such an attitude they have fallen away even from the pretense of impartiality, and have come out as frankly representative of a class interest. But even to assert this class interest efficiently they have been obliged to abandon, in fact if not in word, their correlative principle of national irresponsibility. Whatever the national interest may be, it is not to be asserted by the political practice of non-interference. The hope of automatic democratic fulfillment must be abandoned. The national government must step in and discriminate; but it must discriminate, not on behalf of liberty and the special individual, but on behalf of equality and the average man.

Thus the Jeffersonian principle of national irresponsibility can no longer be maintained by those Democrats who sincerely believe that the inequalities of power generated in the American economic and political system are dangerous to the integrity of the democratic state. To this extent really sincere followers of Jefferson are obliged to admit the superior political wisdom of Hamilton's principle of national responsibility, and once they have made this admission, they have implicitly abandoned their contention that the doctrine of equal rights is a sufficient principle of democratic political action. They have implicitly accepted the idea that the public interest is to be asserted, not merely by equalizing individual rights, but by controlling individuals in the exercise of those rights. The national public interest has to be affirmed by positive and aggressive action. The nation has to have a will and a policy as well as the individual; and this policy can no longer be confined to the merely negative task of keeping individual rights from becoming in any way privileged.

The arduous and responsible political task which a nation in its collective capacity must seek to perform is that of selecting among the various prevailing ways of exercising individual rights those which contribute to national perpetuity and integrity. Such selection implies some interference with the natural course of popular action; and that interference is always costly and may be harmful either to the individual or the social interest must be frankly admitted. He would be a foolish Hamiltonian who would claim that a state, no matter how efficiently organized and ably managed, will not make serious and perhaps enduring mistakes; but he can answer that inaction and irresponsibility are more costly and dangerous than intelligent and responsible interference. The practice of non-interference is just as selective in its effects as the practice of state interference. It means merely that the nation is willing to accept the results of natural selection instead of preferring to substitute the results of artificial selection. In one way or another a nation is bound to recognize the results of selection. The Hamiltonian principle of national responsibility recognizes the inevitability of selection; and since it is inevitable, is not afraid to interfere on behalf of the selection of the really fittest. If a selective policy is pursued in good faith and with sufficient intelligence, the nation will at least be learning from its mistakes. It should find out gradually the kind and method of selection, which is most desirable, and how far selection by non-interference is to be preferred to active selection.

As a matter of fact the American democracy both in its central and in its local governments has always practiced both methods of selection. The state governments have sedulously indulged in a kind of interference conspicuous both for its activity and its inefficiency. The Federal government, on the other hand, has been permitted to interfere very much less; but even during the palmiest days of national irresponsibility it did not altogether escape active intervention. A protective tariff is, of course, a plain case of preferential class legislation, and so was the original Interstate Commerce Act. They were designed to substitute artificial preferences for those effected by unregulated individual action, on the ground that the proposed modification of the natural course of trade would contribute to the general economic prosperity. No less preferential in purpose are the measures of reform recently enacted by the central government. The amended Interstate Commerce Law largely increases the power of possible discrimination possessed by the Federal Commission. The Pure Food Bill forbids many practices, which have arisen in connection with the manufacture of food products, and discriminates against the perpetrators of such practices. Factory legislation or laws regulating the hours of labor have a similar meaning and justification. It is not too much to say that substantially all the industrial legislation, demanded by the "people" both here and abroad and passed in the popular interest, has been based essentially on class discrimination.

The situation which these laws are supposed to meet is always the same. A certain number of individuals enjoy, in the beginning, equal opportunities to perform certain acts; and in the competition resulting there from some of these individuals or associations obtain advantages over their competitors, or over their fellow-citizens whom they employ or serve. Sometimes these advantages and the practices whereby they are obtained are profitable to a larger number of people than they injure. Sometimes the reverse is true. In either event the state is usually asked to interfere by the class whose economic position has been compromised. It by no means follows that the state should acquiesce in this demand. In many cases interference may be more costly than beneficial. Each case must be considered on its merits. But whether in any particular case the state takes sides or remains impartial, it most assuredly has a positive function to perform on the premises. If it remains impartial, it simply agrees to abide by the results of natural selection. If it interferes, it seeks to replace natural with artificial discrimination. In both cases it authorizes discriminations which in their effect violate the doctrine of "equal rights." Of course, a reformer can always claim that any particular measure of reform proposes merely to restore to the people a "Square Deal"; but that is simply an easy and thoughtless way of concealing novel purposes under familiar formulas. Any genuine measure of economic or political reform will, of course, give certain individuals better opportunities than those they have been recently enjoying, but it will reach this result only by depriving other individuals of advantages which they have earned.

Impartiality is the duty of the judge rather than the statesman, of the courts rather than the government. The state which proposes to draw a ring around the conflicting interests of its citizens and interfere only on behalf of a fair fight will be obliged to interfere constantly and will never accomplish its purpose. In economic warfare, the fighting can never be fair for long, and it is the business of the state to see that its

own friends are victorious. It holds, if you please, itself a hand in the game. The several players are playing, not merely with one another, but with the political and social bank. The security and perpetuity of the state, and of the individual in so far as he is a social animal, depend upon the victory of the national interest—as represented both in the assurance of the national profit and in the domination of the nation's friends. It is in the position of the bank at Monte Carlo, which does pretend to play fair, but which frankly promulgates rules advantageous to itself. Considering the percentage in its favor and the length of its purse, it cannot possibly lose. It is not really gambling; and it does not propose to take any unnecessary risks. Neither can a state, democratic or otherwise, which believe in its own purpose. While preserving at times an appearance of impartiality so that its citizens may enjoy for a while a sense of the reality of their private game, it must on the whole make the rules in its own interest. It must help those men to win who are most capable of using their winnings for the benefit of society.

CONSTRUCTIVE DISCRIMINATION

Assuming, then, that a democracy cannot avoid the constant assertion of national responsibility for the national welfare, an all-important question remains as to the way in which and the purpose for which this interference should be exercised. Should it be exercised on behalf of individual liberty? Should it be exercised on behalf of social equality? Is there any way in which it can be exercised on behalf of both liberty and equality?

Hamilton and the constitutional liberals asserted that the state should interfere exclusively on behalf of individual liberty; but Hamilton was no democrat and was not outlining the policy of a democratic state. In point of fact democracies have never been satisfied with a definition of democratic policy in terms of liberty. Not only have the particular friends of liberty usually been hostile to democracy, but democracies both in idea and behavior have frequently been hostile to liberty; and they have been justified in distrusting a political regime organized wholly or even chiefly for its benefit. "La Liberté," says Mr. Emile Faguet, in the preface to his "Politiques et Moralistes du Dix-Neuviéme Siécle" —"La Liberté s'oppose a l'Egalité, car La Liberté est aristocratique par essence. La Liberté ne se donne jamais, ne s'octroie jamais; elle se conquiert. Or ne peuvent la conquérir que des groupes sociaux qui ont su se donne la cohérence, l'organisation et la discipline et qui par conséquent, sont des groupes aristocratiques." The fact that states organized exclusively or largely for the benefit of liberty are essentially aristocratic explains the hostile and suspicious attitude of democracies towards such a principle of political action.

Only a comparatively small minority are capable at any one time to exercising political, economic, and civil liberties in an able, efficient, or thoroughly worthy manner; and a regime wrought for the benefit of such a minority would become at best a state, in which economic, political, and social power would be very unevenly distributed—a state like the Orleans Monarchy in France of the "Bourgeoisie" and the "Intellectuels." Such a state might well give its citizens fairly good government, as did the Orleans Monarchy; but just in so far as the mass of the people had any will of its own, it could not arouse vital popular interest and support; and it could not contribute, except negatively, to the fund of popular good sense and experience. The lack of such popular support caused the death of the French liberal monarchy; and no such regime can endure, save, as in England, by virtue of a somewhat abject popular acquiescence. As long as it does endure, moreover, it tends to undermine the virtue of its own beneficiaries. The favored minority, feeling as they do

tolerably sure of their position, can scarcely avoid a habit of making it somewhat too easy for one another. The political, economic, and intellectual leaders begin to be selected without any sufficient test of their efficiency. Some sort of a test continues to be required; but the standards which determine it drift into a condition of being narrow, artificial, and lax. Political, intellectual, and social leadership, in order to preserve its vitality needs a feeling of effective responsibility to a body of public opinion as wide, as varied, and as exacting as that of the whole community.

The desirable democratic object, implied in the traditional democratic demand for equality, consists precisely in that of bestowing a share of the responsibility and the benefits, derived from political and economic association, upon the whole community. Democracies have assumed and have been right in assuming that a proper diffusion of effective responsibility and substantial benefits is the one means whereby a community can be supplied with an ultimate and sufficient bond of union. The American democracy has attempted to manufacture a sufficient bond out of the equalization of rights: but such a bond is, as we have seen, either a rope of sand or a link of chains. A similar object must be achieved in some other way; and the ultimate success of democracy depends upon its achievement.

The fundamental political and social problem of a democracy may be summarized in the following terms. A democracy, like every political and social group, is composed of individuals, and must be organized for the benefit of its constituent members. But the individual has no chance of effective personal power except by means of the secure exercise of certain personal rights. Such rights, then, must be secured and exercised; yet when they are exercised, their tendency is to divide the community into divergent classes. Even if enjoyed with some equality in the beginning, they do not continue to be equally enjoyed, but make towards discriminations advantageous to a minority. The state, as representing the common interest, is obliged to admit the inevitability of such classifications and divisions, and has itself no alternative but to exercise a decisive preference on behalf of one side or the other. A well-governed state will use its power to promote edifying and desirable discriminations. But if discriminations tend to divide the community, and the state itself cannot do more than select among the various possible cases of discrimination those which it has some reason to prefer, how is the solidarity of the community to be preserved? And above all, how is a democratic community, which necessarily includes everybody in its benefits and responsibilities, to be kept well united? Such a community must retain an ultimate bond of union which counteracts the divergent effect of the discriminations, yet which at the same time is not fundamentally hostile to individual liberties.

The clew to the best available solution of the problem is supplied by a consideration of the precise manner, in which the advantages derived from the efficient exercise of liberties become inimical to a wholesome social condition. The hostility depends, not upon the existence of such advantageous discriminations for a time, but upon their persistence for too long a time. When, either from natural or artificial causes, they are properly selected, they contribute at the time to their selection both to individual and to social efficiency. They have been earned, and it is both just and edifying that, in so far as they have been earned, they should be freely enjoyed. On the other hand, they should not, so far as possible, be allowed to outlast their own utility. They must continue to be earned. It is power and opportunity enjoyed without being earned which help to damage the individual—both the individuals who benefit and the individuals who consent—and which tend to loosen the ultimate social bond. A democracy, no less than a monarchy or an aristocracy, must recognize political, economic, and social

discriminations, but it must also manage to withdraw its consent whenever these discriminations show any tendency to excessive endurance. The essential wholeness of the community depends absolutely on the ceaseless creation of a political, economic, and social aristocracy and their equally incessant replacement.

Both in its organization and in its policy a democratic state has consequently to seek two different but supplementary objects. It is the function of such a state to represent the whole community; and the whole community includes the individual as well as the mass, the many as well as the few. The individual is merged in the mass, unless he is enabled to exercise efficiently and independently his own private and special purposes. He must not only be permitted, he must be encouraged to earn distinction; and the best way in which he can be encouraged to earn distinction is to reward distinction both by abundant opportunity and cordial appreciation. Individual distinction, resulting from the efficient performance of special work, is not only the foundation of all genuine individuality, but is usually of the utmost social value. In so far as it is efficient, it has a tendency to be constructive. It both inserts some member into the social edifice which forms for the time being a desirable part of the whole structure, but it tends to establish a standard of achievement which may well form a permanent contribution to social amelioration. It is useful to the whole community, not because it is derived from popular sources or conforms to popular standards, but because it is formative and so helps to convert the community into a well-formed whole.

Distinction, however, even when it is earned, always has a tendency to remain satisfied with its achievements, and to seek indefinitely its own perpetuation. When such a course is pursued by an efficient and distinguished individual, he is, of course, faithless to the meaning and the source of his own individual power. In abandoning and replacing him a democracy is not recreant to the principle of individual liberty. It is merely subjecting individual liberty to conditions which promote and determine its continued efficiency. Such conditions never have been and never will be imposed for long by individuals or classes of individuals upon themselves. They must be imposed by the community, and nothing less than the whole community. The efficient exercise of individual power is necessary to form a community and make it whole, but the duty of keeping it whole rests with the community itself. It must consciously and resolutely preserve the social benefit, derived from the achievements of its favorite sons; and the most effective means thereto is that of denying to favoritism of all kinds the opportunity of becoming a mere habit.

The specific means whereby this necessary and formative favoritism can be prevented from becoming a mere habit vary radically among the different fields of personal activity. In the field of intellectual work the conditions imposed upon the individual must for the most part be the creation of public opinion; and in its proper place this aspect of the relation between individuality and democracy will receive special consideration. In the present connection, however, the relation of individual liberty to democratic organization and policy can be illustrated and explained most helpfully by a consideration of the binding and formative conditions of political and economic liberty. Democracies have always been chiefly preoccupied with the problems raised by the exercise of political and economic opportunities, because success in politics and business implies the control of a great deal of physical power and the consequent possession by the victors in a peculiar degree of both the motive and the means to perpetuate their victory.

The particular friends of freedom, such as Hamilton and the French "doctrinaires," have always believed that both civil and political liberty depended on the denial of popular Sovereignty and the rigid limitation of the suffrage. Of course, a democrat cannot accept such a conclusion. He should doubtless admit that the possession of absolute Sovereign power is always liable to abuse; and if he is candid, he can hardly fail to add that democratic favoritism is subject to the same weakness as aristocratic or royal favoritism. It tends, that is, to make individuals seek distinction not by high individual efficiency, but by compromises in the interest of useful popularity. It would be vain to deny the gravity of this danger or the extend to which, in the best of democracies, the seekers after all kinds of distinction have been hypnotized by an express desire for popularity. But American statesmen have not always been obliged to choose between Hamilton's unpopular integrity and Henry Clay's unprincipled bidding for popular favor. The greatest American political leaders have been popular without any personal capitulation; and their success is indicative of what is theoretically the most wholesome relation between individual political liberty and a democratic distribution of effective political power. The highest and most profitable individual political distinction is that which is won from a large fiend and from a whole people. Political, even more than other kinds of distinction, should not be the fruit of a limited area of selection. It must be open to everybody, and it must be acceptable to the community as a whole. In fact, the concession of substantially equal political rights is an absolute condition of any fundamental political bond. Grave as are the dangers which a democratic political system incurs, still graver ones are incurred by a rigidly limited electoral organization. A community, so organized, betrays a fundamental lack of confidence in the mutual loyalty and good faith of its members, and such a community can remain well united only at the cost of a mixture of patronage and servility.

The limitation of the suffrage to those who are individually capable of making the best use of it has the appearance of being reasonable; and it has made a strong appeal to those statesmen and thinkers who believed in the political leadership of intelligent and educated men. Neither can it be denied that a rigidly restricted suffrage might well make in the beginning for administrative efficiency and good government. But it must never be forgotten that a limited suffrage confines ultimate political responsibility, not only to a number of peculiarly competent individuals, but to a larger or smaller class; and in the long run a class is never to be trusted to govern in the interest of the whole community. A democracy should encourage the political leadership of experienced, educated, and well-trained men, but only on the express condition that their power is delegated and is to be used, under severe penalties, for the benefit of the people as a whole. A limited suffrage secure governmental efficiency, if at all, at the expense of the political education and training of the disfranchised class, and at the expense, also, of a permanent and radical popular political grievance. A substantially universal suffrage merely places the ultimate political responsibility in the hands of those for whose benefit governments are created; and its denial can be justified only on the ground that the whole community is incapable of exercising the responsibility. Such cases unquestionably exist. They exist wherever the individuals constituting a community, as at present in the South, are more divided by social or class ambitions and prejudices than they are united by a tradition of common action and mutual loyalty. But wherever the whole people are capable of thinking, feeling, and acting as if they constituted a whole, universal suffrage, even if it costs something in temporary efficiency, has a tendency to be more salutary and more formative than a restricted suffrage.

The substantially equal political rights enjoyed by the American people for so many generations have not proved dangerous to the civil liberties of the in-

dividual and, except to a limited extent, not to his political liberty. Of course, the American democracy has been absolutely opposed to the delegation to individuals of official political power, except under rigid conditions both as to scope and duration; and the particular friends of liberty have always claimed that such rigid conditions destroyed individual political independence and freedom. Hamilton, for instance, was insistent upon the necessity of an upper house consisting of life-members who would not be dependent on popular favor for their retention of office. But such proposals have no chance of prevailing in a sensible democracy. A democracy is justified in refusing to bestow permanent political power upon individuals, because such permanent tenure of office relaxes oftener than it stimulates the efficiency of the favored individual, and makes him attach excessive importance to mere independence. The official leaders of a democracy should, indeed, hold their offices under conditions which will enable them to act and think independently; but independence is really valuable only when the officeholder has won it from his own followers. Under any other conditions it is not only peculiarly liable to abuse, but it deprives the whole people of that ultimate responsibility for their own welfare, without which democracy is meaningless. A democracy is or should be constantly delegating an effective share in this responsibility to its official leaders, but only on condition that the power and responsibility delegated is partial and is periodically resumed.

The only Americans who hold important official positions for life are the judges of the Federal courts. Radical democrats have always protested against this exception, which, nevertheless, can be permitted without any infringement of democratic principles. The peculiar position of the Federal judge is symptomatic of the peculiar importance in the American system of the Federal Constitution. A senator would be less likely to be an efficient and public-spirited legislator, in case he were not obliged at regular intervals to prove title to his distinction. A justice of the Supreme Court, on the other hand, can the better perform his special task, provided he has a firm and permanent hold upon his office. He cannot, to be sure, entirely escape responsibility to public opinion, but his primary duty is to expound the Constitution as he understands it; and it is a duty which demands the utmost personal independence. The fault with the American system in this respect consists not in the independence of the Federal judiciary, but in the practical immutability of the Constitution. If the instrument which the Supreme Court expounds could be altered whenever a sufficiently large body of public opinion has demanded a change for a sufficiently long time, the American democracy would have much more to gain than to fear from the independence of the Federal judiciary.

The interest of individual liberty in relation to the organization of democracy demands simply that the individual officeholder should possess an amount of power and independence adequate to the efficient performance of his work. The work of a justice of the Supreme Court demands a power that is absolute for its own special work, and it demands technically complete independence. An executive should, as a rule, serve for a longer term, and hold a position of greater independence than a legislator, because his work of enforcing the laws and attending to the business details of government demands continuity, complete responsibility within its own sphere, and the necessity occasionally of braving adverse currents of public opinion. The term of service and the technical independence of a legislator might well be more restricted than that of an executive; but even a legislator should be granted as much power and independence as he may need for the official performance of his public duty. The American democracy has shown its enmity to individual political liberty, not because it has required its political fa-

vorites constantly to seek re-election, but because it has since 1800 tended to refuse to its favorites during their official term as much power and independence as is needed for administrative, legislative, and judicial efficiency. It has been jealous of the power it delegated, and has tried to take away with one hand what it gave with the other.

Taking American political traditions, ideals, institutions, and practices as a whole, there is no reason to believe that the American democracy cannot and will not combine sufficient opportunities for individual political distinction with an effective ultimate popular political responsibility. The manner in which the combination has been made hitherto is far from flawless, and the American democracy has much to learn before it reaches an organization adequate to its own proper purposes. It must learn, above all, that the state, and the individuals who are temporarily responsible for the action of the state, must be granted all the power necessary to redeem that responsibility. Individual opportunity and social welfare both depend upon the learning of this lesson; and while it is still very far from being learned, the obstacles in the way are not of a disheartening nature.

With the economic liberty of the individual in the case is different. The Federalists refrained from protecting individual political rights by incorporating in the Constitution any limitation of the suffrage; but they sought to protect the property rights of the individual by the most absolute constitutional guarantees. Moreover, American practice has allowed the individual a far larger measure of economic liberty than is required by the Constitution; and this liberty was granted in the expectation that it would benefit, not the individual as such, but the great mass of the American people. It has undoubtedly benefited the great mass of the American people; but it has been of far more benefit to a comparatively few individuals. Americans are just beginning to learn that the great freedom which the individual property-owner has enjoyed is having the inevitable result of all unrestrained exercise of freedom. It has tended to create a powerful but limited class whose chief object it is to hold and to increase the power which they have gained; and this unexpected result has presented the American democracy with the most difficult and radical of its problems. Is it to the interest of the American people as a democracy to permit the increase or the perpetuation of the power gained by this aristocracy of money?

A candid consideration of the foregoing question will, I believe, result in a negative answer. A democracy has as much interest in regulating for its own benefit the distribution of economic power as it has the distribution of political power, and the consequences of ignoring this interest would be as fatal in one case as in the other. In both instances regulation in the democratic interest is as far as possible from meaning the annihilation of individual liberty; but in both instances individual liberty should be subjected to conditions which will continue to keep it efficient and generally serviceable. Individual economic power is not any more dangerous than individual political power provided it is not held too absolutely and for too long a time. But in both cases the interest of the community as a whole should be dominant; and the interest of the whole community demands a considerable concentration of economic power and responsibility, but only for the ultimate purpose of its more efficient exercise and the better distribution of its fruits.

That certain existing American fortunes have in their making been of the utmost benefit to the whole economic organism is to my mind unquestionable the fact. Men like Mr. J. Pierpont Morgan, Mr. Andrew Carnegie, Mr. James J. Hill, and Mr. Edward Harriman have in the course of their business careers contributed enormously to American economic efficiency. They have been overpaid for their services, but that is irrelevant to the question

immediately under consideration. It is sufficient that their economic power has been just as much earned by substantial service as was the political power of a man like Andrew Jackson; and if our country is to continue its prosperous economic career, it must retain an economic organization which will offer to men of this stamp the opportunity and the inducement to earn distinction. The rule which has already been applied to the case of political power applies, also, to economic power. Individuals should enjoy as much freedom from restraint, as much opportunity, and as much responsibility as in necessary for the efficient performance of their work. Opinions will differ as to the extent of this desirable independence and its associated responsibility. The American millionaire and his supporters claim, of course, that any diminution of opportunity and independence would be fatal. To dispute this inference, however, does not involve the abandonment of the rule itself. A democratic economic system, even more than a democratic political system, must delegate a large share of responsibility and power to the individual, but under conditions, if possible, which will really make for individual efficiency and distinction.

The grievance which a democrat may feel towards the existing economic system is that it makes only partially for genuine individual economic efficiency and distinction. The political power enjoyed by an individual American rarely endures long enough to survive its own utility. But economic power can in some measure at least be detached from its creator. Let it be admitted that the man who accumulates $50,000,000 in part earns it, but how about the man who inherits it? The inheritor of such a fortune, like the inheritor of a ducal title, has an opportunity thrust upon him. He succeeds to a colossal economic privilege which he has not earned and for which he may be wholly incompetent. He rarely inherits with the money the individual ability possessed by its maker, but he does inherit a "money power" wholly independent of his own qualifications or deserts. By virtue of that power alone he is in a position in some measure to exploit his fellow-countrymen. Even though a man of very inferior intellectual and moral caliber, he is able vastly to increase his fortune through the information and opportunity which that fortune bestows upon him, and without making any individual contribution to the economic organization of the country. His power brings with it no personal dignity of efficiency; and for the whole material and meaning of his life he becomes as much dependent upon his millions as a nobleman upon his title. The money which was a source of distinction to its creator becomes in the course of time a source of individual demoralization to its inheritor. His life is organized for the purpose of spending a larger income than any private individual can really need; and his intellectual point of view is bounded by his narrow experience and his class interests.

No doubt the institution of private property, necessitating, as it does, the transmission to one person of the possessions and earnings of another, always involves the inheritance of unearned power and opportunity. But the point is that in the case of very large fortunes the inherited power goes far beyond any legitimate individual needs, and in the course of time can hardly fail to corrupt its possessors. The creator of a large fortune may well be its master; but its inheritor will, except in the case of exceptionally able individuals, become its victim, and most assuredly the evil social effects are as bad as the evil individual effects. The political bond which a democracy seeks to create depends for its higher value upon an effective social bond. Gross inequalities in wealth, wholly divorced from economic efficiency on the part of the rich, as effectively loosen the social bond as do gross inequalities of political and social standing. A wholesome social condition in a democracy does not imply uniformity of wealth any more than it implies uniformity of ability and purpose, but

it does imply the association of great individual economic distinction with responsibility and efficiency. It does imply that economic leaders, no less than political ones, should have conditions imposed upon them which will force them to recognize the responsibilities attached to so much power. Mutual association and confidence between the leaders and followers is as much a part of democratic economic organization as it is of democratic political organization; and in the long run the inheritance of vast fortunes destroys any such relation. They breed class envoy on one side, and class contempt on the other; and the community is either divided irremediably by differences of interest and outlook, or united, if at all, by snobbish servility.

If the integrity of a democracy is injured by the perpetuation of unearned economic distinctions, it is also injured by extreme poverty, whether deserved or not. A democracy which attempted to equalize wealth would incur the same disastrous fate as a democracy which attempted to equalize political power; but a democracy can no more be indifferent to the distribution of wealth than it can to the distribution of the suffrage. In a wholesome democracy every male adult should participate in the ultimate political responsibility, partly because of the political danger of refusing participation to the people, and partly because of the advantages to be derived from the political union of the whole people. So a wholesome democracy should seek to guarantee to every male adult a certain minimum of economic power and responsibility. No doubt it is much easier to confer the suffrage on the people than it is to make poverty a negligible social factor; but the difficulty of the task does not make it the less necessary. It stands to reason that in the long run the people who possess the political power will want a substantial share of the economic fruits. A prudent democracy should anticipate this demand. Not only does any considerable amount of grinding poverty constitute a grave social danger in a democratic state, but so, in general, does a widespread condition of partial economic privation. The individuals constituting a democracy lack the first essential of individual freedom when they cannot escape from a condition of economic dependence.

The American democracy has confidently believed in the fatal prosperity enjoyed by the people under the American system. In the confidence of that belief it has promised to Americans a substantial satisfaction of their economic needs; and it has made that promise an essential part of the American national idea. The promise has been measurably fulfilled hitherto, because the prodigious natural resources of a new continent were thrown open to anybody with the energy to appropriate them. But those natural resources have in no large measure passed into the possession of individuals, and American statesmen can no longer count upon them to satisfy the popular hunger for economic independence. An ever larger proportion of the total population of the country is taking to industrial occupations, and an industrial system brings with it much more definite social and economic classes, and a diminution of the earlier social homogeneity. The contemporary wage-earner is no longer satisfied with the economic results of being merely an American citizen. His union is usually of more obvious use to him than the state, and he is tending to make his allegiance to his union paramount to his allegiance to the state. This is only one of many illustrations that the traditional American system has broken down. The American state can regain the loyal adhesion of the economically less independent class only by positive service. What the wage-earner needs, and what it is to the interest of a democratic state he should obtain, is a constantly higher standard of living. The state can help him to conquer a higher standard of living without doing any necessary injury to his employers and with a positive benefit to general economic and social efficiency. If it is to earn the loyalty of the wage-earners, it must recognize the legitimacy of his demand, and make the satisfaction of it an essential part of its public policy.

The American state is dedicated to such a duty, not only by its democratic purpose, but by its national tradition. So far as the former is concerned, it is absurd and fatal to ask a popular majority to respect the rights of a minority, when those rights are interpreted so as to seriously to hamper, if not to forbid, the majority from obtaining the essential condition of individual freedom and development—viz. The highest possible standard of living. But this absurdity becomes really critical and dangerous, in view of the fact that the American people, particularly those of alien birth and descent, have been explicitly promised economic freedom and prosperity. The promise was made on the strength of what was believed to be an inexhaustible store of natural opportunities; and it will have to be kept even when those natural resources are no longer to be had for the asking. It is entirely possible, of course, that the promise can never be kept,—that its redemption will prove to be beyond the patience, the power, and the wisdom of the American people and their leaders; but if it is not kept, the American commonwealth will no longer continue to be a democracy.

THE BRIDGE BETWEEN DEMOCRACY AND NATIONALITY

We are now prepared, I hope, to venture upon a more fruitful definition of democracy. The popular definitions err in describing it in terms of its machinery or of some partial political or economic object. Democracy does not mean merely government by the people, or majority rule, or universal suffrage. All of these political forms or devices are a part of its necessary organization; but the chief advantage such methods of organization have is their tendency to promote some salutary and formative purpose. The really formative purpose is not exclusively a matter of individual liberty, although it must give individual liberty abundant scope. Neither is it a matter of equal rights alone, although it must always cherish the social bond which the principle represents. The salutary and formative democratic purpose consists in using the democratic organization for the joint benefit of individual distinction and social improvement.

To define the really democratic organization as one which makes expressly and intentionally for individual distinction and social improvement is nothing more than a translation of the statement that such an organization should make expressly and intentionally for the welfare of the whole people. The whole people will always consist of individuals, constituting small classes, who demand special opportunities, and the mass of the population who demand for their improvement more generalized opportunities. At any particular time or in any particular case, the improvement of the smaller classes may conflict with that of the larger class, but the conflict becomes permanent and irreconcilable only when it is intensified by the lack of a really binding and edifying public policy, and by the consequent stimulation of class and factional prejudices and purposes. A policy, intelligently informed by the desire to maintain a joint process of individual and social amelioration, should be able to keep a democracy sound and whole both in sentiment and in idea. Such a democracy would not be dedicated either to liberty or to equality in their abstract expressions, but to liberty and equality, in so far as they made for human brotherhood. As M. Faguet says in the introduction to his "Politiques et Moralistes du Dix-Neuviéme Siécle," from which I have already quoted: "Liberté et Egalité sont donc contradictoires et exclusives l'une et l'autre; mais la Fraternité les concilierait. La Fraternité

non seulement concilierait la Liberte et l'Egalité, mais elle les ferait gêneratrices l'une et l'autre." The two subordinate principles, that is, one representing the individual and the other the social interest, can by their subordination to the principle of human brotherhood, be made in the long run mutually helpful.

The foregoing definition of the democratic purpose is the only one which can entitle democracy to an essential superiority to other forms of political organization. Democrats have always tended to claim some such superiority for their methods and purposes, but in case democracy is to be considered merely as a piece of political machinery, or a partial political idea, the claim has no validity. Its superiority must be based upon the fact that democracy is the best possible translation into political and social terms of an authoritative and comprehensive moral idea; and, provided a democratic state honestly seeks to make its organization and policy contribute to a better quality of individuality and a higher level of associated life, it can within certain limits claim the allegiance of mankind on rational moral grounds.

The proposed definition may seem to be both vague and commonplace; but it none the less brings with it practical consequences of paramount importance. The subordination of the machinery of democracy to its purpose, and the comprehension within that purpose of the higher interests both of the individual and society, is not only exclusive of many partial and erroneous ideas, but demands both a reconstructive programme and an efficient organization. A government by the people, which seeks an organization and a policy beneficial to the individual and to society, is confronted by a task as responsible and difficult as you please; but it is a specific task which demands the adoption of certain specific and positive means. Moreover it is a task which the American democracy has never sought consciously to achieve. American democrats have always hoped for individual and social amelioration as the result of the operation of their democratic system; but if any such result was to follow, its achievement was to be a happy accident. The organization and policy of a democracy should leave the individual and society to seek their own amelioration. The democratic state should never discriminate in favor of anything or anybody. It should only discriminate against all sorts of privilege. Under the proposed definition, on the other hand, popular government is to make itself expressly and permanently responsible for the amelioration of the individual and society; and a necessary consequence of this responsibility is an adequate organization and a reconstructive policy.

The majority of good Americans will doubtless consider that the reconstructive policy, already indicated, is flagrantly socialistic both in its methods and its objects; and if any critic likes to fasten the stigma of socialism upon the foregoing conception of democracy, I am not concerned with dodging the odium of the word. The proposed difinition of democracy is socialistic, if it is socialistic to consider democracy inseparable from a candid, patient, and courageous attempt to advance the social problem towards a satisfactory solution. It is also socialistic in case socialism cannot be divorced from the use, wherever necessary, of the political organization in all its forms to realize the proposed democratic purpose. On the other hand, there are some doctrines frequently associated with socialism, to which the proposed conception of democracy is wholly inimical; and it should be characterized not so much socialistic, as unscrupulously and loyally nationalistic.

A democracy dedicated to individual and social betterment is necessarily individualist as well as socialist. It has little interest in the mere multiplication of average individuals, except in so far as such multiplication is necessary to economic and political efficiency; but it has the deepest interest in the development of a higher quality of individual self-expression. There are two indispensable economic conditions of qualitative individual self-expression. One is the preservation of the institution of private property in some form, and the other is the radical transformation of its existing nature and influence. A democracy certainly cannot fulfill its mission without the eventual assumption by the state of many functions now performed by individuals, and without becoming expressly responsible for an improved distribution of wealth; but if any attempt is made to accomplish these results by violent means, it will most assuredly prove to be a failure. An improvement in the distribution of wealth or in economic efficiency which cannot be accomplished by purchase on the part of the state or by a legitimate use of the power of taxation, must be left to the action of time, assisted, of course, by such arrangements as are immediately practical. But the amount of actual good to the individual and society which can be effected *at any one time* by an alteration in the distribution of wealth is extremely small; and the same statement is true of any proposed state action in the interest of the democratic purpose. Consequently, while responsible state action is an essential condition of any steady approach to the democratic consummation, such action will be wholly vain unless accompanied by a larger measure of spontaneous individual amelioration. In fact, one of the strongest arguments on behalf of a higher and larger conception of state responsibilities in a democracy is that the candid, courageous, patient, and intelligent attempt to redeem those responsibilities provides one of the highest types of individuality—viz. the public-spirited man with a personal opportunity and a task which should be enormously stimulating and edifying.

The great weakness of the most popular form of socialism consists, however, in its mixture of a revolutionary purpose with an international scope. It seeks the abolition of national distinctions by revolutionary revolts of the wage-earner against the capitalist; and in so far as its proposes to undermine the principle of national cohesion and to substitute for it an international organization of a single class, it is headed absolutely in the wrong direction. Revolutions may at times be necessary and on the whole helpful, but not in case there is any other practicable method of removing grave obstacles to human amelioration; and in any event their tendency is socially disintegrating. The destruction or the weakening of nationalities for the ostensible benefit of an international socialism would in truth gravely imperil the bond upon which actual human association is based. The peoples who have inherited any share in Christian civilization are effectively united chiefly by national habits, traditions, and purposes; and perhaps the most effective way of bringing about an irretrievable division of purpose among them would be the adoption by the class of wage-earners of the programme of international socialism. It is not too much to say that no permanent good can, under existing conditions, come to the individual and society except through the preservation and the development of the existing system of nationalized states.

Radical and enthusiastic democrats have usually failed to attach sufficient importance to the ties whereby civilized men are at the present time actually united. Inasmuch as national traditions are usually associated with all sorts of political, economic, and social privileges and abuses, they have sought to identify the higher social relation with the destruction of the national tradition and the substitution of an ideal bond. In so doing they are committing a disastrous error; and democracy will never become really constructive until this error is recognized and democracy abandons its former alliance with revolution. The higher human relation must be brought about chiefly by the improvement and the intensification of existing human relations. The only possible foundation for

a better social structure is the existing social order, or which the contemporary system of nationalized states forms the foundation.

Loyalty to the existing system of nationalized states does not necessarily mean loyalty to an existing government merely because it exists. There have been, and still are, governments whose ruin is a necessary condition of popular liberation; and revolution doubtless still has a subordinate part to play in the process of human amelioration. The loyalty which a citizen owes to a government is dependent upon the extent to which the government is representative of national traditions and is organized in the interest of valid national purposes. National traditions and purposes always contain a large infusion of dubious ingredients; but loyalty to them does not necessarily mean the uncritical and unprotesting acceptance of the national limitations and abuses. Nationality is a political and social idea as well as the great contemporary political fact. Loyalty to the national interest implies devotion to a progressive principle. It demands, to be sure, that the progressive principle be realized without any violation of fundamental national ties. It demands that any national action taken for the benefit of the progressive principle be approved by the official national organization. But it also serves as a ferment quite as much as a bond. It bids the loyal national servants to fashion their fellow-countrymen into more of a nation; and the attempt to perform this bidding constitutes a very powerful and wholesome source of political development. It constitutes, indeed, a source of political development which is of decisive importance for a satisfactory theory of political and social progress, because a people which becomes more of a nation has a tendency to become for that very reason more of a democracy.

The assertion that a people which becomes more of a nation becomes for that very reason more of a democracy, is, I am aware, a hazardous assertion, which can be justified, if at all, only at a considerable expense. As a matter of fact, the two following chapters will be devoted chiefly to this labor of justification. In the first of these chapters I shall give a partly historical and partly critical account of the national principle in its relation to democracy; and in the second I shall apply the results, so achieved, to the American national principle in its relation to the American democratic idea. But before starting this complicated task, a few words must be premised as to the reasons which make the attempt well worth the trouble.

If a people, in becoming more of a nation, become for that very reason more of a democracy, the realization of the democratic purpose is not rendered any easier, but democracy is provided with a simplified, a consistent, and a practicable programme. An alliance is established thereby between the two dominant political and social forces in modern life. The suspicion with which aggressive advocates of the national principle have sometimes regarded democracy would be shown to have only a conditional justification; and the suspicion with which many ardent democrats have regarded aggressive nationalism would be similarly disarmed. A democrat, so far as the statement is true, could trust the fate of his cause in each particular state to the friends of national progress. Democracy would not need for its consummation the ruin of the traditional political fabrics; but so far as those political bodies were informed by genuinely national ideas and aspirations, it could await confidently the process of national development. In fact, the first duty of a good democrat would be that of rendering to his country loyal patriotic service. Democrats would abandon the task of making over the world to suit their own purposes, until they had come to a better understanding with their own countrymen. One's democracy, that is, would begin at home and it would for the most part stay at home; and the cause of national well-being

would derive invaluable assistance from the loyal cooperation of good democrats.

A great many obvious objections will, of course, be immediately raised against any such explanation of the relation between democracy and nationality; and I am well aware that these objections demand the most serious consideration. A generation or two ago the European democrat was often by way of being an ardent nationalist; and a constructive relation between the two principles was accepted by many European political reformers. The events of the last fifty years have, however, done much to sever the alliance, and to make European patriots suspicious of democracy, and European democrats suspicious of patriotism. To what extent these suspicions are justified, I shall discuss in the next chapter; but that discussion will be undertaken almost exclusively for obtaining, if possible, some light upon our domestic situation. The formula of a constructive relation between the national and democratic principles has certain importance for European peoples, and particularly for Frenchmen: but, if true, it is of a far superior importance to Americans. It supplies a constructive form for the progressive solution of their political and social problems; and while it imposes on them responsibilities which they have sought to evade, it also offers compensations, the advantage of which they have scarcely expected.

Americans have always been both patriotic and democratic, just as they have always been friendly both to liberty and equality, but in neither case have they brought the two ideas or aspirations into mutually helpful relations. As democrats they have often regarded nationalism with distrust, and have consequently deprived their patriotism of any sufficient substance and organization. As nationalists they have frequently regarded essential aspects of democracy with a wholly unnecessary and embarrassing suspicion. They have been after a fashion Hamiltonian, and Jeffersonian after more of a fashion; but they have never recovered from the initial disagreement between Hamilton and Jefferson. If there is any truth in the idea of a constructive relation between democracy and nationality this disagreement must be healed. They must accept both principles loyally and unreservedly; and by such acceptance their "noble national theory" will obtain a wholly unaccustomed energy and integrity. The alliance between the two principles will not leave either of them intact; but it will necessarily do more harm to the Jeffersonian group of political ideas than it will to the Hamiltonian. The latter's nationalism can be adapted to democracy without an essential injury to itself, but the former's democracy cannot be nationalized without being transformed. The manner of its transformation has already been discussed in detail. It must cease to be a democracy of indiscriminate individualism, and become one of selected individuals who are obliged constantly to justify their selection; and its members must be united not by a sense of joint irresponsibility, but by a sense of joint responsibility for the success of their political and social ideal. They must become, that is, a democracy devoted to the welfare of the whole people by means of a conscious labor of individual and social improvement; and that is precisely the sort of democracy which demands for its realization the aid of the Hamiltonian nationalistic organization and principle.

WORKS BY HERBERT CROLY

Croly, Herbert. *Marcus Alonzo Hanna*. New York: Macmillan, 1923. Hanna, the logical outcome of plutocratic America, reflected and expressed the views of this era, not as a symbol, but as a man filled with human nature.

_____. *Progressive Democracy*. New York: Macmillan, 1914. An essay showing the necessity of replacing the traditional political-economic system with progressivism.

_____. *The Promise of American Life*. New York: Macmillan, 1909. His major work.

MAJOR SOURCES ON HERBERT CROLY

Bliven, Bruce. "The First Forty Years," *The New Republic*, Vol. 131, No. 21 (Nov. 22, 1954), pp. 6-11. A presentation of *The New Republic's* past editorial policy and how it has maintained the Croly philosophy of conserving the old American ideals.

Forcey, Charles B. "Croly and Nationalism," *The New Republic*, Vol. 131, No. 21 (Nov. 22, 1954), pp. 17-23. Portrays Croly as an ardent Realist, moving from a nationalist to an internationalist stance while forsaking the Idealists of the Wilsonian school.

Forcey, Charles. *The Crossroads of Liberalism: Croly, Weyl, Lippmann, and the Progressive Era*. New York: Oxford, 1961. An analysis of Croly in his attempt to preserve both liberty and prosperity by means of a reformist middle class motivated by nationalism.

Frankfurter, Felix. "Croly and Opinion," *The New Republic*, Vol. 131, No. 21 (Nov. 22, 1954), pp. 112-114. Croly, constantly attempting to expand his individual consciousness for societal insight and service, produces *Promise of American Life,* a watershed in early 20th century political thought and activity.

Smith, Henry Ladel. "Editing for the Superior Few," *The New Republic*, Vol. 131, No. 21 (Nov. 22, 1954), pp. 23-26. An essay on Croly's journalistic policy of using the press to lead the nation towards liberal reform through constant agitation.

Straight, Michael. "The Ghost at the Banquet," *The New Republic*, Vol. 131, No. 21 (Nov. 22, 1954), pp. 11-16. The philosophy of Croly is presented as the only meaningful policy for liberals in the post-McCarthy era.

CHAPTER 12

John Dewey

JOHN DEWEY (1859–1952) was born and raised in a small town in Vermont, and graduated from the University of Vermont in 1879. He subsequently received his doctorate from The Johns Hopkins University in 1884. Dewey taught philosophy at the Universities of Michigan, Minnesota, and Chicago until 1904 when he accepted a chair as professor of philosophy at Columbia University, which he held until his retirement from full-time teaching in 1931.

As a philosopher, Dewey was not content to bring forth theories. He was the chief prophet of progressive education, the learning-by-doing method. As a believer in democratic socialism, Dewey was interested in creating an American political party that would represent the American people better than the two major political parties. In 1946, he joined with labor leaders to lay the groundwork for a third, or Peoples', party, for the 1948 election.

At various times, Dewey was president of the American Psychological Association, the American Association of University Professors, and the People's Lobby; and honorary president of the American Philosophical Association, the National Educational Association, and the Progressive Educational Association.

From The Public and Its Problems

We have had occasion to refer in passing to the distinction between democracy as a social idea and political democracy as a system of government. The two are, of course, connected. The idea remains barren and empty save as it is incarnated in human relationships. Yet in discussion they must be distinguished. The idea of democracy is a wider and fuller idea than can be exemplified in the state even at its best. To be realized it must affect all modes of human association, the family, the school, industry, religion. And even as far as political arrangements are concerned, governmental institutions are but a mechanism for securing to an idea channels of effective operation. It will hardly do to say that criticisms of the political machinery leave the believer in the idea untouched. For, as far as they are justified—and no candid believer can deny that many of them are only too well grounded—they arouse him to bestir himself in order that the idea may find a more adequate machinery through which to work. What the faithful insist upon, however, is that the idea and its external organs and structures are not to be identified. We object to the common supposition of the foes of existing democratic government that the accusations against it touch the social and moral aspirations and ideas which underlie the political forms. The old saying that the cure for the ills of democracy is more democracy is not apt if it means that the evils may be remedied by introducing more machinery of the same kind as that which already exists, or by refining and perfecting that machinery. But the phrase may also indicate the need of returning to the idea itself, of clarifying and deepening our apprehension of it, and of employing our sense of its meaning to critize and remake its political manifestations.

Confining ourselves, for the moment, to political democracy, we must, in any case, renew our protest against the assumption that the idea has itself produced the governmental practices which obtain in democratic states; General suffrage, elected representatives, majority rule, and so on. The idea has influenced the concrete political movement, but it has not caused it. The transition from family and dynastic government supported by the loyalties of tradition to popular government was the outcome primarily of technological discoveries and inventions working a change in the customs by which men had been bound

SOURCE. Reprinted from *The Public and Its Problems* (1927), by permission of Swallow Books. Copyright Mrs. John Dewey, 1954.

together. It was not due to the doctrines of doctrinaires. The forms to which we are accustomed in democratic governments represent the cumulative effect of a multitude of events, unpremeditated as far as political effects were concerned and having unpredictable consequences. There is no sanctity in universal suffrage, frequent elections, majority rule, congressional and cabinet government. These things are devices evolved in the direction in which the current was moving, each wave of which involved at the time of its impulsion a minimum of departure from antecedent custom and law. The devices served a purpose; but the purpose was rather that of meeting existing needs which had become too intense to be ignored, than that of forwarding the democratic idea. In spite of all defects, they served their own purpose well.

Looking back, with the aid which *ex posto facto* experience can give, it would be hard for the wisest to devise schemes which, under the circumstances, would have met the needs better. In this retrospective glance, it is possible, however, to see how the doctrinal formulations which accompanied them were inadequate, one-sided and positively erroneous. In fact they were hardly more than political war-cries adopted to help in carrying on some immediate agitation or in justifying some particular practical polity struggling for recognition, even though they were asserted to be absolute truths of human nature or of morals. The doctrines served a particular local pragmatic need. But often their very adaptation to immediate circumstances unfitted them, pragmatically, to meet more enduring and more extensive needs. They lived to cumber the political ground, obstructing progress, all the more so because they were uttered and held not as hypotheses with which to direct social experimentation but as final truths, dogmas. No wonder they call urgently for revision and displacement.

Nevertheless the current has set steadily in one direction: toward democratic forms. That government exists to serve its community, and that this purpose cannot be achieved unless the community itself shares in selecting its governors and determining their policies, are a deposit of fact left, as far as we can see, permanently in the wake of doctrines and forms, however transitory the latter. They are not the whole of the democratic idea, but they express it in its political phase. Belief in this political aspect is not a mystic faith as if in some overruling providence that cares for children, drunkards and others unable to help themselves. It marks a well-attested conclusion from historic facts. We have every reason to think that whatever changes may take place in existing democratic machinery, they will be of a sort to make the interest of the public a more supreme guide and criterion of governmental activity, and to enable the public to form and manifest its purposes still more authoritatively. In this sense the cure for the ailments of democracy is more democracy. The prime difficulty, as we have seen, is that of discovering the means by which a scattered, mobile and manifold public may so recognize itself as to define and express its interests. This discovery is necessarily precedent to any fundamental change in the machinery. We are not concerned therefore to set forth counsels as to advisable improvements in the political forms of democracy. Many have been suggested. It is no derogation of their relative worth to say that consideration of these changes is not at present an affair of primary importance. The problem lies deeper; it is in the first instance an intellectual problem: the search for conditions under which the Great Society may become the Great Community. When these conditions are brought into being they will make their own forms. Until they have come about, it is somewhat futile to consider what political machinery will suit them.

In a search for the conditions under which the inchoate public now extant may function democratically, we may proceed from a statement of the nature of the democratic idea in its generic social sense.[1] From the standpoint of the individual, it consists in having a responsible share according to capacity in forming and directing the activities of the groups to which one belongs and in participating according to need in the values which the groups sustain. From the standpoint of the groups, it demands liberation of the potentialities of members of a group in harmony with the interests and goods which are common. Since every individual is a member of many groups, this specification cannot be fulfilled except when different groups interact flexibly and fully in connection with other groups. A member of a robber band may express his powers in a way consonant with belonging to that group and be directed by the interest common to its members. But he does so only at the cost of repression of those of his potentialities which can be realized only through membership in other groups. The robber band cannot interact flexibly with other groups; it can act only through isolating itself. It must prevent the operation of all interests save those which circumscribe it in its separateness. But a good citizen finds his conduct as a member of a political group enriching and enriched by his participation in family life, industry, scientific and artistic associations. There is a free give-and-take: fullness of integrated personality is therefore possible of achievement, since the pulls and responses of different groups reinforce one another and their values accord.

Regarded as an idea, democracy is not an alternative to other principles of associated life. It is the idea of community life itself. It is an ideal in the only intelligible sense of an ideal: namely, the tendency and movement of some thing which exists carried to its final limit, viewed as completed, perfected. Since things do not attain such fulfillment but are in actuality distracted and interfered

---

[1] The most adequate discussion of this ideal with which I am acquainted is T. V. Smith's *The Democratic Way of Life.*

with, democracy in this sense is not a fact and never will be. But neither in this sense is there or has there ever been anything which is a community in its full measure, a community unalloyed by alien elements. The idea or ideal of a community presents, however, actual phases of associated life as they are freed from restrictive and disturbing elements, and are contemplated as having attained their limit of development. Wherever there is conjoint activity whose consequences are appreciated as good by all singular persons who take part in it, and where the realization of the good is such as to effect an energetic desire and effort to sustain it in being just because it is a good shared by all, there is in so far a community. The clear consciousness of a communal life, in all its implications, constitutes the idea of democracy.

Only when we start from a community as a fact, grasp the fact in thought so as to clarify and enhance its constituent elements, can we reach an idea of democracy which is not utopian. The conceptions and shibboleths which are traditionally associated with the idea of democracy take on a veridical and directive meaning only when they are construed as marks and traits of an association which realizes the defining characteristics of a community. Fraternity, liberty and equality isolated from communal life are hopeless abstractions. Their separate assertion leads to mushy sentimentalism or else to extravagant and fanatical violence which in the end defeats its own aims. Equality then becomes a creed of mechanical identity which is false to facts and impossible of realization. Effort to attain it is divisive of the vital bonds which hold men together; as far as it puts forth issue, the outcome is a mediocrity in which good is common only in the sense of being average and vulgar. Liberty is then thought of as independence of social ties, and ends in dissolution and anarchy. It is more difficult to sever the idea of brotherhood from that of a community, and hence it is either practically ignored

in the movements which identify democracy with Individualism, or else it is a sentimentally appended tag. In its just connection with communal experience, fraternity is another name for the consciously appreciated goods which accrue from an association in which all share, and which give direction to the conduct of each. Liberty is that secure release and fulfillment of personal potentialities which take place only in rich and manifold association with others: the power to be an individualized self making a distinctive contribution and enjoying in its own way the fruits of association. Equality denotes the unhampered share which each individual member of the community has in the consequences of associated action. It is equitable because it is measured only by need and capacity to utilize, not by extraneous factors which deprive one in order that another may take and have. A baby in the family is equal with others, not because of some antecedent and structural quality which is the same as that of others, but in so far as his needs for care and development are attended to without being sacrificed to the superior strength, possessions and matured abilities of others. Equality does not signify that kind of mathematical or physical equivalence in virtue of which any one element may be substituted for another. It denotes effective regard for whatever is distinctive and unique in each, irrespective of physical and psychological inequalities. It is not a natural possession but is a fruit of the community when its action is directed by its character as a community.

Associated or joint activity is a condition of the creation of a community. But association itself is physical and organic, while communal life is moral, that is emotionally, intellectually, consciously sustained. Human beings combine in behavior as directly and unconsciously as do atoms, stellar masses and cells; as directly and unknowingly as they divide and repel. They do so in virtue of their own structure, as man and woman unite, as the baby seeks the breast and the breast is there to supply its need. They do so from external circumstances, pressure from without, as atoms combine or separate in presence of an electric charge, or sheep huddle together from the cold. Associated activity needs no explanation; things are made that way. But no amount of aggregated collective action of itself constitutes a community. For beings who observe and think, and whose ideas are absorbed by impulses and become sentiments and interests, "we" is as inevitable as "I." But "we" and "our" exist only when the consequences of combined action are perceived and become an object of desire and effort, just as "I" and "mine" appear on the scene only when a distinctive share in mutual action is consciously asserted or claimed. Human associations may be ever so organic in origin and firm in operation, but they develop into societies in a human sense only as their consequences, being known, are esteemed and sought for. Even if "society" were as much an organism as some writers have held, it would not on that account be society. Interactions, transactions, occur *de facto* and the results of interdependence follow. But participation in activities and sharing in results are additive concerns. They demand *communication* as a prerequisite.

Combined activity happens among human beings; but when nothing else happens it passes as inevitably into some other mode of interconnected activity as does the interplay of iron and the oxygen of water. What takes place is wholly describable in terms of energy, or, as we say in the case of human interactions, of force. Only when there exist *signs* or *symbols* of activities and of their outcome can the flux be viewed as from without, be arrested for consideration and esteem, and be regulated. Lightning strikes and rives a tree or rock, and the resulting fragments take up and continue the process of interaction, and so on and on. But when phases of the process are represented by signs, a new medium is interposed. As symbols are related to one another, the important relations of a course of events are recorded and are preserved as meanings. Recollection and foresight are possible; the new medium facilitates calculation, planning, and a new kind of action which intervenes in what happens to direct its course in the interest of what is foreseen and desired.

Symbols in turn depend upon and promote communication. The results of conjoint experience are considered and transmitted. Events cannot be passed from one to another, but meanings may be shared by means of signs. Wants and impulses are then attached to common meanings. They are thereby transformed into desires and purposes, which, since they implicate a common or mutually understood meaning, present new ties, converting a conjoint activity into a community of interest and endeavor. Thus there is generated what, metaphorically, may be termed a general will and social consciousness: desire and choice on the part of individuals in behalf of activities that, by means of symbols, are communicable and shared by all concerned. A community thus presents an order of energies and transmuted into one of meanings which are appreciated and mutually referred by each to every other on the part of those engaged in combined action. "Force" is not eliminated but is transformed in use and direction by ideas and sentiments made possible by means of symbols.

The work of conversion of the physical and organic phase of associated behavior into a community of action saturated and regulated by mutual interest in shared meanings, consequences which are translated into ideas and desired objects by means of symbols, does not occur all at once nor completely. At any given time, it sets a problem rather than marks a settled achievement. We are born organic beings associated with others, but we are not born members of a community. The young have to be brought within the traditions, outlook and interests which characterize a community by means of education: by unremitting instruction and by learning in connection with the phenomena of overt association. Everything which is distinctively human is learned, not native, even though it could not be learned without native structures which mark man off from other animals. To learn in a human way and to human effect is not just to acquire added skill through refinement of original capacities.

To learn to be human is to develop through the give-and-take of communication an effective sense of being an individually distinctive member of a community; one who understands and appreciates its beliefs, desires and methods, and who contributes to a further conversion of organic powers into human resources and values. But this translation is never finished. The old Adam, the unregenerate element in human nature, persists. It shows itself wherever the method obtains of attaining results by use of force instead of by the method of communication and enlightenment. It manifests itself more subtly, pervasively and effectually when knowledge and the instrumentalities of skill which are the product of communal life are employed in the service of wants and impulses which have not themselves been modified by reference to a shared interest. To the doctrine of "natural" economy which held that commercial exchange would bring about such an interdependence that harmony would automatically result, Rousseau gave an adequate answer in advance. He pointed out that interdependence provides just the situation which makes it possible and worth while for the stronger and abler to exploit others for their own ends, to keep others in a state of subjection where they can be utilized as animated tools. The remedy he suggested, a return to a condition of independence based on isolation, was hardly seriously meant. But its desperateness is evidence of the urgency of the problem. Its negative character was equivalent to surrender of any hope of solution. By contrast it indicates the nature of the only possible solution: the perfecting of the means and ways of communication of meanings so that genuinely shared interest in the consequences

of interdependent activities may inform desire and effort and thereby direct action.

This is the meaning of the statement that the problem is a moral one dependent upon intelligence and education. We have in our prior account sufficiently emphasized the role of technological and industrial factors in creating the Great Society. What was said may even have seemed to imply acceptance of the deterministic version of an economic interpretation of history and institutions. It is silly and futile to ignore and deny economic facts. They do not cease to operate because we refuse to note them, or because we smear them over with sentimental idealizations. As we have also noted, they generate as their result overt and external conditions of action and these are known with various degrees of adequacy. What actually happens in consequence of industrial forces is dependent upon the presence or absence of perception and communication of consequences, upon foresight and its effect upon desire and endeavor. Economic agencies produce one result when they are left to work themselves out on the merely physical level, or on that level modified only as the knowledge, skill and technique which the community has accumulated are transmitted to its members unequally and by chance. They have a different outcome in the degree in which knowledge of consequences is equitably distributed, and action is animated by an informed and lively sense of a shared interest. The doctrine of economic interpretation as usually stated ignores the transformation which meanings may effect; it passes over the new medium which communication may interpose between industry and its eventual consequences. It is obsessed by the illusion which vitiated the "natural economy": an illusion due to failure to note the difference made in action by perception and publication of its consequences, actual and possible. It thinks in terms of antecedents, not of the eventual; of origins, not fruits.

We have returned, through this apparent excursion, to the question in which our earlier discussion culminated: What are the conditions under which it is possible for the Great Society to approach more closely and vitally the status of a Great Community, and thus take form in genuinely democratic societies and state? What are the conditions under which we may reasonably picture the Public emerging from its eclipse?

The study will be an intellectual or hypothetical one. There will be no attempt to state how the required conditions might come into existence, nor to prophesy that they will occur. The object of the analysis will be to show that *unless* ascertained specifications are realized, the Community cannot be organized as a democratically effective Public. It is not claimed that the conditions which will be noted will suffice, but only that at least they are indispensable. In other words, we shall endeavor to frame a hypothesis regarding the democratic state to stand in contrast with the earlier doctrine which has been nullified by the course of events.

Two essential constituents in that older theory, as will be recalled, were the notions that each individual is of himself equipped with the intelligence needed, under the operation of self-interest, to engage in political affairs; and that general suffrage, frequent elections of officials and majority rule are sufficient to ensure the responsibility of elected rulers to the desires and interests of the public. As we shall see, the second conception is logically bound up with the first and stands or falls with it. At the basis of the scheme lies what Lippman has well called the idea of the "omnicompetent" individual: competent to frame policies, to judge their results; competent to know in all situations demanding political action what is for his own good, and competent to enforce his idea of good and the will to effect it against contrary forces. Subsequent history has proved that the assumption involved illusion. Had it not been for the misleading influence of a false psychology, the illusion

might have been detected in advance. But current philosophy held that ideas and knowledge were functions of a mind or consciousness which originated in individuals by means of isolated contact with objects. But in fact, knowledge is a function of association and communication; it depends upon tradition, upon tools and methods socially transmitted, developed and sanctioned. Faculties of effectual observation, reflection and desire are habits acquired under the influence of the culture and institutions of society, not ready-made inherent powers. The fact that man acts from crudely intelligized emotion and from habit rather than from rational consideration, is now so familiar that it is not easy to appreciate that the other idea was taken seriously as the basis of economic and political philosophy. The measure of truth which it contains was derived from observation of a relatively small group of shrewd business men who regulated their enterprises by calculation and accounting, and of citizens of small and stable local communities who were so intimately acquainted with the persons and affairs of their locality that they could pass competent judgment upon the bearing of proposed measures upon their own concerns.

Habit is the mainspring of human action, and habits are formed for the most part under the influence of the customs of a group. The organic structure of man entails the formation of habit, for, whether we wish it or not, whether we are aware of it or not, every act effects a modification of attitude and set which directs future behavior. The dependence of habit-forming upon those habits of a group which constitute customs and institutions is a natural consequence of the helplessness of infancy. The social consequences of habit have been stated once for all by James:

Habit is the enormout fly-wheel of society, its most precious conservative influence. It alone is what keeps up within the bounds of ordinance, and saves the children of fortune from the uprisings of the poor. It alone prevents the hardest and most repulsive walks of life from being deserted by those brought up to tread therein. It keeps the fisherman and the deck-hand at sea through the winter; it holds the miner in his darkness, and nails the country-man to his log cabin and his lonely farm through all the months of snow; it protects us from invasion by the natives of the desert and the frozen zone. It dooms us all to fight out the battle of life upon the lines of our nurture or our early choice, and to make the best of a pursuit that disagrees, because there is no other for which we are fitted and it is too late to begin again. It keeps different social strata from mixing.

The influence of habit is decisive because all distinctively human action has to be learned, and the very heart, blood and sinews of learning is creation of habitudes. Habits bind us to orderly and established ways of action because they generate ease, skill and interest in things to which we have grown used and because they instigate fear to walk in different ways, and because they leave us incapacitated for the trial of them. Habit does not preclude the use of thought, but it determines the channels within which it operates. Thinking is secreted in the interstices of habits. The sailor, miner, fisherman and farmer think, but their thoughts fall within the framework of accustomed occupations and relationships. We dream beyond the limits of use and wont, but only rarely does revery become a source of acts which break bounds; so rarely that we name those in whom it happens demonic geniuses and marvel at the spectacle. Thinking itself becomes habitual along certain lines; a specialized occupation. Scientific men, philosophers, literary persons, are not men and women who have so broken the bonds of habits that pure reason and emotion undefiled by use and wont speak through them. They are persons of a specialized infrequent habit. Hence the idea that men are moved by an intelligent and calculated regard for their own good is pure mythology. Even if the principle of self-love

actuated behavior, it would still be true that the *objects* in which men find their love manifested, the objects which they take as constituting their peculiar interests, are set by habits reflecting social customs.

These facts explain why the social doctrinaires of the new industrial movement had so little prescience of what was to follow in consequence of it. These facts explain why the more things changed, the more they were the same; they account, that is, for the fact that instead of the sweeping revolution which was expected to result from democratic political machinery, there was in the main but a transfer of vested power from one class to another. A few men, whether or not they were good judges of their own true interest and good, were competent judges of the conduct of business for pecuniary profit, and of how the new governmental machinery could be made to serve their ends. It would have taken a new race of human beings to escape, in the use made of political forms, from the influence of deeply engrained habits, of old institutions and customary social status, with their inwrought limitations of expectation, desire and demand. And such a race, unless of disembodied angelic constitution, would simply have taken up the task where human beings assumed it upon emergency from the condition of anthropoid apes. In spite of sudden and catastrophic revolutions, the essential continuity of history is doubly guaranteed. Not only are personal desire and belief functions of habit and custom, but the objective conditions which provide the resources and tools of action, together with its limitations, obstructions and traps, are precipitates of the past, perpetuating, willy-nilly, its hold and power. The creation of a *tabula rasa* in order to permit the creation of a new order is so impossible as to set at naught both the hope of buyant revolutionaries and the timidity of scared conservatives.

Nevertheless, changes take place and are cumulative in character. Observation of them in the light of their recognized consequences arouses reflection, discovery, invention, experimentation. When a certain state of accumulated knowledge, of techniques and instrumentalities is attained, the process of change is so accelerated, that, as to-day, it appears externally to be the dominant trait. But there is a marked lab in any corresponding change of ideas and desires. Habits of opinion are the toughest of all habits; when they have become second nature, and are supposedly thrown out of the door, they creep in again as stealthily and surely as does first nature. And as they are modified, the alteration first shows itself negatively, in the disintegration of old beliefs, to be replaced by floating, volatile and accidentally snatched up opinions. Of course there has been an enormous increase in the amount of knowledge possessed by mankind, but it does not equal, probably, the increase in the amount of errors and half-truths which have got into circulation. In social and human matters, especially, the development of a critical sense and methods of discriminating judgment has not kept pace with the growth of careless reports and of motives for positive misrepresentation.

What is more important, however, is that so much of knowledge is not knowledge in the ordinary sense of the word, but is "science." The quotation marks are not used disrespectfully, but to suggest the technical character of scientific material. The layman takes certain conclusions which get into circulation to be science. But the scientific inquirer knows that they constitute science only in connection with the methods by which they are reached. Even when true, they are not science in virtue of their correctness, but by reason of the apparatus which is employed in reaching them. This apparatus is so highly specialized that it requires more labor to acquire ability to use and understand it than to get skill in any other instrumentalities possessed by man. Science, in other words, is a highly specialized language, more difficult to learn than any natural language. It is an artificial language, not in the sense of being factitious, but in that of being a work of intricate art, devoted to a particular purpose and not capable of being acquired nor understood in the way in which the mother tongue is learned. It is, indeed, conceivable that sometime methods of instruction will be devised which will enable laymen to read and hear scientific material with comprehension, even when they do not themselves use the apparatus which is science. The latter may then become for large numbers what students of language call a passive, if not an active, vocabulary. But that time is in the future.

For most men, save the scientific workers, science is a mystery in the hands of initiates, who have become adept in virtue of following ritualistic ceremonies from which the profane herd is excluded. They are fortunate who get as far as a sympathetic appreciation of the methods which give pattern to the complicated apparatus: methods of analytic, experimental observation, mathematical formulation and deduction, constant and elaborate check and test. For most persons, the reality of the apparatus is found only in its embodiments in practical affairs, in mechanical devices and in techniques which touch life as it is lived. For them, electricity is *known* by means of the telephones, bells and lights they use, by the generators and magnetos in the automobiles they drive, by the trolley cars in which they ride. The physiology and biology they are acquainted with is that they have learned in taking precautions against germs and from the physicians they depend upon for health. The science of what might be supposed to be closest to them, of human nature, was for them an esoteric mystery until it was applied in advertising, salesmanship and personnel selection and management, and until, through psychiatry, it spilled over into life and popular consciousness, through its bearings upon "nerves," the morbidities and common forms of crankiness which make it difficult for persons to get along with one another and with themselves. Even now, popular psychology is a mass of cant, of slush and of superstition worthy of the most flourishing days of the medicine man.

Meanwhile the technological application of the complex apparatus which is science has revolutionized the conditions under which associated life goes on. This may be known as a fact which is stated in a proposition and assented to. But it is not known in the sense that men understand it. They do not know it as they know some machine which they operate, or as they know electric light and steam locomotives. They do not understand *how* the change has gone on nor *how* it affects their conduct. Not understanding its "how," they cannot use and control its manifestations. They undergo the consequences, they are affected by them. They cannot manage them, though some are fortunate enough—what is commonly called good fortune—to be able to exploit some phase of the process for their own personal profit. But even the most shrewd and successful man does not in any analytic and systematic way—in a way worthy to compare with the knowledge which he has won in lesser affairs by means of the stress of experience—know the system within which he operates. Skill and ability work within a framework which we have not created and do not comprehend. Some occupy strategic positions which give them advance information of forces that affect the market; and by training and an innate turn that way they have acquired a special technique which enables them to use the vast impersonal tide to turn their own wheels. They can dam the current here and release it there. The current itself is as much beyond them as was ever the river by the side of which some ingenious mechanic, employing a knowledge which was transmitted to him, erected his saw-mill to make boards of trees which he had not grown. That within limits those successful in affairs have knowledge and skill is not to be doubted. But such knowledge goes relatively but little further than that of the competent skilled operator who manages a machine. It suffices to employ the conditions which are before him. Skill enables him to turn the flux of events this way or that in his own neighborhood. It gives him no control of the flux.

Why should the public and its officers, even if the latter are termed statesmen, be wiser and more effective? The prime condition of a democratically organized public is a kind of knowledge and insight which does not yet exist. In its absence, it would be the height of absurdity to try to tell what it would be like if it existed. But some of the conditions which must be fulfilled if it is to exist can be indicated. We can borrow that much from the spirit and method of science even if we are ignorant of it as a specialized apparatus. An obvious requirement is freedom of social inquiry and of distribution of its conclusions. The notion that men may be free in their thought even when they are not in its expression and dissemination has been sedulously propagated. It had its origin in the idea of a mind complete in itself, apart from action and from objects. Such a consciousness presents in fact the spectacle of mind deprived of its normal functioning, because it is baffled by the actualities in connection with which alone it is truly mind, and is driven back in secluded and impotent revery.

There can be no public without full publicity in respect to all consequences which concern it. Whatever obstructs and restricts publicity, limits and distorts public opinion and checks and distorts thinking on social affairs. Without freedom of expression, not even methods of social inquiry can be developed. For tools can be evolved and perfected only in operation; in application to observing, reporting and organizing actual subject-matter; and this application cannot occur save through free and systematic communication. The early history of physical knowledge, of Greek conceptions of natural phenomena, proves how inept become the conceptions of the best endowed minds when those ideas are elaborated apart from the closest contact with the events which they purport to state and explain. The ruling ideas and methods of the human sciences are in much the same condition today. They are also evolved on the basis of past gross observations, remote from constant use in regulation of the material of new observations.

The belief that thought and its communication are now free simply because legal restrictions which once obtained have been done away with is absurd. Its currency perpetuates the infantile state of social knowledge. For it blurs recognition of our central need to possess conceptions which are used as tools of directed inquiry and which are tested, rectified and caused to grow in actual use. No man and no mind was ever emancipated merely by being left alone. Removal of formal limitations is but a negative condition; positive freedom is not a state but an act which involves methods and instrumentalities for control of conditions. Experience shows that sometimes the sense of external oppression, as by censorship, acts as a challenge and arouses intellectual energy and excites courage. But a belief in intellectual freedom where it does not exist contributes only to complacency in virtual enslavement, to sloppiness, superficiality and recourse to sensations as a substitute for ideas: marked traits of our present estate with respect to social knowledge. On one hand, thinking deprived of its normal course takes refuge in academic specialism, comparable in its way to what is called scholasticism. On the other hand, the physical agencies of publicity which exist in such abundance are utilized in ways which constitute a large part of the present meaning of publicity: advertising, propaganda, invasion of private life, the "featuring" of passing incidents in a way which violates all the moving logic of continuity, and which leaves us with those isolated intrusions and shocks which are the essence of "sensations."

It would be a mistake to identify the conditions which limit free communication and circulation of facts and ideas, and which thereby arrest and pervert social thought or inquiry, merely with overt forces which are obstructive. It is true that those who have ability to manipulate social relations for their own advantage have to be reckoned with. They have an uncanny instinct for detecting whatever intellectual tendencies even remotely threaten to encroach upon their control. They have developed an extraordinary facility in enlisting upon their side the inertia, prejudices and emotional partisanship of the masses by use of a technique which impedes free inquiry and expression. We seem to be approaching a state of government by hired promoters of opinion called publicity agents. But the more serious enemy is deeply concealed in hidden entrenchments.

Emotional habituations and intellectual habitudes on the part of the mass of men create the conditions of which the exploiters of sentiment and opinion only take advantage. Men have got used to an experimental method in physical and technical matters. They are still afraid of it in human concerns. The fear is the more efficacious because like all deep-lying fears it is covered up and disguised by all kinds of rationalizations. One of its commonest forms is a truly religious idealization of, and reverence for, established institutions; for example in our own politics, the Constitution, the Supreme Court, private property, free contract and so on. The words "sacred" and "sanctity" come readily to our lips when such things come under discussion. They testify to the religious aurole which protects the institutions. If "holy" means that which is not to be approached nor touched, save with ceremonial precautions and by specially anointed officials, then such things are holy in contemporary political life. As supernatural matters have progressively been left high and dry upon a secluded beach, the actuality of religious taboos has more and more gathered about secular institutions, especially those connected with the nationalistic state.[2] Psychiatrists have discovered that one of the commonest causes of mental disturbance is an underlying fear of which the subject is not aware, but which leads to withdrawal from reality and to unwillingness to think things through. There is a social pathology which leads to withdrawal from reality and to unwillingness to think things through. There is a social pathology which works powerfully against effective inquiry into social institutions and conditions. It manifests itself in a thousand ways; in querulousness, in impotent drifting, in uneasy snatching at distractions, in idealization of the long established, in a facile optimism assumed as a cloak, in riotous glorification of things "as they are," in intimidation of all dissenters— ways which depress and dissipate thought all the more effectually because they operate with subtle and unconscious pervasiveness.

The backwardness of social knowledge is marked in its division into independent and insulated branches of learning. Anthropology, history, sociology, morals, economics, political science, go their own ways without constant and systematized fruitful interaction. Only in appearance is there a similar division in physical knowledge. There is continuous cross-fertilization between astronomy, physics, chemistry and the biological sciences. Discoveries and improved methods are so recorded and organized that constant exchange and intercommunication take place. The isolation of the humane subjects from one another is connected with their aloofness from physical knowledge. The mind still draws a sharp separation between the world in which man lives and the life of man in and by that world, a cleft reflected in the separation of man himself into a body and a mind, which, it is currently supposed, can be known and dealt with apart. That for the past three centuries, energy should have gone chiefly into physical inquiry, beginning

with the things most remote from man such as heavenly bodies, was to have been expected. The history of the physical sciences reveals a certain order in which they developed. Mathematical tools had to be employed before a new astronomy could be constructed. Physics advanced when ideas worked out in connection with the solar system were used to describe happenings on the earth. Chemistry waited on the advance of physics; the sciences of living things required the material and methods of physics and chemistry in order to make headway. Human psychology ceased to be chiefly speculative opinion only when biological and physiological conclusions were available. All this is natural and seemingly inevitable. Things which had the most outlying and indirect connection with human interests had to be mastered in some degree before inquiried could competently converge upon man himself.

Nevertheless the course of development has left us of this age in a plight. When we say that a subject of science if technically specialized, or that it is highly "abstract," what we practically mean is that it is not conceived in terms of its bearing upon human life. All *merely* physical knowledge is technical, couched in a technical vocabulary communicable only to the few. Even physical knowledge which does affect human conduct, which does modify what we do and undergo, is also technical and remote in the degree in which its bearings are not understood and used. The sunlight, rain, air, and soil have always entered in visible ways into human experience; atoms and molecules and cells and most other things with which the sciences are occupied affect us, but not visibly. Because they enter life and modify experience in imperceptible ways, and their consequences are not realized, speech about them is technical; communication is by means of peculiar symbols. One would think, then, that a fundamental and ever-operating aim would be to translate knowledge of the subject-matter of physical conditions into terms which are generally understood, into

[2] The religious character of nationalism has been forcibly brought out by Carleton Hayes, in his *Essays on Nationalism*, especially Chapter IV.

signs denoting human consequences of services and disservices rendered. For ultimately all consequences which enter human life depend upon physical conditions; they can be understood and mastered only as the latter are taken into account. One would think, then, that any state of affairs which tends to render the things of the environment unknown and incommunicable by human beings in terms of their own activities and sufferings would be deplored as a disaster; that it would be felt to be intolerable, and to be put up with only as far as it is, at any given time, inevitable.

But the facts are to the contrary. Matter and the material are words which in the minds of many convey a note of disparagement. They are taken to be foes of whatever is of ideal value in life, instead of as conditions of its manifestation and sustained being. In consequence of this division, they do become in fact enemies, for whatever is consistently kept apart from human values depresses thought and renders values sparse and precarious in fact. There are even some who regard the materialism and dominance of commercialism of modern life as fruits of undue devotion to physical science, not seeing that the split between man and nature, artificially made by a tradition which originated before there was understanding of the physical conditions that are the medium of human activities, is the benumbing factor. The most influential form of the divorce is separation between pure and applied science. Since "application" signifies recognized bearing upon human experience and well-being, honor of what is "pure" and contempt for what is "applied" has for its outcome a science which is remote and technical, communicable only to specialists, and a conduct of human affairs which is haphazard, biased, unfair in distribution of values. What is applied and employed as the alternative to knowledge in regulation of society is ignorance, prejudice, class interest and accident. Science is converted into knowledge in its honorable and emphatic sense *only* in application. Otherwise it is trun-

cated, blind, distorted. When it is then applied, it is in ways which explain the unfavorable sense so often attached to "application" and the "utilitarian": namely, use for pecuniary ends to the profit of a few.

At present, the application of physical science is rather *to* human concerns than *in* them. That is, it is external, made in the interests of its consequences for a possessing and acquisitive class. Application *in* life would signify that science was absorbed and distributed; that is was the instrumentality of that common understanding and thorough communication which is the precondition of the existence of a genuine and effective public. The use of science to regulate industry and trade has gone on steadily. The scientific revolution of the seventeenth century was the precursor of the industrial revolution of the eighteenth and nineteenth. In consequence, man has suffered the impact of an enormously enlarged control of physical energies without any corresponding ability to control himself and his own affairs. Knowledge divided against itself, a science to whose incompleteness is added an artificial split, has played its part in generating enslavement of men, women and children in factories in which they are animated machines to tend inanimate machines. It has maintained sordid slums, flurried and discontented career, grinding poverty and luxurious wealth, brutal exploitation of nature and man in times of peace and high explosives and noxious gases in times of war. Man, a child in understanding of himself, has placed in his hands physical tools of incalculable power. He plays with them like a child, and whether they work harm or good is largely a matter of accident. The instrumentality becomes a master and works fatally as if possessed of a will of its own—not because it has a will but because man has not.

The glorification or "pure" science under such conditions is a rationalization of an escape; it marks a construction of an asylum of refuge, a shirking of responsibility. The true purity of knowledge exists not when it is uncontaminated by contact with use and service. It is wholly a moral matter, an affair of honesty, impartiality and generous breadth of intent in search and communication. The adulteration of knowledge is due not to its use, but to vested bias and prejudice, to one-sidedness of outlook, to vanity, to conceit of possession and authority, to contempt or disregard of human concern in its use. Humanity is not, as was once thought, the end for which all things were formed; it is but a slight and feeble thing, perhaps an episodic one, in the vast stretch of the universe. But for man, man is the center of interest and the measure of importance. The magnifying of the physical realm at the cost of man is but an abdication and a flight. To make physical science a rival of human interests is bad enough, for it forms a diversion of energy which can ill be afforded. But the evil does not stop there. The ultimate harm is that the understanding by man of his own affairs and his ability to direct them are sapped at their root when knowledge of nature is disconnected from its human function.

It has been implied throughout that knowledge is communication as well as understanding. I well remember the saying of a man, uneducated from the standpoint of the schools, in speaking of certain matters: "Sometime they will be found out and not only found out, but they will be known." The schools may suppose that a thing is known when it is found out. My old friend was aware that a thing is fully known only when it is published, shared, socially accessible. Record and communication are indispensable to knowledge. Knowledge cooped up in a private consciousness is a myth, and knowledge of social phenomena is peculiarly dependent upon dissemination, for only by distribution can such knowledge be either obtained or tested. A fact of community life which is not spread abroad so as to be a common possession is a contradiction in terms. Dissemination is something other than scattering at large. Seeds are sown, not by virtue of being thrown out at random, but by being so distributed as to take root and have a chance of growth. Communication of the results of social inquiry is the same thing as the formation of public opinion. This marks one of the first ideas framed in the growth of political democracy as it will be one of the last to be fulfilled. For public opinion is judgment which is formed and entertained by those who constitute the public and is about public affairs. Each of the two phases imposes for its realization conditions hard to meet.

Opinions and beliefs concerning the public presuppose effective and organized inquiry. Unless there are methods for detecting the energies which are at work and tracing them through an intricate network of interactions to their consequences, what passes as public opinion will be "opinion" in its derogatory sense rather than truly public, no matter how widespread the opinion is. The number who share error as to fact and who partake of a false belief measures power for harm. Opinion casually formed and formed under the direction of those who have something at stake in having a lie believed can be *public* opinion only in name. Calling it by this name, acceptance of the name as a kind of warrant, magnifies its capacity to lead action astray. The more who share it, the more injurious its influence. Public opinion, even if it happens to be correct, is intermittent when it is not the product of methods of investigation and reporting constantly at work. It appears only in crises. Hence its "rightness" concerns only an immediate emergency. Its lack of continuity makes it wrong from the standpoint of the course of events. It is as if a physician were able to deal for the moment with an emergency in disease but could not adapt his treatment of it to the underlying conditions which brought it about. He may then "cure" the disease—that is, cause its present alarming symptoms to subside—but he does not modify its causes; his treatment may even affect them for the worse.

Only continuous inquiry, continuous in the sense of being connected as well as persistent, can provide the material of enduring opinion about public matters.

There is a sense in which "opinion" rather than knowledge, even under the most favorable circumstances, is the proper term to use—namely, in the sense of judgment, estimate. For in its strict sense, knowledge can refer only to what *has* happened and been done. What is still *to be* done involved a forecast of a future still contingent, and cannot escape the liability to error in judgment involved in all anticipation of probabilities. There may well be honest divergence as to policies to be pursued, even when plans spring from knowledge of the same facts. But genuinely public policy cannot be generated unless it be informed by knowledge, and this knowledge does not exist except when there is systematic, thorough, and well-equipped search and record.

Moreover, inquiry must be as nearly contemporaneous as possible; otherwise it is only of antiquarian interest. Knowledge of history is evidently necessary for connectedness of knowledge. But history which is not brought down close to the actual scene of events leaves a gap and exercises influence upon the formation of judgments about the public interest only by guess-work about intervening events. Here, only too conspicuously, is a limitation of the existing social sciences. Their material comes too late, too far after the event, to enter effectively into the formation of public opinion about the immediate public concern and what is to be done about it.

A glance at the situation shows that the physical and external means of collecting information in regard to what is happening in the world have far outrun the intellectual phase of inquiry and organization of its results. Telegraph, telephone, and now the radio, cheap and quick mails, the printing press, capable of swift reduplication of material at low cost, have attained a remarkable development. But when we ask what sort of material is recorded and how it is organized, when we ask about the intellectual form in which the material is presented, the tale to be told is very different. "News" signifies something which has just happened, and which is new just because it deviates from the old and regular. But its *meaning* depends upon relation to what it imports, to what its social consequences are. This import cannot be determined unless the new is placed in relation to the old, to what has happened and been integrated into the course of events. Without coordination and consecutiveness, events are not events, but mere occurrences, intrusions; an event implies that out of which a happening proceeds. Hence even if we discount the influence of private interests in procuring suppression, secrecy and misrepresentation, we have here an explanation of the triviality and "sensational" quality of so much of what passes as news. The catastrophic, namely, crime, accident, family rows, personal clashes and conflicts, are the most obvious forms of breaches of continuity; they supply the element of shock which is the strictest meaning of sensation; they are the *new* par excellence, even though only the date of the newspaper could inform us whether they happened last year or this, so completely are they isolated from their connections.

So accustomed are we to this method of collecting, recording and presenting social changes, that it may well sound ridiculous to say that a genuine social science would manifest its reality in the daily press, while learned books and articles supply and polish tools of inquiry. But the inquiry which alone can furnish knowledge as a precondition of public judgments must be contemporary and quotidian. Even if social sciences as a specialized apparatus of inquiry were more advanced than they are, they would be comparatively impotent in the office of directing opinion on matters of concern to the public as long as they are remote from application in the daily and unremitting assembly and interpretation of "news." On the other hand, the tools of social inquiry will be clumsy as long as they are forged in places and under conditions remote from contemporary events.

What has been said about the formation of ideas and judgments concerning the public apply as well to the distribution of the knowledge which makes it an effective possession of the members of the public. Any separation between the two sides of the problem is artificial. The discussion of propaganda and propagandism would alone, however, demand a volume, and could be written only by one much more experienced than the present writer. Propaganda can accordingly only be mentioned, with the remark that the present situation is one unprecedented in history. The political forms of democracy and quasi-democratic habits of thought on social matters have compelled a certain amount of public discussion and at least the simulation of general consultation in arriving at political decisions. Representative government must at least seem to be founded on public interests as they are revealed to public belief. The days are past when government can be carried on without any pretense of ascertaining the wishes of the governed. In theory, their assent must be secured. Under the older forms, there was no need to muddy the sources of opinion on political matters. No current of energy flowed from them. To-day the judgments popularly formed on political matters are so important, in spite of all factors to the contrary, that there is an enormous premium upon all methods which affect their formation.

The smoothest road to control of political conduct is by control of opinion. As long as interests of pecuniary profit are powerful, and a public has not located and identified itself, those who have this interest will have an unresisted motive for tempering with the springs of political action in all that affects them. Just as in the conduct of industry and exchange generally the technological factor is obscured, deflected and defeated by "business," so specifically in the management of publicity. The gathering and

sale of subject-matter having a public import is part of the existing pecuniary system. Just as industry conducted by engineers on a factual technological basis would be a very different thing from what it actually is, so the assembling and reporting of news would be a very different thing if the genuine interests of reporters were permitted to work freely.

One aspect of the matter concerns particularly the side of dissemination. It is often said, and with a great appearance of truth, that the freeing and perfecting of inquiry would not have any especial effect. For, it is argued, the mass of the reading public is not interested in learning and assimilating the results of accurate investigation. Unless these are read, they cannot seriously affect the thought and action of members of the public; they remain in secluded library alcoves, and are studied and understood only by a few intellectuals. The objection is well taken save as the potency of art is taken into account. A technical high-brow presentation would appeal only to those technically high-brow; it would not be news to the masses. Presentation is fundamentally important, and presentation is a question of art. A newspaper which was only a daily edition of a quarterly journal of sociology or political science would undoubtedly possess a limited circulation and a narrow influence. Even at that, however, the mere existence and accessibility of such material would have some regulative effect. But we can look much further than that. The material would have such an enormous and widespread human bearing that its bare existence would be an irresistible invitation to a presentation of it which would have a direct popular appeal. The freeing of the artist in literary presentation, in other words, is as much a precondition of the desirable creation of adequate opinion on public matters as is the freeing of social inquiry. Men's conscious life of opinion and judgment often proceeds on a superficial and trivial plane. But their lives reach a deeper level. The function of art has always been to break through the crust of conventionalized and routine consciousness. Common things, a flower, a gleam of moonlight, the song of a bird, not things rare and remote, are means with which the deeper levels of life are touched so that they spring up as desire and thought. This process is art. Poetry, the drama, the novel, are proofs that the problem of presentation is not insoluble. Artists have always been the real purveyors of news, for it is not the outward happening in itself which is new, but the kindling by it of emotion, perception and appreciation.

We have but touched lightly and in passing upon the conditions which must be fulfilled if the Great Society is to become a Great Community; a society in which the ever-expanding and intricately ramifying consequences of associated activities shall be known in the full sense of that word, so that an organized, articulate Public comes into being. The highest and most difficult kind of inquiry and a subtle, delicate, vivid and responsive art of communication must take possession of the physical machinery of transmission and circulation and breathe life into it. When the machine age has thus perfected its machinery it will be a means of life and not its despotic master. Democracy will come into its own, for democracy is a name for a life of free and enriching communion. It had its seer in Walt Whitman. It will have its consummation when free social inquiry is indissolubly wedded to the art of full and moving communication.

WORKS BY JOHN DEWEY

Dewey, John. *Art as Experience.* New York: Milton, Balch, and Co., 1934. Art must be seen as an expression of experience, not as a separate concept.

————. *The Child and the Curriculum.* Chicago: University of Chicago Press, 1902. Shows the necessity of focusing on the makeup of the developing individual.

————. *A Common Faith.* New Haven, Conn.: Yale University Press, 1934. The basic units of a common faith are those ideal ends that are expressed in human relationships.

————. *Essays in Experimental Logic.* Chicago: University of Chicago Press, 1916. A collection of fourteen essays all attempting to show that "inquiry" is an intermediate step in the development of an experience.

Dewey, John, and Tufts, James H. *Ethics.* New York: Holt, 1908. An analysis and criticism of various types of moral theory in terms of theoretical structure and practicality.

Dewey, John. *Experience and Education.* New York: Macmillan, 1938. Criticizing both "traditional" and "Progressive" educational methods, Dewey prescribes a model system based on the principle of experience.

————. *Experience and Nature.* Chicago: Open Court, 1926. Experience is not a superior type of reality, but a methodology to be used in the selective arranging of natural events.

————. *Human Nature and Conduct.* New York: Holt, 1922. A work in social psychology discussing the aspects of ethical change which occur when scientific knowledge is applied to human behavior.

————. *Individualism Old and New.* New York: Milton, Balch, and Co., 1930. Past forms and expressions of individualism are no longer of relevance in the corporate setting of present society which views nature as an ally not an enemy.

————. *The Influence of Darwin on Philosophy.* New York: Holt, 1910. A collection of eleven essays reflecting the pragmatic approach in the reconstruction of intellectual thought.

————. *Liberalism and Social Action.* New York: Putnam's Sons, 1935. The function of liberalism is to mediate social transition through intelligent and meaningful action.

————. *The Quest for Certainty: A Study of the Relation of Knowledge and Action.* New York: Milton, Balch, and Co., 1929. The pragmatic application of natural science to existing societal needs would result in the replacement of the traditional value system with one of increased intellectual maturity.

————. *Reconstruction in Philosophy.* Boston: Beacon Press, 1920. Since the subject material of philosophy must reflect the dominant issues of contemporary society, a reordering of philosophy is needed due to the changes occurring in the contemporary environment.

_____. *The School and Society*. Chicago: The University of Chicago Press, 1899. If education is to be a meaningful experience, it must be kept relevant to changes in society.

Dewey, John, and Dewey, Evelyn. *Schools of Tomorrow*. New York: E. P. Dutton and Co., 1915. An attempt to illustrate what actually occurs when a teacher institutes different types of educational reform methods.

Dewey, John (ed). *Studies in Logical Theory*. Chicago: The University of Chicago Press, 1903. A collection of eleven essays on logical theory including four by the editor.

Dewey, John. *"Theory of Valuation"in the International Encyclopedia of United Science*. Vol. II, No. 4. Chicago: The University of Chicago Press, 1931. The scientific control of cultural factors can regulate manifested behavior since values result from cultural conditioning.

MAJOR SOURCES ON JOHN DEWEY

Blewett, John (ed.). *John Dewey*. New York: Fordham University Press, 1960. A collection of ten essays written by Catholic authors on the philosophy of John Dewey.

Crossed, Paul K. *The Nihilism of John Dewey*. New York: Philosophical Library, 1955. A critical examination and rebuttal of Dewey's philosophical system which the author sees as meaningless and empty.

Hook, Sidney (ed.). *John Dewey*. New York: The Dial Press, 1950. A symposium consisting of twenty essays covering the various aspects of Dewey's works.

Laidler, Harry W. *John Dewey at Ninety*. New York: League for Industrial Democracy, 1950. A collection of addresses and greetings given on Dewey's ninetieth birthday.

Lamont, Corliss (ed.). *Dialogue on John Dewey*. New York: Horizon Press, 1959. An informal dialogue between eleven acquaintances of John Dewey concerning his life and contributions.

Moore, Edward C. *American Pragmatism: Pierce, James and Dewey*. New York: Columbia University Press, 1961. Describes Dewey's philosophical position of pragmatism as having no precedents in Western thought (reality possesses practical character).

Nathanson, Jerome. *John Dewey*. New York: Scribner's, 1951. Admiring commentary on Dewey's views of human nature and society.

Nathanson, Jerome. "John Dewey: Radical," *The Nation*, Vol. 169, No. 17 (Oct. 22, 1949), pp. 392–394. A description of Dewey as a radical Democrat whose extremist ideology can form the basis for all liberal action and thought.

CHAPTER 13

Adolf A. Berle and Gardiner C. Means

Adolf Augustus Berle, Jr. (b. 1895), with bachelor's and law
degrees from Harvard University, served as a professor of corporate law at Columbia University and also as a key member of
Franklin Roosevelt's "brain trust." He went to Washington as
counsel to the Reconstruction Finance Corporation (1933–1938),
moved to the State Department as Assistant Secretary of State, and
has served several administrations since in various capacities. His
special area of expertise is Latin America. A prolific writer, he
has continued to publish in the area of corporate structure and finance
since his first text in 1928. None of his books has had as much
impact or importance, however, as *The Modern Corporation and
Private Property,* written in 1932 with the coauthorship of Gardiner
C. Means, also a Professor of law at Columbia University. Since
that major work, Berle's writings have emphasized the capacity of
American corporate enterprise to adjust to changing conditions in
various ways; the essential analysis made in *The Modern Corporation and Private Property* has never been modified in any major
regard, but an optimistic note has been struck with regard to the
long-term viability of the American system.

Gardiner C. Means (b. 1896), also educated at Harvard, is an
economist whose service at Columbia was followed by several positions in the national government, including the NRA, the National
Resources Commission, and the National Resources Planning Board
He later served both as consultant and as research associate for
both the Committee for Economic Development and the Fund for
the Republic. Like Berle, his published work follows the basic
analysis and argument of *The Modern Corporation and Private
Property,* and reaches essentially optimistic conclusions about the
American economy.

The Traditional Logic of Property

The shifting relationships of property and enterprise in American industry here described, raise in sharp relief certain legal, economic, and social questions which must now be squarely faced. Of these the greatest is the question in whose interests should the great quasi-public corporations (now representing such a large proportion of industrial wealth) be operated. This problem really asks in a different form the question, who should receive the profits of industry?

It is traditional that a corporation should be run for the benefit of its owners, the stockholders, and that to them should go any profits which are distributed.[1] We now know, however, that a controlling group may hold the power to divert profits into their own pockets. There is no longer any certainty that a corporation will in fact be run primarily in the interests of the stockholders.[2] The extensive separation of ownership and control, and the strengthening of the powers of control, raise a new situation calling for a decision whether social and legal pressure should be applied in an effort to insure corporate operation primarily in the interests of the "owners" or whether such pressure shall be applied in the interests of some other or wider group.

The lawyer answers this question in no uncertain terms by applying to the quasi-public corporation the traditional logic of property. The common law, extended to meet the new situation, logically demands the award of the entire profit to the security holders, and in particular to the stockholders. According to this logic a corporation should be operated primarily in their interests.

The legal argument is largely historical; but it has been built up through a series of phases which make this conclusion inevitable. From earliest times the owner of property has been entitled to the full use or disposal of his property,[3] and in these rights the owner has been protected by law. Since the use of industrial property consists primarily of an effort to increase its value—to make a profit—the owner of such property, in being entitled to its full use, has been entitled to all accretions to its value—to all the profits which it could be made to earn. In so far as he had to pay for the services of other men or other property in order to accomplish this increase in value, these payments operated as deductions; the profit remaining to him was the difference between the added value and the cost of securing these services. To this difference, however, the owner has traditionally been entitled. The state and the law have sought to protect him in this right.

From earliest times, also, the stockholder in the corporation has posed both as the owner of the corporation and the owner of its assets. He was removed slightly from legal ownership in the assets in that he did not have legal "title" to them—that was vested in the corporation; but collectively the stockholders, through their participations were entitled to the whole of corporate assets and to the whole of any corporate profits which could be made. The corporation was theirs, to be operated for their benefit.

In the development of the corporation, constantly widening powers over the management of the enterprise have been delegated to groups within the cor-

---

[1] Bonus schemes are usually undertaken with an aim of *increasing* the profit remaining and available to be distributed as dividends. For this reason they must, in general, be regarded as a cost to the stockholders rather than as a sharing or distribution of profit.

[2] While there are other possible groups,—the employees, the consumers, etc., in whose interest a corporation might be run, discussion of them can best be delayed.

SOURCE: Reprinted from *The Modern Corporation and Private Property* by permission of the publisher, The Macmillan Company. Copyright 1932, The Macmillan Company.

---

[3] Except as impaired by the exercise of police power by the state.

poration. At first these powers concerned mainly the technical (profit-making) activity of the enterprise. Later, powers were delegated which had to do with the distribution of profits and interests among the security holders. With the separation of ownership and control, these powers developed to a stage permitting those in control of a corporation to use them against the interests of ownership. Since powers of control and management were created by law, in some measure this appeared to legalize the diversion of profit into the hands of the controlling group.

Following the traditional logic of property, however, it is clear that these powers are not absolute. They are, rather, powers in trust. The controlling group is, in form at least, managing and controlling a corporation for the benefit of the owners. While insertions might be made in corporation statutes and in corporate charters apparently giving power which could be used against the interests of the owners, these were, in the light of the common law, only grants of power to the controlling group, the better to operate the corporation in the interests of its owners. The very multiplication of absolute powers, including power to shift interests in the corporate assets and profits from security holders to those in control threw into bold relief the tacit (but by no means fictitious) understanding that all these powers were designed for the benefit of the corporation as a whole, and not for the individual enrichment of the management or control. While the law fumbled in application of this principle, and developed through a series of rules, sometimes inconsistent and often not clear in application, not a single case on record denies the ultimate trusteeship of the controlling group, nor even faintly implies that such a group may use its power for its individual advantage. Fact-situations can be "rigged" whereby the individual profit of this group is made to appear an advantage to the corporation as a whole; advantage may be taken of emergencies in which the management and control present the

security-holding group with the alternative of permitting profit to the "control" on the one hand or inviting disaster on the other. Sometimes the courts, shielding themselves behind a consideration of the advantage to the "corporation as a whole," have overlooked the fact that apparent advantage to the mythical corporate entity may mean staggering loss to its separate owners; and that it is often necessary to trace *what group within the corporation* receives the ultimate advantage. Despite these situations in many of which the controlling group is able, first, to seize a portion of the corporate profits and, second, to hold them against legal attack, the theory of the law seems clear. All the powers granted to management and control are powers in trust.

Tracing this doctrine back into the womb of equity, whence it sprang, the foundation becomes plain. Wherever one man or a group of men entrusted another man or group with the management of property, the second group became fiduciaries. As such they were obliged to act conscionably, which meant in fidelity to the interests of the persons whose wealth they had undertaken to handle. In this respect, the corporation stands on precisely the same footing as the common-law trust. Since the business problems connected with trusts were relatively restricted, a series of fairly accurate regulations could be worked out by the equity courts constraining the trustee to certain standards of conduct. The corporation, which carried on any and every kind of business, raised a set of problems of conduct infinitely more varied, and calling for expert business judgment which courts were not equipped to render. Fixed standards of conduct, therefore, became impossible of development in the corporate situation; such rigid standards as were worked out, (for instance, the standard that no stock must be issued unless first offered pre-emptively to existing shareholders) became arbitrary or inapplicable in the complex corporate structure of today. But though definite rules could not be laid down, the courts have maintained a supervisory jurisdiction; the fundamental principle of equitable control remains unimpaired; and the only question is how it should be applied in each case. Inability to answer these questions has given ample latitude to the control to absorb a portion of the corporate profits. This does not mean, however, that the law concedes them a right to such absorption. It merely means that legal machinery may not be sufficiently developed to accomplish a remedy.

Underlying all this is the ancient preoccupation of the common law with the rights of property. Primarily, the common law did not undertake to set up ideal schemes of government. It aimed to protect men in their own. Only where the property interests conflicted with some very obvious public policy did the law interfere. Its primary design was protecting individual attributes of individual men,—their right to property, to free motion and locomotion, to protection of individual relationships entered into between them. In this aspect the corporation was merely one more bit of machinery by which the property of individuals was managed by other individuals; and the corporate management took its place in the picture alongside of agents, trustees, ship captains, partners, joint adventurers, and other fiduciaries. As the power of the corporate management has increased, and as the control of the individual has sunk into the background, the tendency of the law has been to stiffen its assertion of the rights of the security holder. The thing that it has not been able to stiffen has been its regulation of the conduct of the business by the corporate management. And this omission has resulted, not from lack of logical justification, but from lack of ability to handle the problems involved. The management of an enterprise is, by nature, a task which courts can not assume; and the various devices by which management and control have absorbed a portion of the profit-stream have been so intimately related to the business conduct of an enterprise, that the courts seem to have felt not only reluctant to interfere, but positively afraid to do so.

The result accordingly is that the profits of the enterprise, so far as the law is concerned, belong to the security holders *in toto*. Division of these profits among the various groups of security holders is a matter of private agreement, but they, between them, have the complete right to all of the profits which the corporation has made. Not only that: they are entitled to those profits which the management in reasonable exercise of its powers ought to make. They have further a right that no one shall become a security holder except upon a suitable contribution to the corporate assets— that is, that the security holding group shall be a group of persons who have committed actual property to the administration of the management and control of the corporation.

Such is the view which the law has developed by extending to the new situation the traditional logic of property. The control group is not in a position openly to combat this logic. Constant appeals are made both to this ideology and to its legal basis when corporations go into the market seeking capital. The expectation of the entire profit is the precise lure used to induce investment in corporate enterprises. The possibilities of the situation are continuously stressed by investment bankers who, in turn, act for the corporate management and control when the latter are bidding for the public investor's savings. Whatever their private views or actual practice, the control groups within corporations have stopped themselves from maintaining any other view. The legal hypothesis has been too much the basis of the financial structure of today.

Yet, while this conclusion may result inevitably when the traditional logic of property is applied to the new situation, are we justified in applying this logic? In the past, the ownership of business enterprise, the only form of property with which we are here concerned, has always, at least in theory, involved two attributes, first the risking of previously collected wealth in profit-seeking enterprise; and, second, the ultimate management of and responsibility for that enterprise. But in the modern corporation, these two attributes of ownership no longer attach to the same individual or group. The stockholder has surrendered control over his wealth. He has become a supplier of capital, a risk-taker pure and simple, while ultimate responsibility and authority are exercised by directors and "control." One traditional attribute of ownership is attached to stock ownership; the other attribute is attached to corporate control. Must we not, therefore, recognize that we are no longer dealing with property in the old sense? Does the traditional logic of property still apply? Because an owner who also exercises control over his wealth is protected in the full receipt of the advantages derived from it, must it *necessarily* follow that an owner who has surrendered control of his wealth should likewise be protected to the full? May not this surrender have so essentially changed his relation to his wealth as to have changed the logic applicable to his interest in that wealth? An answer to this question cannot be found in the law itself. It must be sought in the economic and social background of law.

The Traditional Logic of Profits

The economist, approaching the problems growing out of the shifting relationship of property and enterprise which we have examined, must start from a different background and with a set of interests differing essentially from those of the law. His interest is not primarily in the protection of man in his own, but in the production and distribution of what man desires. He is preoccupied, not with the rights of property, but with the production of wealth and distribution of income. To him property rights are attributes which may be attached to wealth by society and he regards them and their protection, not as the inalienable right of the individual or as an end in themselves, but as a means to a socially desirable end,[1] namely, "a plentiful revenue and subsistence" for the people.

The socially beneficial results to be derived from the protection of property are supposed to arise, not from the wealth itself, but from the efforts to acquire wealth. A long line of economist have developed what might be called the traditional logic of profits. They have held that, in striving to acquire wealth, that is, in seeking profits, the individual would, perhaps unconsciously, satisfy the wants of others. By carrying on enterprise he would employ his energy and wealth in such a way as to obtain more wealth.[2] In this effort, he would tend to make for profit those things which were in most demand. Competition among countless producers could be relied upon in general to maintain profits within reasonable limits while temporarily excessive profits in any one line of production would induce an increase of activity in that line with a consequent drop of profits to more reasonable levels. At the same time it was supposed that the businessman's effort to increase his profits would, in general, result in more eco-

[1] Adam Smith treated property as a "natural right" (following the teachings of Locke) and its protection as a "law of nature." At the same time he analyzed the beneficient results which might be expected to flow from making actual conditions conform to this "law of nature," i.e., from protecting property. The Nineteenth Century has seen the atrophy of the idea of "natural law" and the shift of emphasis to the advantages of the protection of property. See Adam Smith, "Wealth of Nations," Book I, Chap. X, Pt. II.
[2] Since this study is concerned with property rights in the instruments of production, we need not here consider the process of acquiring wealth in the form of wages and salaries or in the form of interest.

nomical use of the factors of production, each enterprise having to compete with others for the available economic resources. Therefore, it has been argued that by protecting each man in the possession of his wealth and in the possession of any profits he could make from its use, society would encourage enterprise and thereby facilitate the production of goods desired by the community at reasonable prices with economic use of labor, capital, and business enterprise. By protecting property rights in the instruments of production, the acquisitive interests of man could thus be more effectively harnessed to the benefit of the community.

It must be seen that under the condition just described, profits act as a return for the performance of two separate functions. First, they act as an inducement to the individual to risk his wealth in enterprise, and, second, they act as a spur, driving him to exercise his utmost skill in making his enterprise profitable.[3] In the case of a private enterprise the distinction between these two functions does not assume importance. The owner of a private business receives any profits made and performs the functions not only of risk-taking but of ultimate management as well.[4] It may be that in the past when industry was in the main carried on by a multitude of small private enterprises the community, through protecting property, has induced a large volume of risk-taking and a vigorous conduct of industry in exchange for the profits derived therefrom.

[3] These two functions have been recognized in the current literature on profits. Some writers have maintained that profits are primarily a return for the taking of risk while others have maintained that they are primarily a return for exercising business judgment and enterprise. See S. H. Nerlove, "Recent Writings on Profits," The Journal of Business of the University of Chicago, Vol II (1929), p. 363.

[4] Even though he employs a manager to carry on the immediate activities of the business, his desire for profits presumably induces him to select the most efficient manager available and to require of him a high standard of performance.

In the modern corporation, with its separation of ownership and control, these two functions of risk and control are, in the main, performed by two different groups of people. Where such a separation is complete one group of individuals, the security holders and in particular the stockholders, performs the function of risk-takers and suppliers of capital, while a separate group exercises control and ultimate management. In such a case, if profits are to be received only by the security holders, as the traditional logic of property would require, how can they perform both of their traditional economic roles? Are no profits to go to those who exercise control and in whose hands the efficient operation of enterprise ultimately rests?

It is clear that the function of capital supplying and risk-taking must be performed and that the security holder must be compensated if an enterprise is to raise new capital and expand its activity just as the workers must be paid enough to insure the continued supplying of labor and the taking of the risks involved in that labor and in the life based on it. But what if profits can be made more than sufficient to keep the security holders satisfied, more than sufficient to induce new capital to come into the enterprise?[5] Where is the social advantage in setting aside for the security holder, profits in an amount greater than is sufficient to insure the continued supplying of capital and taking of risk? The prospect of additional profits cannot act as a spur on the security holder to make him *operate* the enterprise with more vigor in a way to serve the wants of the community, since he is no longer in control. Such extra profits if given to the security holders

[5] "Profits sufficient to keep the security holders satisfied," etc., is a vague expression and not easily defined. In practice, however, it is not necessarily so vague. Dissatisfaction among stockholders is presumably not important if it does not make itself known; and inability to raise new capital with ease is likely to be all too evident to a controlling group.

would seem to perform no useful economic function.

Furthermore, if all profits are earmarked for the security holder, where is the inducement for those in control to manage the enterprise efficiently? When none of the profits are to be received by them, why should they exert themselves beyond the amount necessary to maintain a reasonably satisfied group of stockholders? *If* the profit motive is the powerful incentive to action which it is supposed to be, and *if* the community is best served when each enterprise is operated with the aim of making the maximum profit, would there not be great social advantage in encouraging the control to seize for themselves any profits over and above the amount necessary as a satisfactory return to capital? Would not the prospect of this surplus profit act as an incentive to more efficient management by those in control? Certainly, one cannot escape the conclusion that if profits have any influence as a motivating force, any surplus which can be made over a satisfactory return to the investor would be better employed when held out as an incentive to action by control than when handed over to the "owners" who have surrendered control.

This conclusion is somewhat modified by the fact that the separation of ownership and control has not yet become complete. While a large body of stockholders are not in a position to exercise any degree of control over the affairs of their corporation,[6] those actually in control are usually stockholders though in many cases owning but a very small proportion of the total stock. It may be that the prospect of receiving one or two percent of the total added profit which could be produced by their own more vigorous activity would be sufficient inducement to produce the most efficient operation of which the controlling group

are capable. It remains true, however, the profits over enough to keep the remaining stockholders satisfied and to make possible the raising of new capital would still involve an economically wasteful disposal. Only the one or two percent of profits going to the controlling group would perform both roles traditionally performed by profits.

The traditional logic of profits, when thus applied to the modern corporation, would indicate that *if profits must be distributed either to the owners or to the control,* only a fair return to capital should be distributed to the "owners"; while the remainder should go to the control as an inducement to the most efficient ultimate management. The corporation would thus be operated financially in the interests of control, the stockholders becoming merely the recipients of the wages of capital.

The conclusion runs directly counter to the conclusion reached by applying the traditional logic of property to precisely the same situation—and is equally suspect.

The Inadequacy of Traditional Theory

When such divergent results are obtained by the application of the logic of two major social disciplines to a new fact situation, we must push our inquiry still further back into the assumptions and concepts of those disciplines.

Underlying the thinking of economists, lawyers and business men during the last century and a half has been the picture of economic life so skillfully painted by Adam Smith. Within his treatise on the "Wealth of Nations" are contained the fundamental concepts which run through most modern thought. Though

---

[6] Except under the most unusual conditions as for instance in case of a proxy fight, when the bulk of the stockholders play the role of the populace supporting or refusing to support a palace revolution.

adjustments in his picture have been made by later writers to account for new conditions, the whole has been painted in the colors which he supplied. Private property, private enterprise, individual initiative, the profit motive, wealth, competition,—these are the concepts which he employed in describing the economy of his time and by means of which he sought to show that the pecuniary self-interest of each individual, if given free play, would lead to the optimum satisfaction of human wants. Most writers of the Nineteenth Century build on these logical foundations, and current economic literature is, in large measure, cast in such terms.

Yet these terms have ceased to be accurate, and therefore, tend to mislead in describing modern enterprise as carried on by the great corporations. Though both the terms and the concepts remain, they are inapplicable to a dominant area in American economic organization. New terms, connoting changed relationships, become necessary.

When Adam Smith talked of "enterprise" he had in mind as the typical unit the small individual business in which the owner, perhaps with the aid of a few apprentices or workers, labored to produce goods for market or to carry on commerce. Very emphatically he repudiated the stock corporation as a business mechanism, holding that dispersed ownership made efficient operation impossible. "The directors of such companies. . .," he pointed out, "being the managers rather of other people's money than of their own, it cannot well be expected that they should watch over it with the same anxious vigilance with which the partners in a private copartnery frequently watch over their own. Like the stewards of a rich man, they are apt to consider attention to small matters as not for their master's honour, and very easily give themselves a dispensation from having it. Negligence and profusion, therefore, must always prevail, more or less, in the management of the affairs of such a company. It is upon this account that joint stock companies

for foreign trade [at the time he was writing, the only important manifestation of the corporation outside of banks, insurance companies, and water or canal companies] have seldom been able to maintain the competition against private adventurers. They have, accordingly, very seldom succeeded without an exclusive privilege, and frequently have not succeeded with one. Without an exclusive privilege they have commonly mismanaged the trade. With an exclusive privilege they have both mismanaged and confined it."[1]

Yet when we speak of business enterprise today, we must have in mind primarily these very units which seemed to Adam Smith not to fit into the principles which he was laying down for the conduct of economic activity. How then can we apply the concepts of Adam Smith in discussing our modern economy?

Let us consider each of these concepts in turn.

PRIVATE PROPERTY

To Adam Smith and to his followers, private property was a unity involving possession. He assumed that ownership and control were combined. Today, in the modern corporation, this unity has been broken. *Passive property*,—specifically, shares of stocks or bonds,—gives its possessors an interest in an enterprise but gives them practically no control over it, and involves no responsibility. *Active property*,—plant, good will, organization, and so forth which make up the actual enterprise,—is controlled by individuals who, almost invariably, have only minor ownership interests in it. In terms of relationships, the present situation can be described as including: (1) "passive property," consisting of a set of relationships between an individual and an enterprise, involving rights of the individual toward the enterprise but almost no effective powers over it; and

---

[1] Adam Smith, "The Wealth of Nations." Everyman's Library edition, Vol II, p. 229.

(2) "active property," consisting of a set of relationships under which an individual or set of individuals hold powers over an enterprise but have almost no duties in respect to it which can be effectively enforced. When active and passive property relationships attach to the same individual or group, we have private property as conceived by the older economists. When they attach to different individuals, private property in the instruments of production disappears. Private property in the share of stock still continues, since the owner possesses the share and has power to dispose of it, but his share of stock is only a token representing a bundle of ill-protected rights and expectations. It is the possession of this token which can be transferred, a transfer which has little if any influence on the instruments of production. Whether possession of active property,—power of control over an enterprise, apart from ownership,—will ever be looked upon as private property which can belong to and be disposed of by its possessor is a problem of the future, and no prediction can be made with respect to it.[2] Whatever the answer, it is clear that in dealing with the modern corporation we are not dealing with the old type of private property. Our description of modern economy, in so far as it deals with the quasi-public corporation, must be in terms of the two forms of property, active and passive, which for the most part lie in different hands.

WEALTH

In a similar way, the concept "wealth" has been changed and divided. To Adam Smith, wealth was composed of tangible things,—wheat and land and buildings, ships and merchandise,—and for most people wealth is still thought of in physical terms. Yet in connection with the modern corporation, two essentially different types of wealth exist. To the holder of passive property, the stockholder, wealth consists, not of tangible goods,—factories, railroad stations, machinery,—but of a bundle of expectations which have a market value and which, if held, may bring him income, and, if sold in the market, may give him power to obtain some other form of wealth. To the possessor of active property,—the "control"—wealth means a great enterprise which he dominates, an enterprise whose value is for the most part composed of the organized relationship of tangible properties, the existence of a functioning organization of workers and the existence of a functioning body of consumers.[3] Instead of having control over a body of tangible wealth with an easily ascertainable market value, the group in control of a large modern corporation is astride an organism which has little value except as it continues to function, and for which there is no ready market. Thus, side by side, these two forms of wealth exist: on the one hand passive wealth,—liquid, impersonal and involving no responsibility, passing from hand to hand and constantly appraised in the market place; and on the other hand, active wealth,—great, functioning organisms dependent for their lives on their security holders, their workers and consumers, but most of all on their mainspring,—"control." The two forms of wealth are not different aspects of the same thing, but are essentially and functionally distinct.

[2] Such would be the case, for instance, if by custom the position of director became hereditary and this custom were given legal sanction.

[3] The concept of the consumer as a functioning part of a great enterprise is one which may at first be difficult to grasp. Yet, just as a body of members is essential to the continued existence of a club, so a body of consumers is essential to the continued existence of an enterprise. In each case the members or consumers are an integral part of the association or enterprise. In each case membership is obtained at a cost for the purpose of obtaining the benefits. The advertising slogan, "Join the Pepsodent Family," is perhaps unintended recognition of this fact.

PRIVATE ENTERPRISE

Again, to Adam Smith, private enterprise meant an individual or few partners actively engaged and relying in large part on their own labor or their immediate direction. Today we have tens and hundreds of thousands of owners, of workers and of consumers combined in single enterprises. These great associations are so different from the small, privately owned enterprises of the past as to make the concept of private enterprise an ineffective instrument of analysis. It must be replaced with the concept of corporate enterprise, enterprise which is the organized activity of vast bodies of individuals, workers, consumers and suppliers of capital, under the leadership of the dictators of industry, "control."

INDIVIDUAL INITIATIVE

As private enterprise disappears with increasing size, so also does individual initiative. The idea that an army operates on the basis of "rugged individualism" would be ludicrous. Equally so is the same idea with respect to the modern corporation. Group activity, the coordinating of the different steps in production, the extreme division of labor in large scale enterprise necessarily imply not individualism but cooperation and the acceptance of authority almost to the point of autocracy. Only to the extent that any worker seeks advancement within an organization is there room for individual initiative,—an initiative which can be exercised only within the narrow range of function he is called on to perform. At the very pinnacle of the hierarchy of organization in a great corporation, there alone, can individual initiative have a measure of free play. Yet even there a limit is set by the willingness and ability of subordinates to carry out the will of their superiors. In modern industry, individual liberty is necessarily curbed.

THE PROFIT MOTIVE

Even the motivation of individual activity has changed its aspect. For Adam Smith and his followers, it was possible to abstract one motive, the desire for personal profit, from all the motives driving men to action and to make this the key to man's economic activity. They could conclude that, where true private enterprise existed, personal profit was an effective and socially beneficent motivating force. Yet we have already seen how the profit motive has become distorted in the modern corporation. To the extent that profits induce the risking of capital by investors, they play their customary role. But if the courts, following the traditional logic of property, seek to insure that all profits reach or be held for the security owners, they prevent profits from reaching the very group of men whose action is most important to the efficient conduct of enterprise. Only as profits are diverted into the pockets of control do they, in a measure, perform their second function.

Nor is it clear that even if surplus profits were held out as an incentive to control they would be as effective an instrument as the logic of profits assumes. Presumably the motivating influence of any such huge surplus profits as a modern corporation might be made to produce would be subject to diminishing returns. Certainly it is doubtful if the prospect of a second million dollars of income (and the surplus profits might often amount to much larger sums) would induce activity equal to that induced by the prospect of the first million or even the first hundred thousand. Profits in such terms bear little relation to those envisaged by earlier writers.

Just what motives are effective today, in so far as control is concerned, must be a matter of conjecture. But it is probable that more could be learned regarding them by studying the motives of an Alexander the Great, seeking new worlds to conquer, than by considering the motives of a petty tradesman of the days of Adam Smith.

COMPETITION

Finally, when Adam Smith championed competition as the great regulator of industry, he had in mind units so small that fixed capital and overhead costs played a role so insignificant that costs were in large measure determinate and so numerous that no single unit held an important position in the market. Today competition in markets dominated by a few great enterprises has come to be more often either cut-throat and destructive or so inactive as to make monopoly or duopoly conditions prevail. Competition between a small number of units each involving an organization so complex that costs have become indeterminate does not satisfy the condition assumed by earlier economists, nor does it appear likely to be as effective a regulator of industry and of profits as they had assumed.

In each of the situations to which these fundamental concepts refer, the Modern Corporation has wrought such a change as to make the concepts inapplicable.[1] New concepts must be forged and a new picture of economic relationships created. It is with this in mind that at the opening of this volume the modern corporation was posed as a major social institution; and its development was envisaged in terms of revolution.

The New Concept of the Corporation

Most fundamental to the new picture of economic life must be a new concept of business enterprise as concentrated in the corporate organization. In some measure a concept is already emerging. Over a decade ago, Walter Rathenau wrote concerning the German counterpart of our great corporation:

> No one is a permanent owner. The composition of the thousandfold complex which functions as lord of the undertaking is in a state of flux. . . . This condition of things signifies that ownership has been depersonalized. . . . The depersonalization of ownership simultaneously implies the objectification of the thing owned. The claims to ownership are subdivided in such a fashion, and are so mobile, that the enterprise assumes an independent life, as if it belonged to no one; it takes an objective existence, such as in earlier days was embodied only in state and church, in a municipal corporation, in the life of a guild or a religious order. . . . The depersonalization of ownership, the objectification of enterprise, the detachment of property from the possessor, leads to a point where the enterprise becomes transformed into an institution which resembles the state in character.[1]

The institution here envisaged calls for analysis, not in terms of business enterprise but in terms of social organization. On the one hand, it involves a concentration of power in the economic field comparable to the concentration of religious power in the medieval church or of political power in the national state. On the other hand, it involves the interrelation of a wide diversity of economic interests,—those of the "owners" who supply capital, those of the workers who "create," those of the consumers who give value to the products of enterprise, and above all those of the control who wield power.

Such a great concentration of power and such a diversity of interest raise

---

[1] It is frequently suggested that economic activity has become vastly more complex under modern conditions. Yet it is strange that the concentration of the bulk of industry into a few large units has not simplified rather than complicated the economic process. It is worth suggesting that the apparent complexity may arise in part from the effort to analyze the process in terms of concepts which no longer apply.

[1] "Von Kommenden Dingen," Berlin, 1918, trans. by E. & C. Paul, ("In Days to Come"), London, 1921, pp. 120, 121.

the long-fought issue of power and its regulation—of interest and its protection. A constant warfare has existed between the individuals wielding power, in whatever form, and the subjects of that power. Just as there is a continuous desire for power, so also there is a continuous desire to make that power the servant of the bulk of the individuals it affects. The long struggles for the reform of the Catholic Church and for the development of constitutional law in the states are phases of this phenomenon. Absolute power is useful in building the organization. More slow, but equally sure is the development of social pressure demanding that the power shall be used for the benefit of all concerned. This pressure, constant in ecclesiastical and political history, is already making its appearance in many guises in the economic field.

Observable throughout the world, and in varying degrees of intensity, is this insistence that power in economic organization shall be subjected to the same tests of public benefit which have been applied in their turn to power otherwise located. In its most extreme aspect this is exhibited in the communist movement, which in its purest form is an insistence that *all* powers and privileges of property, shall be used only in the common interest. In less extreme forms of socialist dogma, transfer of economic powers to the state for public service is demanded. In the strictly capitalist countries, and particularly in time of depression, demands are constantly put forward that the men controlling the great economic organisms be made to accept responsibility for the well-being of those who are subject to the organization, whether workers, investors, or consumers. In a sense the difference in all of these demands lies only in degree. In proportion as an economic organism grows in strength and its power is concentrated in a few hands, the possessor of power is more easily located, and the demand for responsible power becomes increasingly direct.

How will this demand be made effective? To answer this question would be to foresee the history of the next century. We can here only consider and appraise certain of the more important lines of possible development.

By tradition, a corporation "belongs" to its shareholders, or, in a wider sense, to its security holders, and theirs is the only interest to be recognized as the object of corporate activity. Following this tradition, and without regard for the changed character of ownership, it would be possible to apply in the interests of the *passive* property owner the doctrine of strict property rights, the analysis of which has been presented above in the chapter on Corporate Powers as Powers in Trust. By the application of this doctrine, the group in control of a corporation would be placed in a position of trusteeship in which it would be called on to operate or arrange for the operation of the corporation for the *sole* benefit of the security owners despite the fact that the latter have ceased to have power over or to accept responsibility for the *active* property in which they have an interest. Were this course followed, the bulk of American industry might soon be operated by trustees for the sole benefit of inactive and irresponsible security owners.

In direct opposition to the above doctrine of strict property rights is the view, apparently held by the great corporation lawyers and by certain students of the field, that corporate development has created a new set of relationships, giving to the groups in control powers which are absolute and not limited by any implied obligation with respect to their use. This logic leads to drastic conclusions. For instance, if, by reason of these new relationships, the men in control of a corporation can operate it in their own interests, and can divert a portion of the asset fund of income stream to their own uses, such is their privilege. Under this view, since the new powers have been acquired on a quasi-contractual basis, the security holders have agreed in advance to any losses which they may suffer by reason of such use. The result is, briefly, that the existence of the legal and economic relationships giving rise to these powers must be frankly recognized as a modification of the principle of private property.

If these were the only alternatives, the former would appear to be the lesser of two evils. Changed corporate relationships have unquestionably involved an essential alteration in the character of property. But such modifications have hitherto been brought about largely on the principle that might makes right. Choice between strengthening the rights of passive property owners, or leaving a set of uncurbed powers in the hands of control therefore resolves itself into a purely realistic evaluation of different results. We might elect the relative certainty and safety of a trust relationship in favor of a particular group within the corporation, accompanied by a possible diminution of enterprise. Or we may grant the controlling group free rein, with the corresponding danger of a corporate oligarchy coupled with the probability of an era of corporate plundering.

A third possibility exists, however. On the one hand, the owners of passive property, by surrendering control and responsibility over the active property, have surrendered the right that the corporation should be operated in their sole interest,—they have released the community from the obligation to protect them to the full extend implied in the doctrine of strict property rights. At the same time, the controlling groups, by means of the extension of corporate powers, have in their own interest broken the bars of tradition which require that the corporation be operated solely for the benefit of the owners of passive property. Eliminating the sole interest of the passive owner, however, does not necessarily lay a basis for the alternative claim that the new powers should be used in the interest of the controlling groups. The latter have not

presented, in acts or words any acceptable defense of the proposition that these powers should be so used. No tradition supports that proposition. The control groups have, rather, cleared the way for the claims of a group far wider than either the owners or the control. They have placed the community in a position to demand that the modern corporation serve not alone the owners or the control but all society.

The third alternative offers a wholly new concept of corporate activity. Neither the claims of ownership nor those of control can stand against the paramount interests of the community. The present claims of both contending parties now in the field have been weakened by the developments described in this book. It remains only for the claims of the community to be put forward with clarity and force. Rigid enforcement of property rights as a temporary protection against plundering by control would not stand in the way of the modification of these rights in the interest of other groups. When a convincing system of community obligations is worked out and is generally accepted, in that moment the passive property right of today must yield before the larger interests of society. Should the corporate leaders, for example, set forth a program comprising fair wages, security to employees, reasonable service to their public, and stabilization of business, all of which would divert a portion of the profits from the owners of passive property, and should the community generally accept such a scheme as a logical and human solution of industrial difficulties, the interests of passive property owners would have to give way. Courts would almost of necessity be forced to recognize the result, justifying it by whatever of the many legal theories they might choose. It is conceivable,— indeed it seems almost essential if the corporate system is to survive,—that the "control" of the great corporations should develop into a purely neutral technocracy, balancing a variety of claims by various groups in the community and assigning to each a portion of the income stream on the basis of public policy rather than private cupidity.

* * *

In still larger view, the modern corporation may be regarded not simply as one form of social organization but potentially (if not yet actually) as the dominant institution of the modern world. In every age, the major concentration of power has been based upon the dominant interest of that age. The strong man has, in his time, striven to be cardinal or pope, prince or cabinet minister, bank president or partner in the House of Morgan. During the Middle Ages, the Church, exercising spiritual power, dominated Europe and gave to it a unity at a time when both political and economic power were diffused. With the rise of the modern state, political power, concentrated into a few large units, challenged the spiritual interest as the strongest bond of human society. Out of the long struggle between church and state which followed, the state emerged victorious; nationalist politics superseded religion as the basis of the major unifying organization of the western world. Economic power still remained diffused.

The rise of the modern corporation has brought a concentration of economic power which can compete on equal terms with the modern state— economic power versus political power, each strong in its own field. The state seeks in some aspects to regulate the corporation, while the corporation, steadily becoming more powerful, makes every effort to avoid such regulation. Where its own interests are concerned, it even attempts to dominate the state. The future may see the economic organism, now typified by the corporation, not only on an equal plane with the state, but possibly even superseding it as

the dominant form of social organization. The law of corporation, accordingly, might well be considered as a potential constitutional law for the new economic state, while business practice is increasingly assuming the aspect of economic statesmanship.

WORKS BY
ADOLF A. BERLE

Berle, Adolf Augustus. *The American Economic Republic*. New York: Harcourt, Brace and World, 1963.

————, and Warren, William C. *Latin America: Diplomacy and Reality*. New York: Harper and Row, 1962.

————, and Means, Gardiner C. *The Modern Corporation and Private Property*. New York: Macmillan and Company, 1932.

————, *Natural Selection of Political Forces*. Lawrence, Kan.: University of Kansas Press, 1950.

————, *New Directions in a New World*. New York: Harper and Bros., 1940.

————, *Power Without Property*. New York: Harcourt, Brace and World, 1959.

————, *The Three Faces of Power*. New York: Harcourt, Brace and World, 1967.

————, *Tides of Crisis*. New York: Reynal, 1957.

————, *The Twentieth Century Capitalist Revolution*. New York: Harcourt, Brace and World, 1954.

WORKS BY
GARDINER C. MEANS

Means, Gardiner C. *The Corporate Revolution in America*. New York: Crowell-Collier Press, 1962.

————, and Ware, Caroline F. *The Modern Economy in Action*. New York: Harcourt, Brace and Co., 1936.

————, *Pricing Power and the Public Interest*. New York: Harper and Row, 1962.

————, *The Structure of the American Economy*. Washington: U.S. Government Printing Office, 1939-1940.

CHAPTER 14

From Past to Present: A Summary View

THE foregoing selections provide a glimpse of the principal features of American political ideas as they have been articulated by representative men of stature and power. Many other currents have flowed through American politics in different time periods, at various levels, and in different regions, but most of the major landmarks are reflected in these authors. Not surprisingly, their work consistently shows the impact of the basic tenets of liberalism; but some thinkers have reached the margins of conservatism and radicalism, and others are distinguishable by their relative priorities between property rights and human rights and equality. Let us briefly summarize their views, as a preliminary to further consideration of contemporary problems in American political thinking. We shall begin with the three thinkers whose work has set the boundaries and formed the substance of the bulk of subsequent political thought in the United States.

I. THE MAINSTREAM: JEFFERSON, MADISON, HAMILTON

Jefferson

Thomas Jefferson, often closely associated with natural rights defined as human rights, participation, and equality, nevertheless balanced his commitment with an equivalent concern for property rights. Jefferson was ever the Lockean, stressing the independence that land ownership yields the stalwart yeoman, emphasizing the limits that property imposes on the scope of government action, and consistently including property among the sources of virtue. He also remained steadfast, however, in insisting upon government by the living, in the sense of right of the people to change their governments or the interpretations of their constitutions at least once per generation—powers that in the eyes of many constituted distinct threats to property. His major principle was, in his words, to "cherish the people"; this was to be done through their maximum participation in the decisions of government. This principle lies behind his strict constructionist view of the Constitution, his opposition to judicial review, and support for interpretation by the states, and his decentralization and ward-republics ideas. Whatever *could* be decided by the people *should* be, and at the lowest possible level. To some extent, his commitment to popular decision making was a relative matter, generated out of his greater fear for what might happen if decisions were made exclusively by elites with various self-serving inclinations. But it was also a matter of principle: he saw innate capacities in the people to make at least some forms of decisions, he was optimistic in general about their trustworthiness, and he cared about individual growth and fulfillment. This did not prevent him from covering his bet somewhat: he carefully prescribed the books to be employed in the curriculum of his University of Virginia so that Republican (as opposed to exclusively Federalist) views would predominate, and in his letters to Adams, particularly, he showed his enduring judgment that a natural aristocracy of talent was a vital component of good government. This was not merely a late view, or one offered for Adams' benefit. A concern for the proper aristocracy lies behind his insistence upon a role for the people in all forms of candidate selection and election; he believed that choice by the people was the best way of recognizing appropriate talents and installing them in positions of governmental responsibility, much to be preferred to the risks of self-appointed leadership or aristocracies of wealth.

Jefferson wrote much in the course of 60 years of public life and yet never produced a coherent summary work. For this reason, and because of his inherent ambivalence between civil rights, limited, decentralized government, and the welfare of the people on the one hand, and property rights and natural aristocracy, to say nothing of a decisive executive branch, on the other, his ideas have given rise to a wealth of conflicting interpretations over the years. Almost every political position in American history has been able to support itself with a quote from Jefferson, and he has been cited on both sides of many sharp conflicts. One example readily visible from the selections here is his view toward construction of the Constitution. His position, evidenced in the

Kentucky Resolution, was that decisions interpreting the powers of the federal government should be kept out of the hands of distant federal judges and opened instead to the people of the states; the situation that provoked the Resolution in the first place was the infamous Alien and Sedition Acts, so that the specific rationale was civil liberties as well as popular participation. To use this precedent in support of state constitutional interpretation per se, or to uphold limitations on government in behalf of slavery (despite Jefferson's explicit attack on slavery), as Calhoun did, is to elevate form over substance and purpose. Sumner did much the same thing in his incorporation of Jeffersonian principles of limits on government. Despite the fact that Jefferson's limits as applied were all in behalf of civil liberties and popular participation, Sumner used his views exclusively to defend property rights. What these two examples illustrate most decisively is the potentially misleading nature of a focus on a thinker's issue position or his (time-and-purpose-specific) attitude toward the use of government. Jefferson held his views concerning interpretation of the Constitution by the people of the states, and wrote the Kentucky Resolution, on behalf of popular participation and civil liberties, and in opposition to government by aristocracies of mere wealth. His principles of limited government were deduced from his more fundamental concerns: they were not first or absolute principles, but rather the means by which desired ends were thought attainable. To cite them as if they were offered as universally applicable principles of government organization is simply erroneous.

It seems clear at the same time that Jefferson was far from the radical that some of his Federalist opponents thought him. He was convinced that there were limits beyond which popular capacity was exhausted and should not be trusted. Men of talent were properly the leaders and governors. Where he differed from his detractors was over the specific qualities to be defined as "talent" for this purpose and over the means of identifying such men of talent. This is an important, perhaps vital, difference, but he still subscribed to government by men who were quite distinct from the common man, and did not hesitate to declare it. We have previously noted his enduring concern for property, both as the basis of political independence and as an educator towards good citizenship. In the context of the times, he could be perceived by nervous Federalists as a populist demagogue, but he was not. The confusion was neither the first nor the last occasion on which property-oriented liberals perceived human or civil rights liberals as radical redistributors of property. On the evidence, Jefferson was very much a man of the center, and Federalist perceptions are more a testimony to the capacity of those who are well off to imagine depredations on their property than to any inherent purposes of Thomas Jefferson. They also would lead one to believe that Jefferson was much further from their own view than was actually the case.

Madison

American thinkers are distinguishable not only by the relative exclusivity of their commitment to property rights, but also by the ways in which they envisioned those values as being best served. Madison, for example, saw property rights in a context that also valued personal and civil rights, and he believed it possible for property to be served through the interplay of relatively gentle and subtle "natural" forces. In *Federalist No. 10,* he made clear that he considered property and economic motivations as the principle sources and determinants of political activity, with the inevitable prospect of popular efforts at redistribution. The whole structure of separation of powers and checks and balances, together with the large size of the republic, is designed to so moderate and frustrate the anticipated popular thrust that it will provide a sense of the people's wishes without really endangering the basic pattern of property holding. This is Madison's famous principle of the "natural limits to numerical majorities"—a republic of sufficient size to insure that the natural diversities of men and interests would so counteract each other as to prevent formation of a cohesive majority. He sought by this device to solve what he acknowledged as "the republican dilemma" by means of a "republican remedy." The dilemma was the problem endemic to all popular governments of enabling the people to take a substantial part and yet, at the same time, assuring that the result would not be intolerable to vested interests. Madison's "republican remedy" consisted first of large size, which would lead to countervailing elements sufficient to prevent single-minded majorities from forming and also increase the probabilities that only well-tested men of uncommon moderation (and probably property) would rise to positions of leadership; and second, of the additional tier of separation of powers and checks and balances. The latter provisions building in intraelite conflict and potential deadlock might well be considered duplicative; one major critique of the Madisonian design concludes that they are inconsistent with each other and with the idea of wide popular participation and control. They demonstrate at least the extent of Madison's concern for the protection of property within the American system.

But Madison's attachment to property was neither absolute nor exclusive. Granting that it did not occur to him to incorporate a Bill of Rights or the equivalent in the original Constitution, he nevertheless was able to perceive how others might desire it (or be quieted by it) and he was a faithful advocate on behalf of his amendments in the first Congress. Perhaps more genuine was his self-generated determination to have the Revolutionary War debts paid back—at least to some extent—to the original holders, whose funds had supported the Congress at critical times, rather than exclusively to the speculators who had taken advantage of the nearly complete depreciation of the bonds resulting from the nation's earlier inability to raise the required revenue. And the carefully reasoned, deeply felt defense of civil liberties presented in his report on the Virginia Resolution indicates that these stands are probably considerably more than merely tactical efforts to build a political party.

One conventional analysis of Madison has it that he was relatively close to Hamilton at the time of the writing of the *Federalist Papers,* but that he drifted away under the spell of Jefferson, shifting finally to become a thoroughgoing Republican Party loyalist. The better argument seems to be that Madison was a property-conscious nationalist whose interests and personality led him to the scholar-activists' tasks of designing and explaining the instruments by which men might attain the goals they sought. He did not himself invest much time in speculation about mens' capacities, concentrating instead on the instrumental or institutional level after the fashion of a technician who accepts the assumptions of others and engineers means for them to realize their goals. As balanced and moderate in values and temperament as the institutional arrangements he advocated, Madison was understandably more successful as scholar and subordinate than as President.

contradiction?

Hamilton

For contrast and for illustration of the exclusivity of property rights among some American thinkers, one need go no further than Hamilton. We should note at the outset that the services performed by Hamilton were probably essential to building a nation in the total context of the times. It was his design that charted the course through successive stages of development, and he successfully fought the battles that established the first tangible milestones of this progress. This is not to say that industrialization and a powerful and productive economy are exclusively due to Hamilton; the country might have reached the same ends in other ways, perhaps even with less harshness and competitiveness to its capitalism. But we have perspective enough on problems of development today to know that very high levels of sacrifice, ruthlessness, and profiteering are frequently associated with the effort to modernize, and that progress is often painfully slow or nonexistent. Hamilton's way *was* successful, with comparatively little suffering, and he is entitled to some personal credit—in company, of course, with due allowances for distinctively more favorable circumstances from those that now obtain elsewhere.

This much acknowledged, we may look more closely at Hamilton's priority of values. Although, as is often noted, he did present the Constitutional Convention with a plan for a not so limited monarchy, Hamilton promptly made accommodations with the republican design that emerged. In this context, the objects of his approval and disapproval become noteworthy: his strongest approval is reserved for the executive branch and for the "energy" it implies. Elsewhere *(Federalist No. 9)* he indicates that this energy might find its best use in crushing domestic insurrection, perhaps foreshadowing his overkill response to the Whiskey Rebellion. To the problems of faction that Madison had sought to ameliorate in such delicate fashion, Hamilton had a simpler answer: the power and majesty of the federal government would crush where it did not overawe and discourage.

Only slightly below the executive in Hamilton's approval was the institution of an independent judiciary with power to declare acts of the other branches unconstitutional. In *Federalist No. 78,* he makes clear that he expects the judges to exercise this power. His rationale for their possession of such power, even though never explicitly granted in the Constitution, was easily refuted by Jefferson and Madison, but nevertheless became a dominant feature of American constitutional development. It is so completely associated with our understanding of the Constitution today that it seems utterly inevitable and appropriate. Such is the power of ideology for us all. Consider it first as a matter of logic, and then of value preferences. A government has been instituted in which the people have delegated certain powers to a legislature. All agree that acts in excess of those powers are void. Does it *nessarily follow*—though not so provided—that the judiciary has been nominated as the appropriate means of declaring that a given act is indeed in excess of the delegated powers? Of course not. The United States is the only country in the world that operates on such a basis, which says something about inevitability. If it is the *people's* delegation of power which is at stake—if it is the *people's* Constitution—then construction might more logically be by the people themselves. Or if there must be an agent for the purpose, should it not be the agent closest to the people? Who is closest to the people, in the logic of the thing, in the context of, say, 1803—five judges appointed for life many years before, or nearly 200 legislators elected a few months previously? If it be conceded that the legislature is in logic closer to the people (and, as may be suspected, the judges are closer to the propertied interests), then it may be asked whether there are not special judicial skills and capacities that make this decision appropriately theirs. This goes to the question of the nature of the intellectual act performed by anyone who interprets the document: for example, what sorts of decisional processes and standards are to be employed in deciding whether Congress has or does not have power to undertake a particular act that some say is a regulation of "commerce"? Are there skills acquired in law school that make it possible objectively to divine the meaning of "commerce" in situations unimagined by the Framers? Or is the decision out of necessity chiefly one of value preference as to what *should* be within Congress' power in the particular context of the times? Clearly, it is the latter, and Jefferson had by far the more logical position; just as clearly, Hamilton (and the justices who followed his teachings) won the argument and succeeded in implanting judicial supremacy of sorts into American political practice and ideology. One need hardly ask for what reason Hamilton was so anxious for the judiciary to be independent and powerful: his purposes were constant, and he was convinced that property needed a further bulwark against the propensities of the popular branches.

Both executive and judicial agencies and powers were, in Hamilton's eyes, vital steps toward an energetic government. An associated principle for him was the institution of a direct relationship between the government and individual citizens. One of the principal defects of the Articles of Confederation in this view was their failure to provide any means by which the laws of the nation could be applied to individuals. Under the Articles, individuals were not bound by the enactment of the Congress, which could act only in the form of imposing obligations on the states, which in their turn might or might not carry out the Congressional purpose by enacting effectuating statutes. A government that could only act upon the states in their corporate capacities, of course, would encounter frequent uncooperativeness from those states when they disapproved of the actions decided upon—and it would be a commensurately less powerful and efficacious government, which fit the purposes of the drafters of the Articles quite well. But to Hamilton a few years later, this appeared a serious obstacle. He insisted that the federal government must have capacity to act directly upon individuals, enabling coercion to be realistically applied and the laws carried out efficiently. Under this arrangement, every individual would be bound by federal laws and nothing required (or permitted) of the states as intermediaries. The individual who did not comply with the federal law would be immediately subject to enforcement by the combined executive and judicial agencies of the national government.

These well-approved innovations were means of making a government that would be energetic and useful. The further question remains, energetic and useful to what ends? Implicit throughout Hamilton's writings is the assumption that the maintenance of stability and order is itself a major accomplishment to be sought as a primary goal of government. But he had more specific purposes in mind.

Hamilton believed, in his own words, that "money is the vital principle of the body politic." A successful economy would produce sufficient revenue for the government to discharge its obligations, maintain order, and foster the expansion of commerce. The reciprocity and mutuality of vested interest here makes it difficult to identify which was primary for Hamilton. His initiative in the Annapolis Convention of 1786 was for the purpose of proposing arrangements that would improve commerce between the states, but he was on record attacking the revenue-raising weaknesses of the Articles of Confederation even before they had been ratified by all the states. Throughout the *Federalist Papers,* he speaks of commerce and revenue together, and it seems clear that he envisioned an inseparable partnership between business and government in which risks, opportunities, and rewards were essentially identical. This union of government with elements in the society is distinctively Hamiltonian and distinctively at odds with the limited-government and laissez-faire views of almost all of his major contemporaries. Hamilton stood ready to make conscious and deliberate use of government wherever it could be a useful instrument for advancing commerce—and, perhaps not incidentally, serving the interests of the businessmen, financiers, and incipient manufacturers whose success Hamilton so desired.

In so employing government, Hamilton was boldly seeking to bring about conditions which would be strikingly different from those which then obtained in the new nation. Financial and commercial considerations dominated his thinking. In an apt characterizing phrase, Clinton Rossiter terms Hamilton of the right, but not conservative.[1] This captures the essence of Hamilton: the exclusiveness of his business and property rights orientation, coupled with his decisive use of government to bring about change to a specific set of economic conditions in which commerce would be greatly facilitated. He cannot be understood as a conservative, under our definition, for he did not begin with a conception of the society as an organism prior to the individual interests with it; he avidly sought change of a totally antitraditional sort, and his motivations were exclusively economic at the cost of concern for the natural aristocracy of men whose talent might be more appropriate for the many facets of governing. A better way of interpreting Hamilton would seem to be as a liberal with an understanding of natural rights in nearly exclusive property rights terms, who saw the furtherance of the material goals of property holders as paramount and an appropriate purpose to which government might be devoted.

II. EARLY RADICAL-INDIVIDUALISTS: PAINE, EMERSON, THOREAU

Paine

Perhaps the most complete and unrestrained advocacy of natural rights conceived as human rights comes from Thomas Paine. Not even Paine is entirely free of concern for property, but most of his attention is devoted to freeing his listeners from their inhibitions and self-limitations in order that they may commit revolution against their king, or to justifying bloodshed by

Clinton Rossiter, *Conservatism in America.* New York: Random House, 1955, 1962, p. 108.

comparing its scope with the extent of other forms of suffering under the status quo or limited alternatives to it. Particularly in his exchange with Burke, he raises explicit questions about the relative priorities to be observed in attaining justice, organizing government, and enforcing traditions. The vision that animated Paine was one of a world free of unnecessary and arbitrary restraints upon men, in which they would come to trust and love one another and learn to enjoy the "simple" satisfactions of peace and natural harmony.

Emerson and Thoreau

It may seem odd at first to find Emerson, a Boston Brahmin, included with the populist Paine and the moralist Thoreau under the rubric of radicalism. But the impact of his teaching was to give a rationale and authority to the individualistic, transcendental strain in American political thinking that has repeatedly led a few dissenters leftward out of the materialist, short run approach of liberalism.

Much less men of the world than Paine or Jefferson, Emerson and Thoreau carried suspicion of government and concern for the inner life of the individual to its fullest point within the American spectrum. Emerson, heir to two centuries of Calvinist theological arguments in New England, saw self-reliance as the key to salvation and had little use for government, particularly that of the Jacksonians. Thoreau—embarrassingly moral and idealistic, then as now—produced America's most eloquent statement of the eternal dilemma between man's conscience and the practical exigencies of government in response to a government which compromised with slavery. His arguments are applicable in many contexts, of course, and every epoch rediscovers them. Together, Emerson and Thoreau display the twin sources of the stream of individualism within American political thought even more clearly than Paine and Jefferson. Reliance upon oneself for attainment of all worthy goals (readily linkable with exclusive concern for property rights, as Sumner illustrates in such gross fashion) is dominant, with the much more fragile moral basis for judging personal and government actions as a secondary contributor. American political thought would not be complete without the latter, but it would not be American without the former.

III. TRACES OF CONSERVATISM: ADAMS, CALHOUN, CROLY

Adams

It is tempting to suggest that conservatism in the post-1787 United States is represented exclusively by John Adams, but a closer look indicates that there is a thin strand of conservative thinking visible from time to time and in sometimes unanticipated places. The elements that are properly identifiable as conservative frequently appear in men identified in their own generations as generally liberal in the change-oriented or use of government sense, and there is no major thinker subsequent to Adams who is clearly and consistently conservative in outlook or program. But the assumption of noblesse oblige for men of talent to watch over the future of the republic, despite pessimism about the nature of men and resignation at the limited successes likely, is a recurring phenomenon. When it is combined with a view that places the enduring society prior to the individuals within it at any given moment, and the conscious effort to conform change to the traditions of the past, we have sufficient indications of conservatism to deserve comment. Adams and Calhoun offer our first illustrations, and then Herbert Croly, and ultimately (in Chapters 17 and 18) Russell Kirk and Peter Viereck pick up the conservative cause in various ways.

Adams is neither consistently nor exclusively conservative. But he is distinctive among postindependence thinkers in his view of society as having "natural" needs and internal determinants, which require a particular form of ordering for their efficient operation. He steps outside the liberal understanding of man as the center of organization to posit society as having separable claims and needs that a balanced form of government can serve. His approach to property is not exclusively in terms of the natural rights of individuals but also includes (more than Jefferson) a sense of the moral authority that stems from property. In other words, property is not for individual satisfaction and aggrandizement, but in a sense a trusteeship that obliges the holder to serve the community. Because of his obligation, and also because of the opportunity that leisure has given him for education and judgment, he has an authority that others cannot match and should obey. For Adams, the idea of an aristocracy of talent is central, and it is also a feature that regularly distinguishes the conservative from the merely self-interested user of some conservative rhetoric. The basis on which men should come to positions of leadership responsibility is their capacity to know what must be done to preserve the essentials of the society and accommodate its past to present conditions and future goals. Such men are not to be identified by their successes in purely economic affairs, though it may be that some appropriately talented men are indeed economically capable as well. Those who, like Hamilton, would identify capacity to govern by means of economic tests are not conservatives and, like Hamilton, would not be congenial in Adams' eyes. Similarly, the uses of government must sometimes be counter to the immediate and short-range interests of holders of economic power—in order to better serve the long-range interests of the society. What is required is the capacity in men who hold responsibility in government to take such temporarily unpopular action, to make the hard and frequently misunderstood choices that fall to the lot of conservatives. Finally, there is the element of purposefulness—the willingness to suffer now that conditions may be better in the future, and to define a societal tradition and seek to hew to it through changing conditions in the environment. Adams would not yield to criticism of the arrangement of the American state constitutions on grounds which would have transgressed against any of these requirements.

Calhoun

Calhoun is both tragic and ambiguous. He sustains and refutes almost any single interpretation that seeks to integrate his ideas into a consistent pattern of thought. The key to understanding Calhoun may lie in his strong attachment to the South as a collection of interests, some national and some local. He sought, sometimes desperately, to evolve a rationale that would serve both national and local necessities. In the course of his career, he shifted from a strong nationalist position to an even stronger states' rights and nullification position, finally offering the "concurrent majority" principle, effectuated through a dual executive, as an alternative to war.

What was conservative about Calhoun was his explicit concept of the organic relationship between society and government, his severe pessimism about the nature of man, and his continual seeking for a means of providing the order that constitutes liberty and permits progress for the civilization it serves. He envisioned no lessening of suffering for those elements of the society who were at its lower levels, and indeed considered this "mud-sill" a prerequisite to progress: they were (as always) available to do the labor, and only their service would enable others to move ahead and release some to have sufficient leisure to assure cultural as well as material progress.

Calhoun's inconsistencies start when, as a conservative-tending thinker, he looks backward and endorses the thoroughly liberal principles of the Declaration of Independence. In the Jeffersonian tradition, as Calhoun was, it was impossible for him to avoid the Declaration, but, having endorsed it is formative, neither could he avoid its implications: all men created equal, with natural rights prior to those of society or government. Calhoun did assert that men's rights came from their society and were not inherent in them—a conservative position—but he had no audience for such an argument; in seeking to put himself on the line of established traditions, he was obliged to accept the Declaration and suffer the consequences of trying to reason toward conservative means and ends from liberal premises. This meant that he could not wholly deny the entitlement of slaves to some form of status, and having once granted some, it was difficult to explain denying others. Acceptance of the Declaration and the Jeffersonian tradition also led him to laissez-faire and limited government positions, with resulting inconsistencies for the availability of government as an instrument of conservative purpose.

The problem for Calhoun was that the South had both national and local interests that were themselves inconsistent. The South needed sufficient power at the national level to assure that it would not be outvoted, in order to protect slavery and is precarious economic posture. But the very values and practices that rationalized slavery rendered economic conditions more precarious and made it more difficult to secure support from Northern states or the newly developing territories. The abortive effort to provide a semifeudal rationale for slavery could succeed only in putting the South further behind a country whose ideology was exclusively Lockean and Jeffersonian, and in opening a gap that was too great to permit Southern attainment of minimum national goals. Calhoun's best work was his evolution of the concurrent majority principle, by which he sought to make it possible for two quite distinctive interests to maintain a tenuous coalition. He attempted through frank acknowledgement of fundamental difference and the granting of veto powers to each to assure each major interest that it could never be threatened by the other. In the course of this argument, he made an attempt to build a bridge to Northern capitalists by arguing that class interests should unite them with the plantation South against the threat of a rising proletariat. The effort earned him the revealing characterization of "the Marx of the master class" from Richard Hofstadter, but little reception from his immediate audience. The concurrent majority principle, to the extent that it is to be considered as a real issue at all and not just an artifact of the slavery controversy, suffers from its unlikely premise that there will always be two major interests and that they will be permanent and cohesive (and apparently, geographically defined). Unless this were the case, the principle would be totally unworkable. Perhaps it is to be taken as a kind of symbolic admonition, to the effect that no dominant group should seek to press its perhaps temporary predominance beyond the limits of endurance of others; this is apparently what is meant by some contemporary commentators who suggest that Calhoun's concurrent majority has found some kind of operational significance at the present time.

Croly

A quite different selection of conservative ideas is found in Herbert Croly's work, *The Promise of American Life*. As the title suggests, Croly extracted a sense of purpose out of the American past and set about to indicate how it might better be achieved. Having identified what was central to the traditions of the society, he considered how government might be employed to serve societal needs. He was distinctive in his willingness to set government in motion in a way which first would require judgments about an overarching national interest and a commitment to serving that societal interest in deliberate and purposeful ways.

Croly saw American political ideas as summarized in the differences between Hamilton and Jefferson, whom he held to be equally unsatisfactory guides for the twentieth century. He interpreted Hamilton as representing nationalism, in the sense of responding to the necessities of building and developing a nation to new levels of greatness and achievement, but as being, unfortunately, too concerned with the interests of a single group of financiers and businessmen and, therefore, anathema to the people. Jefferson he saw as remedying the absence of concern for the people and their individual attainments, but seriously deficient in his unwillingness to accept the role of government as the conscious servant of the society. In the circumstances of the turn of the century, Croly reasoned, there had to be some rationale for the use of government for deliberate and desirable ends; but the followers of Hamilton were too crass and too exclusively profit-oriented, and the followers of Jefferson were laissez-faire and antigovernment. In neither's political principles was there a place for a government that could control burgeoning corporate power and turn it to the maximum social benefit. Croly, therefore, acting in search of "a morally and socially desirable distribution of wealth," evolved a program (the "new nationalism") that neatly combined what to him were the useful features of each set of principles. He called for the acceptance of "a dominant and constructive national purpose" that would legitimate the subordination of both economic power and individuals to efficient governmental regulation which would promote maximum individual and social advancement.

IV. THE EVOLUTION OF LIBERALISM: SUMNER, CROLY, DEWEY, AND BERLE

Sumner

In tracing the process by which many liberals began to come to terms with the power of government and to employ it in behalf of human rights and equality, we may as well first pose the opposite pole of liberalism—nearly exclusive economic and property rights concerns coupled with absolute laissez-faire attitudes toward government. William Graham Sumner exceeded even Hamilton in his commitment to property rights, and he was a purist in his classic liberal laissez-faire position with regard to the use of government.

Sumner deplored all uses of government, not just the ones designed to benefit the poor or the weak; he castigated violations of free trade principles and just the kinds of special considerations for particular economic interests that Hamilton endorsed.

The rationale for Sumner's utter individualism lay in his classical liberal conviction that progress for all was dependent on the economic successes of those specially talented individuals who might be able to amass fortunes amidst truly competitive conditions. If the natural processes of competition were allowed to run their courses, Sumner believed, all would receive their just rewards and the society would eliminate its weaker members. The problems in analogizing from natural selection analyses of biological evolution did not much trouble Sumner or other Social Darwinists of the time, perhaps just because there was so much precedent in the liberal tradition for individualism, laissez-faire, and limited government. Sumner saw a man's failure to attain wealth as solely attributable to his lack of capacity to compete, and not produced by disadvantages of education, birth, environment, or fortune. The success with which this argument was established as a dominant theme in American political thinking has been characterized as "the capture of the American democrat by the Whigs": by use of the Horatio Alger myth and the other accoutrements of the Gospel of Wealth, the possessors of property captured the thinking of the democrats who might otherwise have viewed their successes as illegitimate and sought redistribution by means of government. There is an important point that is to be made by this analysis: much of the fear of the masses that has burdened holders of property in the United States has been wasted, because the masses have been as much imbued with respect for, and motivations toward the possession of, property as the most thoroughgoing capitalist. Redistribution has not occurred primarily because there have never been many who thought it justifiable or appropriate; one of the reasons for the inability of pragmatic politicians to handle the slavery issue in the early nineteenth century was that slaves were property that could not be eliminated without compensation and that involved sums too vast to seem within the range of possibility. The property-oriented American capitalists, the local version of Whiggery, did not succeed in gaining explicit recognition for their paramountcy, and indeed on most occasions when they sought to establish themselves or their interests as supreme by right or entitlement, they were rejected by the aroused American individualist democrat. But the substance of their ends, in its economic dimensions and to a considerable extent in the personal supremacy of representative capitalists, was still fully obtained—under the banner of individualism, limited government, competitive enterprise, laissez-fare, and "democracy." As we shall see in the next section, this analysis is only one of several possible interpretations of these events.

Sumner is a contributor to this "capture," although this was not part of his conscious purposes. Among other places, this contribution is visible in the way that Sumner evolved definitions of familiar terms to fit the conditions of the times and the value preferences that he held. To Sumner, for example, "equality" meant equality of opportunity, narrowly construed as the right to compete if a man was otherwise able to; for him, the balance was in all other respects on the side of "liberty," in the sense of strict prohibitions on any government interference with a man's enjoyment of the rewards he had realized from success in the completion. It was both immoral and ultimately dysfunctional for government to be used for the purpose of taking from those who had succeeded and giving to those who had not. This was more than just a convenient rationale for justifying the possessions of the rich with a moral or social gloss: Sumner followed it consistently to the point of condemning instances where particular interests had enriched themselves through the use of government. He is best understood as marking a high point in the individualist, limited government, liassez-faire, exclusively property rights version of the American liberal tradition. The mainstream nature of his position may be estimated from the very considerable power that it maintains now, nearly a century later in time and drastically removed in circumstances.

Sumner also has another claim to contemporary relevance, and one that further documents the principled nature of his positions. In a consistent application of a view that sought not just to sustain economic aggrandizement but, within the range of its assumptions, improve qualities of life as well, he attacked what he saw as an imperialist foreign policy. His concern was that a nation could not act on one set of principles in regard to other nations and another set of principles at home. Given his assumption that the territories at stake in the Spanish-American War could not and should not be incorporated in the United States, this concern led him to fear for the domestic effects of an essentially colonialist approach to governing the new territories. If not observed abroad, he asked, could democracy be long sustained at home? A rationalization which permitted the exclusion of some from self-determination and opportunity might eventually undermine commitments to those principles generally, or at least sustain exceptions to them. Or, conversely, an active government for foreign policy purposes might soon become an active government for domestic purposes as well. To Sumner, it appeared that there was a choice to be made, and he opted for avoiding both possibilities by not undertaking the acquisition of territories.

Croly

The work of Herbert Croly marks a major watershed in liberal thought. Repelled by the conditions he saw around him, Croly's analysis cut to the core of the early twentieth century liberal problem: What is to be done in circumstances where economic power is concentrated in a relatively few individuals and corporations whose motivations are essentially self-serving, and where there are also associated if not resulting limitations on the opportunity and capacity of many other individuals to compete equally? When the conditions of existence of many citizens are marginal or less, what is to be done? Such a situation can lead directly to the use of government as the instrument of controlling the excesses of private power, restoring opportunity to individuals, and ameliorating suffering. To be consistent with dominant individualist-limited government ideology, such use of government would be interstitial and limited to those instances where it was absolutely necessary. But would it then be timely and sufficient to do more than temporarily patch up the most extreme dislocations—leaving the fundamental causes to continue to generate greater problems for the future? Any attempt to employ government in a manner equal to the problems that existed, Croly argued, would run aground against the residue of Jeffersonian individualism and limited government; thus liberalism was boxed in between conditions and problems on the one hand and a self-limiting set of inhibitions against use of government on the other.

In the six decades since this analysis, environmental conditions have if anything exacerbated this conflict, but there has been only minor change in the substance of liberal political thought or ideology. There has been no retreat from individualism, limited government, natural rights with an emphasis on property rights, or legalistic procedural regularity. Of course, government has been used more and more frequently, under the rationale that some forms of suffering or disadvantage should be ameliorated for humane, social benefit, or economic reasons—but always in a semiillegitimate manner, and in limited and marginal ways.

New social and political problems have arisen and become more intense with each passing decade, without producing major change in the essentials of liberalism. Urbanization and a 300 percent population increase since the publication of Croly's analysis have converted a rural nation into one nearly 80 percent urban with staggering housing, transportation, and social problems. Aspirations for racial equality, temporarily submerged when Croly wrote, have emerged in insistent form, producing formal change in official policy but a hardening of resistance from whites in critical social and economic dimensions. International threats on a scale never conceived by early twentieth century thinkers have added to the pressures on political ideas and ideology.

In this totally changed context, liberal thinking has moved incrementally into a limited welfare-state pattern, without major modification in any basic tenets. Pragmatic adaptations have been made so that the political system has discharged at least its minimum tasks of order and security, but even these returns now appear in jeopardy from the pressures of internal and external forces. Perhaps there is a range within which eighteenth century assumptions and ideas are adaptable; if so, we may be approaching the limits of that adaptive capacity now. There is no question but that the liberal tradition has succeeded in producing a remarkably flexible and resilient political process, one which has admitted new groups and in effect absorbed many thrusts by means of incremental changes within the bounds set by long-established fundamentals. But this achievement is no reason to assume that eighteenth century ideas are infinitely flexible, nor that twentieth century conditions do not raise problems that will cause change at the fundamental level. There is an important developmental point here that bears repeating: ideas that are relevant and appropriate to circumstances of one era may not be equally relevant and appropriate when conditions change in major ways. The question that Croly sought to raise sixty years ago was whether conditions were not sufficiently different as to require fundamental revision rather than incremental refinement of existing political ideas. He received no answer then, nor has he received a response yet; but accelerating change in conditions is pressing the question ever closer to the point where there must be a response of some kind.

The directions that this response may take are many, although it requires a stern act of intellectual self-extrication to see them in all their variety. Croly's own prescription was based on his interpretation of the essentials of the Hamiltonian and Jeffersonian positions. He shared Hamilton's willingness to assume responsibility for achieving specific goals through the use of government, and he converted Hamilton's purposes into the broader one of a prosperous economy managed by an intelligent and public-spirited government. But he also endorsed Jefferson's concern for the individual's attainments and for the general social and economic betterment of all members of the society. Croly proposed to harmonize these two sets of goals through the deliberate employment of government as the agent of the people for the purpose of realizing a "morally and socially desirable distribution of wealth." This meant that long-range goals would be defined and basic policy directions set through popular decision-making processes, and then public officials would use the powers of government in whatever ways necessary to accomplish those ends. It also and emphatically meant the end of limited government and laissez-faire inhibitions on the part of government. Croly was convinced that conditions in the economy were such as to make concentration of capital and certain monopolies inevitable, desirable, and efficient, and for him the problem was not to break them up but to enable that power to be managed so that it would be used for maximum public benefit. He believed that continued individual self-serving in the context of the times would create intolerable conditions where disparities in wealth and opportunity would destroy all sense of community and all hope for realization of the American promise. He saw his proposals as uniting the nationalist vision of Hamilton with the democratic commitments of Jefferson to raise the possibility of a new era of social and economic achievement.

I suggested in the previous section that Croly shows some traces of conservatism in the basis on which he rested these prescriptions. It should be clear from the above that he also retained elements of Jeffersonian liberalism in his tradition-merging prescriptions. Ironically, but consistent with the fate that often befalls American conservatives, to the extent that he has been drawn upon at all by subsequent thinkers and actors it has been as a forerunner of the new liberalism that legitimated certain uses of government for social betterment purposes. Such is the power of orthodox assumptions and ideas to convert fairly drastic proposals to tolerably incremental modifications of the status quo. A similar fate has befallen those few voices that sought to introduce radical populist or Marxist socialist alternatives into the range of American consideration. Those marginal aspects that could be accommodated with the fundamentals of the liberal tradition were absorbed, and the rest successfully ignored. In the case of Croly, implementation of some measure of his proposals for integration of economic and political power gave rise to the kind of semibenevolent welfare capitalism now sometimes derided under the label of "corporate liberalism." The integration, because it was only partial, left initiative in the hands of the managers of corporate power rather than, as Croly had apparently intended, in the government acting as the agent of the people.

Dewey

The multiplication of social problems, technological changes, and environmental pressures threatened to overwhelm the fact-gathering and decision-making capacities of a society only beginning to adjust to the idea of occasional ad hoc uses of government. By what means could some modern form of public participation be developed so that the requisites of democracy would survive in such an age?

John Dewey sought to take account of many of these factors and establish a political process that would enable the public to determine its own ideas and policies. Raising the liberal faith in reason to a new height, he insisted upon comprehensive factual descriptions as the basis for wise decision making under circumstances of rapidly changing environmental conditions and commensurate development of man's knowledge and capacity to understand and manage them. At the same time, he sought to preserve some role for the public; it remained to be seen, however, whether the role he mapped out would be in practice free of the shaping effects of others' interpretations of the meaning of change in conditions.

Dewey's accommodation was to call for a thoroughgoing empirical approach to public problems, with social scientists researching issues in depth and reporting their findings in factual form. He then expected widespread communication to take place, so that the public would have full and frank access to knowledge. Armed with this knowledge, the public would be in a position to act widely, and all that would be required would be a broadly inclusive decisional process. Dewey was content to accept the public's own definition of its needs and wants as a sufficient basis for government action, and defended this on the basis that democracy carried with it an irretrievable right to be wrong. Stated in such summary fashion, Dewey's principles sound naive. In all probability, "facts" would not be such (at least not exclusively), communication would not be complete, issues would be perceived incompletely by some and not at all by others, and people would act on a variety of "irrational" bases. Although Dewey's formulation had the merit of trying to maintain a major role for the people and still come to terms with changing conditions and the need for descriptive accuracy as a basis for public policy making, it also raised the prospect of a technocratic elite of experts and bureaucrats who would feed the "facts" to the waiting public.

Berle

In the first flush of enthusiasm for empirical approaches to coping with the new twentieth century circumstances, Dewey's solution seemed to serve the needs of the democratic side of liberalism. But a rationale for the role of property and the economy and the relationship of both to government was still needed. Writing in 1932, practically simultaneously with Dewey, Adolf Berle developed an analysis that recognized many of the new problems, legitimated marginal government regulation, but still upheld the essential validity of the established economic order.

Berle acknowledged that the economic market was in fact not offering opportunity to all, and that its self-regulatory capacity was undermined by accumulations of power in the hands of a few corporate producers. He rested his analysis on the argument that the distribution of ownership into many hands through public stockholding in major corporations led to inability on the part of owners to effectively control their property; instead, the executive managers of the corporations had become their real directors, with the result that new and less reliable motives animated these accumulations of power. Managers, for example, were interested in their own prerogatives as well as in maximizing profit, and, therefore, they might on occasion act otherwise than in response to market demands or competitive pressures. Or they might act to restrain trade, accept a lower than maximum profit, or resist new technologies and more efficient means—or in any number of other ways violate the standards that supposedly enabled the market to be a reliable autonomous provider of the greatest good for the largest number. Because of this divergence of ownership and control, with its resulting implications for the economy and, ultimately, the society, Berle argued, an external source of direction and control had to apply the restraints and assure the uses of power that would make the maximum contribution to the work of the market. Thus, government should be employed interstitially to remedy corporate errors, promote economic behavior that would keep the market working, and, if necessary, assist some of those who were suffering from the market's inadequacies.

This was an analysis that upheld relatively infrequent government regulation or "intervention" on an ad hoc basis where circumstances seemed to require it. At the same time, it preserved the fundamental values of property rights, limited government, and laissez-faire. The market remained the basic regulator, at least in theory and rhetoric, and government merely a minor supplement. From such an accommodation, little reexamination of fundamental principles was likely to follow, although there could be (and was, of course, in the New Deal days) considerable controversy over any particular use of government to supplement the market.

POSTSCRIPT

The experience of wrestling with several American political thinkers should have enabled us to refine the basic set of central questions of political theory with which we began, and to sharpen skills of analysis and evaluation. For one thing, we should be skilled in searching out relatively slight differences between values and programs. Because American thinkers have frequently assumed ends rather than specifically stating them, they have argued more often over means; this causes their value differences to appear muted, but they are no less important and revealing. The values of American theorists are somewhat less clear and less explicit, but they are operative, and careful analysis is rewarded by increased understanding of thinkers' underlying premises and goals. It should also be possible to state some of our questions concerning institutional arrangements in subtler and more precise terms. For example, there is not much to be learned from asking whether a thinker believes that elites must carry primary responsibility for shaping public policy (all of them do), but what manner of men he envisages in public office, what sorts of processes place them there, and in what ways he sees them as obliged to observe limits upon their actions. The question is not what goals should be sought through this political system, but in what order they are ranked, and how far one is willing to detract from one in order to attain another. The question is not whether the people are to play a part in public policy making, but how much and when and what mechanisms and conditions are prerequisite to such participation. Is it a practical requirement, for example, that elites be divided before popular impact can be decisive? If so, does the composition and selection process for elites suggest that such occasions will be frequent or infrequent? These are questions that will bring us closer to an understanding of political thinkers' values and prescriptions. They are also questions for which empirical findings provide the beginnings of answers. We should be starting to see how much is to be gained in the way of heightened appreciation of the range of the presently possible by inclusion of the findings and inter- pretations of the empirical researchers.

Finally, I should remind the reader that this is not exclusively an analytical venture. Each author or researcher has, at least potentially, something of value to contribute to an understanding of politics, and ultimately to the reader's capacity to make independent evaluations. Normative judgments, informed by a sophisticated understanding of politics, are the ultimate pur- pose of this enterprise.

CHAPTER 15

Liberalism in Midcentury Context

THE evolution in the political thinking of most liberals which occurred in the first three decades of the twentieth century laid a veneer of change upon the basic components and associated values of the formative years. Unchanged were the core values of individualism, natural rights, limited government, and the goal of facilitating the self-fulfillment of the individual. Around these, however, some associated commitments have evolved (some marginally, a few substantially) and others have matured and hardened. Significant among such developments, and illustrative of important characteristics of midcentury liberalism, are attitudes toward the property rights-equality tension, legalism, rationalism, and the role of the economic market.

Property Rights Versus Equality

This enduring source of intraliberal conflict, which once pitted aspiring plutocrat against committed democrat, now ranges the Manchester liberal against the welfare state liberal in repeated argument over the scope and level of uses of government. Still sharing American materialist standards for all spheres of life, the disputants center on whether government action in specific cases will promote or impede the workings of the market, and on whether government "spending" produces a satisfactory return measured in monetary units. Manchester liberals, generally satisfied with the status quo and their place in it, resist increased government regulation or expenditure in the interests of others. Welfare state liberals, perceiving the disadvantages of some members of the society, seek to ameliorate the worst of these through modest government action. Perhaps the moderation of their programs is an accurate and pragmatic accommodation to the political power of the Manchester liberals, or perhaps it represents the boundaries of their equality-property priorities; but in any event the result is action sufficient to blunt demands and still maintain the basic economic structure intact and operating. Both groups of liberals are inclined to be constrained by established distributions of wealth, status, and power among members of the society, to accept property rights based on such distributions as parameters for action, and to judge results in terms of financial returns. Sharing such self-limitations, of course, implies limits to the efforts that can be made on behalf of equality or other human rights; at some point, most liberals will converge and deny the validity of claims that would transgress upon existing property rights or require expenditures that cannot be expected to produce short-term financial successes.

Legalism

Running through all the major American thinkers is the liberal concern for the sanctity of contract and regularity of procedures. Most of the thinkers represented here had some form of legal training, and further, such an approach was congenial to their frequently instrumental and goal-assuming orientations. It is a frankly legalistic concern for the specific and the procedural that animates Americans, from Jefferson's statute drafting to Dewey's concern for the instruments by which the public might be able to make its judgments known. Those who are not lawyers are nevertheless procedurally oriented, spending much more time with the mechanisms than with the substance of what policies might be produced. It is true, of course, that procedural mechanisms bring with them certain implicit goals and exclude others, but these thinkers do not appear to have consciously substituted procedural emphases for concern with the substance of what government does. It appears more likely that they have not realized that they were operating with self-imposed relatively narrow ranges of what might be possible. Broadly shared values and assumptions may have led to argument only over the means by which goals were to be realized, or, in other words, over the legal details of effectuation. Behind this procedural emphasis may also be assumptions about the essential harmony of all major interests within the society, and a view that conflicts are relatively unimportant and therefore soluble through concentration on proper procedures.

Conservation

Progressive

Rationalism

The liberal conviction that man could find his way by gathering the evidence necessary to understand and manage his environment both suffered from and contributed to the conditions of the mid-twentieth century. Liberals who faced up to the works of Darwin, Marx, and Freud, who observed the rise and behavior of fascist and other totalitarian regimes, and who were aware of the social and economic circumstances, domestic and foreign, of midcentury existence, could hardly fail to lose confidence in both the achievements and potential of reason. At the same time, liberal devotion to rationalism in the sense of technical skills and organizational order led to increased bureaucratization and the drift of real power to "experts." Such experts and bureaucrats, of course, operating with their own special set of values and priorities, could and did develop methods and programs that were rational and technically appropriate in their eyes but not necessarily responsive to public preferences or needs. The propensity of the technocrat to employ his skills in the service of accepted values—and to avoid examination of the propriety of those values and goals—leads to rigidification of the status quo and to a reduction of the society's capacity to change in response to new conditions. At some point, it may even become more convenient and practical for the technocrat acting in behalf of the established order to adjust public perception of needs and desires to what the apparatus of government is capable of producing than to discover, develop or respond to felt needs within the society.

The Role of the Economic Market

Since the days of Croly, major voices have articulated the failures of the market to serve adequately as either a regulatory or a distributive mechanism. Most liberals perceive consumer impotency, supplier manufacture of demand through advertising, extensive restraint of trade and competition, aggregations of power that dwarf some states and are unresponsive to any external forces, and government-supplied benefits that aid favored industries or producers over others. These and other failures of the market lead to arbitrary dominance of particular products, corporations, and people—a dominance that finds justification only in the fact that it exists. Croly proposed a relatively fundamental shift of the balance between economic and political power, in which primacy would be accorded to the latter and a defined national purpose would be sought. However, limited implementation of his program led instead to an integration of the two in which initiative and priority remained with accumulations of economic power. Government's role is still subsidary, supplementing and supporting various aspects of the economy, and most liberals continue to acknowledge the inadequacies of the market mechanism. This apparent contradiction has never been resolved. Marginal changes in governmental involvement are made from time to time, and Keynesian-based fiscal and tax policies clearly affect the course of the economy, but few have sought more basic modifications.

Although liberalism has evolved in several respects since its American inception, environmental conditions have changed rapidly in the United States and in the world, and at present there is at least a substantial question as to whether the existing structure of ideas is capable of responding to contemporary conditions. The bitter racial conflicts of the 1960's suggest that some sort of boundary has been reached, and that the flexibility and incremental change potential in liberalism is being severely tested. Indeed, we might ask whether contemporary social and economic circumstances admit a harmony between liberalism and democracy. It all depends on one's definition of democracy, of course, but this is just the point: changing conditions may require revision of such definitions to keep them in contact with realities; but if this is done, there may be implications in other directions. In this case, we have seen that liberalism emphasizes a definition of liberty in terms of limits on government, a major role for property rights of individuals, and acknowledgement of the individual's freedom to amass wealth (and hence power). But if one concludes that the mandates of 20th century democracy require government action to remove social and economic disabilities from the Negro, to aid the poor, and to maintain rough parity of political power, then each of the cited elements of liberalism is in direct conflict with goals and purposes of democracy. Certainly some revision of the concept of democracy is in order under new conditions, but the question of how much and in what ways the definition is to be changed is a critical one involving basic value premises.

The lag between liberal ideas and contemporary conditions seems clear, but the probable consequences are not. Liberalism might absorb the thrusts toward change generated by these new conditions, much as it has absorbed them in the past. Or it might evolve into some new form by means of adapting portions of contemporary conservative or radical ideas. The relationship between conditions and ideas is complex, and conditions themselves are multidimensional. We are readily aware that there are continuing changes in different sectors of social life, such as the economy, the society, and technology, and we may also realize that these are interrelated, i.e., that a change in one may work changes in one or more of the other sectors. Let us add that man's understanding of these relationships is also in a process of change through time. No one familiar with the evolution of political ideas could ignore the impact of the 19th and 20th centuries on political thinking, and specifically on thinkers' assumptions about the capacity of men as rational individuals. We now understand man and the relationships between his various forms of activity in totally different ways than we did in earlier ages.

Not only are our views toward the environment one of the conditions that is in the process of change, but the nature of the relationship between sectors may also change with time. For example, at an early stage of development, the characteristics of the economy may have paramount influence over political ideas and ideology. Under circumstances where existence is marginal, and there are no major outside threats, political ideas may be cast in the image of economic necessities. But at later stages of development, when relatively high levels of affluence have been attained, characteristics of the economy may become much less determinative. At this stage, political ideas may be more responsive to by-now-established ideological factors quite independent of economic origins. It is even possible that, long after economic conditions have changed, the assumptions from earlier days continue to motivate economic behavior and structure political thinking.

These considerations suggest that the relationship between conditions and ideas is time-specific, and in all probability different for each generation. Therefore, it properly becomes one of the analytical inquiries that we should direct at thinkers: how does this particular man understand political ideas to originate, and what structured him in his own particular ideas? But it is also a question for each of us to face as we move toward evaluation and prescription: what are our assumptions about the bases of our society's ideas and ideology? How changeable are these ideas, and by what means?

Two further observations are also pertinent. First, political ideas may reasonably be expected to lag behind changing conditions, partly because of delay in recognizing the facts of relevant changes in conditions, and partly because of the grip that ideology has on man's capacity to perceive change and modify ideas. Second, the act of interpreting conditions as to their political relevance offers a vital opportunity for value-based opinion shaping. Whoever performs the task of describing and interpreting changes in conditions is in a position to exert major influence over the future form of political ideas. He has no choice: the mere act of reporting facts supports or refutes some value-based present policy or idea, and the reporter's own preference-based interpretation is merely a further gloss. But the result is to link the reporting with the future of ideas in irretrievable fashion.

Further problems and possibilities concerning the future evolution of ideas are considered in detail in Chapter 16. For the moment, it is sufficient to have raised the crucial points that ideas are constantly in evolution and that conditions shape ideas, but in different ways at different stages of a nation's development; and to realize that what is accepted and appropriate in preindustrial stages may be wholly out of place in advanced- or postindustrial stages. What we must still do, however, is to speculate on the implications of a political tradition dominated by liberalism, and on the role of such political thought in shaping American politics then and now.

SOME PERSPECTIVES ON TWO CENTURIES OF AMERICAN POLITICAL THOUGHT

The character, consequences, and evolution of American political ideas have been variously understood by different interpreters. Most have analyzed the American political tradition from within, or from very close to it, or with the deliberate purpose of glorifying it; this has meant that they have seen value conflicts between the two sides of liberalism as great struggles over fundamental issues. Interpretations have emphasized the consequences of men, decisions, and elections at various points in history, and stressed the importance of sectional, economic, religious, and ethnic factors in shaping present circumstances. From a more detached perspective, or a wider frame of reference, of course, the substance and development of American ideas may look quite different. I shall briefly examine three of these less familiar interpretations, because each may contain some important insight into contemporary dilemmas.

Excessive Consensus, Unrecognized Coerciveness

Several writers have developed independent and distinctive analyses that lead to the conclusion that American political ideas tend to coalesce around a sharply limited set of principles. What they have in common is the view that there is a considerable but unrecognized consensus among all Americans as to the proper values and goals of political organization and action—and that this consensus is so complete and so pervading as to threaten a gentle but tyrannical compulsion upon potential deviants, forcing them into conformity with it. Louis Hartz,[1] for example, attributes the triumph of liberalism to the absence of challenge from left or right; drawing on the European experience, where three social classes founded on feudalism's residue (aristocrats, middle-class bourgeoisie, and peasant-proletariat working classes) gave rise to distinctive political thought (conservatism, liberalism, socialism), he argued that failure to challenge liberalism led to its uncritical adoption. Liberalism thus lost the self-consciousness and self-examination that it enjoyed in Europe, and devolved instead into a deep slumber of decided opinion.

---

[1] Louis Hartz, *The Liberal Tradition in America*. New York: Harcourt, Brace and World, Inc., 1955.

Hartz sees American liberalism as so dogmatically endorsed that it sets bounds within which all political consideration must take place. Thus, there are so many unrecognized givens in American political thinking that we have more of an illusion of political conflict than is really the case: our divisions are over how much of the economic pie is to be gained by each interest or segment of the population, rather than over more fundamental questions of the method of organizing the economy or principles by which distribution should be guided. Those not like us are viewed with fear and distrust, even belligerence. Without "that sense of relativity, that spark of philosophy"[2] acquired through social diversity and social conflict, Hartz asks, can the United States resist the "deep and unwritten compulsions"[3] liberalism contains and respond rationally to the challenges of foreign and domestic problems? He concludes, ". . . instead of recapturing our past, we have got to transcend it. As for a child who is leaving adolescence, there is no going home again for America."[4]

Earlier in point of time but recently much in vogue is the analysis by the French conservative Alexis de Tocqueville.[5] Writing in 1835 after a brief swing through the newly developing nation, de Tocqueville was most concerned about the possible consequences of equality as a political value. He first noted possible tensions between liberty and equality. If liberty is defined as the right to pursue's one's own ends without restraint, then it means that some men, because of their greater talents or good fortune, will become much wealthier or more powerful than others. This is hardly equality. But if equality is sought, even if only in terms of equality of opportunity, it must be by means of limiting the attainment of some other men—which is (for them) at least a denial of liberty, if not an act of tyranny.[6] His second concern was that emphasis on equality not only made all men believe themselves as capable politically as the next, but also the converse—that all others were as (but only as) competent as oneself—with the consequence that they become incapable of independent judgment and unwilling to tolerate nonconformity, leading to an absolute tyranny of the majority. In his words, "I know of no country in which there is so little independence of mind and real freedom of discussion as in America . . . the majority raises formidable barriers around the liberty of opinion: within these barriers, an author may write what he pleases; but woe to him if he goes beyond them."[7] Worrying openly about the capacity of democratic republics to make repression into an affair of the mind, he sought to find hope in social organizations that would combat atomi-

---

[2] Ibid., p. 14.
[3] Ibid., p. 13.
[4] Ibid., p. 32.
[5] Alexis de Tocqueville, *Democracy in America*. New York: Mentor Editions, 1956.
[6] Ibid., p. 55.
[7] Ibid., pp. 117-118.

zation of individuals. In passages much like those in contemporary "mass so-ciety" writings, he placed his faith in a multitude of voluntary associations ("the substructure of freedom") and decentralization of administration.

We may well suspect that de Tocqueville's sociology was influenced by his political preferences, but that does not detract from the importance of his other projections. There is great importance to the definitions of the concepts of liberty and equality and the high probability of conflict between these values, which political thinking cannot ignore. And the forecast that enforce-ment of conformity with established political principles may be accomplished by subtle, majoritarian routes seems much more tenable now than it may have then.

Further support for the thesis that American political thought is charac-terized by compulsive consensus comes from the analysis of Daniel Boorstin. In *The Genius of American Politics*,[8] Boorstin argues that Americans have felt that they were "born free," and that an articulate political theory has never been necessary. He specifically discourages those who would try to develop a self-conscious rationale for American principles in order to facilitate contrast with other political systems of the world, saying that we are better advised merely to go on as we have in the past without trying to analyze our ideas against the European experience. Explanation of the absence of theory on the grounds that the unique circumstances of our existence have generated their own rationale is, of course, another way of declaring that we all agree fully and at the same time expressing satisfaction with that fact. In his contentment with the American tradition, and in his unwillingness to employ the wider frame of reference inherent in a contrast with European ideas, Boorstin is represen-tative of the majority of American historians referred to in the first paragraph of this section; but in his conclusions concerning the depth and intensity of the existing consensus on political values, he reflects the same convictions as Hartz and de Tocqueville.

The contemporary implications of such a consensus of ideas, if that is indeed the case, would be many. If de Tocqueville is right, the principles of equal-itarianism and majoritarianism may make for subtle tyranny of opinion and/or massive social unease and malaise. If Hartz is right, we may be in danger from unquestioned and irrational endorsement of an unrecognizedly centrist set of ideas, with resulting illusions about the range of political controversy and inability to respond to new challenges. From either analysis, it seems, we would do well to look carefully at the American capacity to develop and seriously consider real alternatives to accepted political ideas.

---

[8] Daniel Boorstin, *The Genius of American Politics* Chicago: University of Chicago Press, 1953.

Internal Contradictions, Pragmatic Accommodations

Many writers have analyzed severe social or economic problems or conditions in the United States and called for their solution through government action. At the same time, the same men, joined by other writers, have extolled the American virtues of self-reliance, individualism, limited government, laissez-faire, private enterprise, and the opportunity and desirability of becoming wealthy. But these unremarkable observations show the fundamental nature of the contradictions in liberalism: the use of government to prevent the suffering of the poor, or to assure the civil rights of Negroes, or to prop up the economic market, is simply inconsistent with and contradictory to the expressed values of laissez-faire, limited government, and private initiative. One cannot develop a powerful state for some purposes, be it national defense, welfare, or civil rights, without creating implications in other spheres of activity, such as revenue raising or expenditure patterns, which have profound effects on economy and society.

This is not to say that the contradictions have been recognized or faced. Americans have gone on with rhetoric about individualism and the dangers of government action while employing government on an ad hoc and pragmatic basis to do what seemed necessary at the moment to alleviate suffering and promote specific goals. Each use of government is viewed as an exception from general rules, and is legitimated on the basis of demonstrated need and inability of other solutions to serve that need. The result is that the rhetoric survives unchanged, continuing to act as a brake on action that is considered in the future, and the actual uses of government may fall short of the kinds of things that would fully resolve the problems involved.

Herbert Croly, as we have seen, is one of the few American thinkers to articulate this contradiction in liberalism and seek a way out of it. His not entirely specific but apparently conservative solution was to put forward a national purpose of a "morally and socially desirable distribution of wealth" and then charge the national government with both full responsibility and full power to bring it about. To break out of the self-limitations of liberalism and abandon individualism, limited government, and laissez-faire in one sweeping act was a major intellectual accomplishment. Few other writers have considered the self-constraining effects of accepting these values or the related commitments to established procedures, legalism, property rights, and the economic market; they have preferred instead to work at the less fundamental level of offering pragmatic instrumental solutions. Such solutions may, of course, serve to eliminate the causes of some problems—but it seems likely that many problems are caused, at least in part, by the very values or practices that these thinkers have adopted as givens, and that solution, therefore, will be simply unattainable within the framework in which they operate. At best, their proposals and actions can only reduce the severity of some of the symptoms, while preserving the problem forever.

For our purposes, we should carefully compare the consistency of the assumptions and premises behind ideas with the specific proposals put forward, and look for the implications of the level of analysis undertaken by a thinker. A fundamental analysis accompanied by an incremental solution, for example, suggests a perhaps unrecognized pragmatic accommodation. Pragmatism has many virtues, of course, but we are at least entitled to identify logical inconsistency when we find it. But we should not underestimate the great dilemma that this section spotlights: in the modern world, government is a necessary instrument; but power in government can be a threat to individual freedom and achievement.

Ideologized Quiescence, Repressive Stability

This set of speculations is more a series of questions than a coherent interpretation. The basic challenge inherent in these questions is addressed to the issue of how fully the admittedly dominant elements of liberal political thought have really been shared among the population generally. Where the consensus school saw practically all men genuinely sharing the values of property rights, individualism, and the free enterprise system (and at times being "captured" by such beliefs), this perspective would leave open the possibility that men at the lower levels of society, in fact, hold quite distinctive values and priorities. It premises distinctive interests along socioeconomic class lines, such that the characteristic posture of major elements within the society is one of conflict rather than consensus. At times, of course, the reality of this conflict may be concealed, either because of diversionary events, dramatic threats, or the success of promulgated ideology that is supportive of the status quo.

Several possibilities flow from the premise of intrasocietal conflicts of interest along socioeconomic lines. If paralleled by value differences, it would suggest that liberalism is not as pervasive within the society as other interpretations assume, and that liberalism is really the doctrine only of the middle and upper classes. As such, the values and priorities of liberalism may be forced upon the lower classes, either through socializing processes for lower class leaders who come to power in some way, through the deliberate promotion of liberal ideology in the media and the public school system, or through occasional uses of physical coercion at moments when important interests of the status quo are threatened. Established leaders may encourage lower classes to be quiescent, either by stressing the hopelessness of efforts to change the situation, or by providing assurances that lower class interests are really being looked after. In an interesting speculative essay, Murray Edelman argues that the manipulation of revered symbols by leaders may suffice to divert and reassure masses, thereby preventing them from developing coherent demands and seeking their satisfaction.

If such conflicts of interest are *not* paralleled by value differences (and/or, if the existence of conflict is not perceived), it may be due to the success of the promulgation of the dominant ideology onto the lower classes. In this regard, the historic emphasis in the United States on the importance of assimilating immigrants, on avoiding things un-American, and the extensive and compulsory public school systems, may all take on new implications: they may have served important functions in the process of homogenizing potentially divergent values and priorities into a single package reflecting the (liberal) preferences of dominant people. Thus, the lower classes are subjected to a kind of "false consciousness" in which they come to believe that there are no alternatives but to go along with their lot.

In either event, the groundwork is laid for leaders to ignore, discourage, or repress (either violently or through the established legal processes) the aspirations of the lower classes. Race relations is often cited as an example of this effect: many Negroes have apparently accepted an essentially "white" value structure, which denigrates the characteristics and qualities of blacks, surrounds them with rationalizations for their deprived state, sets up innumerable barriers to their self-extrication from their situation, offers symbolic satisfactions in the form of rhetoric and statutes on the books, and is ready to employ overwhelming repressive force with complete conviction that it is upholding a neutral "law and order."

These are sobering possibilities, difficult to either prove *or* refute. Extensive empirical research would be required to assess the extent of distinctiveness in relevant values, or to objectively analyze the extent of real conflict of interest between classes. Such research would be difficult to do with reference to the past because of the unavailability of data, and with reference to both past and present because of the intimate involvement of value premises in structuring inquiry and interpretation. But the mere articulation of this distinctive possibility emphasizes the need for careful examination of our assumptions, and the need for a wide frame of reference in analysis.

Finally, even this brief review of three alternative interpretations of the character and role of American political ideas suggests that many questions remain open. We simply do not know how widely shared liberalism has been— whether it is an elite-based political doctrine, or a society-wide ideology; nor in what ways its components have affected political actions—whether they are a rationalization for action in accordance with selfish interest, the true basis for elite behavior, or an instrument manipulated by elites to control masses. But these are questions to which we may aspire to find answers through careful exploration of the facts of the present, and this type of inquiry should form part of our empirical investigations. In short, we should seek evidence as to the extent of sharing of liberal ideas, and the uses of these ideas, through research into contemporary attitudes and behavior. We should also shift toward questions of a different order: a much more concrete assessment of the hard realities of the present distribution of power in the United States, and of the ways in which, given that distribution of power, change may still occur. This is the point at which I would urge readers to make use of the evidence presented in the companion volume *Power and Change in the United States: Empirical Findings and Their Implications.* Those who do not have the time or the inclination to take on such a systematic investigation may nevertheless profit from reviewing such facts about power distribution and usage, political values and ideology, and how change occurs, as they may have gleaned from their observation of American politics.

CHAPTER 16

Contemporary Directions in American Political Thought

4261

WE have come to the crucial stage of this experiment. If we are to realize some returns on the investment made in the preceding sections, it must come from rational and politically sophisticated judgment about prescriptions made by the authors represented in the following chapters. In a sense, this body of ideas is not only the ultimate test for individual students seeking independent convictions about their personal political positions, but also for the future of the United States as a viable polity. Unless, by default, the status quo is to be permitted to shape the future, choices must be made from (or in reaction to) this body of prescriptions; failure to make them promptly, and to act on them decisively, of course, amounts to a choice in favor of the determinism inherent in the status quo. I believe the selections that follow represent a wide range of contemporary American ideas, and that the future (assuming there is to be one) must be found among them.

Up to this point, we have been building a sense of the substance and evolution of liberalism, and a characterization of some salient features of power distribution and usage in the United States. We have seen a central thread of identifiable political ideas, values, and ideology as supporting a set of established institutions and processes that are managed by a relatively small and semipermanent body of people who are socially and economically distinct from the general public; and we have looked at this total structure in a context of late 20th century conditions and circumstances. The following questions are before us now: Where is this whole apparatus heading? Is it producing satisfactory results, either in terms of the quality of life of its citizens, or the problems with which it is confronted? If not, what should properly be its goals, and how can they be realized? In specific terms, can the American political system be modified so as to produce more appropriate results (and, if so, how), or can requisite changes be accomplished only through some more fundamental reconstruction (and, if so, what and how)?

The answers to these questions can be provided only by the independent judgment of concerned individuals. I shall confine my efforts in this chapter to a somewhat personalized consideration of what seem to me to be the kinds of problems and pressures that liberalism faces today, and to some brief speculation about what may lie ahead. The authors included in the following chapters are more than capable of speaking for themselves, as are readers of judging them, and so I shall attempt no synthesis or commentary on their works.

LATE 20TH CENTURY LIBERALISM

As I have suggested in previous chapters, the basic core elements of liberalism have been remarkably resilient, evolving only marginally through the years. The essential components of liberalism today are not very much different from what they were in the formative years of the 18th century. Principal among them are individualism and the concept of property rights in most cases, followed by human rights and particular equality. Flowing from these are the principles of limited government, the sanctity of contract, a heavy emphasis on procedural regularity, and a ubiquitous and tenacious devotion to legalism. Related values include materialism and profit-orientation; historical accompaniments, perhaps not necessarily associated, include religion and racism. This unadorned summary identifies only salient central threads, and major carriers of the liberal tradition range from the human rights side to the more exclusively property-oriented side. The entire package of values has become so thoroughly accepted and merged with the dominant political ideology that its presence often goes unrecognized by members of the society.

While these liberal values have remained roughly constant over the last two centuries, the United States has gone through drastic changes in economic, social, and international circumstances. The pace of change has accelerated to the point where twenty years now brings about technological and socioeconomic changes equivalent to the passage of centuries in the past. The problem of liberalism today is essentially summed up in the contrast between the permanency of its basic values and the increasing rapidity of change in its surrounding environment: ideas emerging from the bucolic days of the mid-18th century may simply be unequal to the conditions and problems of a drastically different country in the last third of the 20th century. As long ago as the first decade of this century, Herbert Croly argued that Jeffersonian individualism, insistence upon limited government, and granting of primacy to property rights made it impossible to cope with the growth of corporate power, the inequities of economic distributions, and the pressures of industrialization; with the passage of another sixty years, such pressures have, if anything, worsened, and they have been supplemented by racial and international crises unimagined by Croly.

Liberalism has shifted ground somewhat, but without altering the fundamental commitments outlined above. Most liberals have accepted the idea of using government where and when essential to relieve the most prominent inequities and dislocations of advancing technology and accompanying social and economic change. Some have not, of course, and there has been a steady criticism directed by the Manchester liberals at what they see as excessive intervention by government into the market economy. A theoretical justification for use of government as an economy-aiding device was provided by the work of John Maynard Keynes, however, and adapted into the vocabulary and practice of most American liberals as a means of legitimating marginal supports for an obviously nonself-regulating capitalist system. What has evolved is a kind of patchwork accommodation, achieved by ad hoc responses to crisis after crisis, producing the series of government programs known under the general rubric of the "welfare state." Each particular government program is spurred by a demonstration of the need and justified by the argument that no other source of amelioration is at hand. But little attention is paid to the overall implications of the assumption of such responsibilities or the general problem of the rationale under which government is to be employed, and the net result is that the basic values of limited government and the paramountcy of property rights remain unaffected. Nor are they without effect: the scope of government action is regularly constrained by traditional limitations of powers and by unwillingness to intrude upon the property rights of individuals or corporations. Thus, the problems that give rise to the perceived need for government action are less than fully dealt with—government, after all, can only act within the parameters set by the limited government/property rights commitments—and the cycle of worsening problems-inadequate action goes on.

This much was foreseen by Croly, who insisted that individualism, limited government, and the paramountcy of property rights would result in the inability to effectively employ the only competent agency of control over the economy and over the processes of industrialization, urbanization, and other areas of social change. He did not foresee the two most pressing problems of the late 20th century, of course: race relations and security in an unstable and threatening international environment. But some of the same basic values of liberalism, together with associated characteristics endemic to the American culture (particularly the racism that liberalism tends to institutionalize), bear upon the capacity of the political system to deal with these problems in much the same way as he marked out in regard to problems of economic distribution and management of social change. Thus, liberalism's problem is not new, but it may perhaps be more acute than in Croly's day. Are the values and ideas of the past still viable today, or has liberalism reached the end of the range of adaptability of its basic values?

Let me say immediately and emphatically that the teachings of American history are all to the effect that liberalism has a resiliency and a flexibility that are simply not known to other political systems. For two hundred years, the basic values of liberalism have sustained and nurtured a political system, which, while favored by conditions and by the growth of a strong and plentiful economy, has still shown an independent capacity to deliver what its members apparently have sought while retaining their loyalty and preserving itself. These are no mean achievements: under the umbrella provided by the stability of the American political system, vast numbers of new participants—women, propertyless men, and immigrants, have been absorbed peacefully; staggering changes have been accommodated; and a comparatively high level of democratic freedom has been maintained throughout. This is a tremendous achievement, deserving of a wholesome respect and the closest analysis. Any set of political values that can provide the flexibility necessary to accomplish these results must be given favorable odds on continuing to do so. It is simply illogical to dismiss liberalism in the face of this history, and it is wrong to deny its achievements to date.

But this is only to say that the question of its continued viability is a worthy and important one, requiring specific analysis of its prior sources and present circumstances. I think there are at least five major reasons why liberalism has survived and remained so completely dominant in the United States. I shall identify them briefly, in order to build a characterization of the bases of liberalism's past flexibility that can serve to assess the prospects for more of the same.

1. *The authority and comprehensiveness with which the basic liberal values are communicated and established as uncontestable.* I think the United States is distinct not only in its material resources and standard of living, but in a popular sense of uniqueness and moral superiority—and I do not think these are 20th century innovations. From the War of Independence on, Americans

have talked and acted as if they had something important to demonstrate to the less fortunate peoples of the world; part empirical fact and part cultural arrogance, this is a repeated phenomenon of every period in American history. It may result, in part, from the perceived need to create a separate identity with which waves of immigrants could be indoctrinated. This self-consciousness is not simple nationalism, although there has been much of that too; nor is it unmixed with uncertainty and fear of being "played for a sucker." But the net result is to lead toward special emphasis on things American, and on the validity and propriety of what we have and do in all matters, economic and political. Add to this the early and extensive availability of a public education system, broad and inclusive communication networks, and finally the great and growing incidence of higher education, and I think there results a highly effective system for instilling established and orthodox beliefs and ideology, perhaps more than any other society has ever known. It is not a coercive, but a voluntary process—made possible by wealth, technology, predisposition, and circumstances. It is greatly aided, of course, by the fact that to most leaders and by most accepted standards, liberalism (or whatever one chooses to call the American system) has apparently worked well. Overall, the result is to create very widely shared and deeply held commitments to particular assumptions and processes. When new needs are felt by individual citizens, they are likely to be unconsciously shaped into the forms and language of liberalism, and thus they can be handled by the established political system. It becomes difficult for Americans to even think of demands or possible products that might be desirable to obtain through politics, outside of the framework provided by liberalism as it has been absorbed into ideology and practice. Those who do, and who articulate their demands, are simply not understood, and may be suspected of being captives of foreign and perhaps, therefore, dangerous beliefs.

    2. *Circumstances which permit issues to be seen in economic terms and, therefore, accommodated.* Conflict between people or groups or other units of power within a political system may arise over a wide number of issues—economic interests, status aspirations, policy goals, political power, etc. Issues are soluble or not according to the nature of the conflict and the resources available to satisfy the parties. I think that conflict has been accommodated relatively easily in this country, and that liberal values have, therefore, endured unchanged, because the materialist orientation of Americans has channeled many issues into chiefly economic terms. Where the demands of a rising group were not originally expressed in economic terms, they were converted into economic dimensions and/or mollified by delivery of economic rewards by the adroit (though perhaps unconscious) action of established elites. In this country in the past two centuries, the easiest conflict to resolve was an

economic conflict because resources were so plentiful and the economic product was constantly growing. This meant that no established group had to be deprived of any significant presently enjoyed rewards in order to deliver on the demands. In other words, one secret of liberalism's success was its capacity to mute conflict by converting demands into economic form, where they could be satisfied by merely increasing the size of the total economic product, thus not taking anything away from the "haves" while delivering tangible rewards to the "have-nots." I do not mean that we have had no serious conflicts, nor that economic conflicts are always politely handled and gently settled; the parties at any given time may well believe that they are fighting for possession of very scarce resources, or those who have may be very reluctant to part with the prospect of getting more, and the battle may be bitter. But overall, and under the conditions of an expanding economic product, it has been possible to resolve a rather large share of the conflict that has developed in the United States in this way, in some cases through the use of government as the agency of transfer of goods and services from one group to another. The success of this route has been aided by the shared property orientation of all Americans, which has meant that the "have-nots" first acknowledge certain self-limitations and then are satisfied with receiving things that are relatively uncostly for the "haves" to yield. The "have-nots," for example, are quite likely to be satisfied with a larger share of the profits, or with higher wages, or unemployment compensation, and their demands stop well short of seeking fundamental alteration of the productive mechanism or basic changes in the allocation of political power.

3. *Articulate leaders representing specific interests, regions, and groups have seen themselves as gaining at least some of their goals, and not as being constant losers.* (This is the principle of cross-cutting cleavages; it ignores the question of whether some inert, discouraged, or inarticulate individuals or classes ever see themselves as gaining their goals, referring only to the apparent fact that accepted leaders of participant groups have found cause to believe they were reaching some of their ends.) This effect may be a product of circumstances, caused by the large size and internal diversity of the United States. But it is also a consistent rationalization of liberalism, and the manifestation of its political style. Leaders are conditioned to the expectation of diversity among interests, so that the balancing of demands of one group with countervailing demands of another—as a means of maintaining the essential status quo—becomes part of the technique of management of the polity that rests on liberal assumptions. Thus interest, diversity, circumstances, and style combine to make for a politics of shifting coalitions. When class-based lines threaten, they may be moderated by, for example, the waving of the "bloody shirt" of the Civil War, and the northern farmers and workers draw away

DIRECTIONS IN AMERICAN POLITICAL THOUGHT

from southern tenant farmers and laborers, as occurred in 1892. Ethnic and religious ties cross political party loyalties, and the cities are ranged against the rural areas on some issues. The electoral system operates to promote these divisions and free-flowing alliances by presenting choices based on state, regional, and national loyalties at the same time and through the same party structure. The result is that a specific person or interest sometimes wins and sometimes loses. The crucial point is that no established participant loses consistently; if they did, they might conclude that the system itself was loaded against them. If most active interests in the society can be prevented from reaching this point by a politics of many and fluid coalitions, the prospect of their satisfaction and consequent attachment to the system itself is greatly enhanced. Most political sociologists see this cross-cutting of cleavages as a key to stability, if not to the attainment of democracy itself. Clearly, where such an effect is really operative, it leads to far less challenge to the fundamental values and assumptions that underlie the polity. Not investigated to any substantial extent, however, is the possibility that substantial segments of the population never win, are not participants, and are discouraged or prevented from voicing their complaints.

An associated effect is the opportunity that this form of support for the status quo provides for a continuing body of persons in key positions to assert their version of what is proper for government to do under all the circumstances. In other words, continued counterbalancing of disparate forces within the polity leads to roughly the status quo. In that context, the long-term, regular players in the process are enabled to influence all the others, either as intermediaries or as actors who have the success of the whole enterprise rather than mere personal aggrandizement at heart. Such regulars constitute an establishment, whose principal concern is to preserve the process and the channels by which negotiation and compromise can proceed and the essential nature of the system be maintained. For both of these reasons, the basic values of liberalism emerge relatively unchallenged and unaffected despite much apparent conflict and adjustment between opposing interests. The establishment succeeds by appearing to support the middle way every time—never too far in one direction or the other. Drawing on established centrist ideology, which endorses behavior according to the regular procedures and methods of the law, the establishment is able to carve out for itself both a key position as influencer of the actual results and an image as defender of the system itself. Over time, this can build up to an impressive credence in the eyes of members of the society and a self-fulfilling capacity as arbiter of the proper way to act.

4. *Political thought and controversy has concentrated on the procedures of politics, to the exclusion of consideration of the substance of what is done*

by government. This is the most important single point to be made about the longevity and flexibility of liberalism. The focus on procedural regularity and on legalism has been noted since our earliest consideration of the elements of liberalism. We have seen that the empiricists too have been fascinated by the processes through which men take part in politics and share in the making of decisions. All of these characteristics are matters about which relatively high levels of agreement may be anticipated. Practically everybody within the political system can be expected to approve, endorse and defend the democratic freedoms of speech, voting, due process, etc. They are both a constant source and reminder of shared loyalties and relatively noncontroversial means of holding people together. They contrast sharply, for example, with the prospect of disagreement over precise specification of the substance of what government should do in regard to a problem. The latter makes for disagreement and discord, the former for solidarity and harmony. For those who do not wish to change from the present substance of what government is doing, and for those who simply wish to avoid discord, it is very tempting to try to cast issues in terms of procedural questions. All the heat and bitterness of argument over the issue of what government should be doing can be diffused into relatively unthreatening discussion of the proper application of agreed and shared procedural means by which the government decision is to be taken. Of course, the availability of means determines the chances of attaining the ends that one may be seeking, and many political actors know this very well, but still it is both tempting and politically successful to convert the issue into one that is essentially procedural. I suggest that perhaps in reaction to the trauma of the Civil War (surely a period when people came to care greatly about the substance of government action), the focus of American political discourse shifted to the processes and means by which government actions were decided upon, rather than the substance of what it did. And, of course, as long as the attention of people and political actors is on the procedures by which decisions are made rather than on the rightness or wrongness of the decisions themselves, there is likely to be little question of the values underlying the system or its decisions.

5. *The focus on procedure to the exclusion of substance leads to a strong emphasis on law and order as a virtue in its own right—and to an insistence upon the making of neutral judgments only.* Closely related to the previous point is the special status accorded to the law and orderly legal processes by liberalism's legalistic commitment. Clearly, a legal system that permits change only in accordance with processes and standards that it sets up is a system that helps to channel the kinds of demands that can legitimately be made. Only certain kinds of claims can be given credence and acted upon and the manner in which they are to be handled is specified. Dominant interests do not go

to the trouble of setting up a legal system that is unfriendly to the status quo. The channeling and exclusions accomplished by the law will operate to the advantage of those who are currently in power; it would be a rare legal system that did *not* operate to defend the status quo. *What we mean by the liberal emphasis on legalism, therefore, is that there is a heavy emphasis on preserving the status quo as such under the guise of a purportedly neutral abidance by the law.* Many citizens never make the connection, of course; but the law is an instrument of social control, adherence to which permits the dominant to condition the opportunities of nonelites to gain a greater share in the control of public policy. The liberal emphasis on the sanctity of the law is a means by which challenges to its basic values can be deflected and rendered illegitimate in the eyes of many. The principle of "law and order," familiar and loyalty-provoking as it is, amounts to not much more (in the absence of other considerations) than a plea to preserve the status quo in all its essential outlines. Granted that change is often said to be possible through orderly processes of the law, those processes are controlled by men least likely to be in favor of change, and the substance of the law itself is designed to protect the property and other rights of the "haves" under the present system. Any set of rules, it should be clear, establishes a range of goals that are attainable through those rules. There is no such thing as an utterly neutral set of rules, for as soon as the rules begin to prescribe who shall be players and how they shall play, the loading of the dice has begun. Thus, what appears to some (usually those advantaged by the established order) as neutral rules of law with a sanctity and essence that transcends the knowledge and capacity of mere man, may be simply a device whereby the "have-nots" are contained. This is not to say that even the "have-nots" are likely to recognize this: the emphasis of liberalism on the law, and on legalism generally, permeats all levels of the society and becomes an independent factor in inducing acceptance of the established order—and, of course, of the existing values and standards of liberalism. On those occasions when, having survived the channeling and blunting effects of the established procedure, new values or priorities are projected into a decision-making arena, dominant elements can still change or violate the rules to assure their own goals. There is thus a double set of defenses for established elements in the society: a first line of procedural barriers, on which much attention focuses; and a second line of substantive values, change in which may be simply resisted or prevented, or else deflected by means of a new or revised rhetorical interpretation unaccompanied by tangible consequences.

These several factors are not intended as a comprehensive catalogue of the reasons for the remarkable longevity and flexibility of liberalism, but they do suggest the scope and depth to which liberalism is rooted and has defenses within the American system. Oddsmakers would be well advised to wager on the continued marginal evolution of liberal values and ideas, with those limited changes necessitated by circumstances. Neither conservatives nor radicals should be optimistic. But, just as any set of values and rules operates to set some limits on the range of goals that can be achieved through them, so does the package that we know as liberalism contain within it inherent limits. *Liberalism establishes boundaries as to what can be done, and how it can be done, within the American political system.* If conditions are perceived to require, or the people or other units of power come to desire, ends that are not attainable without modification of the basic liberal values and practices—then it is at least theoretically possible that substantial modification could be wrought; or after a sustained period of incremental change, quite substantial changes might result in the basic elements of the liberal tradition. But, if it is to evolve with fundamental values intact (disregarding merely rhetorical changes in interpretations of basic values), there would seem to be limits to its flexibility. These alternatives depend upon the nature of the pressures on liberalism today, and the extent to which these pressures cut to the central core of liberal values and/or undermine some of the foregoing bases of flexibility and longevity. In seeking an answer to the question of whether liberalism is still viable in the late 20th century, or whether it is so time-specific and condition-specific that it is simply outmoded, we must examine the kinds of pressures and circumstances that are involved.

THE SCOPE OF THE CONTEMPORARY CHALLENGE TO LIBERALISM: THREE ILLUSTRATIVE DIMENSIONS

This discussion has analyzed *ideas* in a context of *policy problems* and in the light of experience as to the *behavior of political actors.* These are three different, though closely related, dimensions of analysis. Continuing the illustrative rather than comprehensive approach of the previous section, I shall touch on some highlights of the contemporary challenge to liberalism in each of these three dimensions.

1. *Ideas: changes in the level, character, and focus of political thinking.* Starting in the late 1950's, and accelerating rapidly in the 1960's, political analysis and evaluation on the part of the liberal intellectuals and some segments of nonelites as well began to proceed along distinctively new lines. (In some ways, the new approach was an adoption, with certain differences in premises, of the long-standing criteria and orientation of the often-ignored American conservative.) Essentially, both analysis and evaluation were directed at more fundamental levels; they accepted fewer givens, asked more

comprehensive questions, and used more basic standards for judgment. The
new politics refused to see problems in isolation, as mere unfortunate by-products of a benevolent and desirable economic or political system: instead, they
began to see problems in context, as rooted in the very nature of the economy
or the underlying value system that sustained both economy and polity. Instead of assuming that the structure and purposes of American politics were
fixed, inevitable and beneficial to all, they began to ask whether basic changes
might not result in fuller delivery on some of the familiar but in the eyes of
many, clearly unfulfilled promises.

Most important of all, the focus of political thinking began to shift away
from rules and procedures and decision-making processes toward the substance
of government action. For many, the realization came slowly, but when it
came the effect was profound: rules and procedures could be (and frequently
were) used as means of serving the interests of the dominant, and uncritical
devotion to legalism could be eternally self-defeating. The lesson was taught
both openly and subtly, sometimes because the established rules were brazenly
misapplied (southern courts and sheriffs were perhaps the most visible teachers
in this period) and sometimes because they were followed to the letter and used
to legitimate injustice (as the legal permanence of de facto school segregation
in northern cities attests). The new politics, operating with a comprehensive,
fundamental, contextual perspective, began to ask what all these niceties of
procedure meant for the important questions of how people were treated by
their government and the quality of their lives generally. Taking the perspective of consumers, and looking at what was coming out of the governmental
process instead of how things went in, intellectuals and activists developed a
whole new set of standards for evaluation of politics. Deliberately eschewing
the technocratic and range-of-the-possible standards of the liberal establishment, they centered first on the quality of life (How do people *feel?* Are their
legitimate desires served by this system? Are their lives meaningful and productive?) and second, on the extent to which such values as justice and
equality are actually realized. The latter standard implied contrasting the nature of public problems such as ghetto life or the rural poverty cycle or the
deterioration and paralysis of the cities with the scale and substance of public
(government) action. In every case, the product of the American governmental process was seen as so minimal, grudging, and supportive of identifiable causes of the problems themselves, that judgments were inclined to be
harsh and impatient.

If the system is so good, why is its product so bad? This question was the
next step in the growing challenge to the fundamentals underlying liberalism
in the late 1960's. Orthodox liberals who could see no further than the established procedures, and who could not or would not comprehend the basis

for the challenge mounted, became a special target. The ensuing dialogue led many of the new analysts to reexamination of the premises underlying liberalism, and to the rejection of many of them. The horror that many saw in the Vietnam War hastened the process, and provided a cutting edge of self-awareness even after rejection of the war became widely shared: Was the war an error born of miscalculation and magnified by the fact that we have not won, or was it a manifestation of basic American values and processes, seriously out of touch with standards of decency and humanity? Those who reached the latter conclusion, clearly, could no longer accept the standard package of liberal values and ideology. They were led to challenge the process itself, asking whether rules and practices so supportive of the status quo should be perpetuated, and whether there was potential utility in the effort to work within their confines. The research and concepts of social science, so oriented toward "scientific" and technocratic rather than humanistic purposes, were challenged by many. "Law and order" was challenged as an independent value: it too often appeared to be used as an excuse for rigid perpetuation of the status quo, detached from the perceived realities of police repression, creditors' exploitation, and legitimation of injustice.

The critical intellectual shift that produced these challenges was one of level and of focus of attention. Gone were pragmatic efforts to deal with the surface manifestations of social dislocations, as well as past acceptance of established institutions and practices as the parameters within which marginal ameliorations sufficient to reduce complaint to tolerable levels must be achieved. Newly present were sensitivity to the quality of peoples' lives in the absolute, rather than relative or comparative, sense; strong ethical commitments to results that approximate justice and equality; and substantive standards of measurement that contrast the product of the political system with the depth and scope of the problems that confront it. The application of these standards will become obvious in the consideration of the nature of public policy problems that follows.

2. *Policy problems: new problems raise different and deeper-cutting issues.* The problems and conditions of the late 20th century are not just unprecedented in severity and breadth of impact; they are also unique in the way they raise visible challenges to the basic values of liberalism and expose its contradictions. It is in the nature of these problems to cut into the very core of individual values and cause people to take sides on raw fundamentals—a sometimes unappetizing but always educational sight. Let us look at the way some representative examples perform this act.

a. *Race relations.* Perhaps in a class by itself as a problem capable of inciting value-based conflict, race relations resurfaced with the desegregation decision of 1954 and has risen in importance ever since. A probably still moderate stage was reached in the late 1960's with waves of ghetto riots and accompanying black power popularity. Of all groups with self-perceptions of deprivation in the United States, black power advocates make the most fundamental attack on the value structure, procedures, and product of what they see as an implacably hostile white society. It may be a sounder analysis to see black power as a modern version of an enduring but normally suppressed American tradition paralleling liberalism—one that resists racism in the name of fraternity, community, and equality.[1] Wendell Phillips, William H. Garrison, W. E. B. DuBois, and Malcolm X, for all their obvious disparities, share these characteristics. Recent writers have taken increasingly uncompromising stands in behalf of black identity and self-determination, but they retain the hope of coalition with those whites who can shed racist values and condescension, and who need blacks in order to achieve their own goals.

Drawing on revolutionary anticolonial writings from the third world, Stokely Carmichael and Charles Hamilton analogize the situation of American Negroes to that of oppressed black people throughout the world.[2] The colonial analogy carries over to the situation of blacks in the United States only in the most general sense of shared exploitation, of course; the specific circumstances of the American situation are much less favorable to black success than they were for colonial peoples in the post-World War II world. The black population of the United States is a tiny minority, where most colonial countries had nonwhite majorities. Relatively little remains of the indigenous culture of the American black man by comparison with the vitality of native and tribal culture on the other continents—and what there is must contend with a heavy overlay of American culture, with all its white-superiority components. Also, the family structure of American blacks has not yet fully recovered from the systematic decimation that it suffered during two centuries of slavery and another of caste status, so that motivation necessary for sustained self-improvement or purposeful and prideful opposition have been equally difficult to generate.

But although the colonial analogy is not applicable to the American racial situation in specific terms, it does call attention to characteristics that captives of liberal analogy might not otherwise see. Carmichael and Hamilton use it to itemize the characteristics of what they call "institutionalized racism"— the practices by which supposedly neutral rules and legal provisions, supported by language and values, operate to enforce white exploitation and the status quo even in the absence of deliberate intent. Their goal is to create an independent black sense of self-worth, identity, and humanity. They see no alternative for black men but to seek such ends by means of full-scale

---

[1] I am indebted for this suggestion to Professor Robert Pranger of the University of Washington; he is not to be charged with this formulation, however.
[2] Stokely Carmichael and Charles V. Hamilton, *Black Power: The Politics of Liberation in America* (New York: Vintage Books, 1967)

reconstruction of the basic values of the dominant white society. The enormity of this task is acknowledged, but the alternative is seen as guerrilla warfare and race (or societal) suicide.

In the course of developing, articulating, and acting out this position, black power advocates have been blamed for more or less spontaneous riots, attacked by black and white alike for fomenting revolution, and viewed as agents of the communist conspiracy. It is at least clear that their call has reached to the very basic levels of deeply held values on both sides. Although not much understanding is generated during the course of the conflict, it is this exposure of values and attitudes, and the critical awareness of ideology and practice that is spurred, which will in the long run determine the future of liberalism. Both sophisticated observers and daily participants have been forced to ask whether the established practices and limitations can endure these tensions. We may move to a domestic garrison state, or to basic change after reconsideration of the proper nature of fundamental values and priorities; the direction is as yet unclear, but it does not seem likely that we can contrive to remain unaffected.

b. *Distributions of the economic product.* The key problems in the economic sphere center around technology, responsibility, and momentum. With an immensely productive and technologically sophisticated economy, it seems an anomaly to some that there should be literally millions of people apparently bypassed by affluence and instead trapped in a generationally repeated cycle of poverty. It is not just a matter of lack of appropriate training, or temporary unemployment because of changes in productive techniques, but a more or less total detachment from the society and a fundamental unemployability because of lack of both opportunity *and* psychic motivation. But devising means of directing a share of the American abundance toward such people, and of promoting their entrance into the society's affluence, proves to be much more difficult than the definition of their problem.

Several analyses of the American economy in the late 1960's suggest that technological sophistication and the current organizational structure combine to give it a self-fulfilling and semiautonomous character: the capacity of the economy to produce particular goods and services leads to deliberate creation of a demand for such products, a cycle that, if repeated often enough, could result in replacing man's real wants with a substitute package made up of what the economy finds it technically practical and profitable to produce. This spectre of uncontrollability and inevitability is heightened by the realization that the vast expenditures directed by government toward particular sectors of the economy (i.e., military spending) creates employment expectations and other investments that could be severely disrupted by relatively slight shifts in world conditions or government priorities.

There is thus the possibility of a highly productive and technically so-phisticated machine, operating with massive momentum but not responsible to any persons or groups of people with independent judgmental capacity. The corporation acts, but no individuals bear responsibility for what it does; hundreds of times over, the economy rumbles on, creating wants in the image of its technological capacities, and drawing certain people into prearranged slots at comfortable salaries so that they can become proper consumers, while other people are simply ignored. These are images that confront the in-dividualist-capitalist ethic of liberalism with the charge of simple irrelevance and threaten the core values of liberalism at their most sensitive economic origins. The prospect of the subjugation of man to the technostructure leads some to ask whether the rhetoric of capitalism is not hopelessly out of date, necessitating replacement by bold new forms of public ownership and/or control.

An associated concern is that, spurred by the advance of rationalism in the form of technology, the society's standards of judgment and practices become exclusively quantitative, standardized, and profit-oriented. Qualitative, hu-manistic criteria are difficult to operationalize and apply, and perhaps threat-ening to investments in the present manner of doing things, and it may be tempting to ignore them.

c. *Foreign policy.* The Vietnam War operated as a major catalyst, politi-cizing thousands if not millions of people, young and old, and raising basic questions not only about the principles on which foreign policy should be based, but also about the propriety of traditional American if not liberal values. Fear and stringent repression have always been associated with so-cialism and communism in American history, and there is undoubtedly much insight to be gained into the ideology and value structure of Americans from an effort to understand why communism creates such acute anxieties. Whether it develops among nonelites spontaneously out of their property orientations, religious commitments, or personal freedom ethos, or merely because elites find it a convenient social control mechanism, there can be little doubt that communism has been a uniquely frightening and activating stimulus in Ameri-can political behavior. Nevertheless, the trauma of the Vietnam War led some people to openly challenge the prevailing and heretofore unquestioned as-sumption that the communist countries are an unparalleled evil to be dealt with only through overwhelming military superiority. Indeed, some charged the United States with responsibility for starting the Cold War and acting to hold back social change around the world. Other saw a relentless search for markets, inspired by the particular state of the American economy, as the chief thrust behind United States foreign policy.

Criticism of the Vietnam experience took many levels, of course, and some were less fundamental than just described. But questions about the contemporary propriety of the policy of containment, or the tactics of American intelligence agents in other countries, or the existence of a military-industrial complex that promotes defense expenditures at all costs, or the determinism of the search-for-markets argument, also succeed in raising value-conflict issues. Sooner or later, discussion of such questions begins to center around what American premises and priorities and procedures should be, and the relationship between behavior abroad and democracy at home. At some point, clearly, ruthless or unprincipled tactics with regard to other countries and peoples can not be squared with claims to being a great "democratic" nation deserving of the respect of others. It is just not possible to talk about current foreign policy questions without reaching these vital dimensions; nor, under the conditions of the late 20th century, is it possible to ignore foreign policy as an intimate dimension of government activity with direct personal impact.

d. *The sharing of power.* Less well recognized, but increasingly a question that exposes basic divisions, is the issue of citizen participation—or "participatory democracy" or "student power," in its variant forms. The critical question being raised under this rubric is whether forms and processes of government are to remain fixed in their present shape, operated by their current managers with premises and priorities representative chiefly of the status quo. It is thus an issue both of form and of substance; it asks (as always), who is to wield power and in what ways? The thrust toward acquiring a larger share of power in the hands of the currently less powerful—the poor, blacks, students, workers—contains within it the secondary purpose of employing that new power to reshape the actions and priorities of governing bodies. If thwarted in the quest for inclusion within the sphere of present power-wielders, the technique of establishing parallel institutions to which allegiance is given may serve to focus the issue and gain the ultimate goals.

Decentralization and individual involvement have long been cardinal principles of both conservatives and Manchester liberals, and so citizen participation has the capacity to merge left and right. It encounters resistance from many established liberals, partly on the grounds that the national government is an adequate innovator whose intentions will be thwarted by citizen participants, and partly on the grounds that the familiar rules and procedures do not and should not accommodate wide sharing of power. As the argument develops, all parties are forced into examination of both priorities between established methods and desired goals and the substance of the premises and values on which they propose to act. One does not lightly revise power distributions in a polity that reveres established procedures and sees independent validity to the law and the institutions surrounding it; the attempt to do so—and this principle is a major purpose of that thrust—is bound to open up fundamental value questions.

These four policy problems range across the agenda of American politics, from the domestic "gut" issue of race relations to the more abstract question of how to manage the economy, then to foreign policy, hitherto an area of low public salience or concern, and back to a question of governmental structure and purpose. Even in this illustrative use, their scope and substance suggests the variety of contemporary challenges to the operative premises of the American system. Inherent in the problems themselves is the stimulus to reexamine basic liberal values; political dialogue thus proceeds with new and different standards and concerns different and deeper-cutting issues—and, as we shall see, provokes new political alignments and a new kind of conflict pattern.

3. *People and process: the end of cross-cutting cleavages?* It would be remarkable if these new standards and new issues did not yield a new set of political alignments; but what is really distinctive is that they at least threaten to create a kind of politics not known since pre-Civil War days. We may be moving toward a politics resembling a zero-sum game, where everything one party wins comes out of the treasured possessions of the other side, making the latter a loser to the exact extent that the former becomes a winner. Two points must be made. *First,* today's issues, for the first time since the Civil War, are principally noneconomic in character and they do not appear capable of being postponed or muted by delivering economic rewards; even if they were, the conditions and requirements of the present American economy might necessitate dangerous overseas adventures in order to expand enough to do so. *Second,* and partly as a consequence of the first, each of today's issues seem to line up the same people on winning and losing sides, thus causing a shift from a politics of cross-cutting cleavages to one of consistent, rigid divisions. Let us look at each of these possibilities in more detail.

If I am correct in assuming that race relations and foreign policy are two of the most vital issues of the late 20th century—and I am confident that nothing equals race relations as a divisive force in the United States—then the case for the first point is nearly made. Neither of these matters can be dealt with effectively in economic terms. Blacks cannot achieve their goals unless whites are deprived of their sense of racial superiority; whites must yield what they appear to hold in great esteem; one or the other of the two parties will be a loser, the other a winner, and they will both perceive the results as such because they are fighting over a clearly visible matter that they both see in the same terms and rate highly. There is little room for compromise, because as long as whites do not yield fully, blacks will not have, and blacks want badly. In the case of foreign policy, those who want an end to Vietnams cannot achieve their goals unless those who believe that limited wars are the necessary price of preserving the free world are willing to retreat from their convictions. Neither of these issues admits of moderation through delivery of increased economic rewards, although race relations tensions might be muted somewhat by massive infusions; but economic benefits in the amount necessary to make a real difference would be very difficult to obtain from an economy based on a property-rights principle and supported by a limited-taxation, work-oriented ethos, and even then there would be bitter conflict remaining over status and value aspects of racism.

Nor does the issue of economic distributions readily lend itself to resolution through directing increased economic rewards at the deprived sector. Changes of a perhaps drastic nature in basic and strongly held liberal assumptions would be necessary to draw the poverty-level segment of the population into the economy and society. The same is true of the changes sufficient to render the economy more accountable and less free to manage consumers' wants: the issues are not so much the old questions of who gets how much of an existing or potential product, but of the basic framework and control structure of the productive engine itself. The thrust toward broader sharing of power among citizens, of course, is only marginally interested in obtaining economic rewards; it seeks power partly for its own sake and partly as an enabling device toward reshaping the society's motive values and ideology. Finally, the economy may already be dependent upon defense expenditures and foreign investments to such an extent that greater production of domestic and consumer goods and services would create dislocations at home and further tensions abroad.

This noneconomic feature of contemporary issues means that they are less capable of being accommodated without fundamental value conflict. Added to this is the fact that many of the people who raise such issues with particular vehemence—blacks, poor, middle class young activists, some intellectuals—are not only operating with distinctively substantive standards, but *they are articulate leaders who perceive themselves to be on the losing side in every case.* None of these issues places different people, groups, classes, or regions on a side different from that on which they are located by the other issues. Thus any benefits in the way of stability or democratic tolerance derived from having issues that created fluid cross-cutting social cleavages—shifting with each issue—may no longer be realized. Instead, we might anticipate more rigid divisions and the potential for rejection of the system itself which is supposed to accompany such a conflict pattern. In such an event, pressures on the basics of liberalism will probably mount, with repeated challenges to "law and order" followed by repressive responses of various kinds. It seems reasonable to anticipate that a restructuring of values will follow, either toward a domestic garrison state or toward a broader distribution of wealth, status, and power. Perhaps we should briefly consider the odds on each.

THE PROSPECTS OF AMERICAN LIBERALISM

In speculating as to the probable extent and direction of the political change that now seems inevitable, our premises should include the developmental perspective that we have previously employed. In other words, we should eschew judging American conditions by comparison with political or socio-economic circumstances elsewhere in the world; and we should assume inevitability only in regard to the prospect of continuing change in the environment's pressures upon us and our institutions. The American economy and the other characteristics supporting the American political system are not paralleled elsewhere, and they must be seen as generating expectations and demands that are specific to their perceived capabilities and circumstances. We must look to the American present and project it forward into the future. It will help us little to congratulate ourselves on what we have that others do not, to note that their demands are for what we now have, or to compare our present with harsher days of our past. Whether we like it or not, we are in motion, going somewhere. The question is, where?

For change to be significant and fundamental, rather than merely super-ficial or instrumental, it must occur at the basic level of political values and ideology. Change at this level comes about as an end product of a com-prehensive process of change in political practices, leadership, problems, and events—many aspects and determinants of which we have already explored. Following our previous analysis, we would expect that there would have to be fairly extensive changes in elite composition and behavior, a series of focusing events and government actions that eventuate in electoral ratification of new policies and release elites to make new departures and innovations, and that the final result might be some movement in the realm of values and ideology. Only then, after the process had been repeated several times and the necessary time had elapsed to effectuate value change, would there be confirmation that a new set of parameters had been reached, and the established liberal package replaced by a significant modification. The necessary preconditions (events, elite actions, and ratification, repeated continuously enough to bring about value change) are probably not likely to occur or endure long enough; the forces and agents working for change would have to be very strong and well focused to overcome the nearly unyielding sources of stability within this system.

Two alternative patterns of events and reactions seem theoretically pos-sible. The first is a sustained period of incremental change that would in a reasonable time—say, ten years—add up to significant and fundamental change toward affirmative rights for individuals and broad participation in policy making at both national and local levels. By affirmative rights, I mean a transformation of the present liberal view of individual rights as essentially negative prohibitions on government; these would be replaced by a conception of absolute individual entitlement to minimum shares of all societal outputs, economic and noneconomic. The participatory dimension of change would imply management of functions of government and of the economy by citizens themselves, either through their own individual sharing in decision making or by means of broadly representative and inclusive new decision-making units with many of the present powers of government and corporations combined. These changes would require the twin catalysts of drastic events and severe pressure—riots, massive civil disobedience—to create and sustain the perception of dire threat to established possessions that would be necessary to move elites to real action and nonelites to confirmation of such actions. The chances of such a configuration of events and capable leadership, sustained over the necessary period of time, do not seem very great.

The second pattern of events and reactions includes several possibilities which I shall group under the general heading of decadence and decline. The first stage and most likely prospect is relatively slight modification of the status quo, heavier in the area of rhetoric than in substance, which preserves intact all the basic liberal values. In this event, I would anticipate increasing rigidity and bitterness on the part of the two major groupings identified in the previous section; the issues will not go away, even if responses are minimal, and the only prospect in such a case is a widening gulf between those who seek change and those who resist or remain unperceiving. Another very possible first stage is one of rigid adherence to the status quo without even the appearance of efforts to cope with new conditions and demands. Reassertion of the validity of the traditional values and denial of the necessity to question and revise them would have the effect of accelerating the date of arriving at the wide gulf just described, at which point in both cases we might reasonably anticipate widespread rejection of the established system, acts of civil violence, and systematic repression of such behavior. From this stage of societal fragmentation, speculation can run the gamut from provocation of international nuclear cataclysm by reactionary and jingoistic American policies to domestic insurrection and self-destruction, either physically or societally.

No doubt these are vast oversimplifications and exaggerations of the many possible alternatives that lie ahead. They are intended to encompass the range of the possible with illustrative paths emerging from the present crisis, and to emphasize that the present situation is indeed a crisis. The prescriptions that follow differ in their perceptions of the extent of that crisis, which is inevitable; but most envision an immediate future in which decisive choices are to be made, and all are confident that their analyses hold at least the beginnings of answers. Whether they do or not is a matter for the individual reader to determine.

What *is* clear is that these authors have tried to do the difficult but necessary and unavoidable job of applying theory to practical reality in order to emerge with a sense of direction and purpose. With the sophistication and intellectual tools developed in the course of this book, it should be possible for readers to challenge these authors and draw from them some new reflections and directions for personal use. Two organizational approaches have been followed in structuring selections: I have presented leading representatives of particular areas of thought, with the dual intent of covering the best minds and the political spectrum; and I have also sought to focus on contemporary problems and the principal areas where change has been sought. In this latter section, we may best see the relevance of a theoretical dimension to the solving of immediate social problems.

My last exhortation concerns the intellectual demands to be made upon contemporary writers. Readers have a right to expect an author to adjust in some way to the major empirical findings, to deal with most of the questions that are relevant to "democratic" politics, to proceed logically and specifically, to face up to the problems of how change can be brought about, and to maintain some contact with reality and with contemporary issues. And it is fair to demand clear-cut positions. Although this is a field in which no intelligent person can possibly have all the answers, it is, nevertheless, necessary for some men to act as they understand the circumstances to require, and for others to evaluate their actions in the soundest manner they can. Americans must learn to make judgments and act upon them—not in "neutral," generalized terms ("I cannot do it because if I do it for you I must do it for all") but selectively and on the basis of the rights and wrongs of the particular issue. At some point, citizens can no longer avoid responsibility by pleading ignorance or incapacity, nor can they base a claim to affecting action on mere good will or personal preference unaccompanied by intelligent analysis of situational complexity. Both routes amount to escape from the sometimes unpleasant but nevertheless inescapable obligations of intellect: the making of timely judgments about the contemporary world based on the best available (but not complete) facts, the most appropriate (but not definitive) criteria, and the soundest (but not universal) values that we can bring to bear on an issue.

CHAPTER 17

Classic Conservatism: Russell Kirk

RUSSELL Kirk (b. 1918) is currently University Professor at Long Island University and a regular contributor to newspapers and *The National Review.* He has held teaching positions in politics, history, and American civilization at Michigan State College, the New School for Social Research, and C. W. Post College of Long Island University. An articulate and prolific conservative, he has published more than a dozen books, the best known of which are *The Conservative Mind* (1953), *A Program For Conservatives* (1954), *Beyond the Dreams of Avarice* (1956), and *Confessions of a Bohemian Tory* (1963).

Prescription, Authority, and Ordered Freedom

Civilized man lives by authority; without some reference to authority, indeed, no form of human existence is possible. Also man lives by prescription—that is, by ancient custom and usage, and the

SOURCE. Reprinted from Frank S. Meyer (ed.) *What Is Conservatism?* by permission of the publisher, Holt, Rinehart & Winston, Inc. Copyright 1958 by Holt, Rinehart & Winston, Inc.

rights which usage and custom have established. Without just authority and respected prescription, the pillars of any tolerable civil social order, true freedom is not possible.

For some time it has been fashionable to deride authority and prescription—though a good many people have been experiencing a change of heart recently. "Authority," in the vocabulary of what has been called "the Freudian ethic," has meant arbitrary restraint; and prescription has been equated with cultural lag and superstition. But the consequences of these emancipated notions have been unpalatable. A generation of young people reared according to "permissive" tenets has grown up bored, sullen, and in revolt against the very lack of order which was supposed to ensure the full development of their personalities. And a world lulled by slogans about absolute liberty and perpetual peace has found itself devoured by thoroughgoing tyranny and increasing violence. If men are to exist together at all, some authority must govern them; if they throw off traditional authority, the authority of church and precept and old educational disciplines and parents, then very soon they are compelled to submit to some new and merciless authority. "If you will not have God—and he is a jealous God—" Mr. T. S. Eliot observes, "they you should pay your respects to Hitler or Stalin." Authority and prescription lacking, order cannot subsist. If the authority is unjust, and the prescription merely the decree of some new domination, then the social order will have small place for freedom. Genuinely ordered freedom is the only sort of liberty worth having: freedom made possible by order within the soul and order within the state. Anarchic freedom, liberty defiant of authority and prescription, is merely the subhuman state of the wolf and the shark, or the punishment of Cain, with his hand against every man's.

So if people really desire genuine freedom, they need to know genuine authority. "Authority" is not the policeman's baton. "Conscience is an authority," Newman writes in his essay on John Keble; "the Bible is an authority; such is the Church; such is Antiquity; such are the words of the wise; such are historical memories, such are legal saws and state maxims; such are proverbs; such are sentiments, presages, and prepossessions." Authority, in fine, is the ground upon which prudent action must be performed. If a man acknowledges no authority, he sets himself up as Cain, and before long he is struck down by nemesis, which follows upon *hubris*.

Political authority, the claims and powers of a legitimate state, though an important part of this complex of authority which rules our lives, is no more than a part. Sometimes authorities conflict; indeed, most of the great disputes of history have been, in essence, controversies over the higher source of authority. And such debates never are wholly and finally resolved. Now and again, for instance, the authoritative claims of church and state cannot well be reconciled, and then great trouble results. Similarly, the authority of faith and the authority of reason collide from age to age. In such clashes, the conscientious man endeavors, according to what light is given him, to determine what representatives of authority have claimed too much; but he is foolish if, despairing, he forsakes authority altogether.

Human nature being irremediably flawed, so that all of us in some degree rebel against the people and the institutions to which we owe most, there is in every man a certain impulse to make himself God: that is, to cast off all authority but his own lust and whim. From this vice comes the corrupting influence of total power upon even the best of natures. The rebellion of Lucifer is the symbol of this ancient anarchic impulse—the passion for overthrowing the just authority of God, that upon the vacant throne of authority the rebel may make himself absolute. Yet the doom of such risings is as sure as Lucifer's. For a grown man to rebel against all authority is as ludicrous as for a three-year-old child to defy his parents: whether they are good parents or bad, he can live scarcely a day without them.

From its beginnings, the liberal movement of the nineteenth century had within it this fatuous yearning for the destruction of all authority. Liberalism also possessed some good qualities; but it never has recovered from this congenital defiance of authority and prescription. The early liberals were convinced that once they should overthrow established governments and churches, supplanting them by rational and egalitarian and purely secular institutions, the principal problems of the human condition would be near solution. Poverty, ignorance, disease, and woe might then be terminated, once enlightened self-interest, popular suffrage, and utilitarian public policies had triumphed. One had only to fight clear of the Bad Old Days and the dead weight of superstition. Abolish the old Authorities, and sweetness and light will reign.

Yet the triumph of liberalism endured little more than half a century; by the 1880's, the individualism of the early liberals was being transmuted into socialism, a process easily traced in the life of John Stuart Mill. Liberalism had begun, defying authority and prescription, by breaking all sorts of ancient ties and obligations, but the latter day Liberal, in Santayana's phrase, relaxes no bond except the marriage knot. Increasingly, though implicitly, Liberals came to accept a new authority, that of the omnicompetent welfare state; they continued to repudiate authority only in the sphere of private life.

Just how archaic and unreal, politically, latter-day Liberalism has become is sufficiently illustrated by a conference of the English Liberal Party in the summer of 1961. Three principal resolutions were proposed: to abolish the monarchy, to abolish the hereditary element in the House of Lords, and to expand the welfare state. Though the first proposal was defeated after discussion, the other two were adopted enthusiastically; and so the conference adjourned, its members satisfied that they had shown the English nation how to solve its difficulties in the twentieth century. To anyone but a Liberal ideologue, it is clear enough that abolition of the British monarchy would accomplish nothing but to destroy the symbol of justice and order in Britain; that to destroy the hereditary element in the House of Lords would only injure the most serious deliberative body in the world; and that to extend the British welfare state would do no less than to

finish Liberalism altogether, since that would mean certainly complete socialism, and probably the end of the British constitution and of British prosperity. So much for the eccentricities of a dying party.

Though they have abandoned nearly all their original political program, still the Liberals of the twentient century cling to their general detestation of authority; but this detestation has shifted from the political sphere to the moral and social. The writings of an American latter-day Liberal, a disciple of J. S. Mill, Mr. David Riesman, illustrate this. Professor Riesman recognizes the decay of authority among us and is confusedly disturbed by it. He gives up for lost the "tradition-directed individual"—that is, the man with some respect for authority and tradition—and sheds few tears at his passing. What worries Mr. Riesman more, the "inner-directed individual"—that is, the typical active nineteenth-century liberal—also seems to be not long for this world. So there remain the "other directed"—that is, the modern masses who take for their norms whatever their neighbors seem to be doing— and some scattered and harebrained dissidents, "anomics," masterless men who meaninglessly and futilely defy the great tendencies of their time. Mr. Riesman's only hope is in the possibility of a number of "autonomous" men, uncontrolled by tradition, liberal "inner direction," or the fads and foibles of the hour: rootless persons who somehow, by wishing it, may become superior to the crowd of other-directed about them. No hope could be more ridiculous than this last. Also Mr. Riesman would like to see women "deprivatized"—that is, more footloose"—and to see all who would be autonomous spend much time upon "consumership" and other diversions.

One may as well laugh as cry. To such an intellectual and moral bankruptcy have come even the most intelligent of twentiety-century Liberals. Having denied the very existence of sound and just authority, having scoffed

at the wisdom of our ancestors, Liberalism is altogether cut loose from such
moorings as once it had. Without some
principle of authority, life becomes
meaningless, and political and intellectual factions slip into the dust-bin of
history.

If authority, then—however unfash-
ionable in recent years—remains ineluc-
table for civilization and for any truly
human existence, how do men find such
authority? In a number of ways; but
of these, the means for most men is
what we call prescription or tradition.

Prescription, socially and politically
speaking, means those ways and institutions and rights prescribed by long—
sometimes immemorial—usage. Tradition (a word until the end of the
eighteenth century applied almost exclusively to Christian beliefs not set
down in Scripture) means received opinions, convictions religious and moral and
political and aesthetic passed down from
generation to generation, so that they
are accepted by most men as a matter
of course. I have discussed the nature
of tradition and prescription at some
length in my book *Beyond the Dreams
of Avarice.*

Fulbert of Chartres and Gerbert of
Rheims, those two grand Schoolmen,
said that we moderns are dwarfs standing upon the shoulders of giants. We
see so far only because we are elevated
upon the accomplishment of our ancestors; and if we break with ancestral
wisdom, we at once are plunged into
the ditch of ignorance. All that we have
and know is founded upon the experience of the race. As Burke put it, "The
individual is foolish, but the species is
wise." Men have no right, Burke said,
to risk the very existence of their nation
and their civilization upon experiments
in morals and politics; for each man's
private capital of intelligence is petty;
it is only when a man draws upon the
bank and capital of the ages, the wisdom
of our ancestors, that he can act wisely.
Without resort to tradition and prescription, we are left with merely our vanity

and the brief and partial experience of
our evanescent lives. "What shadows we
are, and what shadows we pursue."

G. K. Chesterton expressed much the
same truth when he wrote of "the democracy of the dead." When we decide
great questions in our time, he held, we
ought to count not merely the votes of
our contemporaries, but the opinions of
many generations of men—and particularly the convictions of the wise men
who have preceded us in time. By trial
and error, by revelation, by the insights
of men of genius, mankind has acquired,
slowly and painfully, over thousands of
years, a knowledge of human nature and
of the civil social order which no one
individual possibly can supplant by private rationality.

This is true especially in matters of
morals, politics, and taste; but in considerable degree it is true also even in
modern science and technology. Once
a student objected to me that surely
enlightened modern man could work out
rationally a must better system of morals and politics than the hodgepodge we
have inherited from blundering ancestors. But I asked this student if, without
consulting senior technicians, books, and
authority generally, he thought he could
construct, unaided, an automobile—if
indeed, he thought that he personally,
even with all sorts of advice, could make
an automobile at all. He confessed that
he could not; and it began to be borne
in upon him to construct, *carte blanche,*
a system of morals and politics that
really would work might be an undertaking more difficult still.

So even the most gifted men, and
always the great mass of human beings,
must fall back upon tradition and prescription if they are to act at all in this
world. At the very least, it saves a great
deal of time. It is conceivable that, if
I set myself to it, I might calculate for
myself the circumference of the earthy,
quite independently of previous calculations. But since I have no strong mathematical gifts, it is improbable that my
calculations would be more accurate
than those of the present authorities;

and it seems almost certain that my result would be quite the same as the present calculation of the earth's cir-circumference; so I would have spent months or years of a brief life in trying to gain what I could have had for the asking. If we are to accomplish anything in this life, we must take much for granted; as Newman said, if one had to make the choice, it would be better to believe all things than to doubt all things. In the matter of the earth's circumference, nearly all of us are much better off if we simply accept the "traditional" or "authoritative" calculation.

This is even more true of moral and social first principles. Only through prescription and tradition, only by habitual acceptance of just and sound authority, can men acquire knowledge of the norms for humanity. Authority tells us that murder is wrong; prescription immemorially has visited severe punishments upon murderers; tradition presents us with an ancient complex of tales of the evil consequences of murder. Now a man who thinks his private petty rationality superior to the wisdom of our ancestors may undertake experiments in murder, with a view to testing these old irrational scruples; but the results of such experiments are sure to be disagreeable for everyone concerned, including the researcher; and that experimenter has no right to be surprised if we hang him by the neck until he is quite dead. For if men flout norm and convention, life becomes intolerable. It is through respect for tradition and prescription, and recourse to those sources of knowledge, that the great mass of men acquire a tolerable understanding of norms and conventions, of the rules by which private and social existence is made tolerable.

A norm is an enduring standard. It is a law of our nature, which we ignore at our peril. It is a rule of human conduct and a measure of public virtue. The norm does not signify the average, the median, the mean, the mediocre. The norm is not the conduct of the average sensual man. A norm is not simply a measure of average performance within a group. There exists law for man, and law for thing; the late Alfred Kinsey nothwithstanding, the norm for the wasp and the snake is not the norm for man. A norm has an objective existence: though men may ignore or forget a norm, still that norm does not cease to be, nor does it cease to influence men. A man apprehends a norm or fails to apprehend it, but he does not create or destroy norms.

The sanction for obedience to norms must come from a source other than private advantage and rationality—from a source more than human, indeed. Men do not submit long to their own creations. Standards erected out of expediency will be demolished soon enough, also out of expediency. Either norms have an existence independent of immediate utility, or they are mere fictions. If men assume that norms are merely the pompous fabrications of their ancestors, got up to serve the interests of a faction or an age, then every rising generation will challenge the principles of personal and social order and will learn wisdom only through agony. For half a century, we have been experiencing the consequences of a moral and social neoterism.

"Goodnatured unambitious men are cowards when they have no religion." So, in *Back to Methuselah*, writes Bernard Shaw. "They are dominated and exploited not only by greedy and often halfwitted and half-alive weaklings who will do anything for cigars, champagne, motor cars, and the more childish and selfish uses of money, but by able and sound administrators who can do nothing else with them than dominate and exploit them. Government and exploitation become synonymous under such circumstances; and the world is finally ruled by the childish, the brigands, and the blackguards." (One may acknowledge the acuteness of this insight without subscribing to the curious religion, or quasi-religion, which Shaw sets forth—half soberly, half facetiously—in *Back to Methuselah*.)

As a gloss upon this, one may say also that the average good-natured unambitious men as a coward also if he lacks—even though retaining some religious feelings—"that wise prejudice" by which "a man's virtue becomes his habit," in Burke's phrase. If his life is regulated, almost unconsciously, upon certain received opinions concerning justice and injustice, charity and selfishness, freedom and servitude, truth and falsehood, he will behave habitually with some degree of resolution and courage; but if he is all at sea in a latter-day Liberalism and moral relativism, in which any point of view or mode of conduct has something to be said for it, then he will be unnerved when the test comes. Acting customarily upon tradition and prescription, he will not feel alone; the democracy of the dead will endorse him. But acting without norms, he must be, ordinarily, either a coward or a brute in any personal or civic crisis.

A man who accepts tested authority, and acknowledges the beneficent influence of prescription and tradition, is conventional; but he is not servile. Conventions are the means by which obedience to norms is inculcated in society. Conventions are compacts by which we agree to respect one another's dignity and rights. A high degree of respect for convention is quite consonant with a high development of individual personality, and even of eccentricity. Many of the great "characters," indeed, are the great champions of convention; the names of Samuel Johnson and Benjamin Disraeli, of John Adams, John Randolph, and Theodore Roosevelt may suffice for illustration. There exists no necessary opposition between strong outward indifference to foible and strong inward loyalty to norms. A man of strong character who accepts just authority and its works will be meek—but meek only as Moses: that is, obedient to the will of God, but unflinching against human tyrants.

The good citizen is a law-abiding traditionalist: so the politics of Virgil have been summed up. If men are courageous or virtuous, ordinarily this is because they are persons of good moral *habits:* that is, they act habitually, and almost unthinkingly, upon certain premises they have learnt from infancy, through force of example and through formal instruction. This is what Burke meant when he wrote that prejudice is the wisdom of unlettered men. They draw their strength from acceptance of tradition and prescription.

Now it does not follow that an unquestioning acceptance of received opinions and long-established usage will of itself suffice to solve all personal and public problems. The world does change; a certain sloughing off of tradition and prescription is at work in any vigorous society, and a certain adding to the bulk of received opinion goes on from age to age. We cannot live precisely by the rules of our distant forefathers, in all matters. But, again to employ a phrase of Burke's, the fact that a belief or an institution has long been accepted by men, and seems to have exerted a beneficent influence, establishes in its favor "a legitimate presumption." If we feel inclined to depart from old ways, we ought to do so only after very sober consideration of ultimate consequences. Authority, prescription, and tradition undergo in every generation a certain filtering process, by which the really archaic is discarded; yet we ought to be sure that we actually are filtering, and not merely letting our heritage run down the drain.

Similarly, the general principles and valuable institutions which we have inherited from past generations must be applied and utilized with prudence; there the exercise of right reason by the leaders of any society sets to work. We possess moral norms, the Decalogue, for instance, but the way in which we observe those norms must be determined in our time by the circumstances in which we find ourselves, so that wise men in our age must reconcile exigency and enduring standard. We possess tested political institutions; but for those institutions to endure, now and then reform is essential, lest the institutions atrophy. Thus Burke's model of a statesmen is one who combines with an ability to reform a disposition to preserve.

Prescription and tradition, then, cannot stand forever if the living do not sustain them by vigorous application and prudent reform. But it is equally true that lively action and ingenious reform are mere ropes of sand, unless linked with the wisdom of the ages.

One instance of the abiding value of inherited convictions—beliefs that have their origin both in the experience of the race and in the reasoning of men of genius, but have acquired through subtle processes the status of popular prejudices—is the idea of justice, as expressed by Plato and Cicero. The great classical philosophers of politics argued that justice resides in this: to each his own. Every man, ideally, ought to receive the things that best suit his own nature. Men's talents and appetites vary greatly from individual to individual; therefore a society is unjust which treats all men as if they were uniform, or which allots to one sort of nature rights and duties that properly belong to other sorts of human beings.

This concept of justice has entered deeply into the ethics, the jurisprudence, and even the imaginative literature of what is called "Western civilization." It still is a profound influence upon many men and women who never have read Cicero or Plato. It creates a prejudice against radical egalitarianism, which would reduce all men to a single mode of existence. It has inculcated a sound prejudice in favor of *order:* that is, a society marked by a variety of rewards and duties, a commonwealth in which, as Burke said, all men "have equal rights; but not to equal things." This theory underlies, for example, the British and American constitutions.

Nowadays this classical idea of justice is challenged by the Marxist doctrine that order should be abolished: all human beings should be treated as identical units, and compulsory equality of condi-

tion enforced. When the average American or Englishman is brought face to face with Marxist demands for the overthrow of prescriptive order and the establishment of a society without demarcations, he may not be able to meet the Marxist propagandist with a privately reasoned defense of variety and constitutionalism; but he resists the Marxist doctrine out of a feeling that what the Communist proposes somehow is fundamentally unjust. The average American or Englishman remains a law-abiding traditionalist, even in this day of giddy technological and industrial alteration; he takes it for granted that we were not born yesterday; that we have no right to case away our tested civil social order; that monotonous uniformity of condition is contrary to deep ancient human aspirations; that Communism flies in the face of the nature of things. And because he is the heir to a great tradition, he knows something of the character of justice, and he is resolute despite the threats and seductions of the radical innovator.

"The great mysterious incorporation of the human race" is, as Burke said, a contract of sorts: but a contract between the divine and the human natures, and among the dead, the living, and those yet unborn. We know something of the terms of that eternal contract of society through traditions and prescriptions. Our obedience to norms, to true and just authority in morals and politics, keeps that immortal contract alive. And that obedience secures us all in ordered freedom.

Government is instituted to secure justice and order, through respect for legitimate authority; and if we ask from government more than this, we begin to imperil justice and order. It is one of the saddest illusions of the Liberal era, the notion that political manipulation can make men happy. But some forms of government can succeed in making men miserable. So I venture to suggest here the general lineaments of the kind of government which seems reasonably consonant with the general welfare. I think that here we need to refer to two principles. The first principle is that a good government allows the more energetic natures among a people to fulfill their promise, while ensuring that these persons shall not tyrannize over the mass of men. The second principle is that in every state the best possible—or least baneful—form of government is one in accord with the traditions and prescriptive ways of its people. Beyond these two general principles, there is no rule of politics which may be applied, uniformly and universally, with safety.

Even Mr. Riesman has rediscovered the old truth that men are not created equal; they are created different. Variety, not uniformity, gives any nation vigor and hope. Thus my first principle of good government—for which I am much indebted to Professor Eric Voegelin—has a hearing once more, though the overmastering tendency of the past century and a half has been social egalitarianism. "One man is as good as another, or maybe a little better": this secular dogma has done mischief to the preservation or establishment of good government. Equality in political power has tended to lead to equality of condition. "Everybody belongs to everybody else"—this is the motto of society in Huxley's *Brave New World;* and that society is a life in death. For these assumptions are thorough falsehoods. One man is not as good as another, and everyone does not belong to everyone else. The first fallacy is the denial of Christian morals, the second the denial of the Christian idea of personality.

Aye, men are created different; and a government which ignores this law becomes an unjust government, for it sacrifices nobility to mediocrity; it pulls down the aspiring natures to gratify the inferior natures. This degradation injures humanity in two ways. First, it frustrates the natural longing of talented persons to realize their potentialities; it leaves the better men dissatisfied with themselves and their nation, and they sink into boredom; it impedes any improvement of the moral, intellectual, and material condition, in terms of quality, of mankind. Second, it adversely affects the well-being, late or soon, of the mass of men; for, deprived of responsible leadership and example, the innumerable men and women destined to walk in the routine ways of life suffer in the tone of their civilization, and in their material condition. A government which converts into a secular dogma the Christian mystery of moral equality, in short, is hostile towards human existence.

Remember that there are two parts to this political principle: not only should a just government recognize the rights of the more talented natures, but it should recognize the right of the majority of men not to be agitated and bullied by these aspiring talents. The prudent statesman endeavors to maintain a balance between these two claims. There have been ages in which the aristocracy, natural or hereditary, has usurped the whole governance of life, demanding of the average man a tribute and an obedience which deprive the majority of their desire to live by custom and prescription and often damage their material interests. Such a regime, indifferent to the welfare of the majority, is as bad a government as a domination indifferent to the claims of the talented minority. But nowadays the danger is not that the stronger natures—and I refer to moral and intellectual qualities, not merely to domineering and acquisitive abilities—will lord it over an abused majority; rather, the curse of our time is what Ortega called "the revolt of the masses," the threat that mediocrity may trample underfoot every just elevation of mind and character, every hopeful talent for leadership and improvement. Therefore, the sagacious statesman of our age must be more acutely concerned with the preservation of the rights of the talented minority than with the extension of the rights of the crowd.

A domination which confounds popular government with equality of moral worth, equality of intellect, or equality of condition is a bad government. For a good government respects the claims of extraordinary character. It respects the right of the contemplative to his solitude. It respects the right of the practical leader to take an honest initiative in the affairs of the commonwealth. It respects the right of the inventor to his ingenuity, the right of the manufacturer or merchant to the rewards of his industry, the right of the thrifty man to keep his savings and bequeath them to his heirs. It respects such claims and rights, this good government, because in the enjoyment of these rights, and in the performance of the duties to which these rights are joined, men fulfill themselves; and a considerable measure of justice—"to each his own"—is attained.

Today the balance between the claims of the unusual natures and the ordinary natures, in some ages overthrown to the advantage of aspiring talents, is injured rather by the extortionate demands of a doctrinaire egalitarianism. Communist Russia is the most thorough example of the triumph of this degradation of the democratic dogma. I am aware that Soviet Russia is governed by a clique of party intriguers and successful administrators, paying little more than lip service to their own secular dogma of egalitarianism; yet this does not alter the fact that, obedient to the ideology of dialectical materialism, the Soviets have suppressed the claims of the nobler natures to do the work natural to them. What we see in the new elite of Communism is not a predominance of the higher natures, but a domination of Jacobin fanatics, devoid, nearly all of them, of high moral endowments. This is the regime of a host of squalid oligarchs. Among them are no prophets, and no poets; and only qualification for entry into this elite is ruthless cunning in the struggle for pure power. Not the higher natures, but the lower, in terms of moral attainment and independence of mind, are recognized and rewarded by the Soviets.

Now it is not American "democracy," as such, that stands at the antipodes from the Soviet undertaking; American

moral and political tradition, rather, and American constitutionalism are the forces of resistance. A political democracy may attain a tolerable balance between the rights of the talented natures and the claims of the average natures. But it also is possible for a monarchy to achieve that balance, or an aristocracy, or some other frame of government. Respect for natural and prescriptive rights is peculiar to no single set of political institutions.

Yet the kind of government which seems most likely to appreciate and defend the claims of either interest in the commonwealth is what Aristotle called a "polity," a balancing and checking of classes in society. The United States remain, in considerable degree, a polity; *pure* democracy was not intended by the founders of this Republic, and it has not yet triumphed among us. It ought not to triumph. For the good government does not grow up from mere protection of entrenched property, nor yet from the victory of the proletariat.

A prudent government, within the bounds set by decency and good order, leaves every man to consult his own humor. It does not attempt to force the happiness of the statistical Bentham upon the romantic Coleridge; for one man's happiness, even among the talented natures, is another man's misery. By a salutary neglect, this government allows private happiness to take care of itself. One may call this prudent and tolerant government "democracy," if one wishes, though I think that is twisting the word. I call it simply a government which prefers principle to ideology, variety to uniformity, balance to omnipotence.

Now for my second principle of good government: that a government should accord with the traditions and the prescriptive ways of a people. This is the view of Montesquieu and of Burke. A good government is no artificial contrivance, no invention of coffeehouse philosophers, got up upon *a priori* abstractions to suit the intellectual mood of an hour. Governments hastily designed upon theories of pure reason ordinarily are wretched dominations. The longest-lived of these poor governments has been that of modern France, which never has recovered from the hacking and chopping that the constitution of French society received at the hands of rigid metaphysicians from 1789 onward. Much more evanescent, because they had a smaller reservoir of tradition to exhaust, were the artificial governments set up in central and southern Europe after the First World War. Now the good government, very different from these, is the growth of centuries of social experience. It has been called organic; I prefer the analog "spiritual." Trusting to the wisdom of our ancestors and the experience of the nation, it puts its faith in precedent, prescription, historical trial and error, and consensus of opinion over the generations. Not infatuated with neatness, it prefers the strength and majesty of the Gothic style. The government of Britain, because of its age and success, is our best example of this type. And the government of the United States is nearly as good an instance of the triumph of this principle that society is an august continuity and essence, held together by veneration, prescription, and tradition.

Nominally, of course, we Americans created our Federal Constitution by deliberate action, within the space of a few months. But in actuality that formal constitution, and our state constitutions, chiefly put down on paper what already existed and was accepted in public opinion: beliefs and institutions long established in the colonies, and drawn from centuries of English experience with parliaments, the common law, and the balancing of orders and interests in a realm. Respect for precedent and prescription governed the minds of the Founders of the Republic. We appealed to the prescriptive liberties of Englishmen, not to *liberte, egalite, fraternite;* and the philosophical and moral structure of our civil order was rooted in the Christian faith, not in the worship of Reason.

The success of the American and British governments, I am suggesting, is produced by their preference for growth, experience, tradition, and prescription over a closet-metaphysician's grand design. The great lessons of politics are taught a people through their historical experience; no nation can sever itself from its past and still prosper, for the dead alone give us energy; and whatever constitution has been long accepted in a nation, that constitution—amended, perhaps, but essentially the same—is as good as a people can expect. True, that constitution may be improved, or restored; but if it is discarded altogether, like wastepaper, every order in society suffers terribly.

The American and British constitutions have worked well; but, being living essences, they cannot easily be transplanted to other states. One of the cardinal errors of the French revolutionaries was their endeavor to remake France upon the model of what they thought English politics to be. Though any people have something to learn from the experiences of any other, still there exists no single constitution calculated to work successfully everywhere. For the political institutions of a people grow out of their religion, their moral habits, their economy, even their literature; political institutions are but part of an intricate structure of civilization, the roots of which go infinitely deep. Attempts to impose borrowed institutions upon an alien culture generally are disastrous, though some decades, or even generations, may be required for the experiment to run its unlucky course. Randolph of Roanoke, in opposing Clay's design for encouraging revolutions upon the American pattern, cried out in his sardonic way, "You can no more make liberty out of Spanish matter than you can make a frigate out of a bundle of pine saplings." Though this is somewhat hard upon the Spaniards, it remains true that parliamentary government, Anglo-American style, rarely has been secure in Spanish lands; Spaniards' liberty, when they enjoy it, is secured by different institutions and customs.

Yet still our political theory and our foreign policy are plagued by the delusion that some domination of American constitutions and manners will be established universally—the American Liberal's conviction, in Santayana's sentence, that "the nun must not remain a nun, and China shall not keep its wall." This fond hope never will be realized. For individuals, as Chesterton said, are happy only when they are their own potty little selves; and this is as true of nations. To impose the American constitution upon all the world would not render all the world happy; to the contrary, our constitution would work in few lands and would make many men miserable in short order. States, like men, must find their own paths to order and justice and freedom; and usually those paths are ancient and winding ways, and their signposts are Authority, Tradition, Prescription. Without the legal institutions, rooted in common and Roman law, from which it arose, the American constitutional system would be unworkable. Well, take up this constitutional system, abstractly, and set it down, as an exotic plant, in Persia or Guinea or the Congo, where the common law (English style) and the Roman law are unknown, and where bed of justice rests upon the Koran or upon hereditary chieftainship—why, the thing cannot succeed. Such an undertaking may disrupt the old system of justice, and may even supplant it, for a time; but in the long run, the traditional morals, habits, and establishments of a people, confirmed by their historical experience, will reassert themselves, and the innovation will be undone—if that culture is to survive at all.

The Asiatic or African who attempts to convert himself and his nation, abruptly and wholesale, to Western ways must end disillusioned; we will be fortunate if he does not end in violent reaction. Like the Lebanon Arab in Cunninghame-Graham's story *Sidi bu Zibbula*, he will crouch upon his dung-hill, saying, "I have seen your Western cities; and the dung is better."

Good government is no mass-produced article. Order and justice and freedom are found in diverse ways, but they cannot be divorced from the historical experience of a people. Theory divorced from experience is infinitely dangerous, the plaything of the ideologue, the darling dagger of the energumen. Though their social functions may be similar, the justice of the peace cannot supplant the *cadi;* and no James Mill, however learned, can rightfully make laws for India.

I am saying this: far from being right to revolt against the past, a people are fortunate if their political order maintains a tolerable degree of freedom and justice for the different interests in society. We are not made for perfect things, and if ever we found ourselves under the domination of the "perfect" government, we would make mincemeat of it, from sheer boredom. From just authority, from respect for our cultural and moral and political heritage, comes genuine civil freedom. It was something of this sort, I suppose, that St. Paul meant when he declared, "The powers that be are ordained of God." With authority and prescription, a people may work their way towards the freedom of the true polity. Without authority and prescription, they are afflicted by the devastating "freedom" of the Congo.

WORKS BY RUSSELL KIRK

Kirk, Russell. *Academic Freedom, an Essay in Definition.* Chicago: H. Regnery Co., 1956.

————. *The American Cause.* Chicago: H. Regnery Co., 1957.

————. *Beyond the Dreams of Avarice, Essays of a Social Critic.* Chicago: H. Regnery Co., 1956.

————. *The Conservative Mind, from Burke to Santayana.* Chicago: H. Regnery Co., 1953.

————. *The Intelligent Woman's Guide to Conservatism.* New York: The Devin-Adair Co., 1957.

_____. *The Intemperate Professor, and Other Splinetics.* Baton Rouge: Louisiana State University Press, 1965.

_____. *John Randolph of Roanoke, a Study in American Politics with Selected Speeches and Letters.* Chicago: H. Regnery Co., 1964.

_____. *Old House of Fear.* New York: Fleet Pub. Corp., 1961.

_____. *A Program for Conservatives.* Chicago: H. Regnery Co., 1954.

_____. *The Surly Sullen Bell, Ten Stories and Sketches, Uncanny or Uncomfortable.* New York: Fleet Pub. Corp., 1962.

Kirk, Russell, and McClellan, James. *Political Principles of Robert A. Taft.* New York: Fleet Press Corp., 1967.

CHAPTER 18

Modern Conservatism: Peter Viereck

PETER Viereck (b. 1916) is a professor of modern European history at Mount Holyoke College. A poet as well as a historian, he has published several volumes in each field. Among the best known of his politically oriented books are *Conservatism Revisited* (1949), *The Shame and Glory of the Intellectuals* (1953), *The Unadjusted Man: A New Hero for Americans* (1956), and *Conservatism: From John Adams to Churchill* (1956).

The Philosophical "New Conservatism" (1962)

The author's preceding chapter of 1955, in the symposium book *The New American Right,* treats this new right as mainly the right-wing radicals of

SOURCE. Reprinted from *The Radical Right* (Garden City, N.Y.: Doubleday Anchor, 1964) by permission of the author. Copyright 1963, by Daniel Bell. This essay appears in longer form in the author's *Conservatism Revisited and the New Conservatism: What Went Wrong?* (New York: Macmillan, 1965) and *The Shame and Glory of the Intellectuals* (New York: G. Putnam Sons, 1965), both of which are available in paperback editions.

McCarthyism and of Midwest neopopulist Republicanism. Hence, the 1955 chapter fails to deal with something far more serious intellectually—the non-McCarthyite, non-thought-controlling movement known as "the new conservatism." The latter movement, being non-popular and being burdened with partly merited philosophical pretensions, is restricted mainly to the campuses and the magazine world, even though it sometimes lends ghost-writers and an egghead facade to the popular political arena outside.

The extreme McCarthy emphasis of the 1955 chapter was justified in the exceptional context of the early 1950's. It is perhaps no longer justified in the context of this 1962 edition. As for over-publicized groups like the John Birch Society, fortunately they have no chance of attaining anything like the mass attained by McCarthy, Coughlin, or Huey Long. This is because they lack the demagogic populist or pseudo-socialist economic platform without which chauvinist thought-control movements have no chance of success. Note that Hitler called himself not merely a nationalist but a National Socialist. Note that Huey Long ("every man a king"), Coughlin ("free silver"), and McCarthy ("socialistic" farm subsidies) had a similar rightist-leftist amalgam rather than a purely rightist or nationalist platform.

Though the pseudo-conservatism of Long-Coughlin-McCarthy seems dead for the time being, and though that of the John Birchers seems stillborn, the philosophical "new conservatism" is still —on its admittedly smaller scale—alive. Alive whether for better or worse, its merits and defects being approximately equal. Since the present author furnished the first postwar book of the new conservatism—*Conservatism Revisited: The Revolt Against Revolt* (1949, reprinted by Collier Books, 1962)—he bears a certain responsibility: again, "whether for better or worse." Hence, since the new conservatism is still alive and since it was not included in the preceding chapter of 1955, the following supplementary chapter seems in order.

I

In the 1930's, when the present author, still a student, was writing an article for the *Atlantic Monthly* urging "a Burkean new conservatism in America," and to some extent even as late as his *Conservatism Revisited* of 1949, "conservatism" was an unpopular epithet. In retrospect it becomes almost attractively amusing (like contemplating a dated period piece) to recall how violently one was denounced in those days for suggesting that Burke, Calhoun, and Irving Babbitt were not "Fascist Beasts" and that our relatively conservative Constitution was not really a plot-in-advance, by rich bogeymen like George Washington and the Federalist Party. For example, the author's *Atlantic* article, written in prewar student days, was denounced more because the word used ("conservative") was so heretical than because of any effort by the Popular Frontist denouncers to read what was actually said. It was the first-written and worst-written appeal ever published in America for what is called a "new conservatism ("new" meaning Non-Republican, non-commercialist, non-conformist). This new conservatism it viewed as synthesizing in some future day the ethical New Deal social reforms with the more pessimistic, anti-mass insights of America's Burkean founders. Such a synthesis, argued the article, would help make the valuable anti-Fascist movement among literary intellectuals simultaneously anti-Communist also, leaving behind the Popular Frontist illusions of the 1930's.

As the liberal Robert Bendiner then put it, "Out of some 140,000,000 people in the United States, at least 139,500,000 are liberals, to hear them tell it. . . Rare is the citizen who can bring himself to say, 'Sure I'm a conservative.' . . . Any American would sooner drop dead then proclaim himself a reactionary." In July, 1950, a newspaper was listing the charges against a prisoner accused of creating a public disturbance. One witness charged, "He was using abusive and obscene language, calling people conservatives and all that."

When conservatism was still a dirty word, it seemed gallantly non-conformist to defend it against the big, smug liberal majority among one's fellow writers and professors. In those days, therefore, the author deemed it more helpful to stress the virtues of conservative thought than its faults, and this is what he did in the 1949 edition of *Conservatism Revisited*. But in the mood emerging from the 1950's, blunt speaking about conservatism's important defects no longer runs the danger of obscuring its still more important virtues.

The main defect of the new conservatism, threatening to make it a transient fad irrelevant to real needs, is its rootless nostalgia for roots. Conservatives of living roots were Washington and Coleridge in their particular America and England, Metternich in his special Austria, Donoso Cortes in his Spain, Calhoun in his antebellum South, Adenauer and Churchill in the 1950's. American conservative writings of living roots were the *Federalist* of Hamilton, Madison, Jay, 1787-88; the *Defense of the Constitutions* of John Adams, 1787-88; the *Letters of Pubicola* of John Quincy Adams, 1791; Calhoun's *Disquisition and Discourse,* posthumously published in 1850; Irving Babbitt's *Democracy and Leadership,* 1924. In contrast, today's conservatism of yearning is based on roots either never existent or no longer existent. Such a conservatism of nostalgia can still be of high literary value. It is also valuable as an unusually detached perspective about current social foibles. But it does real harm when it leaves literature and enters short-run politics, conjuring up mirages to conceal sordid realities or to distract from them.

In America, southern agrarianism has long been the most gifted literary form of the conservatism of yearning. Its most important intellectual manifesto was the Southern symposium *I'll Take My Stand* (1930), contrasting the cultivated human values of a lost aristocratic agrarianism with Northern Commercialism and liberal materialism. At their best, these and more recent examples of the conservatism of yearning are needed warnings against shallow practicality. The fact that such warnings often come from the losing side of our Civil War is in itself a merit; thereby they caution a nation of success-worshippers against the price of success. But at their worst such books of the 1930s, and again of today, lack the living roots of genuine conservatism and have only lifeless ones.

The lifeless ones are really a synthetic substitute for roots, contrived by romantic nostalgia. They are a test-tube conservatism, a lab job of powdered Burke or cake-mix Calhoun.

Such romanticizing conservatives refuse to face up to the old and solid historical roots of most or much American liberalism. What is really rootless and abstract is not the increasingly conservatized New Deal liberalism but their own Utopian dream of an aristocratic agrarian restoration. Their unhistorical appeal to history, their traditionless worship of tradition, characterize the conservatism of writers like Russell Kirk.

In contrast, a genuinely rooted, history minded conservative conserves the roots that are *really there,* exactly as Burke did when he conserved not only the monarchist-conservative aspects of William III's bloodless revolution of 1688 but also its constitutional-liberal aspects. The latter aspects, formulated by the British philosopher John Locke, have been summarized in England and America ever since by the word "Lockean."

Via the Constitutional Convention of 1787, this liberal-conservative heritage of 1688 became rooted in America as a blend of Locke's very moderate liberalism and Burke's very moderate conservatism. From the rival Federalists and Jeffersonians through today, all our major rival parties have continued this blend, though with varied proportion and stress. American history is based on the resemblance between moderate liberalism and moderate conservatism; the history of Continental Europe is based on the difference between extreme liberalism and extreme conservatism.

But some American new conservatives import from Continental Europe a conservatism that totally rejects even our moderate native liberalism. In the name of free speech and intellectual gadflyism, they are justified in expounding the indiscriminate anti-liberalism of hothouse Bourbons and czarist serffloggers. But they are not justified in calling themselves American tradition-alists or in claiming any except exotic roots for their position in America. Let them present their case frankly as anti-traditional, rootless revolutionaries of Europe's authoritarian right wing, at-tacking the deep-rooted American tra-dition of liberal-conservative synthesis. Conservative authority, yes; right-wing authoritarianism, no. Authority means a necessary reverence for tradition, law, legitimism; authoritarianism means sta-tist coercion based only on force, not moral roots, and suppressing individual liberties in the Continental fashion of czardom, Junkerdom, Maistrean ultra-royalism.

Our argument is not against importing European insights when applicable; that would be Know-Nothing chauvinism. The more foreign imports the better, when capable of being assimilated: for example, the techniques of French sym-bolism in studying American poetry or the status-resentment theory of Nietz-sche in studying the new American right. But when the European view or insti-tution is neither applicable to the Ameri-can reality nor capable of being assimi-lated therein, as is the case with the sweeping Maistre-style anti-liberalism and tyrannic authoritarianism of many of the new conservatives, then objec-tions do become valid, not on grounds of bigoted American chauvinism but on grounds of distinguishing between what can, what cannot, be transplanted vi-ably and freedom-enhancingly.

The Burkean builds on the conrete existing historical base, not on a vacuum of abstract wishful thinking. When, as in America, that concrete base includes British liberalism of the 1680's and New Deal reforms of the 1930's, then the real American conserver assimilates into con-servatism whatever he finds lasting and good in liberalism and in the New Deal. Thereby he is closer to the Tory Cardi-nal Newman than many of Newman's American reactionary admirers. The latter overlook Newman's realization of the need to "inherit and make the best of" liberalism in certain contexts:

If I might presume to contrast Lacordaire and myself, I should say that we had been both of us inconsistent;—he, a Cath-olic, in calling himself a Liberal; I, a Protestant, in being an Anti-liberal; and moreover, that the cause of this incon-sistency had been in both cases one and the same. That is, we were both of us such good conservatives as to take up with what we happened to find established in our respective countries, at the time when we came into active life. Toryism was the creed of Oxford; he inherited, and made the best of, the French Revolu-tion.[1]

How can thoughtful new conserva-tives, avoiding the political pitfalls that so many have failed to avoid, apply fruitfully to American life today what we have called non-political "cultural conservatism"—the tradition of Mel-ville, Hawthorne, Thoreau, Henry Ad-ams, Irving Babbit, William Faulkner? In order to conserve our classical hu-manistic values against what he called "the impieties of progress," Melville had issued the following four-line warning to both kinds of American material-ists: (1) the deracinating, technology-brandishing industrialists; their so-called freedom and progress is merely the eco-nomic "individualism" of Manchester-liberal pseudo-conservatism; and (2) the leftist collectivists; their unity is not a rooted organic growth of shared values[2] but a mechanical artifact of apriorist blueprint abstractions,[3] imposed gash-ingly upon concrete society by a pro-crustean statist bureaucracy. The last-named distinction—between a unity that is grown and a unity that is made—dif-ferentiates the anti-cash-nexus and anti-rugged-individualism of "Tory Socialists" (in the aristocratic Shaftesbury-Disraeli-F.D.R.-Stevenson tradition) from the anti-capitalism of Marxist Socialists or left-liberal materialists. Here, then, is Melville's little-known warning to both bourgeois and Marxist materialists:

---

[1] From the appendix of the second edition (London, 1865) of Newman's *Apologia Pro Vita Sua*.
[2] Here to be defined as "archetypes."
[3] Here to be defined as "stereotypes."

Not magnitude, not lavishness,
But Form—the site;
Not innovating wilfulness,
But reverence for the Archetype.

A scrutiny of the plain facts of the situation has forced our report on the new conservatives to be mainly negative. But a positive contribution is indeed being made by all those thinkers, novelists, and poets in the spirit of this Melville quotation today (whether or not they realize their own conservatism) who are making Americans aware of the tragic antithesis between archetypes and stereotypes in life and between art and technique literature. Let us clarify this closely related pair of antitheses and then briefly apply them to that technological brilliance which is corrupting our life and literature today. Only by this unpopular and needed task, closer in spirit to the creative imagination of a Faulkner or an Emily Dickson than to the popular bandwagons of politics, can the new conservatism still overcome its current degeneration into either (at best) Manchester-liberal economic materialism or (at worst) right-wing nationalist thought control. And only via this task can America itself humanize and canalize its technological prowess creatively, instead of being dehumanized and mechanized by it in the sense of Thoreau's "We do not ride on the railroad; it rides upon us."

Every outlook has its own characteristic issue of moral choice. For thoughtful conservatives today, the meaningful moral choice is not between conforming and nonconforming but between conforming to the ephemeral, stereotyped values of the moment and conforming to the ancient, lasting, archetypal values shared by all creative cultures.

Archetypes have grown out of the soil of history—slowly, painfully, organically. Stereotypes have been manufactured out of the mechanical processes of mass production—quickly, painlessly, artificially. They have been synthesized in the labs of the entertainment industries and in the blueprints of the social engineers.

The philistine conformist and the ostentatious professional nonconformist are alike in being rooted in nothing deeper than the thin topsoil of stereotypes, the stereotypes of Babbitt Senior and Babbitt Junior respectively.

The sudden uprooting of archetypes was the most important consequence of the worldwide industrial revolution. This moral wound, this cultural shock was even more important than the economic consequences of the industrial revolution. Liberty depends on a substratum of fixed archetypes, as opposed to the arbitrary shuffling about of laws and institutions. The distinction holds true whether the shuffling about be done by the apriorist abstract rationalism of the eighteenth century or by the even more inhuman and metallic mass production of the nineteenth century, producing new traumas and new uprootings every time some new mechanized stereotype replaces the preceding one. The contrast between institutions grown organically and those shuffled out of arbitrary rationalist liberalism was summed up by a British librarian on being asked for the French constitution "Sorry, sir, but we don't keep periodicals."

Every stereotyped society swallows up the diversities of private bailiwicks, private eccentricities, private inner life, and the creativity inherent in concrete personal loyalties and in loving attachments to unique local roots and their rich historical accretions. Apropos the creative potential of local roots, let us recall not only Burke's words on the need for loyalty to one's own "little platoon" but also Synge's words, in the Ireland of 1907, on "the springtime of the local life," where the imagination of man is still "fiery and magnificent and tender." The creative imagination of the free artist and free scientist requires private elbowroom, free from the pressure of centralization and the pressure of adjustment to a mass average. This requirement holds true even when the centralization is benevolent and even when the mass average replaces sub-average diversities. Intolerable is the very concept of some busybody benevolence, whether economic, moral, or psychiatric, "curing" all diversity by making it average."

Admittedly certain kinds of diversity are perfectly dreadful; they threaten everything superior and desirable. But at some point the cure to these threats will endanger the superior and the desirable even more than do the threats themselves. The most vicious maladjustments, economic, moral, or psychiatric, will at some point become less dangerous to the free mind than the overadjustment—the stereotyping—needed to cure them.

In the novel and in the poem, the most corrupting stereotype of all is the substitution of good technique for art. What once resulted from the inspired audacity of a heartbreakingly lonely craftsman is now mass-produced in painless, safe, and uninspired capsules. This process is taking over every category of education and literature. The stream of consciousness for which James Joyce wrestled in loneliness with language; the ironic perspective toward society that Proust attained not as entertainment but as tragedy; the quick, slashing insights for which a Virginia Woolf bled out her heart, all these intimate personal achievements of the unstandardized private life are today the standard props of a hundred hack imitators, mechanically vending what is called "the *New Yorker*-type story." Don't underestimate that type of story; though an imitation job, it is imitation with all the magnificent technical skill of America's best-edited weekly. And think of the advantages: no pain any more, no risk any more, no more nonsense of inspiration. Most modern readers are not even bothered by the difference between such an efficient but bloodless machine job and the living product of individual heart's anguish.

What, then, is the test for telling the coffee from the Nescafe—the true artistic inspiration from the jar of Instant Muse?

The test is pain. Not mere physical pain but the exultant, transcending pain of selfless sacrifice. The test is that holy pain, that brotherhood of sacrifice, that aristocracy of creative suffering of which Baudelaire wrote, *"Je sais que la douleur est l'unique noblesse."* In other words, in a free democracy the only justified aristocracy is that of the lonely creative bitterness, the artistically creative scars of the fight for the inner imagination against outer mechanization—the fight for the private life.

II

Nationalist demagogy, whether McCarthy style or John Birch style, would never have become such a nuisance if liberal intellectuals and New Dealers had earlier made themselves the controlling spearhead of American anti-Communism with the same fervor they shows when spearheading anti-fascism. Only because they defaulted that duty of equal leadership against both kinds of tyranny, only because of the vacuum of leadership created by that default, were the bullies and charlatans enabled partly to fill the vacuum and partly to exploit the cause of anti-Communism. Such had been the thesis of my book *Shame and Glory of the Intellectuals*—a thesis entirely valid for the postwar Yalta era of illusions about Communism among the Henry Wallace kind of liberal and New Dealer.

Today that era is long over. It is ironic that Johnny-come-lately anti-Communists like McCarthy and the Birchers did not attack New Dealers until after the latter had got over the pro-Communist illusions that some of them undoubtedly and disastrously had. Today it is no longer in the interest of our two political camps to go on forever with such recriminations of the past. What is to the co-operative interest of both parties is to make sure that both are not replaced (after an intervening Kennedy era) by the "rejoicing third"—some new movement of nationalist demagogy. Conservatives have no more excuse to refuse to co-operate with liberals and New Dealers against right-wing nationalist threats to our shared liberties than to refuse to co-operate against comparable left-wing threats.

Fortunately, many Burkean new conservatives—Raymond English, Chad Walsh, Thomas Cook, Clinton Rossiter, J. A. Lukacs, August Heckscher, Will Herberg, Reinhold Niebuhr, and other distinguished names—have always been active and effective foes of the thought-control nationalists. Every one of these names achieved a record of all-out, explicit anti-McCarthyism in the days when that demagogue still seemed a danger and when it still took courage, not opportunism, to attack him. The same cannot be said of other, often better-known "new conservatives." They failed the acid test of the McCarthy temptation of the 1950's in the same way that the fellow-traveler kind of liberal failed the acid test of the Communist temptation of the 1930's. Both temptations were not only ethical tests of integrity but also psychological tests of balance and aesthetic tests of good taste.

Apropos such tests, Clinton Rossiter concludes, in his book *Conservatism in America*, "Unfortunately for the cause of conservatism, Kirk has now begun to sound like a man born one hundred and fifty years too late and in the wrong country." But it is pleasanter to see the positive, not only the negative, in a fellow-writer one esteems. Let us partly overlook Kirk's silence about the McCarthy thought-control menace in Chicago. Let us partly overlook his lack of silence in supporting as so-called "conservatives" the Goldwater Manchester liberals of old-guard Republicanism (as if historic Anglo-American conservatism, with its Disraeli-Churchill-Hughes-Roosevelt tradition of humane social reform, could ever be equated with the robber-baron kind of *laisser-faire* capitalism). Fortunately, Kirk's positive contribution sometimes almost balances such embarrassing ventures into practical national politics. His positive contribution consists of his sensitive, perceptive rediscovery of literary and philosophical figures

like Irving Babbitt and George Santayana for a true humanistic conservatism today.

Even at its best, even when avoiding the traps of right-wing radicalism, the new conservatism is partly guilty of causing the emotional deep-freeze that today makes young people ashamed of generous social impulses. New conservatives point out correctly that in the 1930's many intellectuals wasted generous emotions on unworthy causes, on Communist totalitarianism masked as liberalism. True enough—indeed, a point many of us, as "premature" anti-Communists, were making already in those days. But it does not follow, from recognizing the wrong generosities of the past, that we should today have no generous emotions at all, not even for many obviously worthy causes all around us, such as desegregation. Not only liberals but conservatives like Burke (reread his speeches against the slave trade) and John Adams and John Quincy Adams (among America's first fighters for Negro rights) have fought fascism as contradicting our traditional Christian view of man.

The cost of being a genuine Burke-Adams conservative today is that you will be misrepresented in two opposite ways—as being really liberals at heart, hypocritically pretending to be conservatives; as being authoritarian reactionaries at heart, hypocritically pretending to be devoted to civil liberties. So far as the first misrepresentation goes; devotion to civil liberties is not a monopoly of liberals. It is found in liberals and Burkean conservatives alike, as shown in the exchange of letters in their old age between the liberal Thomas Jefferson and his good friend, the conservative John Adams. So far as the second misrepresentation goes: the test of whether a new conservative is sincere about civil liberties or merely a rightist authoritarian is the same as the test of whether any given liberal of the 1930s was sincere about civil liberties or merely a leftist authoritarian. That test (which Senator Goldwater fails) is twofold, involving one question about practice, one question about theory. In practice, does the given conservative or liberal show his devotion to civil liberties in deeds as well as words? In theory, does he show awareness of a law we may here define as the law of compensatory balance? The law of compensatory balance makes the exposure of Communist fellow-traveling the particular duty of liberals, the exposure of right-wing thought-controllers the particular duty of conservatives.

Here are some further implications of the law of compensatory balance. A traditional monarchy is freest, as in Scandinavia, when anticipating social-democracy in humane reforms; an untraditional, centralized mass democracy is freest when encouraging, even to the point of tolerating eccentricity and arrogance, the remnants it possesses of aristocracy, family and regional pride, and decentralized provincial divergencies, traditions, privileges. A conservative is most valuable when serving in the more conservative party. Thus the conservative Burke belonged not to the Tory but to the Whig Party. Similarly Madison, whose tenth *Federalist* paper helped found and formulate our conservative Constitutionalist tradition of distrusting direct democracy and majority dictatorship, joined the liberal Jeffersonian party, not the Federalist Party. Reinhold Niebuhr, conservative in his view of history and anti-modernist, anti-liberal in theology, is not a Republican but a New Dealer in political-party activities.

III

Our distinction between rooted conservatives and rootless, counterrevolutionary doctrinaires is the measure of the difference between two different groups in contemporary America: the humanistic value-conservers and the materialistic old-guard Republicans. The latter are what a wrong and temporary journalistic usage often calls "conservative." It is more accurate to call them

nineteenth-century Manchester liberals with roots no deeper than the relatively recent post-Civil War "gilded age." Already on May 28, 1903, Winston Churchill denied them and their British counterparts the name of conservatives when he declared in Parliament:

> The new fiscal policy (of high tariffs) means a change, not only in the historic English parties but in the conditions of our public life. The old Conservative Party with its religious convictions and constitutional principles will disappear and a new party will arise. . .like perhaps the Republican Party in the United States of America. . .rigid, materialist and secular, whose opinions will turn on tariffs and who will cause the lobbies to be crowded with the touts of protected industries.

The Churchill quotation applies well to Senator Goldwater today. This charming and personable orator is a *laisser-faire* Manchester liberal when humane social reforms are at stake. But, as in Churchill in the above quotation, he is ready to make an exception against *laisser-faire* when protection of privileged industry is involved. The Burkean conservative today cherishes New Deal reforms in economics and Lockean parliamentary liberalism in politics, as traditions that are here to stay. Indeed, it is not the least of the functions of the new conservatism to force a now middle-aged New Deal to realize that it has become conservative and rooted, and that therefore it had better stop parroting the anti-Constitutional, anti-traditional slogans of its youth. These slogans are now being practiced instead, and to a wilder extent than even the most extreme New Deal liberal ever envisaged, by the Republican radicals of the right, with their wild-eyed schemes for impeaching Justice Warren or abolishing taxes.

The best-rooted philosophical conservatives in America derive from the anti-material-progress tradition of Melville and Irving Babbitt; they are found mainly in the literary and educational world, the creative world at its best, the non-political world. Politics will not be ready for their ideas for another generation; they should shed their illusions on that score. The normal time lag of a generation likewise separated the literary and university origin of Coleridge's conservatism from its osmosis into the politics of Disraeli Toryism.

Sir Henry Maine (1822-1888), one of the world's leading authorities on constitutions, called America's Constitution the most successful conservative bulwark in history against majority tyranny and mass radicalism and on behalf of traditional liberties and continuity of framework. Later scholars like Louis Hartz prefer to derive our free heritage not from the Burkean and Federalist ideas of Adams and the Constitution but from eighteenth-century Lockean liberalism. Both sides are partly right and need not exclude each other. For Locke's liberalism is a relatively moderate and tradition-respecting brand when compared with the Continental, anti-traditional liberalism of Rousseau, not to mention the Jacobins. So we come full circle in America's political paradox; our conservatism, in the absence of medieval feudal relica, must grudgingly admit it has little real tradition to conserve except that of liberalism—which then turns out to be a relatively conservative liberalism.

The need for new conservatives to maintain continuity *also* with well-rooted liberal traditions does not mean conservatism and liberalism are the same. Their contrast may be partly and briefly defined[4] as the tragic cyclical view of man, based on a political secularization of original sin, versus the optimistic faith in the natural goodness of man and mass and the inevitability of linear progress. In Coleridgian terms, conservatism is the concrete organic growth of institutions, as if they were trees, while rationalist

liberalism is an abstract, mechanical moving around of institutions as if they were separate pieces of furniture. Conservatism serves "growingness" and moves inarticulately and traditionally, like the seasons; liberalism serves "progress" and moves consciously and systematically, like geometry. The former is a circle, the latter an ever-advancing straight line. Both are equally needed half truths; both are equally inherent in the human condition, liberalism on a more rational level and conservatism on a perhaps deeper level. It may be generalized that the conservative mind does not like to generalize. Conservative theory is anti-theoretical. The liberal and rationalist mind consciously articulates abstract blueprints; the conservative mind unconsciously incarnates concrete traditions. Liberal formulas define freedom; conservative traditions embody it.

Even while philosophical conservatives support liberals in day-to-day measures of social humaneness or of Constitutional liberties against rightist or leftist radicals, the above basic contrast between the two temperaments will always remain. For these contrasts are symbolized by contrasting spokesmen in our history. George Washington, John Adams, and the Federalists are not the same as apriorist egalitarians like Paine, or believers in natural goodness like Jefferson. John Calhoun is not the same as Andrew Jackson. Barrett Wendell, Irving Babbitt, Paul Elmer More are not the same as the spokesmen of our liberal weeklies or of the New York *Post*. Charles Evans Hughes is not the same as La Follette or even Woodrow Wilson. No, the need for conservative continuity with America's institutionalized liberal past does not mean identity with liberalism, least of all with optimism about human nature, or utilitarian overemphasis on material progress, or trust in the direct democracy of the masses. Instead, conservative continuity with our liberal past simply means that you cannot escape from history; history has provided America with a shared liberal-conservative base more liberal than European

---

[4] Longer, more complete definition, with all the needed specific examples in political and intellectual life, is attempted in the first three chapters of the present writer's Anvil paperback, *Conservatism from John Adams to Churchill* (Van Nostrand Company, Princeton, 1956).

Continental conservatives, more conservative than European Continental liberals.

This shared liberal-conservative base is a rooted reality, not a rightist nostalgia for roots, and from it grows the core of the New Deal and of the Kennedy program, as opposed to the inorganic, mechanical abstractions of either a Karl Marx or an Adam Smith. So let new conservatives stop becoming what they accuse liberals of being—rootless doctrinaires.

IV

When asked by President Teddy Roosevelt what the justification was of Austria's supposedly outdated monarchy, the old Hapsburg emperor Francis Joseph replied, "To protect my peoples from their governments." Similarly Disraeli—like Lord Bolingbroke of the early eighteenth century—defended the Crown and the Established Church as bulwarks of the people's rights against Ephemeral politicians. The throne, whether Hapsburg or British, serves to moderate excesses of nationalistic or economic pressure groups against individual rights. In non-monarchic America, this same indispensable protection of liberty against the mob tyranny of transient majorities is performed by the Supreme Court, that similarly hallowed and aloof inheritor of the monarchic aura.

So conservatism fights on two fronts. It fights the atomistic disunity of unregulated capitalism. It fights the merely bureaucratic, merely mechanical unity of modern Socialism. It fights both for the sake of organic unity—but thereby runs the risk of creating a third threat of its own. For within its organic unity lies the totalitarian threat whenever the free individual is sacrificed totally and without guarantees (instead of partly and with constitutional guarantees) to that unity. Such a total sacrifice of individual to society took place in German romanticism; organic unity there became an anti-individual cult of the folk-state (Volk).

This cult took place already in the nineteenth century. It not only unbalanced German conservatism toward extreme statism (via Hegel) but unwittingly prepared the German people psychologically for Hitler's gangster unity.

The proper conservative balance between individual diversity and organic social unity has been best formulated by Coleridge, in 1831:

> The difference between an inorganic and an organic body lies in this: in the first—a sheaf of corn—the whole is nothing more than a collection of the individual parts of phenomena. In the second—a man—the whole is everything and the parts are nothing. A State is an idea intermediate between the two, the whole being a result from, and not a mere total of, the parts,—and yet not so merging the constituent parts in the result, but that the individual exists integrally within it.

Coleridgian conservatism, the height of the conservative philosophy, lies in the above intermediate "and yet", which saves the "individual integrally" while linking him organically. The folk romanticism of Germany and the "Third Rome" heritage of czarist Russia upset that balance in favor of "the whole is everything, the parts nothing," thereby paving the way for Nazism and Communism respectively. On the opposite extreme, America upset that Coleridgian balance in favor of "the whole is nothing" ("a sheaf of corn")—after the chaotic robber-baron individualists emerged as the real victors of the Civil War. So the proper rebalancing ("intermediate between the two") would promote an almost exaggerated individualism in Germany and Russia and an almost exaggerated "socialistic" or New Deal unity in America, not for its own sake but to even the scales.

Therefore in America it is often the free trade unions who unconsciously are our ablest representatives of the word they hate and misunderstand—conservatism. The organic unity they restore to the atomized "proletariat" is the providential Coleridgian "intermediate" between doctrinaire capitalism and doctrinaire Socialism. In the words of Frank Tannenbaum in *A Philosophy of Labor,* 1952

> Trade unionism is the conservative movement of our time. It is the counter-revolution. Unwittingly, it has turned its back upon most of the political and economic ideas that have nourished western Europe and the United States during the last two centuries. In practice, though not in words, it denies the heritage that stems from the French Revolution and from English liberalism. It is also a complete repudiation of Marxism. . . .
>
> In contrast with (Communism, Fascism, and *laisser-faire* capitalism) the trade union has involved a clustering of men about their work. This fusion (the new, medieval-style organic society) has been going on for a long time. It has been largely unplanned. . . .There is a great tradition of humanism and compassion in Europe and American politics, philosophy, and law, which counters, at first ineffectively, the driving forces operating for the atomization of society and the isolation of man. That tradition in England includes such names as Cobbett, Shaftesbury, Romilly, Dickens, Byron, Coleridge, Carlyle, Ruskin, Charles Kingsley. . . .The trade union is the real alternative to the authoritarian state. The trade union is our modern "society", the only true society that industrialism has fostered. As a true society it is concerned with the whole man, and embodies the possibilities of both the freedom and the security essential to human dignity.

This Tannenbaum passage is both conservative and new. Yet it would fill with horror the Kirk-Goldwater kind of mind that today claims to speak for "the new conservatism." Such horror is not an argument against Tannenbaum nor against a new conservatism. It is an argument against the misuse of language. And it is an argument against that old-guard wing of the Republican Party which has yet to learn the anti-rightist warning spoken in 1790 by the conservative Burke: "A state without the means of some change is without the means of its conservation."

What about the argument (very sincerely believed by the *National Review* and old-guard Republicans) that denies the label "conservative" to those of us who support trade unionism and who selectively support many New Deal reforms? According to this argument, our support of such humane and revolution-preventing reforms in *politics*—by New Dealers and democratic Socialists—makes us indistinguishable in *philosophy* from New Dealers and democratic Socialists. Similarly our support of the liberal position on civil liberties in politics supposedly makes us indistinguishable from liberals in philosophy. Shall we then cease to call ourselves philosophical conservatives, despite our conservative view of history and human nature?

The answer is: Children, don't oversimplify, don't pigeonhole; allow for pluralistic overlappings that defy abstract blueprints and labels. Trade unionists (and some of the new humanistic, non-statist Socialists that are evolving in England and West Germany) may be what Frank Tannenbaum calls "the conservative-counter-revolution" despite themselves (a neo-medieval organic society) and against their own conscious intentions. Meanwhile, self-styled conservatives are often unconscious anarchic wreckers and uprooters (from the French O.A.S. to America's second generation of campus neo-McCarthyites). Moreover, the same social reform in politics may be supported for very different philosophical reasons. To cite an old example newly relevant today, the support of the workingman's right to vote and right to strike by both the Chartists and the Tory Disraeli merely means that some support a reform as a first step to mass revolution while others support the same reform to woo the masses away from revolution and to give them a sense of belongingness by changing them from masses to individuals.

Finally, there is the distinction between what is done and how it is done. This distinction differentiates the conservative from the democratic Socialist and from the New Deal bureaucrat even when they all vote the same ticket (as so many of us could not help but do, given the Republican alternative, in the case of Roosevelt, Stevenson, and Kennedy). This distinction, this clarification of the proper use of "conservative," is found in an important and much-discussed essay by August Heckscher, at that time the chief editorial writer of the New York *Herald Tribune* and in 1962 appointed President Kennedy's Consultant for Cultural Affairs. Writing in the Harvard magazine *Confluence* in September, 1953, Mr. Heckscher said:

> The failure to understand the true nature of conservatism has made political campaigns in the United States signally barren of intellectual content. In debate it is difficult at best to admit that you would do the same thing as the opposition, but in a different way. Yet the spirit in which things are done really does make a difference, and can distinguish a sound policy from an unsound one. Social reforms can be undertaken with the effect of draining away local energies, reducing the citizenry to an undifferentiated mass, and binding it to the shackles of the all-powerful state. Or they can be undertaken with the effect of strengthening the free citizen's stake in society. The ends are different. The means will be also, if men have the wit to distinguish between legislation which encourages voluntary participation and legislation which involves reckless spending and enlargement of the federal bureaucracy.
>
> It is easy to say that such distinctions are not important. A conservative intellectual like Peter Viereck is constantly challenged, for example, because in a book like *Shame and Glory of the Intellectuals* he supports a political program not dissimilar in its outlines from that which was achieved during twenty years of social renovation under the Democrats. But the way reforms are undertaken is actually crucial. Concern for the individual, reluctance to have the central government perform what can be done as well by the state or to have the public perform what can be done as well by private enterprise—these priorities involve values. And such values (upheld by writers like Mr. Viereck) are at the

heart of modern conservatism. . . .So conservatism at best remains deeper and more pervasive than any party; and a party that does claim it exclusively is likely to deform and exploit it for its own purposes.

In conclusion, let us broaden the discussion from America into certain worldwide considerations about the nature of despotism. They are considerations about which all men of good will can agree as a strategy of freedom, whether New Deal social democrats or Manchester-liberal Republicans or Burkean conservatives. If there is no such agreement, then the epitaph on the tombstone of freedom may appropriately be these lines of Yeats:

Things fall apart; the center cannot hold. . . .
The best lack all conviction, while the worst
Are full of passionate intensity.

According to the neo-Stalinist wing in Russia today, almost all intellectuals and reformers are secret agents of western capitalism. According to the right wing today in America, almost all intellectuals and reformers are secret agents of eastern Communism. Mirror images, of course. And wrong twice.

Each mirror image needs the other and reflects on the other. They need each other as bogeymen. They reflect on each other because each leftist extreme frightens waverers into the rightist camp; each rightist extreme frightens waverers into the leftist camp. McCarthyism used to frighten European liberals into being fellow-travelers with Communism. Communism frightens American conservatives into being fellow-travelers with the pseudo-conservative nationalist thought controllers.

Neither mirror image is strong enough to destroy freedom by itself. Freedom is destroyed when both attack at the same time. Lenin was able to seize power in November, 1917, only because the new Duma government had been weakened by right-wing authoritarians, the John Birchers of Russia, who slandered it as "Red" and who had undermined it by the Kornilov Putsch in September.

Hitler was able to seize power in 1933 only because the Weimar Republic had been weakened by Communist authoritarians, who slandered it as "social Fascist" and who had undermined it by postwar Putsches. In 1962 in France, the anti-de Gaulle Communists and the O.A.S. rightists are examples of the same process in our own time. So are the Gizenga leftists and Tshombe rightists in the Congo.

In both Congo and California, in France today as in Kerensky's Russia yesterday, the fellow-traveler left and the thought-control right are still needing each other and feeding each other, as against the center. Meanwhile in every country the Burke-style conservatives, who revere a rooted constitution, and the Mill-style liberals, who revere civil liberties, likewise need each other: to unite against what Metternich called "the white radicals" of the right as well as the red radicals. Hence this slogan to end all slogans: "LIBERTARIANS OF THE WORLD, UNITE! YOU HAVE NOTHING TO LOSE BUT ABSTRACTIONS. YOU HAVE A WORLD TO CHAIN."

Liberties versus "liberty." Concrete liberties, preserved by the chains of ethics, versus abstract liberty-in-quotes, betrayed by messianic sloganizing, betrayed into the far grimmer chains of totalitarianism. "Man was born free" (said Rousseau, with his faith in the natural goodness of man) "but is everywhere in chains." "In chains, and so he ought to be," replies the thoughtful conservative, defending the good and wise and necessary chains of rooted tradition and historical continuity, upon which depend the civil liberties, the shared civil liberties of modern liberals and conservatives, and parliamentary monarchists, and democratic Socialists. Without the chaos-chaining, the id-chaining heritage of rooted values, what is to keep man from becoming Eichmann or Nechayev—what is to save freedom from "freedom"?

WORKS BY PETER VIERECK

Viereck, Peter. *Conservatism: From John Adams to Churchill.* Princeton, N.J.: Van Nostrand, 1956.

_____. *Conservatism Revisited and The New Conservatives: What Went Wrong.* New York: The Free Press, 1965.

_____. *Conservatism Revisited—The Revolt Against Revolt 1815-1949.* New York: C. Scribner's Sons, 1949.

_____. *Dream and Responsibility: The Tension between Poetry and Society.* Washington: University Press of Washington, D.C., 1953.

_____. *The First Morning: New Poems.* New York: C. Scribner's Sons, 1952.

_____. *Metapolitics—From the Romantics to Hitler.* New York: A.A. Knopf, 1941.

_____. *Meta-politics, The Roots of the Nazi Mind.* New York: Capricorn Books, 1961.

_____. *New and Selected Poems, 1932-1967.* Indianapolis: Bobbs-Merrill, 1967.

_____. *The Persimmon Tree; New Pastoral and Lyrical Poems.* New York: C. Scribner's Sons, 1956.

_____. *Shame and Glory of the Intellectual.* Boston: Beacon Press, 1953.

_____. *Strike Through the Mask: New Lyrical Poems.* New York: C. Scribner's Sons, 1950.

_____. *Terror and Decorum, 1940-1948.* New York: C. Scribner's Sons, 1950.

_____. *The Tree Witch: A Verse Drama.* New York: C. Scribner's Sons, 1961.

CHAPTER 19

Laissez-Faire Capitalism: Milton Friedman

MILTON Friedman (b. 1912) is a professor of economics at the University of Chicago. He served with the National Resources Commission, the National Bureau of Economic Research, and the U.S. Treasury Department before becoming a full-time teacher of economics. He is best known politically for his advocacy of unfettered free enterprise, as expressed in *Capitalism and Freedom;* other well-known books within the economics field are *Essays in Positive Economics* (1953), *A Theory of the Consumption Function* (1957), and *A Program for Monetary Stability* (1960).

From Capitalism and Freedom

THE RELATION BETWEEN ECONOMIC FREEDOM AND POLITICAL FREEDOM

It is widely believed that politics and economics are separate and largely unconnected; that individual freedom is a political problem and material welfare an economic problem; and that any kind

SOURCE. Reprinted from *Capitalism and Freedom* by permission of the publisher, The University of Chicago Press. Copyright 1962, The University of Chicago.

of political arrangements can be combined with any kind of economic arrangements. The chief contemporary manifestation of this idea is the advocacy of "democratic socialism" by many who condemn out of hand the restrictions on individual freedom imposed by "totalitarian socialism" in Russia, and who are persuaded that it is possible for a country to adopt the essential features of Russian economic arrangements and yet to ensure individual freedom through political arrangements. The thesis of this chapter is that such a view is a delusion, that there is an intimate connection between economics and politics, that only certain combinations of political and economic arrangements are possible, and that in particular, a society which is socialist cannot also be democratic, in the sense of guaranteeing individual freedom.

Economic arrangements play a dual role in the promotion of a free society. On the one hand, freedom in economic arrangements is itself a component of freedom broadly understood, so economic freedom is an end in itself. In the second place, economic freedom is also an indispensable means toward the achievement of political freedom.

The first of these roles of economic freedom needs special emphasis because intellectuals in particular have a strong bias against regarding this aspect of freedom as important. They tend to express contempt for what they regard as material aspects of life, and to regard their own pursuit of allegedly higher values as on a different plane of significance and as deserving of special attention. For most citizens of the country, however, if not for the intellectual, the direct importance of economic freedom is at least comparable in significance to the indirect importance of economic freedom as a means to political freedom.

The citizens of Great Britain, who after World War II was not permitted to spend his vacation in the United States because of exchange control, was being deprived of an essential freedom no less than the citizen of the United States, who was denied the opportunity to spend his vacation in Russia because of his political views. The one was ostensibly an economic limitation on freedom and the other a political limitation, yet there is no essential difference between the two.

The citizen of the United States who is compelled by law to devote something like 10 per cent of his income to the purchase of a particular kind of retirement contract, administered by the government, is being deprived of a corresponding part of his personal freedom. How strongly this deprivation may be felt and its closeness to the deprivation of religious freedom, which all would regard as "civil" or "political" rather than "economic," were dramatized by an episode involving a group of farmers of the Amish sect. On grounds of principle, this group regarded compulsory federal old age programs as an infringement of their personal individual freedom and refused to pay taxes or accept benefits. As a result, some of their livestock were sold by auction in order to satisfy claims for social security levies. True, the number of citizens who regard compulsory old age insurance as a deprivation of freedom may be few, but the believer in freedom has never counted noses.

A citizen of the United States who under the laws of various states is not free to follow the occupation of his own choosing unless he can get a license for it, is likewise being deprived of an essential part of his freedom. So is the man who would like to exchange some of his goods with, say, a Swiss for a watch but is prevented from doing so by a quota. So also is the Californian who was thrown into jail for selling Alka Seltzer at a price below that set by the manufacturer under so-called "fair trade" laws. So also is the farmer who cannot grow the amount of wheat he wants. And so on. Clearly, economic freedom, in and of itself, is an extremely important part of total freedom.

Viewed as a means to the end of political freedom, economic arrangements are important because of their effect on the concentration or dispersion of power. The kind of economic organization that provides economic freedom directly, namely, competitive capitalism, also promotes political freedom because it separates economic power from political power and in this way enables the one to offset the other.

Historical evidence speaks with a single voice on the relation between political freedom and a free market. I know of no example in time or place of a society that has been marked by a large measure of political freedom, and that has not also used something comparable to a free market to organize the bulk of economic activity.

Because we live in a largely free society, we tend to forget how limited is the span of time and the part of the globe for which there has ever been anything like political freedom: the typical state of mankind is tyranny, servitude, and misery. The nineteenth century and early twentieth century in the Western world stand out as striking exceptions to the general trend of historical development. Political freedom in this instance clearly came along with the free market and the development of capitalist institutions. So also did political freedom in the golden age of Greece and in the early days of the Roman era.

History suggests only that capitalism is a necessary condition for political freedom. Clearly it is not a sufficient condition. Fascist Italy and Fascist Spain, Germany at various times in the last seventy years, Japan before World Wars I and II, tzarist Russia in the decades before World War I—are all societies that cannot conceivably be described as politically free. Yet, in each, private enterprise was the dominant form of economic organization. It is therefore clearly possible to have economic arrangements that are fundamentally capitalist and political arrangements that are not free.

Even in those societies, the citizenry had a good deal more freedom than citizens of a modern totalitarian state like Russia or Nazi Germany, in which economic totalitarianism is combined with political totalitarianism. Even in Russia under the Tzars, it was possible for some citizens, under some circumstances, to change their jobs without getting permission from political authority because capitalism and the existence of private property provided some check to the centralized power of the state.

The relation between political and economic freedom is complex and by no means unilateral. In the early nineteenth century, Bentham and the Philosophical Radicals were inclined to regard political freedom as a means to economic freedom. They believed that the masses were being hampered by the restrictions that were being imposed upon them, and that if political reform gave the bulk of the people the vote, they would do what was good for them, which was to vote for *laissez faire*. In retrospect, one cannot say that they were wrong. There was a large measure of political reform that was accompanied by economic reform in the direction of a great deal of *laissez faire*. An enormous increase in the well-being of the masses followed this change in economic arrangements.

The triumph of Benthamite liberalism in nineteenth-century England was followed by a reaction toward increasing intervention by government in economic affairs. This tendency to collectivism was greatly accelerated, both in England and elsewhere, by the two World Wars. Welfare rather than freedom became the dominant note in democratic countries. Recognizing the implicit threat to individualism, the intellectual descendants of the Philosophical Radicals—Dicey, Mises, Hayek, and Simons, to mention only a few—feared that a continued movement toward centralized control of economic activity would prove *The Road to Serfdom,* as Hayek entitled his penetrating analysis of the process. Their emphasis was on economic freedom as a means toward political freedom.

Events since the end of World War II display still a different relation between economic and political freedom. Collectivist economic planning has indeed interfered with individual freedom. At least in some countries, however, the result has not been the suppression of freedom, but the reversal of economic policy. England again provides the most striking example. The turning point was perhaps the "control of engagements" order which, despite great misgivings, the Labour party found it necessary to impose in order to carry out its economic policy. Fully enforced and carried through, the law would have involved centralized allocation of individuals to occupations. This conflicted so sharply with personal liberty that it was enforced in a negligible number of cases, and then repealed after the law had been in effect for only a short period. Its repeal ushered in a decided shift in economic policy, marked by reduced reliance on centralized "plans" and "programs," by the dismantling of many controls, and by increased emphasis on the private market. A similar shift in policy occurred in most other democratic countries.

The proximate explanation of these shifts in policy is the limited success of central planning or its outright failure to achieve stated objectives. However, this failure is itself to be attributed, at least in some measure, to the political implications of central planning and to an unwillingness to follow out its logic when doing so requires trampling roughshod on treasured private rights. It may well be that the shift is only a temporary interruption in the collectivist trend of this century. Even so, it illustrates the close relation between political freedom and economic arrangements.

Historical evidence by itself can never be convincing. Perhaps it was sheer coincidence that the expansion of freedom occurred at the same time as the development of capitalist and market institutions. Why should there be a connection? What are the logical links between economic and political freedom? In discussing these questions we shall consider first the market as a direct component of freedom, and then the indirect relation between market arrangements and political freedom. A by-product will be an outline of the ideal economic arrangements for a free society.

As liberals, we take freedom of the individual, or perhaps the family, as our ultimate goal in judging social arrangements. Freedom as a value in this sense has to do with the interrelations among people; it has no meaning whatsoever to a Robinson Crusoe on an isolated island (without his Man Friday). Robinson Crusoe on his island is subject to "constraint," he has limited "power," and he has only a limited number of

alternatives, but there is no problem of freedom in the sense that is relevant to our discussion. Similarly, in a society freedom has nothing to say about what an individual does with his freedom; it is not an all-embracing ethic. Indeed, a major aim of the liberal is to leave the ethical problem for the individual to wrestle with. The "really" important ethical problems are those that face an individual in a free society—what he should do with his freedom. There are thus two sets of values that a liberal will emphasize—the values that are relevant to relations among people, which is the context in which he assigns first priority to freedom; and the values that are relevant to the individual in the exercise of his freedom, which is the realm of individual ethics and philosophy.

The liberal conceives of men as imperfect beings. He regards the problem of social organization to be as much a negative problem of preventing "bad" people from doing harm as of enabling "good" people to do good; and, of course, "bad" and "good" people may be the same people, depending on who is judging them.

The basic problem of social organization is how to co-ordinate the economic activities of large numbers of people. Even in relatively backward societies, extensive division of labor and specialization of function is required to make effective use of available resources. In advanced societies, the scale on which coordination is needed, to take full advantage of the opportunities offered by modern science and technology, is enormously greater. Literally millions of people are involved in providing one another with their daily bread, let alone with their yearly automobiles. The challenge to the believer in liberty is to reconcile this widespread interdependence with individual freedom.

Fundamentally, there are only two ways of co-ordinating the economic activities of millions. One is central direction involving the use of coercion—the technique of the army and of the modern totalitarian state. The other is voluntary cooperation of individuals—the technique of the market place.

The possibility of coordination through voluntary cooperation rests on the elementary—yet frequently denied—proposition that both parties to an economic transaction benefit from it, *provided the transaction is bi-laterally voluntary and informed.*

Exchange can therefore bring about coordination without coercion. A working model of a society organized through voluntary exchange is a *free private enterprise exchange economy*—what we have been calling competitive capitalism.

In its simplest form, such a society consists of a number of independent households—a collection of Robinson Crusoe, as it were. Each household uses the resources it controls to produce goods and services that it exchanges for goods and services produced by other households, on terms mutually acceptable to the two parties to the bargain. It is thereby enabled to satisfy its wants indirectly by producing goods and services for others, rather than directly by producing goods for its own immediate use. The incentive for adopting this indirect route is, of course, the increased product made possible by division of labor and specialization of function. Since the household always has the alternative of producing directly for itself, it need not enter into any exchange unless it benefits from it. Hence, no exchange will take place unless both parties do benefit from it. Cooperation is thereby achieved without coercion.

Specialization of function and division of labor would not go far if the ultimate productive unit were the household. In a modern society, we have gone much farther. We have introduced enterprises which are intermediaries between individuals in their capacities as suppliers of service and as purchasers of goods. And similarly, specialization of function and division of labor could not go very far if we had to continue to rely on the barter of product for product. In consequence, money has been introduced as a means of facilitating exchange, and of enabling the acts of purchase and of sale to be separated into two parts.

Despite the important role of enterprises and of money in our actual economy, and despite the numerous and complex problems they raise, the central characteristic of the market technique of achieving coordination is fully displayed in the simple exchange economy that contains neither enterprises nor money. As in that simple model, so in the complex enterprise and money-exchange economy, cooperation is strictly individual and voluntary *provided:* (a) that enterprises are private, so that the ultimate contracting parties are individuals and (b) that individuals are effectively free to enter or not to enter into any particular exchange, so that every transaction is strictly voluntary.

It is far easier to state these provisos in general terms than to spell them out in detail, or to specify precisely the institutional arrangements most conducive to their maintenance. Indeed, much of technical economic literature is concerned with precisely these questions. The basic requisite is the maintenance of law and order to prevent physical coercion of one individual by another and to enforce contracts voluntarily entered into, thus giving substance to "private." Aside from this, perhaps the most difficult problems arise from monopoly—which inhibits effective freedom by denying individuals alternatives to the particular exchange—and from "neighborhood effects"—effects on third parties for which it is not feasible to charge or recompense them. These problems will be discussed in more detail in the following chapter.

So long as effective freedom of exchange is maintained, the central feature of the market organization of economic activity is that it prevents one person from interfering with another in respect of most of his activities. The consumer is protected from coercion by the seller because of the presence of other sellers with whom he can deal. The seller is protected from coercion by the consumer because of other consumers to whom he can sell. The employee is protected from coercion by the employer because of other employers for whom he can work, and so on. And the market does this impersonally and without centralized authority.

Indeed a major source of objection to a free economy is precisely that it does this task so well. It gives people what they want instead of what a particular group thinks they ought to want. Underlying most arguments against the free market is a lack of belief in freedom itself.

The existence of a free market does not of course eliminate the need for government. On the contrary, government is essential both as a forum for determining the "rules of the game" and as an umpire to interpret and enforce the rules decided on. What the market does is to reduce greatly the range of issues that must be decided through political means, and thereby to minimize the extent to which government need participate directly in the game. The characteristic feature of action through political channels is that it tends to require or enforce substantial conformity. The great advantage of the market, on the other hand, is that it permits wide diversity. It is, in political terms, a system of proportional representation. Each man can vote, as it were, for the color of tie he wants and get it; he does not have to see what color the majority wants and then, if he is in the minority, submit.

It is this feature of the market that we refer to when we say that the market provides economic freedom. But this characteristic also has implications that go far beyond the narrowly economic. Political freedom means the absence of coercion of a man by his fellow men. The fundamental threat to freedom is power to coerce, be it in the hands of a monarch, a dictator, an oligarchy, or a momentary majority. The preservation of freedom requires the elimination of such concentration of power to the fullest possible extent and the dispersal and distribution of whatever power cannot be eliminated—a system of checks and balances. By removing the organization of economic activity from the control of political authority, the market eliminates this source of coercive power. It enables economic strength to be a check to political power rather than a reinforcement.

Economic power can be widely dispersed. There is no law of conservation which forces the growth of new centers of economic strength to be at the expense of existing centers. Political power, on the other hand, is more difficult to decentralize. There can be numerous small independent governments. But it is far more difficult to maintain numerous equipotent small centers of political power in a single large government than it is to have numerous centers of economic strength in a single large economy. There can be many millionaires in one large economy. But can there be more than one really outstanding leader, one person on whom the energies and enthusiasms of his countrymen are centered? If the central government gains power, it is likely to be at the expense of local governments. There seems to be something like a fixed total of political power to be distributed. Consequently, if economic power is joined to political power, concentration seems almost inevitable. On the other hand, if economic power is kept in separate hands from political power, it can serve as a check and a counter to political power.

The force of this abstract argument can perhaps best be demonstrated by example. Let us consider first, a hypothetical example that may help to bring out the principles involved, and then some actual examples from recent experience that illustrate the way in which the market works to preserve political freedom.

One feature of a free society is surely the freedom of individuals to advocate and propagandize openly for a radical change in the structure of the society—so long as the advocacy is restricted to persuasion and does not include force or other forms of coercion. It is a mark of the political freedom of a capitalist society that men can openly advocate and work for socialism. Equally, political freedom in a socialist society would require that men be free to advocate the introduction of capitalism. How could the freedom to advocate capitalism be preserved and protected in a socialist society?

In order for men to advocate anything, they must in the first place be able to earn a living. This already raises a problem in a socialist society, since all jobs are under the direct control of political authorities. It would take an act of self-denial whose difficulty is underlined by experience in the United States after World War II with the problem of "security" among Federal employees, for a socialist government to permit its employees to advocate policies directly contrary to official doctrine.

But let us suppose this act of self-denial to be achieved. For advocacy of capitalism to mean anything, the proponents must be able to finance their cause—to hold public meetings, publish pamphlets, buy radio time, issue newspapers and magazines, and so on. How could they raise the funds? There might and probably would be men in the socialist society with large incomes, perhaps even large capital sums in the form of government bonds and the like, but these would of necessity be high public officials. It is possible to conceive of a minor socialist official retaining his job although openly advocating capitalism. It strains credulity to imagine the socialist top brass financing such "subversive" activities.

The only recourse for funds would be to raise small amounts from a large number of minor officials. But this is no real answer. To tap these sources, many people would already have to be persuaded, and our whole problem is how to initiate and finance a campaign to do so. Radical movements in capitalist societies have never been financed this way. They have typically been supported by a few wealthy individuals who have become persuaded—by a Federick Van-

derbilt Field, or an Anita McCormick Blaine, or a Corliss Lamont, to mention a few names recently prominent, or by a Friedrich Engels, to go farther back. This is a role of inequality of wealth in preserving political freedom that is seldom noted—the role of the patron.

In a capitalist society, it is only necessary to convince a few wealthy people to get funds to launch any idea, however strange, and there are many such persons, many independent foci of support. And, indeed, it is not even necessary to persuade people or financial institutions with available funds of the soundness of the ideas to be propagated. It is only necessary to persuade them that the propagation can be financially successful; that the newspaper or magazine or book or other venture will be profitable. The competitive publisher, for example, cannot afford to publish only writing with which he personally agrees; his touchstone must be the likelihood that the market will be large enough to yield a satisfactory return on his investment.

In this way, the market breaks the vicious circle and makes it possible ultimately to finance such ventures by small amounts from many people without first persuading them. There are no such possibilities in the socialist society; there is only the all-powerful state.

Let us stretch our imagination and suppose that a socialist government is aware of this problem and is composed of people anxious to preserve freedom. Could it provide the funds? Perhaps, but it is difficult to see how. It could establish a bureau for subsidizing subversive propaganda. But how could it choose whom to support? If it gave to all who asked, it would shortly find itself out of funds, for socialism cannot repeal the elementary economic law that a sufficiently high price will call forth a large supply. Make the advocacy of radical causes sufficiently remunerative, and the supply of advocates will be unlimited.

Moreover, freedom to advocate unpopular causes does not require that such advocacy be without cost. On the contrary, no society could be stable if advocacy of radical change were costless, much less subsidized. It is entirely appropriate that men make sacrifices to advocate causes in which they deeply believe. Indeed, it is important to preserve freedom only for people who are willing to practice self-denial, for otherwise freedom degenerates into license and irresponsibility. What is essential is that the cost of advocating unpopular causes be tolerable and not prohibitive.

But we are not yet through. In a free market society, it is enough to have the funds. The suppliers of paper are as willing to sell it to the *Daily Worker* as to the *Wall Street Journal*. In a socialist society, it would not be enough to have the funds. The hypothetical supporter of capitalism would have to persuade a government factory making paper to sell to him, the government printing press to print his pamphlets, a government post office to distribute them among the people, a government agency to rent him a hall in which to talk, and so on.

Perhaps there is some way in which one could overcome these difficulties and preserve freedom in a socialist society. One cannot say it is utterly impossible. What is clear, however, is that there are very real difficulties in establishing institutions that will effectively preserve the possibility of dissent. So far as I know, none of the people who have been in favor of socialism and also in favor of freedom have really faced up to this issue, or even made a respectable start at developing the institutional arrangements that would permit freedom under socialism. By contrast, it is clear how a free market capitalist society fosters freedom.

A striking practical example of these abstract principles is the experience of Winston Churchill. From 1933 to the outbreak of World War II, Churchill was not permitted to talk over the British radio, which was, of course, a government monopoly administered by the British Broadcasting Corporation. Here was a leading citizen of his country, a Member of Parliament, a former cabinet minister, a man who was desperately trying by every device possible to persuade his countrymen to take steps to ward off the menace of Hitler's Germany. He was not permitted to talk over the radio to the British people because the BBC was a government monopoly and his position was too "controversial."

Another striking example, reported in the January 26, 1959 issue of *Time,* has to do with the "Blacklist Fadeout." Says the *Time* story,

The Oscar-awarding ritual is Hollywood's biggest pitch for dignity, but two years ago dignity suffered. When one Robert Rich was announced as top writer for *The Brave One,* he never stepped forward. Robert Rich was a pseudonym, masking one of about 150 writers. . . blacklisted by the industry since 1947 as suspected Communists or fellow travelers. The case was particularly embarrassing because the Motion Picture Academy had barred any Communist or Fifth Amendment pleader from Oscar competition. Last week both the Communist rule and the mystery of Rich's identity were suddenly rescripted.

Rich turned out to be Dalton *(Johnny Got His Gun)* Trumbo, one of the original "Hollywood Ten" writers who refused to testify at the 1947 hearings on Communism for the movie industry. Said producer Frank King, who had stoutly insisted that Robert Rich was "a young guy in Spain with a beard": "We have an obligation to our stockholders to buy the best script we can. Trumbo brought us *The Brave One* and we bought it". . . .

In effect it was the formal end of the Hollywood black list. For barred writers, the informal end came long ago. At least 15% of current Hollywood films are reportedly written by blacklist members. Said Producer King, "There are more ghosts in Hollywood than in Forest Lawn. Every company in town has used the work of blacklisted people. We're just the first to confirm what everybody knows."

One may believe, as I do, that communism would destroy all of our freedoms, one may be opposed to it as firmly and as strongly as possible, and yet, at the same time, also believe that in a free society it is intolerable for a man to be prevented from making voluntary arrangements with others that are mutually attractive because he believes in or is trying to promote communism. His freedom includes his freedom to promote communism. Freedom also, of course, includes the freedom of others not to deal with him under those circumstances. The Hollywood blacklist was an unfree act that destroys freedom because it was a collusive arrangement that used coercive means to prevent voluntary exchanges. It didn't work precisely because the market made it costly for people to preserve the blacklist. The commercial emphasis, the fact that people who are running enterprises have an incentive to make as much money as they can, protected the freedom of the individuals who were blacklisted by providing them with an alternative form of employment, and by giving people an incentive to employ them.

If Hollywood and the movie industry had been government enterprises or if in England it had been a question of employment by the British Broadcasting Corporation it is difficult to believe that the "Hollywood Ten" or their equivalent would have found employment. Equally, it is difficult to believe that under those circumstances, strong proponents of individualism and private enterprise—or indeed strong proponents of any view other than the status quo—would be able to get employment.

Another example of the role of the market in preserving political freedom, was revealed in our experience with McCarthyism. Entirely aside from the substantive issues involved, and the merits of the charges made, what protection did individuals, and in particular government employees, have against irresponsible accusations and probings into matters that it went against their conscience to reveal? Their appeal of the Fifth Amendment would have been a hollow mockery without an alternative to government employment.

Their fundamental protection was the existence of a private-market economy in which they could earn a living. Here again, the protection was not absolute. Many potential private employers were, rightly or wrongly, averse to hiring those pilloried. It may well be that there was far less justification for the costs generally imposed on people who advocate unpopular causes. But the important point is that the costs were limited and not prohibitive, as they would have been if government employment had been the only possibility.

It is of interest to note that a disproportionately large fraction of the people involved apparently went into the most competitive sectors of the economy—small business, trade, farming—where the market approaches most closely the ideal free market. No one who buys bread knows whether the wheat from which it is made was grown by a Communist or a Republican, by a constitutionalist or a Fascist, or, for that matter, by a Negro or a white. This illustrates how an impersonal market separates economic activities from political views and protects men from being discriminated against in their economic activities for reasons that are irrelevant to their productivity—whether these reasons are associated with their views or their color.

As this example suggests, the groups in our society that have the most at stake in the preservation and strengthening of competitive capitalism are those minority groups which can most easily become the object of the distrust and enmity of the majority—the Negroes, the Jews, the foreign-born, to mention only the most obvious. Yet, paradoxically enough, the enemies of the free market—the Socialists and Communists—have been recruited in disproportionate measure from these groups. Instead of recognizing that the existence of the market has protected them from the attitudes of their fellow countrymen, they mistakenly attribute the residual discrimination to the market.

THE ROLE OF GOVERNMENT
IN A FREE SOCIETY

A common objection to totalitarian societies is that they regard the end as justifying the means. Taken literally, this objection is clearly illogical. If the end does not justify the means, what does? But this easy answer does not dispose of the objection; it simply shows that the objection is not well put. To deny that the end justifies the means is indirectly to assert that the end in question is not the ultimate end, that the ultimate end is itself the use of the proper means. Desirable or not, any end that can be attained only by the use of bad means must give way to the more basic end of the use of acceptable means.

To the liberal, the appropriate means are free discussion and voluntary cooperation, which implies that any form of coercion is inappropriate. The ideal is unanimity among responsible individuals achieved on the basis of free and full discussion. This is another way of expressing the goal of freedom emphasized in the preceding chapter.

From this standpoint, the role of the market, as already noted, is that it permits unanimity without conformity; that it is a system of effectively proportional representation. On the other hand, the characteristic feature of action through explicitly political channels is that it tends to require or to enforce substantial conformity. The typical issue must be decided "yes" or "no"; at most, provision can be made for a fairly limited number of alternatives. Even the use of proportional representation in its explicitly political form does not alter this conclusion. The number of separate groups that can in fact be represented is narrowly limited, enormously so by comparison with the proportional representation of the market. More important, the fact that the final outcome generally must be a law applicable to all groups, rather than separate legislative enactments for each "party" represented, means that

proportional representation in its political version, far from permitting unanimity without conformity, tends toward ineffectiveness and fragmentation. It thereby operates to destroy any consensus on which unanimity with conformity can rest.

There are clearly some matters with respect to which effective proportional representation is impossible. I cannot get the amount of national defense I want and you, a different amount. With respect to such indivisible matters we can discuss, and argue, and vote. But having decided, we must conform. It is precisely the existence of such indivisible matters—protection of the individual and the nation from coercion are clearly the most basic—that prevents exclusive reliance on individual action through the market. If we are to use some of our resources for such indivisible items, we must employ political channels to reconcile differences.

The use of political channels, while inevitable, tends to strain the social cohesion essential for a stable society. The strain is least if agreement for joint action need be reached only on a limited range of issues on which people in any event have common views. Every extension of the range of issues for which explicit agreement is sought strains further the delicate threads that hold society together. If it goes so far as to touch an issue on which men feel deeply yet differently, it may well disrupt the society. Fundamental differences in basic values can seldom if ever be resolved at the ballot box; ultimately they can only be decided, though not resolved, by conflict. The religious and civil wars of history are a bloody testament to this judgment.

The widespread use of the market reduces the strain on the social fabric by rendering conformity unnecessary with respect to any activities it encompasses. The wider the range of activities covered by the market, the fewer are the issues on which explicitly political decisions are required and hence on which it is necessary to achieve agreement. In turn, the fewer the issues on which agreement is necessary, the greater is the likelihood of getting agreement while maintaining a free society.

Unanimity is, of course, an ideal. In practice, we can afford neither the time nor the effort that would be required to achieve complete unanimity on every issue. We must perforce accept something less. We are thus led to accept majority rule in one form or another as an expedient. That majority rule is an expedient rather than itself a basic principle is clearly shown by the fact that our willingness to resort to majority rule, and the size of the majority we require, themselves depend on the seriousness of the issue involved. If the matter is of little moment and the minority has no strong feelings about being overruled, a bare plurality will suffice. On the other hand, if the minority feels strongly about the issue involved, even a bare majority will not do. Few of us would be willing to have issues of free speech, for example, decided by a bare majority. Our legal structure is full of such distinctions among kinds of issues that require different kinds of majorities. At the extreme are those issues embodied in the Constitution. These are the principles that are so important that we are willing to make minimal concessions to expediency. Something like essential concensus was achieved initially in accepting them, and we require something like essential consensus for a change in them.

The self-denying ordinance to refrain from majority rule on certain kinds of issues that is embodied in our Constitution and in similar written or unwritten constitutions elsewhere, and the specific provisions in these constitutions or their equivalents prohibiting coercion of individuals, are themselves to be regarded as reached by free discussion and as reflecting essential unanimity about means.

I turn now to consider more specifically, though still in very broad terms, what the areas are that cannot be handled through the market at all, or can

be handled only at so great a cost that the use of political channels may be preferable.

GOVERNMENT AS RULE-MAKER AND UMPIRE

It is important to distinguish the day-to-day activities of people from the general customary and legal framework within which these take place. The day-to-day activities are like the actions of the participants in a game when they are playing it; the framework, like the rules of the game they play. And just as a good game requires acceptance by the players both of the rules and of the umpire to interpret and enforce them, so a good society requires that its members agree on the general conditions that will govern relations among them, on some means of arbitrating different interpretations of these conditions, and on some device for enforcing compliance with the generally accepted rules. As in games, so also in society, most of the general conditions are the unintended outcome of custom, accepted unthinkingly. At most, we consider explicitly only minor modifications in them, though the cumulative effect of a series of minor modifications may be a drastic alteration in the character of the game or of the society. In both games and society also, no set of rules can prevail unless most participants most of the time conform to them without external sanctions; unless that is, there is a broad underlying social consensus. But we cannot rely on custom or on this consensus alone to interpret and to enforce the rules; we need an umpire. These then are the basic roles of government in a free society: to provide a means whereby we can modify the rules, to mediate differences among us on the meaning of the rules, and to enforce compliance with the rules on the part of those few who would otherwise not play the game.

The need for government in these respects arises because absolute freedom is possible. However attractive anarchy may be as a philosophy, it is not feasible in a world of imperfect men. Men's freedoms can conflict, and when they do, one man's freedom must be limited to preserve another's—as a Supreme Court Justice once put it, "My freedom to move my first must be limited by the proximity of your chin."

The major problem in deciding the appropriate activities of government is how to resolve such conflicts among the freedoms of different individuals. In some cases, the answer is easy. There is little difficulty in attaining near unanimity to the proposition that one man's freedom to murder his neighbor must be sacrificed to preserve the freedom of the other man to live. In other cases, the answer is difficult. In the economic area, a major problem arises in respect of the conflict between freedom to combine and freedom to compete. What meaning is to be attributed to "free" as modifying "enterprise"? In the United States, "free" has been understood to mean anyone is free to set up an enterprise, which means that existing enterprises are not free to keep out competitors except by selling a better product at the same price or the same product at a lower price. In the continental tradition, on the other hand, the meaning has generally been that enterprises are free to do what they want, including the fixing of prices, division of markets, and the adoption of other techniques to keep out potential competitors. Perhaps the most difficult specific problem in this area arises with respect to combinations among laborers, where the problem of freedom to combine and freedom to compete is particularly acute.

A still more basic economic area in which the answer is both difficult and important is the definition of property rights. The notion of property, as it has developed over centuries and as it is embodied in our legal codes, has become so much a part of us that we tend to take it for granted, and fail to recognize the extent to which just what constitutes property and what rights the ownership

of property confers are complex social creations rather than self-evident propositions. Does my having title to land, for example, and my freedom to use my property as I wish, permit me to deny to someone else the right to fly over my land in his airplane? Or does his right to use his airplane take precedence? Or does this depend on how high he flies? Or how much noise he makes? Does voluntary exchange require that he pay me for the privilege of flying over my land? Or that I must pay him to refrain from flying over it? The mere mention of royalties, copyrights, patents; shares of stock in corporations; riparian rights, and the like, may perhaps emphasize the role of generally accepted social rules in the very definition of property. It may suggest also that, in many cases, the existence of a well specified and generally accepted definition of property is far more important than just what the definition is.

Another economic area that raises particularly difficult problems is the monetary system. Government responsibility for the monetary system has long been recognized. It is explicitly provided for in the constitutional provision which gives Congress the power "to coin money, regulate the value thereof, and of foreign coin." There is probably no other area of economic activity with respect to which government action has been so uniformly accepted. This habitual and by now almost unthinking acceptance of government responsibility makes thorough understanding of the grounds for such responsibility all the more necessary, since it enhances the danger that the scope of government will spread from activities that are, to those that are not, appropriate in a free society, from providing a monetary framework to determining the allocation of resources among individuals. We shall discuss this problem in detail in Chapter III.

In summary, the organization of economic activity through voluntary exchange presumes that we have provided, through government, for the maintenance of law and order to prevent coercion of one individual by another, the enforcement of contracts voluntarily entered into, the definition of the meaning of property rights, the interpretation and enforcement of such rights, and the provision of a monetary framework.

ACTION THROUGH GOVERNMENT ON GROUNDS OF TECHNICAL MONOPOLY AND NEIGHBORHOOD EFFECTS

The role of government just considered is to do something that the market cannot do for itself, namely, to determine, arbitrate, and enforce the rules of the game. We may also want to do through government some things that might conceivably be done through the market but that technical or similar conditions render it difficult to do in that way. These all reduce to cases in which strictly voluntary exchange is either exceedingly costly or practically impossible. There are two general classes of such cases: monopoly and similar market imperfections, and neighborhood effects.

Exchange is truly voluntary only when nearly equivalent alternatives exist. Monopoly implies the absence of alternatives and thereby inhibits effective freedom of exchange. In practice, monopoly frequently, is not generally, arises from government support or from collusive agreements among individuals. With respect to these, the problem is either to avoid governmental fostering of monopoly or to stimulate the effective enforcement of rules such as those embodied in our anti-trust laws. However, monopoly may also arise because it is technically efficient to have a single producer or enterprise. I venture to suggest that such cases are more limited than is supposed but they unquestionably do arise. A simple example is perhaps the provision of telephone services within a community. I shall refer to such cases as "technical" monopoly.

When technical conditions make a monopoly the natural outcome of competitive market forces, there are only three alternatives that seem available: private monopoly, public monopoly, or public regulation. All three are bad so we must choose among evils. Henry Simons, observing public regulation of monopoly in the United States, found the results so distasteful that he concluded public monopoly would be a lesser evil. Walter Eucken, a noted German liberal, observing public monopoly in German railroads, found the results so distasteful that he concluded public regulation would be a lesser evil. Having learned from both, I reluctantly conclude that, if tolerable, private monopoly may be the least of the evils.

If society were static so that the conditions which give rise to a technical monopoly were sure to remain, I would have little confidence in this solution. In a rapidly changing society, however, the conditions making for technical monopoly frequently change and I suspect that both public regulation and public monopoly are likely to be less responsive to such changes in conditions, to be less readily capable of elimination, than private monopoly.

Railroads in the United States are an excellent example. A large degree of monopoly in railroads was perhaps inevitable on technical grounds in the nineteenth century. This was the justification for the Interstate Commerce Commission. But conditions have changed. The emergency of road and air transport has reduced the monopoly element in railroads to negligible proportions. Yet we have not eliminated the ICC. On the contrary, the ICC, which started out as an agency to protect the public from exploitation by the railroads, has become an agency to protect railroads from competition by trucks and other means of transport, and more recently even to protect existing truck companies from competition by new entrants. Similarly, in England, when the railroads were nationalized, trucking was at first brought into the state monopoly.

If railroads had never been subjected to regulation in the United States, it is nearly certain that by now transportation, including railroads, would be a highly competitive industry with little or no remaining monopoly elements.

The choice between the evils of private monopoly, public monopoly, and public regulation cannot, however, be made once and for all, independently of the factual circumstances. If the technical monopoly is of a service or commodity that is regarded as essential and if its monopoly power is sizable, even the shortrun effects of private unregulated monopoly may not be tolerable, and either public regulation or ownership may be a lesser evil.

Technical monopoly may on occasion justify a *de facto* public monopoly. It cannot by itself justify a public monopoly achieved by making it illegal for anyone else to compete. For example, there is no way to justify our present public monopoly of the post office. It may be argued that the carrying of mail is a technical monopoly and that a government monopoly is the least of evils. Along these lines, one could perhaps justify a government post office but not the present law, which makes it illegal for anybody else to carry mail. If the delivery of mail is a technical monopoly, no one will be able to succeed in competition with the government. If it is not, there is no reason why the government should be engaged in it. The only way to find out is to leave other people free to enter.

The historical reason why we have a post office monopoly is because the Pony Express did such a good job of carrying the mail across the continent that, when the government introduced transcontinental service, it couldn't compete effectively and lost money. The result was a law making it illegal for anybody else to carry the mail. That is why the Adams Express Company is an investment trust today instead of an operating company. I conjecture that if entry into the mail-carrying business were open to all, there would be a large number of firms entering it and this archaic industry would become revolutionized in short order.

A second general class of cases in which strictly voluntary exchange is impossible arises when actions of individuals have effects on other individuals for which it is not feasible to charge or recompense them. This is the problem of "neighborhood effects." An obvious example is the pollution of a stream. The man who pollutes a stream is in effect forcing others to exchange good water for bad. These others might be willing to make the exchange at a price. But it is not feasible for them, acting individually, to avoid the exchange or to enforce appropriate compensation.

A less obvious example is the provision of highways. In this case, it is technically possible to identify and hence charge individuals for their use of the roads and so to have private operation. However, for general access roads, involving many points of entry and exit, the costs of collection would be extremely high if a charge were to be made for the specific services received by each individual, because of the necessity of establishing toll booths or the equivalent at all entrances. The gasoline tax is a much cheaper method of charging individuals roughly in proportion to their use of the roads. This method, however, is one in which the particular payment cannot be identified closely with the particular use. Hence, it is hardly feasible to have private enterprise provide the service and collect the charge without establishing extensive private monopoly.

These considerations do not apply to long-distance turnpikes with high density of traffic and limited access. For these, the costs of collection are small and in many cases are now being paid, and there are often numerous alternatives, so that there is no serious monopoly problem. Hence, there is every reason why these should be privately owned and operated. If so owned and operated, the enterprise running the highway should receive the gasoline taxes paid on account of travel on it.

Parks are an interesting example because they illustrate the difference between cases that can and cases that cannot be justified by neighborhood effects, and because almost everyone at first sight regards the conduct of National Parks as obviously a valid function of government. In fact, however, neighborhood effects may justify a city park; they do not justify a national park, like Yellowstone National Park or the Grand Canyon. What is the fundamental difference between the two? For the city park, it is extremely difficult to identify the people who benefit from it and to charge them for the benefits which they receive. If there is a park in the middle of the city, the houses on all sides get the benefit of the open space, and people who walk through it or by it also benefit. To maintain toll collectors at the gates or to impose annual charges per window overlooking the park would be very expensive and difficult. The entrances to a national park like Yellowstone, on the other hand, are few; most of the people who come stay for a considerable period of time and it is perfectly feasible to set up toll gates and collect admission charges. This is indeed now done, though the charges do not cover the whole costs. If the public wants this kind of an activity enough to pay for it, private enterprises will have every incentive to provide such parks. And, of course, there are many private enterprises of this nature now in existence. I cannot myself conjure up any neighborhood effects or important monopoly effects that would justify governmental activity in this area.

Considerations like those I have treated under the heading of neighborhood effects have been used to rationalize almost every conceivable intervention. In many instances, however, this rationalization is special pleading rather than a legitimate application of the concept of neighborhood effects. Neighborhood effects cut both ways. They can be a reason for limiting the activities of government as well as for expanding them. Neighborhood effects impede voluntary exchange because it is difficult to identify the effects on third parties and to measure their magnitude; but this difficulty is present in governmental activity as well. It is hard to know when neighborhood effects are sufficiently large to justify particular costs in overcoming them and even harder to distribute the costs in an appropriate fashion. Consequently, when government engages in activities to overcome neighborhood effects, it will in part introduce an additional set of neighborhood effects by failing to charge or to compensate individuals properly. Whether the original or the new neighborhood effects are the more serious can only be judged by the facts of the individual case, and even then, only very approximately. Furthermore, the use of government to overcome neighborhood effects itself has an extremely important neighborhood effect which is unrelated to the particular occasion for government action. Every act of government intervention limits the area of individual freedom directly and threatens the preservation of freedom indirectly for reasons elaborated in the first chapter.

Our principles offer no hard and fast line how far it is appropriate to use government to accomplish jointly what it is difficult or impossible for us to accomplish separately through strictly voluntary exchange. In any particular case of proposed intervention, we must take up a balance sheet, listing separately the advantages and disadvantages. Our principles tell us what items to put on the one side and what items on the other and they give us some basis for attaching importance to the different items. In particular, we shall always want to enter on the liability side of any proposed government intervention, its neighborhood effect in threatening freedom, and give this effect considerable weight. Just how much weight to give to it, as to other items, depends upon the circumstances. If, for example, existing government intervention is minor, we shall attach a smaller weight to the negative effects of additional government intervention. This is an important reason why many earlier liberals, like Henry Simons, writing at a time when government was small by today's standards, were willing to have government undertake activities that today's liberals would not accept now that government has become so overgrown.

ACTION THROUGH GOVERNMENT ON PATERNALISTIC GROUNDS

Freedom is a tenable objective only for responsible individuals. We do not believe in freedom for madmen or children. The necessity of drawing a line between responsible individuals and others is inescapable, yet it means that there is an essential ambiguity in our ultimate objective of freedom. Paternalism is inescapable for those whom we designate as not responsible.

The clearest case, perhaps, is that of madmen. We are willing neither to permit them freedom nor to shoot them. It would be nice if we could rely on voluntary activities of individuals to house and care for the madmen. But I think we cannot rule out the possibility that such charitable activities will be inadequate, if only because of the neighborhood effect involved in the fact that I benefit if another man contributes to the care of the insane. For this reason, we may be willing to arrange for their care through government.

Children offer a more difficult case. The ultimate operative unit in our society is the family, not the individual. Yet the acceptance of the family as the unit rests in considerable part on expediency rather than principle. We believe that parents are generally best able to protect their children and to provide for their development into responsible individuals for whom freedom is appropriate. But we do not believe in the freedom of parents to do what they will with other people. The children are re-

sponsible individuals in embryo, and a believer in freedom believes in protecting their ultimate rights.

To put this in a different and what may seem a more callous way, children are at one and the same time consumer goods and potentially responsible members of society. The freedom of individuals to use their economic resources as they want includes the freedom to use them to have children—to buy, as it were, the services of children as a particular form of consumption. But once this choice is exercised, the children have a value in of themselves and have a freedom of their own that is not simply an extension of the freedom of the parents.

The paternalistic ground for governmental activity is in many ways the most troublesome to a liberal; for it involves the acceptance of a principle—that some shall decide for others—which he finds objectionable in most applications and which he rightly regards as a hallmark of his chief intellectual opponents, the proponents of collectivism in one or another of its guises, whether it be communism, socialism, or a welfare state. Yet there is no use pretending that problems are simpler than in fact they are. There is no avoiding the need for some measure of paternalism. As Dicey wrote in 1914 about an act for the protection of mental defectives, "The Mental Deficiency Act is the first step along a path on which no sane man can decline to enter, but which, if too far pursued, will bring statesmen across difficulties hard to meet without considerable interference with individual liberty."[1] There is no formula that can tell us where to stop. We must rely on our fallible judgment and, having reached a judgment, on our ability to persuade our fellow men that it is a correct judgment, or their ability to persuade us to modify our views. We must

---

[1] A. V. Dicey, *Lectures on the Relation between Law and Public Opinion in England during the Nineteenth Century* 2nd. ed. (London: Macmillan, 1914), p. 1i.

put our faith, here as elsewhere, in a consensus reached by imperfect and biased men through free discussion and trial and error.

CONCLUSION

A government which maintained law and order, difined property rights, served as a means whereby we could modify property rights and other rules of the economic game, adjudicated disputes about the interpretation of the rules, enforced contracts, promoted competition, provided a monetary framework, engaged in activities to counter technical monopolies and to overcome neighborhood effects widely regarded as sufficiently important to justify government intervention, and which supplemented private charity and the private family in protecting the irresponsible, whether madman or child—such a government would clearly have important functions to perform. The consistent liberal is not an anarchist.

Yet it is also true that such a government would have clearly limited functions and would refrain from a host of activities that are now undertaken by federal and state governments in the United States, and their counterparts in other Western countries. Succeeding chapters will deal in some detail with some of these activities, and a few have been discussed above, but it may help to give a sense of proportion about the role that a liberal would assign government simply to list, in closing this chapter, some activities currently undertaken by government in the U.S., that cannot, so far as I can see, validly be justified in terms of the principles outlined above:

1. Parity price support programs for agriculture.

2. Tariffs on imports or restrictions on exports, such as current oil import quotas, sugar quotas, etc.

3. Governmental control of output, such as through the farm program, or through prorationing of oil as is done by the Texas Railroad Commission.

4. Rent control, such as is still practiced in New York, or more general price and wage controls, such as were imposed during and just after World War II.

5. Legal minimum wage rates, or legal maximum prices, such as the legal maximum of zero on the rate of interest that can be paid on demand deposits by commercial banks, or the legally fixed maximum rates that can be paid on savings and time deposits.

6. Detailed regulation of industries, such as the regulation of transportation by the Interstate Commerce Commission. This had some justification on technical monopoly grounds when initially introduced for railroads; it has none now for any means of transport. Another example is detailed regulation of banking.

7. A similar example, but one which deserves special mention because of its implicit censorship and violation of free speech, is the control of radio and television by the Federal Communications Commission.

8. Present social security programs, especially the old-age and retirement programs compelling people in effect (a) to spend a specified fraction of their income on the purchase of retirement annuity, (b) to buy the annuity from a publicly operated enterprise.

9. Licensure provisions in various cities and states which restrict particular enterprises or occupations or professions to people who have a license, where the license is more than a receipt for a tax which anyone who wishes to enter the activity may pay.

10. So-called "public-housing" and the host of other subsidy programs directed at fostering residential construction such as F.H.A. and V.A. guarantee of mortgage, and the like.

11. Conscription to man the military services in peacetime. The appropriate free market arrangement is volunteer military forces; which is to say, hiring

men to serve. There is no justification for not paying whatever price is necessary to attract the required number of men. Present arrangements are inequitable and arbitrary, seriously interfere with the freedom of young men to shape their lives, and probably are even more costly than the market alternative. (Universal military training to provide a reserve for war time is a different problem and may be justified on liberal grounds.)

12. National parks, as noted above.

13. The legal prohibition on the carrying of mail for profit.

14. Publicly owned and operated toll roads, as noted above.

This list is far from comprehensive.

WORKS BY MILTON FRIEDMAN

Friedman, Milton. *Capitalism and Freedom.* Chicago: University of Chicago Press, 1962.

————. *Essays in Positive Economics.* Chicago: University of Chicago Press, 1952.

————. *Inflation: Causes and Consequences.* New York: Asia Pub. House, 1963.

————. *Price Theory, a Provisional Text.* Chicago: Aldine Pub. Co., 1962.

————. *A Program for Monetary Stability.* New York: Fordham University Press, 1959.

————. *A Theory of the Consumption Function.* Princeton: Princeton University Press, 1957.

Friedman, Milton, and Kuznets, Simon. *Income from Independent Professional Practice.* New York: National Bureau of Economic Research, 1954.

Friedman, Milton, and Roosa, Robert V. *The Balance of Payments: Free Versus Fixed Exchange Rates.* Chicago: Chicago University Press, 1957.

Friedman, Milton, and Schwartz, Anna Jacobson. *The Great Contraction, 1929–1933.* Princeton: Princeton University Press, 1965.

————. *A Monetary History of the United States—1867–1960.* Princeton: Princeton University Press, 1963.

Friedman, Milton, Shoup, Carl, and Mack, Ruth P. *Taxing to Prevent Inflation.* New York: Columbia University Press, 1943.

CHAPTER 20

Mainstream Liberalism: Arthur Schlesinger, Jr. and John Kenneth Galbraith

THERE are literally dozens of worthy competitors for inclusion in a chapter that purports to reflect contemporary liberal thought. In narrowing this field for a collection that seeks to touch widely upon many variant strands of thought on both sides of the liberal mainstream, I have sought to represent both the economic and the more broadly political (and foreign policy) dimensions. Within the economic realm, no voice of liberalism is better known than that of John Kenneth Galbraith, Warburg Professor of Economics at Harvard University. Galbraith has served as Ambassador to India, as a leader of Americans for Democratic Action, and as an adviser and consultant to many officials and candidates. He is the author of several books, perhaps the best known of which are *The Affluent Society* (1958) and *The New Industrial State* (1967).

Arthur Schlesinger, Jr., equally well known and a close associate of Galbraith at Harvard and in political activities for many years, provides a broader political and foreign policy emphasis. Although *The Vital Center* from which this selection is taken was written in 1948, Schlesinger makes the point in his preface to the 1962 edition that his ideas are still applicable, and so this excerpt has been used. Schlesinger, who served as a Presidential Assistant from 1961 to 1964, is a distinguished historian now at the City University of New York. His major books include a trilogy on the New Deal under the title of *The Age of Roosevelt* and an account of the Kennedy years entitled *A Thousand Days* (1966).

Not represented in this chapter is contemporary liberalism's emphasis on procedure and legalism. For this purpose, I strongly recommend Supreme Court Justice Abe Fortas' *Concerning Dissent and
Civil Disobedience* (New York: Signet Books, 1968), an inexpensive
paperback that is immensely provocative in many ways.

Arthur M. Schlesinger, Jr.

From The Vital Center

THE REVIVAL OF AMERICAN RADICALISM

The Equalitarianism of the Declaration of Independence was a spontaneous
expression of the American experience.
Life on the frontier was making the
national character intolerant of classes in
the social sense; and the rise of the city
would gradually release the forces which
would carry on the struggle against class
domination in the economic and political
spheres. Born in revolution, "conceived
in liberty and dedicated to the proposition that all men are created equal,"
America from its beginning has charted
its history and its politics by the morning star of equality.

The faith that all men were created
equal brought with it two political
premises: that all men were endowed
with certain unalienable rights; and that,
if government became destructive of
those rights, it was "the right of the
people to alter or to abolish it." Embodied in the more sober language of
the Constitution, these premises assured,
on the one hand, the freedom of the
individual, and, on the other, the right
of the people to control the political and
economic life of the nation. These guarantees have become the basic premises
of American democracy.

Critics of democracy have claimed to
detect an inherent incompatibility in this
marriage of majority rule and minority
rights. Nor can it be said that our democratic philosophers have been at their

most lucid on the point. Thomas Jefferson's formulation is typical. "Absolute
acquiescence in the decisions of the
majority," he said, was the "vital principle of republics"—but he then went
on in the same address to add in apparent contradiction that the will of the
majority, though "in all cases" to prevail, yet "to be rightful must be reasonable." A few lines later he even placed
a whole category of rights out of reach
of the majority for fear that the majority might destroy them. "The minority
possess their equal rights . . . and to violate [them] would be oppression."[1]

The problem of reconciling majority
rule with minority rights is, in terms
of strict logic, insoluble. But the incompatibility exists much more in these
terms than it does in the practice of
society. For any logical decision in favor
of majorities or of minorities would be
fatal to free government. Jefferson's
language, however distressing to logi-
cians, expresses the deep and healthy
instincts of a free people who require
a margin for decision—a margin in
which people, leadership and events can
arrive at concrete solutions in concrete
cases. The Declaration of Independence
and the constitution wove individual
freedom into our democratic fabric;
Alexander Hamilton and Andrew Jackson added the conception of the positive
state. The result has been our success
in preserving a system where, except
for the Civil War, neither majorities nor
minorities have been thwarted to the
point of resorting to revolution.

Our democratic tradition has been at
its best an activist tradition. It has

SOURCE. Reprinted from *The Vital Center*
by permission of the publisher, Houghton
Mifflin Company. Copyright 1949, 1962 by
Arthur M. Schlesinger, Jr.

[1] J. D. Richardson, ed., *Messages and Papers
of the Presidents,* Washington, 1908, vol. I,
pp. 322, 323.

found its fulfillment, not in complaint or in escapism, but in responsibility and decision. In times of crisis, as I mentioned earlier, those who believe deeply in freedom and democracy have generally provided truly national leadership. The Jacksonians were only the first, and the New Dealers the most recent, of a number of rescue parties which radicals have launched to save a beleaguered capitalism. At its best, our left has provided superb political leadership and broadly effective administrative management. It has twice led the nation victoriously, for example, through that most exacting of all tests, twentieth-century war.

Yet the very existence of this activist capacity—this appetite for decision and responsibility—has tended to split the left between those, like Jackson and Roosevelt, who regard liberalism as a practical program to be put into effect; and those, like the Doughface progressives, who use liberalism as an outlet for private grievances and frustrations. On the one hand are the politicians, the administrators, the doers; on the other, the sentimentalists, the utopians, the wailers. For the doer, the essential form of democratic education is the taking of great decisions under the burden of civic responsibility. For the wailer, liberalism is the mass expiatory ritual by which the individual relieves himself of responsibility for his government's behavior.

This split goes to the very heart of the liberal predicament. Where the doer is determined to do what he can to save free society, the wailer, by rejecting practical responsibility, serves the purpose of those who wish free society to fail—which is why the Doughface so often ends up as the willing accomplice of Communism. A liberalism which purports to shape a real world must first accept the limitations and possibilities of that world. It must reconcile itself to a tedious study of detail—less gratifying perhaps than the emotional orgasm of passing resolutions against Franco, monopoly or sin, but probably more likely to bring about actual results.

It must recognize that the great decisions of public policy are not actor's poses, struck with gestures for purposes of dramatic effect; they are decisions made in practical circumstances with real consequences which cannot be separated from the meaning of the decision. Life, in short, is not a form of political soap opera: it is sometimes more complicated than one would gather from the liberal weeklies.

We may feel the conflict between doer and wailer, New Dealer and Doughface, to be relatively new. It is a conflict within each of us; and it is true that only recently have we been forced to choose one side or the other; only recently has the rise of Communism transformed the wailer from a harmless and often beguiling character to a potentially sinister one. But the conflict is an old one—as real in Jackson's day, for example, as in our own. It goes to the essential question of different attitudes toward human nature. For the Jackson-Roosevelt tradition of liberal activism had its roots in a set of assumptions, conscious and unconscious, about man; and these assumptions are flatly denied or ignored by the Doughface progressive.

A century ago in America, men of good will, indifferent to political and economic reform in the real world, disdainful of pragmatic comprimise, sought to transform society by fleeing from it into model communities. The Utopians believed man to be perfectible; and that radiant belief permitted some of them to slide over into the inevitable next step—that is, to believe that they, at least, were already perfect. Men in a conviction of infallibility can sacrifice humanity without compunction on the altar of some abstract and special good.

That tough-minded Jacksonian, Nathaniel Hawthorne, spent a few months at Brook Farm, the showpiece of the Utopians. After his departure he wrote *The Blithedale Romance*, perhaps the most brilliant of American political novels. Into his book he poured the invincible repugnance which a Jacksonian cannot but feel toward a Utopian, a New Dealer toward a Doughface. In Hollingsworth, the Utopian reformer, Hawthorne with the artist's prescience glimpsed the ultimate possibilities of a belief in perfectibility. He created a figure which the twentieth century recognizes more quickly than the nineteenth; we know him well from the pages of Koestler and the transcripts of the Moscow Trials.

Hollingsworth, Hawthorne wrote, had "a stern and dreadful peculiarity"; while avowing his love for humanity, he did not seem himself entirely human. "This is always true of those men who have surrendered themselves to an overruling purpose. It does not so much impel them from without, nor even operate as a motive power within, but grows incorporate with all that they think and feel, and finally converts them into little else save that one principle." When that happens, warns Hawthorne, avoid them like the plague. "They have no heart, no sympathy, no reason, no conscience. They will keep no friend, unless he make himself the mirror of their purpose; they will smite and slay you, and trample your dead corpse under foot, all the more readily, if you take the first step with them and cannot take the second, and the third, and every other step of their terribly strait path."

"They have an idol," Hawthorne continued, "to which they consecrate themselves high-priest, and deem it holy work to offer sacrifices of whatever is most precious; and never once seem to suspect—so cunning has the Devil been with them—that this false deity, in whose iron features, immitigable to all the rest of mankind, they see only benignity and love, is but a spectrum of the very priest himself, projected upon the surrounding darkness. And the higher and purer the original object, and the more unselfishly it may have been taken up, the slighter is the probability that they can be led to recognize the process by which godlike benevo-

lence has been debased into alldevouring egotism."[2]

With his intense conviction of the weakness of man before the temptations of pride and power, Hawthorne extrapolated unerringly from the pretty charades of Brook Farm to the essence of totalitarian man. Yet during the next century the serene course of progress seemed to give little warrant to the violence of Hawthorne's political imagination. The insights into the egotism of power consequently vanished from the mind of the liberal intellectual.

In the placid years before the First War, sin was fading fast into the world of myth. "He moved with such assurance in the realism of light," Louis Jaffe has written of Louis D. Brandeis, "that darkness had ceased for him to be a living reality. The demonic depths and vast violence of men's souls were part of the historical past rather than the smouldering basis of the present. . . Nothing in his system prepared Brandeis for Hitler."[3] Vernon L. Parrington, turning to *The Blithedale Romance*, found its sharp probings "thin and unreal"; "the figure of Hollingsworth," Parrington could remark with sarcasm, "is Hawthorne's reply to the summons of the social conscience of the times."[4]

Parrington evidently thought that in Hollingsworth Hawthorne was portraying a George Norris or a Bob La-Follette. We know today that he was portraying a Zhdanov. And if the Brandeises and the Parringtons were caught off guard, if nothing in their system prepared them for totalitarianism, how much more unprepared were the readers of the liberal weeklies, the great thinkers who sought to combat Nazism by

---

[2] Nathaniel Hawthorne, *The Blithedale Romance*, chap. ix. The same point could be made in terms of Herman Melville; see, for example, the illuminating essay by Richard Chase, "Melville's *Confidence Man*," *Kenyon Review*, Winter, 1949.
[3] Louis Jaffe, *University of Chicago Law Review*, April, 1947.
[4] V. L. Parrington, *Main Currents in American Thought*, New York, 1927, vol. ii, p. 448.

peace strikes, the Oxford oath and disarmament, the ever hopeful who saw in the Soviet Communism merely the lengthened shadow of Brook Farm! . . .This was in a real sense a *trahison des clercs*. For the politicians themselves retained an instinctive and hardy skepticism. Even the most guileless of our democratic leaders have had in their heart a searching doubt about human perfectibility—a conviction that every form of human power requires relentless correction. This, indeed, is the gusto of democracy, the underlying sense of comedy which brooks no worship of authority because it knows that no man is that good.

Communism has been the greatest threat, because Communism draped itself so carefully in the cast-off clothes of a liberalism grown fat and complacent, and because the disguise took in so many of the intellectuals. But John Taylor of Caroline has defined long ago the corrosive skepticism of the American radical who will not be taken in: "The hooks of fraud and tyranny are universally baited with melodious words. . . There is edification and safety in challenging political words and phrases as traitors and trying them rigorously by principles, before we allow them the smallest degree of confidence. As the servants of principles, they gain admission into the family, and thus acquire the best opportunities of assassinating their masters."[5] While the radical intellectual dallied with Communism, the radical politician remained faithful to democracy.

Eugene Debs, for example, had no use for the Communist Party, nor had Bob LaFollette. "I have not sought, I do not seek, I repudiate the support of any advocate of Communism," cried Franklin D. Roosevelt at the height of the period when Communists sought to trap liberals in the steel embrace of the united front. "The Soviet Union," he said, a few years later, "as a matter of

practical fact . . . is a dictatorship as absolute as any other dictatorship in the world."[6] No important New Dealer, except Wallace himself, was involved in in the Wallace movement.*

Today, finally and tardily, the skeptical insights are in process of restoration to the liberal mind. The psychology of Freud has renewed the intellectual's belief in the dark, slumbering forces of the will. The theology of Bart and Niebuhr has given new power to the old and chastening truths of Christianity. More than anything else, the rise of

---

[5] John Taylor, *Inquiry into the Principles and Policy of the Government of the United States,* Fredericksburg, 1814, pp. 558-59.

[6] F. D. Roosevelt, *Public Papers and Addresses,* New York, 1938-41, vol. v, p. 384; *New York Times,* February 11, 1940.

* With the partial exception of Mr. Tugwell, who appeared at the Philadelphia convention, expressed himself unhappily afterward, and then relapsed into silence. He took no active part in the campaign. He differed from the Progressive Party on such crucial issues as the Marshall Plan; and had long opposed the machinations of the Communists. When a Puerto Rican political leader briefly collaborated with the Communists, Tugwell accused him of extending "a dangerous tolerance. . . forgetting that they had no directed interest in Puerto Rico but were only using independence as a means of causing trouble for another 'capitalist' nation. . . . In typical communist fashion they worked night and day, admitted no scruples in making decisions and conducted themselves in ways which indicated their contempt for such burgeois concepts as promises and contracts. . . . It was obvious that the *communistas* were getting ready for the day when the party line of international communism would diverge from policies of the United States. In this there could be no doubt that we were developing a dangerous vulnerability." *The Stricken Land,* New York, 1946, pp. 568, 570. Yet, after the party line of international Communism had diverged from U.S. policies, Tugwell evidently allowed his old friend Henry Wallace to persuade him into lending a kind of support to the Progressives. Apparently Tugwell came himself to feel that Wallace was extending a "dangerous tolerance" and expressed fears that the "wrong people," might get control of the Progressive Party. When asked to identify the "wrong people," he replied enigmatically, "I certainly don't know whether they are Communists but they certainly act like them." *New York Times,* August 11, 1948.

Hitler and Stalin has revealed in terms no one can deny the awful reality of the human impulses toward aggrandizement and destruction—impulses for which the liberal intellectual had left no room in his philosophy. The conceptions of the intellectual are at last beginning to catch up with the instincts of the democratic politician.

When the challenge of Communism finally forced American liberals to take inventory of their moral resources, the inventory resulted in the clear decision that freedom had values which could not be compromised in deals with totalitarianism. Thus America found itself reaching much the same conclusion as the non-Communist left of Europe. In the years after the Second War Americans began to rediscover the great tradition of liberalism—the tradition of Jackson and Hawthorne, the tradition of a reasonable responsibility about politics and a moderate pessimism about man. In Januray, 1947, New Dealers like Eleanor Roosevelt, Wilson Wyatt, Leon Henderson and Paul Porter united with moderate pessimists like Reinhold Niebuhr, Elmer Davis and Marquis Childs to form Americans for Democratic Action (ADA), a new liberal organization, excluding Communists and dedicated to democratic objectives. The formation of ADA marks perhaps as much as anything the watershed at which American Liberalism began to base itself once again on a solid conception of man and of history.

The very necessities of foreign policy—the growing necessity of checking Communism by developing some constructive alternative—speeded the clarification of liberal ideas in 1947 and 1948. For the only realistic hope for a bulwark against Communism in Europe lay in the strengthening of the democratic socialists—a program which could not but rouse the bitter opposition of the Communists. Intelligent State Department officials saw the point and were prepared to take the risk at a time when too many liberals were still deluding themselves with talk of Big Three

unity. The State Department, indeed, was changing fast from the stodgy and inefficient department of the thirties, which Americans had reasonably regarded as a refuge for effete and conventional men who adored countesses, pushed cookies and wore hankerchiefs in their sleeves. Even in the age of Cordell Hull a new breed of American foreign servant had been in the making—the modern professional diplomat, a close student of history and politics, convinced that the desire of men for freedom and economic security may be as legitimate a factor in foreign affairs as strategic bases or the investments of Standard Oil. The leader of this group was Hull's highly able undersecretary, Sumner Welles—a man who could regret that Rosa Luxemburg's friend Karl Liebknecht had not been given the chance to organize Germany, who regarded our attitude toward the Spanish Civil War as "disastrous," and who was to be in private life an influential supporter of the conception of the Third Force.[7]

The mountaineer vindictiveness of Mr. Hull hampered Welles's efforts and eventually drove him from the Department. But Welles was only the most prominent of a new generation of foreign service officers. When James F. Byrnes began to rid the Department of the hacks, the bright younger men assumed new prominence. Byrnes, Dean Acheson, his able undersecretary, and Benjamin V. Cohen, the wise counselor of the Department, were quick to grasp the character of the European problem and to throw United States support to the forces of the center and the non-Communist left. Byrnes was suceeded by George C. Marshall, who had learned from bitter experience in China that United States interests could expect very little more support from the reactionaries than from the Communists. Marshall gave two of the ablest foreign-service officers new positions of authority. Charles E. Bohlen, a brilliant student

---

[7] Sumner Welles, *The Time for Decision,* New York, 1944, pp. 16, 57.

of Russia, became counselor; George Kennan headed the State Department's Policy Planning Group.

Under Byrnes and Marshall the State Department began to understand the significance of the non-Communist left. The very phrase, indeed, was reduced in the Washington manner to its initials; and the cryptic designation "NCL" was constantly to be heard in Georgetown drawing rooms.* The return to Washington of Averell Harriman as Secretary of Commerce strengthened the support for this approach: successive appointments in Moscow and London had fully educated Harriman to the difference between socialism and Communism. By 1948 the State Department could tell Congress that the socialists were "among the strongest bulwarks in Europe against Communism."[8]

This quiet revolution in the attitudes of the State Department was carried out in great part under the guns of the reactionary 80th Congress. It did not affect all State Department officials, especially some serving overseas; and it had no perceptible impact at all on the Department of Defense, which remained a citadel of the non-Communist right. But the State Department of 1949 had changed impressively from Hull's croquet-playing set of a decade earlier.

The emergence of the non-Communist left in Europe eventually had its effect even on the American labor movement. The American Federation of Labor, it is true, under the spur of David Dubinsky, had given generous help to the Socialist parties and free trade-union federations of Europe. But, at a time when young men in the State Department were puzzling how best to support the Third Force, the Congress of Industrial Organizations across the street in Lafayette Place remained apparently indifferent. Men like Walter Reuther and James B. Carey were trying to rally the

CIO in support of European democracy, but their efforts for a long time ran head on into the Communist bloc. Indeed the success in immobilizing the CIO for three crucial years was one of the few Communist triumphs in postwar America. In the end, the successful fight against Communist influence, culminating in Reuther's victory in the United Auto Works and the discharge of Lee Pressman as CIO general counsel, brought the CIO side by side with the AF of L, ADA and the NCL group in the State Department in support of the Third Force in Europe.

The election of 1948 came as a culmination of these various tendencies in domestic and foreign policy. The American people voted with some definiteness against the restoration to power of the business community; at the same time, they repudiated the Wallace movement. America, in other words, was going left—but it was categorically a non-Communist left. The job of liberalism, in other words, was to devote itself to the maintenance of individual liberties and to the democratic control of economic life—and to brook no compromise, at home or abroad, on either of these two central tenets. The American liberal concluded by 1948 that man, being neither perfect morally nor perfect intellectually, cannot be trusted to use absolute power, public or private, either with virtue or with wisdom.

Some perceive dangers in these new directions of liberalism. It is argued that the abandonment of the old faith in the full rationality of man leaves no foothold short of authoritarianism. Yet is it not rather the belief in the perfectibility of man which encourages the belief that a small group of men are already perfect and hence may exercise total power without taint or corruption? It is a moderate pessimism about man which truly fortifies society against authoritarianism—because such pessimism must apply far more strongly to a special elite or a single party, exposed to the temptations of pride and power, than it does to the people in general. "Sometimes it

---

* A full history of the NCL movement would have to include the key role of a brilliant Oxford don, Isaiah Berlin.

[8] *New York Herald Tribune*, January 15, 1948.

is said that man cannot be trusted with the government of himself," Jefferson once wrote. "Can he, then, be trusted with the government of others? Or have we found angels in the form of kings, gauleiters or commissars; and we know too well what happens when mere humand claim angelic infallibility. Depotism is never so much to be dreaded as when it pretends to do good: who would act the angel acts the brute."[9]

The people as a whole are not perfect; but no special group of the people is more perfect: that is the moral and rationale of democracy. Consistent pessimism about man, far from promoting authoritarianism, alone can inoculate the democratic faith against it. "Man's capacity for justice makes democracy possible," Niebuhr has written in his remarkable book on democratic theory; "but man's inclination to injustice makes democracy necessary."[10]

The image of democratic man emerges from the experience of democracy; man is a creature capable of reason and of purpose, of great loyalty and of great virtue, yet also he is vulnerable to material power and to spiritual pride. In our democratic tradition, the excessive self-love which transforms power into tyranny is the greatest of all dangers. But the self-love which transforms radicalism from an instrument of action into an expression of neurosis is almost as great a danger. If irresponsible power is the source of evil, and irresponsible impotence, the source of decadence, then responsible power—power held for limited terms under conditions of strict accountability—is the source of wisdom.

It is the spirit that American democracy faces the future. For the 1948 election solved nothing: it simply gave liberalism a new lease on power. The great challenge still lies ahead. Our industrial organization, as we have seen, overpowers man, unnerves him, de-

moralizes him. The problem remains of ordering society so that it will subdue the tendencies of industrial organization, produce a wide amount of basic satisfaction and preserve a substantial degree of individual freedom.

The campaign against social anxiety has just begun. Before American radicalism prosecutes it any further, it must come to terms with the two problems which have dogged and perplexed it throughout its history: the problem of the role of classes in politics; and the problem of the role of government in social planning.

In spite of the current myth that class conflicts in America were a fiendish invention of Franklin D. Roosevelt, classes have, in fact, played a basic part in American political life from the beginning. The founders of the republic construed politics automatically in terms of classes. No more magistral summation of the economic interpretation of politics exists than James Madison's celebrated Tenth Federalist Paper. "The most common and durable source of factions," Madison wrote, "has been the various and unequal distribution of property. . .The regulation of these various and interfering interests forms the principal task of modern legislation."[11] The Founding Fathers disagreed, not over the reality of class conflict, but over its origin: whether, as Hamilton and John Adams claimed, it was the inevitable result of natural differences in the talents of man, or, as Jefferson and John Taylor of Caroline claimed, it was the result of unnatural tyrannies, imposed by fraud and maintained by force.

The extension of the franchise expelled class conflict as an element in conservative oratory, since there ceased to be political profit in proclaiming the exclusive virtues of a class which was an electoral minority. But the tradition of Jefferson and Jackson firmly anchored class conflict in radical democratic thought. "It is to be regretted, that the

[9] Richardson, ed., *Messages and Papers*, vol. I, p. 332.
[10] Reinhold Niebuhr, *The Children of Light and the Children of Darkness*, New York, 1944, p. xi.

[11] James Madison, *Federalist No. 10*.

rich and powerful too often bend the acts of Government to their selfish purposes," said Jackson, ". . .when the laws undertake. . .to make the rich richer and the potent more powerful, the humble members of society—the farmers, mechanics, and laborers—who have neither the time nor the means of securing like favors to themselves, have a right to complain of the injustice of their Government."[12]

The fight on the part of the "humble members of society" against business domination has been the consistent motive of American liberalism. Far from importing subversive European ideas when he renewed this theme, Franklin Roosevelt was only returning to the political doctrine of the hallowed past. Nor is there anything specifically Marxist about class conflict. "As far as I am concerned," Marx himself wrote, "the honour does not belong to me for having discovered the existence either of classes in modern society or of the struggle between the classes. Bourgeois historians a long time before me expounded the historical development of this class struggle." "To limit Marxism to the teaching of the class struggle," added Lenin, "means to curtail Marxism—to distort it, to reduce it to something which is acceptable to the bourgeoisie. A Marxist is one who *extends the acceptance of the class struggle to the acceptance of the dictatorship of the proletariat.*"[13] It is precisely this extension which American radicalism has refused to make.

The problem of classes is this: Economic conflict is essential if freedom is to be preserved, because it is the only barrier against class domination; yet economic conflict, pursued to excess, may well destroy the underlying fabric of common principle which sustains free society.

[12] Richardson, ed., *Messages and Papers,* Vol. II, p. 590.
[13] Marx to Weydemeyer, March 5, 1852, V. I. Lenin, *State and Revolution,* New York, 1932, pp. 29, 30.

I cannot imagine a free society which has eliminated conflict. So long as there is inequality in the distribution of property and variety in the nature of economic interests, so long will politics center on economic issues; and so long the insurgency of the discontented will provide the best guarantee against the tyranny of the possessors.

Yet this conflict must be kept within bounds, if freedom itself is to survive. The differences among classes in a capitalist democracy are often wide and bitter; but they are much less impassable than the differences between capitalist democracy and authoritarianism; and sometimes in the heat of the battle the warring classes tend to forget their family relationship. It is perhaps fortunate for the continuity of the American development that the Civil War came along to heal the social wounds opened up in the age of Jackson; that one world war closed the rifts created by the New Freedom and another those of the New Deal. But external war is an expensive means of making antagonistic classes suddenly realize how much their agreement outweighs their differences.

Britain has been more successful than the United States in domesticating the class struggle. The British tradition of responsible conservatism has prevented the possessing classes from seeing national disaster in every trifling social reform; while British labor has itself developed a profound sense of national responsibility; and class conflict has consequently become more an instrument of national progress than one of national disruption. We desperately need in this country the revival of responsibility on the right—the development of a nonfascist right to work with the non-Communist left in the expansion of free society. Conservatism, if it is wise, will see in legitimate social protest, not the gratuitous mischief of agitators, but the sign of an evil to be corrected. "The more we condemn unadulterated Marxian Socialsim," Theordore Roosevelt used to say, "the stouter should be our insistence on thoroughgoing social reforms."[14]

This means, in part, that a sense of humility is indispensable to democratic politics. The conservative must not identify a particular *status quo* with the survival of civilization; and the radical equally must recognize that his protests are likely to be as much the expressions of his own self-interest as they are of some infallible dogma about society. People who know they alone are right find it hard to compromise; and compromise is the strategy of democracy. The protagonists in the class conflict must be honest, responsible and, above all, humble, or at least liable to moods of humility.

In the last analysis, however, the best way to prevent class conflict from tearing society apart is to prevent classes themselves from rigidifying into castes. In the past our free economic system has kept our class structure relatively loose. Depressions have been the great leveler; and shirtsleeves have often returned to shirtsleeves by the third generation. But the rise of corporate bigness has tended to give classes a greater fixity. Today we have ruled out depression as a proper means of speeding the circulation of the elites. It may well be that such present expedients as the widening of educational opportunity and the opening up of places for talent in such new industries as government and Hollywood will not be enough to stop the hardening into caste.

Here is one field which calls for bold and imaginative action. President Conant of Harvard has suggested that a genuine American radical "would use the power of government to reorder the 'haves and have nots' every generation to give flux to our social order." Why, for example, should the ownership of industry be passed on by nepotism or patronage and not according to managerial ability? The American radical, says Conant, "will be resolute in his demand to confiscate (by constitutional methods) all property once a generation. He will demand really effective inheritance and gift taxes and the breaking up of trust funds and estates. And this point cannot be lightly pushed aside, for it is the kernel of his radical philosophy."[15]

President Conant's proposal of government intervention to limit the right of inheritance places squarely before the radical his second problem: the role of the state. American democracy emerged in an age which had conquered freedom by limiting the power of the government; American radicalism itself was born in a specific revolt against arbitrary government. This experience had a traumatic effect on the early radicals. The state had given them, so to speak, a prenatal fright, and they never quite recovered. The Jeffersonians concluded with real feeling that the government was best which governed least.

The administration of Andrew Jackson was the first one to govern energetically in the interests of the people. But, in order to combat the power of concentrated wealth, Jackson was obliged to enlarge the power of the state. He was using these enlarged powers, he believed, to restore America to that condition of pristine innocence where Jeffersonian maxims would once more be dominant; but the effect of his administration was less to break up concentrated wealth than it was to strengthen government. Under the banner of anti-statism, Jackson made the state stronger than ever before.

He had no alternative. American anti-statism was the function of a particular economic order. Jefferson had dreamed of a nation of small freeholders and virtuous artisans, united by sturdy independence, mutual respect and the ownership of property. Obviously, strong government would be superfluous in Arcadia. But the Industrial Revolution changed all that. The corporation began

---

[14] Theodore Roosevelt, *The Foes of Our Own Household,* New York, 1917, p. 177.

[15] James B. Conant, "Wanted: American Radicals," *Atlantic Monthly,* May, 1943.

to impersonalize the economic order. It removed the economy, in other words, from the control of a personal code and delivered it to agencies with neither bodies to be kicked nor souls to be damned. Impersonality produced an irresponsibility which was chilling the lifeblood of society. The state consequently had to expand its authority in order to preserve the ties which hold society together. The history of governmental intervention has been the history of the growing ineffectiveness of the private conscience as a means of social control. The only alternative is the growth of the public conscience, whose natural expression is the democratic government.

Alexander Hamilton and John Quincy Adams had conceived of the national government as a purposeful instrument of social progress. But the Whigs and Republicans of the middle period lacked the vision of their Federalist predecessors. The Democrats, for their part, remained under the spell of the Jeffersonian dream. Salvation continued to lie for them in the atomization of economic power, the reduction of government and the return to a self-winding economy. And, in the meantime, the social pressures for affirmative government, accumulating throughout the nation, placed politics in a state of precarious tension.

Theodore Roosevelt was the first modern statesman to note the spirit of irresponsibility which was suffusing industrial society and to call upon positive government to redress the balance. In so doing, he invoked the dream of the benevolent state; and he raised in opposition the last serious resurgence of Jeffersonianism. The campaign of 1912 set the Hamiltonian and Jeffersonian solutions of the social question in vivid contrast. The debate between the New Nationalism of Theodore Roosevelt and the New Freedom of Woodrow Wilson was conducted with uncommon brilliance. American radicals have never been able to decide which side was right.

Theodore Roosevelt, supported by Herbert Croly and Walter Lippmann, spoke for what he called the socialization of democracy. The Socialists, Roosevelt said, were right in regarding trusts as an inevitable stage in the history of capitalism. The competitive era had gone for good; and the only answer, Roosevelt felt, was an expansion of the powers of government to convert business consolidation into a force for the public welfare. Trust-busting, T.R. said, is "madness. As a matter of fact, it is futile madness . . It is preposterous to abandon all that has been wrought in the application of the cooperative idea in business and to return to the era of cutthroat competition." As Croly put it, the philosophy of the Sherman Anti-Trust Act operated as a "fatal bar" to effective national planning.[16]

The New Nationalism was a philosophy of limited collectivism. "Its advocates," said Croly, "are committed to a drastic reorganization of the American political and economic system, to the substitution of a frank social policy for the individualism of the past, and to the realization of this policy, if necessary, by the use of efficient government instruments."[17] The state should incorporate large corporations, regulate them by means of federal commissions, tax their excessive profits and eventually move toward public ownership of natural monopolies.

Against the New Nationalism, Woodrow Wilson unfurled the Jeffersonian standard of the New Freedom. Backed by Louis D. Brandeis and Robert M. LaFollette, Wilson denied that trusts were inevitable or desirable; bigness, as Brandeis said, was a curse; and the solution lay in an unsparing policy of breaking up huge combinations. Wilson had no faith in the positive enlargement of governmental functions. The role of government intervention was, not to plan for the general welfare, but to roll back

---

[16] Theodore Roosevelt, introduction to S. J. Duncan-Clark, *The Progressive Movement,* Boston, 1913, p. xix; Herbert Croly, *The Promise of American Life,* New York, 1909, p. 274.
[17] Herbert Croly, *Progressive Democracy,* New York, 1914, p. 15.

the trend of economic development from consolidation to competition.

Wilson's profound instinct for social freedom gave emotional cogency to what was only a superficial economic case against the trusts. Much of the corporate combination of the day, it is true, was produced, not by the technical necessities of large-scale production, but by the legerdemain of the bankers. Yet Roosevelt was surely right on the long-run tendencies. Large-scale business enterprise, for all its defects, has played an indispensable part in enabling capitalism to achieve its productive miracles. When Wilson was forced to suspend the antitrust act in order to increase war production in 1917, Roosevelt could exult with some justice, "If the Sherman Law hurts our production and business efficiency in war time, it hurts it also in peace time, for the problems of boring for oil, of producing steel, manufacturing and selling agricultural implements, are no different."[18]

Still, a healthy political impulse underlay Wilson's opposition to the New Nationalism. The Wilsonians simply could not see how the enlarged state was to be kept out of the hands of the interests it was supposed to control; and they were at war with those interests. The basic contrast between Wilson and Roosevelt, indeed, was that Wilson's policies were *politically* the more radical, Roosevelt's *economically* the more radical.

Wilson contemplated what was in effect a crusade against big business on behalf of small business and labor. A Jacobin in his politics, he was prepared to whip up emotions against the existing order, but he had no notion of basic social change. He aimed at little except increased opportunities for the small entrepreneur. Roosevelt, on the other hand, contemplated an enormous increase in the power of the state over an increasingly centralized economy. He was laying the foundations for central economic planning and for the welfare state, and

---

[18] Theodore Roosevelt, *The Foes of Our Own Household*, p. 122.

he hoped to maintain political freedom by such extreme devices as the recall of judges. But he relied too much on the painless conversion of the great capitalists to his program, overinfluenced perhaps by the dubious example of George W. Perkins. He was unwilling to stir up the anti-business emotions which alone would prevent his planned economic order from turning into a dictatorship of the trusts. To economic radicalism Roosevelt added political conservatism— a conservatism inadequately concealed by the apparent leftism of some of his political radicalism; and neither combination could solve the large questions of economic policy.

The New Deal drew from both the New Nationalism and the New Freedom. The National Recovery Administration period, for example, was straight out of Roosevelt and Croly, just as the Temporary National Economic Commission period was pure Wilson and Brandeis. Again each tactic demonstrated its limitations. NRA revealed the incredible difficulties of national regulation of business under capitalism. So long as a sense of emergency gave the public interest a chance to win out over special interests, NRA worked fairly well (as the War Production Board would work well a decade later). But, as the conviction of crisis receded, NRA was placed in an intolerable dilemma. The businessmen who staffed it tended increasingly to resolve their doubts in favor of business: and a business-dominated NRA looked more and more like the road to the corporate state. If, on the other hand, the New Dealers had made NRA decisions against the business community, a political storm would either have overthrown NRA or have forced the Government itself in self-defense to march even faster in the direction of statism.

The failure of NRA drove Franklin Roosevelt to the strategy of the New Freedom. If he could not socialize the spirit of business, then he would isolate business and frighten it into good behavior. It was a pragmatist's answer to an almost insoluble dilemma. If you permit business to combine, how can you prevent it from eventually taking over the government agencies set up to regulate the combination? And, if you try to break business down into competitive units, are you not trying to reverse an irreversible economic process? Roosevelt's solution was the TNEC tactic of using trust-busting not so much as an economic solution as a means of keeping big business off binges of restriction. At best, this program could not abolish monopoly but only persuade businessmen, if not to stay on the water-wagon, at least to restrain themselves to about a 3.2 per cent indulgence in monopolistic practices.

Both the New Nationalism and the New Freedom, it should be noted, enhanced the power of the state, the one by rolling out the carpet for new governmental functions, the other by letting them sneak in the back door. The New Deal completed the exorcism of Jeffersonian inhibitions about strong government, committing liberals even after to the Hamilton-T.R. faith in the state as a necessary instrument of the social welfare. Yet the very growth of government contained dangers. As Franklin Roosevelt himself pointed out, "We have built up new instruments of public power. In the hands of a people's government this power is wholesome and proper. But in the hands of political puppets of an economic autocracy such power would provide shackles for the liberty of the people."[19]

But what alternative was there to the expansion of the state? The free market has been decreasingly the main theater of economic decisions. We are changing from a market society to an administrative society; and the problem is which set of administrators is to rule. If the basic decisions are to be made either in a directors' boardroom or in a government agency, then the political process permits us a measure of access, at least, to a government agency. Big government, for all its dangers, remains democracy's

only effective response to big business—especially when big business behaves with such political recklessness as it has behaved in the United States.

Yet experience imposes very definite cautions with respect to the expansion of governmental power. The record of democratic socialism, for example, has already caused a retreat from the notion of government as a play-by-play planner—not only because of the temptations this role presents to a bureaucracy, but because total planners do not have the information or the wisdom to plan successfully. Socialist Britain, someone observed, is more planned against than planning. The consequence has been a revulsion against pinpoint planning, against direct, physical controls and detailed intervention in business decisions (save when emergency conditions, such as war or forced reconstruction, permit no alternative).

The lesson of the experiments with democratic socialism is plainly that the state should aim at establishing conditions for economic decisions, not at making all the decisions itself. It should create an economic environment favorable to private business policies which increase production; and then let the free market carry the ball as far as it can.[*] Keynes, not Marx, is the prophet of the new radicalism.

The function of the state, in other words, is to define the ground rules of the game; not to pitch, catch, hit homers or (just as likely) pop up or throw to the wrong base. The state may acquire total economic power for the most benevolent of motives; but benevolence is no guarantee of wisdom. The danger of the total planner is, first, that his almost inevitable blunders may convulse the entire economy, and, second, that in a panic-stricken effort to cover up his blunders he may multiply his controls

[19] Franklin D. Roosevelt, *Public Papers,* vol. v, p. 16.

[*] "A Socialist Government cannot do everything. What it leaves to private enterprise should not be grudged and sabotaged, but encouraged and aided to reach the highest possible efficiency." G. Bernard Shaw, *London Times,* January 19, 1948.

till they destroy the initiative and free movement of men and finally the free play of political criticism.

The state can do a great deal to set the level of economic activity by policies which at once will be stable enough to create an atmosphere favorable to private investment and adequate consumption and effective enough to prevent economic breakdown. Keynes and his followers have pointed out the great resources of fiscal and monetary policy. When a sag in spending or in demand threatens the economy, then the government through tax reduction and compensatory spending can maintain high levels of employment and production. Taxation and subsidies can be potent means of directing private investment to under-developed industries and regions; and a whole range of general incentives can be used to draw labor and capital into socially beneficial undertakings.

In some cases, as in Britain, the state may well wish to take over basic industries in order to insure that enough steel, coal or power will flow to the economy. The United States wisely nationalized the production of atomic energy; President Truman has suggested the possibility of government-owned steel mills; and the public interest is obviously paramount in such areas as conservation and river development. The public sector of the economy through the use of uniform accounting procedures can serve as a competitive spur to the private sector ·(and vice versa). And anti-trust action may still have its role: some British Socialists today appear to be turning to it, not in the New Freedom spirit of reversing the trend toward concentration, but in the New Deal spirit of scaring businessmen out of the restrictive practices which often (but not always) accompany monopoly.*

---

* The Union for Democratic Action London Letter, October 15, 1948, quotes a Labour M.P. as saying, "We agree that the effect of trust-busting in America isn't permanent. Broken apart, business interests tend to combine again in other forms. It's like painting the Firth of Forth bridge; no sooner do you finish at one end than you

In the meantime, society itself must be safeguarded against the internal evils which would otherwise disrupt it. Legislation has already imposed essential standards for working conditions, wages and hours, the employment of women and children, and so on. Another kind of legislation provides for insurance in case of accidents, sickness, unemployment or old age. We have far to go in the direction of meeting equivalent standards in education, housing and medical care; and the Government must step in to make sure that there standards are high enough for a free people. This drive toward "social security" cannot, of course, be the heart of a radical program. Indeed, an obsession with security may well contain dangers for economic progress. Monopoly, for example, tends to sacrifice production to a sure profit margin; labor, by overdoing seniority rights and apprenticeship, can block the rise of talent; and excessive security for all, in the sense of the provision of comforts without work, may well result in social stagnation. Yet we are far indeed today from risking that result. It is hard to see that a federal program of hot lunches for school children or of medical aid for sick people is going to remove all incentives to economic progress. No one should be allowed to starve for lack of food, or die for lack of doctors; all children should be well and amply fed and educated: when we reach this stage of social security, then we can consider how much farther it is safe to go.

But the state must *not* place its main reliance on a static program of welfare subsidies. Nor should it put much stock in the interminable enterprise of government regulation—an enterprise which only intoxicates the bureaucrat, paralyzes the businessman, and too often

---

have to start again at the other. But it's a lot worse not to paint the bridge at all. British industry would be in a far healthier state today if there had been a constant barrage of government prosecution and public condemnation of trusts and combinations. Price rings and gentlemen's agreements have put British industry to sleep. It's high time we woke it up."

ends in the capture of the regulatory agency by the interests to be regulated. The state should expend its main strength (1) in determining the broad level and conditions of economic activity through indirect means and (2) in making a success of projects clearly its own responsibility.

If the state must have the powers to avert economic collapse, where should they be located? Excessive centralization is obviously the great evil (next to giving the state no powers at all); the instruments of public power must not all be collected in a single hand. David Lilienthal's argument for the independence of the Tennessee Valley Authority put the case for decentralization in classic terms. The fact is that government ownership and control can take many forms. Federal ownership can be direct or (preferably) in the form of the independent public corporation like TVA; and state and municipal ownership can exist alongside it. The co-operative movement can be greatly expanded. And private ownership will have an indispensable role: we talk at present about setting up public plants to provide yardsticks for the efficiency of private management, but in the future we may wish to use the private plants as the yardstick. The more varieties of ownership in the economy, the better. Liberty gets more fresh air and sunlight through the interstices of a diversified society than through the iron curtain of totalitarianism. The recipe for retaining liberty is not doing everything in one fine logical sweep, but muddling through—a secret long known to the British who, as D. W. Brogan has put it, "change anything except the appearance of things."[20]

It would be imprudent for a non-economist to talk about the details of economic policy. But there seems to be no reason to despair over our technical capacity to stay on an even keel. *Saving American Capitalism* (New York, 1948), a collection of essays edited by Professor Seymour Harris, gives an exciting impression of the vitality of our economy and of the strength and variety of tools in our economic kit.

What is equally (or more) important is the vitality of our political leadership. The Democratic Party has performed in recent years the astonishing feat of rejuvenating itself while still in power. Ordinarily power chokes up the paths of advancement within a party and causes an organizational hardening of the arteries. The Republican Party, when it went out of power in 1932, had such a bad case of arteriosclerosis that it did not begin to produce able younger leadership until 1938—the year when Robert A. Taft was elected senator from Ohio, Harold Stassen became governor of Minnesota and Thomas E. Dewey had first try for the governorship of New York.

But the Democratic Party in 1949 has not only its quota of New Deal veterans—such men as Leon Henderson, W. Averell Harriman, Benjamin V. Cohen, Dean Acheson, William O. Douglas, Adolf A. Berle, Jr. It also had a new generation of younger men, who either played minor roles in the original New Deal or were unknown to Washington in those years and have risen to prominence since—Wilson Wyatt, Adlai Stevenson, Paul Porter, Hubert Humphrey, Chester Bowles, Mike Monroney, Paul Douglas, Clark Clifford. All this constitutes a reservoir of vigor and talent which is quite remarkable for a party in power as long as the current Democratic Party.

In addition, the rise of the politicalized labor leader introduces a new and possibly valuable element in American politics. Walter Reuther, the extraordinary able and intelligent leader of the United Auto Workers, may well become in another decade the most powerful man in American politics. Yet political power will impose grave responsibilities on the trade-union movement. If labor uses power as unwisely as the business community has used it, its claims to po-

[20] D. W. Brogan, *The English People,* New York, 1943, p. 108.

litical leadership will be rejected as firmly by the American people. But if labor accepts the role of partnership in government and subordinates its sectional demands to the public welfare, it may become as politically significant as the British Labour Party. The great dilemma will come when irresponsible labor leaders, like John L. Lewis, and the Communists whip up the sectional demands against the national interest in order to entice away the rank-and-file from the responsible leaders. This dilemma will put to test both the skill and capacity of the Reuthers, Dubinskys, Murrays and Rieves, and the maturity of the union member. It will also test the responsibility of the business community; for, if it can restrain itself from forcing the dilemma as part of its own anti-union tactics, it will contribute in the long run to the strength and stability of free society.

Our problem is not resources or leadership. It is primarily one of faith and time: faith in the value of our own freedoms, and time to do the necessary things to save them. To achieve the fullness of faith, we must renew the traditional sources of American radicalism and seek out ways to maintain our belief at a high pitch of vibration. To achieve a sufficiency of time, we must ward off the totalitarian threat to free society—and do so without permitting ourselves to become the slaves of Stalinism, as any man may become the slave of the things he hates.

WORKS BY ARTHUR MEIER SCHLESINGER, JR.:

Schlesinger, Arthur M., *The Age of Jackson*. Boston: Little, Brown and Co., 1939.

——. *The Age of Roosevelt*. Boston: Houghton Mifflin, 1957-1959.

——. *The Bitter Heritage: Vietnam. and American Democracy 1941-1966*. Boston: Houghton Mifflin, 1966.

——. *Kennedy or Nixon, Does It Make Any Difference?* New York: Macmillan, 1960.

——. *Orestes A. Brownson: A Pilgrim's Progress*. Boston: Little, Brown and Co., 1939.

——. *The Politics of Hope*. Boston: Houghton Mifflin, 1962.

——. *A Thousand Days: John F. Kennedy in the White House*. Boston: Houghton Mifflin, 1965.

——. *The Vital Center; The Politics of Freedom*. Boston: Houghton Mifflin, 1949.

Schlesinger, Arthur M. and Revere, R. H. *The General and the President*. New York: Farrar, Straus, and Young, 1951.

John Kenneth Galbraith

The Theory of Social Balance

It is not till it is discovered that high individual incomes will not purchase the mass of mankind immunity from cholera, typhus, and ignorance, still less secure them the positive advantages of educational opportunity and economic security, that slowly and reluctantly, amid prophecies of moral degeneration and economic disaster, society begins to make collective provision for needs which no ordinary individual, even if he works overtime all his life, can provide himself.

R. H. Tawney [1]

I

The final problem of the productive society is what it produces. This manifests itself in an implacable tendency to provide an opulent supply of some things and a niggardly yield of others. This disparity carries to the point where it is a cause of social discomfort and social unhealth. The line which divides our area of wealth from our area of poverty is roughly that which divides privately produced and marketed goods and services from publicly rendered services. Our wealth in the first is not only in startling contrast with the meagerness of the latter, but our wealth in privately produced goods is, to a marked degree, the cause of crisis in the supply of public services. For we have failed to see the importance, indeed the urgent need, of maintaining a balance between the two.

This disparity between our flow of private and public goods and services is no matter of subjective judgment. On the contrary, it is the source of the most extensive comment which only stops short of the direct contrast being made here. In the years following World War II, the papers of any major city—those of New York were an excellent example—told daily of the shortages and shortcomings in the elementary municipal and metropolitan services. The schools were old and overcrowded. The police force was under strength and underpaid. The parks and playgrounds were insufficient. Streets and empty lots were filthy, and the sanitation staff was underequipped and in need of men. Access to the city by those who work there

[1] R. H. Tawney, *Equality*. 4th ed. London: Allen & Unwin, 1952, pp. 134-35.

SOURCE. Reprinted from *The Affluent Society,* chapters 18 and 22. By permission of the publishers, Houghton Mifflin Company, Boston, Mass. Copyright 1958, John Kenneth Galbraith.

was uncertain and painful and becoming more so. Internal transportation was overcrowded, and unhealthful, and dirty. So was the air. Parking on the streets had to be prohibited, and there was no space elsewhere. These deficiencies were not in new and novel services but in old and established ones. Cities have long swept their streets, helped their people move around, educated them, kept order, and provided horse rails for vehicles which sought to pause. That their residents should have a nontoxic supply of air suggests no revolutionary dalliance with socialism.

The discussion of this public poverty competed, on the whole successfully, with the stories of ever-increasing opulence in privately produced goods. The Gross National Product was rising. So were retail sales. So was personal income. Labor productivity had also advanced. The automobiles that could not be parked were being produced at an expanded rate. The children, though without schools, subject in the playgrounds to the affectionate interest of adults with odd tastes, and disposed to increasingly imaginative forms of delinquency, were admirably equipped with television sets. We had difficulty finding storage space for the great surpluses of food despite a national disposition to obesity. Food was grown and packaged under private auspices. The care and refreshment of the mind, in contrast with the stomach, was principally in the public domain. Our colleges and universities were severely overcrowded and underprovided, and the same was true of the mental hospitals.

The contrast was and remains evident not alone to those who read. The family which takes its mauve and cerise, air-conditioned, power-steered, and power-braked automobile out for a tour passes through cities that are badly paved, made hideous by litter, blighted buildings, billboards, and posts for wires that should long since have been put underground. They pass on into a countryside that has been rendered largely invisible by commercial art. (The goods which the latter advertise have an absolute priority in our value system. Such aesthetic considerations as a view of the countryside accordingly come second. On such matters we are consistent.) They picnic on exquisitely packaged food from a portable icebox by a polluted stream and go on to spend the night at a park which is a menace to public health and morals. Just before dozing off on an air mattress, beneath a nylon tent, amid the stench of decaying refuse, they may reflect vaguely on the curious unevenness of their blessings. Is this, indeed, the American genius?

II

In the production of goods within the private economy it has long been recognized that a tolerably close relationship must be maintained between the production of various kinds of products. The output of steel and oil and machine tools is related to the production of automobiles. Investment in transportation must keep abreast of the output of goods to be transported. The supply of power must be abreast of the growth of industries requiring it. The existence of these relationships—coefficients to the economist—has made possible the construction of the input-output table which shows how changes in the production in one industry will increase or diminish the demands in other industries. To this table, and more especially to its ingenious author, Professor Wassily Leontief, the world is indebted for one of its most important of modern insights into economic relationships. If expansion in one part of the economy were not matched by the requisite expansion in other parts—were the need for balance not respected—then bottlenecks and shortages, speculative hoarding of scarce supplies, and sharply increasing costs would ensue. Fortunately in peacetime the market system operates easily and effectively to maintain this balance, and this together with the existence of stocks and some flexibility in the coefficients as a result of substitution, insures that no serious difficulties will arise. We are reminded of the existence of the problem only by noticing how serious it is for those countries—Poland or, in a somewhat different form, India—which seek to solve the problem by planned measures and with a much smaller supply of resources.

Just as there must be balance in what a community produces, so there must also be balance in what the community consumes. An increase in the use of one product creates, ineluctably, a requirement for others. If we are to consume more automobiles, we must have more gasoline. There must be more insurance as well as more space on which to operate them. Beyond a certain point more and better food appears to mean increased need for medical services. This is the certain result of the increased consumption of tobacco and alcohol. More vacations require more hotels and more fishing rods. And so forth. With rare exceptions—shortages of doctors are an exception which suggests the rule—this balance is also maintained quite effortlessly so far as goods for private sale and consumption are concerned. The price system plus a rounded condition of opulence is again the agency.

However, the relationships we are here discussing are not confined to the private economy. They operate comprehensively over the whole span of private and public services. As surely as an increase in the output of automobiles puts new demands on the steel industry so, also, it places new demands on public services. Similarly, every increase in the consumption of private goods will normally mean some facilitating or protective step by the state. In all cases if these services are not forthcoming, the consequences will be in some degree ill. It will be convenient to have a term which suggests a satisfactory relationship between the supply of privately produced goods and services and those of the state, and we may call it social balance.

The problem of social balance is ubiquitous, and frequently it is obtrusive. As noted, an increase in the consumption of automobiles requires a facilitating supply of streets, highways, traffic control, and parking space. The protective services of the police and the highway patrols must also be available, as must those of the hospitals. Although the need for balance here is extraordinarily clear, our use of privately produced vehicles has, on occasion, got far out of line with the supply of the related public services. The result has been hideous road congestion, an annual massacre of impressive proportions, and chronic colitis in the cities. As on the ground, so also in the air. Planes collide with disquieting consequences for those within when the public provision for air traffic control fails to keep pace with private use of the airways.

But the auto and the airplane, versus the space to use them, are merely an exceptionally visible example of a requirement that is pervasive. The more goods people procure, the more packages they discard and the more trash that must be carried away. If the appropriate sanitation services are not provided, the counterpart of increasing opulence will be deepening filth. The greater the wealth the thicker will be the dirt. This indubitably describes a tendency of our time. As more goods are produced and owned, the greater are the opportunities for fraud and the more property that must be protected. If the provision of public law-enforcement services do not keep pace, the counterpart of increased well-being will, we may be certain, be increased crime.

The city of Los Angeles, in modern times, is a near-classic study in the problem of social balance. Magnificently efficient factories and oil refineries, a lavish supply of automobiles, a vast consumption of handsomely packaged products, coupled with the absence of a municipal trash collection service which forced the use of home incinerators, made the air nearly unbreathable for an appreciable part of each year. Air pollution could be controlled only by a complex and highly developed set of public services—by better knowledge stemming from more research, better policing, a municipal trash collection service, and possibly the assertion of the priority of clean air over the production of goods. These were long in coming. The agony of a city without usable air was the result.

The issue of social balance can be identified in many other current problems. Thus an aspect of increasing private production is the appearance of an extraordinary number of things which lay claim to the interest of the young. Motion pictures, television, automobiles, and the vast opportunities which go with the mobility, together with such less enchanting merchandise as narcotics, comic books, and pornographia, are all included in an advancing gross national product. The child of a less opulent as well as a technologically more primitive age had far fewer such diversions. The red schoolhouse is remembered mainly because it had a paramount position in the lives of those who attended it that no modern school can hope to attain.

In a well-run and well-regulated community, with a sound school system, good recreational opportunities, and a good police force—in short a community where public services have kept pace with private production—the diversionary forces operating on the modern juvenile may do no great damage. Television and the violent mores of Hollywood and Madison Avenue must contend with the intellectual discipline of the school. The social, athletic, dramatic, and like attractions of the school also claim the attention of the child. These, together with the other recreational opportunities of the community, minimize the tendency to delinquency. Experiments with violence and immorality are checked by an effective law-enforcement system before they become epidemic.

In a community where public services have failed to keep abreast of private consumption things are very different. Here, in an atmosphere of private opulence and public squalor, the private goods have full sway. Schools do not compete with television and the movies. The dubious heroes of the latter, not Miss Jones, become the idols of the young. The hot rod and the wild ride take the place of more sedentary sports for which there are inadequate facilities of provision. Comic books, alcohol, narcotics, and switch-blade knives are, as noted, part of the increased flow of goods, and there is nothing to dispute their enjoyment. There is an ample supply of private wealth to be appropriated and not much to be feared from the police. An austere community is free from temptation. It can be austere in its public services. Not so a rich one.

Moreover, in a society which sets large store by production, and which has highly effective machinery for synthesizing private wants, there are strong pressures to have as many wage earners in the family as possible. As always all social behavior is part of a piece. If both parents are engaged in private production, the burden on the public services is further increased. Children, in effect, become the charge of the community for an appreciable part of the time. If the services of the community do not keep pace, this will be another source of disorder.

Residential housing also illustrates the problem of the social balance, although in a somewhat complex form. Few would wish to contend that, in the lower or even the middle-income brackets, Americans are munificently supplied with housing. A great many families would like better located or merely more houseroom, and no advertising is necessary to persuade them of their wish. And the provision of housing is in the private domain. At first glance at least, the line we draw between private and public seems not to be preventing a satisfactory allocation of resources to housing.

On closer examination, however, the problem turns out to be not greatly different from that of education. It is improbable that the housing industry is greatly more incompetent or inefficient in the United States than in those countries—Scandinavia, Holland, or (for the most part) England—where slums have been largely eliminated and where *minimum* standards of cleanliness and comfort are well above our own. As the experience of these countries shows, and as we have also been learning, the housing industry functions well only in combination with a large, complex, and costly array of public services. These include land purchase and clearance for redevelopment; good neighborhood and city planning, and effective and well-enforced zoning; a variety of financing and other aids to the housebuilder and owner; publicly supported research and architectural services for an industry which, by its nature, is equipped to do little on its own; and a considerable amount of direct or assisted public construction for families in the lowest-income brackets. The quality of the housing depends not on the industry, which is given, but on what is invested in these supplements and supports.

III

The case for social balance has, so far, been put negatively. Failure to keep public services in minimal relation to private production and use of goods is a cause of social disorder or impairs economic performance. The matter may now be put affirmatively. By failing to exploit the opportunity to expand public production we are missing opportunities for enjoyment which otherwise we might have had. Presumably a community can be as well rewarded by buying better schools or better parks as by buying bigger automobiles. By concentrating on the latter rather than the former it is failing to maximize its satisfactions. As with schools in the community, so with public services over the country at large.

It is scarcely sensible that we should satisfy our wants in private goods with reckless abundance, while in the case of public goods, on the evidence of the eye, we practice extreme self-denial. So, far from systematically exploiting the opportunities to derive use and pleasure from these services, we do not supply what would keep us out of trouble.

The conventional wisdom holds that the community, large or small, makes a decision as to how much it will devote to its public services. This decision is arrived at by democratic process. Subject to the imperfections and uncertainties of democracy, people decide how much of their private income and goods they will surrender in order to have public services of which they are in greater need. Thus there is a balance, however rough, in the enjoyments to be had from private goods and services and those rendered by public authority.

It will be obvious, however, that this view depends on the notion of independently determined consumer wants. In such a world one could with some reason defend the doctrine that the consumer, as a voter, makes an independent choice between public and private goods. But given the dependence effect—given that consumer wants are created by the process by which they are satisfied—the consumer makes no such choice. He is subject to the forces of advertising and emulation by which production creates its own demand. Advertising operates exclusively, and emulation mainly, on behalf of privately produced goods and services.[2] Since management and emulative effects operate on behalf of private production, public services will have an inherent tendency to lag behind. Automobile demand which is expensively synthesized will inevitably have a much larger claim on income than parks or public health or even roads where no such influence operates. The engines of mass communication, in their highest state of development, assail the eyes and ears of the community on behalf of more beer but not of more schools. Even in the conventional wisdom it will scarcely be contended that this leads to an equal choice between the two.

The competition is especially unequal for new products and services. Every corner of the public psyche is canvassed by some of the nation's most talented citizens to see if the desire for some merchantable product can be cultivated. No similar process operates on behalf of the nonmerchantable services of the state. Indeed, while we take the cultivation of new private wants for granted we would be measurably shocked to see it applied to public services. The scientist or engineer or advertising man who devotes himself to developing a new carburetor, cleanser, or depilatory for which the public recognizes no need and will feel none until an advertising campaign arouses it, is one of the valued members of our society. A politician or a public servant who dreams up a new public service is a wastrel. Few public offenses are more reprehensible.

So much for the influences which operate on the decision between public and private production. The calm decision between public and private consumption pictured by the conventional wisdom is, in fact, a remarkable example of the error which arises from viewing social behavior out of context. The inherent tendency will always be for public services to fall behind private production. We have here the first of the causes of social imbalance.

[2] Emulation does operate between communities. A new school or a new highway in one community does exert pressure on others to remain abreast. However, as compared with the pervasive effects of emulation in extending the demand for privately produced consumer's goods there will be agreement, I think, that this intercommunity effect is probably small.

IV

Social balance is also the victim of two further features of our society—the truce on inequality and the tendency to inflation. Since these are now part of our context, their effect comes quickly into view.

With rare exceptions such as the post office, public services do not carry a price ticket to be paid for by the individual user. By their nature they must, ordinarily, be available to all. As a result, when they are improved or new services are initiated, there is the ancient and troublesome question of who is to pay. This, in turn, provokes to life the collateral but irrelevant debate over inequality. As with the use of taxation as an instrument of fiscal policy, the truce on inequality is broken. Liberals are obliged to argue that the services be paid for by progressive taxation which will reduce inequality. Committed as they are to the urgency of goods (and also, as we shall see in a later chapter, to a somewhat mechanical view of the way in which the level of output can be kept most secure) they must oppose sales and excise taxes. Conservatives rally to the defense of inequality—although without ever quite committing themselves in such uncouth terms—and oppose the use of income taxes. They, in effect, oppose the expenditure not on the merits of the service but on the demerits of the tax system. Since the debate over inequality cannot be resolved, the money is frequently not appropriated and the service not performed. It is a casualty of the economic goals of both liberals and conservatives for both of whom the questions of social balance are subordinate to those of production and, when it is evoked, of inequality.

In practice matters are better as well as worse than this statement of the basic forces suggests. Given the tax structure, the revenues of all levels of government grow with the growth of the economy. Services can be maintained and sometimes even improved out of this automatic accretion.

However, this effect is highly unequal. The revenues of the federal government, because of its heavy reliance on income taxes, increase more than proportionately with private economic growth. In addition, although the conventional wisdom greatly deplores the fact, federal appropriations have only an indirect bearing on taxation. Public services are considered and voted on in accordance with their seeming urgency. Initiation or improvement of a particular service is rarely, except for purposes of oratory, set against the specific effect on taxes. Tax policy, in turn, is decided on the basis of the level of economic activity, the resulting revenues, expediency, and other considerations. Among these the total of the thousands of individually considered appropriations is but one factor. In this process the ultimate tax consequence of any individual appropriation is *de minimus,* and the tendency to ignore it reflects the simple mathematics of the situation. Thus it is possible for the Congress to make decisions affecting the social balance without invoking the question of inequality.

Things are made worse, however, by the fact that a large proportion of the federal revenues are pre-empted by defense. The increase in defense costs has also tended to absorb a large share of the normal increase in tax revenues. The posi-balance has also been weakened since World War II by the strong, although receding, conviction that its taxes were at artificial wartime levels and that a tacit commitment exists to reduce taxes at the earliest opportunity.

In the states and localities the problem of social balance is much more severe. Here tax revenues—this is especially true of the General Property Tax—increase less than proportionately with increased private production. Budgeting too is far more closely circumscribed than in the case of the federal government—only the monetary authority enjoys the pleasant privilege of underwriting its own loans. Because of this, increased services for states and localities regularly pose the question of more revenues and more taxes. And here, with great regularity, the question of social balance is lost in the debate over equality and social equity.

Thus we currently find by far the most serious social imbalance in the services performed by local governments. The F.B.I. comes much more easily by funds than the city police force. The Department of Agriculture can more easily keep its pest control abreast of expanding agricultural output than the average city health service can keep up with the needs of an expanding industrial population. One consequence is that the federal government remains under constant pressure to use its superior revenue position to help redress the balance at the lower levels of government.

V

Finally, social imbalance is the natural offspring of persistent inflation. Inflation by its nature strikes different individuals and groups with highly discriminatory effect. The most nearly unrelieved victims, apart from those living on pensions or other fixed provision for personal security, are those who work for the state. In the private economy the firm which sells goods has, in general, an immediate accommodation to the inflationary movement. Its price increases are the inflation. The incomes of its owners and proprietors are automatically accommodated to the upward movement. To the extent that wage increases are part of the inflationary process, this is also true of organized industrial workers. Even unorganized white-collar workers are in a milieu where prices and incomes are moving up. The adaption of their incomes, if less rapid than that of the industrial workers, is still reasonably prompt.

The position of the public employee is at the other extreme. His pay scales are highly formalized, and traditionally they have been subject to revision only at lengthy intervals. In states and localities inflation does not automatically bring added revenues to pay higher salaries and incomes. Pay revision for all public workers is subject to the temptation to wait and see if the inflation isn't coming to an end. There will be some fear—this seems to have been more of a factor in England than in the United States—that advances in public wages will set a bad example for private employers and unions.

Inflation means that employment is pressing on the labor supply and that private wage and salary incomes are rising. Thus the opportunities for moving from public to private employment are especially favorable. Public employment, moreover, once had as a principal attraction a high measure of social security. Industrial workers were subject to the formidable threat of unemployment during depression. Public employees were comparatively secure, and this security was worth an adverse salary differential. But with improving economic security in general this advantage has diminished. Private employment thus has come to provide better protection against inflation and little worse protection against other hazards. Though the dedicated may stay in public posts, the alert go.

The deterioration of the public services in the years of inflation has not gone unremarked. However, there has been a strong tendency to regard it as an adventitious misfortune—something which, like a nasty shower at a picnic, happened to blight a generally good time. Salaries were allowed to lag, which was a pity. This is a very inadequate view. Discrimination against the public services is an organic feature of inflation. Nothing so weakens government as persistent inflation. The public administration of France for many years, of Italy until recent times, and of other European and numerous South American countries have been deeply sapped and eroded by the effects of long-continued inflation. Social imbalance reflects itself in inability to enforce laws, including significantly those which protect and advance basic social services. One outgrowth of the resulting imbalance has been frustration and pervasive discontent. Over much of the world there is a rough and not entirely accidental correlation between the strength of indigenous communist parties or the frequency of revolutions and the persistence of inflation.

VI

A feature of the years immediately following World War II was a remarkable attack on the notion of expanding and improving public services. During the depression years such services had been elaborated and improved partly in order to fill some small part of the vacuum left by the shrinkage of private production. During the war years the role of government was vastly expanded. After that came the reaction. Much of it, unquestionably, was motivated by a desire to rehabilitate the prestige of private production and therewith of producers. No doubt some who joined the attack hoped, at least tacitly, that it might be possible to sidestep the truce on taxation vis-a-vis equality by having less taxation of all kinds. For a time the notion that our public services had somehow become inflated and excessive was all but axiomatic. Even liberal politicians did not seriously protest. They found it necessary to aver that they were in favor of public economy too.

In this discussion a certain mystique was attributed to the satisfaction of privately supplied wants. A community decision to have a new school means that the individual surrenders the necessary amount, willy-nilly, in his taxes. But if he is left with that income, he is a free man. He can decide between a better car or a television set. This was advanced with some solemnity as an argument for the TV set. The difficulty is that this argument leaves the community with no way of preferring the school. All private wants, where the individual can choose, are inherently superior to all public desires which must be paid for by taxation and with an inevitable component of compulsion.

The cost of public services was also held to be a desolating burden on private production, although this was at a time when the private production was burgeoning. Urgent warnings were issued of the unfavorable effects of taxa-

tion on investment—"I don't know of a surer way of killing off the incentive to invest than by imposing taxes which are regarded by people as punitive."[3] This was at a time when the inflationary effect of a very high level of investment was causing concern. The same individuals who were warning about the inimical effects of taxes were strongly advocating a monetary policy designed to reduce investment. However, an understanding of our economic discourse requires an appreciation of one of its basic rules: men of high position are allowed, by a special act of grace, to accommodate their reasoning to the answer they need. Logic is only required in those of lesser rank.

Finally it was argued, with no little vigor, that expanding government posed a grave threat to individual liberties. "Where distinction and rank is achieved almost exclusively by becoming a civil servant of the state . . . it is too much to expect that many will long prefer freedom to security."[4]

With time this attack on public services has somewhat subsided. The disorder associated with social imbalance has become visible even if the need for balance between private and public services is still imperfectly appreciated.

Freedom also seemed to be surviving. Perhaps it was realized that all organized activity requires concessions by the individual to the group. This is true of the policeman who joins the police force, the teacher who gets a job at the high school, and the executive who makes his way up the hierarchy of Du Pont. If there are differences between public and private organization, they are of kind rather than of degree. As this is written the pendulum has, in fact, swung back. Our liberties are now menaced by the conformity, exacted by the large corpo-

---

[3] Arthur F. Burns, Chairman of the President's Council of Economic Advisers, *U.S. News & World Report,* May 6, 1955.
[4] F. A. Hayek, *The Road to Serfdom.* London: George Routledge & Sons, 1944, p. 98.

ration and its impulse to create, for its own purposes, the organization man. This danger we may also survive.

Nonetheless, the postwar onslaught on the public services left a lasting imprint. To suggest that we canvass our public wants to see where happiness can be improved by more and better services has a sharply radical tone. Even public services to avoid disorder must be defended. By contrast the man who devises a nostrum for a nonexistent need and then successfully promotes both remains one of nature's noblemen.

The Redress of Balance

Our next task is to find a way of obtaining and then of maintaining a balance in the great flow of goods and services with which our wealth each year rewards us. In particular, we must find a way to remedy the poverty which afflicts in public services and which is in such increasingly bizarre contrast with our affluence in private goods. This is necessary to temper and, more hopefully, to eliminate the social disorders which are the counterpart of the present imbalance. It is necessary in the long run for promoting the growth of private output itself. Such balance is a matter of elementary common sense in a country in which need is becoming so exiguous that it must be cherished where it exists and nurtured where it does not. To create the demand for new automobiles we must contrive elaborate and functionless changes each year and then subject the consumer to ruthless psychological pressures to persuade him of their importance. Were this process to falter or break down, the consequences would be disturbing. In the meantime there are large ready-made needs for schools, hospitals, slum clearance and urban redevelopment, sanitation, parks, playgrounds, police, and a thousand other things. Of these needs almost no one must be persuaded. They are unavailable only because, as public officials of all kinds and ranks explain each day with practiced skill, the money to provide them is unavailable. So it has come about that we get growth and increased employment along the dimension of private goods only at the price of increasingly frantic persuasion. We exploit but poorly the opportunity along the dimension of public services. The economy is geared to the least urgent set of human wants. It would be far more secure if it were based on the whole range of need.

II

The problem will not be settled by a resolve to spend more for schools and streets and other services and to tax accordingly. Such decisions are made every day, and they do not come to grips with the causes of the imbalance. These lie much deeper. The most important difference between private and public goods and services is a technical one. The first lend themselves to being sold to individuals. The second do not. As noted above, in the evolution of economic enterprise, the things which could be produced and sold for a price were taken over by private producers. Those that could not, but which were in the end no less urgent for that reason, remained with the state. Bread and steel went naturally to private enterprise, for they could readily be produced and marketed by individuals to individuals. Police protection, sanitation, and sewer systems remained with public authority for, on the whole, they could not. Once the decision was taken to make education universal and compulsory, it ceased to be a marketable commodity. With the rise of the national state so did national defense. The line between public and private activity, as we view it at any given moment, is the product of many forces— tradition, ideological preference, and social urgency all play some part. But to a far greater degree than is commonly supposed, functions accrue to the state because, as a purely technical matter, there is no alternative to public management.

The goods and services which are marketable at a price have a position of elementary strategic advantage in the economy. Their price provides the income which commands labor, capital, and raw materials for production. This is inherent in the productive process. In the absence of social intervention, private production will monopolize all resources. Only as something is done about it will resources become available for public services. In Anglo-Saxon constitutional history, the requirement of an affirmative act to divert resources from private to public use was the key weapon of parliament in contending for power with the sovereign. The king had no— or, more precisely, but few—recurring revenues. Hence all taxes for public purposes had to be specifically voted. Gradually it became settled that there must be redress of grievances before supply. Apart from the use of the power of the purse as the protector of popular liberty, there was much else to be said for the practice. In poor and ill-governed societies private goods meant comfort and life itself. Food, clothing, and shelter, all technically subject to private purchase and sale, had an urgency greater than any public service with the possible exception of the provision of law and order. The burden of proof was on any step that diverted resources from the satisfaction of these simple biological requirements to the almost invariably spendthrift services of the state.

Recurring revenues are now commonplace. The control of the purse is still an element in the distribution of power between the legislative and executive authority. But it is only one element in a complex relationship and, unlike England under the Stuarts, the approval of expenditures, not the voting of taxes, is the linchpin of the legislature's power. Yet a good deal remains unchanged. We still seek to synthesize, on behalf of private goods, an urgency that was once provided not by Madison Avenue but by the even more effective importunities of hunger and cold. And for a very large part of our public activity, revenues are relatively static. Although aggregate income increases, many tax systems return a comparatively fixed dollar amount. Hence new public needs, or even the increase in the requirements for old ones incident on increasing population, require affirmative steps to transfer resources to public use. There must first be a finding of need. The burden of proof lies with those who propose the expenditure. Resources do not automatically accrue to public authority for a decision as to how they may best be distributed to schools, roads, police, public housing, and other claimant ends. We are startled by the thought. It would lead to waste.

But with increasing income, resources do so accrue to the private individual. Nor when he buys a new automobile out of increased income is he required to prove need. We may assume that many fewer automobiles would be purchased than at present were it necessary to make a positive case for their purchase. Such a case must be made for schools.

III

The solution is a system of taxation which automatically makes a pro rata share of increasing income available to public authority for public purposes. The task of public authority, like that of private individuals, will be to distribute this increase in accordance with relative need. Schools and roads will then no longer be at a disadvantage as compared with automobiles and television sets in having to prove absolute justification.

The practical solution would be much eased were the revenues of the federal government available for the service of social balance. These, to the extent of about four-fifths of the total, come from personal and corporation income taxes. Subject to some variations, these taxes rise rather more than proportionately with increases in private income. Unhappily they are presently pre-empted in large measure by the requirements of national defense and the competition of arms. In the mid-fifties defense expenditures were rather more than half of all the expenditures of the federal government and rather more than the total expenditures of states and localities combined. Were this sum to become available in any considerable part for the civilian services of governments in the years ahead, social balance could be quickly restored. And present income taxes would admirably keep the balance and without formally upsetting the present compromise on the question of equality. The word "formally" should perhaps be stressed, for in one articulate and influential branch of the conventional wisdom high tax rates are justifiable for military purposes but immoral and confiscatory if used for civilian purposes.

Perhaps the time will come when federal revenues and the normal annual increase will not be pre-empted so extensively for military purposes. Conventional attitudes hold otherwise; on all prospects of mankind there is hope for betterment save those having to do with an eventual end, without war, to the arms race. Here the hard cold voice of realism warns there is no hope. Perhaps things are not so utterly hopeless.

But meanwhile the problem of social balance must be faced. So far as the federal government is concerned, it must be accomplished while relying primarily on the personal and corporate income taxes. As we shall see presently, there are other taxes with a high claim to consideration, but there are other units of government with higher claim to their use. As usual, the solution is implicit in the alternatives. The test is not that high military costs make reductions in other public outlays necessary. Rather it is whether, given these military outlays, we are more in need of the services that improve social balance or the additional private goods with which we are more affluently supplied than ever before. When the issue is so presented and faced, there can be but one conclusion.[1]

However, even though the higher urgency of the services for social balance are conceded, there is still the problem of providing the revenue. And since it is income taxes that must be used, the question of social balance can easily be lost sight of in the reopened argument over equality. The truce will be broken and liberals and conservatives will join battle on this issue and forget about the poverty in the public services that awaits correction and, as we shall see presently, the poverty of people which can only be corrected at increased public cost. All this—schools, hospitals, even the scientific research on which increased production depends—must wait while we debate the ancient and unresolvable question of whether the rich are too rich.

The only hope—and in the nature of things it rests primarily with liberals—is to separate the issue of equality from that of social balance. The second is by far the more important question. The fact that a tacit truce exists on the issue of inequality is proof of its comparative

---

[1] This discussion assumes a satisfactory level of employment. Taxes and expenditures may be respectively lowered and increased to correct an insufficiency in demand. When social imbalance is great it will be clear that there is a strong case for correcting a shortage of demand by increased spending for needed public services rather than by a tax reduction which allows of increased spending for less needed private goods.

lack of social urgency. In the past the liberal politician has countered the conservative proposal for reduction in top-bracket income taxes with the proposal that relief be confined to the lower brackets. And he has insisted that any necessary tax increase be carried more than proportionately by the higher-income brackets. The result has been to make him a co-conspirator with the conservative in reducing taxes, whatever the cost in social balance; and his insistence on making taxes an instrument of greater equality has made it difficult or impossible to increase them. Meanwhile, the individual with whom he sympathizes and whom he seeks to favor are no longer the tax-ridden poor of Bengal or the first Empire but people who, by all historical standards, are themselves comparatively opulent citizens. In any case, they would be among the first beneficiaries of the better education, health, housing, and other services which would be the fruits of improved social balance, and they would be the long-run beneficiaries of more nearly adequate investment in people.

The rational liberal, in the future, will resist tax reduction, even that which ostensibly favors the poor, if it is at the price of social balance. And, for the same reason, he will not hesitate to accept increases that are neutral as regards the distribution of income. His classical commitment to greater equality can far better be kept by attacking as a separate issue the more egregious of the loopholes in the present tax laws. These loopholes—preferential treatment of capital gains and the special depletion allowances for mineral, including in particular oil, recovery—are strongly in conflict with traditional liberal attitudes, for this is inequality sanctioned by the state. There is work enough here for any egalitarian crusader.

IV

While there is much that the federal government must do by way of re-

dressing balance, as Chapter XVIII has suggested, it is in state and local services that the imbalance is most striking. Here, however, the solution—although it involves another wrench in liberal attitudes—is most clear. It involves much expanded use of the sales tax.

So long as social balance is imperfect there should be no hesitation in urging high rates. Coverage should be general on consumer products and services. In the affluent society no useful distinction can be made between luxuries and necessaries. Food and clothing are as difficult as ever to do without. But they can be and frequently are among the most opulent of expenditures.

The relation of the sales tax to the problem of social balance is admirably direct. The community is affluent in privately produced goods. It is poor in public services. The obvious solution is to tax the former to provide the latter—by making private goods more expensive, public goods are made more abundant. Motion pictures, electronic entertainment, and cigarettes are made more costly so that schools can be more handsomely supported. We pay more for soap, detergents, and vacuum cleaners in order that we may have cleaner cities and less occasion to use them. We have more expensive cars and gasoline so that we may have highways and streets on which to drive them. Food being comparatively cheap and abundant, we tax it in order to have better medical services and better health in which to enjoy it. This forthright solution has the further advantage that sales taxation can be employed with fair efficiency by states and even by cities. It is in the services rendered by these governments that the problem of social balance is especially severe. The yield of the sales tax increases with increasing production. As wants are contrived for private goods more revenues are provided for public use. The general property tax, the principal alternative to the sales tax, is rigid and inflexible. Since its rates must ordinarily be raised for additional services, including those that are associated with increasing income and product, the burden of proving need is especially heavy. This tax is a poor servant of social balance.

During the present century the use of sales taxation by states and cities has been growing. Liberals have ordinarily resisted its use. At a minimum they have viewed it with grave misgiving. This has again made the liberal the effective enemy of social balance. The reasons for this opposition provide an interesting example of how ideas, as they remain stereotyped in face of change, can force those who hold them into roles inconsistent with their own professions. The American liberal has been, all things considered, the opponent of better schools, better communities, better urban communications, and indeed even of greater economic stability.

The effect of a sales tax varies greatly as between a poor and an affluent country, and the difference is one not of degree but of kind. Under the *ancien regime* in France the tax on salt achieved an enduring reputation for its oppressiveness which it retains in parts of modern India to this day. In the United States a tax on salt, even one that doubled or trebled its price, would work no perceptible hardship. It is not that salt is more dispensable now than in the day of the *gabelle*. But where it was then a major object of expenditure it is now an insignificant one. And where the price of salt once affected visibly and directly what remained for other use, it is now too small to have a noticeable effect.

As with salt so with other things. In a family which can buy only bread and cloth, a tax on bread and clothing means that children will be hungrier and less well clad. In a family which can buy many things the adjustment comes at the margin in spending for gasoline, in stallment payments, the races, or the quality of the ceremonial steak.

Thus does affluence alter the case against sales taxation. It will be argued that some people are still very poor. The sales tax, unlike the income tax, weighs heavily on the small consumption of such individuals. But if the income tax is unavailable or in service or other ends, the only alternative is to sacrifice social balance. A poor society rightly adjusts its policy to the poor. An affluent society may properly inquire whether, instead, it shouldn't remove the poverty. As we shall see in the next chapter, moreover, improved social balance is one of the first requisites for the elimination of poverty. The modern liberal rallies to protect the poor from the taxes which in the next generation, as the result of a higher investment in their children, would eliminate poverty.

V

There is another objection to greatly multiplied use of the sales tax which is that, unlike the personal and corporation income taxes, it makes no positive contribution to economic stability. The latter do so in two respects. Falling on the corporations and the well-to-do, they weigh most heavily on income that is on its way to be saved rather than on income that is on its way to be spent for consumers' goods. The investment of saved income has long been considered the most mercurial and hence the least certain link between the receipt of income and its return to the spending stream. The income tax thus taps and insures spending where this is intrinsically the least certain. Income taxes and especially the personal income tax have, in addition, their role as built-in stabilizers of the economy. As incomes fall the personal tax, through the mechanism of the progressive rates, automatically reduces itself. As a result, and not without reason, it has come to be regarded as central to the strategy of economic management.

However, it is of the essence of the present argument that other goals share in urgency with protection and maximization of total output. One is the social balance that is served by sales taxation. Moreover, the principal purpose of the measures outlined in the last chapter was to make possible the escape from the commitment to maximum production without doing damage to individual economic security.

But social balance also adds to the stability and security of production along another dimension, for we have seen that exploitation of the solid needs of the public sector of the economy, as distinct from the tenuous and expensively synthesized wants for private goods, will almost certainly contribute to stability and orderly economic growth. Production will then be based on the whole range of human wants, not a part. As such it will be more secure.

Finally, with better social balance, investment in human resources will be kept more nearly abreast of that in material capital. This, we have seen, is the touchstone for technological advance. As such it is a most important and possibly the most important factor in economic growth. Such are the paradoxes of economic policy.

The much increased use of the sales tax, as here suggested, is obviously not intended as a substitute for the income tax. This has long been the fond dream of conservatives. The present intention, which is to break the deadlock imposed by the extraneous relation of the income tax to equality and divert a much increased share of resources to public need, accords with the conventional wisdom of neither conservatives nor liberals.

Nonetheless, it is the latter who will be most reluctant. Apart from the ancient commitment to equality, the Keynesian system is, pre-eminently, the conventional wisdom of liberals. And here support for the income tax is categorical. Keynes did not foresee that the rapid expansion in output which was implicit in his ideas would soon bring us to the time when not total output but its composition would become the critical matter. Had he survived, he would no doubt have been perturbed by the tendency of his followers to concentrate their policy on the single goal of increased output. He did not lack discrimination. But his followers or some of them will almost certainly continue to protect the Keynesian system, with its concentration on aggregate demand and output, from ideas which Keynes might have been disposed to urge. Such is the fate of anyone who becomes a part of the conventional wisdom.

VI

Given a sufficiency of demand, the responding production of goods in the modern economy is almost completely reliable. We have seen in the early chapters of this essay why men once had reason to regard the economic system as a meager and perilous thing. And we have seen how these ideas have persisted after the problem of production was conquered. There will be some who will still suggest that to divert more resources to public use will be to imperil private production. There is not the slightest ground for this suggestion; and we have seen, in fact, that the risk lies in another direction—that our reliance on private goods is by methods that threaten the stability of demand, and that social imbalance imperils the prospect for long-run economic growth. Still the fear will be expressed.

Here is the last advantage of sales taxation as a technique for diverting resources to public use. This tax has been recommended for years by the most impeccable of conservatives. Such august audiences as the National Association of Manufacturers have repeatedly heard and applauded speeches reciting its virtues. It has been made clear that it does not damage incentives or interfere with production. It is true that the sales tax has been given these credentials as an alternative to other taxes. But it has received this blessing from those who speak with the prestige of producers. As a political point this is not negligible.

One final observation may be made. There will be question as to what is the test of balance—at what point may we conclude that balance has been achieved in the satisfaction of private and public needs. The answer is that no test can be applied, for none exists. The traditional formulation is that the satisfaction returned to the community from a marginal increment of resources devoted to public purposes should be equal to the satisfaction of the same increment in private employment. These are incommensurate, partly because different people are involved, and partly because it makes the cardinal error of comparing satisfaction of wants that are synthesized with those that are not.

But a precise equilibrium is not very important. For another mark of an affluent society is the opportunity for the existence of a considerable margin for error on such matters. The present imbalance is clear, as are the forces and ideas which give the priority to private as compared with public goods. This being so, the direction in which we move to correct matters is utterly plain. We can also assume, given the power of the forces that have operated to accord a priority to private goods, that the distance to be traversed is considerable. When we arrive, the opulence of our private consumption will no longer be in contrast with the poverty of our schools, the unloveliness and congestion of our cities, our inability to get to work without struggle, and the social disorder that is associated with imbalance. But the precise point of balance will never be defined. This will be of comfort only to those who believe that any failure of definition can be made to score decisively against a larger idea.

CHAPTER 21

Democratic Socialism: Michael Harrington

MICHAEL Harrington (b. 1928) is an author and journalist, and currently serves as Chairman of the Board of the League for Industrial Democracy and as a member of the National Executive Committee of the Socialist Party. His major works of social criticism include *The Other America* (1963), *The Accidental Century* (1965), and *Towards a Democratic Left* (1968).

From The Accidental Century

CAPITALISM: THE COLD DECADENCE

The average nineteenth-century prophet thought that capitalism would end volcanically. Its contradictions, it was said, would one day burst the system asunder.

Now, another metaphor may have become more apt: Capitalism is moving towards its end massively, imperceptibly, like a glacier. Its decadence is cold, not hot.

SOURCE. Reprinted from *The Accidental Century,* by permission of the Macmillan Company. Copyright 1965 by Michael Harrington.

Thomas Mann's images of disorder were, from World War I on, evoked by the violent apocalypse. But in *Buddenbrooks,* he wrote of a less dramatic change, the defeat of the merchant oligarchs by the new businessmen. That development, which Mann only glimpsed, was but the beginning of a process: the pacific war of capitalism against capitalism, the gentle apocalypse. This quiet decadence persisted as a possibility when the economic breakdowns, revolutions, and counterrevolutions did not destroy the established order. And since its progress is recorded by statistical increments rather than by masses in the street, since it is gradual enough to allow the old rhetoric to mask the new reality, it is more difficult to observe than the collapse of a nation or the disintegration of a social class.

Three aspects of the cold decadence of capitalism suggest its character. The capitalist economy is destroying the capitalist civilization and personality; in the process, businessmen are building a collective society for private profit; and, as a result, it is the corporation rather than the Communist Party which is the major Western institution moving toward a convergence with the Soviet example.

I

The civilization of capitalism—not its economic mechanism, but its culture, its morality, its idealism—is being destroyed by the capitalist economy. The expropriation of traditional values is thus being carried out by unwitting businessmen rather than by revolutionary proletarians.

Historically, capitalism appeared as an ethic as well as a system of production. The competitive individual with his absolute right to private property served his fellowmen by seeking his own profit. It was the free market, an invisible hand fixing prices, allocating resources to their best use and so on, which victored all the antagonistic personal greeds into a common good. In such a theory, the making of money was a virtue since it promoted individualism, innovation, and the wealth of the entire society.

In the Protestant version of the capitalist morality, riches were the reward of the righteously ascetic. In the French Physiocrat's view, private property was the very basis of freedom itself. As A. A. Berle summarized this doctrine, "if a man was to be free, able to speak his own mind, depict his own thought and develop his own personality, he would have to have a base apart from one that was politically or ecclesiastically organized and controlled." That base was private property.

The idyll described in these visions did not, of course, exist. The millions who were degraded in the teeming new cities were the victims of the accident of their birth rather than the products of an economic selection of the fit and unfit. They demonstrated this fact when they formed the labor and socialist movement and educated the wealthy in some of the fundamentals of humanity. And yet, there was some relationship between the workings of the economy and the righteousness felt by the entrepreneur. If business early learned the value of state subsidy and tariff protection, there was still competition. The invisible hand of the market regularly misallocated resources and precipitated depressions, but over the long run (with the modifications imposed upon it by the supposedly incompetent majority), more and more goods were manufactured and distributed.

Under such circumstances, it did not take utter hypocrisy or ignorance to profess the capitalist faith sincerely.

At the same itme, the predictions of violent capitalist breakdown were tenable enough to corroborate the traditional socialist expectation. For most of the twentieth century it did indeed seem that the system would end apocalyptically. In the thirty-one years between 1914 and 1945, there were two world wars, the Russion Revolution, aborted revolutions throughout Central Europe, the Great Depression, Italian fascism, and the barbaric retrogression of Nazism. The data gave comfort to the "catastrophic optimism" of Karl Marx (the phrase is Raymond Aron's).

After World War II, however, events altered the classic perspective. The United States did not undergo its scheduled depression and instead reconverted to prosperity. This allowed it to subsidize the reorganization of capitalism in Western Europe. The renaissance of the Continental economy profoundly affected the labor and socialist movements. They largely abandoned the doctrine of the class struggle and accepted the welfare state and mixed economy as their ideal.

Capitalism enjoyed an unprecedented internal security from everything but itself.

It was in this period that the capitalist economy took the most vigorous measures against the capitalist ideology. And perhaps the twenty years of postwar capitalist success destroyed more of the capitalist ethic than the thirty-one years of intrawar capitalist failure. This was the process of the cold decadence.

The capitalist destruction of the capitalist ethic took place primarily through the private collectivization of the Western economy for minority profit.

A few anticipated this process and many have described it after the fact. The industrialist and mystic, Walter Rathenau, talked as early as 1917 (in a book entitled *Von Kommenden Dingen—Of Coming Things*) of an economy in which corporations would generate their own resources, free themselves from any real relation to the individual investor or the market, and become anonymous, self-sufficient automatons. Vatican sociology has often expressed a similar fear. In *Mater et Magistra,* John XXIII wrote, "In fact, by its own deep-seated and, as it were, intrinsic tendencies, free competition has almost destroyed itself. It has brought about a great accumulation of wealth and a corresponding concentration of economic power in the hands of a few 'who are frequently not the owners but only the trustees and managers of invested funds, which they administer at their own pleasure.'" (The quotation is from Pious XI in 1931.)

There are many statistical descriptions of this process and there is no point in rehearsing them at any length here. A few figures should suffice to outline a reality which is daily becoming more and more unmistakable. Their relevance to this chapter is that each one of these changes in economic structure marks an ethical event, the passing of a virtue.

In the place of the old competition, there is now a "corporate socialism" (the phrase is Estes Kefauver's) or a "collective capitalism" (Gardiner C. Means). Instead of a multiplicity of producers confronting one another in the market, there were in 1962 in America 500 corporations with $229.1 billion in sales—or more than half the sales and 70 percent of the total profit of the economy. The United States, as the most advanced industrial nation, became the most anticapitalist without knowing it.

This enormous concentration of corporate power had been particularly dynamic in the post-World War II period. Between 1947 and 1954, the 100 largest companies had increased their share of manufacturing from 23 percent to 30 percent; and the 200 top units controlled fully 37 percent of manufacturing. In American slang, one spoke of the Big Three in automobiles (actually, the Big Two and nearly the Big One), of the Big Four in steel, the Big Three in chemicals, and so on.

In 1964 the *U.S. News & World Report,* a conservative business magazine, announced that 25 percent of all American profit had gone to seven companies: General Motors, the American Telephone and Telegraph Company, Standard Oil of New Jersey, Texaco, Ford, Gulf Oil, and International Business Machines. In 1956, the same seven corporations had cornered "only" 16.6 percent of the profits. In short, the concentration of the rewards of production was even more acute than the concentration of the volume of production.

There were attempts to explain this development away by arguing that it had been accompanied by the diffusion of stock ownership. In part, this was simply much less true than the proponents of the thesis thought. In a 1963 National Bureau of Economic Research study, Robert J. Lampmann pointed out that 1.6 percent of the adult population of the United States held 82.4 percent of the publicly held shares. Insofar as a larger number of people did hold some stock, this represented a growth in the total of helpless, impotent small stockholders whose fragmented "ownings" had little to do with how corporations acted.

As a result of this concentration of corporate power, more and more companies were freed from the law of supply and demand. The most dramatic form of this development was the "administered price," in which the cost of an item on the market was determined, not by how much how many buyers were willing to pay, but in order to return a set profit. So it was that a Senate Committee in the 1950's revealed that General Motors "targeted" its profits for a "20% rate of return on the net worth after taxes at a predetermined level of production, or standard volume." Actually, the intention in this case was modest, since the company in question regularly reached profit levels of 25 percent and above.

Gardiner C. Means, one of the first American economists to theorize about this transformation, estimates that General Electric and Du Pont also have target rates of 20 percent after taxes, that Union Carbide seeks a 15 percent, and that U. S. Steel in the fifties increased its target from a traditional 8 percent to a goal of perhaps as high as 15 percent.

There is a most instructive irony in all of this, one which reveals how much a businessman can be a revolutionist without noticing it.

During the New Deal, when much of management was talking of the destruction of cherished values, the Administration set up a National Planning Board. It explored the possibilities of "facilitative planning" (a rough equivalent of the "indicative planning" practiced in France, to be described shortly). In the course of its work, the Board developed production-consumption patterns which indicated how people would spend their money at different levels of economic activity and

what the production and employment requirements would be at these levels.

Gardiner Means, who was the Board's Director of Research, notes that the main practical use of this technique by the Government was made during World War II. The military sector was analyzed in terms of production-consumption relationships, and input-output analysis was employed in one of the vastest industrial efforts of all time. After the war, some of these ideas survived, but modestly, in the Employment Act of 1946 and the activities of the Council of Economic Advisers.

But, and here the irony surfaces, the large corporations had become so huge that they could take up these methods which had been worked out for the national economy. Thus, General Electric estimated the demand for electrical appliances at full employment, and then decided what proportion of the market it would plan to supply. This same company is one of the most politically conservative in the United States, and would be appalled if the Government were to emulate the planning techniques of the profit-making corporations, techniques which the Government itself had developed. General Electric, and many giants like it, had emancipated itself from most of the capitalist verities but not the capitalist rhetoric.

This contradiction in which businessmen consciously violate the economic laws that they proclaim is not limited to a few of the largest corporations. Texas oilmen, the most aggressive of America's millionaire conservatives, invest mightily in the propagation of *laissez-faire*, pure and simple, and especially simple. They are able to do so because they operate in an industry in which production is strictly controlled under law and with their support. The Farm Bureau, the organization which represents the wealthy American farmers who receive over $4 billion in annual subsidy, predictably opposes degrading "handouts" to poor farmers. This near-comic opposition of greed and principle is only one aspect of the historic corruption of capitalism by capitalism. Occasionally, though, someone does talk of the *Emperor's Clothes.*

In the thirties, Russell Leffingwell of Morgan's told an investigating committee, "The growth of corporate enterprise has been drying up individual independence and initiative. . . . We are becoming a nation of hired men. Hired by great aggregates of capital."

With the corporate giants able to remove price and profit from the vagaries of the free market, they were also able to collectivize inventiveness. In the United States, where military research and development played such a major role in the postwar economy, some two-thirds of this technological pioneering was financed directly or indirectly by the Government. In every Western nation, inventive genius had become rationalized through research bureaucracies.

A similar process took place in another area where business was theoretically supposed to submit to the judgment of the free economy; the money market. In fulfillment of Rathenau's 1917 prophecy that the corporation would be able to divorce itself from the individual investor, the American companies more and more raised their capital from themselves. A. A. Berle has estimated that, from 1947 to 1956, the United States economy raised $292 billion in investment funds. Of this enormous sum, 60 percent was financed from retain profits, and 40 percent from "outside" the corporations. But even this latter figure was deceptive, since the "outside" was not primarily composed of thinking, judging risktakers, but of insurance companies, mutual funds, pension trusts, and other institutions whose adventurousness is limited by law or tradition.

Some of the elements of capitalist collectivization, then, are the concentration of economic power, the consequent ability to "administer" prices to an economy rather than responding to the law of supply and demand, the utilization of profit targets and planning techniques, the statification of inventiveness, and the abolition of risk in the money market. Making money had been declared virtuous because it promoted individualism, inventiveness, and the productive taking of chances. Now, each one of these qualities had been largely negated by the system. Adam Smith had thought that the corporation was hopelessly medieval, since it represented the anonymous control of someone else's money, and this contradicted the spiritual essence and genius of capitalism. By the mid-twentieth century, the corporation was capitalism.

This developing new system created new kinds of people.

In *The Lonely Crowd*, David Riesman perceptively described the personality evoked by the old reality and ethic. The "inner-directed" entrepreneur lived on a social frontier between feudalism and capitalism. He therefore consciously chose his individualism and his values, operating on a sort of internal gyroscope. In the twentiety century, however, wealth had become a function of manipulation and organization. There appeared the "other-directed" man, the team player who needed radar rather than a gyroscope, who took his values from others—when he could find them.

C. A. R. Crosland described a similar change in England. "The old style capitalist was by instinct a tyrant and an aristocrat who cared for no one's approval. The new style executive prides himself on being a good committee man, and subconsciously longs for the approval of the sociologist." In France, Pierre Bauchet has documented the way in which the new directors, bureaucrats of capital rather than entrepreneurs, find it natural and useful to integrate their "private" activities into a state plan.

But perhaps the most poignant case in point came to light in William H. Whyte's study of *The Organization*

Man. Whyte wrote his book while working for *Fortune,* a business magazine. Though honest about the reality of capitalism, he is hardly its ideological opponent, and this led him to a hopeless contradiction. Whyte candidly described the way in which the corporation was invading, and consciously rationalizing, the very lives of its employees. Even the romantic concept of marriage, one of the great moral accomplishments of capitalist civilization, is bureaucratized as the company calculates a man's wife along with the rest of the assets and liabilities.

Having described this relentless progress of the organization, Whyte can recommend no resistance more profound than an interior aloofness. He counsels the young executive to be a sort of good businessman Schweik, defeating the system by disloyally playing its game. This individual act of disaffiliation is as far as Whyte can go, and thus the true believer in the individualistic truths of the old capitalist ethic becomes a fifth columnist within the actual capitalist economy.

In American, then, one can watch the cold decadence of capitalism as it transforms and collectivizes the executive personality. In Europe, however, these changes have become explicitly political.

France is the most illuminating example of this juridical denial of capitalist laws by capitalist economies. In the Paris of the early sixties, a conservative and nationalist general presided over the Fourth Plan and prepared the Fifth. His prime minister was a banker. They were both committed to a directed economy in which state planning is a means of mobilizing the entire society behind politically determined goals. They were also in favor of capitalism or at least of extracting private profit from public effort. In this dual purpose of state plan and corporate gain, De Gaulle and Pompidou presented one of the most advanced instances of private collectivization.

The French Plan began immediately after the Second World War. In part, it was a culmination of the social consciousness of the Resistance; in part, it was a necessity imposed upon a wartorn nation which had to restore the very structure of its economy. By the mid-fifties, French planning had transcended both of the motives that presided over its birth. It had become conservative, or at least technocratic, rather than militant and plebian as in the Resistance ideal. And it was starting to plan in a context of relative affluence rather than that of poverty.

Even during the extreme parliamentary instability of the last days of the Fourth Republic, the French economy continued to register high rates of growth (annual increments of over 5 percent were common in the mid-fifties). When General de Gaulle took power, he inherited the accomplishments of the Plan and turned them into a vision of paternalistic, directed, and planned economy which would restore grandeur to the nation. (He also developed a curious thesis of a classless France in which workers, peasants, and the bourgeoisie would no longer contend among themselves but be tutored, on television, by the Leader.)

The Plan which was at the center of this philosophy does not in any way change the system of ownership or profit in France. It is "indicative" rather than compulsory, and the businessman is free to ignore its suggestions. Indeed, as critics of the Plan like Pierre Mendes-France have documented, even the nationalized enterprises, like Renault or the public banks, often violate the very guidelines of the Government which "owns" them. (In a society dominated by private corporations, public corporations absorb the former's methods, morality, and immorality.) Yet, the Government's control of 50 percent of new investment is a powerful lever with which to secure conformity to the Plan.

On paper, there is a wide participation of all classes in the society in the planning process (this is the basis for

De Gaulle's claim to a classless, co-operative France). In fact, the Fourth Plan was elaborated by commissions which were weighted over 90 percent toward businessmen and state functionaries—the distinction between the two categories is not always clear—and about 8 percent for worker and peasant unionists. Still, even if there were numerical equality between corporate and popular representatives, the businessmen would be at an enormous advantage. They command professional, paid research staffs and are thus in a position to understand and shape the Plan. The unions, by virtue of the very income and power structure of the society, count for less in these deliberations, whatever the representational mathematics.

The chief concept of the French Plan was, and is, a denial of one of the basic propositions of capitalist economics. Rather than allowing the "invisible hand" of the marketplace to determine the allocation of resources and rewards, the planners make a conscious and political choice of a growth rate to be achieved over a period of several years. Supply and demand are then adjusted to this decision, rather than the other way around. The result was a more harmonious development of the entire economy and an increase in the profit of the corporations that now have the state as a center for market research. But, as Gilbert Mathieu, the economic correspondent of *Le Monde,* noted in 1963, the relative inequities of income distribution increased between 1956 and 1961.

Indeed, there is a sense in which this maldistribution of income under the Plan is inevitable. When the state intervenes in an economy in which rewards are still assigned on the basis of private profit, than an increase in the general integration and efficiency of the society will benefit the rich. This might be offset by a vigorous and progressive tax policy, but this is certainly not the case in France (which, if anything, provides more scope for tax avoidance by the wealthy than the United States). As it is, one comes up with a system that combines the collective mode of planning with the private appropriation of money, a hybrid that moves away from both capitalism and socialism. And in terms of the distribution of wealth, the effect is for the entire community to subsidize those who are best off.

In American discussions, the embarrassing French example is usually countered with the German "miracle." In that country, it is said, the "social market economy" has observed the classic rules and prospered accordingly. However, as *Business Week* noted in the early sixties, the reality is a little less Adam Smithian than the claim: 55 percent of all investment in plant, equipment, and construction was financed by the state, and more than 40 percent of aluminum and more than 40 percent of auto, lead, and zinc production were also statified. (According to a high official of the French Commissariat du Plan, conversations between French and German planners in 1963 indicated that the two nations had an equal government intervention, albeit in different forms.)

Given such facts, it becomes somewhat more understandable that the British Conservative Party, in the name of anti-socialism, should introduce national planning in their country. As George Lichtheim concluded from this case and others, the directed economies of Europe "may still be capitalist" but they "cannot any longer be described as bourgeois." Capitalism is destroying capitalist motivation, ideology, and even personality.

In the United States, however, this process has been somewhat more disguised than in Europe. In the absence of open government planning, America has preferred to carry out its collectivizations in the name of something called "free enterprise." Ironically, the French Commissariat du Plan sends a technician to America in order to learn planning methods from the corporations. For in this country, the exigencies of production demand planning as much as in

Europe, only the piety of tradition will not allow the work to be spoken openly.

Even so, in the mid-sixties there were signs that American theory would at least begin to catch up with American practice. A majority report of the Senate Subcommittee on Employment and Manpower in 1964 urged conscious planning. And in the Housing Message of 1964, President Lyndon B. Johnson declared, "By 1970, we shall have to build at least two million new homes a year to keep up with the growth of our population. We will need many new classrooms, uncounted miles of new streets and utility lines, and an unprecedented volume of water and sewage facilities. We will need stores and churches and libraries, distribution systems for goods, transportation systems for people and communications systems for ideas. . . .

Now is the time to direct the productive capacity of our home building industry to the great needs of the neglected segments of our population. . . . In the tradition of the long-established partnership between private industry and community development, the Federal Government should encourage and facilitate these new and desirable approaches."

Such a statement recognized that the housing needs of the nation were so complex and interrelated that they required both anticipation and planning. But, significantly, after the Federal Government had accomplished what the free market was once supposed to do—direct a broad allocation of resources—and after it had laid down the plans for the new communities and provided their infrastructure, they would be turned over to private builders for their profit. Here again, innovation is collectivized and profit privatized.

While the Europeans were carrying out frank social planning for private profit, America was doing the same thing shamefacedly. As a result, a conservative movement could arise in the United States and, in the logical name of all the hallowed truths, make the preposterous proposal to go back to *laissez-faire*. And many of the wealthiest businessmen who supported this fantasy were themselves the most successful practitioners of the capitalist anticapitalism. The spectacle would be humorous were it not dangerous, yet clearly a society cannot long pay such an astronomical price for its rhetoric. Along with the old-fashioned virtues, the old-fashioned vocabulary will have to vanish.

In short, in the spiritual name of courageous, inventive, and risk-taking individuals, bureaucratized corporations, supported and subsidized by governments, were planning in increasing independence of the laws of supply and demand or the judgments of investors. Economic life was more and more dominated by anonymous collectivities, and a relatively few directors were making decisions that effected the existence of almost every citizen. The civilization of capitalism, its ethics, its morality, its philosophy, was being destroyed by the practice of capitalism.

And businessmen, without giving too much thought to the matter, were shaping new environments and new types of men.

II

If Karl Marx was the great prophet of the apocalyptic decadence of capitalism, of its violent breakdown, it was Joseph Schumpeter who most profoundly expressed its cold decadence. His feat was all the more remarkable in that he was a partisan, not a foe, of the system whose strange doom he described. He was, as Daniel Bell has said, that rare being, an economist with a sense of the tragic.

Indeed, one of the most remarkable things about Schumpeter is that he wrote his *Capitalism, Socialism and Democracy* in a time of the worldwide breakdown of the capitalist economy, yet he predicted that the system would be destroyed, not by its failures, but by its very accomplishments. Capitalism, he said, "through its very success undermines the social institutions which protect it, and 'inevitably' creates conditions in which it will not be able to live and which strongly point to socialism as the heir 'apparent.'" Setting aside for the moment Schumpeter's prediction of the coming of socialism, let's examine the thesis of the evolutionary subversion of capitalism.

Perhaps Schumpeter's most poetic statement of the theme is contained in an analogy between the medieval warrior and the modern businessman. Among other things, the knight was rendered obsolete by a weapons technology, by guns which democratized the battlefield and made a peasant or an artisan as lethal as a prince. Similarly, the capitalist is the victim of a technological change which, and the notion has a poignance, he himself brings about. "Since capitalist enterprise, by its very achievements, tends to automate progress, we conclude that it tends to make itself superfluous—to break into pieces under the pressure of its own success. The perfectly bureaucratized giant industrial unit only ousts the small or medium-sized firm, but in the end it also ousts the entrepreneur and expropriates the bourgeoisie as a class which in the process stands to lose not only its income but also what is infinitely more important, its function."

Like the social psychologists who came after him. Schumpeter understood that these changes in structure implied transformations of personal and ethical values as well: "The capitalist process, by substituting a mere parcel of shares for the walls of, and machines in, a factory, takes the life out of the idea of property. It loses the grip that was once so strong—the grip in the sense of the legal right and the actual ability to do as one pleases with one's own. . . . And this evaporation of what we may term the material substance of property—its visible and touchable reality—affects not only the attitudes of the holder but also that of the workmen and public in general. Denatured, defunctionalized

and absentee ownership does not impress and call forth moral allegiance as the vital form of property did."

The capitalist economy, Schumpeter realized, expropriated the capitalist civilization. "The scheme of values in capitalist society," he wrote, "though casually related to economic success, is losing its hold not only upon the public mind but also upon the 'capitalist' stratum itself."

At this moment in his analysis, Schumpeter developed a profound insight in the form of a confused prophecy and a bad definition. Socialism, he said, was the successor to that capitalist system which destroyed itself by accomplishing too much.

For Schumpeter, any society which centralized economic decision and in which the public sphere dominated the private was socialist. By reducing the term to a simple description of a way of organizing an economy, he narrowed, and radically so, the meaning that the socialist movement itself had given to its ideal. In Western European history and, above all, in the American socialist version of Eugene Victor Debs, socialism stood for equality, solidarity, the elimination of class distinction, cooperation, and the fulfillment of democracy at least as much for the nationalization of the means of production.

What Schumpeter did was to confuse socialism, which was and is a democratic program for a collectivist age, with collectivism itself (after the triumph of Joseph Stalin, the world Communist movement propagandized in favor of this same error). And yet, his very imprecision contains an important understanding on his part. "A society," Schumpeter wrote, "may be fully and truly socialist and yet be led by an absolute ruler or be organized in the most democratic of all possible ways." If one takes Schumpeter's "socialism" as a reference, not to the historical socialist dream of a democratic life, but to the collectivism which emerges out of capitalism, a significant truth appears.

Schumpeter understood that the political issue was not *whether* the future was to be collective, but *how* it was to be so. Collectivism could be the basis of the "most democratic" organization. It was not, as conservatives had held, inevitably cruel and totalitarian. But then, it could also support absolutism and authoritarianism. It was not, as some socialists had thought, inevitably benign and libertarian.

And so Schumpeter concluded on a note of profound ambiguity. Collectivism was inexorably being created by the "Banderbilts, Carnegies and Rockefellers" more than by the revolutionary proletariat. But the social content of this irresistible trend, whether it would be egalitarian or dictatorial, humane or antihumanist, was not predetermined. The quality of the life of the future was still to be fashioned, and by men and not by economic patterns. In short, the question of freedom had been posed, not settled, by contemporary history.

III

Schumpeter's insight can be deepened by way of a further irony. The *laissez-faire* ideologists had always charged that any form of collectivism would inevitably be bureaucratic and unfree. Today in the West there is indeed the possibility for the emergency of such an anthill society. It is promoted by unwitting businessmen, the spiritual children of *laissez-faire*.

The basis for this paradox is fairly simple to describe. Capitalists are now in control of the transition to a non- and anticapitalist order. Their training and background prepare them to carry out such a transition in the most confused and self-contradictory way. Left to themselves, the managers will create a bureaucratic form of collectivism and thus emphasize the convergence of the Western and Soviet systems much more effectively than any of the Communist parties of Europe and America.

The potential of this development comes more and more to the surface in the discussions of corporate "responsibility." A section of the business community, disturbed by the disappearance of any clear management responsibility to stockholders or to the law of supply and demand or to owners—or any other classic source of legitimacy for economic power—has been trying to decide to whom, or to what, the corporations owe fealty. For if the classic morality of private property no longer describes who rules, and should rule, what does?

Some of these theorists have come up with a most revealing answer, usually put affirmatively, happily. The corporation, they argue, is becoming responsible to the public. But if this is so, then the managers no longer fulfill the virtue of making money. Now, they are making public policy. And then, as an insightful observer put it, one is watching "the frightening spectacle of a powerful economic group whose future and perceptions are shaped in a tight materialistic context of money and things but which imposes its narrow ideas about a broad spectrum of unrelated non-economic subjects on the mass of men and society."

The ambiguities of this corporate collectivism are perhaps most accessible in the writings of A. A. Berle.

Berle's analysis is particularly important in that he writes as a friend of the capitalist order and proponent of the notion that the corporation must develop a conscience. In 1932, he had joined Gardiner C. Means in writing *The Modern Corporation and Private Property*, one of the very first empirical studies to hold that in the capitalist society the capitalist himself—the property owner—no longer managed his enterprise. In his place stood an administrator, an executive, who made decisions but did not own. Since this seminal analysis, many writers have developed aspects of the Berle and Means thesis of the separation of ownership and control in advanced capitalist society. And Berle has attempted to come to legal and ethical grips with the consequences of the system of ("power without property") which he had helped define.

To whom are the managers responsible if ownership is no longer the source of their authority? Under the developed ideology of capitalism, it was possible for the manager not to own his enterprise, but then he was the agent of the stockholders and thus ultimately responsive to the claims of property. But if Berle is right in his factual description, the stockholders have become passive, have been excluded from the decision process, and the manager disposes of millions, and even billions, of dollars without being practically accountable to anyone.

Berle's answer to the theoretical problem inherent in this situation is straightforward. The corporation should, he affirms, develop a conscience. And in one way or another, major segments of American business have taken up this rhetoric, proclaiming through institutional advertisements that they are somehow trustees of the commonweal. One company, General Electric, raised this theme to the level of a corporate philosophy (called "Boulwareism") which combined community education with a concerted attempt to destroy trade unionism.

But then there is a basic anomaly in Berle's position, one which F. A. Hayek, among the best known of the contemporary defenders of the traditional capitalist wisdom, put bluntly: "So long as management is supposed to serve the interests of the stockholder, it is reasonable to leave control of its action to the stockholders. But if management is supposed to serve wider public interests, it becomes merely a logical consequence of this conception that the appointed representatives of the public interest should control management."

Hayek is right as against Berle in that latter attempts to give a democratic legitimacy to the corporation—it is supposed to become an instrument of the people—but leaves it in the hands of a bureaucratic elite which is neither elected nor controlled by the people. Berle is right as against Hayek in that the traditional theory of the corporate rule of the stockholder applies less and less every day. In short, Berle's description of new forms of property is much more compelling than his vision of a new corporate ethic.

This confusion over the theoretical justification of the current system of production points to the kind of world which the corporation is, in fact, creating. It is not socialist, for, as Hayek notes, it is run by a managerial elite. It is increasingly not capitalist in the historically understood definition of the term, since it does not rest upon private property. It is a society whose trends are collectivist, and therefore anticapitalist, and bureaucratic and elitist and therefore antisocialist.

One might say that the corporation is moving toward a bureaucratic collectivist order, neither capitalist nor socialist. When one leaves the ethical questions about this system of "power without property" and moves on to more empirical description, the issues become clearer. Here it is possible to determine the responsibility of the corporation as it actually manifests itself in day-to-day operation. A public corporation, for instance, would show a political struggle in its decision process. A corporation with a conscience would demonstrate situations in which ethical considerations overrode a calculus of gain. What, in fact, has been the conduct of the corporation?

Predictably, all of these changes in the structure of the economy have affected the way in which corporate decisions are made. In his authoritative *La Planification Francaise,* Pierre Bauchet describes the separation of ownership and control in France. Then, in an analysis which applies to the United States, he states some of the consequences of this fact. The managers, he says, "seek less a profit of the capitalist than a profit of the enterprise. The capitalist's profit is traditionally identified with immediate financial gain, while that of the enterprise develops over a long period of activity: the first is based upon the conservation and increase of the wealth of the owners, the second upon augmenting the power of the firm. . ." It is, Bauchet believes, because of this development that the corporations engage in long-term planning and are even willing to integrate their policies with those of the state. Their power is no longer personal; it has become collective.

Gardiner C. Means has a similar description of the mode of operation of the American corporation where "the directors. . .try to run it well for the same reasons that the trustees of a great university seek to run the university well. . ."

And yet, even though the old robber-baron psychology no longer operates, even though the aim is no longer a personal profit, the goal is still a private profit. Only now, the private recipient is not an individual or a family but the collective of managers itself. And the way in which this power has actually been exercised provides no warrant for the discovery of a corporate conscience.

Between 1958 and 1962, for instance, American manufacturers spent $13.3 billion on new investment—and let 18 percent of their productive capacity stand idle. Socially, one result of this pattern was to promote a high, chronic rate of unemployment. On a public or conscientious basis it would be impossible to justify such a squandering of resources, both human and material. But with their targeted profit rates, the corporations go on strike whenever they cannot gain their predetermined return. More than that, their targets are established on a long-run volume of production so they can make their money even while allowing their plants to work far under capacity.

The steel industry is an excellent example of this process. Dominated by a small group of corporations, it spent a fair portion of the 1950's running well under its capacity—and sometimes 50 percent under capacity. It was not that

society had satisfied its social appetite for steel. Far from it. In the very same periods, unmet needs desperately required steel: low-cost housing, schools, hospitals, transportation systems, etc. According to the hallowed laws of the free market, the steel giants should have taken advantage of this demand by lowering prices, increasing volume, and thus creating a new market.

In reality, the steel corporations, particularly the industry leader, U. S. Steel, used this period to increase their targeted profits, as Gardiner C. Means suggests. They also increased prices, recommended wage restraint to workers whom they accused of being recklessly inflationary in their demands, and, when this curious concept of the public interest was mildly challenged by a Democratic President, reacted as if America had suddenly become a totalitarian society. All this took place in a sector of the economy whose decisions affect more of the life of the United States than most state governments and many acts of Federal legislation.

In short, the structures, techniques, and direction of the corporation have been more and more collectivized, and its policies are generally no longer made to further the interest of an individual or family. But the old principle of profit survives the passing of its ethical justifications and itself becomes collective, anonymous, and even more powerful. In the heart of the process, it is difficult to discern a conscience.

So far, the focus has been upon the collectivization of corporate production, personality, and decision-making. But there is another important collectivization: that of mass opinion and taste. This, of course, is accomplished by the most successful educational institution of contemporary capitalism, the advertising industry.

Much of the rage directed against advertising by intellectuals is unfair. These critics note that this industry has a systematic habit of degrading language, truth, and culture in general. They generally assume that this is primarily due to the personal corruption of those who direct the communications media in America. Yet this misses the more profound functions of advertising and implies the too simple theory that one is confronted by a conspiracy of traitorous college graduates. The reality goes much more deeply into the American economic system and the new, private collectivism.

The advertising industry now accounts for an expenditure of approximately $15 billion a year which puts it on a par with formal education as a social activity. As a standard text by S. Watson Dunn describes the situation, "Since the end of World War II, advertising expenditures have been rising faster than Gross National Product, national income, carloadings, or almost any barometer of business activity one might choose." Such a massive investment is clearly not made out of a Philistine hatred of culture.

Rather, this development takes place because the rationalization and collectivization of production require the rationalization and collectivization of taste. The child, in David Riesman's apt phrase, is turned into a "consumer trainee." And, as David M. Potter, one of the most perceptive commentators on the subject, has written, "advertising now competes with such long-standing institutions as the school and the church in the magnitude of its social influence." Just as the "free market" no longer allocates resources, determines prices, or raises the bulk of new investment funds, it no longer provides an open confrontation of buyer and seller. The consumer is taxed so that his own desires may be standardized enough to be run through a computing machine.

Even more basically, it is the role of advertising to make the misallocation of resources characteristic of corporate collectivism appear as the free choice of the society.

For example, the public sector of American life—health, governmentally financed housing, education, transportation, and the like—is considered a great burden by most Americans. Yet, this sector contains some of the most important necessities of modern life and is a fundamental constituent of a standard of living. The private sector, on the other hand, is thought of as an area of freedom. Here one may bid for competing detergents made by the same firm, purchase planned obsolescence in automobiles and household appliances, and pay interest rates which are carefully designed for maximum deception. The private sector advertises; the public sector, by far and large, does not.

It takes money and ingenuity to convince people to invest in luxuries which they do not need and to ignore their necessities. It also makes money to do so. And it is the advertising industry that makes this misallocation of resources seem rational and freely chosen.

This instance, and the other cases of planned waste for profit, should serve to throw light on Berle's hopes for the coming of a corporate conscience. Whatever the institutional advertisements about the public responsibilities of business, the corporation acts to promote its private, but collective, profit. It imposes itself upon the people rather than responding to their needs, producing on a basis of targeted greed. It no longer follows the classic capitalist virtues, but it has managed to retain the classic capitalist vice of irresponsibility.

It is a somewhat confused recognition of this reality that leads Berle to one of his most surprising statements. Again, it must be emphasized that he writes as a defender of capitalism (and, in foreign-policy terms, as one of the more rigid American opponents of the Soviet Union). Yet he asserts, "The private property system in production, which began with our great grandfather's farm and forge, has almost vanished in the vast area of the American economy dominated by this system (retained-profits financing and institutional investment—

author's note). Instead, we have something which differs from the Russian or socialist system *mainly in its philosophic content*" (emphasis added).

Even if one takes Berle's statement of the present convergence of the communist and capitalist systems as extreme, as I do, how is it that one can even talk of such a comparison? For if this were even a major tendency in the West, then the role of the Communist parties is being usurped by businessmen. To deal with this bizarre possibility, it is necessary to go back to some of the implications of Schumpeter's definition of "socialism."

In the Marxian version of the hot decadence of capitalism, the working class of the most advanced, technologically developed nations would seize power from owners who could no longer resolve the contradiction between the social character of the productive process and the private character of the system that directed it. History would make the capitalists weak and the workers desperately strong. Yet, it is quite possible that the movement toward collectivism (not socialism) in this century took place under the opposite conditions from the ones envisioned by Marx: in Russia, where the workers were weak; in the West, where the capitalists were strong.

If Russia in 1917 was ripe for socialist revolution, it was almost totally unripe for socialism. Industrially backward, its tiny working class could, for specific historic reasons, lead the overthrow of the old order, but it did not have the numbers or the economic resources to build a new order. Lenin and Trotsky felt that their Revolution was only the beginning, that it was going to be rescued by socialist victories in the heart of Europe. That did not happen.

Instead, the first attempt actually to institute socialism was based upon the socialization of poverty rather than abundance. As Marx had predicted long before, such a project could not succeed democratically. The material basis for socialism was an already existent wealth, which was precisely what the Russians did not have. Stalin forced the restriction of consumption, feeding heavy industry rather than people. To exact such a sacrifice from the masses, he expropriated their political power and concentrated it in the hands of a bureaucratic elite with social and economic privileges.

The Russian rhetoric was socialist, the Russian reality was not. The state owned the means of production—but the people did not "own" the state. They could exercise such an "ownership" over the nationalized means of production only if they could determine who would direct them and with what policies. For them, democracy was the only title to social wealth, their equivalent of the capitalist stock certificate. Thus, the destruction of democratic freedoms by Stalin was not simply a denial of political rights but the end of the social and economic power of the people as well.

The new bureaucracy established its privileges through its totalitarian monopoly of political power. The bureaucrat played politics as the businessman plays the market—as a means to gain economic and social position. When the industrial backwardness of Russia was overcome, the wealth created by the labor of the many was concentrated in the hands of a few. This was a collectivization in the absence of a strong working class.

In the West, the bureaucratic and collectivist tendencies emerged from riches rather than from scarcity. The capitalist system automated and collectivized the old-fashioned capitalist out of existence, replacing him with a manager. The corporation bureaucrat became more powerful, but not as in Russia through a process of forced industrialization. His power grew as society was backing leisurely and unthinkingly into the future. The executive was a revolutionist but did know it. The resulting structure—and it is still far from finished—was not identical to the Soviet system or anything like it. In Russia there was totalitarianism; in the West, limited democracy; under communism, resources were allocated by direct and centralized political decision; under capitalism, by indirect, though increasingly centralized, economic decision.

And yet, there is a possible convergence of these utterly different histories. As the West becomes more collectivized under a managerial elite and Russia becomes wealthier under a political elite, the conscious, self-seeking decisions of a minority could become the basis of both economies. In terms of their evolution, there would be tremendous contrasts between General Motors and a Commissariat of Transportation. In terms of economic function and practice, the two entities could come to resemble one another more and more.

And what the two cases would share, above all, would be that their collectivization would have been accomplished without the active, directing participation of the great mass of the people.

Marx, and the early socialist movement, had based the hope for a liberating collectivism on the way in which socialization would take place; through the revolutionary struggle of the democratic majority. It would be humane, he argued, because the people, and the workers in particular, would be driven to brotherhood out of a daily necessity which they would turn into a social virtue. They would join together in unions, in a political movement; they would counterpose their superior numbers and ethic to the superior funds and egotism of business. The secret of their triumph, and consequently of the society they would fashion, would be free cooperation.

But assuming the very real possibility that Western collectivism will be introduced by businessmen, then Marx's method would point toward dark consequences. The conditions of life, the practical necessities, of the executive are material gain, authority, direction. The

capitalist who accidently stumbled into the revolutionizing of society would imbue it with the only values he knows, and the worst traditions of the past and the grimmest potential of the future would be united.

IV

But one need not look so far into the distance in order to discern the cold decadence of capitalism.

Practically every ethical, moral, and cultural justification for the capitalist system has now been destroyed by capitalism. The idyll of the free market, risktaking, inventiveness, the social virtue of making money, all these have been abolished by the very success of capitalism itself. In some cases, most particularly in the United States, this contradiction between rhetoric and reality has led to the appearance of an atavistic "conservatism" which seeks to repeal the modern world. As a social and economic program, this is preposterous; as a political movement, it might threaten the very peace of the earth.

But, most basically, the problem of the cold decadence of capitalism is not that it represents the decline of the values and ideologies of the past. It is that this system will transform itself without really noticing the fact, and that the businessman as revolutionist will corrupt, not simply himself, but the society of the future as well.

WORKS BY
MICHAEL HARRINGTON

Harrington, Michael. *The Accidental Century.* New York: Macmillan, 1965.
————. *The Other America.* New York: Macmillan, 1962.
————. *The Retail Clerks.* New York: John Wiley and Sons, Inc., 1962.
————. *Toward a Democratic Left.* New York: Macmillan, 1968.

CHAPTER 22

Philosophical Radicalism:
Herbert Marcuse

HERBERT Marcuse, born in Germany in 1898 and naturalized as an
American citizen in 1940, is a professor of philosophy and politics
who has taught at Harvard, Columbia, Brandeis, and the University
of California at San Diego. An authority on Hegel and Marx, he
has sought to apply their teachings to an analysis of modern
industrialized societies. His major books include *Reason and Revolution* (1941), *Eros and Civilization* (1954), *Soviet Marxism* (1958),
One Dimensional Man (1964), and (with Barrington Moore and
Robert Paul Wolff) *A Critique of Pure Tolerance* (1965).

From One Dimensional Man

THE NEW FORMS OF CONTROL

A comfortable, smooth, reasonable,
democratic unfreedom prevails in advanced industrial civilization, a token of
technical progress. Indeed, what could be
more rational than the suppression of
individuality in the mechanization of socially necessary but painful performances; the concentration of individual
enterprises in more effective, more pro-

SOURCE. Reprinted from *One Dimensional
Man* by permission of the publisher, Beacon
Press. Copyright 1964, Beacon Press.

ductive corporations; the regulation
of free competition among unequally
equipped economic subjects; the curtail-
ment of prerogatives and national sovereignties which impede the international organization of resources. That
this technological order also involves a
political and intellectual coordination
may be a regrettable and yet promising
development.

The rights and liberties which were
such vital factors in the origins and
earlier stages of industrial society yield
to a higher stage of this society: they
are losing their traditional rationale and
content. Freedom of thought, speech, and
conscience were—just as free enterprise,

which they served to promote and protect—essentially *critical* ideas, designed to replace an obsolescent material and intellectual culture by a more productive and rational one. Once institutionalized, these rights and liberties shared the fate of the society of which they had become an integral part. The achievement cancels the premises.

To the degree to which freedom from want, the concrete substance of all freedom, is becoming a real possibility, the liberties which pertain to a state of lower productivity are losing their former content. Independence of thought, autonomy, and the right to political opposition are being deprived of their basic critical function in a society which seems increasingly capable of satisfying the needs of the individuals through the way in which it is organized. Such a society may justly demand acceptance of its principles and institutions, and reduce the opposition to the discussion and promotion of alternative policies *within* the status quo. In this respect, it seems to make little difference whether the increasing satisfaction of needs is accomplished by an authoritarian or a non-authoritarian system. Under the conditions of a rising standard of living, non-conformity with the system itself appears to be socially useless, and the more so when it entails tangible economic and political disadvantages and threatens the smooth operation of the whole. Indeed, at least in so far as the necessities of life are involved, there seems to be no reason why the production and distribution of goods and services should proceed through the competitive concurrence of individual liberties.

Freedom of enterprise was from the beginning not altogether a blessing. As the liberty to work or to starve, it spelled toil, insecurity, and fear for that vast majority of the population. If the individual were no longer compelled to prove himself on the market, as a free economic subject, the disappearance of this kind of freedom would be one of the greatest achievements of civilization.

The technological processes of mechanization and standardization might release individual energy into a yet uncharted realm of freedom beyond necessity. The very structure of human existence would be altered; the individual would be liberated from the work world's imposing upon him alien needs and alien possibilities. The individual would be free to exert autonomy over a life that would be his own. If the productive apparatus could be organized and directed toward the satisfaction of the vital needs, its control might well be centralized; such control would not prevent individual autonomy, but render it possible.

This is a goal within the capabilities of advanced industrial civilization, the "end" of technological rationality. In actual fact, however, the contrary trend operates: the apparatus imposes its economic and political requirements for defense and expansion on labor time and free time, on the material and intellectual culture. By virtue of the way it has organized its technological base, contemporary industrial society tends to be totalitarian. For "totalitarian" is not only a terroristic political coordination of society, but also a non-terroristic economic-technical coordination which operates through the manipulation of needs by vested interests. It thus precludes the emergence of an effective opposition against the whole. Not only a specific form of government or party rule makes for totalitarianism, but also a specific system of production and distribution which may well be compatible with a "pluralism" of parties, newspapers, "countervailing powers," etc.

Today political power asserts itself through its power over the machine process and over the technical organization of the apparatus. The government of advanced and advancing industrial societies can maintain and secure itself only when it succeeds in mobilizing, organizing, and exploiting the technical, scientific, and mechanical productivity available to industrial civilization. And this productivity mobilizes society as a whole, above and beyond any particular individual or group interests. The brute fact that the machine's physical (only physical?) power surpasses that of the individual, and of any particular group of individuals, makes the machine the most effective political instrument in any society whose basic organization is that of the machine process. But the political trend may be reversed; essentially the power of the machine is only the stored-up and projected power of man. To the extent to which the work world is conceived of as a machine and mechanized accordingly, it becomes the *potential* basis of a new freedom for man.

Contemporary industrial civilization demonstrates that it has reached the stage at which "the free society" can no longer be adequately defined in the traditional terms of economic, political, and intellectual liberties, not because these liberties have become insignificant, but because they are too significant to be confined within the traditional forms. New modes of realization are needed, corresponding to the new capabilities of society.

Such new modes can be indicated only in negative terms because they would amount to the negation of the prevailing modes. Thus economic freedom would mean freedom *from* the economy—from being controlled by economic forces and relationships; freedom from the daily struggle for existence, from earning a living. Political freedom would mean liberation of the individuals *from* politics over which they have no effective control. Similarly, intellectual freedom would mean the restoration of individual thought now absorbed by mass communication and indoctrination, abolition of "public opinion" together with its makers. The unrealistic sound of these propositions is indicative, not of their utopian character, but of the strength of the forces which prevent their realization. The most effective and enduring form of warfare against liberation is the implanting of material and intellectual needs that perpetuate obsolete forms of the struggle for existence.

The intensity, the satisfaction and even the character of human needs, beyond the biological level, have always been preconditioned. Whether or not the possibility of doing or leaving, enjoying or destroying, possessing or rejecting something is seized as a *need* depends on whether or not it can be seen as desirable and necessary for the prevailing societal institutions and interests. In this sense, human needs are historical needs and, to the extent to which the society demands the repressive development of the individual, his needs themselves and their claim for satisfaction are subject to overriding critical standards.

We may distinguish both true and false needs. "False" are those which are superimposed upon the individual by particular social interests in his repression: the needs which perpetuate toil, aggressiveness, misery, and injustice. Their satisfaction might be most gratifying to the individual, but this happiness is not a condition which has to be maintained and protected if it serves to arrest the development of the ability (his own and others) to recognize the disease of the whole and grasp the changes of curing the disease. The result then is euphoria in unhappiness. Most of the prevailing needs to relax, to have fun, to behave and consume in accordance with the advertisements, to love and hate what others love and hate, belong to this category of false needs.

Such needs have a societal content and function which are determined by external powers over which the individual has no control; the development and satisfaction of these needs is heteronomous. No matter how much such needs may have become the individual's own, reproduced and fortified by the conditions of his existence; no matter how much he identifies himself with them and finds himself in their satisfaction, they continue to be what they were from the beginning—products of a society whose dominant interest demands repression.

The prevalence of repressive needs is an accomplished fact, accepted in ignorance and defeat, but a fact that must be undone in the interest of the happy individual as well as all those whose misery is the price of his satisfaction. The only needs that have an unqualified claim for satisfaction are the vital ones—nourishment, clothing, lodging at the attainable level of culture. The satisfaction of these needs is the prerequisite for the realization of *all* needs, of the unsublimated as well as the sublimated ones.

For any consciousness and conscience, for any experience which does not accept the prevailing societal interest as the supreme law of thought and behavior, the established universe of needs and satisfactions is a fact to be questioned—questioned in terms of truth and falsehood. These terms are historical throughout, and their objectivity is historical. The judgment of needs and their satisfaction, under the given conditions, involves standards of *priority*—standards which refer to the optimal development of the individual, of all individuals, under the optimal utilization of the material and intellectual resources available to man. The resources are calculable. "Truth" and "falsehood" of needs designate objective conditions to the extent to which the universal satisfaction of vital needs and, beyond it, the progressive alleviation of toil and poverty, are universally valid standards. But as historical standards, they do not only vary according to area and stage of development, they also can be defined only in (greater or lesser) *contradiction* to the prevailing ones. What tribunal can possibly claim the authority of decision?

In the last analysis, the question of what are true and false needs must be answered by the individuals themselves, but only in the last analysis, that is, if and when they are free to give their own answer. As long as they are kept incapable of being autonomous, as long as they are indoctrinated and manipulated (down to their very instincts), their answer to this question cannot be taken as their own. By the same token, however, no tribunal can justly arrogate to itself the right to decide which needs should be developed and satisfied. Any such tribunal is reprehensible, although our revulsion does not do away with the question: how can the people who have been the object of effective and productive domination by themselves create the conditions of freedom?

The more rational, productive, technical, and total the repressive administration of society becomes, the more unimaginable the means and ways by which the administered individuals might break their servitude and seize their own liberation. To be sure, to impose Reason upon an entire society is a paradoxical and scandalous idea—although one might dispute the rightcousness of a society which ridicules this idea while making its own population into objects of total administration. All liberation depends on the consciousness of servitude, and the emergency of this consciousness is always hampered by the predominance of needs and satisfactions which, to a great extent, have become the individual's own. The process always replaces one system of preconditioning by another; the optimal goal is the replacement of false needs by true ones, the abandonment of repressive satisfaction.

The distinguishing feature of advanced industrial society is its effective suffocation of those needs which demand liberation—liberation also from that which is tolerable and rewarding and comfortable—while it sustains and absolves the destructive power and repressive function of the affluent society. Here, the social controls exact the overwhelming need for the production and consumption of waste; the need for stupefying work where it is no longer a real necessity; the need for modes of relaxation which soothe and prolong this stupefication; the need for maintaining such deceptive liberties as free competition at administered prices, a free press which censors itself, free choice between brands and gadgets.

Under the rule of a repressive whole, liberty can be made into a powerful instrument of domination. The range of choice open to the individual is not the decisive factor in determining the degree of human freedom, but *what* can be chosen and what *is* chosen by the individual. The criterion for free choice can never be an absolute one, but neither is it entirely relative. Free election of masters does not abolish the masters or the slaves. Free choice among a wide variety of goods and services does not signify freedom if these goods and services sustain social controls over a life of toil and fear—that is, if they sustain alienation. And the spontaneous reproduction of superimposed needs by the individual does not establish autonomy; it only testifies to the efficacy of the controls.

Our insistence on the depth and efficacy of these controls is open to the objection that we overrate greatly the indoctrinating power of the "media," and that by themselves the people would feel and satisfy the needs which are now imposed upon them. The objection misses the point. The preconditioning does not start with the mass production of radio and television and with the centralization of their control. The people enter this stage as preconditioned receptacles of long standing; the decisive difference is in the flattening out of the contrast (or conflict) between the given and the possible, between the satisfied and the unsatisfied needs. Here, the so-called equalization of class distinctions reveals its ideological function. If the worker and his boss enjoy the same television program and visit the same resort places, if the typist is as attractively made up as the daughter of her employer, if the Negro owns a Cadillac, if they all read the same newspaper, then this assimilation indicates not the disappearance of classes, but the

extent to which the needs and satisfactions that serve the preservation of the Establishment are shared by the underlying population.

Indeed, in the most highly developed areas of contemporary society, the transplantation of social into individual needs is so effective that the difference between them seems to be purely theoretical. Can only really distinguish between the mass media as instruments of information and entertainment, and as agents of manipulation and indoctrination? Between the automobile as nuisance and as convenience? Between the horrors and the comforts of functional architecture? Between the work for national defense and the work for corporate gain? Between the private pleasure and the commercial and political utility involved in increasing the birth rate?

We are again confronted with one of the most vexing aspects of advanced industrial civilization: the rational character of its irrationality. Its productivity and efficiency, its capacity to increase and spread comforts, to turn waste into need, and destruction into construction, the extent to which this civilization transforms the object world into an extension of man's mind and body makes the very notion of alienation questionable. The people recognize themselves in their commodities; they find their soul in their automobile, hi-fi set, split-level home, kitchen equipment. The very mechanism which ties the individual to his society has changed, and social control is anchored in the new needs which it has produced.

The prevailing forms of social control are technological in a new sense. To be sure, the technical structure and efficacy of the productive and destructive apparatus has been a major instrumentality for subjecting the population to the established social division of labor throughout the modern period. Moreover, such integration has always been accompanied by more obvious forms of compulsion: loss of livelihood, the administration of justice, the police, the armed forces. It still is. But in the contemporary period, the technological controls appear to be the very embodiment of Reason for the benefit of all social groups and interests—to such an extent that all contradiction seems irrational and all counteraction impossible.

No wonder then that, in the mode advanced areas of this civilization, the social controls have been introjected to the point where even individual protest is affected at its roots. The intellectual and emotional refusal "to go along" appears neurotic and impotant. This is the socio-psychological aspect of the political event that marks the contemporary period: the passing of the historical forces which, at the preceding stage of industrial society, seemed to represent the possibility of new forms of existence.

But the term "introjection" perhaps no longer describes the way in which the individual by himself reproduces and perpetuates the external controls exercised by his society. Introjection suggests a variety of relatively spontaneous processes by which a Self (Ego) transposes the "outer" into the "inner." Thus introjection implies the existence of an inner dimension distinguished from and even antagonistic to the external exigencies—an individual consciousness and an individual unconscious *apart from* public opinion and behavior.[1] The idea of "inner freedom" here has its reality: it designates the private space in which man may become and remain "himself."

Today this private space has been invaded and whittled down by technological reality. Mass production and mass distribution claim the *entire* individual, and industrial psychology has long since ceased to be confined to the factory. The manifold process of introjection seem to be ossified in almost mechanical reactions. The result is, not adjustment but *mimesis:* an immediate identification

of the individual with *his* society and, through it, with the society as a whole.

This immediate, automatic identification (which may have been characteristic of primitive forms of association) reappears in high industrial civilization; its new "immediacy," however, is the product of a sophisticated, scientific management and organization. In this process, the "inner" dimension of the mind in which opposition to the status quo can take root is whittled down. The loss of this dimension, in which the power of negative thinking—the critical power of Reason—is at home, is the ideological counterpart to the very material process in which advanced industrial society silences and reconciles the opposition. The impact of progress turns Reason into submission to the facts of life, and to the dynamic capability of producing more and bigger facts of the same sort of life. The efficiency of the system blunts the individuals' recognition that it contains no facts which do not communicate the repressive power of the whole. If the individuals find themselves in the things which shape their life, they do so, not by giving, but by accepting the law of things—not the law of physics but the law of their society.

I have just suggested that the concept of alienation seems to become questionable when the individuals identify themselves with the existence which is imposed upon them and have in it their own development and satisfaction. This identification is not illusion but reality. However, the reality constitutes a more progressive stage of alienation. The latter has become entirely objective; the subject which is alienated is swallowed up by its alienated existence. There is only one dimension, and it is everywhere and in all forms. The achievements of progress defy ideological indictment as well as justification; before their tribunal, the "false consciousness" of their rationality becomes the true consciousness.

This absorption of ideology into reality does not, however, signify the

---

[1] The change in the function of the family here plays a decisive role: its "socializing" functions are increasingly taken over by outside groups and media. See my *Eros and Civilization,* Boston: Beacon Press, 1955, p. 96 ff.

"end of ideology." On the contrary, in a specific sense advanced industrial culture is *more* ideological than its predecessor, inasmuch as today the ideology is in the process of production itself.[2] In a provocative form, this proposition reveals the political aspects of the prevailing technological rationality. The productive apparatus and the goods and services which it produces "sell" or impose the social system as a whole. The means of mass transportation and communication, the commodities of lodging, food, and clothing, the irrestible output of the entertainment and information industry carry with them prescribed attitudes and habits, certain intellectual and emotional reactions which bind the consumers more or less pleasantly to the producers and, through the latter, to the whole. The products indoctrinate and manipulate; they promote a false consciousness which is immune against its falsehood. And as these beneficial products become available to more individuals in more social classes, the indoctrination they carry ceases to be publicity; it becomes a way of life. It is a good way of life—much better than before—and as a good way of life, it militates against qualitative change. Thus emerges a pattern of *one-dimensional thought and behavior* in which ideas, aspirations, and objectives that, by their content, transcend the established universe of discourse and action are either repelled or reduced to terms of this universe. They are redefined by the rationality of the given system and of its quantitative extension.

The trend may be related to a development in scientific method: operationalism in the physical, behaviorism in the social sciences. The common feature is a total empiricism in the treatment of concepts; their meaning is restricted to the representation of particular operations and behavior. The operational point of view is well illustrated by P. W.

Bridgman's analysis of the concept of length:[3]

> We evidently know what we mean by length if we can tell what the length of any and every object is, and for the physicist nothing more is required. To find the length of an object, we have to perform certain physical operations. The concept of length is therefore fixed when the operations by which length is measured are fixed: that is, the concept of length involves as much and nothing more than the set of operations by which length is determined. In general, we mean by any concept nothing more than a set of operations; *the concept is synonymous with the corresponding set of operations.*

Bridgman has seen the wide implications of this mode of thought for the society at large:[4]

> To adopt the operational point of view involves much more than a mere restriction of the sense in which we understand "concept," but means a far-reaching change in all our habits of thought, in that we shall no longer permit ourselves to use as tools in our thinking concepts of which we cannot give an adequate account in terms of operations.

Bridgman's prediction has come true. The new mode of thought is today the predominant tendency in philosophy, psychology, sociology, and other fields. Many of the most seriously troublesome concepts are being "eliminated" by showing that no adequate account of them in terms of operations or behavior can be given. The radical empiricist onslaught (I shall subsequently, in chapters VII and VIII, examine its claim to

---

[2] Theodor W. Adorno, *Prismen. Kulturkritik und Gesellschaft,* Frankfurt: Suhrkamp, 1955, p. 24 f.

[3] P. W. Bridgman, *The Logic of Modern Physics,* New York: Macmillan, 1928, p. 5. The operational doctrine has since been refined and qualified. Bridgman himself has extended the concept of "operation" to include the "paper-and-pencil" operations of the theorist (in Philipp J. Frank, *The Validation of Scientific Theories,* Boston: Beacon Press, 1954, Chap. II). The main impetus remains the same: it is "desirable" that the paper-and-pencil operations "be capable of eventual contact, although perhaps indirectly, with instrumental operations."

[4] P. W. Bridgman, *The Logic of Modern Physics,* loc. cit., p. 31.

be empiricist) thus provides the methodological justification for the debunking of the mind by the intellectuals—a positivism which, in its denial of the transcending elements of Reason, forms the academic counterpart of the socially required behavior.

Outside the academic establishment, the "far-reaching change in all our habits of thought" is more serious. It serves to coordinate ideas and goals with those exacted by the prevailing system, to enclose them in the system, and to repel those which are irreconcilable with the system. The reign of such a one-dimensional reality does not mean that materialism rules, and that the spiritual, metaphysical, and bohemian occupations are petering out. On the contrary, there is a gread deal of "Worship together this week," "Why not try God," Zen, existentialism, and beat ways of life, etc. But such modes of protest and transcendence are no longer contradictory to the status quo and no longer negative. They are rather the ceremonial part of practical behaviorism, its harmless negation, and are quickly digested by the status quo as part of its healthy diet.

One-dimensional thought is systematically promoted by the makers of politics and their purveyors of mass information. Their universe of discourse is populated by self-validating hypotheses which, incessantly and monopolistically repeated, become hypnotic definitions or dictations. For example, "free" are the institutions which operate (and are operated on) in the countries of the Free World; other transcending modes of freedom are by definition either anarchism, communism, or propaganda. "Socialistic" are all encroachments on private enterprises not undertaken by private enterprise itself (or by government contracts), such as universal and comprehensive health insurance, or the protection of nature from all too sweeping commercialization, or the establishment of public services which may hurt private profit. This totalitarian logic of accomplished facts has its Eastern counterpart. There, freedom is the way of life instituted by a communist regime, and all other transcending modes of freedom are either capitalistic, or revisionist, or leftist sectarianism. In both camps, non-operational ideas are non-behavorial and subversive. The movement of thought is stopped at barriers which appear as the limits of Reason itself.

Such limitation of thought is certainly not new. Ascending modern rationalism, in its speculative as well as empirical form, shows a striking contrast between extreme critical radicalism in scientfic and philosophic method on the one hand, and an uncritical quietism in the attitude toward established and functioning social institutions. Thus Descartes' *ego cogitans* was to leave the "great public bodies" untouched, and Hobbes held that "the present ought always to be preferred, maintained, and accounted best." Kant agreed with Locke in justifying revolution *if and when* it has succeeded in organizing the whole and in preventing subversion.

However, these accommodating concepts of Reason were always contradicted by the evident misery and injustice of the "great public bodies" and the effective, more or less conscious rebellion against them. Societal conditions existed which provoked and permitted real dissociation from the established state of affairs; a private as well as political dimension was present in which dissociation could develop into effective opposition, testing its strength and the validity of its objectives.

With the gradual closing of this dimension by the society, the self-limitation of thought assumes a larger significance. The interrelation between scientific-philosophical and societal processes, between theoretical and practical Reason, asserts itself "behind the back" of the scientists and philosophers. The society bars a whole type of oppositional operations and behavior; consequently, the concepts pertaining to them are rendered illusory or meaningless. Historical transcendence appears as metaphysical transcendence, not acceptable to science and scientific thought. The operational and behavioral point of view, practiced as a "habit of thought" at large, becomes the view of the established universe of discourse and action, needs and aspirations. The "cunning of Reason" works, as it so often did, in the interest of the powers that be. The insistence on operational and behavioral concepts turns against the efforts to free thought and behavior *from* the given reality and *for* the suppressed alternatives. Theoretical and practical Reason, academic and social behaviorism meet on common ground: that of an advanced society which makes scientific and technical progress into an instrument of domination.

"Progress" is not a neutral term; it moves toward specific ends, and these ends are defined by the possibilities of ameliorating the human condition. Advanced industrial society is approaching the stage where continued progress would demand the radical subversion of the prevailing direction and organization of progress. This stage would be reached when material production (including the necessary services) becomes automated to the extent that all vital needs can be satisfied while necessary labor time is reduced to marginal time. From this point on, technical progress would transcend the realm of necessity, where it served as the instrument of domination and exploitation which thereby limited its rationality; technology would become subject to the free play of faculties in the struggle for the pacification of nature and of society.

Such a state is envisioned in Marx's notion of the "abolition of labor." The term "pacification of existence" seems better suited to designate the historical alternative of a world which—through an international conflict which transforms and suspends the contradictions within the established societies—advanced on the brink of a global war. "Pacification of existence" means the development of man's struggle with man and with nature, under conditions where the competing needs, desires, and aspirations are no longer organized by vested interests in domination and scarcity—an organization which perpetuates the destructive forms of this struggle.

Today's fight against this historical alternative finds a firm mass basis in the underlying population, and finds its ideology in the rigid orientation of thought and behavior to the given universe of facts. Validated by the accomplishments of science and technology, justified by its growing productivity, the status quo defies all transcendence. Faced with the possibility of pacification on the grounds of its technical and intellectual achievements, the mature industrial society closes itself against this alternative. Operationalism, in theory and practice, becomes the theory and practice of *containment*. Underneath its obvious dynamics, this society is a thoroughly static system of life: self-propelling in its oppressive productivity and in its beneficial coordination. Containment of technical progress goes hand in hand with its growth in the established direction. In spite of the political fetters imposed by the status quo, the more technology appears capable of creating the conditions for pacification, the more are the minds and bodies of man organized against this alternative.

The most advanced areas of industrial society exhibit throughout these two features: a trend toward consummation of technological rationality, and intensive efforts to contain this trend within the established institutions. Here is the internal contradiction of this civilization: the irrational element in its rationality. It is the token of its achievements. The industrial society which makes technology and science its own is organized for the ever-more-effective domination of man and nature, for the ever-more-effective utilization of its resources. It becomes irrational when the success of these efforts opens new dimensions of human realization. Organization for peace is different from organization for war; the institutions which served the struggle for existence cannot serve the pacification of existence. Life as an end is qualitatively different from life as a means.

Such a qualitatively new mode of existence can never be envisaged as the mere by-product of economic and political changes, as the more or less spontaneous effect of the new institutions which constitute the necessary prerequisite. Qualitative change also involves a change in the *technical* basis on which this society rests—one which sustains the economic and political institutions through which the "second nature" of man as an aggressive object of administration is stabilized. The techniques of industrialization are political techniques; as such, they prejudge the possibilities of Reason and Freedom.

To be sure, labor must precede the reduction of labor, and industrialization must precede the development of human needs and satisfactions. But as all freedom depends on the conquest of alien necessity, the realization of freedom depends on the *techniques* of this conquest. The highest productivity of labor can be used for the perpetuation of labor, and the most efficient industrialization can serve the restriction and manipulation of needs.

When this point is reached, domination—in the guise of affluence and liberty—extends to all spheres of private and public existence, integrates all authentic opposition, absorbs all alternatives. Technological rationality reveals its political character as it becomes the great vehicle of better domination, creating a truly totalitarian universe in which society and nature, mind and body are kept in a state of permanent mobilization for the defense of this universe.

Ethics and Revolution

I propose to discuss the relation between ethics and revolution by taking as guidance the following question: Can a revolution be justified as right, as good, perhaps even as necessary, and justified not merely in political terms (as expedient for certain interests) but in ethical terms, that is to say, justified with respect to the human condition as such, to the potential of man in a given historical situation? This means that ethical terms such as "right" or "good" will be applied to political and social movements, with the hypothesis that the moral evaluation of such movements is (in a sense to be defined) more than subjective, more than a matter of preference. Under this hypothesis, "good" and "right" would mean serving to establish, to promote, or to extend human freedom and happiness in a commonwealth, regardless of the form of government. This preliminary definition combines individual and personal, private and public welfare. It tries to recapture a basic concept of classical political philosophy which has been all too often repressed, namely, that the end of government is not only the greatest possible freedom, but also the greatest possible happiness of man, that it is to say, a life without fear and misery, and a life in space.

Here we encounter the first vexing question, namely, who determines, who can and by what right determine the general interest of a commonwealth, and thereby determine the range and limits of individual freedom and happiness, and the sacrifices imposed upon individual freedom and happiness in the name and on behalf of the commonwealth? For as long as the general and individual welfare do not immediately coincide, the latter will be *made* to conform with the former. And if we ask this question we are at once confronted with an equally serious and embarrassing problem: granted even that freedom is not only an individual and private affair, that it is rather determined by the society, by the state in which we live,

SOURCE. Reprinted from Richard T. De-George, ed. *Ethics and Society* by permission of the publisher, Doubleday & Co. Copyright 1966 by the Kansas University Endowment Association.

what about happiness? Is the happiness of an individual his own private affair, or is it too, in a very definite sense, subject to the limitations and even the definitions imposed upon it by a commonwealth? The extreme position that human happiness is and must remain individual and the individual's own affair cannot be defended if we give it only a few minutes' thought. There are certainly modes and types of individual happiness which cannot be tolerated by any kind of commonwealth. It is perfectly possible—as a matter of fact we know it to be the fact—that people who were the master torturers in the Hitler concentration camps were often quite happy doing their job. This is one of the many cases of individual happiness where we do not hesitate to say that it is not merely the individual himself who can be and who can remain the judge of his own happiness. We assume a tribunal which is (actually or morally) entitled to "define" individual happiness.

Now after these preliminary clarifications, let me define what I mean by "revolution." By "revolution" I understand the overthrow of a legally established government and constitution by a social class or movement with the aim of altering the social as well as the political structure. This definition excludes all military coups, palace revolutions, and "preventive" counterrevolutions (such as Fascism and Nazism) because they do not alter the basic social structure. If we define revolution in this way we can move one step forward by saying that such a radical and qualitative change implies violence. Peaceful revolutions, if there are such things, if there can be such things, do not present any problem. We can therefore reformulate the initial question by asking: Is the revolutionary use of violence justifiable as a means for establishing or promoting human freedom and happiness? The question implies a very important assumption, namely, that there are rational criteria for determining the possibilities of human freedom and happiness available to a society in a specific historical situation. If there are no such rational criteria, it would be impossible to evaluate a political movement in terms of its chances to attain a greater extent or a higher degree of freedom and happiness in society.

But postulating the availability of rational standards and criteria for judging the given possibilities of human freedom and happiness means assuming that the ethical, moral standards are *historical* standards. If they are not, they remain meaningless abstractions. Applied to our question, this means that to claim an ethical and moral right, a revolutionary movement must be able to give rational grounds for its chances to grasp real possibilities of human freedom and happiness, and it must be able to demonstrate the adequacy of its means for obtaining this end. Only if the problem is placed in such a historical context, is it susceptible to rational discussion. Otherwise, only two positions remain open, namely, to reject *a priori* or to endorse *a priori* all revolution and revolutionary violence. Both positions, the affirmative as well as the negative one, offend against historical facts. It is, for example, meaningless to say that modern society *could* have come about without the English, American, and French Revolutions. It is also meaningless to say that all revolutionary violence had the same social function and consequences. The violence of the Civil Wars in seventeenth century England, the violence of the first French Revolution certainly had effects and consequences very different from those of the Bolshevik Revolution, and very different from the counterrevolutionary violence perpetrated by the Nazi and Fascist regimes. Moreover, the positions of *a priori* rejecting or *a priori* approving social and political violence would amount to sanctioning any change brought about in history, regardless of whether it would be in a progressive or regressive, liberating or enslaving direction.

A very brief glance at the historical development of our problem may facilitate the discussion. In classical political philosophy, revolutions were not considered as breaks of the historical continuum. Plato as well as Aristotle believed that revolutions were built into the very dynamic of politics, that they belonged to the historical and at the same time natural cycle of birth, growth and decay of political forms. In medieval and early modern philosophy the idea of a natural and divine order either outlawed all resistance to established government, or made resistance against tyranny not only a right but a moral duty and obligation. Then, in the sixteenth and seventeenth centuries, the practically unlimited right to resist a government, even to overthrow a government, was normally claimed by Protestant against Catholic, and by Catholic against Protestant regimes. A most characteristic reaction against these doctrines may be seen in the attitude towards revolution which we find in such different figures as Hobbes and Descartes, namely, that change is always to the worst. Leave the established social and political institutions as they are, for, no matter how bad they may be, the risk of overthrowing them is too great. Descartes, the great revolutionary in thought, was extremely conservative with respect to the "great public bodies." To them, doubt is not supposed to be extended, they are supposed to be left alone. At the same time, philosophers are strongly inclined to endorse a revolution once it has proved to be successful. Representative of this attitude is the case of Kant—certainly not a paragon of opportunism and expedience—who rejected the right of resistance and condemned revolt against established government, but added that, once a revolution has succeeded, a new legal government is established, and man owes obedience to the new revolutionary government just as he owed it to the government which was overthrown by the revolution.

On the other side of the fence, political theory and practice recognize historical situations in which violence becomes the necessary and essential element of progress. This concept it instrumental in the political theory and practice of totalitarian democracy. Robespierre calls for the "despotism of liberty" against the despotism of tyranny: in the fight for freedom, in the interest of the whole against the particular interests of oppression, terror may become a necessity and an obligation. Here, violence, revolutionary violence, appears not only as a political means but as a moral duty. The terror is defined as *counter*violence: it is "legitimate" only in defense against the oppressors and until they are defeated. Similarly, the Marxian concept of proletarian dictatorship is that of a transitional self-cancelling dictatorship: self-cancelling because it is supposed to last only as long as the power of the old ruling classes still combats the construction of the socialist society; after their defeat, the engines of repression were to be stopped. Here, too, revolutionary violence is defined as counterviolence. The Marxian concept assumes that the old ruling classes would never voluntarily abdicate their position, that they would be the first to use violence against the revolution, and that revolutionary violence would be the defense against counterrevolutionary violence.

The theory of an educational, transitional dictatorship implies the paradoxical proposition that man must be "forced to be free." Political philosophy has always recognized the moral function of coercion (the coercive power of law, either above the sovereign or identical with the sovereign), but Rousseau provides a radically new justification. Coercion is necessitated by the immoral, repressive conditions under which men live. The basic idea is: how can slaves who do not even know they are slaves free themselves? How can they liberate themselves by their own power, by their own faculties? How can the spontaneously accomplish liberation? They must be taught and must be led to be free, and this the more so the more the society in which they live uses all available means in order to shape and pre-form their consciousness and to make it immune against possible alternatives. This idea of an educational, prepara-tory dictatorship has today become an integral element of revolution and of the justification of the revolutionary oppression. The dictatorships which be-gan as revolutionary dictatorships and then perpetuated themselves claim to be in their very essence and structure tran-sitional and preparatory for a stage at which they can be abolished by virtue of their own achievements.

The main argument against the notion of the transitional dictatorship is usually condensed in the question: who edu-cates the educators? By what right do those who actually exercise the dicta-torship speak in the name of freedom and happiness as general conditions? This argument by itself is not sufficient, because in a lesser degree it applies even to non-authoritarian societies, where the policy-making top layer is not constantly and effectively controlled from below. However, even if we con-cede that the majority of men are not yet free today, and that their liberation cannot be spontaneous, the question still remains whether the dictatorial means are adequate to attain the end, namely, liberation. In other words the question of a transitional dictatorship cannot be separated from the general question of whether there can be such a thing as a moral justification of sup-pression and violence in a revolution. I shall now briefly discuss this question.

The historical revolutions were usu-ally advocated and started in the name of freedom, or rather in the name of greater freedom for more strata of the population. We must first examine this claim strictly on empirical grounds. Hu-man freedom is not and never has been a static condition but an historical con-dition, a process which involves the radi-cal alteration, and even negation, of established ways of life. The form and content of freedom change with every new stage in the development of civiliza-tion, which is man's increasing mastery

of man and nature. In both modes, mastery means domination, control; more effective control of nature makes for more effective control of man. Ob-viously, the possibilities of human free-dom and happiness in advanced indus-trial society today are in no way comparable with those available, even theoretically available, at preceding stages of history. Thus, with respect to the form, extend, degree and content of human freedom, we deal with strictly historical and changing conditions. We can say even more. Measured against the real possibilities of freedom, we al-ways live in a state of relative unfree-dom. The wide gap between real possi-bility and actuality, between the rational and the real has never been closed. Freedom always presupposes liberation, or a step from one state of freedom and unfreedom to a subsequent state. With the advance of technical progress, the later state is *potentially* (but by no means actually!) a *higher* stage, that is, quantitatively and qualitatively. But if this is the case, if freedom always presup-poses liberation from unfree and un-happy conditions, it means that this liberation always offends against and ul-timately subverts established and sanc-tioned institutions and interests. In his-tory, they never abdicated voluntarily. Consequently, if and when freedom is a process of liberation, a transition from lower, more restricted forms of freedom to higher forms of freedom, then it al-ways, no matter how, offends against the existing and established state of affairs. And precisely on this ground revolu-tionary violence has been most effectively justified as counter-violence, that is, as violence necessary in order to secure higher forms of freedom against the re-sistance of the established forms.

The ethics of revolution thus testi-fies to the clash and conflict of two historical rights: on the one side, the right of that which *is*, the established commonwealth on which the life and perhaps even the happiness of the in-dividuals depend; and on the other side, the right of that which *can* be and perhaps even *ought* to be because it may reduce toil, misery, and injustice, provided always that this chance can be demonstrated as a real possibility. Such a demonstration must provide rational criteria; we can now add: these must be *historical* criteria. As such, they amount to an "historical calculus," namely, calculation of the chances of a future society as against the chances of the existing society with respect to human progress, that is to say, technical and material progress used in such a way that it increases individual freedom and happiness. Now if such an historical calculus is to have any rational basis, it must, on the one side, take into account the sacrifices exacted from the living generations on behalf of the established society, the established law and order, the number of victims made in defense of this society in war and peace, in the struggle for existence, individual and national. The calculus would further have to take into account the intellectual and material resources available to the society and the manner in which they are actually used with respect to their full capacity of satisfying vital human needs and pacifying the struggle for existence. On the other side, the historical calculus would have to project the chances of the contesting revolutionary movement of improving the prevailing conditions, namely, whether the revolutionary plan or program demonstrates the technical, material, and mental possibility of reducing the sacrifices and the number of victims. Even prior to the question as to the possibility of such a calculus (which, I believe, does exist), its inhuman quantifying character is evident. But its inhumanity is that of history itself, token of its empirical, rational foundation. No hypocrisy should from the beginning distort the examination. Nor is this brutal calculus an empty intellectual abstraction; in fact, at its decisive turns, history became such a calculated experiment.

The ethics of revolution, if there is such a thing, will therefore be in accordance not with absolute, but with historical standards. They do not cancel the validity of those general norms which formulate requirements for the progress of mankind toward humanity. No matter how rationally one may justify revolutionary means in terms of the demonstrable chance of obtaining freedom and happiness for future generations, and thereby justify violating existing rights and liberties and life itself, there are forms of violence and suppression which no revolutionary situation can justify because they negate the very end for which the revolution is a means. Such are arbitrary violence, cruelty, and indiscriminate terror. However, within the historical continuum, revolutions establish a moral and ethical code of their own and in this way become the origin, the fountainhead and source of new general norms and values. In fact some of today's most generally-professed values originated in revolutions, for example, the value of tolerance in the English Civil Wars, the inalienable rights of man in the American and French Revolutions. These ideas become an historical force, first as partial ideas, instruments of a revolutionary movement for specific political ends. Their realization originally involved violence; they then assumed not only partial political but general ethical validity and rejected violence. In this way, revolutions place themselves under ethical standards.

Violence *per se* has never been made a revolutionary value by the leaders of the historical revolutions. His contemporaries rejected Georges Sorel's attempt to cut the link between violence and reason, which was at the same time the attempt to free the class struggle from all ethical considerations. In comparing the violence of the class struggle in its revolutionary phase with the violence of military operations in war, he made the former subject to strategic calculations only: the end was the total defeat of the enemy; violence a means to attain this end—the relation between means and end was a technical one. Sorel's defense of violence this side of good and evil remained isolated from the revolutionary

reality of his time; if he had any influence, it was on the side of the counter-
revolution. Otherwise, violence was defended, not *per se,* but as a part of
rational suppression, suppression of counterrevolutionary activity, of established
rights and privileges, and, for the society
at large, of material and intellectual
needs, that is, enforcement of austerity,
rationing, censorship.

Now this suppression which includes
violence is practiced in the interest of
the objectives of the revolution, and
these objectives are presented not only
as political but also as moral values,
ethical imperatives, namely greater freedom for the greater number of people.
And in this sense the objectives and the
ends of the revolution itself claim general validity and become subject to
moral standards and evaluation.

Here we are confronted with the problem of all ethics, namely, the question
as to the ultimate sanction of moral
values. Or, in plain language, who or
what determines the validity of ethical
norms? The question becomes acute only
with the secularization of the West; it
was no problem in the Middle Ages as
long as a transcendent sanction of ethics
was accepted. The infidels could justly
be exterminated, heretics could justly be
burned—in spite of all protest. This was
justice in terms of the prevailing values,
which in turn were those of transcendent
ethics. But today, where is the sanction
of ethical values—sanction not in terms
of the enforcement but in terms of the
acceptance of ethical values, the proof of
their validity? Sanction today, it seems,
rests mainly in a precarious and flexible
syndrome of custom, fear, utility, and
religion; flexible because, within the
syndrome, there is a large range of
change. I refer, for example, to the high
degree of liberalization in sexual morality which we have witnessed during the
last thirty years, or, to the easy suspension of practically all ethical values in
so-called emergency situations. The sanction and validity of ethical norms is
thus restricted to the normal state of
affairs in social and political relations.

Now in terms of the normal established state of affairs, a revolution is
by definition immoral; it offends against
the right of the existing commonwealth;
it permits and even demands deception,
cunning, suppression, destruction of life
and property, and so on. But a judgment
by definition is an inadequate judgment.
Ethical standards by virtue of their imperative claim transcend any given state
of affairs, and they transcend it, not to
any metaphysical entities but to the historical continuum in which every given
state of affairs has emerged, by which
every given state of affairs is defined,
and in which every given state of affairs
will be altered and surpassed by other
states. And in the historical continuum
which defines its place and function, the
ethics of revolution appeal to an historical calculus. Can the intended new society, the society intended by the revolution, offer better chances for progress
in freedom than the existing society? In
the historical continuum, these chances
can only be measured by going beyond
the given state of affairs, going beyond
it not simply into an abstract vacuum
of speculation, but going beyond it by
calculating the resources, intellectual as
well as material, scientific as well as
technical, available to a given society,
and projecting the most rational ways
of utilizing these resources. Now if such
projection is possible, then it can yield
objective criteria for judging revolutions
as to their historical function in terms
or progress or regression, in terms of
the development of *humanitas.*

A preliminary answer is suggested by
a glance at the historical process itself.
Historically, the objective tendency of
the great revolutions of the modern period was the enlargement of the social
range of freedom and the enlargement
of the satisfaction of needs. No matter
how much the social interpretations of
the English and French Revolutions may
differ, they seem to agree in that a
redistribution of the social wealth took
place, so that previously less privileged
or under-privileged classes were the
beneficiaries of this change, economically

and/or politically. In spite of subsequent periods of reaction and restoration, the result and objective function of these revolutions was the establishment of more liberal governments, a gradual democratization of society, and technical progress. I said "objective function" because this evaluation of the revolution is obviously a judgment *ex post facto*. The intention and ideology of the leaders of the revolution, and the drives of the masses may have had quite different aims and motives. By virtue of their objective function, these revolutions attained progress in the sense defined, namely, a demonstrable enlargement of the range of human freedom; they thus established, in spite of the terrible sacrifices exacted by them, an ethical right over and above all political justification.

But if such ethical right and its criteria are always and necessarily after the fact, it serves for nought and leaves us with the irrational choice of either *a priori* accepting or *a priori* rejecting all revolution. Now I submit that, while the historical function of a revolution becomes identifiable only after the fact, its prospective direction, progressive or regressive is, with the certainty of a reasonable *chance,* demonstrable *before* the fact—to the same degree to which the historical conditions of progress are demonstrable. For example, it could be demonstrated—and it was demonstrated before the fact—that the French Revolution of 1789 would give, in terms of the historical calculus, a better chance for the development of human freedom than the Ancien Régime. Contrariwise, it could be demonstrated, and was demonstrated long before the fact, that Fascist and National-Socialist regimes would do the exact opposite, namely, necessarily restrict the range of human freedom. Moreover, and I think this is a very important point, such demonstration of the historical *chances* before the fact becomes increasingly rational with the development of our scientific, technical, and material resources and capabilities, with out progress in the scientific mastery of man and nature. The possibilities

and contents of freedom today are coming more and more under the control of man: they are becoming increasingly calculable. And with this advance in effective control and calculability, the inhuman distinction between violence and violence, sacrifice and sacrifice become increasingly rational. For throughout history, the happiness and freedom, and even the life of individuals, have been sacrificed. If we consider human life *per se* sacred under all conditions, the distinction is meaningless, and we have to admit that history is *per se* amoral and immoral, because it has never respected the sanctity of human life as such. But in fact we do distinguish between sacrifices which are legitimate and sacrifices which are not legitimate. This distinction is an historical one, and with this qualification, ethical standards are also applicable to violence.

Let me now recapitulate and reformulate. In absolute ethical terms, that is to say, in terms of suprahistorical validity, there is no justification for any suppression and sacrifice for the sake of future freedom and happiness, revolutionary or otherwise. But in historical terms we are confronted with a distinction and a decision. For suppression and sacrifice are daily exacted by all societies, and one cannot start—indeed I would like to say this with all possible emphasis—one cannot start becoming moral and ethical at an arbitrary but expedient point of cut off: the point of revolution. Who can quantify and who can compare the sacrifices exacted by an established society and those exacted by its subversion? Are ten thousand victims more ethical than twenty thousand? Such is in fact the inhuman arithmetic of history, and in this inhuman historical context operates the historical calculus. Calculable are the material and intellectual resources available, calculable are the productive and distributive facilities in a society, and the extent of unsatisfied vital needs and of satisfied non-vital needs. Quantifiable and calculable are the quantity and size of the labor force and of the population as a whole. That is the empirical material at the disposal of the historical calculus. And on the basis of this quantifiable material the question can be asked whether the available resources and capabilities are utilized most rationally, that is to say, with a view to the best possible satisfaction of needs under the priority of vital needs and with a minimum of toil, misery and injustice. If the analysis of a specific historical situation suggests a negative answer, if conditions exist in which technological rationality is impeded or even superseded by repressive political and social interests which define the general welfare, then the reversal of such conditions in favor of a more rational and human use of the available resources would also be a maximalization of the chance of progress in freedom. Consequently, a social and political movement in this direction would, in terms of the calculus, allow the presumption of historical justification. It can be no more than a presumption, subject to correction as the movement actually develops, reveals its potential and establishes new facts, or in other words, as it sustains or as it cuts the links between the means which the revolution employs and the end which it professes to attain.

And this leads to the last question which I want to raise here, namely, can the revolutionary end justify *all* means? Can we distinguish between rational and irrational, necessary and arbitrary, suppression? When can such suppression be called rational in terms of the objective of a respective revolution? I shall briefly illustrate the scope of this question by the Bolshevik Revolution. The professed objective of the Bolshevik Revolution was socialism. It implied the socialization of the means of production, the dictatorship of the proletariat as preparatory to a classless society. In the specific historical situation in which the Bolshevik Revolution occurred, socialism called for industrialization in competition with the advanced capitalist countries of the West, for the building

up of the armed forces, and for propaganda on a global scale. Now can we apply a distinction between rational and irrational to these objectives and to the degree of suppression involved in them? In terms of the revolution, rational would be accelerated industrialization, the elimination of non-cooperative layers of management from the economy, the enforcement of work discipline, sacrifices in the satisfaction of needs imposed by the priority of heavy industry in the first stages of industrialization, and suspension of civil liberties if they were used for sabotaging these objectives. And we can reject, without long discussion, as not justifiable, even in terms of the revolution, the Moscow trials, the permanent terror, the concentration camps, and the dictatorship of the Party over the working classes. Further examination would require introducing into the discussion the situation of global coexistence; but time forbids us to do so. We have also made abstraction from the human element in the leadership of the revolution, that is to say, from the so-called historical individuals.

And here I want to add one remark. It seems to me characteristic that, the more calculable and the more controllable the technical apparatus of modern industrial society becomes, the more does the chance of human progress depend on the intellectual and moral qualities of the leaders, and on their willingness and ability to educate the controlled population and to make it recognize the possibility, nay, the necessity of pacification and humanization. For today, the technical apparatus of advanced industrial society is in itself authoritarian, requiring service, submission, subordination to the objective mechanism of the machine system, that is to say, submission to those who control the apparatus. Technology has been made into a powerful instrument of streamlined domination—the more powerful the more it proves its efficiency and delivers the goods. And as such, it serves the politics of domination.

I come to the conclusion. The means-end relation is the ethical problem of revolution. In one sense, the end justifies the means, namely, if they demonstrably serve human progress in freedom. This legitimate end, the only legitimate end, demands the creation of conditions which would facilitate and expediate its realization. And the creation of these conditions may justify sacrifices, as it has justified sacrifices throughout history. But this relation between means and ends is a dialectical one. The end must be operative in the repressive means for attaining the end. But no matter how rational, how necessary, how liberating —revolution involves violence. The nonviolent history is the promise and possibility of a society which is still to be fought for. At present, the triumphant violence seems to be on the other side.

WORKS BY HERBERT MARCUSE

Marcuse, Herbert. *Eros and Civilization, a Philosophical Inquiry into Freud.* Boston: Beacon Press, 1955.

_____. *Negations.* Boston: Beacon Press, 1968.

_____. *One Dimensional Man, Studies in the Ideology of Advanced Industrial Society.* Boston: Beacon Press, 1964.

_____. *Reason and Revolution: Hegel and the Rise of Social Theory.* London: Oxford University Press, 1941.

_____. *Soviet Marxism, a Critical Analysis.* New York: Columbia University Press, 1958.

CHAPTER 23

The New Left: Tom Hayden

Tom Hayden (b. 1939) was one of the founders of the Students for a Democratic Society, a New Left organization active in spurring social and political change by a variety of means. He wrote the "Port Huron Statement" in 1962, and it served as a founding manifesto. His other writings provide a summary of the rapid changes of the subsequent years. *Rebellion in Newark* (1967) is an on-the-spot report of the Newark ghetto riots of 1967, and *The Other Side* (with Staughton Lynd) is a report on a trip to North Vietnam. Other occasional writings may be found in *The New York Review of Books, Ramparts,* and *Dissent.*

The "Port Huron Statement" of Students for a Democratic Society*

INTRODUCTION: AGENDA FOR A GENERATION

We are the people of this generation, bred in at least modest comfort, housed now in universities, looking uncomfortably to the world we inherit.

When we were kids the United States was the wealthiest and strongest country in the world; the only one with the atom bomb, least scarred by modern war, an initiator of the United Nations that we thought would distribute Western influence throughout the world. Freedom and equality for each individual, government of, by, and for the people—these American values we found good, principles by which we could live as men. Many of us began maturing in complacency.

As we grew, however, our comfort was penetrated by events too troubling to dismiss. First, the permeating and victimizing fact of human degradation, symbolized by the Southern struggle against racial bigotry, compelled most of us from silence to activism. Second, the enclosing fact of the Cold War, symbolized by the presence of the Bomb, brought awareness that we ourselves,

---

* Although this document is not exclusively the work of Hayden, he was its principal author; it is an early (1962) statement of the organization's goals.

and our friends, and millions of abstract "others" we knew more directly because of our common peril, might die at any time. We might deliberately ignore, or avoid, or fail to feel all other human problems, but not these two, for these were too immediate and crushing in their impact, too challenging in the demand that we as individuals take the responsibility for encounter and resolution.

While these and other problems either directly oppressed us or rankled our consciences and became our own subjective concerns, we began to see complicated and disturbing paradoxes in our surrounding America. The declaration "all men are created equal. . ." rang hollow before the facts of Negro life in the South and the big cities of the North. The proclaimed peaceful intentions of the United States contradicted its economic and military investments in the Cold War status quo.

We witnessed, and continue to witness, other paradoxes. With nuclear energy whole cities can easily be powered, yet the dominant nation-states seem more likely to unleash destruction greater than that incurred in all wars of human history. Although our own technology is destroying old and creating new forms of social organization, men still tolerate meaningless work and idleness. While two-thirds of mankind suffers undernourishment, our own upper classes revel admist superfluous abundance. Although world population is expected to double in forty years, the nations still tolerate anarchy as a major principle of international conduct and uncontrolled exploitation governs the sapping of the earth's physical resources. Although mankind desperately needs revolutionary leadership, America rests in national stalemate, its goals ambigious and tradition-bound instead of informed and clear, its democratic system apathetic and manipulated rather than "of, by and for the people."

Not only did tarnish appear on our image of American virtue, not only did disillusion occur when the hypocrisy of American ideals was discovered, but we began to sense that what we had originally seen as the American Golden Age was actually the decline of an era. The worldwide outbreak of revolution against colonialism and imperialism, the entrenchment of totalitarian states, the menace of war, overpopulation, international disorder, supertechnology—these trends were testing the tenacity of our own commitment to democracy and freedom and our abilities to visualize their application to a world in upheaval.

Our work is guided by the sense that we may be the last generation in the experiment with living. But we are a minority—the vast majority of our people regard the temporary equilibriums of our society and world as eternally functioning parts. In this is perhaps the outstanding paradox: we ourselves are imbued with urgency, yet the message of our society is that there is no viable alternative to the present. Beneath the reassuring tones of the politicians, beneath the common opinion that America will "muddle through," beneath the stagnation of those who have closed their minds to the future, is the pervading feeling that there simply are no alternatives, that our times have witnessed the exhaustion not only of Utopias, but of any new departures as well. Feeling the press of complexity upon the emptiness of life, people are fearful of the thought that at any moment things might be thrust out of control. They fear change itself, since change might smash whatever invisible framework seems to hold back chaos for them now. For most Americans, all crusades are suspect, threatening. The fact that each individual sees apathy in his fellows perpetuates the common reluctance to organize for change. The dominant institutions are complex enough to blunt the minds of their potential critics, and entrenched enough to swiftly dissipate or entirely repel the energies of protest and reform, thus limiting human expectancies. Then, too, we are a materially improved society, and by our own improvements we seem to have weakened the case for further change.

Some would have us believe that Americans feel contentment amidst prosperity—but might it not better be called a glaze above deeply felt anxieties about their role in the new world? And if these anxieties produce a developed indifference to human affairs, do they not as well produce a yearning to believe there *is* an alternative to the present, that something *can* be done to change circumstances in the school, the workplaces, the bureaucracies, the government? It is to this latter yearning, at once the spark and engine of change, that we direct our present appeal. The search for truly democratic alternatives to the present, and a commitment to social experimentation with them, is a worthy and fulfilling human enterprise, one which moves us and, we hope, others today. On such a basis do we offer this document of our convictions and analysis: as an effort in understanding and changing the conditions of humanity in the late twentieth century, an effort rooted in the ancient, still unfulfilled conception of man attaining determining influence over his circumstances of life.

VALUES

Making values explicit—an initial task in establishing alternatives—is an activity that has been devalued and corrupted. The conventional moral terms of the age, the politician moralities— "free world," "people's democracies"— reflect realities poorly, if at all, and seem to function more as ruling myths than as descriptive principles. But neither has our experience in the universities brought us moral enlightenment. Our professors and administrators sacrifice controversy to public relations; their curriculums change more slowly that the living events of the world; their skills and silence are purchased by investors in the arms race; passion is called unscholastic. The questions we might want raised—what is really important? Can we live in a different and better way? If we wanted to change society, how would we do it?—are not thought to be questions of a "fruitful, empirical nature," and thus are brushed aside.

Unlike youth in other countries we are used to moral leadership being exercised and moral dimensions being clarified by our elders. But today, for us, not even the liberal and socialist preachments of the past seem adequate to the forms of the present. Consider the old slogans: Capitalism Cannot Reform Itself, United Front Against Fascism, General Strike, All Out on May Day. Or, more recently, No Cooperation with Commies and Fellow Travelers, Ideologies are Exhausted, Bipartisanship, No Utopias. These are incomplete, and there are few new prophets. It has been said that our liberal and socialist predecessors were plagued by vision without program, while our own generation is plagued by program without vision. All around us there is astute grasp of method, technique—the committee, the ad hoc group, the lobbyist, the hard and soft sell, the make, the projected image—but, if pressed critically, such expertise is incompetent to explain its implicit ideals. It is highly fashionable to identify oneself by old categories, or by naming a respected political figure, or by explaining "how we would vote" on various issues.

Theoretic chaos has replaced the idealistic thinking of old—and, unable to reconstitute theoretic order, men have condemned idealism itself. Doubt has replace hopefulness—and men act out a defeatism that is labeled realistic. The decline of utopia and hope is in fact one of the defining features of social life today. The reasons are various: the dreams of the older left were perverted by Stalinism and never recreated; the congressional stalemate makes men narrow their view of the possible; the specialization of human activity leaves little room for sweeping thought; the horrors of the twentieth century, symbolized in the gas ovens and concentration camps and atom bombs, have blasted hopefulness. To be idealistic is to be considered apocalyptic, deluded. To have no serious aspirations, on the contrary, is to be "tough-minded."

In suggesting social goals and values, therefore, we are aware of entering a sphere of some disrepute. Perhaps matured by the past, we have no sure formulas, no closed theories—but that does not mean values are beyond discussion and tentative determination. A first task of any social movement is to convince people that the search for orienting theories and the creation of human values is complex but worthwhile. We are aware that to avoid platitudes we must analyze the concrete conditions of social order. But to direct such an analysis we must use the guideposts of basic principles. Our own social values involve conceptions of human beings, human relationships, and social systems.

We regard *men* as infinitely precious and possessed of unfulfilled capacities for reason, freedom, and love. In affirming these principles we are aware of countering perhaps the dominant conceptions of man in the twentieth century: that he is a thing to be manipulated, and that he is inherently incapable of directing his own affairs. We oppose the depersonalization that reduces human beings to the status of things—if anything, the brutalities of the twentieth century teach that means and ends are intimately related, that vague appeals to "posterity" cannot justify the mutilations of the present. We oppose, too, the doctrine of human incompetence because it rests essentially on the modern fact that men have been "competently" manipulated into competence—we see little reason why men cannot meet with increasing skill the complexities and responsibilities of their situation, if society is organized not for minority, but for majority, participation in decision-making.

Men have unrealized potential for self-cultivation, self-direction, self-understanding, and creativity. It is this potential that we regard as crucial and to which we appeal, not to the human potentiality for violence, unreason, and submission to authority. The goal of man and society should be human independence: a concern not with image of popularity but with finding a meaning in life that is personally authentic; a quality of mind not compulsively driven by a sense of powerlessness, nor one which unthinkingly adopts status values, nor one which represses all threats to its habits, but one which has full spontaneous access to present and past experiences, one which easily unites the fragmented parts of personal history, one which openly faces problems which are troubling and unresolved; one with an intuitive awareness of possibilities, an active sense of curiosity, an ability and willingness to learn.

This kind of independence does not mean egotistic individualism—the object is not to have one's way so much as it is to have a way that is one's own. Nor do we deify man—we merely have faith in his potential.

Human relationships should involve fraternity and honesty. Human interdependence is contemporary fact; human brotherhood must be willing, however, as a condition of future survival and as the most appropriate form of social relations. Personal links between man and man are needed, especially to go beyond the partial and fragmentary bonds of function that bind men only as worker to worker, employer to employee, teacher to student, American to Russian.

Loneliness, estrangement, isolation describe the vast distance between man and man today. These dominant tendencies cannot be overcome by better personnel management, nor by improved gadgets, but only when a love of man overcomes the idolatrous worship of things by man. As the individualism we affirm is not egoism, the selflessness we affirm is not self-elimination. On the contrary, we believe in generosity of a kind that imprints one's unique individual qualities in the relation to other men, and to all human activity. Further, to dislike isolation is not to favor the abolition of privacy; the latter differs from isolation in that it occurs or is abolished according to individual will.

We would replace power rooted in possession, privilege, or circumstance by power and uniqueness rooted in love, reflectiveness, reason and creativity. As a *social system* we seek the establishment of a democracy of individual participation, governed by two central aims: that the individual share in those social decisions determining the quality and direction of his life; that society be organized to encourage independence in men and provide the media for their common participation.

In a participatory democracy, the political life would be based on several root principles:

that decision-making of basic social consequence be carried on by public groupings;

that politics be seen positively, as the art of collectively creating an acceptable pattern of social relations;

that politics has the function of bringing people out of isolation and into community, thus being a necessary, though not sufficient, means of finding meaning in personal life;

that the political order should serve to clarify problems in a way instrumental to their solution; it should provide outlets for the expression of personal grievance and aspiration; opposing views should be organized so as to illuminate choices and facilitate the attainment of goals; channels should be commonly available to relate men to knowledge and to power so that private problems—from bad recreation facilities to personal alienation—are formulated as general issues.

The economic sphere would have as its basis the principles:

that work should involve incentives worthier than money or survival. It should be educative, not stultifying; creative, not mechanical; self-directed, not manipulated, encouraging independence, a respect for others, a sense of dignity

and a willingness to accept social responsibility, since it is this experience that has crucial influence on habits, perceptions and individual ethics;

that the economic experience is so personally decisive that the individual must share in its full determination;

that the economy itself is of such social importance that its major resources and means of production should be open to democratic participation and subject to democratic social regulation.

Like the political and economic ones, major social institutions—cultural, educational, rehabilitative, and others—should be generally organized with the well-being and dignity of man as the essential measure of success.

In social change or interchange, we find violence to be abhorrent because it requires generally the transformation of the target, be it a human being or a community of people, into a depersonalized objective of hate. It is imperative that the means of violence be abolished and the institutions—local, national, international—that encourage nonviolence as a condition of conflict be developed.

These are our central values, in skeletal form. It remains vital to understand their denial or attainment in the context of the modern world.

THE STUDENTS

In the last few years, thousands of American students demonstrated that they at least felt the urgency of the times. They moved actively and directly against racial injustices, the threat of war, violations of individual rights of conscience and, less frequently, against economic manipulation. They succeeded in restoring a small measure of controversy to the campuses after the stillness of the McCarthy period. They succeeded, too, in gaining some concessions from the people and institutions they opposed, especially in the fight against racial bigotry.

The significance of these scattered movements lies not in their success or failure in gaining objectives—at least not yet. Nor does the significance lie in the intellectual "competence" or "maturity" of the students involved—as some pedantic elders allege. The significance is in the fact the students are breaking the crust of apathy and overcoming the inner alienation that remain the defining characteristics of American college life.

If student movements for change are still rareties on the campus scene, what is commonplace there? The real campus, the familiar campus, is a place of private people, engaged in their notorious "inner emigration." It is a place of commitment to business-as-usual, getting ahead, playing it cool. It is a place of mass affirmation of the Twist, but mass reluctance toward the controversial public stance. Rules are accepted as "inevitable," bureaucracy as "just circumstances," irrelevance as "scholarship," selflessness as "martyrdom," politics as "just another way to make people, and an unprofitable one, too."

Almost no students value activity as citizens. Passive in public, they are hardly more idealistic in arranging their private lives: Gallup concludes they will settle for "low success, and won't risk high failure." There is not much willingness to take risks (not even in business), no setting of dangerous goals, no real conception of personal identity except one manufactured in the image of others, no real urge for personal fulfillment except to be almost as successful as the very successful people. Attention is being paid to social status (the quality of shirt collars, meeting people, getting wives or husbands, making solid contacts for later on); much, too, is paid to academic status (grades, honors, the med school rat race). But neglected generally is real intellectual status, the personal cultivation of the mind.

"Students don't even give a damn about the apathy," one has said. Apathy toward apathy begets a privately constructed universe, a place of systematic study schedules, two nights each week

for beer, a girl or two, and early marriage; a framework infused with personality, warmth and under control, no matter how unsatisfying otherwise.

Under these conditions university life loses all relevance to some. Four hundred thousand of our classmates leave college every year.

But apathy is not simply an attitude; it is a product of social institutions, and of the structure and organization of higher education itself. The extracurricular life is ordered according to *in loco parentis* theory, which ratifies the administration as the moral guardian of the young.

The accompanying "let's pretend" theory of student extracurricular affairs validates student government as a training center for those who want to spend their lives in political pretense, and discourages initiative from the more articulate, honest, and sensitive students. The bounds and style of controversy are delimited before controversy begins. The university "prepares" the student for "citizenship" through perpetual rehearsals and, usually, through emasculation of what creative spirit there is in the individual.

The academic life contains reinforcing counterparts to the way in which extracurricular life is organized. The academic world is founded on a teacher-student relation analogous to the parent-child relation which characterizes *in loco parentis*. Further, academia includes a radical separation of the student from the material of study. That which is studied, the social reality, is "objectified" to sterility, dividing the student from life—just as he is restrained in active involvement by the deans controlling student government. The specialization of function and knowledge, admittedly necessary to our complex technological and social structure, has produced an exaggerated compartmentalization of study and understanding. This has contributed to an overly parochial view, by faculty, of the role of its research and scholarship, to a discontinuous and truncated understanding, by students, of the surrounding social order; and to a loss of personal attachment, by nearly all, to the worth of study as a humanistic enterprise.

There is, finally, the cumbersome academic bureaucracy extending throughout the academic as well as the extracurricular structures, contributing to the sense of outer complexity and inner powerlessness that transforms the honest searchings of many students to a ratification of convention and, worse, to a numbness to present and future catastrophes. The size and financing systems of the university enhance the permanent trusteeship of the administrative bureaucracy, their power leading to a shift within the university toward the value standards of business and the administrative mentality. Huge foundations and other private financial interests shape the under-financed colleges and universities, not only making them more commercial, but less disposed to diagnose society critically, less open to dissent. Many social and physical scientists, neglecting the liberating heritage of higher learning, develop "human relations" or "morale-producing" techniques for the corporate economy, while others exercise their intellectual skills to accelerate the arms race. . . .

There are no convincing apologies for the contemporary malaise. While the world tumbles toward the final war, while men in other nations are trying desperately to alter events, while the very future qua future is uncertain— America is without community, impulse, without the inner momentum necessary for an age when societies cannot successfully perpetuate themselves by their military weapons, when democracy must be viable because of the quality of life, not its quantity of rockets.

The apathy here is, first, *objective*— the felt powerlessness of ordinary people, the resignation before the enormity of events. But subjective apathy is encouraged by the *objective* American situation—the actual structural separation of people from power, from relevant knowledge, from pinnacles of de-cision-making. Just as the university influences the student way of life, so do major social institutions create the circumstances in which the isolated citizen will try hopelessly to understand his world and himself.

The very isolation of the individual— from power and community and ability to aspire—means the rise of a democracy without publics. With the great mass of people structurally remote and psychologically hesitant with respect to democratic institutions, those institutions themselves attenuate and become, in the fashion of the vicious circle, progressively less accessible to those few who aspire to serious participation in social affairs. The vital democratic connection between community and leadership, between the mass and the several elites, has been so wretched and perverted that disastrous policies go unchallenged time and again.

POLITICS WITHOUT PUBLICS

The American political system is not the democratic model of which its glorifiers speak. In actuality it frustrates democracy by confusing the individual citizen, paralyzing policy discussion, and consolidating the irresponsible power of military and business interests.

A crucial feature of the political apparatus in America is that greater differences are harbored within each major party than the differences existing between them. Instead of two parties presenting distinctive and significant differences of approach, what dominates the system is a natural interlocking of Democrats from Southern states with the more conservative elements of the Republican Party. This arrangement of forces is blessed by the seniority system of Congress which guarantees Congressional committee domination by conservatives— ten of seventeen committees in the Senate and thirteen of twenty-one in the House of Representatives are chaired currently by Dixiecrats.

The party overlap, however, is not the only structural antagonist of democracy in politics. First, the localized nature of the party system does not encourage discussion of national and international issues: thus problems are not raised by and for people, and political representatives usually are unfettered from any responsibilities to the general public except those regarding parochial matters. Second, whole constituencies are divested of the full political power they might have: many Negroes in the South are prevented from voting, migrant workers are disenfranchised by various residence requirements, some urban and suburban dwellers are victimized by gerrymandering, and poor people, are too often without the power to obtain political representation. Third, the focus of political attention is significantly distorted by the enormous lobby force, composed predominantly of business interests, spending hundreds of millions each year in an attempt to conform facts about productivity, agriculture, defense, and social services, to the wants of private economic groupings.

What emerges from the party contradiction and insulations of privately held power is the organized political stalemate: calcification dominates flexibility as the principle of parliamentary organization, frustration is the expectancy of legislators intending liberal reform, and Congress becomes less and less central to national decision-making, especially in the area of foreign policy. In this context, confusion and blurring is built into the formulation of issues, long-range priorities are not discussed in the rational manner needed for policy-making, the politics of personality and "image" become a more important mechanism than the construction of issues in a way that affords each voter a challenging and real option. The American voter is buffeted from all directions by pseudo-problems, by the structurally initiated sense that nothing political is subject to human mastery. Worried by his mundane problems which never get solved, but constrained by the common

belief that politics is an agonizingly slow accommodation of views, he quits all pretense of bothering.

A most alarming fact is that few, if any politicians are calling for changes in these conditions. Only a handful even are calling on the President to "live up to" platform pledges; no one is demanding structural changes, such as the shuttling of Southern Democrats out of the Democratic Party. Rather than protesting the state of politics, most politicians are reinforcing and aggravating that state. While in practice they rig public opinion to suit their own interests, in word and ritual they enshrine "the sovereign public" and call for more and more letters. Their speeches and campaign actions are banal, based on a degrading conception of what people want to hear. They respond not to dialogue, but to pressure: and knowing this, the ordinary citizen sees even greater inclination to shun the political sphere. The politician is usually a trumpeter to "citizenship" and "service to the nation," but since he is unwilling to seriously rearrange power relationships, his trumpetings only increase apathy by creating no outlets. Much of the time the call to "service" is justified not in idealistic terms, but in the crasser terms of "defending the free world from Communism"—thus making future idealistic impulses even harder to justify in anything but Cold War terms.

In such a setting of status quo politics, where most if not all government activity is rationalized in Cold War anti-Communist terms, it is somewhat natural that discontented, super-patriotic groups would emerge through political channels and explain their ultra-conservatism as the best means of Victory over Communism. They have become a politically influential force within the Republican Party, at a national level through Senator Goldwater, and at a local level through their important social and economic roles. Their political views are defined generally as the opposite of the supposed views of Communists: complete individual freedom in the economic sphere, non-participation by the government in the machinery of production. But actually "anti-Communism" becomes an umbrella by which to protest liberalism, internationalism, welfareism, the active civil rights and labor movements. It is to the disgrace of the United States that such a movement should become a prominent kind of public participation in the modern world—but ironically, it is somewhat to the interests of the United States that such a movement should be a public constituency pointed toward realignment of the political parties, demanding a conservative Republican Party in the South and an exclusion of the "leftist" elements of the national GOP. . . .

The Politics of "The Movement"

My own disenchantment with American society was not caused by its racial bigotry, its warlike posturing, its supreme respect for money. All these might be understood as irrationalities which could be struck from the national character if only rational men were mobilized more effectively. But when events prove this assumption false, then disenchantment really begins: with the understanding that the most respected and enlightened Americans are among the most barbarous.

Take just two examples. There is a conventional notion that the Southern racial crisis is caused and prolonged by "white trash"—an isolated and declining

SOURCE. Reprinted from *Dissent,* Vol. 13, January-February 1966, by permission of the author and publisher. Copyright 1966 by Tom Hayden.

remnant in our society. We are told that rational men are attempting, within the framework of due process, to educate these minority elements to a more progressive social outlook. But this picture is shattered every day by events in the Black Belt. There the murderers of civil rights workers again and again include men like Byron De la Beckwith, the respected downtown businessman who shot Medgar Evers in the back. They are middle class and enjoy the broad support of their local communities.

When this is pointed out, of course, we are told that respectable men are murderers only in places like Mississippi. By national standards, the Black Belt killers are not respectable. But is Mississippi an isolated part of America? If not, who at the national level is responsible for the state of terror in Mississippi? Part of the answer, I am afraid, is that leading Northerners buttress the Southern status quo. Without dozens of companies owned from the North, plus the billions provided by defense contracts and agricultural subsidies, Mississippi could not have survived the postwar period as a racist state. Mississippi Power and Light, for example, many of whose personnel are connected with the White Citizens Council, is owned and controlled by the same men who play leading roles in another corporation known for its enlightenment, Harvard University.

A second example: we are told that the United States is on the side of the new nations and the exploited and impoverished peoples of the third world. But, once again, the facts have nothing to do with this happy picture—as the affairs of an American businessman like Charles Engelhard of New Jersey suggest. In his mid-forties, Engelhard is already renowned in business circles and has become an important political figure in the liberal wing of the Democratic party. He was sent by the President to represent the U.S. at occasions as vital as the celebration of Algerian independence. He was a friend of John

F. Kennedy; Lyndon Johnson praises him as a "great humanitarian." How did he become so famous? Presumably because he owns the controlling shares in the mines of the Republic of South Africa. But aren't those mines a blasphemy against the values of the Free World? And is Engelhard an isolated and unrespectable member of that world?

This is civilized barbarism—pernicious, sophisticated, subtly concealed from public view, massively protected from political attack. The barbaric America is invisible to the majority of its people, who are lodged in occupations and social positions which form a desensitizing trap. They are at the bottom, or in the middle, of organizations whose official purposes are justified in abstract terms. Their views, inherited from their families or implanted by the school system, and fed every day by the mass media, permit them to screen out threatening information or alternative ways of seeing the world.

The usual way to "escape" the trapped condition of ordinary Americans is to ascend to higher levels of influence and knowledge in some key institution. But while an overview of society is gained from these positions, a new trap is waiting. For entry into higher organizational circles depends upon accepting their general design and purpose. This means that people in "responsible" positions are most often blind to immoral consequences of their work. Their blindness is intensified by the belief that they are close to people's problems and that administrative remedies exist for whatever arises. This is the usual attitude among public servants, from police to administrators of the war-on-poverty.

II

This national trance depends upon one crucial assumption: that American society is being improved domestically. The legitimacy gained by the industrial unions, the liberal welfare legislation which was passed in the thirties and forties, and now the civil rights and anti-poverty reforms of the sixties—these are seen as part of a long sweep toward a society of economic and social justice. But there is, in fact, little evidence to justify the view that the social reforms of the past thirty years actually improved the quality of American life in a lasting way. And there is much evidence which suggests that the reforms gained were illusory or token, serving chiefly to sharpen the capacity of the system for manipulation and oppression.

Look closely for a moment at the social legislation upon which the notion of domestic improvement is based. The Wagner Act was supposed to effect unionization of workers; but today the unionized labor force is shrinking with the automation of the mass-production industries, and millions of other workers, never organized, are without any protection. The social security laws were supposed to support people in distress, but today many are still not covered, and those with coverage can barely make ends meet. Unemployment compensation policies were supposed to aid men in need of jobs, but today many are still without coverage, while benefits represent a smaller and smaller share of the cost of living. The 1946 Full Employment Act was supposed to guarantee federal action to provide a job for every American who needed one, but today the official (understated) unemployment rate is close to six per cent. The 1949 Public Housing Act, sponsored by conservative Robert Taft, was to create 800,000 low-cost units by 1953, but today less than half that number are constructed, many of them beyond reach of the poor. The difficult struggle to enact even a token policy of public medical care, the hollow support for public education, the stagnation and starvation of broader programs for health, recreation, and simple city services—all this is evidence for a simple truth. *The welfare state is a myth.*

Seen in the context of a history of unkept promises, the 1965 anti-poverty program should evoke no optimism. The amount of money allocated is a pittance; most of it is going to local politicians, school boards, welfare agencies, housing authorities, professional personnel, and even to the police; its main thrust is to shore up sagging organizational machinery, not to shift the distribution of income and influence in the direction of the poor. Some of the more sophisticated liberals understand that the "involvement of the poor" is essential to an effective program, but this is seen in capitalist-psychological terms, stressing the need to "repair" the defeatist self-image which supposedly exludes the poor from sharing in the enterprise system. A few people, including members of the Administration, see "involvement" in political terms as well. But this participation is frustrated by the poverty planners' undeviating allegiance to existing power centers. In reality, then, the poor only *flavor* the program. A few are co-opted into it, but only as atomized individuals. They do not have independent organizational strength, as do the machines and social agencies.

But the quality of the welfare state is best illustrated by the sluggish way in which it responds to pressure for civil rights reform. It required the slaughter of little girls, a near bloodbath in Birmingham, violence toward Northern whites, students and ministers, an outbreak of riots across the North, and the organization of an independent political party in Mississippi before the Administration began to move on the civil rights front. And that motion gives little hope of real progress. Indeed, the present (1965) voting rights bill actually shrinks the existing powers of the Federal government (as established in such codes as Section 242, Title 18, which provides for criminal prosecution of people acting under cover of law to violate others' constitutional rights). It leaves the decision to take action to the Attorney General; it involves complicated and time-consuming procedures for local

Negroes; it provides no protection against intimidation for civil rights workers or local people.

In all these areas, from the Wagner Act to the newest civil rights legislation, my criticism has been narrowed to the question: did the legislation achieve, or does it offer some hope of achieving, its stated purposes? The tragedy, however, is not simply that these programs fall short of their goals. Rather, the goals themselves are far from desirable to anyone interested in greater democracy and a richer quality of social life. Welfare and public housing policies, for instance, are creating a new and public kind of authoritarianism. Public relief clients and tenants, lacking any protective organizations, are subject to the caprice and cruelty of supervisors, investigators, and local machine politicians. Similarly, labor and civil rights legislation creates tools for government intervention at moments of sharp social conflict, without really changing the tyrannical conditions in which millions of workers and Negroes live. The full employment and anti-poverty acts, along with the relief measures of the thirties, give the government power to cushion the economic situation just short of the point of mass unemployment. Programs such as urban renewal serve as the major domestic outlet for investment capital and, consciously or not, as a means of demoralizing and politically fragmenting the poor. The national government thus becomes the chief force for stabilizing the private economy and for managing social crisis. Its interests, institutions and personnel have merged with those of high finance and industry.

The traditional Left expectation of irreconcilable and clashing class interests has been defied. Still assuming such antagonism, however, many Leftists tend to view each piece of social legislation as a victory which strengthens the "progressive" forces. They see a step-by-step transformation of society as the result of pushing for one "politically acceptable" reform after another. But it appears that the American elite has discovered a long-term way to stabilize or cushion the contradictions of our society. It does this through numerous forms of state intervention, the use of our abundant capacity for material gratification, and the ability to condition nearly all the information which people receive. And if this is the case, then more changes of the New Deal variety will not be "progressive" at all. Except for temporarily booting income for a few people, this entire reformist trend has weakened the poor under the pretense of helping them and strengthened elite rule under the slogan of curbing private enterprise. In fostering a "responsible" Negro and labor leadership and bringing it into the pseudo-pluralist system of bargaining and rewards, a way has been found to contain and paralyze the disadvantaged and voiceless people.

III

Why have liberal strategies failed to secure substantial reforms over the last three decades? The answer can only be grasped by looking at the general organizing concepts of American liberal and labor leaders. These begin with the view that the American masses are "apathetic" and can only be roused because of simple material needs or during short periods of great enthusiasm. The masses most likely to move, it is said, are those who have gained something already: the unionized workers, registered voters, property owners. Those less likely to move are the people on the absolute bottom with nothing to lose, for they are too damaged to be the real motor of change.

From this rough description of the masses, liberals go on to argue the need for certain sorts of organizations. The masses need skilled and responsible leaders, they insist. It is best if these leaders have rank-and-file experience and operate within a formally democratic system. But this grass-roots flavor must not obscure the necessity for leaders to lead, that is, put forward a program, a set of answers that guides the movement. And because they monopolize leadership experience, it soon appears to these leaders that they alone are qualified to maintain the organization.

The perilous position of the movement, due to attacks from centralized business and political forces, adds a further incentive for a top-down system of command. The need for alliances with other groups, created in large part through the trust which sets of leaders develop for each other, also intensified the trend toward vertical organization. Finally, the leaders see a need to screen out anyone with "Communist-oriented" views, since such individuals are presumably too skilled to be allowed to operate freely within the movement. Slowly an elite is formed, calling itself the liberal-labor community. It treats the rank-and-file as a mass to be molded; sometimes thrust forward into action, sometimes held back. A self-fulfilling pattern emerges: because the nature of the organization is elitist, many people react to it with disinterest or suspicion, giving the leadership the evidence it needs to call the masses apathetic.

The pressures which influence these leaders come, not primarily from below, but from the top, from the most powerful men in the country. Sometimes bluntly and sometimes subtly, the real elite grooms responsible trade union and civil rights leaders. The leaders' existence comes to depend upon the possibility of receiving attention from the President or some top aide, and they judge organizational issues with an eye on this possibility. There is usually no question about the leaders' primary loyalty to the "national interest" as defined by the Administration, even though they always believe their judgments are independently made. Thus most of the civil rights leadership in 1964, fearing the Goldwater movement and hoping for civil rights legislation from a victorious Johnson Administration, called for a "moratorium" on mass demonstrations. The labor leadership performed the same function for the same reasons during World War II; the irony is that their critics in that period included A. Philip Randolph and Bayard Rustin, two Negroes who pushed for the 1964 moratorium.

A recent incident clarified the political role of this leadership and pointed toward the possibility of an alternative strategy. This was the challenge posed by the Mississippi Freedom Democratic party and the Student Nonviolent Coordinating Committee at the 1964 Democratic National Convention.

Members of the FDP trooped into Atlantic City to argue for their rightful control of the Mississippi Democratic seats. They found substantial support from rank-and-file members of Northern delegations who favored their modest demand for at least equal treatment with the racist party at the convention. Here was a chance, it was thought, to end Southern obstruction of the Johnson Administration's program. But when the Democratic leadership let its position be known: the FDP was morally sound, but "illegal" and "not qualified." Support within the delegations wavered. The FDP's last chance for success depended on rallying national liberal-labor leaders to support its demand for a floor debate, in front of the television camers. But some Negro leaders worked against the Mississippi party, others took a vacillating position and no one would stand firmly with them. To do so, the leaders claimed, would jeopardize Humphrey's chance at the vice-presidency, strengthen Goldwater's hand, and split the FDP from its "allies" in the liberal-labor world. The FDP members decided that the fate of Humphrey and Goldwater depended in fact upon the same power structure that was determining their own fate. Not wanting the kind of "allies" and "victories" being offered, they went home. Their real allies were the poor people waiting in the Delta; and their real victory was in being able to main-

tain fidelity to those allies. This was a victory because it kept the movement alive and gave its members some real understanding of what was needed to change the national situation.

IV

The Mississippi Convention challenge points towards a new kind of politics and a new kind of organizing, which has at least an outside chance of truly changing American society. This stirring we call the Movement.

The Movement tries to oppose American barbarism with new structures and opposing identities. These are created by people whose need to understand their society and govern their own existence has somehow now been cancelled out by the psychological damage they have received. For different reasons such needs survive among the poor, among students and other young people, and finally among millions of other Americans not easily grouped except by their modest individual resistance to the system's inhumanity. It is from these ranks that the Movement is being created. What kind of people, more exactly, are they, and what kind of organization strategy might they develop?

1. AN INTERRACIAL MOVEMENT OF THE POOR

The Mississippi sharecroppers are the most visible and inspiring representations of an awakening that is taking place among the poor in America. Their perspective centers on Negro freedom, of course, but they are committed deeply to the idea of a movement of all the powerless and exploited. In certain ways theirs is a radicalism unique because of Black Belt conditions. Their strength comes from a stable system of family life and work. Politics is new and fresh for them; they have not experienced the hollow promises of an opportunistic liberal-Negro machine. Their opposition's naked brutality keeps them constantly in a crisis framework. The broadening of their movement into Arkansas, Alabama, Louisiana, Georgia, the Carolinas and Virginia, already underway, can be expected to challenge fundamentally the national coalition directing the Democratic party. Already the Democrats are trying to groom moderate and liberal politicians to provide an "alternative" to the segregationists and the independent FDP. Probably this effort will succeed, in the sense that political moderates will begin to compete for electoral power and leadership of the civil rights forces, mostly basing their strength in the cities, among privileged Negroes. The FDP, as a structure, may be absorbed into the national party, if only because it has no other, more effective place to go. But since the new Southern power structure will not solve the problems of poverty and race which have plagued the North for generations, there is very little chance that this movement of poor people will be entirely co-opted or crushed.

In the black ghettoes of the North, the Movement faces heavier obstacles. There work is often deadening, family life distorted: "proper" political channels are sewers; people are used to, and tired of, party organizers exploiting them. The civil rights movement does not touch these hundreds of ghettoes in any significant way because of the middle class nature of its program and leadership. However, the Harlem rent strikes and the activities of Malcolm X are clear evidence that there are in the ghettoes people prepared to take action. Some of them are of Southern background; some are housewives with wasted talents; some are youth with no future for their energy; some are junkies and numbers men with little loyalty to their particular game. Different as the forms of their discontent may be, the discontent itself is general to the ghetto and can be the spring for action. Under present conditions, political movements among these people are likely to be based on a race consciousness which is genuine and militant—and which is also vital because of the failure of whites to act in favor of

equal rights. The ghetto race consciousness, however, is intertwined with the consciousness of being both poor and powerless. Almost of necessity, the demands that the ghetto poor put forward are also in the interest of the white poor, as well as of middle class professionals who depend on the expansion of the public sectors of the economy.

But will white working class and poor people take up these issues, which the "Negro problem" by its nature tends to raise? The negative evidence is plentiful. Poor whites, such as those in parts of the South who are truly irrelevant to the modern economy, tend to see their plight (sometimes with accuracy) as personal rather than social: a function of sickness, bad luck, or psychological disorder. Poverty is not seen clearly as the fate of a whole interracial class, but only as the fate of individuals, each shamed into self-blame by their Protestant ideology. Working class whites, on the other hand, are more likely to be conscious of their problems as a group, but they tend to defend their scarce privileges—jobs, wages, education for their children—against what they see as the onslaught of Negro competition. While "backlash" did not split the alliance of white working people with the Democratic party in 1964, it does serve as a barrier to an alliance with the Negro poor. But it is foolish to be rigid about these notions. Whites *are* being organized, on a mass basis, in areas of Appalachia where there exists a common culture and an industrial union tradition, and where the blame for misery can be laid to the coal operators, the conservative United Mine Workers, and the government. They also have been organized in Cleveland, where they face the "welfare situation" together.

But these organizing efforts were led by local people or independent organizers outside the structure of the labor movement. Today there are millions of workers trapped by the organizational framework of the AFL-CIO. Their unrest at times moves the international unions slightly, but the internations are more dependent on government and business than on their own members, and, in addition, they seem to posess effective techniques for curbing shop revolts. It is not simply the "better objective conditions" which split the white from the Negro poor, but the existence of trade unions which actively distort the better aspirations of their members. Economic and social conditions, of course, are not improving and workers discontent is evidenced by the recent wave of rank-and-file revolts. But whether this discontent spurs a coalition of poor whites with Negroes depends, most of all, on whether a way can be found to organize workers independent of AFL-CIO routines. Concretely, that means democratic control by the workers of their union locals, and the entry of those locals into political activities and coalitions on the community level. It also means community action and organization among the millions of low-paid workers presently outside the labor movement.

The crucial importance of community work can only be grasped if one understands the sorts of ideas the American poor have about themselves. They operate with a kind of split consciousness. On the one hand, poor people know they are victimized from every direction. The facts of life always break through to expose the distance between American ideals and personal realities. This kind of knowledge, however, is kept undeveloped and unused because of another knowledge inposed on the poor, a keen sense of dependence on the oppressor. This is the source of that universal fear which leads poor people to act and even to think subserviently. Seeing themselves to blame for their situation, they rule out the possibility that they might be qualified to govern themselves and their own organizations. Besides fear, it is their sense of inadequacy and embarrassment which destroys the possibility of revolt. At the same time, this set of contradictory feelings results in indirect forms of protest all the time: styles of dress and language, withdrawal from political life, defiance of the boss's or the welfare worker's rules and regulations.

There can be no poor people's movement in any form unless the poor can overcome their fear and embarrassment. I think the release comes from a certain kind of organizing which tries to make people understand their own worth and dignity. This work depends on the existence of "material issues" as a talking and organizing point—high rents, voting rights, unpaved roads, and so on—but it moves from there into the ways such issues are related to personal life. The organizer spends hours and hours in the community, listening to people, drawing out their own ideas, rejecting their tendency to depend on him for solutions. Meetings are organized at which people with no "connections" can be given a chance to talk and work out problems together—usually for the first time. All this means fostering in everyone that sense of decision-making power which American society works to destroy. Only in this way can a movement be built which the Establishment can neither buy off nor manage, a movement too vital ever to become a small clique of spokesmen.

An organization form that suggests the style of such a movement is the "community union," involving working-class and poor people in working insurgency. Open and democratic, the community union offers a real alternative to the kind of participation permitted in civil rights groups, trade unions, and Democratic party machines. It might take a variety of forms: block clubs, housing committees, youth groups, etc. The union's insistence on the relevance of "little people," as well as its position outside and against the normal channels, would create a rooted sense of independence among the members.

The problem of politics among the poor is severe. In the first place, their potential electoral power is low because of their location in gerry-mandered political districts, their rapid movement from house to house, and the complicated and discriminatory electoral procedures in many cities. Beyond these problems lies the obvious and well-grounded cynicism of the poor about elections. Given all these conditions, it is barely conceivable that a poor person could be elected to an important political office. Even were this possible, it would be on a token basis, and the elected official would be under strong pressure to conform to the rules of the game. Thus, the orthodox idea of politics is contradictory to building a movement. The movement needs to discover a politics of its own. This might be done by electing people who will see their office as a community organizing tool, letting community people participate directly in decisions about how the office should be used. This experiment is being made in Atlanta where a SNCC field secretary, Julian Bond, was elected in June 1965 to the State Legislature. Or what might be done is to contest the basic class and racial injustices of American politics, demanding that poverty areas be granted political representation, or running freedom elections to dramatize the lack of representation for the boxed-in poor. This sort of thing would probably mobilize more poor people than orthodox electoral activity. The mobilization would be "practical" from the standpoint of getting modest reforms; more important, it would point toward the need to rearrange American political institutions to fit the needs of excluded people.

2. A STUDENT MOVEMENT

If poor people are in the movement because they have nothing to gain in the status system, students are in it because, in a sense, they have gained too much. Most of the active student radicals today come from middle to upper-middle class professional homes. They were born with status and affluence as facts of life, not goals to be striven for. In their upbringing, their parents stressed the right of children to question and make judgments, producing perhaps the first generation of young people both affluent and independent of mind. And then these students so often encountered social institutions that denied them their independence and betrayed the democratic ideals they were taught. They saw that men of learning were careerists; that school administrators and ministers almost never discussed the realities the students lived with; that even their parents were not true to the ideals they taught the young.

It was against this background that young people became concerned about war, racism and inequality in the early sixties. By now, the empty nature of existing vocational alternatives has pushed several hundreds of these students into community organizing. Working in poor communities is a concrete task in which the split between job and values can be healed. It is also a position from which to expose the whole structure of pretense, status and glitter that masks the country's real human problems. And, finally, it is a way to find people who want to change the country, and possibly can do so.

When a student comes into a community, there are countless obstacles in his way. He is an outsider, he is over-educated, he has nothing concrete to offer people, and often, he is white in a Negro ghetto. At the same time, however, he brings something with him: the very presence of students suggests to the poor that their more activist notions may be right after all. The student alone can say, "Look, I come from the world that says you are not qualified, and I know that is a lie. I come to you because you can teach me as much as I can teach you." Students can also make the poverty problem visible and threatening because they create resources previously unimaginable. Parents and universities become energized; money can be raised; contacts can be set up with other people's organizations around the country. Finally, students and poor people make each other feel real. What has flowed from this connection is most of the vitality of the civil rights and anti-poverty movements over the past five years.

Now it appears that students are finding ways to organize effectively around other problems too: university reform and peace. The Berkeley "uprising" and the April march of 20,000 against the war in Vietnam were major departures from the inconsequential student politics of the old days. On many campuses students are beginning to form unions of their own, as well as independent seminars pointed toward the eventual organization of a "free university." In addition, they are beginning to mobilize community action against the Vietnamese war—thereby encountering their friends already at work among the poor. These efforts may thread the several protest movements in the country into a grass-roots coalition.

3. MIDDLE-CLASS INSURGENTS

A centralized and commercial society wastes the talents and energies of millions of individuals. Some of these are women who are excluded from Male-dominated vocations. Some are people with human values who cannot assert them effectively within organizations attached to the cold war consensus. Some were politically active in the thirties, but faded away when popular movements declined. Some are part of the postwar generation which missed the experience of a radical movement altogether, and who are lodged uncomfortably in publishing houses, universities, and labor bureaucracies.

The new movements are opening great possibilities for participation by such middle class people. Their activity often includes vital financial support, but it can and does go farther. Insurgency within American institutions is spreading: professors fighting their administrations, lawyers against the bar association, welfare workers against the political machine, muckrakers against the press establishments. This insurgency is bound to increase as the new generation of student activists graduates into the professions. And it is an insurgency which

needs a movement of poor people, insistently demanding new social purposes from the professionals.

To summarize: the Movement is a community of insurgents sharing the same radical values and identity, seeking an independent base of power wherever they are. It aims at a transformation of society led by the most excluded and "unqualified" people. Primarily, this means building institutions outside the established order which seek to become the genuine institutions of the total society. Community unions, freedom schools, experimental universities, community-formed police review boards, people's own anti-poverty organizations fighting for federal money, independent union locals—all can be "practical" pressure points from which to launch reform in the conventional institutions while at the same time maintaining a separate base and pointing towards a new system. Ultimately, this movement might lead to a Continental Congress called by all the people who feel excluded from the higher circles of decision-making in the country. This Congress might even become a kind of second government, receiving taxes from its supporters, establishing contact with other nations, holding debates on American foreign and domestic policy, dramatizing the plight of all groups that suffer from the American system.

If it is hard to imagine this kind of revolutionary process in the United States, it might be because no previous model of revolution seems appropriate to this most bloated and flexible of the advanced societies. There may be no way to change this country. At least there is no way we can bank on. Both technological change and social reform seem to rationalize the power of the system to drain the heart of protest. The Movement at least suggests that we bank on our own consciousness, what there is of our own humanity, and begin to work.

From "Two, Three, Many Columbias" (1968)

The goal written on the university walls was "Create two, three, many Columbias"; it meant expand the strike so that the U.S. must either change or send its troops to occupy American campuses.

At this point the goal seems realistic; an explosive mix is present on dozens of campuses where demands for attention to student views are being disregarded by university administrators.

The American student movement has continued to swell for nearly a decade: during the semi-peace of the early 1960's as well as during Vietnam; during the token liberalism of John Kennedy as well as during the bankrupt racism of Lyndon Johnson. Students have responded most directly to the black movement of the '60's: from Mississippi Summer to the Free Speech Movement; from "Black Power" to "Student Power"; from the seizure of Howard University to the seizure of Hamilton Hall. As the racial crisis deepens so will the campus crisis. But the student protest is not just an offshoot of the black protest—it is based on authentic opposition to the middle-class world of manipulation, channeling, and careerism. The students are in opposition to the fundamental institutions of society.

The students' protest constantly escalates by building on its achievements and legends. The issues being considered by seventeen-year-old freshmen at Columbia would not have been within the imagination of most "veteran" student activists five years ago.

Columbia opened a new tactical stage in the resistance movement which began last fall: from the overnight occupation of buildings to permanent occupation; from mill-ins to the creation

of revolutionary committees; from symbolic civil disobedience to barricaded resistance. Not only are these tactics already being duplicated on other campuses, but they are sure to be surpassed by even more militant tactics. In the future it is conceivable that students will threaten destruction of buildings as a last deterrent to police attacks. Many of these tactics learned can also be applied in smaller hit-and-run operations between strikes: raids on the offices of professors doing weapons research could win substantial support among students while making the university more blatantly repressive.

In the buildings occupied at Columbia, the students created what they called a "new society" or "liberated area" or "commune," a society in which decent values would be lived out even though university officials might cut short the communes through use of police. The students had fun, they sang and danced and wisecracked, but there was continual tension. There was no question of their constant awareness of the seriousness of their acts. Though there were a few violent arguments about tactics, the discourse was more in the form of endless meetings convened to explore the outside political situation, defense tactics, maintenance and morale problems within the group. Debating and then determining what leaders should do were alternatives to the remote and authoritarian decision-making of Columbia's trustees.

The Columbia strike represented more than a new tactical movement, however. There was a political message as well. The striking students were not holding onto a narrow conception of students as a priviliged class asking for inclusion in the university as it now exists. This kind of demand could easily be met by administrators by opening minor opportunities for "student rights" while cracking down on campus radicals. The Columbia students were instead taking an internationalist and revolutionary view of themselves in opposition to the imperialism of the very institutions in which they have been groomed and educated. They did not even want to be included in the decision-making circles of the military-industrial complex that runs Columbia: *they want to be included only if their inclusion is a step toward transforming the university.* They want a new and independent university standing against the mainstream of American society, or they want no university at all. They are, in Fidel Castro's words, "guerrillas in the field of culture."

How many other schools can be considered ripe for such confrontations? The question is hard to answer, but it is clear that the demands of black students for cultural recognition rather than paternalistic tolerance, and radical while students' awareness of the sinister paramilitary activities carried on in secret by the faculty on many campuses, are hardly confined to Columbia. Columbia's problem is the American problem in miniature—the inability to provide answers to widespread social needs and the use of the military to protect the authorities against the people. This process can only lead to greater unity in the movement.

Support from outside the university communities can be counted on in many large cities. A crisis is foreseeable that would be too massive for police to handle. It can happen; whether or not it will be necessary is a question which only time will answer. What is certain is that we are moving toward power—the power to stop the machine if it cannot be made to serve humane ends.

American educators are fond of telling their students that barricades are part of the romantic past, that social change today can only come about through the processes of negotiation. But the students at Columbia discovered that barricades are only the beginning of what they call "bringing the war home."

CHAPTER 24

Black Liberation: Martin Luther King and Stokely Carmichael

No issue has cut so deeply into the American consciousness as that of the status of the black man in American society. Martin Luther King was the first great leader of the modern movement for black liberation. Through his actions as well as his writings, he helped give form and eloquence to the civil rights movement of the 1950's and 1960's. His belief in nonviolence, sorely tried in the last years before his assassination, is eloquently expressed in its most revolutionary form in his "Letter From a Birmingham Jail." Most notable of his many other books are *Why We Can't Wait* (1964) and *Stride Toward Freedom* (1962).

As the black power movement began to compete for prominence with King's nonviolent emphasis, Stokely Carmichael rose to leadership. In a sense falling heir to the black nationalist spirit that was unquenched by the premature death of Malcolm X, Carmichael served as executive director of the Student Nonviolent Coordinating Committee for a time and then struck out on his own. His book *Black Power: The Politics of Liberation in America* (written in collaboration with Charles V. Hamilton) is the fullest single statement of the black power analysis and prescription. The essay reprinted here is an earlier statement of the same argument.

Martin Luther King, Jr.

Letter From Birmingham Jail*

April 16, 1963

My Dear Fellow Clergymen:

While confined here in the Birmingham city jail, I came across your recent statement calling my present activities "unwise and untimely." Seldom do I pause to answer criticism of my work and ideas. If I sought to answer all the criticisms that cross my desk, my secretaries would have little time for anything other than such correspondence in the course of the day, and I would have no time for constructive work. But since I feel that you are men of genuine good will and that your criticisms are sincerely set forth, I want to try to answer your statement in what I hope will be patient and reasonable terms. I think I should indicate why I am here in Birmingham, since you have been influenced by the view which argues against "outsiders coming in." I have the honor of serving as president of the Southern Christian Leadership Conference, an organization operating in every southern state, with headquarters in Atlanta, Georgia. We have some eighty-five affiliated organizations across the South, for Human

* *Author's Note.* This response to a published statement by eight fellow clergymen from Alabama (Bishop C. C. J. Carpenter, Bishop Joseph A. Durick, Rabbi Hilton L. Grafman, Bishop Paul Hardin, Bishop Holan B. Harmon, the Reverend George M. Murray, the Reverend Edward V. Ramage and the Reverend Earl Stallings) was composed under somewhat constricting circumstances. Begun on the margins of the newspaper in which the statement appeared while I was in jail, the letter was continued on scraps of writing paper supplied by a friendly Negro trusty, and concluded on a pad my attorneys were eventually permitted to leave me. Although the text remains in substance unaltered, I have indulged in the author's prerogative of polishing it for publication.

Rights. Frequently we share staff, educational and financial resources with our affiliates. Several months ago the affiliate here in Birmingham asked us to be on call to engage in a nonviolent direct-action program if such were deemed necessary. We readily consented, and when the hour came we lived up to our promise. So I, along with several members of my staff, am here because I was invited here. I am here because I have organizational ties here.

But more basically, I am in Birmingham because injustice is here. Just as the prophets of the eighth century B.C. left their villages and carried their "thus saith the Lord" far beyond the boundaries of their home towns, and just as the Apostle Paul left his village of Tarsus and carried the gospel of Jesus Christ to the far corners of the Greco-Roman world, so am I compelled to carry the gospel of freedom beyond my own home town. Like Paul, I must constantly respond to the Macedonian call for aid.

Moreover, I am cognizant of the interrelatedness of all communities and states. I cannot sit idly by in Atlanta and not be concerned about what happens in Birmingham. Injustice anywhere is a threat to justice everywhere. We are caught in an inescapable network of mutuality, tied in a single garment of destiny. Whatever affects one directly, affects all indirectly. Never again can we afford to live with the narrow, provincial "outside agitator" idea. Anyone who lives inside the United States can never be considered an outsider anywhere within its bounds.

You deplore the demonstrations taking place in Birmingham. But your statement, I am sorry to say, fails to express a similar concern for the conditions that brought about the demonstrations. I am sure that none of you would want to rest content with the superficial kind of social analysis that deals merely with effects and does not grapple with underlying causes. It is unfortunate that demonstrations are taking place in Birmingham, but it is even more unfortunate that the city's white power structure left the Negro community with no alternative.

In any nonviolent campaign there are four basic steps: collection of the facts to determine whether injustices exist; negotiation; self-purification; and direct action. We have gone through all these steps in Birmingham. There can be no gainsaying the fact that racial injustice engulfs this community. Birmingham is probably the most thoroughly segregated city in the United States. Its ugly record of brutality is widely known. Negroes have experienced grossly unjust treatment in the courts. There have been more unsolved bombings of Negro homes and churches in Birmingham than in any other city in the nation. These are the hard, brutal facts of the case. On the basis of these conditions, Negro leaders sought to negotiate with the city fathers. But the latter consistently refused to engage in good-faith negotiation.

Then, last September, came the opportunity to talk with leaders of Birmingham's economic community. In the course of the negotiations, certain promises were made by the merchants—for example, to remove the stores' humiliating racial signs. On the basis of these promises, the Reverend Fred Shuttlesworth and the leaders of the Alabama Christian Movement for Human Rights agreed to a moratorium on all demonstrations. As the weeks and months went by, we realized that we were the victims of a broken promise. A few signs, briefly removed, returned; the others remained.

As in so many past experiences, our hopes had been blasted, and the shadow of deep disappointment settled upon us. We had no alternative except to prepare for direct action, whereby we would present our very bodies as a means of laying our case before the conscience of the local and the national community. Mindful of the difficulties involved, we decided to undertake a process of self-purification. We began a series of workshops on nonviolence, and we repeatedly asked ourselves: "Are you able to accept blows without retaliating?" "Are you able to endure the ordeal of jail?" We decided to schedule our direct-action program for the Easter season, realizing that except for Christmas, this is the main shopping period of the year. Knowing that a strong economic-withdrawal program would be the by-product of direct action, we felt that this would be the best time to bring pressure to bear on the merchants for the needed change.

Then it occurred to us that Birmingham's mayoralty election was coming up in March, and we speedily decided to postpone action until after election day. When we discovered that the Commissioner of Public Safety, Eugene "Bull" Connor, had piled up enough votes to be in the run-off, we decided again to postpone action until the day after the run-off so that the demonstrations could not be used to cloud the issues. Like many others, we waited to see Mr. Connor defeated, and to this end we endured postponement after postponement. Having aided in this community need, we felt that our direct-action program could be delayed no longer.

You may well ask: "Why direct action? Why sit-ins, marches and so forth? Isn't negotiations a better path?" You are quite right in calling for negotiation. Indeed, this is the very purpose of direct action. Nonviolent direct action seeks to create such a crisis and foster such a tension that a community which has constantly refused to negotiate is forced to confront the issue. It seeks so to dramatize the issue that it can no longer be ignored. My citing the creation of tension as part of the work of the nonviolent-resister may sound rather shocking. But I must confess that I am not afraid of the word "tension." I have earnestly opposed violent tension, but there is a type of constructive, non-violent tension which is necessary for growth. Just as Socrates felt that it was necessary to create a tension in the mind so that individuals could rise from the bondage of myths and half-truths to the unfettered realm of creative analysis and objective appraisal, so must we see the need for nonviolent gadflies to create the kind of tension in society that will help men rise from the dark depths of prejudice and racism to the majestic heights of understanding and brotherhood.

The purpose of our direct-action program is to create a situation so crisis-packed that it will inevitably open the door to negotiation. I therefore concur with you in your call for negotiation. Too long has our beloved Southland been bogged down in a tragic effort to live in monologue rather than dialogue.

One of the basic points in your statement is that the action that I and my associates have taken in Birmingham is untimely. Some have asked: "Why didn't you give the new city administration time to act?" The only answer that I can give to this query is that the new Birmingham administration must be prodded about as much as the outgoing one, before it will act. We are sadly mistaken if we feel that the election of Albert Boutwell as mayor will bring the millennium to Birmingham. While Mr. Boutwell is a much more gentle person than Mr. Connor, they are both segregationists, dedicated to maintenance of the status quo. I have hope that Mr. Boutwell will be reasonable enough to see the futility of massive resistance to desegregation. But he will not see this without pressure from devotees of civil rights. My friends, I must say to you that we have not made a single gain in civil rights without determined legal and nonviolent pressure. Lamentably, it is an historical fact that privileged groups seldom give up their privileges voluntarily. Individuals may see the moral light and voluntarily give up their unjust posture; but, as Reinhold

Niebuhr has reminded us, groups tend to be more immoral than individuals.

We know through painful experience that freedom is never voluntarily given by the oppressor; it must be demanded by the oppressed. Frankly, I have yet to engage in a direct-action campaign that was "well timed" in the view of those who have not suffered unduly from the disease of segregation. For years now I have heard the word "Wait!" It rings in the ear of every Negro with piercing familiarity. This "Wait" has almost always meant "Never." We must come to see, with one of our distinguished jurists, that "justice too long delayed is justice denied."

We have waited for more than 340 years for our constitutional and God-given rights. The nations of Asia and Africa are moving with jetlike speed toward gaining political independence, but we still creep at horse-and-buggy pace toward gaining a cup of coffee at a lunch counter. Perhaps it is easy for those who have never felt the stinging darts of segregation to say, "Wait." But when you have seen vicious mobs lynch your mothers and fathers at will and drown your sisters and brothers at whim; when you have seen hate-filled policemen curse, kick and even kill your black brothers and sisters; when you see the vast majority of your twenty million Negro brothers smothering in an airtight cage of poverty in the midst of an affluent society; when you suddenly find your tongue twisted and your speech stammering as you seek to explain to your six-year-old daughter why she can't go to the public amusement park that has just been advertised on television, and see tears welling up in her eyes when she is told that Funtown is closed to colored children, and see ominous clouds of inferiority beginning to form in her little mental sky, and see her beginning to distort her personality by developing an unconscious bitterness toward white people; when you have to concoct an answer for a five-year-old son who is asking: "Daddy, why do white people treat colored people so mean?"; when you take a cross-country drive and find it necessary to sleep night after night in the uncomfortable corners of your automobile because no motel will accept you; when you are humiliated day in and day out by nagging signs reading "white" and "colored"; when your first names becomes "nigger," your middle name becomes "boy" (however old you are) and your last name becomes "John," and your wife and mother are never given the respected title "Mrs."; when you are harried by day and haunted by night by the fact that you are a Negro, living constantly at tiptoe stance, never quite knowing what to expect next, and are plagued with inner fears and outer resentments; when you are forever fighting a degenerating sense of "nobodiness"—then you will understand why we find it difficult to wait. There comes a time when the cup of endurance runs over, and men are no longer willing to be plunged into the abyss of despair. I hope, sirs, you can understand our legitimate and unavoidable impatience.

You express a great deal of anxiety over our willingness to break laws. This is certainly a legitimate concern. Since we so diligently urge people to obey the Supreme Court's decision of 1954 outlawing segregation in the public schools, at first glance it may seem rather paradoxical for us consciously to break laws. One may well ask: "How can you advocate breaking some laws and obeying others?" The answer lies in the fact that there are two types of laws: just and unjust. I would be the first to advocate obeying just laws. One has not only a legal but a moral responsibility to obey just laws. Conversely, one has a moral responsibility to disobey unjust laws. I would agree with St. Augustine that "an unjust law is no law at all."

Now, what is the difference between the two? How does one determine whether a law is just or unjust? A just law is a man-made code that squares with the moral law or the law of God. An unjust law is a code that is out of harmony with the moral law. To put it in the terms of St. Thomas Aquinas: An unjust law is a human law that is not rooted in eternal law and natural law. Any law that uplifts human personality is just. Any law that degrades human personality is unjust. All segregation statutes are unjust because segregation distorts the soul and damages the personality. It gives the segregator a false sense of superiority and the segregated a false sense of inferiority. Segregation, to use the terminology of the Jewish philosopher Martin Buber, substitutes an "I-it" relationship for the "I-thou" relationship and ends up relegating persons to the status of things. Hence segregation is not only politically, economically and sociologically unsound, it is morally wrong and sinful. Paul Tillich has said that sin is separation. Is not segregation an existential expression of man's tragic separation, his awful estrangement, his terrible sinfulness? Thus it is that I can urge men to obey the 1954 decision of the Supreme Court, for it is morally right; and I can urge them to disobey segregation ordinances, for they are morally wrong.

Let us consider a more concrete example of just and unjust laws. An unjust law is a code that a numerical or power majority group compels a minority group to obey but does not make binding on itself. This is *difference* made legal. By the same token, a just law is a code that a majority compels a minority to follow and that it is willing to follow itself. This is *sameness* made legal.

Let me give another explanation. A law is unjust if it is inflicted on a minority that, as a result of being denied the right to vote, had no part in enacting or devising the law. Who can say that the legislature of Alabama which set up that state's segregation laws was democratically elected? Throughout Alabama all sorts of devious methods are used to prevent Negroes from becoming registered voters, and there are some counties in which, even though Negroes constitute a majority of the population, not a single Negro is registered. Can any law enacted under such circumstances be considered democratically structured?

Sometimes a law is just on its face and unjust in its application. For instance, I have been arrested on a charge of parading without a permit. Now, there is nothing wrong in having an ordinance which requires a permit for a parade. But such an ordinance becomes unjust when it is used to maintain segregation and to deny citizens the First-Amendment privilege of peaceful assembly and protest.

I hope you are able to see the distinction I am trying to point out. In no sense do I advocate evading or defying the law, as would the rabid segregationist. That would lead to anarchy. One who breaks an unjust law must do so openly, lovingly, and with a willingness to accept the penalty. I submit that an individual who breaks a law that conscience tells him is unjust, and who willingly accepts the penalty of imprisonment in order to arouse the conscience of the community over its injustice, is in reality expressing the highest respect for law.

Of course, there is nothing new about this kind of civil disobedience. It was evidence sublimely in the refusal of Shadrach, Meshach and Abednego to obey the laws of Nebuchadnezzar, on the ground that a higher moral law was at stake. It was practiced superbly by the early Christians, who were willing to face hungry lions and the excruciating pain of chopping blocks rather than submit to certain unjust laws of the Roman Empire. To a degree, academic freedom is a reality today because Socrates practiced civil disobedience. In our own nation, the Boston Tea Party represented a massive act of civil disobedience.

We should never forget that everything Adolf Hitler did in Germany was "legal" and everything the Hungarian

freedom fighters did in Hungary was "illegal." It was "illegal" to aid and comfort a Jew in Hitler's Germany. Even so, I am sure that, had I lived in Germany at the time, I would have aided and comforted my Jewish brothers. If today I lived in a Communist country where certain principles dear to the Christian faith are suppressed, I would openly advocate disobeying that country's antireligious laws.

I must make two honest confessions to you, My Christian and Jewish borthers. First, I must confess that over the past few years I have been gravely disappointed with the white moderate. I have almost reached the regrettable conclusion that the Negro's great stumbling block in his strike toward freedom is not the White Citizen's Counciler or the Ku Klux Klanner, but the white moderate, who is more devoted to "order" than to justice; who prefers a negative peace which is the absence of tension to a positive peace which is the presence of justice; who constantly says: "I agree with you in the goal you seek, but I cannot agree with your methods of direct action"; who paternalistically believes he can set the timetable for another man's freedom; who lives by a mythical concept of time and who constantly advises the Negro to wait for a "more convenient season." Shallow understanding from people of good will is more frustrating than absolute misunderstanding from people of ill will. Lukewarm acceptance is much more bewildering than outright rejection.

I had hoped that the white moderate would understand that law and order exist for the purpose of establishing justice and that when they fail in this purpose they become the dangerously structured dams that block the flow of social progress. I had hoped that the white moderate would understand that the present tension in the South is a necessary phase of the transition from an obnoxious negative peace, in which the Negro passively accepted his unjust plight, to a substantive and positive peace, in which all men will respect the dignity and worth of human personality. Actually, we who engage in nonviolent direct action are not the creators of tension. We merely bring to the surface the hidden tension that is already alive. We bring it out in the open, where it can be seen and dealt with. Like a boil that can never be cured so long as it is covered up but must be opened with all its ugliness to the natural medicines of air and light, injustice must be exposed, with all the tension its exposure creates, to the light of human conscience and the air of national opinion before it can be cured.

In your statement you assert that our actions, even though peaceful, must be condemned because they precipitate violence. But is this a logical assertion? Isn't this like condemning a robbed man because his possession of money precipitated the evil act of robbery? Isn't this like condemning Socrates because his unswerving commitment to truth and his philosophical inquiries precipitated the act by the misguided populace in which they made him drink hemlock? Isn't this like condemning Jesus because his unique God-consciousness and never-ceasing devotion to God's will precipitated the evil act of crucifixion? We must come to see that, as the federal courts have consistently affirmed, it is wrong to urge an individual to cease his efforts to gain his basic constitutional rights because the quest may precipitate violence. Society must protect the robbed and punish the robber.

I had also hoped that the white moderate would reject the myth concerning time in relation to the struggle for freedom. I have just received a letter from a white brother in Texas. He writes: "All Christians know that the colored people will receive equal rights eventually, but it is possible that you are in too great a religious hurry. It has taken Christianity almost two thousand years to accomplish what it has. The teachings of Christ take time to come to earth." Such an attitude stems from a tragic misconception of time, from the strangely irrational notion that there is something in the very

flow of time that will inevitably cure all ills. Actually, time itself is neutral; it can be used either destructively or constructively. More and more I feel that the people of ill will have used time much more effectively than have the people of good will. We will have to repent in this generation not merely for the hateful words and actions of the bad people but for the appalling silence of the good people. Human progress never rolls in on wheels of inevitability; it comes through the tireless efforts of men willing to be co-workers with God, and without this hard work, time itself becomes an ally of the forces of social stagnation. We must use time creatively, in the knowledge that the time is always ripe to do right. Now is the time to make real the promise of democracy and transform our pending national elegy into a creative psalm of brotherhood. Now is the time to lift our national policy from the quicksand of racial injustice to the solid rock of human dignity.

You speak of our activity in Birmingham as extreme. At first I was rather disappointed that fellow clergymen would see my nonviolent efforts as those of an extremist. I began thinking about the fact that I stand in the middle of two opposing forces in the Negro community. One is a force of complacency, made up in part of Negroes who, as a result of long years of oppression, are so drained of self-respect and a sense of "somebodiness" that they have adjusted to segregation; and in part of a few middleclass Negroes who, because of a degree of academic and economic security and because in some ways they profit by segregation, have become insensitive to the problems of the masses. The other force is one of bitterness and hatred, and it comes perilously close to advocating violence. It is expressed in the various black nationalist groups that are springing up across the nation, the largest and best-known being Elijah Muhammad's Muslin movement. Nourished by the Negro's frustration over the continued existence of racial discrimination, this movement is made up of people who have lost faith in America, who have absolutely repudiated Christianity, and who have concluded that the white man is an incorrigible "devil."

I have tried to stand between these two forces, saying that we need emulate neither the "do-nothingism" of the complacent nor the hatred and despair of the black nationalist. For there is the more excellent way of love and nonviolent protest. I am grateful to God that, through the influence of the Negro church, the way of nonviolence became an integral part of our struggle.

If this philosophy had not emerged, by now many streets of the South would, I am convinced, be flowing with blood. And I am further convinced that if our white brothers dismiss as "rabble-rousers" and "outside agitators" those of us who employ nonviolent direct action, and if they refuse to support our nonviolent efforts, millions of Negroes will, out of frustration and despair, seek solace and security in black-nationalist ideologies—a development that would inevitably lead to a frightening racial nightmare.

Oppressed people cannot remain oppressed forever. The yearning for freedom eventually manifests itself, and that is what has happened to the American Negro. Something within has reminded him of his birthright of freedom, and something without has reminded him that it can be gained. Consciously, or unconsciously, he has been caught up by the *Zeitgeist,* and with his black brothers of Africa and his brown and yellow brothers of Asia, South America and the Caribbean, the United States Negro is moving with a sense of great urgency toward the promised land of racial justice. If one recognizes this vital urge that has engulfed the Negro community, one should readily understand why public demonstrations are taking place. The Negro has many pent-up resentments and latent frustrations, and he must release them. So let him march; let him make prayer pilgrimages to the city hall; let him go on freedom rides—and try to

understand why he must do so. If his repressed emotions are not released in nonviolent ways, they will seek expression through violence; this is not a threat but a fact of history. So I have not said to my people: "Get rid of your discontent." Rather, I have tried to say that this normal and healthy discontent can be channeled into the creative outlet of nonviolent direct action. And now this approach is being termed extremist.

But though I was initially disappointed at being categorized as an extremist, as I continued to think about the matter I gradually gained a measure of satisfaction from the label. Was not Jesus an extremist for love: "Love your enemies, bless them that curse you, do good to them that hate you, and pray for them which despitefully use you, and persecute you." Was not Amos an extremist for justice: "Let justice roll down like waters and righteousness like an ever-flowing stream." Was not Paul an extremist for the Christian gospel: "I bear in my body the marks of the Lord Jesus." Was not Martin Luther an extremist: "Here I stand; I cannot do otherwise, so help me God." And John Bunyan: "I will stay in jail to the end of my days before I make a butchery of my conscience." And Abraham Lincoln: "This nation cannot survive half slave and half free." And Thomas Jefferson: "We hold these truths to be self-evident, that all men are created equal. . ." So the question is not whether we will be extremists, but what kind of extremists we will be. Will we be extremists for hate or for love? Will we be extremists for the preservation of injustice or for the extension of justice? In that dramatic scene on Calvary's hill three men were crucified. We must never forget that all three were crucified for the same crime—the crime of extremism. Two were extremists for immorality, and thus fell below their environment. The other, Jesus Christ, was an extremist for love, truth and goodness, and thereby rose above his environment. Perhaps the South, the nation and the world are in dire need of creative extremists.

I had hoped that the white moderate would see this need. Perhaps I was too optimistic; perhaps I expected too much. I suppose I should have realized that few members of the oppressor race can understand the deep groans and passionate yearnings of the oppressed race, and still fewer have the vision to see that injustice must be rooted out by strong, persistent and determined action. I am thankful, however, that some of our white brothers in the South have grasped the meaning of this social revolution and committed themselves to it. They are still all too few in quantity, but they are big in quality. Some—such as Ralph McGill, Lillian Smith, Harry Golden, James McBride Dabbs, Ann Braden and Sarah Patton Boyle—have written about our struggle in eloquent and prophetic terms. Others have marched with us down nameless streets of the South. They have languished in filthy, roach-infested jails, suffering the abuse and brutality of policemen who view them as "dirty nigger-lovers." Unlike so many of their moderate brothers and sisters, they have recognized the urgency of the moment and sensed the need for powerful action" antidotes to combat the disease of segregation.

Let me take note of my other major disappointment. I have been so greatly disappointed with the white church and its leadership. Of course, there are some notable exceptions, I am not unmindful of the fact that each of you has taken some significant stands on this issue. I commend, you, Reverend Stallings, for your Christian stand on this past Sunday, in welcoming Negroes to your worship service on a nonsegregated basis. I commend the Catholic leaders of this state for integrating Spring Hill College several years ago.

But despite these notable exceptions, I must honestly reiterate that I have been disappointed with the church. I do not say this as one of those negative critics who can always find something wrong with the church. I say this as a minister of the gospel, who loves the church; who was nurtured in its bosom; who has been sustained by its spiritual blessings and who will remain true to it as long as the cord of life shall lengthen.

When I was suddenly catapulted into the leadership of the bus protest in Montgomery, Alabama, a few years ago, I felt we would be supported by the white church. I felt that the white ministers, priests and rabbis of the South would be among our strongest allies. Instead, some have been outright opponents, refusing to understand the freedom movement and misrepresenting its leaders; all too many others have been more cautious than courageous and have remained silent behind the anesthetizing security of stained-glass windows.

In spite of my shattered dreams, I came to Birmingham with the hope that the white religious leadership of this community would see the justice of our cause and, with deep moral concern, would serve as the channel through which our just grievances could reach the power structure. I had hoped that each of you would understand. But again I have been disappointed.

I have heard numerous southern religious leaders admonish their worshippers to comply with a desegregation decision because it is the law, but I have longed to hear white ministers declare: "Follow this decree because integration is morally right and because the Negro is your brother." In the midst of blatant injustices inflicted upon the Negro, I have watched white churchmen stand on the sideline and mouth pious irrelevancies and sanctimonious trivialities. In the midst of a mighty struggle to rid our nation of racial and economic injustice, I have heard many ministers say: "Those are social issues, with which the gospel has no real concern." And I have watched many churches commit themselves to a completely other-worldly religion which makes a strange, un-Biblical distinction between body and soul, between the sacred and the secular.

I have traveled the length and breadth of Alabama, Mississippi and all the other southern states. On sweltering summer days and crisp autumn mornings I have looked at the South's beautiful churches with their lofty spires pointing heavenward. I have beheld the impressive outlines of her massive religious-education buildings. Over and over I have found myself asking: What kind of people worship here? Who is their God? Where were their voices when the lips of Governor Barnett dripped with words of interposition and nullification? Where were they when Governor Wallace gave a clarion call for defiance and hatred? Where were their voices of support when bruised and weary Negro men and women decided to rise from the dark dungeons of complacency to the bright hills of creative protest?"

Yes, these questions are still in my mind. In deep disappointment I have wept over the laxity of the church. But be assured that my tears have been tears of love. There can be no deep disappointment where there is not deep love. Yes, I love the church. How could I do otherwise? I am in the rather unique position of being the son, the grandson and the great-grandson of preachers. Yes, I see the church as the body of Christ. But, oh! How we have blemished and scarred that body through social neglect and through fear of being nonconformists.

There was a time when the church was very powerful—in the time when the early Christians rejoiced at being deemed worthy to suffer for what they believed. In those days the church was not merely a thermometer that recorded the ideas and principles of popular opinion; it was a thermostat that transformed the mores of society. Whenever the early Christians entered a town, the people in power became disturbed and immediately sought to convict the Christians for being "disturbers of the peace" and "outside agitators." But the Christians pressed on, in the conviction that they were "a colony of heaven," called to obey God rather than man. Small in number, they were big in commitment. They were too God-intoxicated to be "astronomically intimidated." By their effort and example they brought an end

to such ancient evils as infanticide and gladiatorial contests.

Things are different now. So often the contemporary church is a weak, ineffectual voice with an uncertain sound. So often it is an archdefender of the status quo. Far from being disturbed by the presence of the church, the power structure of the average community is consoled by the church's silent—and often even vocal—sanction of things as they are.

But the judgment of God is upon the church as never before. If today's church does not recapture the sacrificial spirit of the early church, it will lose its authenticity, forfeit the loyalty of millions, and be dismissed as an irrelevant social club with no meaning for the twentieth century. Every day I meet young people whose disappointment with the church has turned into outright disgust.

Perhaps I have once again been too optimistic. Is organized religion too inextricably bound to the status quo to save our nation and the world? Perhaps I must turn my faith to the inner spiritual church, the church within the church, as the true *ekklesia* and the hope of the world. But again I am thankful to God that some noble souls from the ranks of organized religion have broken loose from the paralyzing chains of conformity and joined us as active partners in the struggle for freedom. They have left their secure congregations and walked the streets of Albany, Georgia, with us. They have gone down the highways of the South on tortuous rides for freedom. Yes, they have gone to jail with us. Some have been dismissed from their churches, have lost the support of their bishops and fellow ministers. But they have acted in the faith that right defeated is stronger than evil triumphant. Their witness has been the spiritual salt that has preserved the true meaning of the gospel in these troubled times. They have carved a tunnel of hope through the dark mountain of disappointment.

I hope the church as a whole will meet the challenge of this decisive hour. But even if the church does not come to the aid of justice, I have no despair about the future. I have no fear about the outcome of our struggle in Birmingham, even if our motives are at present misunderstood. We will reach the goal of freedom in Birmingham and all over the nation, because the goal of America is freedom. Abused and scorned though we may be, our destiny is tied up with America's destiny. Before the pilgrims landed at Plymouth, we were here. Before the pen of Jefferson etched the majestic words of the Declaration of Independence across the pages of history, we were here. For more than two centuries our forebears labored in this country without wages; they made cotton king; they built the homes of their masters while suffering gross injustice and shameful humiliation—and yet out of a bottomless vitality they continued to thrive and develop. If the inexpressible cruelties of slavery could not stop us, the opposition we now face will surely fail. We will win our freedom because the sacred heritage of our nation and the eternal will of God are embodied in our echoing demands.

Before closing I feel impelled to mention one other point in your statement that has troubled me profoundly. You warmly commended the Birmingham police force for keeping "order" and "preventing violence." I doubt that you would have so warmly commended the police force if you had seen its dogs sinking their teeth into unarmed, nonviolent Negroes. I doubt that you would so quickly commend the policemen if you were to observe their ugly and inhumane treatment of Negroes here in the city jail; if you were to watch them push and curse old Negro women and young Negro girls; if you were to see them slap and kick old Negro men and young boys; if you were to observe them, as they did on two occasions, refuse to give us food because we wanted to sing our grace together. I cannot join you in your praise of the Birmingham police department.

It is true that the police have exercised a degree of discipline in handling the demonstrators. In this sense they have conducted themselves rather "nonviolently" in public. But for what purpose? To preserve the evil system of segregation. Over the past few years I have consistently preached that nonviolence demands that the means we use must be as pure as the ends we seek. I have tried to make clear that it is wrong to use immoral means to attain moral ends. But now I must affirm that it is just as wrong, or perhaps even more so, to use moral means to preserve immoral ends. Perhaps Mr. Connor and his policemen have been rather nonviolent in public, as was Chief Pritchett in Albany, Georgia, but they have used the moral means of nonviolence to maintain the immoral end of racial injustice. As T. S. Eliot has said: "The last temptation is the greatest treason: To do the right deed for the wrong reason."

I wish you had commended the Negro sit-inners and demonstrators of Birmingham for their sublime courage, their willingness to suffer and their amazing discipline in the midst of great provocation. One day the South will recognize its real heroes. They will be the James Merediths, with the noble sense of purpose that enables them to face jeering and hostile mobs, and with the agonizing loneliness that characterizes the life of the pioneer. They will be old, oppressed, battered Negro women, symbolized in a seventy-two-year-old women in Montgomery, Alabama, who rose up with a sense of dignity and with her people decided not to ride segregated buses, and who responded with ungrammatical profundity to one who inquired about her weariness: "My feets is tired, but my soul is at rest." They will be the young high school and college students, the young ministers of the gospel and a host of their elders, courageously and nonviolently sitting in at lunch counters and willingly going to jail for conscience' sake. One day the South will know that when these disinherited children of God sat down at lunch counters, they were in reality standing up for what is best in the American dream and for the most sacred values in our Judaeo-Christian heritage, thereby bringing our nation back to those great wells of democracy which were dug deep by the founding fathers in their formulation of the Constitution and the Declaration of Independence.

Never before have I written so long a letter. I'm afraid it is much too long to take your precious time. I can assure you that it would have been much shorter if I had been writing from a comfortable desk, but what else can one do when he is alone in a narrow jail cell, other than write long letters, think long thoughts and pray long prayers?

If I have said anything in this letter that overstates the truth and indicates an unreasonable impatience, I beg you to forgive me. If I have said anything that understates the truth and indicates my having a patience that allows me to settle for anything less than brotherhood, I beg God to forgive me.

I hope this letter finds you strong in the faith. I also hope that circumstances will soon make it possible for me to meet each of you, not as an integrationist or a civil-rights leader but as fellow clergyman and a Christian brother. Let us all hope that the dark clouds of racial prejudice will soon pass away and the deep fog of misunderstanding will be lifted from our fear-drenched communities, and in some not too distant tomorrow the radiant stars of love and brotherhood will shine over our great nation with all their scintillating beauty.

Yours for the cause of Peace and Brotherhood,

Martin Luther King, Jr.

WORKS BY MARTIN LUTHER KING, JR.

King, Martin Luther, Jr. *The Measure of a Man.* Philadelphia: Christian Education Press, 1959.

————. *Strength to Love.* New York: Harper and Row, 1963.

————. *Strike Toward Freedom.* New York: Congress of Racial Equality, 1957.

————. *Where Do We Go from Here: Chaos or Community?* New York: Harper and Row, 1967.

————. *Why We Can't Wait.* New York: Harper and Row, 1967.

Stokely Carmichael

Toward Black Liberation

One of the most pointed illustrations of the need for Black Power, as a positive and redemptive force in a society degenerating into a form of totalitarianism, is to be made by examining the history of distortion that the concept has

SOURCE. From *The Massachusetts Review,* Autumn 1966. Reprinted by permission of The Massachusetts Review, Amherst, Mass.

received in national media of pubicity. In this "debate," as in everything else that affects our lives, Negroes are dependent on, and at the discretion of, forces and institutions within the white society which have little interest in representing us honestly. Our experience with the national press has been that where they have managed to escape a meretricious special interest in "Git Whitey" sensationalism and race-war mongering, individual reporters and commentators have been conditioned by the enveloping racism of the society to the point where they are incapable even of objective observation and reporting of racial *incidents,* much less the analysis of *ideas.* But this limitation of vision and perceptions is an inevitable consequence of the dictatorship of definition, interpretation and consciousness, along with the censorship of history that the society has inflicted upon the Negro—and itself.

Our concern for black power addresses itself directly to this problem, the necessity to reclaim our history and our identity from the cultural terrorism and depredation of self-justifying white guilt.

To do this we shall have to struggle for the right to create our own terms through which to define ourselves and our relationship to the society, and to have these terms recognized. This is the first necessity for a free people, and the first right that any oppressor must suspend. The white fathers of American racism knew this—instinctively it seems—as is indicated by the continuous record of the distinction and omission in their dealings with the red and black men. In the same way that southern apologists for the "Jim Crow" society have so obscured, muddied and misrepresented the record of the reconstruction period, until it is almost impossible to tell what really happened, their contemporary counterparts are busy doing the same thing with the recent history of the civil rights movement.

In 1964, for example, the National Democratic Party, led by L. B. Johnson and Hubert H. Humphrey, cynically undermined the efforts of Mississippi's Black population to achieve some degree of political representation. Yet, whenever the events of that convention are recalled by the press, one sees only that version fabricated by the press agents of the Democratic Party. A year later the House of Representatives in an even more vulgar display of political racism made a mockery of the political rights of Mississippi's Negroes when it failed to unseat the Mississippi Delegation to the House which had been elected through a process which methodically and systematically excluded over 450,000 voting-age Negroes, almost one half of the total electorate of the state. Whenever this event is mentioned in print it is in terms which leaves one with the rather curious impression that somehow the oppressed Negro people of Mississippi are at fault for confronting the Congress with a situation in which they had no alternative but to endorse Mississippi's racist political practices.

I mention these two examples because, having been directly involved in them, I can see very clearly the discrepancies between what happened, and the versions that are finding their way into general acceptance as a kind of popular mythology. Thus the victimization of the Negro takes place in two phases—first it occurs in fact and deed, then, and this is equally sinister, in the official recording of those facts.

The "Black Power" program and concept which is being articulated by SNCC, CORE, and a host of community organizations in the ghettoes of the North and South has not escaped that process. The white press has been busy articulating their own analyses, their own interpretations, and criticisms of their own creations. For example, while the press had given wide and sensational dissemination to attacks made by figures in the Civil Rights movement—foremost among which are Roy Wilkins of the NAACP and Whitney Young of the Urban League—and to the hysterical ranting about black racism made by the political chameleon that now serves as Vice-President, it has generally failed to give accounts of the reasonable and productive dialouge which is taking place in the Negro community, and in certain important areas in the white religious and intellectual community. A national committee of influential Negro Churchmen affiliated with the National Council of Churches, despite their obvious respectability and responsibility, had to resort to a paid advertisment to articulate their position, while anyone shouting the hysterical yappings of "Black Racism" got ample space. Thus the American people have gotten at best a superficial and misleading account of the very terms and tenor of this debate. I wish to quote briefly from the statement by the national committee of Churchmen which I suspect that the majority of Americans will not have seen. This statement appeared in the *New York Times* of July 31, 1966.

We an informal group of Negro Churchmen in America are deeply disturbed about the crisis brought upon our country by historic distortions of important human realities in the controversy about "black power." What we see shining through the variety of rhetoric is not anything new but the same old problem of power and race which has faced our beloved country since 1619.

. . . The conscience of black men is corrupted because, having no power to implement the demands of conscience, the concern for justice in the absence of justice becomes a chaotic self-surrender. Powerlessness breeds a race of beggars. We are faced now with a situation where powerless conscience meets conscience-less power, threatening the very foundations of our Nation.

. . . We deplore the overviolence of riots, but we feel it is more important to focus on the real sources of these eruptions. These sources may be abetted inside the Ghetto, but their basic cause lies in the silent and covert violence which white middleclass America inflicts upon the victims of the inner city.

. . . In short; the failure of American leaders to use American power to create equal opportunities *in life* as well as *law,* this is the real problem and not the anguished cry for black power.

. . . Without the capacity to *participate with power, i.e.,* to have some organized political and economic strength to really influence people with whom one interacts—integration is not meaningful.

. . . America has asked its Negro citizens to fight for opportunity as *individuals,* whereas at certain points in our history what we have needed most has been opportunity for the *whole group,* not just for selected and approved *Negroes.*

. . . We must not apologize for the existence of this form of group power, for we have been oppressed as a group and not as individuals. We will not find our way out of that oppression until both we and America accept the need for Negro Americans, as well as for Jews, Italians, Poles, and while Anglosaxon Protestants, among others to have and to wield group power.

Traditionally, for each new ethnic group, the route to social and political integration into America's pluralistic society, has been through the organization of their own institutions with which to represent their communal needs within the larger society. This is simply stating what the advocates of black power are saying. The strident outcry, *particularly* from the liberal community, that has been evoked by this proposal can only be understood by examining the historic relationship between Negro and White power in this country.

Negroes are defined by two forces, their blackness and their powerlessness. There have been traditionally two communities in America. The White community, which controlled and defined the forms that all institutions with the society would take, and the Negro community which has been excluded from participation in the power decisions that shaped the society, and has traditionally been dependent upon, and subservient to the White community.

This has not been accidental. The history of every institution of this society indicates that a major concern in the ordering and structuring of the society has been the maintaining of the Negro community in its condition of dependence and oppression. This has not been on the level of individual acts of discrimination between individual whites against individual Negroes, but as total acts by the White community against the Negro community. This fact cannot be too strongly emphasized—that racist assumptions of white superiority have been so deeply ingrained in the structure of the society that is infuses its entire functioning, and is so much a part of the national subconscious that it is taken for granted and is frequently not even recognized.

Let me give an example of the difference between individual racism and institutionalized racism, and the society's response to both. When unidentified white terrorists bomb a Negro Church and kill five children, that is an act of individual racism, widely deplored by most segments of the society. But when in that same city, Birmingham, Alabama, not five but 500 Negro babies die each year because of a lack of proper food, shelter and medical facilities, and thousands more are destroyed and maimed physically, emotionally and intellectually because of conditions of poverty and deprivation in the ghetto, that is a function of institutionalized racism. But the society either pretends it doesn't know of this situation, or is incapable of doing anything meaningful about it. And this resistance to doing anything meaningful about conditions in that ghetto comes from the fact that the ghetto is itself a product of a combination of forces and special interests in the white community, and the groups that have access to the resources and power to change that situation benefit, politically and economically, from the existence of that ghetto.

It is more than a figure of speech to say that the Negro community in America is the victim of white imperialism and colonial exploitation. This is in practical economic and political terms true. There are over 20 million black people comprising ten percent of this nation. They for the most part live in well-defined areas of the country—in the shanty-towns and rural black belt areas of the South, and increasingly in the slums of northern and western industrial cities. If one goes into any Negro community, whether it be in Jackson, Miss., Cambridge, Md. or Harlem, N.Y., one will find that the same combination of political, economic, and social forces are at work. The people in the Negro community do not control the resources of that community, its political decisions, its law enforcement, its housing standards; and even the physical ownership of the land, houses, and stores lie *outside that community.*

It is white power that makes the laws, and it is violent white power in the form of armed white cops that enforces those laws with guns and nightsticks. The vast majority of Negroes in this country live in these captive communities and must endure these conditions of oppression because, and only because, *they are black and powerless.* I do not suppose that at any point the men who control the power and resources of this country ever sat down and designed these black enclaves, and formally articulated the terms of their colonial and dependent status, as was done, for example, by the Apartheid government of South Africa. Yet, one can not distinguish between one ghetto and another. As one moves from city to city it is as though some malignant racist planning-unit had done precisely this—designed each one from the same master blueprint. And indeed, if the ghetto had been formally and deliberately planned, instead of growing spontaneously and inevitably from the racist functioning of the various institutions that combine to make the society, it would be somehow less frightening. The situation would be less frightening because, if these ghettoes were the result of design and conspiracy, one could understand their similarity as being artificial and consciously imposed, rather than the result of identical patterns of white racism which repeat themselves in cities as distant as Boston and Birmingham. Without bothering to list the historic factors which contribute to this pattern—economic exploitation, political impotence, discrimination in employment and education—one can see that to correct this pattern will require far-reaching changes in the basic power-relationships and the ingrained social patterns within the society. The question is, of course, what kinds of changes are necessary, and how is it possible to bring them about?

In recent years the answer to these questions which has been given by most articulate groups of Negroes and their white allies, the "liberals" of all stripes, has been in terms of something called "integration." According to the advocates of integration, social justice will be accomplished by "integrating the Negro into the mainstream institutions of the society from which he has been traditionally excluded." It is very significant that each time I have heard this formulation it has been in terms of "the Negro," the individual Negro, rather than in terms of the community.

This concept of integration had to be based on the assumption that there was nothing of value in the Negro community and that little of value could be created among Negroes, so the thing to do was to siphon off the "acceptable" Negroes into the surrounding middle-class white community. Thus the goal of the movement for integration was simply to loosen up the restrictions barring the entry of Negroes into the white community. Goals around which the struggle took place, such as public accommodation, open housing, job opportunity on the executive level (which is easier to deal with than the problem of semi-skilled and blue jobs which involve more far-reaching economic adjustments), are quite simply middle-class goals, articulated by a tiny group of Negroes who had middle-class aspirations. It is true that the student demonstrations in the South during the early sixties, out of which SNCC came, had a similar orientation. But while it is hardly a concern of a black sharecropper, dishwasher, or welfare recipient whether a certain fifteen-dollar-a-day motel offers accommodations to Negroes, the overt symbols of white superiority and the imposed limitations on the Negro community had to be destroyed. Now, black people must look beyond these goals, to the issue of collective power.

Such a limited class orientation was reflected not only in the program and goals of the civil rights movement, but in its tactics and organization. It is very significant that the two oldest and most "respectable" civil rights organizations have constitutions which *specifically* pro-

hibit partisan political activity. CORE once did, but changed that clause when it changed its orientation toward black power. But this is perfectly understandable in terms of the strategy and goals of the older organizations. The civil rights movement saw its role as a kind of liaison between the powerful white community and the dependent Negro one. The dependent status of the black community apparently was unimportant since—if the movement were successful—it was going to blend into the white community anyway. We made no pretense of organizing and developing institutions of community power in the Negro community, but appealed to the conscience of white institutions of power. The posture of the civil rights movement was that of the dependent, the suppliant. The theory was that without attempting to create any organized base of political strength itself, the civil rights movement could, by forming coalitions with various "liberal" pressure organizations in the white community—liberal reform clubs, labor unions, church groups, progressive civic groups—and at time one or other of the major political parties—influence national legislation and national social patterns.

I think we all have seen the limitations of this approach. We have repeatedly seen that political alliances based on appeals to conscience and decency are chancy things, simply because institutions and political organizations have no consciences outside their own special interests. The political and social rights of Negroes have been and always will be negotiable and expendable the moment they conflict with the interests of our "allies." If we do not learn from history, we are doomed to repeat it, and that is precisely the lesson of the Reconstruction. Black people were allowed to register, vote and participate in politics because it was to the advantage of powerful white allies to promote this. But this was the result of white decision, and it was ended by other white men's decision before any political base powerful enough to challenge that decision could be established in the southern Negro community. (Thus at this point in the struggle Negroes have no assurance—save a kind of idiot optimism and faith in a society whose history is one of racism—that if it were to become necessary, even the painfully limited gains thrown to the civil rights movement by the Congress will not be revoked as soon as a shift in political sentiments should occur.)

The major limitation of this approach was that it tended to maintain the traditional dependence of Negroes, and of the movement. We depended upon the good-will and support of various groups within the white community whose interests were not always compatible with ours. To the extent that we depended on the financial support of other groups, we were vulnerable to their influence and domination.

Also the program that evolved out of this coalition was really limited and inadequate in the long term and one which affected only a small select group of Negroes. Its goal was to make the white community accessible to "qualified" Negroes and presumably each year a few more Negroes armed with their passport—a couple of university degrees—would escape into middle-class America and adopt the attitudes and life styles of that group; and one day the Harlems and the Watts would stand empty, a tribute to the success of integration. This is simply neither realistic nor particularly desirable. You can integrate communities, but you assimilate individuals. Even if such a program were possible its result would be, not to develop the black community as a functional and honorable segment of the total society, with its own cultural identity, life patterns, and institutions, but to abolish it—the final solution to the Negro problem. Marx said that the working class is the first class in history that ever wanted to abolish itself. If one listens to some of our "moderate" Negro leaders it appears that the American Negro is the first race that ever wished to abolish itself. The fact is that

what must be abolished is not the black community, but the dependent colonial status that has been inflicted upon it. The racial and cultural personality of the black community must be preserved and the community must win its freedom while preserving its cultural integrity. This is the essential difference between integration as it is currently practised and the concept of black power.

What has the movement for integration accomplished to date? The Negro graduating from M.I.T. with a doctorate will have better job opportunities available to him than to Lynda Bird Johnson. But the rate of unemployment in the Negro community is steadily increasing, while that in the white community decreases. More educated Negros hold executive jobs in major corporations and federal agencies than ever before, but the gap between white income and Negro income has almost doubled in the last twenty years. More suburban housing is available to Negroes, but housing conditions in the ghetto are steadily declining. While the infant mortality rate of New York City is at its lowest rate ever in the city's history, the infant mortality rate of Harlem is steadily climbing. There has been an organized national resistance to the Supreme Court's order to integrate the schools, and the federal government has not acted to enforce that order. Less than fifteen percent of black children in the South attend integrated schools; and Negro schools, which the vast mamority of black children still attend, are increasingly decrepit, overcrowded, under-staffed, inadequately equipped and funded.

This explains why the rate of school dropouts is increasing among Negro teenagers, who then express their bitterness, hopelessness, and alienation by the only means they have—rebellion. As long as people in the ghettoes of our large cities feel that they are victims of the misuse of white power without any way to have their needs represented—and these are frequently simple needs:

to get the welfare inspectors to stop kicking down your doors in the middle of the night, the cops from beating your children, the landlord to exterminate the vermin in your home, the city to collect your garbage—we will continue to have riots. These are not the products of "black power," but of the absence of any organization capable of giving the community the power, the black power, to deal with its problems.

SNCC proposes that it is now time for the black freedom movement to stop pandering to the fears and anxieties of the white middle class in the attempt to earn its "good-will," and to return to the ghetto to organize these communities to control themselves. This organization must be attempted in northern and southern urban areas as well as in the rural black belt counties of the South. The chief antagonist to this organization is, in the South, the overtly racist Democrat party, and in the North the equally corrupt big city machines.

The standard argument presented against independent political organization is "But you are only 10%." I cannot see the relevance of this observation, since no one is talking about taking over the country, but taking control over our own communities.

The fact is that the Negro population, 10% or not, is very strategically placed because—ironically—of segregation. What is also true is that Negroes have never been able to utilize the full voting potential of our numbers. Where we could vote, the case has always been that the white political machine stacks and gerrymanders the political subdivisions in Negro neighborhoods so the true voting strength is never reflected in political strength. Would anyone looking at the distribution of political power in Manhattan, ever think that Negroes represented 60% of the population there?

Just as often the effective political organization in Negro communities is absorbed by tokenism and patronage—the time honored practice of "giving" certain offices to selected Negroes. The

machine thus creates a "little machine," which is subordinate and responsive to it, in the Negro community. These Negro political "leaders" are really vote deliverers, more responsible to the white machine and the white power structure, than to the community they allegedly represent. Thus the white community is able to substitute patronage control for audacious black power in the Negro community. This is precisely what Johnson tried to do even before the Voting Rights Act of 1966 was passed. The National Democrats made it very clear that the measure was intended to register Democrats, not Negroes. The President and top officials of the Democratic Party called in almost 100 selected Negro "leaders" from the Deep South. Nothing was said about changing the policies of the racist state parties, nothing was said about repudiating such leadership figures as Eastland and Ross Barnett in Mississippi or George Wallace in Alabama. What was said was simply "Go home and organize your people into the local Democratic Party—*then* we'll see about poverty money and appointments." (Incidentally, for the most part the War on Poverty in the South is controlled by local Democratic ward heelers—and outspoken racists who have used the program to change the form of the Negroes' dependence. People who were afraid to register for fear of being thrown off the farm are not afraid to register for fear of losing their Head-Start jobs.)

We must organize black community power to end these abuses, and to give the Negro community a chance to have its needs expressed. A leadership which is truly "responsible"—not to the white press and power structure, but to the community—must be developed. Such leadership will recognize that its power lies in the unified and collective strength of that community. This will make it difficult for the white leadership group to conduct its dialogue with individuals in terms of patronage and prestige, and will force them to talk to the community's representatives in terms of real power.

The single aspect of the black power program that has encountered most criticism is this concept of independent organization. This is presented as third-partyism which has never worked, or a withdrawal into black nationalism and isolationism. If such a program is developed it will not have the effect of isolating the Negro community but the reverse. When the Negro community is able to control local office, and negotiate with other groups from a position of organized strength, the possibility of meaningful political alliances on specific issues will be increased. This is a rule of politics and there is no reason why it should not operate here. The only difference is that we will have the power to define the terms of these alliances.

The next question usually is, "So—can it work, can the ghettoes in fact be organized?" The answer is that this organization must be successful, because there are no viable alternatives—not the War on Poverty, which was at its inception limited to dealing with effects rather than causes, and has become simply another source of machine patronage. And "Integration" is meaningful only to a small chosen class within the community.

The revolution in agricultural technology in the South is displacing the rural Negro community into northern urban areas. Both Washington, D.C. and Newark, N.J. have Negro majorities. One third of Philadelphia's population of two million people is black. "Inner city" in most major urban areas is already predominantly Negro, and with the white rush to suburbia, Negroes will in the next three decades control the heart of our great cities. These areas can become either concentration camps with a bitter and volatile population whose only power is the power to destroy, or organized and powerful communities able to make constructive contributions to the total society. Without the power to control their lives and their communities, without effective political institutions through which to relate to the total society, these communities will exist in a constant state of insurrection. This is a choice that the country will have to make.

SELECTED BIBLIOGRAPHY OF MATERIALS ON PRE-WORLD WAR II POLITICAL DEVELOPMENTS

Adams, D.K. *America in the Twentieth Century: A Study of the United States Since 1917.* Cambridge: Cambridge University Press, 1967. A social-political history of the United States noting the increased power of the state through a reinterpretation of the Constitution.

Adams, Henry. *The Education of Henry Adams.* Boston: Houghton Mifflin, 1918.

Allen, Frederick Lewis. *Only Yesterday: An Informal History of the Nineteen-Twenties.* New York: Harper, 1931. A lively, well-written account of the politics, morals, finances, arts, and crimes of the 1920's.

Arnold, Thurman W. *The Folklore of Capitalism.* New Haven: Yale University Press, 1937. An examination and repudiation of the economic and political faiths current in the early General Grant period, and an expression of faith in vigorous action.

Beard, Charles A. *The Economic Basis of Politics, and Other Related Writings.* New York: Vintage, 1957. A series of essays demonstrating the influence of economics in the formation of political ideologies.

Berle, Adolf A., Jr., and Means, Gardiner C. *The Modern Corporation and Private Property.* New York: Commerce Clearing House, 1932.

Chamberlain, John. *Farewell to Reform.* New York: Liveright, 1932.

Commager, Henry Steele. *The American Mind.* New Haven: Yale University Press, 1950. An analysis and interpretation of American ideas and character since 1800.

Corey, Lewis. *The Decline of American Capitalism.* New York: Covici, Friede, 1934. A Marxian proclamation describing the uselessness of attempting to prop up the capitalist system since the forces of economic change necessitate its destruction.

Cronon, Edward David. *Black Moses.* Madison: University of Wisconsin Press, 1955. The story of Marcus Garvey and the attempt to reject white society by a program of Negro nationalism.

Davenport, Russell W. *U.S.A.: The Permanent Revolution.* New York: Prentice-Hall, 1951. The editors of *Fortune* magazine in collaboration with Davenport defend and expound their interpretation of the American way of life.

Drucker, Peter. *Concept of the Corporation.* New York: John Day, 1946. Valuable exposition of some of the ways that a corporation, like General Motors, goes at its problems; the book treats the corporation in terms of politics and sociology instead of economics and law.

Dulles, Foster Rhea. *Twentieth Century America.* Boston: Houghton, Mifflin, 1945. A discussion of the twofold increase of democracy and American foreign activity since 1900.

Faulkner, Harold U. *From Versailles to the New Deal.* New Haven: Yale University Press, 1950. A well-written, objective political history of the 1920's.

Freeman, Joseph. *An American Testament: A Narrative of Rebels and Romantics.* New York: Farrar and Rinehart, 1936.

Friedal, Frank. *America in the Twentieth Century.* New York: A.A. Knopf, 1960. A political and economic survey of the factors that shaped America's present foreign and domestic policy.

Girvetz, Harry K. *The Evolution of Liberalism.* New York: Collier Book, 1963.

————. *From Wealth to Welfare: The Evolution of Liberalism.* Stanford: Stanford University Press, 1950. Simply and plainly sets forth the significant historical changes that have altered the content of liberal doctrine.

Goldman, Eric F. *Rendezvous with Destiny.* New York: A. A. Knopf, 1952. A classic but elementary history of reform movements since the Civil War.

Greer, Thomas H. *What Roosevelt Thought: The Social and Political Ideas of Franklin D. Roosevelt.* East Lansing: Michigan State University Press, 1958.

Hicks, John D. *The American Nation.* Boston: Houghton, Mifflin, 1941. A political history of the United States from 1865 to 1940.

Hofstadter, Richard. *Social Darwinism in America.* Boston: Beacon Press, 1944. A secular philosophy used as a rationale for conservatism, Social Darwinism was to remain the dominant force up to the New Deal.

————. *The Age of Reform.* New York: A.A. Knopf, 1966. A study of the political thought of American reformers from Bryan to F.D.R., noting the cohabitation of reform and antiliberalism within the various movements.

Krock, Arthur. *In the Nation: 1932–1936.* New York: McGraw-Hill, 1966. A journalist's narrative explanation of the political happenings in Washington from the New Deal to the Great Society.

Nyrdal, Gunnar. *An American Dilemma.* New York: Harper and Bros., 1944.

Schumpeter, Joseph A. *Capitalism, Socialism and Democracy.* 3rd Ed. New York: Harper Bros., 1950.

Shannon, David A. *The Socialist Party of America.* New York: Macmillan, 1955. Readable and thoughtful study of the history of the Socialist Party from its beginning to its "decline and death" in the 1950's.

Spitz, David. *Patterns of Anti-Democratic Thought.* New York: Macmillan, 1949. An incisive analysis of antidemocratic political philosophies, as developed by their American exponents.

Steffens, Lincoln. *The Autobiography of Lincoln Steffens.* New York: Harcourt, Brace & World, 1931. The life story of an American reporter; a good picture of the times through which the reporter lived.

White, Morton G. *Social Thought in America: The Revolt Against Formalism.* New York: Viking Press, 1949. A history of liberal 20th century philosophy as expressed through the works of several of its leading representatives.

Wilson, Woodrow. *The New Freedom.* Garden City, N.Y.: Doubleday, 1933.

SELECTED BIBLIOGRAPHY OF POST-WORLD WAR II POLITICAL THOUGHT

Adler, William (ed.). *A New Day: Robert Kennedy.* New York: Signet, 1968. Kennedy's views on contemporary sociopolitical issues as expressed in his speeches from 1962.

Alinsky, Saul D. *Reveille for Radicals.* Chicago: University of Chicago Press, 1946. A description of the program and tactics necessary for a grassroots movement to obtain control over its own affairs.

Ball, George W. *The Discipline of Power: Essentials of a Modern World Structure.* Boston: Little, Brown, 1968.

Bell, Daniel. *The End of Ideology.* Glencoe, Ill.: The Free Press, 1960.

Bell, Daniel (ed.). *The Radical Right.* Garden City, N.Y.: Doubleday, 1963.

Bowles, Chester. *Ideas, People and Peace.* New York: Harper and Bros., 1958. The author calls for dynamic American leadership to exert a program of peace and development in the world through selective economic aid and technical assistance.

Buckley, William Frank. *God and Man at Yale.* Chicago: Regnery, 1951.

_____. *Up from Liberalism.* New York: McDowell, Obolensky, 1959.

Buckley, William Frank and Bozell, L. Brent. *McCarthy and his Enemies.* Chicago: Regnery, 1954

Cash, W. J. *The Mind of the South.* New York: A.A. Knopf, 1941.

Caplovitz, David. *The Poor Pay More.* New York: The Free Press, 1967. The author presents evidence that the spending policy of the poor, which results in their paying more than the worth of the goods consumed, is the direct result of their state of poverty.

Caudill, Harry M. *Night Comes to the Cumberlands.* Boston: Little, Brown, 1962. Through a social history of the Kentucky Appalacians, the author brings out the need for a meaningful conservation program for both the land and the humans who live on it.

Cleaver, Eldridge. *Soul on Ice.* New York: McGraw-Hill, 1968. A series of essays noting American society's imprisonment of the human soul.

Conot, Robert. *Rivers of Blood, Years of Darkness.* New York: Bantam, 1967. The Watts riot, marking the end of Negro passivity, is analyzed by the author followed by recommendations for reform measures (primarily educational reforms).

Cottrell, W. F. *Energy and Society*. New York: McGraw-Hill, 1955. One of the most suggestive works on the relationship of technology and social life.

Cremin, Lawrence A. *The Transformation of the School*. New York: A.A. Knopf, 1961. A history of American education.

Crick, Bernard. *The American Science of Politics*. Berkely: The University of California Press, 1959. An analysis of the thoughts of the leading 20th century political scientists.

Cruse, Harold. *The Crisis of the Negro Intellectual*. New York: Morrow, 1968. Through a history of the Negro Left since World War I, the author presents the best single analysis of the origins, central themes, and intellectual and contextual difficulties of Black Power.

Dewhurst, Frederick and associates. *America's Needs and Resources*. New York: Twentieth Century Fund, 1955.

Dulles, John Foster. *War or Peace*. New York: Macmillan, 1950.

Egbert, Donald D. and Persons, Stow, (eds.). *Socialism and American Life*. 2 Vols. Princeton: Princeton University Press, 1952. A scholarly appraisal of American socialism and its impact upon American society. Volume II offers a detailed critical bibliography which is extremely valuable to students of American socialism.

Ekrich, Arthur A. Jr. *The Decline of American Liberalism*. New York: Longmans, Green, 1955.

Elman, Richard M. *The Poorhouse State: The American Way of Life on Public Assistance*. New York: Pantheon, 1967. The author condemns the existing welfare policy, a system created by the moral ambiguity of the middle class, and calls for a program of mass economic assistance.

Evans, M. Staunton. *The Politics of Surrender*. New York: The Devin-Adair Co., 1966. America's liberal-based foreign policy has failed to protect our national interests due to its unwillingness to define policy in terms of the enemy (Communism).

Fager, Charles E. *White Reflections on Black Power*. Grand Rapids: W. B. Eerdmans Pub. Co., 1967. Showing how the 1964 Civil Rights Act is both meaningless and misused, the author comments on the resulting emergence of the Black Power Movement.

Fainsod, Merle, Gordon, Lincoln and Palamountain, J. C., Jr. *Government and the American Economy*. New York: W. W. Norton, 1959.

Fisher, Sydney (ed.). *New Horizons for the United States in World Affairs*. Columbus, Ohio: Ohio State University Press, 1966. A collection of eight essays attempting to present new perspectives in United States foreign policy.

Fromm, Erich. *Escape From Freedom*. New York: Farrar and Rinehart, 1941. Fromm attempts to show how men, not free to build a meaningful life in society, are attracted to totalitarian states in their search for security.

————. *The Sane Society*. New York: Rinehart, 1955. An analytic study showing the necessity of the simultaneous growth of all aspects of culture in order to create a meaningful and relevant social system.

Fulbright, J. William. *The Arrogance of Power*. New York: Random House, 1967.

————. *Old Myths and New Realities*. New York: Random House, 1964.

George, Wesley Critz. *The Biology of the Race Problem*. (Prepared by Commission of the Governor of Alabama),

1962. The author argues against integration and intermarriage due to the Negroes' biological (and consequently social) inferiority.

Gettleman, Marvin E., and Mermelstein, David (eds.). *The Great Society Reader.* New York: Random House, 1967. A collection of radical essays condemning the Great Society and the failure of American liberalism.

Goldwin, Robert A. (ed.). *Beyond the Cold War: Essays on American Foreign Policy in a Changing World Environment.* Chicago: Rand McNally and Co., 1965. Eleven essays presenting viable alternatives in United States foreign and military policy formulation as necessitated by the end of the Cold War.

Goodman, Paul. *Like a Conquered Province.* New York: Random House, 1967. A collection of six lectures in which the author announces redemption is possible in this empty society only through small personal victories.

Goldwater, Barry M. *The Conscience of a Conservative.* Shepherdsville, Ky.: Victor Pub. Co., 1960.

The Governor's Commission on the Los Angeles Riots. *Violence in the City. . . An End or a Beginning?* Los Angeles, 1965. Concluding that the Watts riot was a multicausal disorder, the commission recommends a series of institutional reforms.

Greer, Scott. *The Emerging City.* New York: The Free Press of Glencoe, 1962.

Grimes, Alan P. *Equality in America: Religion, Race, and the Urban Majority.* New York: Oxford University Press, 1964.

Hartz, Louis. *The Liberal Tradition in America.* New York: Harcourt, Brace, 1955.

Heilbroner, Robert L. *The Making of Economic Society.* Englewood Cliffs, N.J.: Prentice-Hall, 1962.

————. *The Future as History.* New York: Harper and Bros., 1959. In order to respond to a changing world situation, the author proclaims the necessity for Americans to adopt an attitude that will recognize the historic evolution of progress.

Hoffer, Eric. *The Temper of Our Times.* New York: Harper and Row, 1967. Five essays by the longshoreman-intellectual on the sociopsychological condition of American society, with rich condemnation of intellectuals, Negroes, youth, and revolutions.

Horowitz, David. *The Free World Colossus.* New York: Hillad Warg, 1965. Through a study of American foreign policy during the Cold War, the author describes how the United States, having near complete control over strategic decisions in the early Cold War era, has continually supported a policy of oppression and tyranny.

Hough, Joseph C. *Black Power and White Protestants* (A Christian response to the new Negro pluralism). New York: Oxford University Press, 1968. Viewing Black Power as an attempt to be rid of the stigma inherent in a minority position, the author believes eventual equality necessitates Black-White cooperation.

Howe, Irving (ed.). *The Radical Imagination.* New York: New American Library, 1967. A collection of articles taken from *Dissent* of which Howe is the editor.

Jacobs, Paul. *Prelude to Riot: A View of Urban America from the Bottom.* New York: Random House, 1968. The author presents a study in the treatment of minority groups by government institutions.

Jacobs, Paul, and Landau, Saul. *The New Radicals: A Report with Documents.* New York: Random House, 1966. Viewing the New Left as an attempt to formulate an ideology which will combine individual existential values and mass movements, the authors present a series of original documents and add commentary and analysis.

Kaufman, Arnold. *The Radical Liberal: New Man in American Politics.* New York: Atherton, 1968. The author states that only through a nonrevolutionary radicalism can liberalism and a progressive American society be preserved.

Kempner, Alan H. Jr. *The Liberal Syndrome.* New York: Exposition Press, 1966. A psyhcological examination of America's sellout to the Communists caused by the liberals' neurotic desire for security.

Kennan, George F. *Realities of American Foreign Policy.* Princeton: Princeton University Press, 1954. A series of lectures elucidating the author's point that foreign policy is merely a means by which to obtain the goals of American society.

Kennedy, Edward M. *Decisions for a Decade.* New York: Signet, 1968.

Kennedy, John F. *The Strategy of Peace.* New York: Harper and Bros., 1960.

Kennedy, Robert F. *To Seek a Newer World.* Garden City, N.Y. Doubleday, 1967.

Krosney, Herbert. *Beyond Welfare: Poverty in the Supercity.* New York: Holt, Rinehart, and Winston, 1967. Rejecting the welfare system and its denial of human rights through its policy of "colonialism," the author calls for a strengthening of Black political power as a vehicle for reform.

Lazer, Harry. *The American Political System in Transition.* New York: Thomas Y. Crowell and Co., 1967. An analysis of the adaptation of 20th century American political structure to the forces of social and economic change.

Lerner, Max. *America as a Civilization.* New York: Simon and Schuster, 1957. A comprehensive analysis and interpretation of the American way of life, including the history, the culture, the people, economy, politics, society, art, and world power of our country; the book is perhaps too big and too comprehensive.

Lichtheim, George. *The Concept of Ideology and Other Essays.* New York: Random House, 1967. The author calls for the Hegelian synthesis of liberal and Marxian ideologies in order to achieve a comprehensive understanding of contemporary society.

Lindsay, John V. *Journey into Politics.* New York: Dodd, Mead, 1967.

Lippman, Walter. *Essays in the Public Philosophy.* Boston: Little, Brown, 1955. A comprehensive statement of the author's political views.

Loweke, George P. *The Political Plague in America.* Boston: Forum, 1964. The author claims government interference in the capitalist socioeconomic system has resulted in the continual weakening of American society.

Lumer, Hyman. *Poverty: Its Roots and Its Future.* New York: International, 1965. The author proclaims socialism as the only program that can end poverty.

McCarthy, Eugene J. *A Liberal Answer to the Conservative Challenge.* New York: MacFadden, 1964.

————. *The Limits of Power.* New York: Holt, Rinehart, and Winston, 1967.

Mailer, Norman. *The Armies of the Night; History as Novel; The Novel as History.* New York: New American Library. 1968. A description of contemporary emotional and moral sentiments as expressed in middle class protest movements (particularly the March on the Pentagon).

Marx, Gary T. *Protest and Prejudice.* New York: Harper and Row, 1968. Through opinion research, the author presents a survey of belief patterns in the Black community.

Meehan, Eugene J. *Contemporary Political Thought: A Critical Study.* Homewood, Ill.: Dorsey Press, 1967. A critical analysis of the methodology and content of various schools of political thought.

Mills, C. Wright. *The Causes of World War Three.* New York: Simon and Schuster. 1958. The author argues for the adoption of a radical politics of responsibility since both the liberal and conservative ideologies are based upon rationality without reason.

Mills, C. Wright. *The Power Elite.* New York: Oxford University Press, 1956.

Morgan, Thomas B. *The Anti-Americas.* London: M. Joseph, 1967. The author sees anti-Americanism as resulting from the outmoded foreign policy of postwar interventionism.

Morganthau, Hans J. (ed.). *The Crossroad Papers: A Look into the American Future.* New York: W. W. Norton, 1965. Initiated by ADA, this series of essays discusses pragmatic approaches to the various political and social problems facing America.

Mrydal, Gunnar. *Asian Drama.* 3 Vols. New York: Twentieth Century Fund, 1968. A study of the economic and social factors that underlie poverty in Asian countries.

_____. *Challenge to Affluence.* New York: Pantheon, 1962. The author emphasizes the need for America to increase its economic growth as a means for ending racial discrimination and providing international leadership.

Newfield, Jack. *A Prophetic Minority.* New York: New American Library, 1966. An analysis of the New Left, portraying its attempts to add an existential dimension to American politics.

Nixon, Richard M. *The Challenge We Face.* New York: McGraw-Hill, 1960.

Oglesby, Carl, and Shaull, Richard. *Containment and Change.* New York: Macmillan, 1967. Two essays critically condemning American society and foreign policy for its imperialistic quest for economically fertile frontiers.

Osgood, Charles E. *An Alternative to War or Surrender.* Urbana: University of Illinois Press, 1962. The author holds hope of eventual world disarmament through a policy of GRIT (graduated reciprocation in tension-reduction).

_____. *Perspective in Foreign Policy.* Palo Alto: Pacific, 1966. By placing current foreign crises in long-range perspective, the author illustrates the need for patience by the United States in its search for a free world.

Palamountain, Joseph C., Jr. *The Politics of Distribution.* Cambridge: Harvard University Press, 1955.

Pennock, J. Roland. *Liberal Democracy: Its Merits and Prospects.* New York: Rinehart, 1950.

Potter, David M. *People of Plenty: Economic Abundance and the American Character.* Chicago: The University of Chicago Press, 1955.

Powledge, Fred. *Black Power-White Resistance: Notes on the New Civil War.* New York: World Pub. Co., 1968. Viewing separatism as resulting in eventual genocide, the author proposes integration without assimilation.

Rand, Ayn. *The Fountainhead.* Philadelphia: Blakiston, 1943.

_____. *Capitalism, The Unknown Ideal.* New York: New American Library. 1966.

Reischauer, Edwin O. *Beyond Vietnam.* New York: A.A. Knopf, 1968. The author calls for a reevaluation of American interests in Asia and our role on the mainland.

Reisman, David. *The Lonely Crowd.* New Haven: Yale University Press, 1950. Interesting analysis of American character and society.

Reuss, Henry S. *The Critical Decade: An Economic Policy for America and the Free World.* New York: McGraw-Hill, 1964. Avoiding rhetorical cliches, Reuss expounds a bold program of a free world community allowing for mutual aid and economic growth.

Roosevelt, James (ed.). *The Liberal Papers.* Garden City, N.Y.: Doubleday Anchor Books, 1962.

Severeid, Eric. *Small Sounds in the Night.* New York: A.A. Knopf, 1956. A collection of commentaries by the stalwart old journalist on aspects of American society and its politics.

Stanley, C. Maxwell. *Waging Peace: A Businessman Looks at United States Foreign Policy.* New York: Macmillan, 1956. An engineer by trade, the author calls for world armament control through effective use of the United Nations.

Talmon, J. *The Origins of Totalitarian Democracy.* London: Secker and Warburg, 1952.

Theoibald, Robert (ed.). *Social Policies for America in the Seventies: Nine Divergent Views.* Garden City, N.Y.: Doubleday, 1968. Each of the essays presented assumes that economic growth must be seen not in terms of its maximazation, but in the existing social and environmental needs.

Thomas, Norman M. *The Test of Freedom.* New York: Norton, 1954.

————. *A Socialist's Faith.* New York: Norton, 1951.

Warburg, James P. *The United States in the Post-war World.* New York: Athenum, 1967. Viewing the past twenty years of foreign policy as irrational and without pattern, the author calls for an informed and expressive electorate as a means of restoring reason.

Weinstein, James. *The Decline of Socialism in America, 1912–1925.* New York: Monthly Review Press, 1967.

Whyte, William H. *The Organization Man.* New York: Simon and Schuster, 1956.

Williams, Robin. *American Society.* New York: A.A. Knopf, 1960.

Wilson, John. *Equality.* New York: Harcourt, Brace, and World, 1967. An Englishman's analysis of "natural" and "artificial" equality for a slave-master relationship.

Wood, Robert C. *1400 Governments.* Cambridge: Harvard University Press, 1961.

Index